ANXIETY DISORDERS IN CHILDREN AND ADOLESCENTS

Edited by
JOHN S. MARCH

Foreword by *Dennis P. Cantwell*

The Guilford Press
New York London

© 1995 The Guilford Press
A Division of Guilford Publications, Inc.
72 Spring Street, New York, NY 10012

Printed in the United States of America

This book is printed on acid-free paper.

Last digit is print number: 9   8   7   6   5   4   3

Library of Congress Cataloging-in-Publication Data

Anxiety disorders in children and adolescents / edited by John S. March.
   p.   cm.
   Includes bibliographical references and index.
   ISBN 0-89862-834-2
   1. Anxiety in children.   2. Anxiety in adolescence.   I. March, John S., MD
   [DNLM: 1. Anxiety Disorders—in infancy & childhood. 2. Anxiety Disorders—in adolescence.   WM 172 A63732 1995]
   RJ506.A58A58 1995
   618.92'8522—dc20
   DNLM/DLC
   for Library of Congress   94-30107
                                        CIP

To my friend Kaj Lohmann,
and to my parents,
Ralph and Robin March,
whose love and support
rendered all this imaginable

Contributors

Adrian Angold, MRCPsych, Department of Psychiatry and Behavioral Sciences, Duke University Medical Center, Durham, North Carolina

Deborah Beidel, Ph.D., Department of Psychiatry and Behavioral Sciences, Medical University of South Carolina, Charleston

Joseph Biederman, M.D., Massachusetts General Hospital, Boston

Laura Bennett Murphy, Ph.D., Department of Psychology, Duke University Medical Center, Durham, North Carolina

Bruce Black, M.D., Department of Psychiatry, Tufts University School of Medicine and New England Medical Center, Boston, Massachusetts

Jonathan Chaloff, B.A., Clinical Psychopharmacology Unit, Massachusetts General Hospital, Boston

C. Keith Connors, Ph.D., Program in Child and Adolescent Anxiety Disorders, Department of Psychiatry, Duke University Medical Center, Durham, North Carolina

Phillip Costanzo, Ph.D., Department of Psychology: Social Health and Sciences, Duke University, Durham, North Carolina

E. Jane Costello, Ph.D., Department of Psychiatry and Behavioral Sciences, Department of Psychology, Duke University Medical Center, Durham, North Carolina

John F. Curry, Ph.D., Department of Psychiatry and Behavioral Sciences, Duke University Medical Center, Durham, North Carolina

Sara Dow, B.A., Child Psychiatry Branch, National Institutes of Mental Health, Bethesda, Maryland

Drew Erhardt, Ph.D., Program in Child and Adolescent Anxiety Disorders, Department of Psychiatry, Duke University Medical Center, Durham, North Carolina

Greta Francis, Ph.D., Department of Psychiatry and Human Behavior, Brown University School of Medicine, Providence, Rhode Island

David Gardner, B.Sc.Phm., Pharmacy Services in Psychiatry, Department of Pharmacy, Sunnybrook Health Science Centre, University of Toronto, Ontario, Canada

Golda S. Ginsburg, Ph.D., Department of Psychology, Florida International University, Miami

Joanne Greenawald, M.D., Department of Child Psychiatry, Medical University of South Carolina, Charleston

Stephen R. Hooper, Ph.D., Department of Psychiatry, Clinical Center for the Study of Development and Learning, Child and Adolescent Neuropsychology Consultation Program, Univeristy of North Carolina School of Medicine, Chapel Hill

Lisa Amaya-Jackson, M.D., M.P.H., Deparment of Psychiatry and Behavioral Sciences, Duke University Medical Center, Durham, North Carolina

Shara Miller-Johnson, Ph.D., Department of Psychology: Social and Health Sciences, Duke University, Durham, North Carolina

Jerome Kagan, Ph.D., Department of Psychology, Harvard University, Cambridge, Massachusetts

Charles Keith, M.D., Division of Child and Adolescent Psychiatry, Duke University Medical Center, Durham, North Carolina

Stan Kutcher, M.D., F.R.C.P.(C), Division of Adolescent Psychiatry, Sunnybrook Health Science Centre, Department of Psychiatry, University of Toronto, Ontario, Canada

Henrietta Leonard, M.D., Child Psychiatry Branch, National Institutes of Mental Health, Bethesda, Maryland

John S. March, M.D., M.P.H., Program in Child and Adolescent Anxiety Disorders, Department of Psychiatry, Duke University Medical Center, Durham, North Carolina

Tracy L. Morris, Ph.D., Department of Psychology, West Virginia Univeristy, Morgantown

Karen Mulle, R.N., Program in Child and Adolescent Anxiety Disorders, Department of Psychiatry, Duke University Medical Center, Durham, North Carolina

Sharon Reiter, M.D., F.R.C.P.(C), Adolescent Anxiety Disorders Program, Division of Adolescent Psychiatry, Sunnybrook Health Science Centre; Department of Psychiatry, University of Toronto, Ontario, Canada

Jerrold F. Rosenbaum, M.D., Clinical Psychopharmacology Unit, Massachusetts General Hospital, Boston

Randy Sallee, M.D., Department of Psychiatry and Pharmacology, Medical University of South Carolina, Charleston

Wendy K. Silverman, Ph.D., Department of Psychology, Florida International University, Miami

Patricia Stallings, M.A., Program in Child and Adolescent Anxiety Disorders, Department of Psychiatry, Duke University Medical Center, Durham, North Carolina

Susan E. Swedo, Ph.D., Child Psychiatry Branch, National Institutes of Mental Health, Bethesda, Maryland

Karen C. Wells, Ph.D., Department of Psychiatry and Behavioral Sciences, Duke Univeristy Medical Center, Durham, North Carolina

Heidi Wencel, M.A., Department of Psychology: Social and Health Sciences, Duke University, Durham, North Carolina

Foreword

It is a pleasure to write the Foreword for this book, which is the first to deal comprehensively with the major issues of anxiety disorders in children and adolescents. It has long been recognized that *symptoms* of anxiety and true anxiety *disorders* are quite common in children and adolescents. Several recent epidemiologic studies have suggested an overall prevalence rate of anxiety disorders in children and adolescents of between 8 and 10%. There are different rates for specific disorders such as generalized anxiety, social phobia, panic disorder, obsessive–compulsive disorder, separation anxiety disorder, and others. Although our knowledge base about anxiety disorders in childhood and adolescence has increased over time and there has been a renewed interest in research in this area, this book attempts to bring together this body of knowledge.

The scientific study of child and adolescent psychopathology does not have a very long history, for a variety of reasons, but one of the most important was the long-held view that specific diagnostic categorization of childhood and adolescent problems was not of clinical importance for differential treatment interventions. With the publication of the third edition of the *Diagnostic and Statistical Manual of Mental Disorders* (DSM-III) in 1980 and the subsequent publications of DSM-III-R in 1987 and DSM-IV in 1994 this view has changed. However, our understanding of some disorders of childhood and adolescence is much greater than of others. For example, we know a substantial amount about the clinical picture, subtypes, outcome, biological correlates, and response to various types of treatment of some of the rarer disorders such as infantile autism. We know even more about some of the more common disruptive behavior disorders, such as attention-deficit/hyperactivity disorder (ADHD) and conduct disorder, and, in recent years, the base of knowledge on mood disorders in childhood and adolescence has increased exponentially. However, the scientific study of the anxiety disorders has lagged behind.

Several years ago, I proposed a multistage model for the scientific study of psychiatric disorders of childhood and adolescence. The stages of that model are clinical phenomenology, psychosocial factors, demographic factors, biologic factors, family–genetic factors, family–environmental factors, natural history, and intervention response. At the starting point of clinical investigation in my model, clinical phenomenology, each of the specific anxiety disorders has to be described in terms of its core features and associated features (subtypes and comorbidities). This entails categorical and dimensional ways of describing anxiety symptomatology, which the DSM publications and the ICD-10 provide. Factor and cluster analysis of dimensional measures of anxiety are alternative and complementary ways of describing the anxiety disorders. Chapter 6 of this book details the difficulties inherent in assessing anxiety disorders in children and adolescents, and the chapters on individual disorders amplify how difficult it is to assess those specific disorders and delineate the clinical phenomenology of each of them in some detail.

Once the clinical phenomenology of any disorder has been clearly defined and subtyped, meaningful investigations of the following stages of the model can be undertaken. These include the study of demographic factors, such as incidence, prevalence, morbidity risk, and lifetime expectancy rates, along with the effects of age, gender, social class, ethnicity, and culture on the prevalence and manifestations of the disorder. Chapter 5 on epidemiology outlines these issues.

The study of psychosocial factors includes looking at the level of acute and chronic life stress, such as would be affected by early childhood experiences of physical and sexual abuse and separation and attachment difficulties. Psychosocial correlates are discussed in each of the chapters on specific disorders.

Biological factors, according to the multistage model, include associated brain damage and dysfunction; physical handicaps and disorders; neurological disorders; and laboratory measures of disorders in neurophysiology, neuroendocrinology, biochemistry, neuropharmacology, brain imaging, and neuropsychology. The chapters on the neurobiology and neuropsychology of anxiety disorders of childhood and adolescence in this book are unique. It is in the area of laboratory studies, particularly biological laboratory studies, that child psychiatry is lacking compared with studies of psychiatric disorders in adults and of medical disorders in children.

In the multistage model, family–environmental factors include parenting styles, parent–child interaction, and the presence of parental mental illness. The study of genetic factors includes consideration of patterns of psychopathology against a background of such potentially influential factors as family aggregation, adoption, twins, linkage, segregation, gene maps, and high-risk. Some of these points are discussed in the chapters in this book that deal with individual disorders and in Chapter 3 on "behavioral inhibition," which is a possible inborn characteristic that predisposes the development of childhood and adolescent anxiety disorder.

The study of the natural history of anxiety disorders would choose among true prospective, true retrospective, catch-up prospective, antero-spective, and high-risk studies to explore continuities and discontinuities between childhood, adolescent, and adult anxiety disorders. Mechanisms for these continuities and discontinuities are important for prevention and treatment planning. Chapters in this book on individual disorders discuss the developmental pathways of these disorders, their differential courses, and their outcomes.

The last stage of the multistage model is intervention response. What is needed are controlled studies of different therapeutic "packages" of the same disorders and the efficacy of the same specific therapeutic packages for *different* disorders. The therapies discussed include psychopharmaco-logical intervention and psychosocial interventions ranging from dynamic psychotherapy, to family therapy, to cognitive-behavioral therpay. Chapters 14–17 indicate how far we have to go in the way of controlled and comparative studies of the effectiveness of these interventions. Chapter 18, on setting up an anxiety disorders clinic, presents an excellent model for service delivery that can also be used for research purposes.

This book is the starting point for all clinicians and researchers work-ing with children and adolescents with anxiety disorders.

—DENNIS P. CANTWELL, M.D.
UCLA Neuropsychiatric Institute

Preface

Where there is charity and wisdom, there is neither fear nor ignorance. Where there is patience and humility, there is neither anger nor vexation. Where there is poverty and joy, there is neither greed nor avarice. Where there is peace and meditation, there is neither anxiety nor doubt.
—The Counsels of the Holy Father St. Francis

In 1986, The Guilford Press published *Anxiety Disorders of Childhood* under the able editorship of Rachel Gittelman-Klein. At the time, the revolution in descriptive psychopathology that had been initiated with the third edition of the *Diagnostic and Statistical Manual of Mental Disorders* (DSM-III) provided the stimulus for a text on anxiety disorders in young persons. Since then we have seen considerable progress in recognizing and treating anxiety across the lifespan, and many researchers now believe that the childhood-onset anxiety syndromes foreshadow adult anxiety disorders. Thus the time again seems favorable for a text on this topic, especially since DSM-IV introduces nosologic refinements that bring child and adult disorders into closer alignment.

As shown in Part I, Foundations, interesting and scientifically credible models concerning the nature and genesis of anxiety disorders in youth are now available. In Chapter 1 Randy Sallee surveys the rapidly expanding body of scientific evidence suggesting that the anxiety disorders are neurobehavioral conditions. I join Steve Hooper in extending this discussion in Chapter 2 to the neuropsychological level, noting that the application of models of brain function borrowed from cognitive neuroscience promises to bridge the behavioral and neuroanatomic levels of analysis. In Chapter 3 Joe Biederman and his colleagues, whose seminal work in this area needs no introduction, describe their thought provoking application of Jerome Kagan's construct of behavioral inhibition (Hirshfeld, Rosenbaum, Biederman, et al., 1992)—which is closely linked to neuropsychological models of brain activation and inhibition—to children and adults with anxiety disorders. Phil Costanzo and his colleague Shari Johnson discuss in Chapter 4 the role of social psychological factors in the genesis and maintenance of anxiety in children; Jane

Costello and Adrian Angold go on to teach us in Chapter 5 about the changes in anxiety symptomatology that occur over time, presumably in response to developmental imperatives. One feature of skilled clinical care and research is careful assessment. In Chapter 6, the concluding chapter of Part I, Pat Stallings and I address assessment issues, pointing out that, with a few conspicuous exceptions, we are strongly constrained at present by a lack of reliable and valid instruments keyed to modern concepts of anxiety in children. The chapters in Part I are not linked across levels of analysis, methodologies, populations, or even disorders— a glance at the largely nonoverlapping references illustrates the point. I hope that the imaginative reader will speculate that the next edition of this text will be driven by hypotheses originating in integrated models about the etiopathogeneis of anxiety disorders in children. I certainly expect it will be so.

Integrated models will of course depend on expanded knowledge about individual disorders and their cross-sectional and longitudinal comorbidities. In Part II, Disorders, we ask, "What is known about the DSM-IV childhood-onset anxiety disorders?" We know a great deal more than we did in 1986, in part because of work by the authors in this section. For example, the senior authors were without exception involved in one or more of the DSM-IV advisory subcommittees, so the information in these chapters on the latest nosologic refinements and specific treatments for the childhood-onset anxiety disorders is up to date. Wendy Silverman, who has successfully pushed the boundaries of assessment methodologies, and Golda Ginsburg discuss the simple phobias and generalized anxiety disorder in Chapter 7. Drawing on their own research, much of it conducted with Sam Turner, Deborah Beidel and Tracy Morris provide in Chapter 8 an overview of the generalized and specific social phobias; Henrietta Leonard and Sarah Dow review research about one such social phobia, namely selective mutism, in Chapter 10. In contrast to selective mutism, about which we know relatively little, Henrietta Leonard, Susan Swedo, and I review the literature on obsessive–compulsive disorder in youth, a disorder about which we know a great deal, in Chapter 11. The contributions to this area by the National Institutes of Mental Health (NIMH) group need little acknowledgment, and it was a great privilege for me to collaborate with Henri and Sue on this chapter. Bruce Black reviews in Chapter 9 the literature on separation anxiety and panic disorders, making a convincing, albeit appropriately cautious, case for linking the two conditions. Drawing in part on our work with the children of Hamlet, North Carolina, my colleague Lisa Amaya-Jackson and I discuss posttraumatic stress disorder as it occurs in younger patients in Chapter 12. Finally, since most children presenting with one anxiety disorder have another, and many have additional externalizing and internalizing symptoms as well, John Curry and Laura Murphy summarize both cross-sectional and longitudinal comorbidity in Chapter 13.

While each of the chapters in Part II includes a discussion of disorder-specific treatments (the interested reader will find helpful pointers to additional information among the references), Part III, Treatment, features the leading treatment modalities that have been applied to anxiety in young persons. Besides discussing general principles, the authors in Part III endeavor to communicate the "flavor" of treatment and consequently also some of the subtleties that differentiate excellent from merely adequate clinicians.

Ideally, all children with anxiety symptoms should first receive a disorder-specific cognitive-behavioral intervention since, of the available interventions, cognitive-behavioral psychotherapy clearly shows the most empirical support. Deborah Beidel and Greta Francis eloquently describe in Chapter 14 the theoretical framework supporting a large number of applied cognitive-behavioral treatments (CBT), in the process providing cogent examples of how to implement CBT in multiply anxious youngsters. Unfortunately, not all children do well with CBT alone, even when compliance is maximized (March, Mulle, & Herbel, 1994). Drawing on clinical lore, age-downward extension of adult pharmacotherapies, and a small but growing body of empirical evidence, Stan Kutcher and colleagues discuss psychopharmacological treatment approaches to anxiety disorders in young persons in Chapter 15. Despite the promise of CBT and pharmacotherapy, we do well to remember that every child with an anxiety disorder has a unique story to tell. And, as wise clinicians also know, these disorders influence and are influenced by the youngster's family. Drawing on years of accumulated wisdom with anxious children, Charles Keith presents in Chapter 16 an "experience-near" view of psychodynamic therapy for anxiety in children, implicitly revealing that exposure is at the heart even of psychodynamic treatment (Foa & Kozak, 1985). In a comprehensive and thoughtful review of family therapy models as applied to anxiety disorders in youth, Karen Wells provides in Chapter 17 a framework for conducting CBT in the family setting and a means of addressing family psychopathology when family dysfunction interferes with the application of cognitive-behavioral and/or pharmacotherapies. In Chapter 18, my colleagues and I conclude Part III with a discussion of the practicalities of organizing an anxiety disorders subspecialty program.

It is of course traditional to acknowledge the debt one owes to those without whom the text at hand could not have been written. This is my first edited book, and, before now, I unknowingly treated this segment of the preface as a custom akin to the best kind of gossip; I now realize how necessary and meaningful are these acknowledgments. Every chapter in this book builds on work by others. Thus, as I write these words, I am aware of the need to honor the contributions of the many colleagues—some known, others unknown to me—whose purpose has been to ease the suffering of children with anxiety disorders by extending the frontier of scientific knowledge about pathological anxiety. In this context, I especially wish to thank three exemplary clinician/researchers who have influenced me greatly: John Greist for his ongoing and deeply appreciated personal and collegial support; Edna Foa, whose remarkably coherent and impressive body of work is a continuing inspiration; and Keith Conners, whose mentoring of child and adolescent psychiatric researchers has indelibly shaped our field for the better. I also wish to express my appreciation to the authors in this volume; other than personal satisfaction, there is lamentably little reward in academic circles for writing book chapters. As the book took shape, the able and patient support of Seymour Weingarten, Editor-in-Chief at The Guilford Press, and Jodi Creditor, my production editor and patient supporter, have been invaluable. Their wise counsel and honest desire to see wider dissemination of scientific knowledge are primary causes for the publication of this text. Thanks as well to the many patients and their families who have taught me so much about anxiety disorders in children. Without you this book would not have been written. Finally, I want to acknowledge that this work was supported in part by an NIMH Scientist Development Award for Clinicians (1 K20 MH00981-01), without which my research career to this point would have been far less productive.

There is of course more to life than academia, and I want to thank my wife, Kathleen, and my children, Matthew and Maggie, for their good humor as I put this volume together. Their love and support make all other things, including the varied tasks of academic life, possible. At a somewhat greater distance, I am deeply appreciative of my parents, Ralph and Robin March, and my close friend and first psychotherapist, Kaj Lohmann. We often do a poor job these days of honoring and supporting those who supported and taught us as we were growing up. Thus it is with great appreciation that I dedicate this book to my parents and to Kaj; they truly share credit for its realization.

Finally, as in most areas of psychiatry and psychology, controversy abounds. Thus these chapters, while rich in information, will in some instances not do justice to the leading edge of the field, nor perhaps will the reader agree with all he or she finds herein. The errors of fact are mine; the controversies will eventually yield to good science. In editing this book, my goal, like yours, has been to help anxious children and adolescents author a more normal and agreeable story. May this text assist clinicians and researchers alike on this path.

—JOHN S. MARCH

REFERENCES

Foa, E., & Kozak, M. (1985). Emotional processing of fear: exposure to corrective information. *Psychological Bulletin, 90,* 20–35.

Hirshfeld, D. R., Rosenbaum, J. F., Biederman, J., et al. (1992). Stable behavioral inhibition and its association with anxiety disorder. *Journal of the American Academy of Child and Adolescent Psychiatry, 31*(1), 103–111.

Klein, R. (1986). *Anxiety disorders of childhood.* New York: Guilford Press.

March, J., Mulle, K., & Herbel, B. (1994). Behavioral psychotherapy for children and adolescents with obsessive–compulsive disorder: An open trial of a new protocol driven treatment package. *Journal of the American Academy of Child and Adolescent Psychiatry, 33*(3), 333–341.

Contents

PART I
Foundations

Chapter 1

Neurobiology

Randy Sallee
Joanne Greenawald

onsiderable progress has been made in our understanding of the neurobiology of anxiety, with momentum stemming from unique and specific pharmacologic agents and the recent cloning of their presumptive central nervous system (CNS) receptors. Attention to the ontogeny of panic and generalized anxiety disorder (GAD) in the adult has stimulated interest in the "behaviorally inhibited" subjects of Kagan, Resnick, and Snidman (1988) and has focused on the neurobiologic factors associated with children at risk for anxiety syndromes as adults. Much of the work described in this chapter deals with discoveries of underlying neurobiology from the adult literature or with childhood-onset disorder studied in adult life (e.g., obsessive–compulsive disorder [OCD]). Often similar investigations are lacking from the work on childhood anxiety disorders so that direct comparison of challenge tests or experimental paradigms is impossible. If childhood anxiety is thought of as a risk factor or prodromal condition to the fully expressed adult conditions, then the adult neurobiology studies have much to suggest about work to be done with children. A continuum is assumed from the behaviorally inhibited children of Kagan et al. (1988) to disorders in the adolescent that more closely resemble adult conditions. Klein (1981) suggests a continuum between a subgroup of separation-anxiety-disordered children to panic-disordered adults, but the relationship of other childhood anxiety disorders to adult syndromes (e.g., the relationship of child overanxious disorder to adult GAD) is unknown.

The premise of this chapter concerning neurobiology is that neural pathways involved in adult anxiety are to some extent reflected in childhood syndromes. The neurochemical and neuroanatomic studies that most

fully elicidate adult anxiety states are either absent from or too preliminary in the child literature to be directly helpful but are discussed here to
suggest their application to childhood disorders. The ethological work presented is meant to underscore the continuum between anxiety states in
animal models and man by elucidating the developmental aspects gleaned
from the animal literature, with particular emphasis on the work of Higley
and Suomi (1989) and others in nonhuman primates. Animal models may
help to sort out the environmental and genetic risks through key developmental periods that lead to full expression of anxiety syndromes in the
infant, juvenile, and adult animal. In an excellent review of the subject,
Harris (1989) suggests that such developmental models of anxiety focus
on constitutionally vulnerable animals to work out the genetics and neurobiology of these behavioral syndromes.

STUDIES OF NEUROTRANSMITTER SYSTEMS

Major neurotransmitter systems associated with anxiety include the
γ-aminobutyric acid-ergic (GABAergic), noradrenergic, and serotonergic
diatheses; recent evidence suggests involvement of neuropeptides cholecystokinin, neuropeptide Y, and corticotropin-releasing factor (CRF). Recent advances in knowledge about their involvement in the pathophysiology of anxiety will be briefly explored, with emphasis on relevant work
in the child literature where applicable. The neurochemical correlates of
anxiety (Rogeness, Maas, Javors, et al., 1988) in relationship to concepts
of stress system homeostasis (Chrousos & Gold, 1992) are presented to
elucidate sympathetic system vulnerability put forth by Kagan et al. (1988)
in behaviorally inhibited children. The hypothalamic–pituitary–adrenal
(HPA) axis and the locus ceruleus/sympathetic system appear to work in
concert to provide this homeostasis, the dysregulation of which is likely
to manifest itself in anxiety states in children. Though psychophysiologic
studies of these stress responses in children are limited, the evidence points
to continuity with the adult literature and suggests a biologic basis for
childhood anxiety.

Because much of our present understanding of OCD is being advanced
by structural studies utilizing magnetic resonance imaging (MRI) and functional studies both before and after treatment with positron emission
tomography (PET), we present this work as being relevant to childhood
anxiety disorder. Electroencephalographic studies and psychosurgery findings relevant to the neural pathways implicated in anxiety are also briefly
discussed, with emphasis directly on child/adolescent patients or childhood-
onset syndromes.

Noradrenergic System

The neurobiology of fear, anxiety, and alarm points to a key role for the noradrenergic system, with much support from animal studies and animal models of anxiety (Redmond & Huang, 1979; Uhde, Boulenger, Siever, et al., 1982). Increased noradrenergic system function has been associated with state anxiety measures in depressed patients (Post, Ballenger, & Goodwin, 1980) and with measures of anxiety (levels of 3-methoxy-4-hydroxyphenyl glycol [MHPG]) in normal volunteers (Ballenger, Post, Zimmerman, et al., 1981; Ballenger, Post, Jimerson, et al., 1984) and in panic patients (Ko, Elsworth, Roth, et al., 1983). The locus ceruleus is the major nucleus for brain noradrenergic activity. The overactivation of the locus ceruleus is proposed as a common pathway to the production of fear response, while underactivity may lead to inattentiveness, impulsivity, and risk-taking behavior (Charney & Redmond, 1983). The locus ceruleus has been hypothesized as the common pathway for acute panic attacks whose hypothesized brainstem origin (Gorman, Liebowitz, Fyer, et al., 1989) is greatly modulated by descending pathways from higher cortical centers as well as input from the periphery (e.g., vagal afferents to the nucleus solitarius) and serotonergic input from the midbrain raphe nuclei.

The functioning of the noradrenergic system is highly regulated, with important feedback monitoring attributed to the α_2-adrenergic auto-receptor. Altered central α_2-adrenoreceptor sensitivity has been implicated in panic and in GAD. Stimulation of growth hormone release by clonidine action at the α_2-adrenergic receptor is blunted in panic and GAD patients (Charney & Heninger, 1986, Abelson, Glitz, Cameron, et al., 1991), suggesting receptor subsensitivity. Yohimbine, an α_2-adrenergic receptor antagonist, produces anxietylike symptoms in humans (Charney, Heninger, & Brier, 1984) and tends to precipitate profound anxiety and panic attacks in panic disorder patients. Yohimbine increases locus ceruleus activity, increasing MHPG, systolic blood pressure, and symptom ratings in panic patients (Heninger, Charney, & Price, 1988; Charney et al., 1984).

Peripheral markers for central α_2-adrenergic receptors have been investigated using the platelet α_2-adrenergic receptor indexed by tritiated ligands such as [^{3}H]clonidine and [^{3}H]yohimbine. Lowered α_2-adrenergic receptor densities are found in platelets of panic-disordered patients (Cameron, Smith, Lee, et al., 1990; Charney, Woods, & Heninger, 1989). These peripheral markers appear to distiguish anxiety-disordered from depressed patients. The [^{3}H]clonidine-determined B_{max} for the platelet α_2-adrenergic receptor appears to be associated with symptom severity in panic (Cameron et al., 1990), although correlations with physiologic markers such as blood pressure, pulse, and circulating catecholamines are often elusive.

Examination of the peripheral markers for noradrenergic activity in children and adolescents is scant. Kagan, Reznick, and Snidman (1987) compared urinary catecholamine levels with indices of behavioral inhibition at 21 months, 4 years, and 5.5 years at longitudinal follow-up. Though correlations were modest, the noradrenergic activity index was associated with the behavioral inhibition index at age 4 and 5.5 years. Rogeness et al. (1990) compared boys with high and low levels of plasma dopamine β-hydroxylase (DBH), a marker for central and peripheral noradrenergic activity. The low-DBH group had fewer anxiety and depressive disorder diagnoses, while the high-DBH group showed significantly lower MHPG/ VMA (vanillylmandelic acid) and MHPG/NA-R ratios in a separation-anxiety-disordered subset.

According to Rogeness, Javors, Maas, et al. (1990), higher ratios of MHPG/VMA or MHPG/NA indicate lower efficiency of the noradrenergic system, while the lower ratios as found in separation anxiety disorder are indicative of increased noradrenergic function. Physiologic variables associated with increased activation of the noradrenergic system, such as increased heart rate and blood pressure, tend to be increased in behaviorally inhibited children (Kagan et al., 1987) and in separation-anxiety-disordered children (Rogeness, Cepada, Macedo, et al., 1990). Kagan et al. (1988) have postulated that behaviorally inhibited children exhibit greater sympathetic reactivity, manifested by greater cardiac accelerations and postural blood pressure changes. These authors speculate that higher central norepinephrine levels, greater density of adrenergic receptors, or both may be causal for greater limbic–hypothalamic arousal in the inhibited children. The same behaviorally inhibited children have higher rates of multiple anxiety disorder and accounted for high rates of anxiety disorder (overanxious and phobic) in a longitudinal follow-up study (Biederman, Rosenbaum, Hirshfeld, et al., 1990).

The functional status of various neurotransmitter systems involved in anxiety may be assessed by evaluating the psychobiologic response to selective agents. Pharmacologic probes offer a dynamic assessment of the various systems involved in anxiety and have been used extensively in adults (Table 1.1), but to date this type of information is lacking for anxiety-disordered children. The most robust probe for the noradrenergic system has been the use of clonidine stimulation of growth hormone secretion, presumably by its action as an α_2-adrenergic agonist. Patients with panic disorder have a blunted response to both situationally induced and pharmacologically induced growth hormone stimulation (Charney & Heninger, 1986; Uhde, Vittone, Siever, et al., 1986). Abnormal growth hormone release is not unique to panic; it is also abnormally regulated in

TABLE 1.1. Pharmacologic Probes of CNS Function in Adults with Anxiety Disorder

Reference	Drug	Neurotransmitter receptor mechanism	Anxiety disorder	Results
Charney and Heninger (1986)	Clonidine	α_2-Adrenergic agonist	Panic	↓anxiety
Rasmussen, Goodman, Woods, et al. (1987)	Yohimbine	α_2-Adrenergic antagonist	OCD	No effect
Charney, Heninger, and Brier (1984)	Yohimbine	α_2-Adrenergic antagonist	Panic	↑anxiety, ↑panic attacks
Klein, Zohar, Geraci, et al. (1991)	Caffeine	Adenosine antagonist	Panic	↑anxiety, ↑panic attacks
Breslow, Fankhauser, Potter, et al. (1989)	Baclofen	GABA agonist	Panic	↓anxiety, ↓panic attacks
Nutt, Glue, Lawson, et al. (1990)	Flumazenil	GABA antagonist	Panic	↑panic attacks
Dorow, Horowski, Paschleke, et al. (1983)	β-Carboline	GABA inverse agonist	Controls	↑anxiety
Bradwejn, Koszycki, and Shriqui (1991)	CCK-4 neuropeptide	CCK_B agonist	Panic	↑anxiety, ↑panic attacks in dose-dependent manner
Kahn, Asnis, Wetzler, et al. (1988); Kahn, Wetzler, Van Praag, et al. (1988)	m-CPP (oral)	$5\text{-}HT_{1c-2}/5\text{-}HT_3$	Panic	↑anxiety, induced panic
Germine, Goddard, Woods, et al. (1992)	m-CPP (oral)	$5\text{-}HT_{1c-2}/5\text{-}HT_3$	GAD	↑anxiety
Zohar and Insel (1987); Hollander, Fay, Cohen, et al. (1988)	m-CPP (oral)	$5\text{-}HT_{1c-2}/5\text{-}HT_3$	OCD	↑anxiety, ↑OC symptoms
Charney, Goodman, Price, et al. (1988)	m-CPP (i. v.)	$5\text{-}HT_{1c-2}/5\text{-}HT_3$	OCD	No change
Charney, Woods, Goodman, et al. (1987)	m-CPP (i. v.)	$5\text{-}HT_{1c-2}/5\text{-}HT_3$	Panic	Induced panic attacks
Targum and Marshall (1989)	Fenfluramine	Serotonin agonist	Panic	↑anxiety, ↑panic attacks
Den Boer and Westenberg (1990)	5-HTP	Serotonin precursor	Panic	No change

GAD (Abelson et al., 1991), prepubertal depression (Puig-Antich, 1987) and OCD (Siever, Insel, Jimmerson, et al., 1983).

Serotonin

Serotonin (5-hydroxytryptamine [5-HT]) is a modulatory neurotransmitter with generally inhibitory effects, acting through three major receptor types (5-HT$_1$, 5-HT$_2$, or 5-HT$_3$). Both 5-HT$_1$ and 5-HT$_2$ receptors are G-protein related and found in the frontal cortex and limbic system of the CNS, while 5-HT$_3$, an ionic channel receptor, is found predominantly in the area postrema, with sites in the amygdala and hippocampus (Zifa & Fillian, 1992). 5-HT$_{1A}$ receptors are located both presynaptically, in the raphe nuclei of the brainstem, and postsynaptically, predominantly in the limbic area. Activation of presynaptic 5-HT$_{1A}$ results in inhibition of cell firing and generally decreased serotonin neurotransmission, while activation of the postsynaptic 5-HT$_{1A}$ receptor results in specific limbic inhibition. It has been suggested that the postsynaptic 5-HT$_{1A}$ receptor and the postsynaptic 5-HT$_2$ receptor work in opposition to one another (Schreiber & De Vry, 1993) and that activation of the postsynaptic 5-HT$_{1A}$ receptor may precipitate downregulation of the 5-HT$_2$ receptor. Downregulation of 5-HT$_2$ receptors has been postulated as a common mechanism of action for both 5-HT$_2$-acting drugs (e.g., ritanserin) and 5-HT$_{1A}$-acting drugs (e.g., buspirone) in anxiolytic activity.

Several lines of evidence from animal studies (Chopin & Briley, 1987) and treatment studies of patients with anxiety disorders indicate that the serotonin system plays an important role in the mediation of fear and anxiety (Heninger & Charney, 1988). Overactivity of the serotonin pathways may contribute to the production of pathological anxiety (File, 1984), as inhibition of serotonin synthesis produces an anxiolytic effect. Neurobiologic probes of the serotonin system involve assessment of both presynaptic cerebrospinal fluid 5-hydroxyindoleacetic acid (CSF 5-HIAA, [³H]imipramine binding, fenfluramine challenge, serotonin depletion) and postsynaptic (m-chlorophenylpiperazine [m-CPP], buspirone, ipsapirone) components. Table 1.1 summarizes the serotonergic challenge studies in adult OCD and panic using m-CPP, fenfluramine, and 5-HTP (a serotonin precursor).

m-Chlorophenylpiperazine is a direct 5-HT$_{1c-2}$/5-HT$_3$ agonist that produces anxiety in controls and is used to selectively induce symptoms in panic and OCD. When interpreting m-CPP challenge data, it is important to note that m-CPP may act preferentially at serotonin subreceptors in a dose and route of administration dependent manner and that 5-HT$_2$ and 5-HT$_{1c}$ receptors are similar in pharmacology and molecular structure (78% identity in transmembranal domains). Oral m-CPP administration in OCD produced increased anxiety and obsessions compared to normal controls in one study (Zohar & Insel, 1987); however, parenteral m-CPP and tryptophan (a serotonin precursor) failed to exacerbate OCD symtoms in some studies (Charney, Goodman, Price, et al., 1988) and was found to be provocative in others (Pigott, Hill, Grady, et al., 1993). Challenge with m-CPP after treatment with a serotonin reuptake inhibitor (SRI) is ineffective, suggesting downregulation of postsynaptic serotonin receptors (Zohar, Insel, Zohar-Kadouch, et al., 1988) as a mechanism of action of SRIs in OCD. The addition of metergoline (5-HT$_2$ antagonist) in the course of SRI treatment, however, exacerbates anxiety and OCD symptoms (Benkelfat, Murphy, Zohar, et al., 1989), which suggests that serotonin availability and not receptor downregulation is responsible for the treatment effects of the SRI agents in OCD.

Much of the investigation of serotonin's involvement in anxiety disorders is stimulated by treatment studies showing efficacy of serotonin agents, which have only recently become available. Serotonergic mechanisms have been invoked in the production of anxiety in both GAD and panic patients (Westenberg, den Boer, & Kahn, 1987). Thoren, Asberg, Bertilsson, et al. (1980) first suggested involvement of the serotonin system in OCD by examining the metabolite 5-HIAA in CSF, which decreased in association with symptom reduction after chlorimipramine. 5-HT$_{1A}$ partial agonist buspirone and 5-HT$_2$ antagonist ritanserin are both effective in GAD (Ross & Matas, 1987), and SRIs have proven effective in OCD and panic. Panic, however, may be nonresponsive to both 5-HT$_{1A}$ (Sheehan, Raj, Sheehan, et al., 1988) and 5-HT$_2$ antagonists (Westenberg & den Boer, 1989). Symptom exacerbation on m-CPP challenge (Table 1.1) in both panic disorder and OCD suggests hypersensitivity of 5-HT$_{1c-2}$ or 5-HT$_3$ postsynaptic receptors in these disorders. Serotonin release appears to be normal in panic, based on data from serotonin precursor 5-HTP challenge (den Boer & Westenberg, 1990). However, 5-HT$_{1A}$ receptors are hyporesponsive in panic disorder, as measured by the hypothermic and adrenocorticotropic hormone (ACTH) cortisol increase induced by ipsapirone at 5-HT$_{1A}$ receptors (Lesch, Hoh, Disselkamp-Tietze, et al., 1991). Subsensitivity of the presynaptic 5-HT$_{1A}$ autoreceptor has therefore been postulated in panic disorder perhaps as an adaptive response to lowered available synaptic serotonin levels. 5-HT$_{1A}$-receptor response is normal in OCD (Lesch, Weisman, Hoh, et al., 1992).

Serotonin system abnormalities in children with OCD have been identified using peripheral markers such as imipramine binding in platelets and whole blood serotonin. Whole blood serotonin declines with age to a stable adult level by age 12 (Ritvo, Yuwiler, Geller, et al., 1971), but the relationship between blood serotonin and CNS serotonin activity remains uncertain. Hanna, Yuwiler, and Cantwell (1991) assessed whole blood serotonin concentrations in 16 children and adolescents with severe OCD and detected no differences compared to normal controls. OCD patients with a positive family history of OCD had significantly higher levels of serotonin than either normal controls or OCD patients without such a history. Flament, Rapaport, Murphy, et al. (1987) found no difference between adolescent OCD patients and normal controls in platelet serotonin levels but a significant negative correlation between platelet serotonin content and symptom severity in the OCD group. Flament et al. (1987) found plasma amine oxidase to be negatively correlated with age, with girls having more platelet monoamine oxidase (MAO) activity than boys. There appeared to be a positive correlation between platelet serotonin concentration and platelet MAO activity ($r = .47$, $p < .002$). Only in the OCD group did systolic standing blood pressure correlate with plasma norepinephrine values. After treatment for 5 weeks with clomipramine, OCD patients experienced a marked reduction in platelet serotonin concentration and a smaller reduction in platelet MAO activity. A favorable clinical response to clomipramine was associated with pretreatment serotonin level and a relatively greater decrease in serotonin concentration during treatment. In patients with OCD and comorbid Tourette disorder, the serotonin reuptake transporter in platelets as measured by [^{3}H]imipramine was found to be less abundant compared to controls as well as to patients with Tourette disorder only (Weizman, Mandel, Barber, et al., 1992).

Hypothalamic–Pituitary–Adrenal Axis

The HPA axis has been extensively associated with stress and anxiety in humans. Cortisol is identified as the "stress" hormone and corticotropin CRF has been implicated in the pathogenesis of panic disorder. Blunted ACTH but normal cortisol response to CRF stimulation is present in panic (Hollander, Levin, & Liebowitz, 1990). Few anxiety patients exhibit nonsuppression after dexamethasone (Sheehan, Claycomb, Surman, et al., 1986; Coryell, Black, Kelly, et al., 1989), but the response to CRF stimulation indicates a hyperactive HPA axis. The link between the HPA axis and locus ceruleus/sympathetic system is found in CRF stimulation of locus ceruleus activity as CRF may play a role in stress-produced anxiety (Owens & Nemeroff, 1991). Serotonin systems may also be involved as 5-HT$_{1A}$-agonist antianxiety drugs stimulate HPA axis activity and CRF release in particular.

Perhaps the most neurobiologic data found in childhood anxiety deal with HPA axis involvement. Studies of 1-year-old infants showing extreme distress when separated from their mothers demonstrate that urinary cortisol is elevated (Tennes, Downey, & Vernadakis, 1977). Urinary free cortisol predicts anxiety and inhibition of social behavior in a school-age population (Tennes & Kreye, 1985). Tennes and Kreye found that normal second-graders had higher cortisol on test days than nontest days, but the variance in cortisol was better accounted for by personality and behavioral variables than by test stress itself. Salivary cortisol is elevated in young children showing extreme inhibition in social situations, defined by Kagan et al. (1988) as behavioral inhibition. At longitudinal follow-up, high levels of salivary cortisol correctly predicted the original 21-month behavioral classification for 78% of Kagan's sample. Inhibited children had significantly higher cortisol levels than uninhibited children both in the home and in the laboratory. Kagan et al. (1987) theorize that the HPA axis of inhibited children is tonically at a higher level of activity even in minimal stress situations. Anxiety syndromes in the presence of comorbid disorders have recently been studied by McBurnett, Lahey, Frick, et al. (1991). Salivary cortisol was significantly elevated in conduct-disordered children with comorbid anxiety disorder (McBurnett et al., 1991), and anxiety symptoms exhibited a dose–response effect with increasing cortisol levels.

Neuropeptides

Two important peptide modulators of anxious behavior appear to be neuropeptide Y (NPY) and cholecystokinin (CCK). NPY is abundant in the hypothalamus, limbic system, and cortex and seems to have a regulatory function in neuroendocrine and autonomic systems. Disturbed NPY transmission has been implicated in clinical symptoms of anxiety (Helig & Widerlov, 1990). In rodents, central administration of NPY produces an anxiolytic effect. Modulation of anxiety in rodents has recently been achieved through use of an antisense oligodeoxynucleotide aimed at mimicking the NPY-Y1-receptor mRNA and rendering these receptors nonfunctional (Wahlestedt, Pich, Koob, et al., 1993). NPY-Y1-receptor binding was decreased by 60% while NPY-Y2 receptors were unaffected by antisense NPY-Y1 mRNA. After 2 days of direct intracerebroventricular (i. c. v.) injection, rodents were tested using an elevated plus maze (a pharmacologically validated animal model of anxiety); antisense-treated animals sustained a dramatic anxiolytic effect similar to that produced by benzodiazepines.

These provocative findings are sure to stimulate interest in NPY in anxiety states. The difficulty for direct examination of the effect of peptides on CNS function is that half-life is extremely short (a few minutes), and few exogenously administered peptides effectively penetrate the blood–brain barrier after parenteral administration. A new approach to this problem is mimicking either pharmacologically or through molecular engineering the active site of peptides and attaching them to molecules that both resist peptidase and penetrate the blood–brain barrier. One such small peptide that may play a role in anxiety is CCK-4 tetrapeptide (the active moiety of CCK). In recent challenge studies in humans (controls and panic patients), parenteral CCK-4 has elicited panic in a dose-dependent fashion and therefore can be used to selectively differentiate panic patients from controls (Bradwejn, Koszycki, & Shriqui, 1991).

CCK functions both as a neurotransmitter and as a modulator for classical neurotransmitters such as dopamine, serotonin, GABA, and excitatory amino acids. In the forebrain, CCK is localized in GABA neurons and its release is under tonic GABAergic control. The number of CCK receptors in the forebrain correlates with anxiety states induced by anxiogenic β-carboline or noncompetitive GABA antagonism, causing an upregulation of CCK binding sites. CCK effects can also be blocked by 5-HT$_3$-receptor antagonism, and chronic imipramine treatment protects patients with panic disorder from the effects of CCK-4 challenge.

Animal and human data point to CCK as an anticipatory stress modulator whose abnormal regulation may play a role in anxiety disorder. Lydiard, Ballenger, Laraia, et al. (1992) have reported decreased concentrations of CSF CCK-8S in panic patients compared to nonpanic patients and normal controls. Most direct investigation comes from the use of CCK-related peptides as challenge agents to induce anxiety states in patients and normal controls. In recent studies of patients with panic disorders, CCK-4 (25–50 µg) and CCK-5 (pentagastrin) (0.6 µg/kg) have consistently elicited paniclike symptoms under a challenge paradigm and in a dose-dependent fashion (Bradwejn, Koszycki, Annable, et al., 1992a; Abelson & Nesse, 1990). The attacks provoked by CCK-4 were rated by patients as very similar or identical to those experienced spontaneously. CCK-4 is a selective CCK$_B$ agonist, thereby implicating CCK$_B$ receptors in panic-attack generation, though CCK$_A$ may also be involved in animal models. In primates (African green monkey), parenteral administration of 0.5–4 µg/kg elicits a series of fear behaviors (Palmour, Ervin, Bradwejn, et al., 1991). The ability of CCK-4 to elicit these behaviors in primates depended on the baseline anxiety of the animal and the animal's hierarchical position in its social group. Anxious monkeys who were more restless, submissive to threat, and excessively reactive to their environment were most sensitive to CCK-4. They reacted to lower doses than did conspecifics, and they reacted to higher doses with frozen immobility, cowering, and withdrawal. In patients with panic disorder, the new CCK$_B$ antagonist L-365,260, as well as imipramine, effectively blocks CCK-4-induced panic attacks (Bradwejn, Koszycki, Couetoux du Tertre, et al., 1992), while pretreatment with flumazenil (GABA antagonist) does not (Couetoux du Tertre, Bradwejn, Koszycki, et al., 1992). CCK-4 infusion is associated with increased cerebral blood flow as measured by $H_2^{15}O$ PET scans bilatemporally in panic patients and controls with selective increases in cerebral blood flow in the anterior cingulum, putamen, and vermis in nonpanickers only (Benkelfat, Bradwejn, Meyer, et al., 1992).

Neuropeptides studied in child populations include CSF somatostatin (Kruesi, Swedo, Leonard, et al., 1990). Somatostatin itself may stimulate serotonin release, and somatostatin analog "Sandostatin" reduces paniclike attacks in patients with "idiopathic flushing" (Abelson, Neese, & Vinik, 1990). Kruesi et al. (1990) found decreased somatostatin levels in OCD patients with disruptive behavior disorders, but a direct comparison to normal controls was not possible. Leckman, Riddle, Berrettini, et al. (1988) examined dynorphin A in Tourette disorder patients with comorbid OCD and found that dynorphin levels correlated with severity of OCD symptoms. Swedo, Leonard, Kruesi, et al. (1992) studied dynorphin A in CRF of children and adolescents with primary OCD. These authors found no relationship between dynorphin A and OCD symptoms but a significant and negative association between arginine vasopressin concentration and OCD symptom severity. Dynorphin-related peptides may impact on the HPA axis in that they are cotransmitters within populations of hypothalamic neurons secreting CRF. CRF and dynorphin-related peptides have reciprocal actions on the release of each other, with CRF stimulating dynorphin secretion and dynorphin inhibiting CRF release. Dynorphin 17 significantly inhibits the activating actions of CRF on the locus ceruleus (Overton & Fisher, 1989). From the adult literature, a study by Uhde, Tanar, Rubinow, et al. (1992) has demonstrated hypothalamic–growth hormone dysfunction in panic disorder. Growth hormone responses to clonidine, yohimbine, caffeine, and growth-hormone-releasing factor were blunted in panic patients compared to normal controls. Drug or neuroendocrine challenge in these patients, even if associated with enhanced anxiety, failed to stimulate growth hormone levels over that of controls. Uhde et al. (1992) discuss two adolescent patients with short-stature and panic disorder and speculate whether a common hypothalamic dysfunction in growth hormone responsiveness may be responsible. These findings support a hyporesponsive hypothalamic–growth hormone system in panic disorder and argue for continued investigations of the responsiveness of the hypothalamic tracts involved in both CRF and growth hormone release in childhood anxiety.

ANIMAL MODELS OF ANXIETY

Animal models of childhood anxiety focus on attachment behavior and associated distress on separation. The shorter life span of the animal models allows for full exploration of psychopathology from the developmental perspective. Animal models can be examined for underlying neurobiology at critical periods for exhibiting anxious behaviors. In a recent review of the anxiety invoked in primates by social separation, Kalin (1993) describes the stages of an increasing fear response in young rhesus monkeys as vocalization and activation followed by a motionless "freeze" to avoid detection and hostile grimacing in its most extreme form. The ontogeny of these anxious responses (fully developed in 9- to 12-week-old animals) corresponds to the maturation of the prefrontal cortex, amygdala, and hypothalamus. An analogous time period in humans is 7 to 12 months, when the prefrontal cortex activity increases and marked stranger anxiety is present. Kalin describes a similar maturational time frame for the hypothalamic region: After maternal separation, ACTH-level increases are most profound at 9 to 12 weeks in rhesus monkeys. An earlier study by Breese, Smith, Mueller, et al. (1973) of rhesus monkeys also implicated the hypothalamic serotonin system: Elevations were noted after infant–mother separation. Hypothalamus-related physiologic changes on separation in the infant pigtail macaque include increased heart rate and temperature (Reite & Capitanio, 1985). Hypothalamic neurochemistry is related to the behavioral fear repertoire; animals with relatively lower levels of cortisol "freeze" for shorter periods compared to high-cortisol peers. These stress responses are heritable, and by 5 months the stress responses of the young rhesus mimic those of the mother in both duration of behavior and ACTH level. In children, those with high basal cortisol levels are likely to show greater behavioral inhibition in a novel situation (Kagan et al., 1988). In nonhuman primates, a high CSF concentration of serotonin metabolite 5-HIAA is associated with increased anxiety and fear (Higley, Suomi, & Linnoila, 1988, 1990), and the turnover of monoamine neurotransmitters appears to be relatively stable and highly heritable (Higley, Thompson, Champoux, et al., 1993). Maternal separation also increases CSF 5-HIAA (Higley, Suomi, Linnoila, 1992).

Early postnatal handling and social isolation affect the HPA axis stress response by altering feedback mechanisms (e.g., glucocorticoid receptor) in the hippocampus and the frontal cortex (Meaney, Aitken, Bodnoff, et al., 1985). In the adult animal, environmental factors such as social rank work in concert with underlying neurobiology (temperament) to determine stress response (Sapolsky, 1990). In rhesus infants the interaction with a nurturing mother influences subsequent fear behaviors (Higley & Suomi, 1989); peer-raised animals have increased fear-related behaviors, higher cortisol and ACTH, and increased alcohol consumption (Higley, Hasert, Suomi, et al., 1991; Higley, Suomi, & Linnoila, 1991) compared to maternal-reared animals. Peer-reared rhesus monkeys also have higher levels of CSF 5-HIAA and MHPG than maternal-reared animals. Upon separation, the MHPG concentration increases and remains elevated throughout the separation, while 5-HIAA returns to baseline within 4 weeks. These findings in the rhesus separation-anxiety model suggest involvement of the locus ceruleus–noradrenergic/sympathetic system as well as the HPA stress-response system (Chrousos & Gold, 1992) in modulating the effects of separation.

Animal models of anxiety provide an opportunity to test complex neurochemical theories and to directly assess the role of certain neurochemical pathways in the pathogenesis of anxiety. Evidence for such utility is found in work of Ninan et al. (1982), which explored the role of endogenous ligands for benzodiazepine receptors (e.g., β-carbolines; inverse benzodiazepine agonists) that may play a role in anxiety. The study found that inverse agonists with high affinity for the benzodiazepine receptor cause an acute anxiety syndrome associated with increased heart rate, blood pressure, plasma cortisol, and catecholamines. When Kalin, Shelton, and Turner (1992) administered a β-carboline immediately after maternal separation in infant rhesus monkeys, the animals' anxious responses (e.g., freezing) were augmented. This physiologic fear-type response is blocked by benzodiazepines. Though such studies implicate the benzodiazepine receptor, other compounds also elicit similar behavioral syndromes (e.g., lactate, CCK-4, CO_2).

Other animal models of anxiety disorder include the work of Mineka (1985) that focused on the induction and behavioral treatment of phobic conditions in rhesus monkeys. Animal models of OCD such as canine acral lick dermatitis or "zoo stereotypies" of primates have helped to elucidate neural pathways and treatments for the disorder. The neuroethological similarity of acral lick and OCD has been exploited in studies showing the efficacy of clomipramine (Goldberger & Rapoport, 1991) and fluoxetine (Stein, Shoulberg, Helton, et al., 1992) and suggests a common serotonergic involvement in animals and humans. The neuroethologic approach and animal models applied to child psychiatry have recently been reviewed elsewhere (Harris, 1989).

PHYSIOLOGIC STUDIES

Potential underlying vulnerability of children at risk for anxiety most likely is localized to the locus ceruleus/sympathetic system and the HPA axis. Noninvasive measures of these systems have utilized the physiologic parameters in the cardiovascular (e.g., blood pressure, heart rate variability) and the neuroendocrine systems. Psychophysiologic assessment of anxious children was recently reviewed by Beidel (1989). Heart rate data were found to be stable and predictive in follow-up studies of behaviorally inhibited children (Resnick, Kagan, Sniderman, et al., 1986). High heart rate and low heart rate variability both were correlated with an index of inhibition. In adults with panic, low variance of heart rate (R–R variability) is a reproducible discriminator that tends to indicate either decreased cholinergic activity or increased adrenergic activity (Yeragani, Balon, Pohl, et al., 1990). The heart rate of nonanxious children tends to habituate to stress while that of vulnerable, behaviorally inhibited children tends to accelerate and, at least in the Resnick et al. (1986) sample, to suggest "anticipatory anxiety" at age 5.5 years. When an aggregate index of combined physiologic variables is compared with the index of inhibition, the correlation is substantial ($r = .70$ with the index at 21 months of age and $r = .64$ with the index at 7.5 years of age; Kagan et al., 1988). In general, behavioral inhibition, whatever the relationship to diagnosed anxiety, is similar physiologically to adult diagnosed disorder and is characterized by a higher heart rate, less R–R variability, and increasing heart rate over time during a complex cognitive task. A speculative relationship between behavioral inhibition as a construct and diagnosed anxiety disorder is suggested by recent follow-up data of behaviorally inhibited children.

In clinical samples of children, studies have correlated psychophysiologic responses to a feared stimulus (Beidel, 1988). In general, significant heart rate changes correlate most with extent of fear. Beidel (1988) found that test-anxious children (60% met *Diagnostic and Statistical Manual of Mental Disorders*, third edition [DSM-III] criteria for anxiety disorder) maintained a high and nonvariable heart rate with less adaptation to task. In a nonclinical population anxious adolescents also react to the stress of public speaking with higher heart rate and systolic blood pressure elevations than nonanxious adolescents (Matthews, Manuck, & Saab, 1986).

Risk factors for anxiety may include mitral valve prolapse, at least as suggested by some adult studies. Arkfen, Lachman, McLaren, et al. (1990), however, examined a group of children with mitral valve prolapse and found no increased incidence of anxiety compared to normal children. In a study of children at risk for panic determined solely by panic disorder found in their parent, Reichler, Sylvester, and Heide (1988) could find no distinguishing neurobiologic variable that differed from controls. These asymptomatic children at risk for panic were evaluated for mitral valve prolapse, lactate levels after exercise, 24-hour urinary catecholamines, and platelet MAO activity. A trend toward elevated catecholamines and increased MAO activity was found but did not reach statistical significance.

In a different approach to studying the relationship between childhood anxiety and autonomic dysfunction, Childress, Rock, Oslizlok, et al. (1992) studied children with known autonomic dysfunction to see if they had a higher incidence of anxiety disorders than children without autonomic dysfunction. They compared 34 subjects (age 13.9 ± 3 years) with known vasodepressor syncope (a syndrome characterized by abnormal autonomic regulation of blood pressure and cardiac output) with 33 subjects (age 13.3 ± 1.9 years) with insulin-dependent diabetes mellitus (to control for anxiety associated with chronic illness and clinic visits). Among the syncope patients, 37% had DSM-III-R anxiety disorders, compared to 16% of diabetic subjects (Childress et al., 1992). Positive response to orthostatic challenge in the syncopal group correlated with the physiologic instrument of the Revised Children's Manifest Anxiety Scale, and syncopal patients with positive autonomics endorsed significantly higher physiological anxiety than those with diabetes. These results indicate that autonomic dysfunction itself may be a risk factor for the development of anxiety in children and adolescents.

STRUCTURAL AND FUNCTIONAL BRAIN STUDIES

A growing body of literature aims at delineating specific structural and functional abnormalities in anxiety disorders (Table 1.2). The childhood anxiety disorder that has been most thoroughly studied in this regard is childhood-onset OCD. Techniques and strategies used have been structural brain imaging (computed tomography [CT] and MRI), functional brain imaging (PET and single photon emission computerized tomography [SPECT]), electrophysiologic studies (electroencephalography [EEG], evoked potential stimulation studies), and neuropsychological and psychosurgical mapping. Complementing this information are lesion studies, studies of related disorders (Tourette's syndrome, Syndenham's chorea, postencephalitic syndromes), and animal models. These approaches have led to the identification of potential neuroanatomic substrates for OCD. Attention has focused primarily on the orbitofrontal cortex, the basal ganglia (specifically the caudate nucleus), and related areas such as the cingulum. Some investigators have proposed pathology in the frontal cortex (Insel, 1992; Khanna, 1988) and the basal ganglia (Wise & Rapoport, 1989), while others have suggested that these regions form a circuit that is abnormally hyperactive (Baxter, 1990; Modell, Mountz, Curtis, et al., 1989). While structural and functional studies of OCD have been limited primarily to adult forms, we focus here on studies that address childhood onset or adolescents and children.

Structural Brain Imaging

Computed Tomography

Luxenberg, Swedo, Flament, et al. (1988) performed quantitative volumetric CT scans on 10 young adults with childhood-onset OCD. Bilaterally smaller caudate nuclei were found in patients versus normal controls.

TABLE 1.2. Structural and Functional Studies of Children with OCD/Childhood-Onset OCD

Study	Sample size (N)	Age range/mean age (years)	Scan type	Results
Behar, Rapoport, Berg, et al. (1984)	16	9–18 / 13.7 ± 1.6	CT	↑ventricular size
Rapoport, Elkins, Langer, et al. (1981)	9	13–17 / 14.2	CT	Normal
Insel, Donnelly, Lalakea, et al. (1983)	10	[a]	CT	Normal
Luxenberg, Swedo, Flament, et al. (1988)	10	17–24 / 20.7 ± 2.1	Quantitative CT	↓caudate size
Garber, Ananth, Chiu, et al. (1989)	32	[a]	MRI	Abnormality of orbitol frontal cortex, frontal white matter, cingulate gyrus, and lenticular nuclei
Swedo, Schapiro, Grady, et al. (1989)	18	[b]	PET	↑metabolism in right prefrontal and left anterior cingulate regions
Swale, Hymas, Lees, et al. (1991)	6	[a]	PET	↑metabolism in bilateral orbital, premotor, and midfrontal cortex
Martinot, Allilaire, Mazoyer, et al. (1990)	16	[a]	PET	↓metabolism in global grey matter and prefrontal lateral cortex
Machlin, Harris, Pearlson, et al. (1991)	10	[a]	SPECT	↑medial–frontal blood flow

[a]Adults with mixed childhood/adult onset.
[b]Adults with childhood-onset OCD.

An earlier planimetric study of 16 adolescents with OCD revealed a significantly higher mean ventricular/brain ratio (i.e., larger ventricles) among patients versus matched controls (Behar, Rapaport, Berg, et al., 1984). However, these findings were not supported in three studies that found normal ventricular size in patients (Rapoport, Elkins, Langer, et al., 1981; Luxenberg et al., 1988; Insel, Donnelly, Lalakea, et al., 1983).

Magnetic Resonance Imaging

No overt structural abnormalities were found in a study of 32 adults with mixed childhood- and adult-onset OCD (Garber, Ananth, Chiu, et al., 1989). However, subtle regional tissue abnormalities suggestive of pathology in the orbital frontal cortex, frontal white matter, cingulate gyrus, and lenticular nuclei were found using quantitative analysis of the relaxation parameter T1 for hydrogen. The authors (Garber et al., 1989) note that they did not perform morphologic measurements that might have confirmed previous CT findings of ventricular enlargement or caudate atrophy.

A later study of adults did not find gross structural abnormalities. Kellner, Jolley, Holgate, et al. (1991) performed limited measurements on 12 adults with OCD versus healthy controls. No significant differences between groups were found in the head of the caudate nucleus, cingulate gyrus thickness, intracaudate/frontal horn ratio, and area of the corpus callosum. Significantly, this study also does not confirm previous CT findings of caudate atrophy (Luxenberg et al., 1988). This may be due to measurement differences (direct MRI measurements compared to calculated CT volumes) or study group differences (older adults in the MRI study [mean age 35 ± 9 years] compared to young adults with childhood-onset OCD [mean age 20.7 ± 2.1 years] in the CT study; Kellner et al., 1991).

Functional Brain Imaging

Brain function has been studied in adults with PET and SPECT scanning. These techniques permit the study of dynamic biochemistry in a living subject. The most consistent findings of these studies is hypermetabolism of the orbitofrontal region in OCD patients, regardless of whether OCD is of childhood or adult onset.

Positron Emission Tomography

In the only study that specifically addresses childhood-onset OCD (Swedo, Schapiro, Grady, et al., 1989), left orbital frontal hypermetabolism was found in 18 OCD patients (mean age 27.8 ± 7.4 years; mean age of onset of OCD 8.9 ± 2.6 years). Increased glucose metabolism was also found in the right sensorimotor and bilateral prefrontal and anterior cingulate regions of the patients compared to controls. Normalized values (compared to the ipsilateral hemisphere) were increased in the right prefrontal and left anterior cingulate regions. Of note, Swedo et al. (1989) showed correlations between increased glucose metabolism and symptom severity.

Swale, Hymas, Lees, et al. (1991) measured cerebral metabolism in six adults with mixed childhood- and adult-onset OCD who exhibited obsessional slowness (extreme slowness in executing some everyday tasks). In addition to corroborating hypermetabolism in the orbital cortex, hypermetabolism in the premotor and midfrontal cortex was also found. These findings, unique to PET studies, may be due to differences in scanner resolution or technique, methods of analysis, or patient differences (Swale et al., 1991). Of note is that this is the only study to measure oxygen rather than glucose metabolism.

These findings in childhood-onset OCD have been corroborated in three adult studies. Baxter, Phelps, Maziotta, et al. (1987) studied 14 adult OCD patients and found hypermetabolism in the whole cerebral hemispheres, the heads of the caudate nuclei, and the left orbital gyrus, with a trend toward hypermetabolism in the right orbital gyrus. When the metabolic rates were normalized, significant increases were found only in the left orbital gyrus. Limitations of this earlier study include comorbid depression and potential interference from medication. In a follow-up study of 10 adult drug-free nondepressed OCD patients, similar results were found but included elevated normalized metabolic rates in the right as well as left orbital gyrus (Baxter, Schwartz, Maziotta, et al., 1988). Nordahl, Benkelfat, Semple, et al. (1989) also found elevated normalized regional glucose metabolism in the orbital frontal cortex of 8 nondepressed OCD adults compared to 30 normal controls. However, no significant differences in basal ganglia structures were found.

In contrast to these studies, Martinot, Allilaire, Mazoyer, et al. (1990) found global grey matter hypometabolism and prefrontal lateral cortex hypometabolism (normalized) in 16 mixed adult- and childhood-onset OCD adults. The researchers suggest several reasons for the differences between their results and those of other studies, including differences in age and anxiety level of the patients and control sample differences. An interesting finding of their study was a negative correlation between prefrontal cortex metabolism and performance on a neuropsychological task requiring intact frontal lobe function (Stroop Test). This finding again suggests frontal lobe involvement in OCD. Also potentially important to this seemingly divergent study are the findings of Zohar, Insel, Berman, et al. (1989), who studied regional cerebral blood flow in 10 OCD adults with the xenon inhalation technique. They found that during imaginal flooding of a feared stimulus, regional cerebral blood flow increased slightly in the temporal cortex, but it decreased markedly in several cortical regions during actual exposure to the feared stimulus.

Though these PET studies suggested abnormalities in the orbital frontal cortex, the caudate nucleus, and the anterior cingulate regions in OCD patients, a correlational analysis by Horwitz, Swedo, Grady, et al. (1991) was unable to substantiate these findings.

Interesting additional findings of PET studies are the changes in regional metabolism in OCD patients after successful treatment. Swedo, Leonard, Kruesi, et al. (1992) rescanned 13 of their adults with childhood-onset OCD at least a year after treatment with either clomipramine, fluoxetine, or no drug. As a group, there were significant improvements in OCD and anxiety ratings. Rescanning revealed a significant bilateral decrease in normalized orbitofrontal glucose metabolism. The patients were divided into responders and nonresponders to drug treatment. The patients who responded to pharmacotherapy showed a greater decrease in normalized left orbitofrontal metabolism than nonresponders. In addition, among the treated patients, the decrease in right orbitofrontal metabolism was directly correlated with two measures of OCD improvement.

No other posttherapy studies have been done in childhood onset OCD, but the findings of Swedo et al. (1992) are supported in an adult study by Benkelfat, Nordahl, Semple, et al. (1990) that suggests that clomipramine-induced improvement in OCD symptoms is associated with a relative normalization of previously elevated regional brain metabolism in the orbital frontal cortex and the left caudate nucleus. In a recent study, Baxter, Schwartz, Bergman, et al. (1992) performed PET scans on nine OCD patients before and after either fluoxetine hydrochloride or behavior therapy. Patients who responded to either therapy showed a decrease in normalized right caudate nucleus activity. Responders to drug therapy also showed a decrease in normalized right cingulate cortex and left thalamus activity. Though posttherapy studies are not consistent with one another, they may reflect differences in duration of treatment with early changes appearing in the caudate nucleus and later changes in the orbitofrontal region (Baxter et al., 1992).

Single Photon Emission Computerized Tomography

SPECT scanning allows direct measurement of active physiologic processes and is generally more available and less expensive than PET scanning. Most SPECT studies measure regional cerebral blood flow. Xenon-133 is a noninvasive blood flow technique in which trace amounts of xenon gas are inhaled and its clearance from the brain measured by extracranial head probes. Since brain activity is tightly coupled with blood flow, these are indirect methods of studying functional brain activity.

In a SPECT study by Machlin, Harris, Pearlson, et al. (1991), of 10 OCD patients (in 9 of whom onset was in childhood), the patients had a significantly higher ratio of medial–frontal to whole cortex blood flow, but no differences were found between patients and controls in orbito-frontal blood flow. Though this does not support the general consensus of orbitofrontal hypermetabolism seen in PET studies, it is consistent with frontal lobe involvement in OCD and does support the only childhood-onset study (Swedo et al., 1989), which found prefrontal and anterior cingulate involvement. One explanation for not finding orbitofrontal involvement specifically may be that, compared to PET scans, SPECT scan slices are thicker and of lower resolution, making the orbitofrontal cortex more difficult to locate (Machlin et al., 1991). Hoehn-Saric, Pearlson, Harris, et al. (1991) studied 6 childhood-onset OCD patients 3 to 4 months after fluoxetine treatment and found a significant decrease in the medial–frontal cerebral blood flow ratio as well as in their OCD symptomatology.

A recent SPECT study in adults (Rubin, Villanueva-Meyer, Ananth, et al., 1992) revealed increased activity in the high dorsal parietal cortex bilaterally, the left posterofrontal cortex, and in the orbito-frontal cortex bilaterally. There was also reduced activity in the head of the caudate bilaterally.

Zohar et al. (1989) studied 10 OCD adults with the xenon inhalation technique during relaxation, imaginal flooding, and actual exposure to a phobic stimulus. They found that during imaginal flooding, regional cerebral blood flow increased slightly in the temporal cortex, but surprisingly it decreased markedly in several cortical regions during actual exposure to the feared stimulus when the patients' subjective anxiety, heart rate, and blood pressure were the highest. It should be noted that neither the orbital gyri nor the caudate nuclei could be visualized by this technique. Thus the authors raised the possibility that decreased cortical blood flow might reflect a shunting of blood to other cortical or subcortical regions (Zohar et al., 1989).

Electrophysiologic Brain Studies

Electroencephalography

The few EEG studies that have been done in children with OCD have failed to show specific abnormalities. Flament and Rapoport (1984) studied 27 subjects with a mean age of 14.4 years. Four of the EEGs (15%) were found to be mildly abnormal, but the findings were nonspecific. Routine EEGs on 9 adolescents with primary OCD were all normal except one, which showed diffuse nonlocalized slowing (Rapoport et al., 1981). These researchers also made sleep-EEG recordings and found short rapid-eye-movement (REM) latency and total sleep times and a trend toward increased sleep latency and reduced sleep efficiency. These abnormalities are similar to those of adult patients with primary depression. The finding of decreased REM latency was supported in a study by Zohar and Insel (1987) of 10 OCD patients, 5 of whom had childhood onset.

EEG studies of OCD in adults date from as early as the1940s. Varying rates of EEG abnormalities have been shown, and they have been largely nonspecific but with a predominance of abnormalities in the frontal and temporal regions. For reviews of this literature, see Khanna (1988), Flament and Rapoport (1984), and Kettl and Marks (1986).

Recently, computerized EEG has allowed quantitative or power spectral analysis of recordings from patients with OCD. The first of these studies (Flor-Henry, Yeudall, Koles, et al., 1979) looked at 10 adults with OCD, 2 of whom had childhood onset. Results revealed reduced left temporal variability in beta frequencies. Frontal leads were not studied. Khanna, Mukundan, Channabasavanna (1987) found decreased power in the nondominant frontomedial and posterior temporal regions. The most recent study by Perros, Young, Ritson, et al. (1992) of 13 OCD adults showed predominantly left frontotemporal quantitative EEG abnormalities in the theta frequencies. The utility of this new technique in research and clinical applications remains to be determined.

Evoked Potential Studies

The second type of electrophysiologic evidence considered is evoked potential abnormalities in OCD. Most of the studies have been done on adults. Abnormalities in the amplitude and latencies of evoked potential measures have suggested cortical overarousal and left hemisphere involvement in OCD (Towey, Bruder, Hollnader, et al., 1990).

In a study of nine adolescents with primary OCD, visual evoked responses to four intensities of light and visual and auditory evoked-response single trials were recorded (Rapoport et al., 1981). Few significant differences between patients and controls were found. OCD children had a tendency to have shorter latencies and less decrease in latency with increasing stimulus intensity in the N120 and P200 components, but this is probably not unique to OCD children, as similar results have been found in hyperactive children (Buchsbaum & Wender, 1973).

In the first evoked potential study to address topographical mapping in OCD (Malloy, Rasmussen, Braden, et al., 1989), the evidence once again points to orbital frontal dysfunction. The authors compared the P300 of 18 adult OCD patients to 18 normal controls during a cognitive go–no-go task. Amplitudes of P300 in patients were found to be significantly lower in orbital frontal areas during the no-go trials. Of note is that surface electrodes do not accurately measure differences in deeper areas, such as limbic and basal ganglial structures, which have also been implicated in OCD.

Neuropsychological and Psychosurgical Studies

A large neuropsychological testing study in OCD adolescents has been done at the National Institute of Mental Health. Initially Behar et al. (1984) compared 16 adolescents with 16 matched controls and found spatial–perceptual deficits suggesting frontal dysfunction. Cox, Fedio, and Rapoport (1989) extended this study and published the results of 10 neuropsychological tests in 42 OCD adolescents compared to 35 matched controls. Results revealed significant differences in a subset of neuropsychological tests known to be sensitive to frontal and/or caudate abnormalities. These differences were not correlated with measures of OCD severity, which would point to stable cerebral dysfunction rather than distraction by OCD symptoms. These neuropsychological findings in OCD children have been supported in some studies of OCD adults (Flor-Henry, et al., 1979) but not in others (Insel, Donnelly, Lalakea, 1983). For a recent review of the neuropsychological literature in OCD adults, see Christensen, Kim, Dysken, et al. (1992).

The literature on psychosurgical interventions for intractable OCD in adults is extensive, and several reviews exist (Chiocca & Martuza, 1990; Khanna, 1988; Yaryura-Tobias & Neziroglu, 1983). In general, significant improvement occurs when surgical lesions interrupt frontal or cingulate fibers or related regions (Garber et al., 1989). Psychosurgery tends to interrupt potentially abnormal circuits, lending support to a model of cortical–striatal–thalamic–cortical hyperactivity in OCD (Insel, 1992).

Supporting this theory in children is an interesting case report of an 11-year-old right-handed girl with cingulate epilepsy who exhibited severe OCD symptomatology. Scalp EEG and neuropsychological tests suggested right frontal lobe dysfunction. Intracranial EEG showed a focal seizure origin in the right anterior cingulate gyrus. Due to the intractability of her symptoms, a right anterior cingulotomy was performed, which led to a significant improvement in her obsessive thoughts and compulsive behaviors (Levin & Duchowny, 1991).

Involvement of the anterior cingulum in OCD is corroborated by studies of electrical stimulation of this region, which typically causes stereotypic repetitive motions that patients found difficult to resist (Talairach, Bancaud, Geier, et al., 1973).

SUMMARY

Perhaps the most useful tool in exploring the neurobiology of childhood anxiety has been the construct of behavioral inhibition in children provided by Kagan and associates. At present their studies involve the HPA axis and physiologic parameters, which may be suggestive of syndromes in later life but do not fully elucidate the underlying neural pathways that may be involved. For this type of information we await challenge and provocative studies of childhood anxiety syndromes that may directly compare to adult studies. Animal studies of nonhuman primates shed new light on the ontogeny of these syndromes and the relative stability of biologic variables that reflect the HPA axis and locus ceruleus/sympathetic system. A new generation of specific serotonergic agents appears poised to clarify the relationship between childhood syndromes and adult anxiety, although at present no double-blind treatment trials have been completed (Kutcher, Reiter, Gardner, et al., 1992). Structural and functional data in children with anxiety are limited. New magnetic resonance spectroscopy could allow the determination of regional specific brain metabolism through determination of ^{31}P-containing compounds where for ethical reasons PET and SPECT are unavailable. Zametkin, Liebenauer, Fitzgerald, et al. (1993) have demonstrated, however, that PET may be used safely in young adolescents, and so studies of OCD adults need to be replicted with adolescent subjects, extending the technology to other anxiety disorders of childhood.

REFERENCES

Abelson, J. L., Glitz, D., Cameron, O. G., et al. (1991). Blunted growth hormone response to clonidine in patients with generalized anxiety disorder. *Archives of General Psychiatry, 48*, 157–162.

Abelson, J. L., & Nesse, R. M. (1990). Cholecystokinin-4 and panic. *Archives of General Psychiatry, 47*, 395.

Abelson, J. L., Neese, R. M., & Vinik, A. (1990). Treatment of panic-like attacks with a long-acting analogue of somatostatin. *Journal of Clinical Psychopharmocology, 10*, 128–132.

Arkfen, C. L., Lachman, A. S., McLaren, M. J., et al. (1990). Mitral valve prolapse: Associations with symptoms and anxiety. *Pediatrics, 85(3)*, 311–315.

Ballenger, J. C., Post, R. M., Jimerson, D. C., et al. (1981). Cerebrospinal fluid (CSF) noradrenergic correlations with anxiety in normals. *Scientific Proceedings of the American Psychiatric Association, 134*, 235.

Ballenger, J. C., Post, R. M., Jimerson, D. C., et al. (1984). Neurobiological correlates of depression and anxiety in normal individuals. In R. M. Post & J. C. Ballenger (Eds.), *Neurobiology of mood disorders* (pp. 481–501). Baltimore: Williams & Wilkins.

Baxter, L. R. (1990). Brain imaging as a tool in establishing a theory of brain pathology in obsessive–compulsive disorder. *Journal of Clinical Psychiatry, 51* (Suppl. 2), 22–25.

Baxter, L. R., Phelps, M. E., Mazziotta, J. C., et al. (1987). Local cerebral glucose metabolic rates in obsessive–compulsive disorder: A comparison with rates in unipolar depression and in normal controls. *Archives of General Psychiatry, 44,* 211–218.

Baxter, L. R., Schwartz, J. M., Bergman, K. S., et al. (1992). Caudate glucose metabolic rate changes with both drug and behavior therapy for obsessive–compulsive disorder. *Archives of General Psychiatry, 49,* 681–689.

Baxter, L. R., Schwartz, J. M., Mazziotta, J. C., et al. (1988). Cerebral glucose metabolic rates in nondepressed patients with obsessive–compulsive disorder. *American Journal of Psychiatry, 145,* 1560–1563.

Behar, D., Rapoport, J. L., Berg, C. J., et al. (1984). Computerized tomography and neuropsychological test measures in adolescents with obsessive–compulsive disorder. *American Journal of Psychiatry, 141,* 363–369.

Beidel, D. (1988). Psychophysiological assessment of anxious emotional states in children. *Journal of Abnormal Psychology, 97,* 80–82.

Beidel, D. C. (1989). Assessing anxious emotion: A review of psychophysiological assessment in children. *Clinical Psychology Review, 9,* 717–736.

Benkelfat, C., Bradwejn, J., Meyer, E., et al. (1992, July 2). Neuroanatomical correlates of CCK-4-induced-panic in normals. *Proceedings of the 18th C.I.N.P. Congress, Nice, France, 15* (Suppl. 1, Part B), 223.

Benkelfat, C., Murphy, D. L., Zohar, J., et al. (1989). Clomipramine in obsessive–compulsive disorder. *Archives of General Psychiatry, 46,* 23–28.

Benkelfat, C., Nordahl, T. E., Semple, W. E., et al. (1990). Local cerebral glucose metabolic rates in obsessive–compulsive disorder: Patients treated with clomipramine. *Archives of General Psychiatry, 47,* 840–848.

Biederman, J., Rosenbaum, J. F., Hirshfeld, D. R., et al. (1990). Psychiatric correlates of behavioral inhibition in young children of parents with and without psychiatric disorders. *Archives of General Psychiatry, 47,* 21–26.

Bradwejn, J., Koszycki, D., Annable, L., et al. (1992). A dose-ranging study of the behavorial and cardiovascular effects of CCK-tetrapeptide in panic disorder. *Biological Psychiatry, 32,* 903–912.

Bradwejn, J., Koszycki, D., Couetoux du Tertre, A., et al. (1992). L-365,260: A CCK-B antagonist blocks CCK-4-panic. In *New research program and abstracts,* 145th Meeting of the American Psychiatric Association, Washington, DC, NR138, p. 9.

Bradwejn, J., Koszycki, D., & Shriqui, C. (1991). Enhanced sensitivity to cholescystokinin tetrapeptide in panic disorder-clinical and behavioral findings. *Archives of General Psychiatry, 48,* 603–610.

Breese, G. R., Smith, R. D., Mueller, R. A., et al. (1973). Induction of adrenal catecholamine synthesizing enzymes following mother–infant separation. *Nature, 246,* 94.

Breslow, M. F., Fankhauser, M. P., Potter, R. L., et al. (1989). Role of gamma-aminobutyric acid in antipanic drug efficacy. *American Journal of Psychiatry, 146*(3), 353–356.

Buchsbaum, M. S., & Wender, P. (1973). Average evoked responses in normal and minimally brain dysfunctioned children treated with amphetamines. *Archives of General Psychiatry, 29,* 764–770.

Cameron, O. G., Smith, C. B., Lee, M. A., et al. (1990). Adrenergic status in anxiety disorders: Platelet alpha2-adrenergic receptor binding, blood pressure, pulse, and plasma catecholamines in panic and generalized anxiety disorder patients and in normal subjects. *Biological Psychiatry, 28,* 3–20.

Charney, D. S., Goodman, W. K., Price, L. H., et al. (1988). Serotonin function in obsessive–compulsive disorder: A comparison of the effects of tryptophan and m-chlorophenylpiperazine in patients and healthy subjects. *Archives of General Psychiatry, 45,* 177–185.

Charney, D. S., & Heninger, G. B. (1986). Abnormal regulation of noradrenergic function in panic disorders. *Archives of General Psychiatry, 43,* 1042–1054.

Charney, D. S., Heninger, G. R., & Brier, A. (1984). Noradrenergic function in panic anxiety: Effects of yohimbine in healthy subjects and patients with agoraphobia and panic disorder. *Archives of General Psychiatry, 41,* 751–763.

Charney, D. S., & Redmond, D. E. (1987). Neurobiologic mechanisms in human anxiety: Evidence supporting central noradrenergic hyperactivity. *Neuropharmacology, 22,* 1531–1536.

Charney, D. S., Woods, S. W., Goodman, W. K., et al. (1987). Serotonin function in anxiety: Vol. II. Effects of the serotonin agonist mCPP in panic disorder patients and healthy subjects. *Psychopharmocology, 92,* 14–24.

Charney, D. S., Woods, S. W., & Heninger, G. R. (1989). Noradrenergic function in generalized anxiety disorder: Effects of yohimbine in healthy subjects and patients with generalized anxiety disorder. *Psychiatry Research, 27,* 173–182.

Childress, A. C., Rock, C. M., Oslizlok, M. B., et al. (1992). Vasodepressor syncope and anxiety: Is there a relationship? In *Proceedings of the Annual Meeting of the American Academy of Child and Adolescent Psychiatry,* Washington, DC.

Chiocca, E. A., & Martuza, R. L. (1990). Neurosurgical therapy of the obsessive compulsive disorder. In M. A. Jenike, L. Baer, & W. E. Minichiellow (Eds.), *Obsessive compulsive disorders: Theory and management.* St. Louis, MO: Mosby–Year Book.

Chopin, P., & Briley, M. (1987). Animal models of anxiety: The effect of compounds that modify 5-HT neurotransmission. *Trends in Pharmacological Science, 8,* 383.

Christensen, K. J., Kim, S. W., Dysken, M. W., et al. (1992). Neuropsychological performance in obsessive–compulsive disorder. *Biological Psychiatry, 31,* 4–18.

Chrousos, G. P., & Gold, P. W. (1992). The concepts of stress and stress system disorders overview of physical and behavioral homeostasis. *Journal of the American Medical Association, 267,* 1244–1252.

Coryell, W. H., Black, D. W., Kelly, M. W., et al. (1989). HPA axis disturbance in obsessive–compulsive disorder. *Psychiatry Research, 30,* 243–251.

Couetoux du Tertre, A., Bradwejn, J., Koszycki, D., et al. (1992, May 4). Lack of effect of flumazenil on CCK-4-panic. In *New research program and abstracts,* 145th Meeting of the American Psychiatric Association, Washington, DC, NR138, p. 81.

Cox, C. S., Fedio, P., & Rapoport, J. L. (1989). Neuropsychological testing of obsessive–compulsive adolescents. In J. L. Rapoport (Ed.), *Obsessive com-*

pulsive disorder in children and adolescents (pp. 73–85). Washington, DC: American Psychiatric Press.

Den Boer, J. A., & Westenberg, H. G. M. (1990). Behavioral, neuroendocrine and biochemical effects of 5-hydroxytryptophan administration in panic disorder. *Psychiatry Research, 31,* 267–278.

Dorow, R., Horowski, R., Paschleke, G., et al. (1983). Severe anxiety induced by FG 7142, a beta-carboline ligand for benzodiazepine receptors. *Lancet, i,* 98–99.

File, S. F. (1984). The neurochemistry of anxiety. In G. D. Burrows, T. R. Norman, & B. Davis (Eds.), *Anti-anxiety agents.* Amsterdam, The Netherlands: Elsevier.

Flament, M., & Rapoport, J. L. (1984). Childhood obsessive compulsive disorder. In T. R. Insel (Ed.), *New findings in obsessive compulsive disorder* (pp. 24–43). Washington, DC: American Psychiatric Press.

Flament, M. F., Rapoport, J. L., Murphy, D. L., et al. (1987). Biochemical changes during clomiprimine treatment of childhood obsessive–compulsive disorder. *Archives of General Psychiatry, 44,* 219–225.

Flor-Henry, P., Yeudall, L. T., Koles, Z. J., et al. (1979). Neuropsychological and power spectral EEG—Investigations of the obsessive–compulsive syndrome. *Biological Psychiatry, 14,* 119–130.

Garber, H. J., Ananth, J. V., Chiu, L. C., et al. (1989). Nuclear magnetic resonance study of obsessive compulsive disorder. *American Journal of Psychiatry, 146,* 1001–1005.

Germine, M., Goddard, A. W., Woods, S. W., et al. (1992). Anger and anxiety responses to m-chlorophenylpiperazine in generalized anxiety disorder. *Biological Psychiatry, 32,* 457–461.

Gorman, J. M., Liebowitz, M. R., Fyer, A. J., et al. (1989). A neuroanatomical hypothesis for panic disorder. *American Journal of Psychiatry, 146,* 148–161.

Goldberger, E., & Rapoport, J. L. (1991). Canine acral lick dermatitis: Response to the anti-obsessional drug clomipramine. *Journal of the American Animal Hospital Association, 27,* 179–182.

Hanna, G. L., Yuwiler, A., Cantwell, D. P. (1991). Whole blood serotonin in juvenile obsessive–compulsive disorder. *Biological Psychiatry 29,* 738–744.

Harris, J. C. (1989). Experimental animal modeling of depression and anxiety. *Psychiatric Clinics of North America, 12,* 815–836.

Heilig, M., & Widerlov E. (1990). Neuropeptide Y: An overview of central distribution, functional aspects, and possible involvement in neuropsychiatric illnesses. *Acta Psychiatrica Scandinavica, 82,* 95–114.

Heninger, G. R., & Charney, D. S. (1988). Monoamine receptor systems and anxiety disorders. In G. Winokur & W. Coryell (Eds.), *Psychiatric clinics of North America: Vol. 11. Biologic systems: Their relationship to anxiety* (pp. 309–326). Philadelphia: Saunders.

Heninger, G. R., Charney, D. S., & Price, L. H. (1988). Alpha2-adrenergic receptor sensitivity in depression: The plasma MHPG, behavioral, and cardiovascular responses to yohimbine. *Archives of General Psychiatry, 45,* 718–726.

Higley, J. D., Hasert, M. F., Suomi, S. J., et al. (1991). Nonhuman primate model of alchohol abuse: Effects of early experience, personality, and stress on alchohol consumption. *Proceedings of the National Academy of Science, USA, 88,* 7261–7265.

Higley, J. D., & Suomi, S. J. (1989). Temperamental reactivity in nonhuman primates. In D. Kohnstamm, J. E. Bates, & M. K. Rothbart (Eds.), *Temperament in childhood* (pp. 153–167). Chichester, England: Wiley.

Higley, J. D., Suomi, S. J., & Linnoila, M. (1988). Central amine correlates of timidity and affective disturbances in rhesus monkeys. *American Journal of Primatology, 14,* 425.

Higley, J. D., Suomi, S. J., & Linnoila, M. (1990). Developmental influences on the serotonin system and timidity in the nonhuman primate. In E. F. Coccaro & D. L. Murphy (Eds.), *Serotonin in major psychiatric disorders* (pp. 29–46). Washington, DC: American Psychiatric Press.

Higley, J. D., Suomi, S. J., & Linnoila M. (1991). CSF monoamine metabolite concentrations vary according to age, rearing, and sex, and are influenced by the stressor of social separation in rhesus monkeys. *Psychopharmacology, 103,* 551–556.

Higley, J. D., Suomi, S. J., & Linnoila, M. (1992). A longitudinal study of CSF monoamine metabolite and plasma cortisol concentrations in young rhesus monkeys: Effects of early experience, age, sex, and stress on continuity of interindividual differences. *Biological Psychiatry, 32,* 127–145.

Higley, J. D., Thompson, W. W., Champoux, M., et al. (1993). Paternal and maternal genetic and environmental contributions to cerebrospinal fluid monoamine metabolites in Rhesus monkeys (*Macaca mulatta*). *Archives of General Psychiatry, 50,* 615–623.

Hoehn-Saric, R., Pearlson, G. D., Harris, G. J., et al. (1991). Effects of fluoxetine on regional cerebral blood flow in obsessive compulsive patients. *American Journal of Psychiatry, 148,* 1243–1245.

Hollander, E., Fay, M., Cohen, B., et al. (1988). Serotonergic and noradrenergic sensitivity in obsessive–compulsive disorder: Behavioral findings. *American Journal of Psychiatry, 145,* 1015–1018.

Hollander, E., Levin, A. P., & Liebowitz, M. R. (1990). Biological tests in the differential diagnosis of anxiety disorders. In J. C. Ballenger (Ed.), *Clinical aspects of panic disorder* (pp. 31–46). New York: Wiley–Liss.

Horwitz, B., Swedo, S. E., Grady, C. L., et al. (1991). Cerebral metabolic pattern in obsessive compulsive disorder: Altered intercorrelations between regional rates of glucose utilization. *Psychiatry Research, 40,* 221–237.

Insel, T. R. (1992). Toward a neuroanatomy of obsessive compulsive disorder. *Archives of General Psychiatry, 49,* 739–744.

Insel, T. R., Donnelly, E. F., Lalakea, M. L., et al. (1983). Neurological and neuropsychological studies of patients with obsessive compulsive disorder. *Biological Psychiatry, 18,* 741–751.

Kagan, J., Reznick, J. S., & Snidman, N. (1987). The physiology and psychology of behavioral inhibition in children. *Child Development, 58,* 1459–1473.

Kagan, J., Reznick, J. S., & Snidman, N. (1988). Biological bases of childhood shyness. *Science, 240,* 167–171.

Kahn, R. S., Asnis, G. M., Wetzler, S., et al. (1988). Neuroendocrine evidence for serotonin receptor hypersensitivity in patients with panic disorder. *Psychopharmacology*, 96, 360–364.

Kahn, R. S., Wetzler, S., van Praag, H. M., et al. (1988). Behavioral indications of serotonergic supersensitivity in patients with panic disorder. *Psychiatry Research*, 25, 101–104.

Kalin, N. H. (1993). The neurobiology of fear. *Scientific American*, 268, 94–101.

Kalin, N. H., Shelton, S. E., & Turner, J. G. (1992). Effects of beta-carboline on fear-related behavioral and neurohormonal responses in infant rhesus monkeys. *Biological Psychiatry*, 31(10), 1008–1019.

Kellner, C. H., Jolley, R. R., Holgate, R. C., et al. (1991). Brain MRI in obsessive compulsive disorder. *Psychiatry Research*, 36, 45–49.

Kettl, P. A., & Marks, I. M. (1986). Neurological factors in obsessive compulsive disorder—Two case reports and a review of the literature. *British Journal of Psychiatry*, 149, 315–319.

Khanna, S. (1988). Obsessive compulsive disorder: Is there a frontal lobe dysfunction? *Biological Psychiatry*, 24, 602–613.

Khanna, S., Mukundan, C. R., & Channabasavanna, S. M. (1987, April). *Computerized electroencephalogram in obsessive compulsive disorder*. Presented at the International Conference on New Directions in Affective Disorders, Jerusalem, Israel.

Klein, D. F. (1981). Anxiety reconceptualized. In D. F. Klein & J. Rabkin (Eds.), *Psychopharmocology: A generation of research*. New York: Raven.

Klein, E., Zohar, J., Geraci, M., et al. (1991). Anxiogenic effects of m-CPP in patients with panic disorder: Comparison to caffeine's anxiogenic effects. *Biological Psychiatry*, 30, 973–984.

Ko, G. N., Elsworth, J. D., Roth, R. H., et al. (1983). Panic-induced elevation of plasma MHPG levels in phobic–anxious patients. *Archives of General Psychiatry*, 40, 425–430.

Kruesi, M. J., Swedo, S., Leonard, H., et al. (1990). CSF somatostatin in childhood psychiatric disorders: A preliminary investigation. *Psychiatry Research*, 33, 277–284.

Kutcher, S. P., Reiter, S., Gardner, D. M., et al. (1992). The pharmocotherapy of anxiety disorders in children and adolescents. *Psychiatric Clinics of North America*, 15, 41–67.

Leckman, J. F., Riddle, M. A., Berrettini, W. H., et al. (1988). Elevated CSF dynorphin A[1-8] in Tourette's syndrome. *Life Science*, 43, 2015–2023.

Lesch, K. P., Hoh, A., Disselkamp-Tietze, J., et al. (1991). 5-Hydroxytryptamine1A (5-HT1A) receptor responsivity in obsessive–compulsive disorder: Comparison of patients and controls. *Archives of General Psychiatry*, 48, 540–547.

Lesch, K. P., Wiesmann, M., Hoh, A., et al. (1992). 5HT1A receptor–effector system responsivity in panic disorder. *Psychopharmocolgy*, 106, 111–117.

Levin, B., & Duchowny, M. (1991). Childhood obsessive compulsive disorder and cingulate epilepsy. *Biological Psychiatry*, 30, 1049–1055.

Luxenberg, J. S., Swedo, S. E., Flament, M. F., et al. (1988). Neuroanatomical abnormalities in obsessive compulsive disorder detected with quantitative x-ray computed tomography. *American Journal of Psychiatry*, 145, 1089–1093.

Lydiard, R. B., Ballenger, J. C., Laraia, M. T., et al. (1992). CSF cholescystokinin in patients with panic disorder and in normal comparison subjects. *American Journal of Psychiatry, 149*(5), 691–693.

Machlin, S. R., Harris, G. J., Pearlson, G. D., et al. (1991). Elevated medial–frontal cerebral blood flow in obsessive compulsive patients: A SPECT study. *American Journal of Psychiatry, 148*, 1240–1242.

Malloy, P., Rasmussen, S., Braden, W., et al. (1989). Topographic evoked potential mapping in obsessive compulsive disorder: Evidence of frontal lobe dysfunction. *Psychiatry Research, 28*, 63–71.

Martinot, J. L., Allilaire, J. F., Mazoyer, B. M., et al. (1990). Obsessive compulsive disorder: A clinical, neuropsychological, and positron emission tomography study. *Acta Psychiatrica Scandinavica, 82*, 233–242.

Matthews, K. A., Manuck, S. B., & Saab, P. G. (1986). Cardiovascular responses of adolescents during a naturally occurring stressor and their behavioral and psychophysiological predictors. *Psychophysiology, 23*, 198–209.

McBurnett, K., Lahey, B. B., Frick, P. J., et al. (1991). Anxiety, inhibition, and conduct disorder in children: Vol. II. Relation to salivary cortisol. *Journal of the American Academy of Child and Adolescent Psychiatry, 30*, 192–196.

Meaney, M. J., Aitken, D. H., Bodnoff, S. R., et al. (1985). Early postnatal handling alters glucocorticoid receptor concentrations in selected brain regions. *Behavioral Neuroscience, 99*, 765–770.

Mineka, S. (1985). Animal models of anxiety-based disorders: Their usefulness and limitations. In A. H. Tuma & J. Maser (Eds.), *Anxiety and anxiety disorders* (pp. 199–244). Hillsdale, NJ: Erlbaum.

Modell, J., Mountz, J., Curtis, G., et al. (1989). Neurophysiologic dysfunction in basal ganglia/limbic striatal and thalamocortical circuits as a pathogenetic mechanism of obsessive compulsive disorder. *Journal of Neuropsychiatry, 1*, 27–36.

Ninan, P. T., Insel, T. M., Cohen, R. M., et al. (1982). Benzodiazepine receptor mediated experimental "anxiety" in primates. *Science, 218*, 1332–1334.

Nordahl, T. E., Benkelfat, C., Semple, W. E., et al. (1989). Cerebral glucose metabolic rates in obsessive compulsive disorder. *Neuropsychopharmacology, 2*, 23–28.

Nutt, D. J., Glue, P., Lawson, C., et al. (1990). Flumazenil provocation of panic attacks: Evidence for altered benzodiazepine receptor sensitivity in panic disorder. *Archives of General Psychiatry, 47*, 917–925.

Overton, J. M., & Fisher, L. A. (1989). Modulation of central nervous system actions of corticotropin-releasing factor by dynorphin-related peptides. *Brain Research, 488*, 233–240.

Owens, M. J., & Nemeroff, C. B. (1990). Neurotransmitter regulation of CRF secretion *in vitro*. In E. B. De Souza & C. B. Nemeroff (Eds.), *Corticotropin-releasing factor: Basic and clinical studies of a neuropeptide* (pp. 107–114). Boca Raton, FL: CRC Press.

Palmour, R., Ervin, R., Bradwejn, J., et al. (1991). The anxiogenic and cardiovascular effects of CCK-4 are blocked by the CCK-B antagonist LY262,691. *Neuroscience, 17*, 1602.

Perros, P., Young, E. S., Ritson, J. J., et al. (1992). Power spectral EEG analysis and EEG variability in obsessive compulsive disorder. *Brain Topography*, *4*, 187–191.

Pigott, T. A., Hill, J. L., Grady, T. A., et al. (1993). A comparison of the behavioral effects of oral versus intravenous mCPP administration in OCD patients, and the effect of metergoline prior to IV mCPP. *Biological Psychiatry, 33*, 3–14.

Post, R. M., Ballenger, J. C., & Goodwin, F. K. (1980). Cerebrospinal fluid studies of neurotransmitter function in manic and depressive illness. In J. H. Wood (Ed.), *Neurobiology of cerebrospinal fluid* (pp. 755–759). New York: Plenum Press.

Puig-Antich, J. (1987). Affective disorders in children and adolescents: Diagnostic validity and psychobiology. In H. Y. Meltzer (Ed.), *Psychopharmacology: The third generation of progress.* New York: Raven.

Rapoport, J., Elkins, R., Langer, D. H., et al. (1981). Childhood obsessive compulsive disorder. *American Journal of Psychiatry, 138*, 1545–1554.

Rasmussen, S. A., Goodman, W. K., Woods, S. W., et al. (1987). Effects of yohimbine in obsessive compulsive disorder. *Psychopharmocology, 93*, 308–313.

Redmond, D. E., & Huang, Y. H. (1979). Current concepts II. New evidence for a locus coeruleus-norepinephrine connection with anxiety. *Life Science, 25*, 2149–2162.

Reichler, R. J., Sylvester, C. E., & Hyde, T. S. (1988). Biological studies on offspring of panic disorder probands. In D. J. Dunner, E. S. Gershon, & J. E. Barrett (Eds.), *Relatives at risk for mental disorder* (pp. 103–125). New York: Raven.

Reite, M., & Capitanio, J. P. (1985). On the nature of social separation and social attachment. In M. Reite & T. Field (Eds.), *Psychology of attachment.* New York: Academic Press.

Resnik, J. S., Kagan, J., Sniderman, N., et al. (1986). Inhibited and uninhibited children: A follow-up study. *Child Development, 57*, 660–680.

Ritvo, E. R., Yuwiler, A., Geller, E., et al. (1971). Maturational changes in blood serotonin levels and platelet counts. *Biochemical Medicine, 5*, 90–96.

Rogeness, G. A., Cepeda, C., Macedo, C. A., et al. (1990). Differences in heart rate and blood pressure in children with conduct disorder, major depression, and separation anxiety. *Psychiatric Research, 33*, 199–206.

Rogeness, G. A., Javors, M. A., Maas, J. W., et al. (1990). Catecholamines and diagnoses in children. *Journal of the American Academy of Child and Adolescent Psychiatry, 29*, 234–241.

Rogeness, G. A., Maas, J. W., Javors, M. A., et al. (1988). Diagnosis, catecholamine metabolism, and plasma dopamine-beta-hydroxylase. *Journal of the American Academy of Child and Adolescent Psychiatry, 27*, 121–125.

Ross C. A., & Matas, M. (1987). A clinical trial of busiprone and diazepam in the treatment of generalized anxiety disorder. *Canadian Journal of Psychiatry, 32*, 351–355.

Rubin, R. T., Villanueva-Meyer, J., Ananth, J., et al. (1992). Regional xenon133 cerebral blood flow and cerebral 99m technetium HMPAO uptake in unmedicated patients with obsessive compulsive disorder and matched normal control subjects—Determination by high-resolution single photon emission computed tomography. *Archives of General Psychiatry, 149,* 695–702.

Sapolsky, R. M. (1990). Adrenocortical function, social rank, and personality among wild baboons. *Biological Psychiatry, 28,* 862–878.

Schreiber, R., & De Vry, J. (1993). 5-HT1A receptor ligands in animal models of anxiety, impulsivity and depression: Multiple mechanisms of action? *Progress in Neuro-Psychopharmacology and Biological Psychiatry, 17,* 87–104.

Sheehan, D. V., Claycomb, J. B., Surman, O. S., et al. (1986). Panic attacks and the sexamethasone suppression test. *American Journal of Psychiatry, 140,* 1063–1064.

Sheehan, D. V., Raj, A. B., Sheehan, K. H., et al. (1988). The relative efficacy of busiprone, imipramine and placebo in panic disorder: A preliminary report. *Pharmacology, Biochemistry, and Behavior, 29,* 815–817.

Siever, L. J., Insel, T. R., Jimerson, D. C., et al. (1983). Growth hormone response to clonidine in obsessive–compulsive patients. *British Journal of Psychiatry, 142,* 184–187.

Stein, D. J., Shoulberg, N., Helton, K., et al. (1992). The neuroethnological approach to obsessive–compulsive disorder. *Comprehensive Psychiatry, 33,* 274–281.

Swale, G. V., Hymas, N. F., Lees, A. J., et al. (1991). Obsessional slowness—Functional studies with positron emission tomography. *Brain, 114,* 2191–2202.

Swedo, S. E., Leonard, H. L., Kruesi, M. J., et al. (1992). Cerebrospinal fluid neurochemistry in children and adolescents with obsessive–compulsive disorder. *Archives of General Psychiatry, 49,* 29–36.

Swedo, S. E., Pietrini, P., Leonard, H. L., et al. (1992). Cerebral glucose metabolism in childhood onset obsessive compulsive disorder—Revisualization during pharmacotherapy. *Archives of General Psychiatry, 49,* 690–694.

Swedo, S. E., Schapiro, M. B., Grady, C. L., et al. (1989). Cerebral glucose metabolism in childhood onset obsessive compulsive disorder. *Archives of General Psychiatry, 46,* 518–523.

Talairach, J., Bancaud, J., Geier, S., et al. (1973). The cingulate gyrus and human behavior. *Electroencephalography and Clinical Neurophysiology, 34,* 45–52.

Targum, S. D., & Marshall, L. E. (1989). Fenfluramine provocation of anxiety in patients with panic disorder. *Psychiatry Research, 28,* 295–306.

Tennes, K., & Kreye, M. (1985). Children's adrenocortical responses to classroom activities and tests in elementary school. *Psychosomatic Medicine, 47,* 451–460.

Tennes, K., Downey, K., & Vernadakis, A. (1977). Urinary cortisol excretion rates and anxiety in normal one-year-old infants. *Psychosomatic Medicine, 39,* 178–187.

Thoren, P., Asberg, M., Bertilsson, L., et al. (1980). Clomipramine treatment of obsessive–compulsive disorder: Vol. II. Biochemical aspects. *Archives of General Psychiatry, 37,* 1289–1295.

Towey, J., Bruder, G., Hollnader, E., et al. (1990). Endogenous event-related potentials in obsessive compulsive disorder. *Biological Psychiatry, 28,* 92–98.

Uhde, T. W., Boulenger, J. P., Siever, L. J., et al. (1982). Animal models of anxiety: Implications for research in humans. *Psychopharmacology Bulletin, 18,* 47–52.

Uhde, T. W., Vittone, B. J., Siever, L. J. et al. (1986). Blunted growth hormone response to clonidine in panic disorder patients. *Biological Psychiatry, 21,* 1077–1081.

Uhde, T. W., Tancer, M. E., Rubinow, D. R., et al. (1992). Evidence for hypothalamo-growth hormone dysfunction in panic disorder: Profile of growth hormone (GH) responses to clonidine, yohimbine, caffeine, glucose, GRF and TRH in panic disorder patients versus healthy volunteers. *Neuropsychopharmocolgy, 6,* 101–118.

Wahlestedt, C., Pich, E. M., Koob, G. F., et al. (1993). Modulation of anxiety and neuropeptide Y-Y1 receptors by antisense oligodeoxynucleotides. *Science, 259,* 528–531.

Weizman, A., Mandel, A., Barber, Y., et al. (1992). Decreased platelet imiprimine binding in Tourette's syndrome children with obsessive–compulsive disorder. *Biological Psychiatry, 31,* 705–711.

Westenberg, H. G., & den Boer, J. A. (1989). Serotonin-influencing drugs in the treatment of panic disorder. *Psychopathology, 22,* 68–77.

Westenberg, H. G. M., den Boer, J. A., & Kahn, R. S. (1987). Psychopharmacology of anxiety disorders: On the role of serotonin in the treatment of anxiety states and phobic disorders. *Psychopharmacology Bulletin, 23,* 145–149.

Wise, S. P., & Rapoport, J. L. (1989). Obsessive compulsive disorder: Is it basal ganglia dysfunction? In J. L. Rapoport (Ed.), *Obsessive compulsive disorder in children and adolescents* (pp. 327–344). Washington, DC: American Psychiatric Press.

Yaryura-Tobias, J. A., & Neziroglu F. (1983). *Obsessive compulsive disorders.* New York: Marcel Dekker.

Yeragani, V. K., Balon, R., Pohl, R., et al. (1990). Decreased R-R variance in panic disorder patients. *Acta Psychiatrica Scandinavica, 81,* 554–559.

Zametkin, A. J., Liebenauer, L. L., Fitzgerald, G. A., et al. (1993). Brain metabolism in teenagers with attention-deficit hyperactivity disorder. *Archives of General Psychiatry, 50,* 33–340.

Zifa, E., & Fillion, G. (1992). 5-Hydroxytryptamine receptors. *Pharmacological Reviews, 44,* 401–458.

Zohar, J., & Insel, T. R. (1987). Obsessive compulsive disorder: Psychobiological approaches to diagnosis, treatment, and pathophysiology. *Biological Psychiatry, 22,* 667–687.

Zohar, J., Insel, T. R., Berman, K. F., et al. (1989). Anxiety and cerebral blood flow during behavioral challenge: Dissociation of central from peripheral and subjective measures. *Archives of General Psychiatry, 46,* 505–510.

Zohar, J., Insel, T. R., Zohar-Kadouch, R. C., et al. (1988). Serotonergic responsivity in obsessive–compulsive disorder effects of chronic clomipramine treatment. *Archives of General Psychiatry, 45,* 167–172.

Chapter 2

Neuropsychology

Stephen R. Hooper
John S. March

The clinical and experimental study of childhood anxiety disorders has had a long history, dating back at least to the early conceptualizations of Kraepelin (1883; cited in Walk, 1964), Emminghaus (1887; cited in Harms, 1967), and Kierkegaard (1844/1944) and to Freud's early "Little Hans" case (Freud, 1909/1955) and Watson and Rayner's "Little Albert" case (Watson & Rayner, 1920). It really was not until the publication of the third edition of the *Diagnostic and Statistical Manual of Mental Disorders* (DSM-III; American Psychiatric Association, 1980), however, that the category of childhood and adolescent anxiety disorders was operationalized in a way that spurred increased, systematic study of this group of disorders. DSM-III and its subsequent revisions (DSM-III-R, DSM-IV; American Psychiatric Association, 1987, 1994) have provided specific criteria for clinical and research endeavors, and consequently they have contributed to the increased examination of the reliability, validity, and clinical utility of diagnoses of anxiety disorders in children and adolescents.

Despite this increased interest in child and adolescent anxiety disorders, child psychiatry and related fields (e.g., psychology) are only beginning to uncover some of the biological and biobehavioral correlates of these disorders. In particular, while findings about biological bases of anxiety disorders are emerging at a rapid rate (Chapter 3), there are relatively few findings related to the neuropsychology of child and adolescent anxiety disorders. This chapter provides an overview of several key aspects of the neuropsychological foundations of anxiety disorders in children and adolescents. First, we explore the effects of neuropsychological deficits on manifest anxiety. Second, we present several key models examining the interface between neuropsychology and anxiety disorders. Third, we rotate the conceptual axis and examine some of the findings on the effects of anxiety on neurocognitive performance, and in the fourth section we present available neuropsychological findings in DSM categories of child and adolescent anxiety. The chapter concludes with discussion about the use of a neuropsychological perspective for contributing to our understanding of anxiety disorders in children and adolescents.

NEUROLOGICALLY BASED DEFICITS AND MANIFEST ANXIETY

Although other contributing agents have been implicated in the manifestation of anxiety (e.g., neuroendocrine disturbances, psychogenic factors), the presence of brain dysfunction in childhood generally has been associated with a greater risk for the development of psychiatric disorders, particularly internalizing disorders, and this risk appears to be far greater than risks for other physical handicaps (Brown, Chadwick, Shaffer, et al., 1981; Rutter, Graham, & Yule, 1970; Shaffer, Schonfeld, O'Connor, et al., 1985). Moreover, the effects appear to persist and impede the child's long-term adjustment in many important respects (Breslau & Marshall, 1985; Shaffer et al., 1985).

One of the best investigations on this topic comes from the well-known Isle of Wight epidemiological studies of school-age children by Rutter and his colleagues, conducted a quarter of a century ago (Rutter et al., 1970). Using multiple assessment procedures and controlling for rater bias, Rutter et al. found that about 6 to 7% of the general population of children studied manifested a psychiatric disorder consisting of some persistent emotional, behavioral, or social disability. The rate was nearly two times (11.5%) that for children having chronic handicapping physical conditions not involving the central nervous system. This group consisted of children with disorders such as asthma, diabetes, heart disease, and orthopedic deformities. In contrast, the rate of psychiatric disorder was more than five times higher (34.5%) in their neuroepileptic group, consisting of all children ranging from 5 to 14 years of age with cerebral palsy, epilepsy, or some other frank neurological disorder above the brain stem. Even after eliminating all cases with an IQ ≤ 85 (low IQ was found to be associated with an increased risk for psychiatric disorder), the rate of psychiatric disorder was still twice as high in the neuroepileptic group as in the "other physical handicap" group.

Among children in the neuroepileptic group, both the severity and the nature of the neurological condition appeared to be related to the risk of psychiatric disorder. Thus, psychiatric disorders were more likely in children with bilateral as opposed to unilateral brain lesions. Among children with cerebral palsies, psychiatric disorders were more likely in those with strabismus, impaired language, or specific reading difficulties; among the children with epilepsy, the risk was greater in those with low IQ or psychomotor seizures. However, the prevalence was actually less among children with the most severe debilitating handicaps, suggesting that these children may be spared from psychiatric difficulties by having conditions that unambiguously free them from competing in otherwise stressful pursuits.

The Isle of Wight study (Rutter et al., 1970) provides a strong case for the association of increased risk of psychiatric disorder with the presence of brain damage in childhood. However, this and other studies fail to demonstrate a causal relationship. Although the neurological conditions of the brain-damaged groups typically had an early onset that probably preceded the appearance of any psychiatric disorder, one still can argue that the relationship was merely coincidental. That is, some common vulnerability (e.g., genetic, congenital, environmental) that may have predisposed a child to cerebral damage also may have led independently to psychiatric difficulties. A more convincing case for the existence of a causal relationship comes from studies demonstrating that previously normal children with *acquired* brain injuries are more likely to develop subsequent psychiatric disorders.

Children suffering from head injury represent an excellent choice for examining this question, provided that it is recognized that they do not constitute a random sample of the general population. These children, especially those suffering from mild as opposed to severe injuries, often show preexisting problems with impulsivity, aggression, and attention-seeking behaviors that make them more susceptible to accidental injury. The families of these children also differ from the general population in that they show more parental illness and psychiatric distress, more social disadvantages, and less adequate supervision of the child's play activities (Klonoff, 1971). Nonetheless, an examination of the psychiatric manifestations following head injury can be constructive in developing an understanding of the relationship between neurological impairment and anxiety disorders.

Probably the best controlled examination of this topic comes from the prospective studies of head-injured children by Rutter and colleagues (Brown et al., 1981; Chadwick, Rutter, Brown, et al., 1981; Chadwick, Rutter, Shaffer, et al., 1981; Rutter, Chadwick, Shaffer, et al., 1980). Children ranging from 5 to 14 years of age who had experienced closed head injuries of sufficient severity to result in a posttraumatic amnesia (PTA) of 7 days or more were compared with a group of children with less severe head injuries (those with a PTA $\leq$ 7 days but a duration of at least 1 hour). In addition, these groups were compared with a matched control group of hospital-treated children suffering from accidental orthopedic rather than cranial injuries. All children were studied prospectively at 4 months, 12 months, and 30 months after injury. An important feature of this study was the care taken to determine the children's behavior before their accidents. This was done in an unbiased fashion by interviewing parents immediately after their child's injury but *before* the child's post-injury psychiatric condition could be known.

The children with severe head injuries did not differ from controls in their preinjury behavior, but they showed more than double the rate of psychiatric disorder at 4 months after injury and at each subsequent follow-up period. This was true even when children who had psychiatric disorders before their accidents were eliminated from the study, thereby focusing specifically on the comparative rate of new psychiatric disorders arising over the course of the follow-up period. There was a rather high threshold for an effect, however, because definite cognitive or psychiatric sequelae were found only in head-injured children having a PTA of at least 1 week. Whereas persistent psychiatric sequelae were quite common once this range of severity was reached, cognitive impairment lasting for more than 2 years generally required a PTA of at least 3 weeks. Children with head injuries showed an increased risk for psychiatric disorder, particularly internalizing symptoms, regardless of the age, sex, or social class of the child—factors that ordinarily show a striking mediating effect in the general population.

In addition to frank neurological impairments, a history of soft signs (e.g., mirror movements, dysdiadochokinesis) also has been related to internalizing behavior problems, such as anxiety, depression, and withdrawal (Shaffer et al., 1985). Soft signs typically are believed to be neurological indicators that tend not to be related to neuroanatomical abnormalities but to reflect nonfocal brain dysfunction. Although they are rather prevalent among otherwise normal children, ranging from 8 to 14%, they are more prevalent among children with psychiatric and neurodevelopmental disorders, and they have been related to indices of emotional immaturity and dependency in childhood.

In a well-controlled prospective study, Shaffer et al. (1985) examined the comparative outcomes in adolescence of children with early soft neurological signs. Children with ($n = 83$) and without ($n = 79$) documented soft signs at age 7 received a careful follow-up assessment at age 17. Compared with controls, adolescents with early soft signs had lower IQs and were five to six times more likely to have a psychiatric disorder with symptoms of anxiety, withdrawal, and depression. These findings mainly pertained to boys, but all of the girls in the study with an anxiety–withdrawal diagnosis in adolescence showed early soft signs. The relationship was independent of IQ and, when taken together with the presence of anxious–dependent behavior at age 7, the presence of early soft signs strongly predicted persistent problems with anxiety and withdrawal. No relationship was found with attention-deficit disorder or conduct disorder.

Whether the neurologically based deficits are frankly obvious as in the case of closed head injury or more subtle as seen in neurological soft signs, it is clear that there is a relationship between these findings and manifest psychopathology, particularly internalizing symptoms. These findings are consistent with more recent evidence showing internalizing symptoms to be associated with neurological (Breslau & Marshall, 1985) and neuropsychological (Tramontana, Hooper, & Nardolillo, 1988) impairment. Consequently, it is clear that the classic dissociation between psychiatric and neurologic disorders is not tenable and that brain dysfunction in childhood is associated with at least an increased vulnerability for psychiatric disorders, with much of the emergent evidence arguably (see Szatmari, Offord, Siegel, et al., 1990, for a contrasting viewpoint) indicating the presence of internalizing symptoms such as anxiety.

MODELS FOR THE INTERFACE BETWEEN NEUROPSYCHOLOGY AND ANXIETY

Several theoretical positions and models have been advanced to explain the presence of anxiety during childhood and adolescence. These positions have included psychoanalytic (Freud, 1926/1948), developmental (Achenbach & Edelbrock, 1981), behavioral (Bandura, 1969), and cognitive-behavioral (Meichenbaum, Bream, & Cohen, 1985) perspectives. Despite Eysenck's (1967) theorizing about the biological basis of anxiety disorder, there is a lengthy tradition of dichotomizing psychiatric and neurologic disorders, and anxiety disorders have been one of the diagnostic groups typically viewed from a more functional standpoint. This exclusive dissociation of neurologic from psychiatric behavioral manifestations does not lend itself to a thorough clinical view of an individual's presentation and may actually hinder clinical efforts with the patient. More recent conceptualizations have attempted to address this concern.

For example, Gainotti (1989) presented a theoretical model examining the neurobiological basis of emotion and psychopathology. Within this theoretical perspective, psychopathology is believed to originate from neuroanatomical, neurophysiological, and/or neuroendocrine dysfunction via acquired and/or neurodevelopmental etiological mechanisms. This is consistent with the work of Gray (1982) and Tucker (1989), who addressed this issue directly with respect to anxiety disorders. More recently, neuropsychological factors also have been implicated in the manifestation of psychopathology in children and adolescents, particularly internalizing disorders (Rourke, 1989). The models of Gray, Tucker, and Rourke are briefly presented, with a particular emphasis on their application to anxiety disorders in children and adolescents.

Gray's Model

Gray (1982) provides one of the most well-rounded neurobiological models for understanding anxiety and fear. Not only has this model been applied to the manifestation of anxiety symptoms, but it has been applied to anxiety disorders and to normal variations in personality characteristics that suggest anxiousness. It is largely based on data from experimental findings with animals, including pharmacological efforts, environmental studies (the effects of infantile stress on adult behaviors), and genetic investigations (selective breeding to create reactive and nonreactive genotypes). In general, these separate lines of investigation produced a convergence of data that Gray used to hypothesize a separate subsystem in the brain for mediating anxiety.

In addition to these three lines of research, Gray noted that two behavioral systems were intimately tied to this brain subsystem: the behavioral inhibition system and the fight/flight system. The behavioral inhibition system mediates the reaction of an organism to anxiety-producing stimuli, such as signs of punishment, nonreward, and novel situations, as well as the responses to these stimuli (behavioral inhibition, hypervigilance, increased arousal). This behavioral system has been intimately linked to Papez's (1937) circuit, or the limbic system, which has been implicated in the elaboration of emotional experiences, with particular emphasis on the septohippocampal neural connections.

More specifically, damage to the septal area or to the hippocampal formation, which maintains bidirectional connections with the septum, creates reactions that mirror behavioral inhibition. In fact, it has been hypothesized that the antianxiolytic drugs create their effects by impacting on this neural system, although these effects have been deemed indirect (Gray & Rawlins, 1986). This neural system also involves noradrenergic neurons in the locus ceruleus (they assist in the determination of the behavioral output of the behavioral inhibition system), serotonergic neurons in the raphe nuclei (they assist in determining the behavioral inhibition output), and the neuronal projections that interconnect these various cell groups. Activity in these fibers is increased by anxiety-type stimulation and stress, providing further neural clarification of manifestations of anxiety.

The second behavioral system, the fight/flight system, mediates an organism's response (e.g., in laboratory animals, striking, biting, jumping, hissing, defensive posturing) to stimuli associated with unconditioned pain or nonreward. It is a motivation system designed to suppress feelings of anxiety and to protect the organism. The major neural components of this system are the amygdala, the ventromedial hypothalamus, and the midbrain central gray matter.

Taken together, these two behavioral systems and their corresponding neural networks interact to account for nearly all of the manifestations of anxiety—and perhaps treatment responses—that can be seen in animals and humans. Given the neurotransmitters involved in the neuronal systems, evidence also has emerged to implicate effects on the developing brain and subsequent responses to anxiety-producing stimuli. In general, Gray's model involves the behavioral aspects of anxiety, the cognitive aspects of anxiety via the information-processing activities of the septohippocampal system, and the autonomic signs of anxiety via connections into the spinal cord. Although a scientifically robust model, its application to humans, particularly children and adolescents, will require further investigation.

Tucker's Model

Tucker's (1989) model of emotional functioning and its application to anxiety disorders is also scientifically robust. While many models, such as the nonverbal learning disability model (Rourke, 1989), deal with cortex-to-subcortex, anterior-to-posterior cortex, and left-to-right hemisphere relationships, the Tucker model proposes these relationships and the involvement of neurophysiological control mechanisms as well. Tucker and Frederick (1986) noted that these relationships influence not only types of emotional behaviors but the quality of these behaviors. For example, the disruption of the thalamus has potential impact on emotions and behavior if the thalamocortical projections are impaired. The exact nature of these relationships requires further exploration.

Tucker and Williamson (1984) speculated that the underlying cognitive functional systems of the right hemisphere provide control mechanisms for the perceptual arousal system. As attention is regulated by these systems, an individual's emotional responsivity on the depression–elation and/or hypervigilance dimensions are determined. Disruption of these regulatory systems is likely to contribute to variability in an individual's emotional tone and responsiveness. In contrast, although not without some involvement in the generation of emotion, the left hemisphere apparently maintains cognitive homeostasis via its language specialization and propositional qualities.

Tucker's model holds promise for increasing our understanding of normal and abnormal emotional functioning. The complexity of this model in its involvement of a multitude of neurobiological systems (cortex, subcortex, neurotransmitters) contributes to its robust nature. However, like most other neurobiological models of psychopathology, its application to children and adolescents remains unknown at this time, although efforts to apply a developmental perspective have been made (Tucker, 1991). In particular, the discussion of neurotransmitters in the evolution of emotional function and dysfunction and of their interrelationships with cortical and subcortical regions necessitates the study of children with anxiety symptoms and anxiety disorders over a longitudinal course.

Rourke's Nonverbal Learning Disability Model

Although Rourke (1989) has popularized the nonverbal learning disability model, work by Johnson and Myklebust (1971) over two decades ago provided accurate descriptions of children with this disability. Johnson and Myklebust stated that children with this disorder typically were unable to comprehend the significance of many aspects of the environment, could not pretend or anticipate, and failed to learn and appreciate the implications of gestures, facial expressions, caresses, and other expressions of emotion. Johnson and Myklebust noted that this disorder constituted a fundamental distortion of the total perceptual experience of the child. They labeled it a social perception disability, and Myklebust (1975) later coined the term *nonverbal learning disability*. The findings of Borod, Koff, and Caron (1983) and Ross and Mesulam (1979) in their studies of right-brain-damaged adult patients were consistent with those of Johnson and Myklebust. Although the linkage of nonverbal learning disability to brain damage/dysfunction had been emerging in the adult literature, it remained for Denckla (1983) to compare children with right hemisphere damage to similar adults. She described such children as experiencing a social (emotional) learning disability.

Rourke (1987, 1988b, 1989) has proposed a model for understanding anxiety that is psychometrically instead of neurologically derived. It uses selected aspects of his neuropsychologically based learning disability subtypes and a theory of differential hemispheric functioning advanced by Goldberg and Costa (1981). Relying primarily on data and speculative evidence derived from adult samples, Goldberg and Costa asserted that the right hemisphere is relatively more specialized for intermodal integration, whereas the left hemisphere is more specialized for intramodal integration. Neuroanatomically, these investigators postulated that intramodal integration may be related to the higher ratio of gray matter (neuronal mass and short nonmyelinated fibers) to white matter (long myelinated fibers) characteristic of the left hemisphere, whereas intermodal integration may be related to the lower ratio characteristic of the right hemisphere.

Rourke extended this model by applying a developmental perspective and, given his previous findings on learning disability subtypes (see Rourke, 1985, 1989), extended it to account for nonverbal learning disabilities. Rourke hypothesized that lesioned, excised, or dysfunctional white matter of the right hemisphere interacts with developmental parameters, resulting in nonverbal learning disabilities. He reasoned that, although a significant lesion in the right hemisphere may be sufficient to produce a nonverbal learning disability, it is the destruction of white matter—matter associated with intermodal functions—that is necessary to produce these types of learning disabilities. Furthermore, it is important to note that the white matter fibers are an integral part of the three principal neural axes: commissural fibers (right-to-left interhemispheric connections), association fibers (anterior-to-posterior intrahemispheric connections), and projection fibers (superior-to-inferior connections). Generally, the nonverbal learning disability syndrome would be expected to develop under any significant interference with the functioning of right hemispheric functional systems or with access to those systems (e.g., agenesis of the corpus callosum). Functionally, the characteristics of this type of learning disability, which Rourke noted should be observable by approximately ages 7 to 9 years (Rourke, 1988a; Rourke, Young, & Leenaars, 1989), implicate neuropsychological academic and social–emotional/adaptive domains.

Neuropsychologically, individuals with nonverbal learning disabilities tend to present a distinct profile of strengths and weaknesses. Relative strengths include auditory perception, simple motor functions, and intact rote verbal learning. Selective auditory attention, phonological skills, and auditory–verbal memory also appear intact. Neuropsychological deficits include bilateral tactile-perception problems and motor difficulties that usually are more marked on the left than on the right side of the body, visual–spatial organization problems, and nonverbal problem-solving difficulties. Paralinguistic aspects of language also are impaired (e.g., prosody, pragmatics).

Academically, such individuals show adequate word decoding and spelling, with most spelling errors reflecting good phonetic equivalents. Graphomotor skills eventually appear age-appropriate but are delayed early in development. Marked academic deficits tend to be manifested in mechanical arithmetic, mathematical reasoning, and reading comprehension. Learning of academic subjects such as science also tends to be impaired, largely due to reading comprehension deficiencies and deficits in nonverbal problem solving.

Perhaps one of the most interesting aspects associated with this syndrome is that there appears to be a strong relationship with social–

emotional and adaptive behavior deficits. Individuals with nonverbal learning disabilities present great difficulty adapting to novel situations and manifest poor social perception and judgment. These difficulties, in turn, result in poor social interaction skills. These individuals tend to engage in social withdrawal and social isolation as age increases, and consequently they are at risk for internalized forms of psychopathology such as depression and anxiety. In fact, Rourke et al. (1989) and Bigler (1989) noted the increased risk that these individuals seem to have for depression and suicide. Earlier work by Porter and Rourke (1985) and more recently by Fuerst, Fisk, and Rourke (1990) also suggests possible application of this model to children with anxiety disorders. In fact, given its neuroanatomical and neuropsychological bases, this model is noteworthy for the conjecture that social–emotional disturbances, particularly internalizing disorders (e.g., anxiety, depression), typically are associated with impairments in nonverbal information processing. While ongoing examination of these hypotheses is required, this model provides the opportunity to study neurological and neuropsychological interactions as they may contribute directly and/or indirectly to manifestations of anxiety.

Social–Emotional Learning Disabilities Model

While Rourke's model begins to approximate a developmentally based neuropsychological framework for the association between academic impairments and right hemisphere information-processing deficits, it is less specific about the genesis of internalizing psychopathology. Voeller and colleagues assert that one of the primary determinants of emotional disturbances in children is impaired neuropsychological processing of social–emotional information and not, strictly speaking, impaired visual–spatial–organizational skills. In 1986, Voeller described 15 children exhibiting visual–spatial deficits, math disabilities, and chronic social problems (Voeller, 1986). All the children had left-sided neurological signs, implying right hemispheric dysfunction, and all but one had attentional disturbances. Similar children have been described by Weintraub and Mesulam (1983), Denckla (1983), and others too numerous to list here (Semrud-Clikeman & Hynd, 1990). Not surprisingly, given the emphasis on neuropsychologically based deficits in nonverbal affective communication, they proposed the term "social–emotional learning disabilities" (SELD), borrowed from Denckla, for children presenting with these symptoms.

A growing body of evidence suggests that defects in communicating facial affects (Blonder, Bowers, & Heilman, 1991) and emotional speech prosody (Ross & Mesulam, 1979) may be localizable to the right temporal–parietal cortex, in contrast to language functions, which are lateralized largely to the left temporal–parietal cortex (Pennington, 1991). In adults, recognition of facial affect is separable from the recognition of facial identity. Similarly, recognition of emotional content is separable from recognition of ideational content in written or oral language (Voeller, Hanson, & Wendt, 1988; Blonder et al., 1991). Moreover, the receptive and expressive aspects of affective facial, gestural, and prosodic communication may also be dissociable (Bowers, Bauer, Coslett, et al., 1985). Impairments in processing affective signals place children at high risk for social dysfunction, possibly including disturbances in attachment and peer interactions, which in turn may increase the risk for internalizing psychopathology (Szatmari, Bremner, & Nagy, 1989; Pennington, 1991). We have found that children with anxiety disorders sometimes exhibit results on neurocognitive tests that suggest impairments in visual–spatial–organizational skills and, less commonly, impairments in nonverbal social–emotional communication (March & Conners, unpublished data). However, it remains to be seen if these impairments, while logically attractive as candidates for abnormal information processing in anxiety disorders, are essential to the etiopathogenesis of the conditions or whether they are simply risk factors for an important and interesting subgroup that partially overlaps Asperger's syndrome (Szatmari et al., 1989; Voeller, 1990; American Psychiatric Association, 1994).

EFFECTS OF ANXIETY
ON NEUROCOGNITIVE PERFORMANCE

Given that individuals with brain impairment or dysfunction appear more vulnerable to internalizing disorders, and given the proposed neurobiological models of anxiety, it now becomes important to review how anxiety effects neurocognitive performance in children. Does it improve a child's performance or hinder it? How much anxiety is too much? Are there specific neurocognitive functions that may be especially vulnerable to the effects of anxiety? Relatedly, are there particular situations and/or materials that may be stress-inducing? For whom? While it may not be possible to answer all of these questions in detail, this section and the following section review emerging scientific findings on the effects of anxiety on neurocognitive functioning.

One of the most influential of these findings was presented by Yerkes and Dodson (1908) at the beginning of this century. The Yerkes–Dodson Law addressed the issue of how much arousal/anxiety on what kind of task was necessary for cognitive efficiency and effectiveness. Yerkes and Dodson reported improvements in performance on easy tasks with increasing anxiety. As task difficulty increased, however, they reported that the relationship between anxiety and performance began to take on the form of an inverted U curve. That is, better performances were obtained with medium levels of anxiety whereas poorer performances were demonstrated with low and high levels of anxiety. Since that time, additional findings on the impact of anxiety of neurocognitive functions have been reported.

Anxiety and IQ

While there is no clear reason why the IQ of children with anxiety disorders should be lower than that of other children, there is some mixed evidence that anxiety can disrupt children's general intellectual functioning. Rutter, Tizard, and Whitmore (1981) found that IQ was lower in a neurotic sample of British 11-year-olds than in controls. This finding was particularly evident in females. Kaufman (1979) reported lower performance IQ in anxiety-disordered patients, with increased field dependence being present. In contrast, a study by Richman, Stevenson, and Graham (1982) found higher performance IQs in the neurotic females when compared to match controls. No differences in IQ were noted between school phobic children and hospitalized children (Berg, Collins, McGuire, et al., 1975) or school phobic children and controls (Hersov, 1960). While these data certainly do not suggest a strong relationship between anxiety and intellectual functions, they also do not allow for examination of more detailed aspects of this relationship.

Anxiety and Memory

In his review of the literature on anxiety and task performance, Eysenck (1982) concluded that two primary factors contribute to the effects of anxiety on neurocognitive performance: the worry associated with the anxiety state and motivational factors. The first factor, the worry associated with the anxiety state, encroaches on neurocognitive performance largely by reducing the capacity of an individual's working memory available for performing a selected task. This may be more crucial for a child or adolescent with specific neurocognitive deficits in the working memory domain. The second factor, motivation, is crucial to whether an individual passes or fails any given task. In general, increased anxiety tends to lead to increased motivation. How these two factors interact ultimately determine whether a task is performed in a satisfactory fashion. Consequently, when a task requires little working memory, anxiety actually may improve performance by increasing motivational effort. In contrast, if working memory is overloaded, then task performance probably will be impaired because increased motivational effort may not be able to compensate for the effects of anxiety. In many respects, Eysenck's finding is similar to the reasoning underlying the Yerkes–Dodson Law.

The interaction of anxiety and memory performance also has been examined via another line of inquiry, namely, the accuracy of memory under state-dependent and mood-congruent conditions. State dependence is the theory that what an individual learns in any given mood is recalled most effectively when he or she is in that same mood. Mood congruence is the idea that an individual learns information most effectively if its content is consistent with the individual's mood. While most of the work in this domain has focused on depression (Blaney, 1986), some attempts have been made to apply these findings to anxiety. For example, Nunn, Stevenson, and Whalan (1984) found that when presented with a list of neutral and phobia-related words, agoraphobic patients recalled more phobia-related words than neutral words, whereas controls showed the opposite pattern. Similarly, using a self-referent technique with anxious patients (several words on the word list described the patient), Mogg and Mathews (1989) found that their patients recalled more of the self-referent anxiety-related words. These findings, however, have not been universally upheld in the literature (e.g., Pickles & Van den Broek, 1988), and some investigators have not found any support for them (e.g., Foa, McNally, & Murdock, 1989).

It is important to note that no anxiety and memory studies have been attempted with children and adolescents, and when they are, it will be important for all of the described conditions to be taken into account. In addition, functional issues related to domain-specific knowledge (e.g., recalling math facts versus baseball card statistics) also will need to be considered in these studies. Further, many school-related functions tend to involve new learning for most children, and these developmental factors will need to be considered when studying the effects of anxiety on school performance.

Anxiety and Attention

For adult patients, Beck and Emery (1985) argued that the anxious individual taxes his or her attentional system to a greater extent than a nonanxious patient. They noted that anxious patients tend to be hypervigilant and, consequently, engage in constant scanning of the environment for threats or harmful situations. Indeed, such findings have been documented in auditory attention (Eysenck, MacLeod, & Mathews, 1987) as well as visual attention (MacLeod, Mathews, & Tata, 1986). Further, these findings were found not in depressed patients but in individuals high on trait anxiety. This group also has been observed to be more distractible than normal individuals (Eysenck & Graydon, 1989).

Allocation of selective attention resources probably increases an individual's neurocognitive vulnerability. Indeed, Eysenck (1990) speculated that individuals who are distractible (1) have relatively poor attentional control and, consequently, find it difficult to prevent intrusive thoughts, including those related to self-preservation, and/or (2) find that the resultant disorganizing effects on thinking and behavior make it difficult to cope with life's demands.

As with memory, the study of the effects of anxiety on attentional performance has not been studied in children. Clinically, it seems clear that children who are anxious mimic many of the behaviors and symptoms indicative of a primary attention-deficit disorder; however, the degree of impact of this anxiety is no doubt overlooked in many instances and, in some respects, may be a partial contributor to the lack of the expected response from stimulant medication interventions common in such cases. These questions require further examination in children and adolescents, particularly given their clinical relevance.

Anxiety and Speech/Language

Children with speech and/or language disorders clearly are at risk for the development of social and emotional difficulties (Baker & Cantwell, 1985). For example, case studies of children with speech and language disturbances have revealed many of the same symptoms that have been used to describe anxiety, namely, shyness, withdrawal, thumb-sucking, tension, fears, worries, sleep problems, motor restlessness, and tension. Beitchman, Nair, Clegg, et al. (1986) conducted an epidemiological study to determine the prevalence of DSM-III diagnoses in kindergarten children. These investigators found anxiety disorders, specifically avoidant disorder and separation anxiety disorder, to be more prevalent in children with speech and/or language impairments than in normal controls. Similarly, Cantwell and Baker (1987) showed that both anxiety symptoms and DSM-III anxiety disorders were quite prevalent in a sample of children with speech and language disorders. In fact, 10% of their school-age sample qualified for at least one DSM-III anxiety disorder (separation anxiety 3.2%, avoidant disorder 4.8%, overanxious disorder 2%, simple phobia 0.2%). In addition, studies examining children with speech disturbances (e.g., stuttering, articulation disorders, voice problems) also have shown the presence of anxiety symptoms, such as specific fears (Baumgartner, 1980), social withdrawal (Lingholm & Touliatos, 1979), self-consciousness (Itoh & Kamada, 1981), feelings of inferiority (Yanagawa, 1973), and sleep difficulties (Solomon, 1961).

Whether these findings are related to the impact of anxiety on vulnerable speech and language functions in children or to the impact of speech and language dysfunctions on manifest anxiety remains to be determined. The findings do suggest, however, that these neurocognitive functions have the potential to interact negatively with anxiety.

NEUROPSYCHOLOGICAL FINDINGS IN ANXIETY DISORDERS

Studies specifically designed to assess the impact of anxiety on specific neurocognitive functions in children and adolescents are only beginning to be conducted. For example, Benjamin, Costello, and Warren (1990) reported that teachers described children with anxiety disorders as having increased school dysfunction, suggesting the possible presence of neurologically based learning disabilities. In a more detailed study, Frost, Moffitt, and McGee (1989) examined members of a birth cohort at age 13. Individuals were grouped into a single-disorder group, a multiple-disorder group, and a no-disorder group and assessed for psychopathology and neuropsychological dysfunction. As might be expected, the multiple-disorder group showed the highest rate of neuropsychological dysfunction and performed significantly worse than the no-disorder group across verbal, visual–spatial, verbal memory, and visual–motor neuropsychological parameters. More specifically, the investigators found the single-disorder group to perform significantly worse than the no-disorder group on visual–motor integration. There were no other neuropsychological differences noted between the single-disorder group and the other groups. The identification of neuropsychological patterns in children and adolescents with specific anxiety disorders is only beginning to be pursued, and limited information is available about obsessive–compulsive disorder and conversion reaction.

Obsessive–Compulsive Disorder

Studies investigating the neuropsychological correlates of child and adolescent obsessive–compulsive disorder (OCD) present mixed findings. Adults with OCD not infrequently exhibit left-sided soft signs on neurological examination and poor visual–spatial processing on neuropsychological testing, presumably implicating right-hemisphere dysfunction in OCD (Hollander, Schiffman, Cohen, et al., 1990; Hollander, DeCaria, Aronowitz, et al., 1991). Boone, Ananth, Philpott, et al. (1991) also found subtle deficits in visual–spatial abilities and visual memory, with intact verbal memory, attention, intelligence, and frontal lobe abilities in adults with OCD. Current thinking about the functional neuroanatomy of OCD posits abnormalities in cortical–striatal–thalamic–cortical circuitry (CSTC;

Swedo, Schapiro, Grady, et al., 1989; Baxter, Schwartz, Bergman, et al., 1992; Insel, 1992). Neuroanatomic investigations in adults with OCD have shown EEG abnormalities over the temporal lobes (Jenike, 1984; Jenike & Brotman, 1984); altered middle-latency somatosensory evoked potentials (Malloy, Rasmussen, Braden, et al., 1989); disturbances in the interconnection of the basal ganglia, thalamus, and orbitofrontal and anterior cingulate cortex (Modell, Mountz, Curtis, et al., 1989; Wise & Rapoport, 1989); orbitofrontal and striatal dysfunction on positron emission tomography (PET; Azari, Pietrini, Horwitz, et al., 1993). Interestingly, CSTC circuits receive dense serotonergic innervation (March, Gutzman, Jefferson, et al., 1989; Insel, 1992), and PET abnormalities have been shown to return toward normal in adult patients who respond positively to a serotonin reuptake inhibitor (Baxter et al., 1992).

In the first report of neuropsychological abnormalities in children with OCD, Kaufman (1979) reported lower WISC-R Performance IQ in patients with OCD compared to matched controls. Kaufman observed that many OCD patients exhibited cognitive rigidity in problem solving and that their incessant need to check and recheck their efforts interfered with the efficiency of their performance and, ultimately, their obtained scores on timed tests (subtests on the WISC-R Performance Scale). Rapoport, Elkins, Langer, et al. (1981) later observed that children and adolescents with OCD failed to demonstrate the expected right ear advantage on a dichotic listening task, and although visual–perceptual abilities were largely intact, these children demonstrated impairment in planning and efficiently evaluating their behavior. Consistent with the adult literature (e.g., Flor-Henry, 1979), Rapoport interpreted these findings as implicating frontal and dominant hemispheric functions.

More recent studies (Behar, Rapoport, Berg, 1984; Cox, Fedio, & Rapoport, 1989) implicate frontal lobe involvement and basal ganglia dysfunction, while other studies have generated findings showing visual–spatial deficits and left hemibody signs suggesting possible right hemisphere involvement (Behar et al., 1984; Denckla, 1989; Cox et al., 1989). The patients in these studies also demonstrated significantly higher ventricular/brain ratios and a greater frequency of age-inappropriate synkinesias when compared to a matched control group. Memory, reaction time, and decision time did not differ from those of the normal counterparts (Behar et al., 1984). Finally, March and colleagues (March, Johnston, Jefferson, et al., 1990) reporting the results of a placebo-controlled trial of clomipramine in outpatient children with OCD, speculated that subtle impairments in neurological status may adversely influence the outcome of pharmacotherapy. Hollander and coworkers (1990) also noted that neuropsychiatric abnormalities were positively correlated with a poor response to treatment with serotonin uptake inhibitors in adults with OCD. Conversely, impaired neuropsychological test performance was not associated with specific aspects of OCD phenomenology in the National Institute of Mental Health studies nor did it predict the outcome of treatment with clomipramine (Swedo, Leonard, & Rapoport, 1990; Leonard & Rapoport, 1989). Thus the significance of neuropsychological findings vis-à-vis treatment response is unclear.

Conversion Disorder

To date, only one study has been done on children and adolescents with conversion disorder. Regan and LaBarbera (1984) presented case study evidence indicating a strong lateralization of symptoms in conversion disorders in hospitalized child and adolescent patients. This is in direct opposition to the adult literature, in which symptoms are typically manifested on the nondominant side of the body. Regan and LaBarbera speculated that there may be a developmental component in the manifestation of conversion phenomena. In the adult, the nondominant hemisphere has been recognized as the primary mediator of emotional content, which, in turn, determines somatic manifestations. In the child, these functions may still be mediated, in part, by the dominant hemisphere, and consequently the conversion symptoms may be associated with the dominant side of the body.

Other Anxiety Disorders

To date, no other studies have been conducted to examine the neuropsychological functioning of children and/or adolescents with various types of anxiety disorder or selective types of anxious symptoms. For example, no efforts have examined neuropsychological issues in posttraumatic stress disorder, social phobia, simple phobias, separation anxiety, or avoidant disorder. Further, while some initial neurocognitive correlates have been advanced for children and adolescents with elective mutism, largely involving speech and language deficits, the relatively small prevalence of this disorder has hindered group investigations of these claims (Hooper & Linz, 1992).

Similarly, although some neurologically based theories for panic disorder have emerged (e.g., George & Ballenger, 1992), largely implicating the right parahippocampal region, and related biological findings (e.g., those implicating neuroendocrine and sleep-related abnormalities) also been presented (Roy-Byrne, Mellman, & Uhde, 1988), none of these conjectures have been applied to children. Neuropsychological findings suggesting selective memory deficits (Norton, Schaefer, Cox, et al., 1988) and problems with visual learning, visual recall, and verbal recall (Lucas, Telch,

& Bigler, 1991) in adult panic disorder patients also are surfacing, but, again, none of these relationships has yet to be examined in children or adolescents.

CONCLUSIONS AND DIRECTIONS

The relationship between neuropsychology and manifest anxiety is bi-directional, although clearly there can be situations in which specific anxiety disorders and symptoms can influence neurocognitive functioning and, conversely, in which impaired neurocognitive functioning can create increased anxiety. Although the relationship between brain dysfunction and manifest anxiety in childhood may be nonspecific (Boll & Barth, 1981; Tramontana & Hooper, 1989), its presence may contribute to a lowered adaptive capacity and a greater likelihood of exposure to adverse experiences. The effects of anxiety on neurocognition, however, may be more specific; recent findings show a direct impact of anxiety on selected aspects of attention, memory, and language functions. These situations also can be influenced by personality features (e.g., state vs. trait anxiety, anxious personality tendencies), task demands (e.g., easy vs. difficult tasks), and general learning conditions (e.g., mood congruence and state-dependent learning).

A cursory review of the neuropsychological findings on childhood anxiety disorders, however, only whets one's appetite for more since there is a paucity of evidence on this interface. This appears to be not an oversight on the part of the field but rather a result of many of the factors inherent in doing such research. Perhaps given the high co-occurence of the anxiety disorders with each other as well as with other affective disorders (Benjamin et al., 1990; Brooks, Baltazar, & Munjack, 1989), this type of investigation remains difficult to perform.

Nonetheless, the neurobiological foundations for examining the neuropsychology of manifest anxiety in childhood have been firmly laid; many of the more robust adult theoretical models can be applied to a younger population. For example, in addition to its proposed role in anxiety, the hippocampal formation is considered essential to new learning and memory (e.g., Squire, 1986), and these associations hold enormous potential for study in children. Relatedly, however, these models will require a developmental reframing in order to be applied appropriately to child clinical efforts. For example, what will be the effect of neuropsychological deficits on the developmental gradients of anxious symptoms in children? Will the normal emergence of selected fears in children change (e.g., fear of the dark, fear of monsters)? How about the situational factors involved in the interaction between anxiety and task performance as applied to children and adolescents? Given the school-based setting, many of these factors will be able to be examined in much more detail, especially in relation to content-specific areas (e.g., arithmetic and associated math anxiety). Further, given recent findings suggesting that anxiety symptoms change over time (Rettew, Swedo, Leonard, et al., 1992), is there associated neuropsychological change as well? A developmental framework will be crucial to increasing our understanding of the interface between neuropsychology and childhood anxiety. Last, it will be important for the neuropsychological measurement used in these studies to adhere to the theoretical models proposed for the neurobiological bases of anxiety.

The study of the interface between neuropsychology and anxiety in children and adolescents should continue to provide insights into this realm of disorders. In particular, such studies should increase our knowledge of the correlates and possible etiologies of these disorders. These studies also hold the potential to enhance the validity of childhood anxiety disorders, and they should provide us with greater clinical utility in comprehensively and effectively diagnosing and treating children and adolescents with anxiety disorders.

ACKNOWLEDGMENTS

This chapter was supported by grants awarded to the Center for Development and Learning from the Maternal and Child Health Bureau (MCJ-379154-02-0) and the Administration on Developmental Disabilities (90DD0207) and by an NIMH Scientist Development Award for Clinicians (1 K20 MH00981-01) to Dr. March.

REFERENCES

Achenbach, T. M., & Edelbrock, C. S. (1981). Behavioral problems and competencies reported by parents of normal and disturbed children aged 4 through 16. *Monographs of the Society of Research in Child Development, 46* (Serial No. 188).

American Psychiatric Association. (1980). *Diagnostic and statistical manual of mental disorders* (3rd ed.). Washington, DC: Author

American Psychiatric Association. (1987). *Diagnostic and statistical manual of mental disorders* (3rd ed., rev.). Washington, DC: Author.

American Psychiatric Association. (1994). *Diagnostic and statistical manual of mental disorders* (4th ed.). Washington, DC: Author.

Azari, N. P., Pietrini, P., Horwitz, B., et al. (1993). Individual differences in cerebral metabolic patterns during pharmacotherapy in obsessive–compulsive disorder: A multiple regression/discriminant analysis of positron emission tomographic data. *Biological Psychiatry, 34*(11), 798–809.

Baker, L., & Cantwell, D. P. (1985). Psychiatric and learning disorders in children with speech and language disorders: A critical review. *Advances in learning and behavioral disabilities, 4,* 1–28.

Bandura, A. (1969). *Principles of behavior modification.* New York: Holt, Rinehart, & Winston.

Baumgartner, S. (1980). The social behavior of speech disordered children as viewed by parents. *International Journal of Rehabilitation Research, 3,* 82–84.

Baxter, L. J., Schwartz, J. M., Bergman, K. S., et al. (1992). Caudate glucose metabolic rate changes with both drug and behavior therapy for obsessive–compulsive disorder. *Archives of General Psychiatry, 49*(9), 681–689.

Beck, A. T., & Emery, G. (1985). *Anxiety disorders and phobias: A cognitive perspective.* New York: Basic Books.

Behar, D., Rapoport, J. L., Berg, C. J., et al. (1984). Computerized tomography and neuropsychological test measures in adolescents with obsessive–compulsive disorder. *American Journal of Psychiatry, 141,* 363–369.

Beitchman, J. H., Nair, R., Clegg, M., et al. (1986). Prevalence of psychiatric disorders in children with speech and language disorders. *Journal of the American Academy of Child Psychiatry, 25,* 528–535.

Benjamin, R., Costello, E. J., & Warren, M. (1990). Anxiety disorder in a pediatric sample. *Journal of Anxiety Disorders, 4,* 293–316.

Berg, I., Collins, T., McGuire, R., et al. (1975). Educational attainment in adolescent school phobia. *British Journal of Psychiatry, 126,* 435–438.

Bigler, E. D. (1989). On the neuropsychology of suicide. *Journal of Learning Disabilities, 22,* 180–185.

Blaney, P. H. (1986). Affect and memory: A review. *Psychological Bulletin, 99,* 229–246.

Blonder, L. X., Bowers, D., & Heilman, K. M. (1991). The role of the right hemisphere in emotional communication. *Brain, 114,* 1115–1127. (Published erratum appears in *Brain, 115,* 645)

Boll, T., & Barth, J. (1981). Neuropsychology of brain damage in children. In S. B. Filskov, & T. J. Boll (Eds.), *Handbook of clinical neuropsychology* (pp. 418–452). New York: Wiley.

Boone, K. B., Ananth, J., Philpott, L., et al. (1991). Neuropsychological characteristics of nondepressed adults with obsessive–compulsive disorder. *Neuropsychiatry, Neuropsychology, and Behavioral Neurology, 4,* 96–109.

Borod, J. C., Koff, E., & Caron, H. S. (1983). Right hemispheric specialization for the expression and appreciation of emotion: A focus on the fact. In E. Perecman (Ed.), *Cognitive processing in the right hemisphere* (pp. 83–110). New York: Academic Press.

Bowers, D., Bauer, R., Coslett, H., et al. (1985). Dissociation between the processing of affective and nonaffective faces in patients with unilateral brain lesions. *Brain and Cognition, 4,* 258–272.

Breslau, N., & Marshall, I. A. (1985). Psychological disturbance in children with physical disabilities: Continuity and change in a 5-year follow-up. *Journal of Abnormal Child Psychology, 13,* 199–216.

Brooks, R. B., Baltazar, P. L., & Munjack, D. J. (1989). Co-occurrence of personality disorder with panic disorder, social phobia, and generalized anxiety disorder: A review of the literature. *Journal of Anxiety Disorders, 1,* 259–285.

Brown, G., Chadwick, O., Shaffer, D., et al. (1981). A prospective study of children with head injuries: Vol. III. Psychiatric sequelae. *Psychological Medicine, 11,* 63–78.

Cantwell, D. P., & Baker, L. (1987). The prevalence of anxiety in children with communication disorders. *Journal of Anxiety Disorders, 1,* 239–248.

Chadwick, O., Rutter, M., Brown, G., et al. (1981). A prospective study of children with head injuries: Vol. II. Cognitive sequelae. *Psychological Medicine, 11,* 49–61.

Chadwick, O., Rutter, M., Shaffer, D., et al. (1981). A prospective study of children with head injuries: Vol. IV. Specific cognitive deficits. *Journal of Clinical Neuropsychology, 3,* 101–120.

Cox, C. S., Fedio, P., & Rapoport, J. L. (1989). Neuropsychological testing of obsessive–compulsive adolescents. In J. L. Rapoport (Ed.), *Obsessive–compulsive disorder in children and adolescents* (pp. 73–86). Washington, DC: American Psychiatric Association Press.

Denckla, M. B. (1983). The neuropsychology of social–emotional learning disabilities. *Archives of Neurology, 40,* 461–462.

Denckla, M. B. (1989). Neurological examination. In J. L. Rapoport (Ed.), *Obsessive–compulsive disorders in children and adolescents* (pp. 107–115). Washington, DC: American Psychiatric Association Press.

Eysenck, H. J. (1967). *The biological basis of personality.* Springfield, IL: Charles C. Thomas.

Eysenck, M. W. (1982). *Attentional and arousal: Cognition and performance.* Berlin: Springer.

Eysenck, M. W. (1990). Anxiety and cognitive functioning. In G. D. Burrows, M. Roth, & R. Noyes (Eds.), *Handbook of Anxiety: Vol. 2. The neurobiology of anxiety* (pp. 419–435). New York: Elsevier.

Eysenck, M. W., & Graydon, J. (1989). Susceptibility to distraction as a function of personality. *Personality and Individual Differences.*

Eysenck, M. W., MacLeod, C., & Mathews, W. (1987). Cognitive functioning and anxiety. *Psychological Research, 49,* 189.

Flor-Henry, P. (1979). On certain aspects of the localization of the cerebral systems regulating and determining emotion. *Biological Psychiatry, 14,* 677–698.

Foa, E. B., McNally, R., & Murdock, T. B. (1989). Anxious mood and memory. *Behavioral Research and Therapy, 27,* 141–147.

Freud, S. (1948). Inhibitions, symptoms and anxiety. In J. Strachey (Ed.), *The standard edition of the complete psychological works of Sigmund Freud* (Vol. 20, pp. 87–174). London: Hogarth Press. (Original work published 1926)

Freud, S. (1955). Analysis of a phobia in a five-year-old boy. In J. Strachey (Ed.), *The standard edition of the complete psychological works of Sigmund Freud*

(Vol. 10, pp. 1–149). London: Hogarth Press. (Original work published 1909)

Frost, L. A., Moffitt, T. E., & McGee, R. (1989). Neuropsychological correlates of psychopathology in an unselected cohort of young adolescents. *Journal of Abnormal Psychology, 98, 307–313.*

Fuerst, D. R., Fisk, J. D., & Rourke, B. P. (1990). Psychosocial functioning of learning-disabled children: Relations between WISC Verbal IQ-Performance IQ discrepancies and personality subtypes. *Journal of Consulting and Clinical Psychology, 58,* 657–660.

Gainotti, G. (1989). Features of emotional behavior relevant to neurobiology and theories of emotions. In G. Gainotti & C. Caltagirone (Eds.), *Emotions and the dual brain* (pp. 9–27). New York: Springer-Verlag.

George, M. S., & Ballenger, J. C. (1992). The neuroanatomy of panic disorder: The emerging role of the right parahippocampal region. *Journal of Anxiety Disorders, 6,* 181–188.

Goldberg, E., & Costa, L. D. (1981). Hemisphere differences in the acquisition and use of descriptive systems. *Brain and Language, 14,* 144–173.

Gray, J. A. (1982). *The neuropsychology of anxiety: An enquiry into the functions of the septo-hippocampal system.* Oxford: Oxford University Press.

Gray, J. A., & Rawlins, J. N. P. (1986). Comparator and buffer memory: An attempt to integrate two models of hippocampal function. In R. L. Isaacson & K. H. Pribram (Eds.), *The hippocampus* (Vol. 4). New York: Plenum Press.

Harms, E. (1967). *Origins of modern psychiatry.* Springfield, IL: Charles C. Thomas.

Hersov, L. A. (1960). Persistent non-attendance at school. *Child Psychology and Psychiatry, 1,* 130–136.

Hollander, E., DeCaria, C. M., Aronowitz, B., et al. (1991). A pilot follow-up study of childhood soft signs and the development of adult psychopathology. *Journal of Neuropsychiatry and Clinical Neurosciences, 3*(2), 186–189.

Hollander, E., Schiffman, E., Cohen, B., et al. (1990). Signs of central nervous system dysfunction in obsessive–compulsive disorder [see comments]. *Archives of General Psychiatry, 47*(1), 27–32.

Hooper, S. R., & Linz, T. D. (1992). Elective mutism. In S. R. Hooper, G. W. Hynd, & R. E. Mattison (Eds.), *Child psychopathology: Diagnostic criteria and clinical assessment* (pp. 409–459). Hillsdale, NJ: Erlbaum.

Insel, T. R. (1992). Toward a neuroanatomy of obsessive-compulsive disorder [see comments] [Review]. *Archives of General Psychiatry, 49*(9), 739–744.

Itoh, N., & Kamada, Y. (1981). An analytical study of self-consciousness in stutterers. *Japanese Journal of Child and Adolescent Psychiatry, 22,* 193–202.

Jenike, M. A. (1984). Obsessive–compulsive disorder: A question of a neurologic lesion. *Comprehensive Psychiatry, 25,* 298–304.

Jenike, M. A., & Brotman, A. W. (1984). The EEG in obsessive–compulsive disorder. *Journal of Clinical Psychiatry, 45,* 122–124.

Johnson, D. J., & Myklebust, H. R. (1971). *Learning disabilities.* New York: Grune & Stratton.

Kaufman, A. S. (1979). *Intelligent testing with the WISC-R*. New York: Wiley.

Kierkegaard, S. (1944). *The concept of dread* (W. Lownie, Trans.). Princeton, NJ: Princeton University Press. (Original work published 1844)

Klonoff, H. (1971). Head injuries in children: Predisposing factors, accident conditions, and sequelae. *American Journal of Public Health, 61,* 2405–2417.

Leonard, H. L., & Rapoport, J. L. (1989). Pharmacotherapy of childhood obsessive–compulsive disorder. *Psychiatric Clinics of North America, 12*(4), 963–970.

Lindholm, B. W., & Touliatos, J. (1979). Behavior problems of children in regular classes and those diagnosed as requiring speech therapy. *Perceptual and Motor Skills, 49,* 459–463.

Lucas, J. A., Telch, M. J., & Bigler, E. D. (1991). Memory functioning in panic disorder: A neuropsychological perspective. *Journal of Anxiety Disorders, 5,* 1–20.

MacLeod, C. Mathews, A., & Tata, P. (1986). Attentional bias in emotional disorders. *Journal of Abnormal Psychology, 95,* 15.

Malloy, P., Rasmussen, S., Braden, W., & Haier, R. J. (1989). Topographic evoked potential mapping in obsessive–compulsive disorder: Evidence of frontal lobe dysfunction. *Psychiatry Research, 28,* 63–71.

March, J. S., Gutzman, L. D., Jefferson, J. W., et al. (1989). Serotonin and treatment in obsessive–compulsive disorder. *Psychiatric Development, 7*(1), 1–18.

March, J., Johnston, H., Jefferson, J., et al. (1990). Do subtle neurological impairments predict treatment resistance in children and adolescents with obsessive–compulsive disorder? *Journal of Child and Adolescent Psychopharmacology, 1,* 133–140.

Meichenbaum, D. H., Bream, L. A., & Cohen, J. C. (1985). A cognitive-behavioral perspective of child psychopathology: Implications for assessment and training. In R. J. McMahon & R. D. Peters (Eds.), *Childhood disorders: Behavioral–developmental approaches* (pp. 36–52). New York: Brunner/Mazel.

Modell, J. G., Mountz, J. M., Curtis, G. C., et al. (1989). Neurophysiologic dysfunction in basal ganglia/limbic striatal and thalamocortical circuits as apathogenetic mechanism of obsessive–compulsive disorder. *Journal of Neuropsychiatry and Clinical Neuroscience, 1,* 27–36.

Mogg, K., & Mathews, A. (1989). Is there a self-referent mood-congruent recall bias in anxiety? *Behaviour Research and Therapy, 28,* 91–92.

Myklebust, H. R. (1975). Nonverbal learning disabilities: Assessment and intervention. In H. R. Myklebust (Ed.), *Progress in learning disabilities* (Vol. 3, pp. 85–121). New York: Grune & Stratton.

Norton, G. R., Schaefer, E., Cox, B. J., et al. (1988). Selective memory effects in nonclinical panickers. *Journal of Anxiety Disorders, 2,* 169–177.

Nunn, J. D., Stevenson, R. J., & Whalan, G. (1984). Selective memory effects in agoraphobic patients. *British Journal of Clinical Psychology, 23,* 195–201.

Papez, J. W. (1937). A proposed mechanism of emotion. *Archives of Neurology and Psychiatry, 38,* 725–743.

Pennington, B. (1991). *Diagnosing learning disorders*. New York: Guilford Press.

Pickles, A., & Van den Broek, M. (1988). Failure to replicate evidence for phobic schemata in agoraphobic patients. *British Journal of Clinical Psychology, 27*, 271–272.

Porter, J., & Rourke, B. P. (1985). Socioemotional functioning of learning-disabled children: A subtypal analysis of personality patterns. In B. P. Rourke (Ed.), *Neuropsychology of learning disabilities: Essentials of subtype analysis* (pp. 257–279). New York: Guilford Press.

Rapoport, J. L., Elkins, R., Langer, D. H., et al. (1981). Childhood obsessive–compulsive disorder. *American Journal of Psychiatry, 138*, 1545–1554.

Regan, J., & LaBarbera, J. D. (1984). Lateralization of conversion symptoms in children and adolescents. *American Journal of Psychiatry, 14*, 1279–1280.

Rettew, D. C., Swedo, S. E., Leonard, H. L., et al. (1992). Obsessions and compulsions across time in 79 children and adolescents with obsessive–compulsive disorder. *Journal of the American Academy of Child and Adolescent Psychiatry, 31*, 1050–1056.

Richman, N., Stevenson, J., & Graham, P. J. (1982). *Preschool to school: A behavioral study*. London: Academic Press.

Ross, E. D., & Mesulam, M. M. (1979). Dominant language functions of the right hemisphere? Prosody and emotional gesturing. *Archives of Neurology, 36*(3), 144–148.

Rourke, B. P. (Ed.) (1985). *Neuropsychology of learning disabilities: Essentials of subtype analysis*. New York: Guilford Press.

Rourke, B. P. (1987). Syndrome of nonverbal learning disabilities: The final common pathway of white-matter disease/dysfunction. *Clinical Neuropsychologist, 1*, 209–234.

Rourke, B. P. (1988a). Socio-emotional disturbances of learning-disabled children. *Journal of Consulting and Clinical Psychology, 56*, 801–810.

Rourke, B. P. (1988b). The syndrome of nonverbal learning disabilities: Developmental manifestations in neurological disease, disorder, and dysfunction. *Clinical Neuropsychologist, 2*, 293–330.

Rourke, B. P. (1989). *Nonverbal learning disabilities. The syndrome and the model*. New York: Guilford Press.

Rourke, B. P., Young, G. C., & Leenaars, A. A. (1989). A childhood learning disability that predisposes those afflicted to adolescent and adult depression and suicide risk. *Journal of Learning Disabilities, 22*, 169–175.

Roy-Byrne, P. P., Mellman, T. A., & Uhde, T. W. (1988). Biologic findings in panic disorder: Neuroendocrine and sleep-related abnormalities. *Journal of Anxiety Disorders, 2*, 17–29.

Rutter, M., Chadwick, O., Shaffer, D., et al. (1980). A prospective study of children with head injuries: Vol. I. Design and methods. *Psychological Medicine, 10*, 633–645.

Rutter, M., Graham, P., & Yule, W. (1970). *A neuropsychiatric study in childhood (Clinics in Developmental Medicine Nos. 35–36)*. London: Spastics International Medical Publications/Heinemann Medical Books.

Rutter, M., Tizard, J., & Whitmore, K. (1981). *Education, health, and behaviour*. New York: Krieger.

Semrud-Clikeman M., & Hynd, G. W. (1990). Right hemispheric dysfunction in nonverbal learning disabilities: Social, academic, and adaptive functioning in adults and children [Review]. *Psychological Bulletin, 107*(2), 196–209.

Shaffer, D., Schonfeld, I., O'Conner, P. A., et al. (1985). Neurological soft signs. *Archives of General Psychiatry, 42,* 342–351.

Solomon, A. I. (1961). Personality and behavior patterns of children with functional defects of articulation. *Child Development, 32,* 731–737.

Squire, L. R. (1986). Mechanisms of memory. *Science, 232,* 1612–1619.

Swedo, S., Leonard, H., & Rapoport, J. (1990). Childhood-onset obsessive–compulsive disorder. In M. Jenike, L. Baer, & Minichello (Eds.), *Obsessive–compulsive disorder.* Littleton, MA: PSG.

Swedo, S. E., Schapiro, M. B., Grady, C. L., et al. (1989). Cerebral glucose metabolism in childhood-onset obsessive–compulsive disorder. *Archives of General Psychiatry, 46*(6), 518–523.

Szatmari, P., Bremner, R., & Nagy, J. (1989). Asperger's syndrome: A review of clinical features. *Canadian Journal of Psychiatry, 34*(6), 554–560.

Szatmari, P., Offord, D. R., Siegel, L. S., et al. (1990). The clinical significance of neurocognitive impairments among children with psychiatric disorders: Diagnosis and situational specificity. *Journal of Child Psychology, Psychiatry, and Allied Disciplines, 31,* 287–299.

Tramontana, M. G., & Hooper, S. R. (1989). Neuropsychology of child psychopathology. In C. R. Reynolds & E. Fletcher-Janzen (Eds.), *Handbook of clinical child neuropsychology* (pp. 87–106). New York: Plenum Press.

Tramontana, M. G., Hooper, S. R., & Nardolillo, E. M. (1988). Behavioral manifestations of neuropsychological impairment in children with psychiatric disorders. *Archives of Clinical Neuropsychology, 7,* 281–294.

Tucker, D. M. (1989). Neural substrates of thought and affective disorders. In G. Gainotti & C. Caltagirone (Eds.), *Emotions and the dual brain* (pp. 225–234). New York: Springer-Verlag.

Tucker, D. M. (1991). Development of emotion and cortical networks. In M. Gunnar & C. Nelson (Eds.), *Minnesota Symposium on Child Development: Developmental neuroscience.* New York: Oxford University Press.

Tucker, D. M., & Frederick, S. L. (1986). Emotion and brain lateralization. In H. Wagner & T. Manstead (Eds.), *Handbook of psychophysiology: Emotion and social behaviour.* New York: Wiley.

Tucker, D. M., & Williamson, P. A. (1984). Asymmetric neural control systems in human self-regulation. *Psychological Review, 91,* 185–215.

Voeller, K. K. (1986). Right-hemisphere deficit syndrome in children. *American Journal of Psychiatry, 143*(8), 1004–1009.

Voeller, K. (1990). Right hemisphere deficit syndrome in children: A neurological perspective. *International Journal of Pediatrics, 5,* 163–170.

Voeller, K. K., Hanson, J. A., & Wendt, R. N. (1988). Facial affect recognition in children: A comparison of the performance of children with right and left hemisphere lesions. *Neurology, 38*(11), 1744–1748.

Walk, A. (1964). The pre-history of child psychiatry. *British Journal of Psychiatry, 110,* 754–767.

Watson, J., & Rayner, R. (1920). Conditioned emotional reactions. *Journal of Experimental Psychology, 3,* 1–22.

Weintraub, S., & Mesulam, M. M. (1983). Developmental learning disabilities of the right hemisphere. Emotional, interpersonal, and cognitive components. *Archives of Neurology, 40*(8), 463–468.

Wise, S. P., & Rapoport, J. L. (1989). Obsessive–compulsive disorder: Is it basal ganglia dysfunction? In J. L. Rapoport (Ed.), *Obsessive–compulsive disorder in children and adolescents* (pp. 327–344). Washington, DC: American Psychiatric Association Press.

Yanagawa, M. (1973). On the etiology of stuttering and personality tendencies in mothers and children. *Japanese Journal of Child Psychiatry, 15,* 22–28.

Yerkes, R. M., & Dodson, J. D. (1908). The relation of strength of stimulus to rapidity of habit-formation. *Journal of Comparative and Neurological Psychology, 1908,* 459–482.

Chapter 3

Behavioral Inhibition as a Risk Factor for Anxiety Disorders

Joseph Biederman
Jerrold F. Rosenbaum
Jonathan Chaloff
Jerome Kagan

A nxiety disorders cause symptomatic distress, social dysfunction, school and occupational disability, and financial loss. They include a wide range of disorders with varying levels of severity and functional impairment. These disorders may be different manifestations of a common underlying diathesis, or they may be distinct clinical entities with varying patterns of familial aggregation, course, and treatment outcome. In examining this question, our research focused on panic disorder and agoraphobia (PDAG) because it is a reliably diagnosable condition, typically offering the most severe expression of the anxiety disorders. It is commonly associated with high levels of morbidity, incapacitation, and at times suicidal behavior (Weissman, 1988). An extensive literature documents its pattern of familial aggregation, clinical correlates, nosology, and treatment responses.

Longitudinal studies of anxiety disorders suggest that, for many, these conditions do not arise *de novo* (Pollack, Otto, Rosenbaum, et al., 1990). Instead, they evolve from preexisting traits or tendencies influenced by a variety of factors to produce the full expression of an illness. Although several investigators have looked at the association between early temperamental traits and behavioral disorders (Carey, Fox, & McDevitt, 1977; Earls & Jung, 1987; Graham, Rutter, & George, 1973; Graham &

Stevenson, 1987; Maziade, Capéraà, Laplante, et al., 1985; Maziade, Côté, Bernier, et al., 1989; Maziade, Côté, Thivierge, et al., 1989; Maziade, Caron, Côté, et al., 1990a, 1990b; McDevitt & Carey, 1978) the association between early temperamental traits and anxiety disorders has not been investigated.

Our studies of children at risk for anxiety disorders evolved from the longitudinal studies of behavioral inhibition at the Harvard Infant Study laboratory (Garcia-Coll, Kagan, & Reznick, 1984; Kagan, Reznick, Clarke, et al., 1984; Gersten, 1986, 1989; Reznick, Kagan, Snidman, et al., 1986; Kagan, Reznick, & Snidman, 1987, 1988; Kagan, Reznick, Snidman, et al., 1988; Kagan, 1989, Kagan, Reznick, & Gibbons, 1989; Snidman, 1989; Kagan & Snidman, 1991; Kagan, Snidman, Julia-Sellers, et al., 1991). Kagan and colleagues at the Harvard laboratory have reported that 15 to 20% of Caucasian American children are born predisposed to be irritable as infants, shy and fearful as toddlers, and cautious, quiet, and introverted when they reach school age. In contrast, 25 to 30% of the population show an opposing profile: bold, gregarious, and unperturbed by novelty. Over a 7-year period, Kagan and colleagues followed two independent cohorts of children, both classified at 21 or 31 months of age, are as behaviorally inhibited, the other as behaviorally uninhibited, when exposed to unfamiliar settings, people, and objects. The differences in behavior were substantially preserved from infancy to the later assessments (at 4, 5, and 7.5 years of age). These data indicate that the tendency to approach or to withdraw from novelty is an enduring temperamental trait. Although Kagan's original work was conducted without hypotheses regarding psychopathology, his descriptions of inhibited children at school age were strikingly similar to descriptions of children of agoraphobics who manifested anxiety disorders and to reports of agoraphobic adults about their own childhoods (Klein, 1964; Berg, Marks, McGuire, et al., 1974; Berg, 1976; Deltito, Perugi, Maremmani, et al., 1986). Inhibited children, for example, were avoidant on the first days of school and manifested symptoms of separation anxiety (Gersten, 1986) similar to the symptoms of agoraphobics as children.

Kagan postulated that inhibited children, compared with uninhibited children, have a low threshold for arousal in the amygdala and hypothalamic circuits, especially to unfamiliar events (Kagan et al., 1987; Davis, 1992). As a result, the inhibited children react with specific behaviors and sympathetic activation. High heart rate, low heart-rate variability, and acceleration of heart rate to mild stress imply increased sympathetic activity. Inhibited children have higher and more stable heart rates when young and show an acceleration of heart rate when presented with events requiring effortful assimilation or cognitive work. Further, from 4 to 8 years, inhibited children show a greater increase in diastolic blood pressure when their posture changes from a sitting to a standing position, suggesting increased noradrenergic tone. These data imply a more reactive sympathetic influence on cardiovascular functioning in inhibited children. The behavioral response of retreat and avoidance shown by children with behavioral inhibition, along with evidence of increased arousal in the limbic–sympathetic axes, fit well with current hypotheses of the neurophysiological underpinnings of anxiety disorders, particularly panic disorder (Insel & Murphy, 1984; Reiman, Raichle, Butler, et al., 1984; Charney & Heninger, 1986; Margraf, Ehlers, & Roth, 1986; Gorman, Liebowitz, Fyer, et al., 1989). This suggests that measures developed to assess behavioral inhibition may serve as early identifiers of anxiety proneness in young children.

Primate work by Suomi and colleagues supports the hypothesis of early behavioral and physiological characteristics representing anxiety proneness (Suomi, Kraemer, Baysinger, et al., 1981; Suomi, 1984, 1986). These studies of rhesus monkeys reveal that environmental manipulations such as separation generate persisting "anxietylike" behaviors in monkeys. These anxietylike syndromes are much more easily generated in some monkeys than in others. The factors most predictive of which monkeys will display persisting separation anxiety appear to be under genetic control. Suomi describes the anxiety-prone monkeys as "high reactive." High-reactive infant monkeys, like behaviorally inhibited children, react to novelty with diminished exploration, retreat, and increased markers of limbic–sympathetic arousal. Like Kagan's estimate of behavioral inhibition in a population of normal children, Suomi estimated that 15% of his monkey population is born with the quality of "high reactivity" (Suomi, 1986). The phenomenon of behavioral inhibition in the presence of novel stimuli has also been observed in other species, including rats, cats, and dogs (Adamec & Stark-Adamec, 1989). This is consistent with hypotheses that would link behavioral inhibition to neural substrates that emerged relatively early during the evolution of the human central nervous system.

Based on the work of Kagan and colleagues, our group investigated the value of assessing behavioral inhibition in high-risk children of parents with PDAG. We posited that behavioral inhibition in young children at risk for PDAG could be a risk factor for the development of later psychopathology that may persist, abate, or vary in its expression with development.

An important question in this research is whether behavioral inhibition is an independent behavioral state or merely another expression of anxiety that is identifiable earlier in life than is possible with current psychiatric assessment methods. It is possible that behavioral inhibition reflects a mild version of psychopathology. However, even if behavioral inhibition were to reflect a mild version of psychopathology, it still has heuristic clinical value since it can be detected at a very early age (21 months). Thus, regardless of whether it is an expression or a predictor of psychopathology, behavioral inhibition can help identify children at very high risk. Such an early indicator of anxiety disorders is not currently available.

STUDIES OF BEHAVIORAL INHIBITION AND ANXIETY DISORDERS

In our work on anxiety disorders and behavioral inhibition, we studied samples of children from two different ascertainment sites (Rosenbaum, Biederman, Gersten, et al., 1988; Rosenbaum, Biederman, Hirshfeld, 1991a; Biederman, Rosenbaum, Hirshfeld, et al., 1990; Biederman, Rosenbaum, Bolduc-Murphy, et al., 1993; Biederman, Rosenbaum, Bolduc, et al., 1991; Hirshfeld, Rosenbaum, Biederman, et al., 1992). One sample consisted of 56 children whose parents were in treatment for psychiatric disorders at the Massachusetts General Hospital (MGH). The second sample comprised inhibited and uninhibited children who had originally been selected from birth registries to take part in a longitudinal study of behavioral inhibition conducted by Kagan and colleagues.

All assessments of behavioral inhibition were performed by Kagan and colleagues at his laboratory, blind to knowledge of parental diagnoses. On the basis of these observations, the MGH children were classified into one of two mutually exclusive categories, inhibited and not-inhibited, whereas the Kagan sample was classified as inhibited or uninhibited. The uninhibited children from the Kagan cohort were characterized as consistently bold and fearless in new situations, (hence, uninhibited), whereas children in the MGH at risk sample who were not characterized as inhibited were classified not as uninhibited, but merely as not-inhibited.

Rates of psychopathology in children were determined by structured diagnostic interviews with parents using the Diagnostic Interview for Children and Adolescents–Parent Version (DICA-P; Herjanic & Reich, 1982). Parental psychopathology was rated with the National Institute of Mental Health Diagnostic Interview Schedule (NIMH-DIS; Robins, Helzer, Croughan, et al., 1981) and the Structured Clinical Interview for the DSM-III (SCID; Spitzer & Williams, 1986). Since the DIS does not cover childhood psychopathology, unmodified sections from the DICA-P were used to assess history of childhood psychopathology in the parents. All diagnoses were made blind to the behavioral inhibition assessment of the children. Families of children attending routine pediatric outpatient clinic visits at MGH served as a normal comparison group for rates of psychopathology in the families of children at risk and of Kagan's nonclinical cohort.

Potential normal comparison children were excluded if they had a known history of anxiety disorder or major depressive disorder. In all studies, diagnostic uncertainties were resolved by review of available information by Biederman and Rosenbaum following the best-estimate diagnostic approach (Leckman, Sholomskas, Thompson, et al., 1982). Rates of illness are reported as lifetime prevalences of definite diagnoses (i.e., all DSM-III criteria were unequivocally met).

We found that the rates of behavioral inhibition in children of adults with PDAG, with or without comorbid major depressive disorder (MDD), were significantly higher than in children of parents in our psychiatric comparison group without PDAG or MDD (Rosenbaum et al.). Children of parents with PDAG and children of parents with PDAG and MDD were rated as behaviorally inhibited in 85% and 70% of the cases respectively (Figure 3.1). In contrast, children of parents with MDD alone and without MDD or PDAG had rates of behavioral inhibition of 50% and 15.4% respectively. The distribution of behavioral inhibition scores appeared bimodal in the PDAG and PDAG–MDD groups, suggesting a discontinuity in this trait among these children. Inhibited children also manifested an

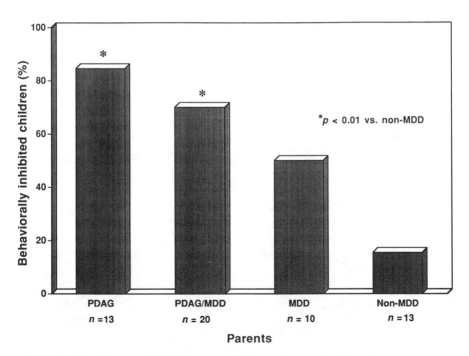

FIGURE 3.1. Behavioral inhibition in children of agoraphobic and comparison parents.

accelerated heart rate and higher salivary cortisol levels over the course of the testing session.

To discern whether behavioral inhibition predicted increased risk for anxiety disorders in children originally classified as inhibited, we conducted psychiatric assessments of both groups of children, the MGH sample of high-risk children and Kagan's longitudinal cohort (Figure 3.2; Biederman et al., 1990).

In the MGH sample, the incidence of all evaluated disorders (anxiety disorders and nonanxiety disorders) was higher in inhibited children than in the not-inhibited and the normal control children. Significant differences were detected in comparisons between inhibited children and normal controls in rates of ≥ 4 disorders per child (27.8% vs. 0%, by Fisher's Exact Test [F.E.T.], $p = .02$), ≥ 2 anxiety disorders per child (22.2% vs. 0%, $p = .04$), and oppositional disorder (33.3% vs. 5.0%, $p = .04$). Although the rates in the not-inhibited and normal control children were exactly the same for both ≥ 4 disorders (both 0%) and ≥ 2 anxiety disorders (both 0%) and very similar for oppositional disorder (8% and 5%, respectively), the comparisons between inhibited and not-inhibited children failed to attain statistical significance, most likely due to the small

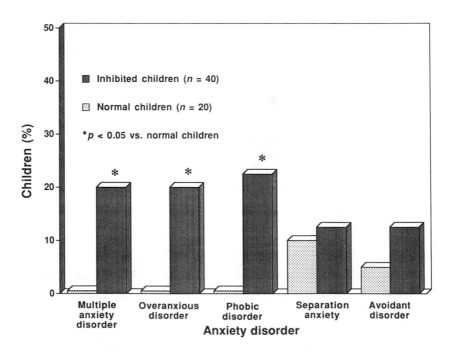

FIGURE 3.2. Anxiety disorders in inhibited and normal children.

numbers in these cells. Similarly, the rates of major depressive disorder (16.7% vs. 0% vs. 0%) and attention-deficit disorder (33.3% vs. 16.7% vs. 10.0%) were higher in inhibited children than in not-inhibited children and normal controls, but differences also failed to attain statistical significance.

In Kagan's longitudinal cohort, the inhibited children had a substantially higher rate of multiple (≥ 2) anxiety disorders when compared with uninhibited children, but this difference fell short of attaining statistical significance (18.2% vs. 0%, F.E.T., p = .07). The rate of oppositional disorder, on the other hand, was significantly lower in inhibited children than in uninhibited children (0% vs. 21.1%, p = .04). Although not statistically significant, the rate of ≥ 4 disorders was higher in inhibited than in uninhibited children (13.6% vs. 10.5%) while the rates of major depression (0% vs. 10.5%) and attention-deficit disorder (18.2% vs. 31.6%) were lower. Overall these results indicate that behavioral inhibition is associated with an increased risk for anxiety disorders in children.

If behavioral inhibition is an expression of vulnerability to anxiety disorders, we also predicted that we should find high rates of anxiety disorders in parents and siblings of inhibited children. To test this hypothesis, we conducted structured psychiatric interviews of the parents and siblings of children from Kagan and colleagues' longitudinal cohort (Figure 3.3; Rosenbaum, Biederman, Hirshfeld, et al., 1991b). As mentioned earlier, these children had been identified as inhibited and uninhibited at 21 months without regard to issues of psychopathology in the child or the family. When compared to parents of uninhibited and normal children, parents of inhibited children had significantly higher rates of social phobia, a history of childhood anxiety disorder, a history of avoidant and overanxious disorders, and a history of continuing anxiety disorder (anxiety in childhood continuing into adulthood in the same individual). Although the number of siblings meeting criteria for anxiety disorder was small, siblings of inhibited children had higher rates of phobias than siblings of comparison children. The finding that behavioral inhibition predicted increased rates of anxiety disorders in biological relatives strengthened our belief that this characteristic of children is linked to the familial predisposition to anxiety disorders.

Although our work suggested that children of parents with PDAG were likely to be classified as behaviorally inhibited and that behaviorally inhibited children were likely to develop anxiety disorders, the factors determining which inhibited children were at risk for childhood onset of anxiety disorders remained unknown. We hypothesized that greater anxiety loading in parents would increase the risk for anxiety disorders in children with behavioral inhibition. To this end, we examined the patterns of aggregation of anxiety disorders in the parents of the MGH at-risk

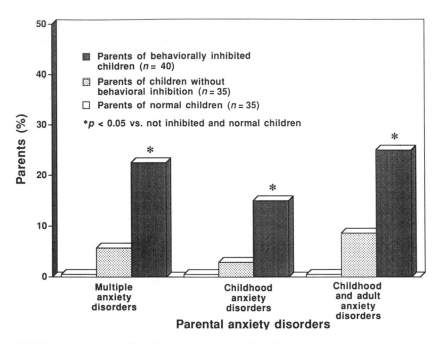

FIGURE 3.3. Anxiety disorders in in parents of children with and without behavioral inhibition from Kagan's sample and comparisons.

sample and the Kagan and colleagues longitudinal cohort sample (MGH at-risk sample, 31 children, 60 parents; Kagan and colleagues longitudinal cohort, 40 children, 75 parents) (Rosenbaum et al., 1992). Within each sample, parents were classified into three groups based on the presence (behavioral inhibition plus anxiety) or absence (behavioral inhibition only or no behavioral inhibition/no anxiety) of behavioral inhibition plus multiple ($\geq$ 2) anxiety disorders in their child. Parents of children with behavioral inhibition plus anxiety, from both the clinical and nonclinical samples, had significantly higher rates of multiple ($\geq$ 2) anxiety disorders compared with parents of children with behavioral inhibition only and parents of children with no behavioral inhibition/no anxiety (Figure 3.4). Our results indicate that the presence of parental loading for anxiety disorders may help identify the subgroup of inhibited children at very high risk for developing childhood-onset anxiety disorders.

In their research, Kagan and colleagues have shown that some children initially identified as inhibited did not maintain this profile over time (Reznick et al., 1986). This suggested that there may be differences between children who consistently remain inhibited (stable behavioral inhibition) and those who do not (unstable behavioral inhibition), thus leading us to the hypothesis that children with stable and unstable behavioral inhibition may differ in antecedents as well as psychiatric outcome. To test this hypothesis, we evaluated the stability of behavioral inhibition of children in Kagan's cohort. These analyses revealed that the high rates of anxiety disorders in children with behavioral inhibition (Biederman et al., 1990, 1993) and in the parents of Kagan's epidemiologically derived children with behavioral inhibition (Rosenbaum et al., 1991b) were accounted for by the group of children with stable behavioral inhibition from 21 months to 7.5 years (Figure 3.5; Hirshfeld et al., 1992). This suggests that there may be two different phenotypes of behavioral inhibition. Stable behavioral inhibition appears to be associated with (1) stable inhibition at least through 7 years of age, (2) a high and stable heart rate during laboratory batteries early in childhood (Kagan et al., 1987), (3) a tendency to develop anxiety disorder, and (4) anxiety disorder in parents. Unstable behavioral inhibition (1) appears to be more variable, (2) is not associated with anxiety disorder early in childhood, and (3) is less strongly associated with parental psychopathology. Although this work is preliminary until confirmed in a larger sample, the data argue strongly for the

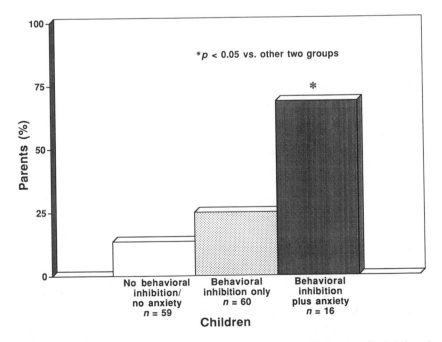

FIGURE 3.4. Multiple (≥2) anxiety disorders in parents of behaviorally inhibited children with and without anxiety disorders.

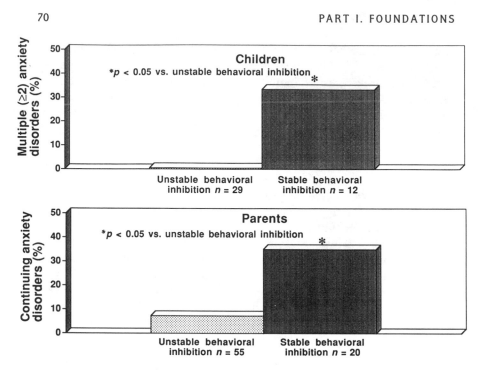

FIGURE 3.5. Anxiety disorders in children with stable and unstable behavioral inhibition and in their parents.

importance of assessing stability of behavioral inhibition in children at risk for anxiety disorders. Children with stable behavioral inhibition may be the subgroup at highest risk. Further, identifying a child as behaviorally inhibited based on a single assessment may be premature, sacrificing specificity for sensitivity and generating more "false positives" of high-risk children. These findings have important clinical implications. They suggest that children consistently inhibited throughout early childhood may be at higher risk for developing anxiety disorders than children without this characteristic and may therefore be more in need of intervention.

Although these results suggested that behavioral inhibition to the unfamiliar may be associated with risk for anxiety disorders in children, longitudinal data were needed to confirm the initial impressions. Using DSM-III structured interviews, we examined psychiatric disorders at 3-year follow-up in both the Massachusetts General Hospital at-risk sample and the Kagan and colleagues longitudinal cohort (Biederman et al., 1993). Analyses of follow-up findings revealed significant differences between all inhibited and all not-inhibited children in the rates of multiple (≥ 4) psychiatric disorders, multiple (≥ 2) anxiety disorders, avoidant disorder, separation anxiety disorder, and agoraphobia (Figure 3.6). Of those who had separation anxiety at baseline, 75% were found to have agoraphobia at follow-up. In addition, when we limited analyses to children who did not have all disorders, we found that the probability of each disorder occurring in children who were well at baseline is greater for the inhibited children. Also, the rates of illness were greatest among children who had stable behavioral inhibition, as defined in our previous study (Hirshfeld et al., 1992). These results are consistent with our previous reports. Furthermore, by using a longitudinal design, they strongly support the hypothesis that behavioral inhibition is a predictor of subsequent anxiety disorders. Table 3.1 highlights the essential questions addressed by this research.

COMMENT

The principal findings of our studies are the following.

1. PDAG in parents, either alone or comorbid with MDD, but not MDD alone, is associated with behavioral inhibition in their children.

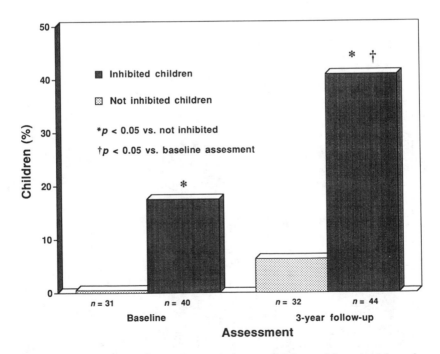

FIGURE 3.6. Multiple (≥2) anxiety disorders in children with and without behavioral inhibition at baseline and at 3-year follow-up.

TABLE 3.1. Summary of Evidence Supporting an Association between Behavioral Inhibition and Anxiety Disorders

Hypothesis	Results	Comments	Study
Children of parents with PDAG will have high rates of behavioral inhibition.	Compared to children of parents with MDD only and children of psychiatric controls, children of parents with PDAG, regardless of comorbid MDD, had significantly higher rates of behavioral inhibition.	Rates of behavioral inhibition in the MDD group fell in between the PDAG and no PDAG/no MDD groups, making it difficult to determine if behavioral inhibition is associated specifically with PDAG.	Rosenbaum, Biederman, Gersten, et al. (1988)
Inhibited children will have higher rates of anxiety disorders than not-inhibited children.	In both clinical and nonclinical samples, inhibited children showed an increased risk for anxiety disorders.	Adult-type anxiety disorders were not assessed.	Biederman, Rosenbaum, Hirshfeld, et al. (1990)
Rates of anxiety disorders will be higher in parents and siblings of inhibited children from the nonclinical cohort than in parents and siblings of uninhibited children.	Parents of inhibited children showed significantly higher rates of anxiety disorders: social phobia; any childhood anxiety; and avoidant, overanxious, and continuing anxiety disorders. Siblings of inhibited children also had higher rates of phobias.	Parents had lower than expected rates of PDAG, possibly because the study, conducted on the 15th floor of a building, screened out subjects with PDAG.	Rosenbaum, Biederman, Hirshfeld, et al. (1991b)
Children remaining stably inhibited during childhood, and their parents, will have elevated rates of anxiety disorder.	Children with stable behavioral inhibition had rates of any anxiety, multiple anxiety, and phobic disorders significantly higher than those of children without stable inhibition. Higher rates of multiple childhood anxiety, continuing anxiety, and avoidant disorder were found in the parents of children with stable behavioral inhibition.	Stability of behavioral inhibition was not assessed in the MGH high-risk sample.	Hirshfeld, Rosenbaum, Biederman, et al. (1992)

72

Hypothesis	Findings	Limitations	Reference
Parents of children who have behavioral inhibition and multiple anxiety disorders will have higher rates of multiple anxiety disorders.	Parents of children with both behavioral inhibition and multiple anxiety disorders had higher rates of multiple anxiety disorders than did parents of children who had only behavioral inhibition and parents of children who had neither behavioral inhibition nor multiple anxiety disorders.	Data did not distinguish parental psychopathology as a genetic or an environmental risk factor for children with behavioral inhibition.	Rosenbaum, Biederman, Bolduc, et al. (1992)
Children with behavioral inhibition will have higher rates of anxiety disorders than will children without behavioral inhibition when reexamined after 3 years.	After 3 years, inhibited children had an increased risk for anxiety disorders. The rates of illness were highest among those who were stably inhibited.	The relatively small sample size plus attrition limited statistical power.	Biederman, Rosenbaum, Bolduc-Murphy, et al. (1993)
	The rates of anxiety disorders in inhibited children increased significantly between the two assessments.		
	The probability of an anxiety disorder (multiple anxiety or avoidant or separation anxiety) appearing in children who, at baseline, were well was greater for inhibited children.		
	Of children with separation anxiety disorder at baseline, 75% had agoraphobia at follow-up.		

2. Behavioral inhibition in children is associated with anxiety disorders.
3. Behavioral inhibition in children predicts increased rates of anxiety disorders in their biological relatives.
4. The subset of inhibited children who show the most stable and consistent behavioral inhibition are more likely than other inhibited children to have a family history of anxiety disorder and are at greater risk for developing anxiety disorders themselves.
5. Parental PDAG, either alone or comorbid with MDD, increases the risk for both anxiety and depressive disorders in their children.
6. The presence of parental loading for anxiety disorders may help identify the subgroup of inhibited children at very high risk for developing childhood onset anxiety disorders.
7. These results hold true at a 3-year follow-up.

Our studies suggest that behavioral inhibition is an early manifestation of a familial predisposition to anxiety disorders. This line of research has raised the question of the potential tautology of the assertion that behavioral inhibition and anxiety disorders may be different reflections of the same diathesis. An alternative interpretation is that behavioral inhibition is simply a laboratory measure of anxiety disorders. However, our results suggest that inhibition and psychopathology are not identical. Most telling is the fact that many (approximately 70%) of the inhibited children are free of anxiety disorder (Biederman et al., 1990). Indeed, Kagan's longitudinal studies in nonclinical populations and our work in high-risk children of clinically referred parents concur that behavioral inhibition is much more prevalent than are anxiety disorders. This is exactly what one would expect if behavioral inhibition measures some factor that is one of several required for the development of an anxiety disorder. We expect that our continuing work in this area will clarify this issue, especially as longer-term follow-up data become available.

Although our work does not resolve the question whether behavioral inhibition is an expression of anxiety disorder or a marker of its potential emergence, it does show that behavioral inhibition can be reliably and validly assessed at a very early age, whereas psychopathology cannot. Indeed, in the data from Kagan and colleagues' longitudinal cohort, behavioral inhibition assessed at 21 months of age predicted anxiety disorders 5 to 6 years later (Biederman et al., 1990, 1993). This lays the groundwork for future studies of preventive intervention programs by giving them a means of identifying children at highest risk for anxiety disorders.

While preliminary, our work provides some information about the specificity of behavioral inhibition. We found that parental PDAG, with and without comorbid MDD, places children at risk for behavioral inhibition, but parental MDD without PDAG apparently does not (Rosenbaum et al., 1988). In addition, the findings of high rates of parental anxiety in children with behavioral inhibition followed by Kagan and colleagues suggest that behavioral inhibition may be specifically associated with anxiety disorders.

Our data from Kagan's epidemiological sample suggest that behavioral inhibition may also be associated with social phobia (Biederman et al., 1990; Rosenbaum et al., 1991a, 1991b; Hirshfeld et al., 1992). One family history study indicates that social phobia is familial (Reich & Yates, 1988), as do two family studies using direct interviews of relatives (Fyer, Mannuzza, Gallops, et al., 1990). All of these studies suggest that social phobia is familially distinct from panic disorder. This is consistent with family studies of panic disorder. Several family studies of phobias directly examined the relationship of social phobia to panic disorder (Crowe, Noyes, Pauls, et al., 1983; Harris, Noyes, Crowe, et al., 1983; Noyes, Crowe, Harris, et al., 1986). Both panic and social phobia tended to breed true, and proband groups with combined social phobia and panic disorder tended to have relatives with panic disorder but not social phobia. These findings, however, may be pertinent only to discrete social phobias. For generalized forms of social phobia, social phobia associated with panic attacks, and social phobia occurring comorbidly with panic disorder, emerging data suggest the possibility of a familial link with panic disorder and thus a common substrate vulnerability.

Important differences exist between behavioral inhibition and emergent anxiety disorders that may suggest a causal association. While behavioral inhibition is a profile of laboratory-based measures, it is not necessarily maladaptive. In contrast, the emergence of anxiety disorders reflects the presence of a group of abnormal symptoms and behaviors with associated distress and disability. Our work to date suggests, moreover, that not all children with behavioral inhibition develop anxiety disorders and that only a minority meet our criterion for a clinically meaningful anxiety state (more than two anxiety disorders; Biederman et al., 1990). Furthermore, behavioral inhibition reflects a persistent trait, identifiable prior to the emergence of diagnostically valid anxiety disorders. This line of thought is consistent with the existing literature on the subject. Maziade and colleagues (Maziade, et al., 1990a) recently reported findings from a study of referred 3- to 12-year-old children assessed for temperamental traits and psychopathology and showed that extreme temperamental characteristics and clinical disorders are not equivalent.

This work argues that clinicians should consider an inhibited young child of a parent with an anxiety disorder as likely to develop an anxiety disorder over time. In the absence of parental disorders, however, behavioral inhibition may not have implications for later pathology. In that case, the inhibited child may simply be more likely to be shy and less inclined to participate in social activities, with no negative ultimate developmental outcome. Alternatively, the inhibited child may be challenged by unique needs and risks for which caregivers need to be aware. The increased autonomic arousal observed with behavioral inhibition may increase the risk for children to be "conditioned" by adverse experience. This heightened dysphoric arousal in the child may also generate increased demands on parents for comfort, with these children behaving in a more dependent fashion and more likely to be distressed by a challenge such as separation. Thus, caregivers should be more alert to the inhibited child's increased needs for support, reassurance, and nurturing when young; when the child is older, caregivers should consider employing behavioral strategies such as rehearsal, cognitive preparation, and explanation before confronting new or challenging situations.

Other work from our center (Pollack et al., 1990; Pollack, Otto, Rosenbaum, et al., 1992) indicates that for adult patients with PDAG, a history of childhood anxiety disorders correlated with a chronic course. Therefore, caregivers should be alert for evolving symptoms of anxiety disorder in inhibited children. To minimize dysfunction, parents can learn cognitive and behavioral principles for managing anxiety symptoms. The inhibited child may need greater preparation for new challenges. When avoidant symptoms do emerge, systematic graduated exposure to feared situations for the child, combining understanding, reassurance, soothing, and cognitive tools (e.g., anticipatory explanation, realistic appraisals), are all indicated. The most basic intervention strategy is, of course, to treat the parental disorder. An anxious, depressed, or agoraphobic parent may be overprotective, impeding separation and self-confidence, or alternatively may be dysfunctional and unsupportive. For the child who remains symptomatic despite effort, recovery may require pharmacotherapy (Biederman, 1987). Pharmacotherapy, then, as well as cognitive-behavioral treatment for the parent and family interventions where indicated, are part of early preventive intervention for the child.

Longitudinal studies are required to resolve whether these early response patterns are specifically linked to risk for anxiety disorders across the life cycle. For now, high rates of behavioral inhibition in children of parents with PDAG (Rosenbaum et al., 1988), high rates of anxiety psychopathology in childen previously identified as behaviorally inhibited (whether from a clinical or nonclinical population; Biederman et al., 1990, 1993), and the presence of increased anxiety psychopathology, especially social phobia, in the parents of inhibited children from a nonclinical sample (Rosenbaum et al., 1991b) argue that a neurophysiologically based anxiety proneness exists. Such a diathesis, manifested early in life, interacts with developmental experience and life events to determine ultimate risk of onset of anxiety disorder.

THE FUTURE

Although it is well established that children of parents with PDAG are at high risk for anxiety disorders, only some of these children develop psychopathology. The identification of predictors would facilitate primary prevention by delineating a group of young children at very high risk for anxiety disorders among those already at risk by having a PDAG parent. While our initial studies indicate that behavioral inhibition is likely to be a powerful predictor of future anxiety disorders in these children (Rosenbaum et al., 1988, 1991a, 1991b, 1992; Biederman et al., 1990, 1991, 1993; Hirshfeld et al., 1992), these initial findings should be considered preliminary until replicated in larger samples. To this end we will be conducting a 5-year study of behavioral inhibition in a large cohort of children of parents with PDAG. This will form the foundation of a long-term follow-up study aimed at demonstrating the usefulness of behavioral inhibition as a predictor of anxiety disorders from childhood through adulthood.

Since our work shows that children who remain inhibited over time (stable behavioral inhibition) have the highest risk for the later development of anxiety disorders (Hirshfeld et al., 1992; Biederman et al., 1993), the assessment of stable behavioral inhibition can further refine our efforts to identify children at highest risk for development of anxiety disorders in later life. We will assess the stability of behavioral inhibition and the onset of psychopathology over time by reassessing the children at regular follow-up evaluations.

Prospective evaluation of individual and familial factors, identified in the initial assessment, will allow us to examine predictors of outcome for children at risk in general and for those with behavioral inhibition and stable behavioral inhibition in particular. By identifying predictors of vulnerability to disorder in young children at risk, this work will facilitate the design of intervention strategies. This research can lead to the design of pertinent treatment strategies, which may include interventions aimed at stabilization of the parental disorder, dealing more effectively with family conflict, or cognitive approaches aimed at desensitization of the vulnerable behaviorally inhibited child to novelty and other challenges.

While the hypothesis of a link between behavioral inhibition and anxiety is particularly compelling given the phenomenological and theoretical connection between inhibition and anxiety (Gray, 1982), an additional potential research issue is the specificity of this association: Is behavioral inhibition in children specifically or exclusively antecedent to anxiety disorder as opposed to other psychopathology, such as unipolar or bipolar mood disorder, schizophrenia, or other anxiety disorders (social phobia, posttraumatic stress disorder, generalized anxiety disorder)? Although our preliminary studies of children at risk focused on children of parents with PDAG, we could not exclude an independent association with parental depression as well. Thus, behavioral inhibition may be antecedent to depression (or subtypes of depression) or other disorders not yet studied. Once a relationship is established for PDAG, establishing associations between behavioral inhibition and other psychopathologic states could go forward.

REFERENCES

Adamec, R. E., & Stark-Adamec, C. S. (1989). Behavioral inhibition and anxiety: Dispositional, developmental, and neural aspects of the anxious personality of the domestic cat. In J. S. Reznick (Ed.), *Perspectives on behavioral inhibition* (pp. 93–124). Chicago: University of Chicago Press.

Berg, I. (1976). School phobia in the children of agoraphobic women. *British Journal of Psychiatry, 128,* 86–89.

Berg, I., Marks, I., McGuire, R., et al. (1974). School phobia and agoraphobia. *Psychological Medicine, 4,* 428–434.

Biederman, J. (1987). Clonazepam in the treatment of prepubertal children with panic-like symptoms. *Journal of Clinical Psychiatry, 48,* 38–41.

Biederman, J., Rosenbaum, J. F., Bolduc, E. A., et al. (1991). A high risk study of young children of parents with panic disorder and agoraphobia with and without comorbid major depression. *Psychiatry Research, 37,* 333–348.

Biederman, J., Rosenbaum, J. F., Bolduc-Murphy, E. A., et al. (1993). A three year follow-up of children with and without behavioral inhibition. *Journal of the American Academy of Child and Adolescent Psychiatry, 32,* 814–821.

Biederman, J., Rosenbaum, J. F., Hirshfeld, D. R., et al. (1990). Psychiatric correlates of behavioral inhibition in young children of parents with and without psychiatric disorders. *Archives of General Psychiatry, 47,* 21–26.

Carey, W. B., Fox, M., & McDevitt, S. C. (1977). Temperament as a factor in early school adjustment. *Pediatrics, 60,* 621–624.

Charney, D. S., & Heninger, G. R. (1986). Noradrenergic function and the mechanism of action of antianxiety treatment: The effects of long-term alprazolam treatment. *Archives of General Psychiatry, 43,* 1042–1054.

Crowe, R. R., Noyes, R., Pauls, D. L., et al. (1983). A family study of panic disorder. *Archives of General Psychiatry, 40,* 1065-1069.

Davis, M. (1992). The role of the amygdala in fear and anxiety. *Annual Review of Neuroscience, 15,* 353–375.

Deltito, J. A., Perugi, G., Maremmani, I., et al. (1986). The importance of separation anxiety in the differentiation of panic disorder from agoraphobia. *Psychiatric Development, 4,* 227–236.

Earls, F., & Jung, K. G. (1987). Temperament and home environment characteristics as casual factors in the early development of childhood psychopathology. *Journal of the American Academy of Child and Adolescent Psychiatry, 26,* 491–498.

Fyer, A. J., Mannuzza, S., Gallops, M. S., et al. (1990). Familial transmission of simple phobias and fears. A preliminary report. *Archives of General Psychiatry, 47,* 252–256.

Garcia-Coll, C., Kagan, J., & Reznick, J. S. (1984). Behavioral inhibition in young children. *Child Development, 55,* 1005–1019.

Gersten, M. (1986). *The contribution of temperament to behavior in natural contexts.* Unpublished doctoral dissertation, Harvard Graduate School of Education, Cambridge, MA.

Gersten, M. (1989). Behavioral inhibition in the classroom. In J. S. Reznick (Ed.), *Perspectives on behavioral inhibition.* (pp. 71–91). Chicago: University of Chicago Press.

Gorman, J. M., Liebowitz, M. R., Fyer, A. J., et al. (1989). A neuroanatomical hypothesis for panic disorder. *American Journal of Psychiatry, 146,* 148–161.

Graham, P., Rutter, M., & George, S. (1973). Temperamental characteristics as predictors of behavior disorders in children. *American Journal of Orthopsychiatry, 43,* 328–339.

Graham, P., & Stevenson, J. (1987). Temperament and psychiatric disorders: The genetic contribution to behavior in childhood. *Australia–New Zealand Journal of Psychiatry, 21,* 267–274.

Gray, J. A. (1982). Précis of the neuropsychology of anxiety: An inquiry into the functions of the septo-hippocampal system. *Behavior and Brain Sciences, 5,* 469–534.

Harris, E. L., Noyes, R., Crowe, R. R., et al. (1983). A family study of agoraphobia: Report of a pilot study. *Archives of General Psychiatry, 40,* 1061–1064.

Herjanic, B., & Reich, W. (1982). Development of a structured psychiatric interview for children: Agreement between child and parent. *Journal of Abnormal Child Psychology, 10,* 307–324.

Hirshfeld, D. R., Rosenbaum, J. F., Biederman, J., et al. (1992). Stable behavioral inhibition and its association with anxiety disorder. *Journal of the American Academy of Child and Adolescent Psychiatry, 31,* 103–111.

Insel, T. R., & Murphy, D. L. (1984). Pharmacologic response and subgroups of patients with affective illness. In R. M. Post & J. C. Ballenger (Eds.), *Neurobiology of mood disorders.* (pp. 60–75). Baltimore, MD: Williams & Wilkins.

Kagan, J. (1989). Temperamental contributions to social behavior. *American Psychologist, 44,* 668–674.

Kagan, J., Reznick, J. S., Clarke, C., et al. (1984). Behavioral inhibition to the unfamiliar. *Child Development, 55,* 2212–2225.

Kagan, J., Reznick, J. S., & Gibbons, J. (1989). Inhibited and uninhibited types of children. *Child Development, 60,* 838–845.

Kagan, J., Reznick, J. S., & Snidman, N. (1987). The physiology and psychology of behavioral inhibition in children. *Child Development, 58,* 1459–1473.

Kagan, J., Reznick, J. S., & Snidman, N. (1988). Biological bases of childhood shyness. *Science, 240,* 167–171.

Kagan, J., Reznick, J. S., Snidman, N., et al. (1988). Childhood derivatives of inhibition and lack of inhibition to the unfamiliar. *Child Development, 59,* 1580–1589.

Kagan, J., & Snidman, N. (1991). Infant predictors of inhibited and uninhibited profiles. *Psychological Science, 2,* 40–44.

Kagan, J., Snidman, N., Julia-Sellers, M., et al. (1991). Temperament and allergic symptoms. *Psychosomatic Medicine, 53,* 332–340.

Klein, D. (1964). Delineation of two-drug responsive anxiety syndromes. *Psychopharmacologia, 5,* 397–408.

Leckman, J. F., Sholomskas, D., Thompson, D., et al. (1982). Best estimate of lifetime psychiatric diagnosis: A methodological study. *Archives of General Psychiatry, 39,* 879–883.

Margraf, J., Ehlers, A., & Roth, W. T. (1986). Biological models of panic disorder and agoraphobia: A review. *Behaviour Research and Therapy, 24,* 553–567.

Maziade, M., Capéraà, P., Laplante, B., et al. (1985). Value of difficult temperament among 7-year-olds in the general population for predicting psychiatric diagnosis at age 12. *American Journal of Psychiatry, 142,* 943–946.

Maziade, M., Caron, C., Côté, R., et al. (1990a). Extreme temperament and diagnosis. *Archives of General Psychiatry, 47,* 477–484.

Maziade, M., Caron, C., Côté, R., et al. (1990b). Psychiatric status of adolescents who had extreme temperaments at age 7. *American Journal of Psychiatry, 147,* 1531–1536.

Maziade, M., Côté, R., Bernier, H., et al. (1989). Significance of extreme temperament in infancy for clinical status in preschool years: Vol. I. Value of extreme temperament at 4-8 months for predicting diagnosis at 4.7 years. *British Journal of Psychiatry, 154,* 533–543.

Maziade, M., Côté, R., Thivierge, J., et al. (1989). Significance of extreme temperament in infancy for clinical status in preschool years: Vol. II. Patterns of temperament change and implications for the appearance of disorders. *British Journal of Psychiatry, 154,* 544–551.

McDevitt, S., & Carey, W. (1978). The measurement of temperament in 3-7 year old children. *Journal of Child Psychology and Psychiatry, 19,* 245–253.

Noyes, R. Jr., Crowe, R. R., Harris, E. L., et al. (1986). Relationship between panic disorder and agoraphobia: A family study. *Archives of General Psychiatry, 43,* 227–232.

Pollack, M. H., Otto, M. W., Rosenbaum, J. F., et al. (1990). Longitudinal course of panic disorder: Findings from the Massachusetts General Hospital Naturalistic Study. *Journal of Clinical Psychiatry, 51*(Suppl. A), 12–16.

Pollack, M. H., Otto, M. W., Rosenbaum, J. F., et al. (1992). Personality disorders in patients with panic disorder: Association with childhood anxiety disorders, early trauma, comorbidity, and chronicity. *Comprehensive Psychiatry, 33,* 78–83.

Reich, J., & Yates, W. (1988). Family history of psychiatric disorders in social phobia. *Comprehensive Psychiatry, 29,* 72–75.

Reiman, E. M., Raichle, M. E., Butler, F. K., et al. (1984). A focal brain abnormality in panic disorder, a severe form of anxiety. *Nature, 310,* 683–685.

Reznick, J. S., Kagan, J., Snidman, N., et al. (1986). Inhibited and uninhibited children: A follow-up study. *Child Development, 57,* 660–680.

Robins, L. N., Helzer, J. E., Croughan, J., et al. (1981). The National Institute of Mental Health Diagnostic Interview Schedule: Its history, characteristics, and validity. *Archives of General Psychiatry, 38,* 381–389.

Rosenbaum, J. F., Biederman, J., Bolduc, E. A., et al. (1992). Comorbidity of parental anxiety disorders as risk for childhood-onset anxiety in inhibited children. *American Journal of Psychiatry, 149,* 475–481.

Rosenbaum, J. F., Biederman, J., Gersten, M., et al. (1988). Behavioral inhibition in children of parents with panic disorder and agoraphobia. A controlled study. *Archives of General Psychiatry, 45,* 463–470.

Rosenbaum, J. F., Biederman, J., Hirshfeld, D. R., et al. (1991a). Behavioral inhibition in children: A possible precursor to panic disorder or social phobia. *Journal of Clinical Psychiatry, 52*(Suppl. 5), 5–9.

Rosenbaum, J. F., Biederman, J., Hirshfeld, D. R., et al. (1991b). Further evidence of an association between behavioral inhibition and anxiety disorders: Results from a family study of children from a non-clinical sample. *Journal of Psychiatric Research, 25,* 49–65.

Snidman, N. (1989). Behavioral inhibition and sympathetic influence on the cardiovascular system. In J. S. Reznick (Ed.), *Perspectives on behavioral inhibition* (pp. 51–70). Chicago: University of Chicago Press.

Spitzer, E., & Williams, J. B. W. (1986). *The structured clinical interview for DSM-III-R.* New York: New York State Psychiatric Institute.

Suomi, S. J. (1984). The development of affect in rhesus monkeys. In N. Fox & R. Davidson (Eds.), *The psychobiology of affective disorders* (pp. 119–159). Hillsdale, NJ: Erlbaum.

Suomi, S. J. (1986). Anxiety-like disorders in young nonhuman primates. In R. Gittelman (Ed.), *Anxiety disorders of childhood* (pp. 1–23). New York: Guilford Press.

Suomi, S. J., Kraemer, G. W., Baysinger, C. M., et al. (1981). Inherited and experiential factors associated with individual differences in anxious behavior displayed by Rhesus monkeys. In D. F. Klein & J. Rabkin (Eds.), *Anxiety: New research and changing concepts* (pp. 179–200). New York: Raven.

Weissman, M. M. (1988). The epidemiology of anxiety disorders: Rates, risks and familial patterns. *Journal of Psychiatric Research, 22,* 99–114.

Chapter 4

Social Development

Philip Costanzo
Shari Miller-Johnson
Heidi Wencel

I n the face of the increasing prevalence of childhood anxiety disorders, storybook prototypes of happy, untroubled, and playful children seem more an escape from painful reality than symbols of normative childhood experiences. As we come to know more about childhood development and the impact of social contingencies on children's affective and behavioral reactivity, the myth of a blissful childhood seems to be coming apart at its metaphoric seams. It could well be that the increasing pressures of day-to-day coping over the past several decades have conspired to compromise what was once a comparatively blissful developmental stage.

Alternatively and probably more realistically, increased attention to the study of childhood anxiety and distress over the past decade may have revealed that we (as a culture) had been underestimating its prevalence and impact in the past. As we become more vigilant in constructing the meaning of child behavior, the night terrors, specific phobic avoidances, or bursts of unexplained activity (for examples) that might have once been benignly thought of as "Kinderspiel" take on credibility as symptomatic patterns of anxiety disorder. It is not as if "Kinderspiel" or normal developmental crises have ceased to exist. Rather, the organization of pieces of behavioral symptomatology into recurrent patterns with predicted adaptive consequences is now recognizable as anxiety rather than normal developmental challenges.

What accounts for anxiety disorders in children? What "natural" factors buffer children against diagnosable symptomatic panic and anxiety? How can preventative programs for anxiety disorders be constructed in developmentally meaningful ways? What "unnatural" or therapeutic approaches to intervention in the case of anxiety in children might show the greatest promise of efficacy? These are pivotal, difficult, and complex questions. To begin searching the knowledge base to arrive at even provisional answers, one must go beyond the domains of clinical research and theory to the broader venue of social developmental studies. While one must certainly acknowledge the constitutional, biological, and neural bases for at least a subset of the symptom patterns classified as anxiety disorders (Chapters 1, 2, and 3), the potentiation of socially embedded patterns of anxious reaction must at least partially inhere in life course processes as they arise in development. Indeed for a subset of disorders that fit under the rubric of anxiety, social experience, interpersonal processes, and their cognitive sequelae may be primary.

If these presuppositions are valid, there is a gap in our understanding of the connections between social developmental processes and clinical anxiety in children. Most researchers in both social and developmental psychology employ relatively discrete and short-term indices of anxiety arousal and behavior when exploring plausible causes. Clinical researchers, on the other hand, generally center their causal analyses on connected patterns of diagnosable anxious distress in children. Thus, while there is a clear literature depicting the social psychology of anxiety, it generally does not intersect with the clinical literature in patterned manifestations of anxious distress. This is unfortunate, both for clinical knowledge and for our general understanding of adaptive development.

The intent of this chapter is to close this gap between clinical research and theory on anxiety disorders in children and social developmental perspectives and data on anxious reactivity and related phenomena. Perhaps through an understanding of the factors that produce anxious patterns of behavior and cognition in "normal" development, we can come closer to mapping the social correlates of clinically relevant and diagnosable anxiety states in children.

This chapter has two general goals:

1. Examination of the lines of social/developmental theory and research that bear a relationship to the study of anxiety disorders in children.
2. Proposal of generalizations from the literature that have clear implicative value for the diagnosis, prevention, and treatment of anxiety disorders.

SOCIAL PSYCHOLOGY
OF CHILDREN'S DEVELOPMENT

The domain of study that explores social influences on developmental processes has grown rapidly over the past two decades. Both social and developmental psychologists have contributed to this growth (Costanzo, 1992; Dweck & Leggett, 1988; Ruble & Thompson, 1992). While the specific questions asked by researchers in this domain are many, research and theory focus on two general concerns. First, social and developmental researchers are interested in understanding how variations in socialization processes affect the developing behavioral and affective repertoires of children. Second (and of more current emphasis), investigators of social development are interested in tracking the transmission of social expectancies and social constructions in the course of childhood development. Both the behavioral and social-cognitive consequences of socialization are centrally involved in particular developments—including the development of anxiety. Childhood anxiety comprises both symptomatic behavioral components and a set of generalized cognitive expectancies and "fears" about self and the social world. Indeed, the behavioral manifestations of anxiety in children can be portrayed as deriving from the socialized constructions and cognitions chronically held by children. For example, separation anxiety is more than the reflexive experience of "panic" or agitation based on the absence of the prime socializer. It is also a state predicated on the child's acquired belief systems concerning the nature of self and social connections. In turn, this system of beliefs is acquired in the context of experienced relationships and evolve from the relationships and the socialization contingencies that accompany them.

It is in this sense that the study of social development becomes pivotal to our understanding of clinical manifestations of phenomena such as anxiety and depression. Social developmentalists have been keenly interested in the manner and processes by which agents of socialization communicate expectancies about stimuli and circumstances in the environment and in the capacity of the self to master and adapt to those circumstances. This is more than a one-way process, since it has become clear that the targets of socialization also have effects on the agents' behaviors and socialization approaches (Maccoby & Martin, 1983). Thus, constitutional and biological variations in children (such as temperament, for example) can partially effect how parents rear and respond to their children. It is further presumed that the processes socializers use in rearing children are connected to the emergence of meaning structures and resultant behavior of children.

The processes through which socialization "translates" into internalized structures of meaning are the focuses of much contemporary social developmental research. As noted, both social and developmental psychologists are pursuing these questions. From the standpoint of social psychology, the focus is on the way in which variations in processes of social influence affect internalization of schemes and meaning structures in the targets of socialization (Costanzo, 1992; Ruble & Thompson, 1992). Developmental psychologists, while interested in process variation, are further concerned with the particular roles of parents and social structures in the natural world as they connect to such processes (Maccoby & Martin, 1983). Both fields converge on three recurrent lines of research that bear critical relevance to the development of childhood anxiety disorders:

1. Study of the emergence of self-efficacy, perceptions of internal control, and self-regulation in children.
2. Impact of childhood socialization on the development of self-knowledge, self-esteem and chronic patterns of self and other attributions.
3. Emergence of social relationship expectancies in childhood. Of particular interest here is the impact of processes of socializer–child attachment on the development of security and interpersonal trust.

These three lines of research are reviewed as they bear on the phenomena associated with childhood anxiety and its amelioration.

DEVELOPMENT OF SELF-EFFICACY AND SELF-REGULATION IN CHILDREN

From the earliest moments of infancy, a child confronts a world in which the volume of stimuli impinging on the senses requires patterned organization. Such organization is a necessary antecedent to adaptive action—particularly self-initiated adaptive action. In the social world, the organization of "disconnected" stimuli is aided by the infant and toddler's acquisition of context-relevant standards for behavior. In the literature of developmental psychology, early milestones in the child's attainment of such mastery are explored in the work on developing self-regulation. As noted by Kopp (1987), "One of the most demanding aspects of the socialization process requires children to become aware and to conform to standards of socially appropriate behavior and to assume responsibility for their own behavior" (p. 34). In the earliest phases of development, caregivers quite naturally assume control via a variety of social, facial, and nonverbal signals indicating appropriate behavioral accommodation to contexts and stimuli. During this normative socialization sequence, caregiver control gives way to child self-control and finally to child self-regulation.

In the self-control phase, children are able to enact caregiver standards without external monitoring. This obviously implies the development of representational thinking skills and memory, as well as at least a primitive notion of how elements of stimuli in the immediate context are organized. In the self-regulation phase, the child becomes capable of adapting to the changing situational demands of naturalistically fluid circumstances by the use of self-constructed strategic plans and behavior (see Kopp, 1982, for a thoughtful theoretical discussion of this transition). Numerous studies of everyday behaviors, such as feeding, compliance activities, safety-relevant behaviors, and play behaviors (Holden, 1983; Rogoff, Malkin, & Gilbride, 1984; Schaffer, 1984; Vaughn, Kopp, & Krakow, 1984; many others), illustrate the natural flow of the socialized self-regulation cycle.

The particulars of emergent self-control in young children are just beginning to be understood. The comparative gap in the literature on early self-regulation and its development is understandable, given the tediousness and difficulty of observational research that relies on nonverbal transactions between caregivers and children and between children and objects. Nevertheless, the generalized sequence intuited by Kopp plays itself out in numerous research studies of postverbal children and their caregivers, as well as in the study of adaptive and maladaptive control orientations in adults.

Before we illustrate the line of research that defines the acquisition of self-perceived control and self-initiated efficacy in children, it is important both to express the general outcomes of this work and to be clear about why we view it as so pivotal to an understanding of the developmental emergence of anxiety. As we noted at the outset of this section, a prime task from the earliest phases of development is the organization and subsequent mastery of the flow of events in the environment. Constructing the meaning of contexts and developing standards for enacting adaptive behaviors in the face of the events can be viewed as the key processes in the emergence of internalized control over anxiety arousal. More specifically, the inability to cognitively construct frames for understanding how stimuli and contexts "go together" increases the individual's dependence on the whims of a noisy world and accordingly reduces the probability that noxious external stimuli (and the internal arousal they occasion) can be behaviorally terminated or pleasant stimuli can be behaviorally approached.

In essence, the cognitive and behavioral components of organization and behavioral control are the seminal tools that permit the child to reduce uncertainty and ameliorate fear and thus to enact adaptive behavior. Early experiences with an uncontrollable world are likely to be particularly pivotal, since the young child has very few a priori cognitive structures and principles that can account for changes in the environment. In short, a clear definition of anxiety is: *a state induced in individuals when events are conceived as haphazard, when the environment is unstructured and unpredictable, and when adaptive strategies to control either the stimuli or the internal state of arousal they induce are absent.* Given the conditions of socialization, the emergence and chronicity of this kind of state can be specifically attached to a single category of stimuli or circumstances (e.g., separation from caregiver) or can be relatively undifferentiated and diffuse with cross-situational properties.

The capacity to organize environmental events and to predict and control their onset has certain neurobiological and constitutional antecedents that have a particular impact on the development of attentional processes. At the same time, however, it is clear that caregiver–child social interactions are pivotal events that both exacerbate underlying constitutional problems and also function independently to produce difficulties in self-regulation. The social psychology of these transactions in development thus constitutes an important source for understanding the emergence, prevention, and treatment of anxiety disorders in children.

As indicated earlier, the acquisition of self-regulation and its cognitive mediators is a staged process across development. Caregivers vary in their sensitivity to their children's need for external guidance, standards, and directives. In the early phases of development, considerable caregiver control is normative and necessary in the first steps the child takes in constructing the environment. However, caregiver control beyond the cognitive and organizational needs of the child in later phases will forestall the child's acquisition of self-monitored behavioral and cognitive repertoires (see Kopp, 1987, for a discussion). Furthermore, extreme caregiver control will inhibit in later childhood the development of flexible strategic skills that permit the child to organize and master novel environments. The absence of such self-constructions and adaptive skills is likely to vastly increase the probability of an anxious adjustment during childhood.

When the literatures giving rise to the above propositions are examined, several generalizations can be deduced that illustrate the social psychological processes underlying the emergence of self-efficacy and self-regulation:

1. As the child shows capacity for increasingly autonomous functioning, optimally caregiver external control should decline and child self-control be enhanced.
2. Superfluous levels of caregiver control undermine the child's acquisition of a sense of agency and increase the child's dependence on others for mastery over stimuli.

3. Superfluous incentives or controls by caregivers also undermine intrinsic motivation in the child: They make the association between a child's unique intentions and behavioral outcomes more ambiguous.
4. Anxiety and depression result from low self-perceived efficacy and low expectations for control.

These are a few among a number of generalizations that emerge from the social psychological research literature on the development of efficacy and control expectations in children. Initial research exhibiting the consequences of superfluous control on children's acquisition of intrinsic motivation was primarily process-directed and did not explicitly examine actual child-rearing strategies of particular parents and caregivers. Some of the earliest systematic research derived from the cognitive dissonance framework. In particular, Lepper and associates (Lepper, Greene, & Nisbett, 1973) conducted a series of laboratory analogue studies on third-grade children. They did not directly explore the relations to childhood anxiety, but they nevertheless illustrated the powerful role superfluous extrinsic control can play in reducing a child's sense of agency and self-interest.

In Lepper's studies, the typical paradigm involved an *a priori* exposure condition in which children were given the opportunity to solve interesting math puzzles. Directly after the puzzle-solving activity, half the children were provided with a rather substantial reward for their participation and the other half were offered no reward. After a delayed interval of 1 to 2 weeks, children were again exposed to similar math puzzles but as one among a number of interesting activities they could choose to engage in. When the researchers measured the relative time spent with the math puzzles, they found that the previously unrewarded children spent significantly more time and exhibited greater interest in the math puzzles than the rewarded children. Lepper's interpretation was that rewards can undermine a child's interest in initially self-selected interesting activities. In short, oversufficient rewards interfered with children's tendency to see prior choices as governed by their own interest: The reward alone could be viewed as the reason for playing with the puzzles. Therefore, intrinsic motivation and resultant behavioral output were reduced when external rewards were provided.

Later investigators seized on this paradigm in studying the socialization of ambiguous self-efficacy and self-uncertainty. Boggiano and Ruble (1986), for example, explored the implications of extrinsic socializer rewards and sanctions on the self-related cognitions associated with anxiety and motivation. She found that young elementary-school-age children showed high evaluation anxiety in achievement domains in which intrinsic interest was compromised by superfluous sanctions. The consequence of social arousal anxiety was conjectured to be the development of an extrinsic motivational orientation to learning. This kind of orientation includes (1) the need for socializer guides and rules to promote achievement, (2) the avoidance of achievement feedback, and (3) a sense of helplessness with regard to cognitions of competence in a domain. In essence, Boggiano expanded Lepper's focus on undermined interest in children to the particulars of achievement anxiety and evaluation apprehension in children.

Along similar lines, Dweck and Legget (1988) found that children's beliefs about their own capabilities and "control" over the achievement domain had pervasive effects on cognitive processes, affective arousal, and motivation. These investigators discriminated two groups of children, based on performance-oriented style. One group viewed competence as a fixed and unchanging attribute, while the other group connected increases in effect with changes in ability. Again, the origins of the "fixed" style were presumed to be oversufficient adult sanction and feedback and the child's subsequent avoidance of evaluation feedback because of resulting frustration and anxiety. Simultaneously, the child's tendency to connect effortful behaviors with altered negative self-cognitions is undermined by the internalized notion that ability is fixed and outcomes unchanging.

This emergent theme from the achievement-orientation literature plays itself out in multiple domains of the child's activity. The developing belief that action, effort, and strategy have little effect on altering either outcomes or noxious stimuli increases the child's vulnerability to anxious experience. The presumed "structure" underlying these developments is ramified by more clinically inclined theorists (e.g., Harter, Connell, and Bandura) to include generalized low self-efficacy, disrupted self-systems, and pervasively reduced conceptions of competence and/ or effectiveness.

Bandura (1988a, 1990) defines the dimension of self-efficacy as a child's (or person's) belief in his or her capacity to mobilize cognitive resources, motivation, and behavior to control the demands of a situation or task. While deriving his approach from the social learning perspective, Bandura also employed in his theoretical model components of Seligman's learned helplessness theory (Seligman, Abramson, Semmel, & Von Baeyer, 1970) and the aforementioned work on achievement-related control perceptions. The kernel process in Bandura's model is children's socialized expectancy concerning the utility or power of their behavior to alter important effects in their lives. High self-perceived efficacy has been found to be associated with efficient, analytic thinking in complex situations,

increased levels of performance, and increased abilities to visualize success scenarios that further promote effective courses of action. In contrast,
low self-efficacy has been associated with performance-related concerns,
stress, and internalized symptoms such as anxiety and depression. More
intriguingly, individuals low in self-perceived efficacy are more likely to
experience increased autonomic arousal, increases in plasma catecholo-
mine levels, and accelerated opiod secretion when confronted with challenges (Bandura, 1988b). In essence, children who have acquired a reduced
sense of their own capacity to control important outcomes experience
escalations in apprehension when confronting new or frightful experiences,
coupled with a clear inefficiency either to reduce internal arousal or to
change or alter outside obstacles. As we shall see shortly, this kind of
control-mediated anxiety is probably ameliorated by therapeutic interventions that provide children with strategies to master and resources for
offsetting threat. Such interventions are at the heart of much cognitive-
behavioral treatment. Given the degree to which the development of low
self-efficacy beliefs is embedded in a history of socialization where self-
regulation has been coopted by external regulation, the therapeutic res-
toration task is quite a difficult one.

With Bandura's work, we see the expansion of studies in achievement
styles to general efficacy in multiple domains. Harter's (1992) notion of
self-perceived competence serves a similar expansion role in the literature.
From Harter's perspective, there are multiple domains of self-perceived
competence. The lower an individual child's self-perceived competence in
a domain (e.g., achievement or social), the more extrinsic his or her motivational orientation in the domain. The more extrinsic the motivational
orientation, the more reliant the child becomes on external resources to
effect positive outcomes and avoid negative ones. One's perceived inability to competently encounter important events in social and achievement
domains is related to the probability of both anxiety arousal and depression. Specifically, the more pervasive and invariable the perceived lack of
competence, the more chronic these affect states will be. For example,
Harter (1987) has found that depression in children is highly correlated
(approximately $r = .60$) with a construct she defines as low self-worth. Low
self-worth is represented by the discrepancy between the level of importance a child attaches to a competence domain and the child's level of self-
perceived ability in the domain.

The likely root of anxiety in this formulation relates to a child's affective reaction to enact behavior in a domain of low perceived competence. In the life course of the child and adolescent, social-structural demands naturally increase the need for the child to behave competently in
many domains. For example, if a child values achievement but his or her
perceived competence in this domain is low, the natural demands of school

will force the child to encounter this discrepancy often. Anticipatory achievement anxiety and test anxiety are likely results of such exposure. Such states can be accompanied by symptoms such as sleeplessness and worry, trivial anxious behaviors such as nail biting, sweating, and autonomic arousal, and even the inhibition of performance because of over-arousal, thereby justifying the next bout of achievement anxiety. To the extent that children and adolescents find themselves structurally embedded in school contexts, instances of achievement anxiety for those who both value achievement and perceive themselves as lacking control over achievement are likely to be frequent. In addition, the symptoms accompanying such pervasive exposure to anxiety inducers may trigger an attributional pattern that leaves the child with conceptions of self not only as lacking competence but also of being "anxious." This self-perception is likely to promote the spread of anxiety to other domains of the child's life.

In using achievement anxiety as an example, a paradigm for the connections between efficacy expectations, domain importance, and anxious experience is clearly drawn. What is notable in the analysis is the degree to which the inducers of anxiety in children may be partly embedded in characteristics of the social structure accompanying "normal development." As pointed out by Harter (1992) and Eccles, Midgley, and Adler (1984), the effects of adaptation to school culture on extrinsic motivation and efficacy beliefs can be quite considerable, particularly for children with vulnerabilities to appraisal anxiety that might derive from earlier developmental experiences with self-regulatory deficits.

To be more specific, the emergence of achievement-based anxieties is likely to become more evident as the child moves from elementary to secondary school. The school environment becomes more impersonal, formal, and evaluative, and competence activity becomes less supported by teacher or socializer supervision. The very use of external resources (such as teacher support) becomes normatively less acceptable with increasing age. This renders an extrinsic motivational style that is particularly hazardous with respect to anxiety produced by low efficacy. Perceptions of low control over academic performance become more evident as a child moves into adolescence, and internalizing symptoms such as worry, low self-esteem, and anxiety become increasingly apparent during early adolescence as a response to change in school context (see Harter, 1992; Eccles et al., 1984; Simmons & Blyth, 1987). Interestingly, the impact of altered school structure on low perceived efficacy in latency-age children is found to be most evident in developing girls (see Simmons & Blyth, e.g.). One would expect, then, that clinical manifestations of anxiety are likely to increase more markedly for girls than for boys as they move from childhood to adolescence. The epidemiological data for both depression and anxiety appear to bear this out. Paradoxically, the more successful socializers are in convincing children to internalize strong values pertaining to achievement, the more likely it is that the natural factors producing an extrinsic orientation to achievement will result in anxiety or generalize beyond the achievement domain. The thrust of this perspective is that when goals or values are perceived to be important and internal controls are simultaneously perceived to be low, then anxiety and depression are likely results.

While our discussion of Harter's notion of self-perceived competence and its relation to motivational orientation and arousal is confined to achievement, one should not confine application of these principles to this domain alone. For example, a person's self-perceived efficacy in social relationships has more variable standards for individual self-evaluation. However, the dynamics governing the construction of efficacy expectations and perceived internal control in these more "subjective" domains are presumed to follow principles similar to those operative in the case of achievement. Furthermore, efficacy expectations have been shown to generalize across domains. Thus, a child (or adult, for that matter) can be viewed in a typological sense as possessing a generalized expectation of low control for self, with moderate-to-strong relationships to both anxiety and depression.

In at least one recent treatment of the interplay between perceived intrinsic control and anxiety (Connell, 1990), the construct of a "self-system" was refashioned in contemporary terms (it was originally a strong component of Sullivanian theory). The implication of this construct is that developmentally emergent motivational and cognitive schema of intrinsic control comprise the structure of chronic self-conceptions and, in turn, influence both behavior and affective expectations. While control varies across domains of experience, overall perceived self-efficacy predicts vulnerability to anxiety. Self-constructions of efficacy within a domain (e.g., social relationships) should allow for the prediction of delimited and specific anxiety and/or phobias. As we shall see in the subsequent section on attribution, self-knowledge, and social comparison, it appears that the stabilization of self-conception is developmentally completed during the child's latency (e.g., ages 10 to 12). There are a number of developmental, cultural, and cognitive bases for this transition to stable schema. One of the most compelling is the alteration in the societal appropriateness of adult guidance. That is, at latency, parental, teacher, or other adult controls are no longer appropriate compensatory mechanisms for self-regulation and self-perceived efficacy—the child is expected to master the environment with fewer instances of adult surveillance and support. Furthermore, the child becomes increasingly embedded in a peer culture and is exposed to comparative standards of self-evaluation. Finally, the child's capacity to formulate abstract self-categorizations is enhanced by changes in underlying cognitive skills in the domains of language and thought. The clinical implications of this developmental transition are quite rich:

1. Anxious expectations in young children (prior to age 10) are likely to be more situationally delimited and controllable by adult supports than they are in older children.

2. The treatment of anxiety disturbances in young, prelatency children should follow two courses: (a) while self-constructions are still formative, the use of behavioral exposure to manipulations would be sufficient even in the absence of cognitive interventions; (b) the alteration in reward or control contingencies in parents and other socializers is an important aspect of behavioral treatments because the generalization of self-expectancies to day-to-day experience is critical.

3. In older, latency-age children, the treatment of anxiety must take greater account of internal self-representations. As such, the use of cognitive-behavioral strategies as opposed to solely behavioral ones should become more evident. Collateral work with parents and socializers, while a reasonable adjunct, is not a pivotal aspect of the cognitive-behavioral intervention approach. In this developmental period, the clinician is treating anticipatory internal constructions that give rise to anxiety and is less focused on altering external guides that compose the socialization context. This approach is further warranted by the increasing importance of peer standards of evaluation in mid-childhood and latency. If the cultural context is at all relevant to treatment, efforts need to be more strongly focused on peer than authority contexts. Most clearly, however, therapeutic interventions related to anxiety in latency-age children (and beyond) require careful attention to internalized beliefs about self-efficacy, control, and the stability of perceived environmental structures surrounding and mediating these beliefs. Thus, a "critical period" for the initiation of cognitive-behavioral treatment of anxiety in children should ensue at latency. Perhaps an example derived from social developmental literature will illuminate this supposition. In early cases of school phobia and school refusal (prekindergarten through second grade) behavioral exposure and working with socializers are most important. It is important to "get the child to school," and the expectation is that anxiety will dissipate with exposure. When school phobia either emerges or persists beyond third grade, simple exposure does not suffice, and the treatment of underlying cognitions concerning self and the school environment becomes important.

4. Finally, the literature on the development of efficacy beliefs im-

plies that the early instances of anxiety are likely to be situationally de-limited rather than cross-situational or free floating. Furthermore, early developmental instances of specific fears and anxiety that go untreated are likely to eventuate into more generalized belief structures and resultant anxiety. Although this is an empirical issue, the literature on the development of self and social cognitions briefly considered in the next section firmly suggests this conclusion.

ATTRIBUTIONS, SOCIAL COMPARISONS, AND SELF-KNOWLEDGE

In the preceding section of this chapter, we feature the work on efficacy beliefs and expectations. It should be noted once again that this work constituted the primary core of social developmental theory and research with regard to the study of child psychopathology, including childhood anxiety. In this section and the next, our goal is to briefly articulate the underlying process base for examining the origins of efficacy expectations and affectively mediated self-systems. In this section we consider the development of social-cognitive processes from early to later childhood; in the final section we consider the early interpersonal origins of beliefs about the self and the social world, particularly the implications of early attachment relationships for the development of anxiety.

As can be intuited from our coverage of self-efficacy beliefs, the development of anxiety across the life span depends on the individual's construction of the meaning of events in the social world and the role of the self in such constructions. Across development, children come to schematize the world along dimensions crucial to the level of anxiety they chronically experience. In the most general terms, the environment can be construed as a benign place or a threatening place; outcomes can be viewed as predictable or unpredictable; self can be viewed as an "origin" or "pawn" in the attainment of outcomes (including the warding off of negative affect). The combination of the schematization of the world (or components of it) as threatening with beliefs in the unpredictability of events and "pawnship" (or low efficacy) of the self in mastering aspects of that world is the complex meaning struc-ture that is likely to give rise to the experience of anxiety in a child. The more chronic the complex scheme, the more repetitive and pervasive the anxiety.

Attributions

The historical bases of current social-cognition work evolves from the marriage of interpersonal psychiatry (e.g., Sullivan, 1965) and person-perception perspectives (Heider, 1944). These models combine to form the contemporary foundation for examination of the relationship between attributions and maladaptive behavior in children. The literature on the development of attribution processes is voluminous, and we touch on only those facets that bear a relevance to anxiety and the development of anxiety-prone constructions.

The most interesting work on attribution from the standpoint of psychopathology has been the study of systematic biases and consistent "illusions" in social and self-attribution processes (see Ross & Nisbett, 1982). Despite the apparent simplicity and obviousness of logically grounded processes of attribution, human social and self-inference is literally dominated by biases, or "errors" in attributional process. Many of the biases of attribution are viewed as quite natural and adaptive despite their *a priori* illogicality. Some generally adaptive biases include such phenomena as *correspondence error* (Jones & McGillis, 1976), the tendency for behavior to flood the field of perception and attribution. Because of their objectivity, behavior and outcomes are more prepotent forms of attributional evidence. This leads perceivers to often discount their own and actors' intentions or environmental inductions to action in inferring traits of the actor. While young children show a greater tendency toward correspondence error than do older children and adults, it functions as a frequent socially shared illusion for all of us.

Another example of a frequent and natural error of perceivers is the *self-serving bias*. This is a self-favoring attributional tendency that explains either our failures as externally caused or our successes as ones of intrinsic ability. This bias promotes a stance of positive expectancy and buffers the self against declines in esteem. Both correspondence error and self-serving bias are prominent in human social and self-perception because they generally favor adaptation. Thus, through correspondence error, we are in a position to get a quick read on social circumstances and others in the environment through the use of readily accessible cues. In the flow of social transactions, such a quick read promotes the kind of rapid adjustments that move us to approach or avoid others and select situations suited to the self. Self-serving bias, while frequently illusory, promotes positive anticipation, optimism, and continued motivation in domains of achievement.

A third example of a bias that is relevant to the developing experience of anxiety is the "belief in a just world" (Lerner, 1980). Through socialization, we come to the construction that "people get what they deserve and deserve what they get." This *justice bias* results in distortion in our perception of the causes of a variety of outcomes that accrue to self and others in the environment. In young children, it is clear that despite antecedent circumstances, people who are punished are viewed as bad, those rewarded as good. This bias becomes more subtle with development and results in phenomena like blaming the victim. Indeed, a breakdown in the justice bias is most likely to be found in victims of traumatic experience who are confronted with such a challenge to their just world schema that they frame a new ideology. To illustrate, victims of trauma (e.g., rape) frequently blame themselves in order to reestablish the perception of justice, stability, and control. In short, justice biases buffer individuals against the view of the world as threatening and unpredictable but can lead to dysfunctional constructions (e.g., self-blame, fear). Children, in particular, are set to perceive order and justice in the environment because of a generally positive view of authority. Socializers promote such views, and in most instances, they bring about adaptive illusions.

How do psychopathology and anxiety relate to social-cognitive illusions and biases? In general, researchers of social cognition have found two general forms of negatively adaptive social perception related to such illusions. The first relates to the rigid and overly pervasive application of biases and the second relates to the generalized chronic failure of "normal" illusions and biases (see Costanzo, 1991).

The two domains of psychopathology that have received greatest focus among social cognition researchers are antisocial aggression and depression. In the first domain, Dodge and Feldman (1990) present convincing data to indicate that antisocial aggression in children is mediated by faulty information processing in social cognition. The fault they explicitly find in such children is an overly strong correspondence bias in the case of aggression. That is, aggressive children are more likely than their normal counterparts to infer that others' negative behaviors "correspond" to their underlying hostile intentions (when indeed intentions are ambiguous at most). Such children then aggress to ward off anticipated hostility from others and retaliate for perceived wrongs. Considerable evidence indicates that this hostile attributional bias (or negative correspondence bias) is quite prevalent in children diagnosed as antisocial. Furthermore, contemporary research suggests that social-cognitive interventions designed to alter specific correspondence bias in children successfully reduce antisocial adjustments in children (see Asher & Coie, 1990, and Dodge & Feldman, 1990, for discussions).

In the case of depression, social-cognitive researchers most generally find a breakdown in both adaptive correspondence biases and self-serving biases. In depressed individuals, the buffers provided by optimistic self-serving biases and simple behavioral correspondence bias are less evident than they are in nondepressed individuals (Alloy & Abramson, 1979). In essence, those prone to depression are realistic in intuiting the level of positive control they exert over their own outcomes; such realism seems to be an antecedent to depression (Alloy & Abramson, 1979). The data in support of this cognitive buffering hypothesis are intriguing. Depressed individuals have been found to be less likely to distort or enhance the degree of control they exert over their positive outcomes. Indeed, in experimental settings, they have been found to be more accurate in their inferences of personal control. In short, self-serving bias can be viewed as an adaptive illusion buffering the individual against depression. Models for the cognitive-behavioral treatment of depression generally seek to reestablish positive and illusory biases. In the case of depression in children, what becomes particularly important is the socialization context. At this point in this developing literature, it appears a defensible conclusion that depressed parents "share" their schema with the child, leading to shared cognitive styles that militate against the development of adaptive or self-serving biases.

The relationship between social-cognitive biases and anxiety has not been subjected to the same intensity of study as the relationship of anti-social aggression and depression. Nevertheless, the research discussed earlier on self-efficacy beliefs and their role in stabilizing a child's expectations is clearly relevant to the attributional basis of anxiety. From the standpoint of social-cognitive research on children, anxiety would flow from styles of attribution that increase rather than decrease uncertainty and unpredictability in domains of perceived threat. Cognitive-behavioral approaches to complex forms of anxiety (e.g., undefined and free-floating varieties) must attend to therapeutic processes that are focused on reattribution training in which the child is assisted in locating stable causes that account for his or her arousal and sense of threat. Even if these perceived causes represent illusory foreclosures on cause, they should drive a social construction system that is more ordered. Simpler cases of anxiety in children such as phobias, in which particular objects have already been identified as sources of arousal, are best dealt with by the use of exposure treatments alone. In these cases, the child has located stable and predictable causes for affect arousal such that reorientation of attribution is probably a superfluous therapeutic step. In short, the social-cognitive treatment of anxiety should be selectively applied to arousal states for which environmental or personal causes are unlabeled by the individual.

Peer Social Comparison

In middle childhood, the ongoing process of information seeking and self-evaluation broadens its social reference point from the family to the peer group. This change in social reference is a pivotal aspect of the transition from early childhood to adolescence. This transition is also associated with

profound cognitive changes in the child's ability to abstract and generalize from prior experience to anticipations and expectations of subsequent
experience. Because both the social referential transition and the cognitive transition is so evident in middle childhood, it is important to recognize changes in the child's experience of anxiety and therapeutic distinctions in younger versus older children. As we noted earlier in this chapter,
because of the ideological schema that develop and are internalized during early socialization with parents, the latency-age child's experience of
anxiety-based symptoms is likely to be predicated on relatively fixed and
general meaning structures that have wide applicability. As a consequence,
the treatment of anxiety in the latency-age child requires attention to the
cognitive structures guiding affect. Simple flooding and exposure, then,
are likely to become a much less effective approach to treatment (except
in cases in which relatively primitive, specified fears and phobias are carried forward into adolescence and beyond).

One of the more perplexing natural paradoxes of development is
brought about by the child's gradual adoption of the peer group as a prime
reference group. The paradox is fostered by the temporal overlap between
the cognitive solidification of meaning structures from early childhood and
the introduction of new sources of belief flowing from newly empowered
peer influence (Costanzo, 1970). In short, at about the time the child develops fixed and stable self- and social expectations, the peer group assumes
a powerful role in creating new and perhaps conflictual self- and social
cognitions. As the peer group becomes part of the child's appraisal system, old anxieties can be somewhat naturally ameliorated and new anxieties introduced. That is, the latency-age child can find clear social support for discarding vulnerable, early learned belief structures that could
have occasioned anxiety in the past. At the same time, he or she adopts a
new set of standards and beliefs that result in the introduction of new bases
for anxiety (Gore, 1992).

Two general forms of appraisal flowing from peer contexts are *comparative appraisal* and *reflected appraisal*. In *comparative appraisal*, the
child employs others as benchmarks for the evaluation of his or her own
abilities and traits, particularly competence-related attributes. One important way in which children discover whether they are good at math or in
social friendships, for example, is to compare themselves to their peers.
This form of appraisal has a couple of developmental consequences. First,
the child gains knowledge about elements that distinguish self from other
and thereby fosters unique identity. A more negative consequence is that
the child is exposed to new sources of appraisal and evaluative anxiety,
which can result in reduced self-esteem, lowered motivation, and negative
self-expectancies (Ruble & Frey, 1991). *Reflected appraisal* is the process

by which children become attentive to the attitudes of others toward them. This process is critical in the child's reformulation of self-concept and is discussed briefly in the next subsection.

A considerable body of research has been done recently on *comparative appraisal*—children's reactions to social comparison. Ruble and colleagues (e.g., Ruble & Frey, 1991; Ruble & Thompson, 1992; Frey & Ruble, 1990) have done a number of interesting experimental demonstrations of the effects of social comparison. Among their findings:

1. Children compare their own performances to others' from a very early age. However, they are not affectively aroused by the comparisons until approximately age 10, and they do not incorporate the results of these comparisons into a self-evaluation until after age 10. In short, peers and their behavior are of interest to children from toddlerhood, but by middle childhood, curiosity gives way to self-evaluative anxiety.

2. Some children develop overly rigid standards of comparison during latency and on this basis raise comparative competence failures to a kind of "moral" anxiety (i.e., a general sense of being a "bad" and generally incompetent person). Indeed, in adolescence, rigid and distorted comparison standards constitute clear bases for bouts of anxiety, low self-esteem, and negative self-expectancy.

3. Since in many instances latency-age children develop distorted as well as rigid comparison standards (Gore, 1992; Ruble & Thompson, 1992), it is frequently important for clinicians to augment cognitive–behavioral approaches with the kind of "peer feedback" comparison circumstances that issue from group treatment. That is, part of the cognitive reformulation of anxiety-inducing negative self-standards should employ the child's emerging orientation toward the peer group. Indeed, if the literature on relative peer and adult social influence is relied on (Costanzo, 1970; Costanzo, Coie, & Dorval, 1985), clinical approaches to ameliorating anxiety and depression in latency through adolescence must at least partly employ peer feedback systems. Therapists, like parents, lose a measure of their effectiveness in peer-centered developmental eras. To the extent that cognitive-behavioral approaches are important to the treatment of anxiety, it is important that reformulated "cognitions" about self and the social world should be formed in peer group contexts.

4. Negative social/self comparisons are self-perpetuating and frequently result in "self-fulfilling prophesies." That is, since negative comparison increases performance anxiety and performance anxiety increases the probability of poor performance, the child who is prone to such comparisons frequently confirms their negative expectations in behaviors (Harter, 1990; Ruble & Thompson, 1992). Breaking this cycle of nega-

tive comparison to negative behavioral confirmation involves the introduction of new standards for self-evaluation. The alleviation of social anxiety and fears of rejection depend upon the interposition of such standards
in the course of counseling and therapy (Crick & Ladd, 1993).

In summary, the peer social comparison pressures that naturally
emerge in development through the middle childhood years embed anxieties in the social context. Children who acquire vulnerable meaning structures relating to their efficacy and to their view of threat are very likely to
suffer with the natural elements of peer social comparison. Gore (1992)
and others point out that early social support in the context of family tends
to buffer the child from the anxiety-inducing properties inherent in peer
comparison and comparative self-appraisal.

Revisiting Self-Cognition

Throughout this chapter, we have referred to the involvement of formative self-schemas in the emergence of anxiety in childhood. Beliefs about
one's efficacy (Bandura, 1990) or one's competence and worth (Harter,
1990) or one's standing relative to others (Ruble & Frey, 1991) have been
discussed as significant components of the cognitive underbelly of anxiety in children (as well as adults). Mental constructions of the social world
are not simply developing objective intellectual categories but are most
compelling in the context of cognitive systems also containing emotionally
loaded constructions of the self. From the standpoint of social-cognitive
research and theory, the combination of low self-evaluation, high environmental unpredictability, and high perception of chronic environmental threat begets the kinds of expectancies that give rise to dysfunctional
anxiety.

Although additional treatment of the domain of self-concept would
be largely redundant with the foregoing discussions of efficacy, competence, and social cognitive structures in anxiety, it is important to introduce an emerging framework in social development that further elucidates
the relationship of self-concept to anxiety. Higgins (1987, 1989) has recently developed a theory of the reorganization of self-states that is highly
relevant to clinical phenomena such as anxiety and depression in children.
Higgins partitions the structures that develop to promote self-schemati-
zation into three categories: (1) the "real self," or the way a child actually
characterizes his or her own attributes; (2) the "ought self," or the socialized standards that children portray as guiding their behavior; and (3) the
"ideal self," or the goals the child seeks to achieve for self. By its very
nature, the real self always falls short of both the ought self and the ideal

self. The magnitude of these discrepancies is an important factor in the child's anxious and depressed adaptation. Employing an open-ended self-endorsement questionnaire to assess the three components of self, Higgins has found that children who show large discrepancies between real and ideal self-constructions also score high in scales of clinical depression. Children who show large discrepancies between their constructions of real self and ought self score high on clinical scales of anxiety. In essence, from Higgins's perspective, anxiety is a product of the child's internalization of standards for self that far exceed self-concepts.

These findings reveal a similarity with the data on social comparison discussed earlier. Reflected appraisal, like comparative appraisal, sets conditions for self-evaluation. The source of anxiety that derives from self-concept appears to inhere in the failure of self to meet the standards set in transactions with socializers. Therapeutic approaches to address discrepancies in self-perceptions can help the child reformulate standards for behavior or reformulate his or her perceived adherence to such standards. These types of cognitive-behavioral interventions would be most effective in the case of anxiety-prone self-cognitions.

It is interesting to note that the ought self/real self discrepancies that Higgins found to relate to anxiety are the products of socialized relationships with caretakers. That is, the standards we internalize for self are ones that are likely to emerge from developmentally early interactions. When such relationships are supportive and secure, discrepancies should be less frequent and more "buffered" when they do occur. In the last section of this chapter, we take a close look at the context of early relationship formation as it relates to social and self-construction.

SOCIAL PSYCHOLOGY OF ATTACHMENT
AND EARLY RELATIONSHIPS

Given current knowledge of social development, the importance of attributional styles, self-efficacy, and self-esteem in the development of anxiety is primary. Yet it is worth briefly discussing the implications of a newly emerging direction in the study of social development that bears on anxiety.

One of the most promising new areas in the study of social development is the psychological consequences of early socializer–child relationships. The concerted study of the centrality of early attachment relationships was initiated by John Bowlby's (1969, 1988) ecological–evolutionary perspective, which asserted that the attachment behavioral system between mother and infant is biologically predicated as a basis for protection from predators and for safe exploration of the environment. With evolution and the alteration in the social contexts of human behavior over time, the survival of the attachment behavioral system now manifests itself in dimensions like trust and general safety rather than in protection from predatory intraspecies and/or interspecies' rivalry.

In many ways, the attachment behavioral system constitutes the origin for the cognitive schema we have discussed in relation to "predictability" and threat. As Ainsworth (1982, 1990) proposed:

1. Parents who are responsive to infant communication in the early stages of life imbue a child with a sense of control and predictability over the environment.
2. With secure attachment, an infant is unlikely to exhibit anxiety as long as he or she possesses working models of reassurance that a parent will be available if the child experiences needs.
3. Insecurely attached infants have low expectations about parent availability and demonstrate high-intensity attachment-seeking behaviors (that are frequently disorganized).

In pursuing these propositions, Ainsworth designed a research paradigm that moved the study of attachment forward. In the "Stranger Paradigm," babies are brought to a laboratory playroom with their mothers. After a period of play with mothers in the room, the mothers leave the babies alone with an experimenter–stranger and play objects. The critical measures of attachment style are collected when the mothers return to the setting and rejoin their babies. Using this general paradigm, Ainsworth and numerous other researchers found three types of attachment–reunion patterns. The first is referred to as *secure attachment* and occurs in approximately 50% of the infants; reunion styles included reapproach to the mothers and low levels of anxious behaviors such as crying and/or protest. The researchers found two patterns of insecure attachment. One was referred to as *anxious–ambivalent attachment*: On reunion, babies approached, protested, hugged, and hit their mothers and exhibited intensive clinging behaviors (approximately 25%). The other pattern found was an *avoidant* style in which the baby totally ignored the returning mother and focused on other individuals and/or activities (approximately 25% of tested babies).

While these results are interesting in their own right, what is more pertinent to the study of developing anxiety is the durability and continuity of these effects beyond infancy. A number of researchers have found that the early attachment classifications of infants persist across development and constitute the roots of the child's ideology concerning trust and the development of self-system components (Cicchetti & Beeghly, 1990; Cicchetti, Cummings, Greenberg, et al., 1990). The mechanism for the continuity of attachment style has been conceived to be the child's internalization of working models of social relationships. The work of Main, Kaplan, and Cassidy (1985), as well as that of Bretherton (1985), indicates that these attachment patterns are equally discernible in middle childhood. Indeed, there is a suggestion that such patterns are reintensified in later developmental contexts (e.g., the child's entry into school or day care) that elicit attachment constructions. Early dynamics of attachment should have a profound influence on specified anxiety disorders such as separation anxiety in the school years. It would seem important to examine whether attachment history is a predictor of separation anxiety in children. Specifically, secure early attachment should be a buffer against the experience of separation and relationship-based anxieties in later childhood. Conversely, insecure anxious or avoidant attachment histories should increase a child's vulnerability to such disorders.

There is both clinical evidence and implicative research evidence that vulnerability to anxiety-based interpersonal disorders in childhood and adolescence follows from early attachment-based anxieties. For example, Raush and colleagues' (Raush, Barry, Hertel, & Swain, 1974) clinical data suggest that severe anxiety deriving from early life relationships inhibits the recognition of new experiences because anxiety-provoking experiences in the current world become assimilated to schema from earlier life situations. Furthermore, a number of researchers (e.g., LaFreniere & Sroufe, 1985; Sroufe, 1990) have found that children who demonstrated anxious attachments in infancy displayed less competent peer relations in preschool than those with secure attachment histories. Finally, evidence shows that early acquired relationship-based anxiety is associated with aggressive conflict-resolution tactics in adolescence.

From the standpoint of our discussion of the social-cognitive and efficacy-based components of childhood anxiety, these preliminary data begin to support an origin for underlying schema that give rise to anxiety. Clearly, much remains to be done in linking the dynamics of early attachment to psychological disorder in clinical populations of children. The implications of attachment for states such as anxiety are clear, particularly in considering the important role of socially based mental models. A child's initial exposure to exchanges of trust, predictability, and support are important starting points for the internalization of ideologies that guide self-attribution, self-efficacy, and social comparison, for examples. By finding ways to assess early instances of attachment difficulty, one might find that a primary step in the prevention of childhood disorder is the remediation of early disruptions in attachment relationships. Indeed, the therapeutic "correction" of anxiety arousal in children would involve measured exposure to new relationships and cognitions concerning trust.

POSTSCRIPT

In this chapter we discuss the possibilities for the linkage of social developmental research with clinical research on anxiety. It often seems that basic research and clinical research operate in parallel. We must remember, however, that both clinical researchers and basic researchers of child behavior observe the same organisms and many of the same determinants and outcomes.

Anxiety is a dimensional as well as categorical phenomena. That is, it is a form of psychopathology with which all "normal" and "disordered" individuals have experience. In social science such states as anxiety are generated by momentary inductions (e.g., of unpredictability or low efficacy). In life, such inductions are real and pervasively consistent. One must have faith that there is a continuity between lab creations of anxious experience and real-life creations of anxiety disorder for this chapter to have meaning. In that respect, we must be clear on several points:

1. Anxiety is a socialized state and/or trait in children.
2. Anxiety depends on cognitive representations of self and the social world.
3. Cognitive representations and constructions themselves can be traced to socialization contingencies.
4. Such contingencies can be altered and restructured by therapeutic and preventive steps.
5. What we know about the things that alter anxious experience in the child research context should affect the therapeutic inductions we employ in real-life clinical phenomena.
6. No aspect of development can be disconnected from its conceptual "neighbors" when one is searching out the determinants of pressing and difficult psychopathological states.

If we did not believe all that, the disciplines of developmental psychopathology, child psychiatry, and child clinical psychology would be anxious ones indeed. They would be possessed of the same lack of predictability, pessimism about success, and "pawnship" that seem critical components of a child's anxious experience. If we cannot find the means to control a phenomenon, we become victim to it. We the writers hope that the study of social development helps decrease our "victimization" and helps advance knowledge about the nature of childhood anxiety.

REFERENCES

Ainsworth, M. C. S. (1982). Attachment: Retrospect and prospect. In C. M. Parkes & J. Stevenson-Hinde (Eds.), *The place of attachment in human behavior* (pp. 3–30). New York: Basic Books.

Ainsworth, M. C. S. (1990). Some considerations regarding theory and assessment relevant to attachments beyond infancy. In M. T. Greenberg, D. Cicchetti, & E. M. Cummings (Eds.), *Attachment in the preschool years* (pp. 463–488). Chicago: University of Chicago Press.

Alloy, L. B., & Abramson, L. Y. (1979). Judgment of contingency in depressed and nondepressed students: Sadder but wiser? *Journal of Experimental Psychology, 108,* 441–485.

Asher, S. R., & Coie, J. D. (1990). *Peer rejection in childhood.* Cambridge, MA: Cambridge University Press.

Bandura, A. (1988a). Self-regulation of motivation and action through goal systems. In V. Hamilton, G. H. Bower, & N. H. Frijda (Eds.), *Cognitive perspectives on emotion and movitation* (pp. 37–61). Dordrecht: Kluwer.

Bandura, A. (1988b). Self-efficacy mechanism in physiological activation and health-promoting behavior. In J. Madden IV, S. Matthysse, & J. Barchas (Eds.), *Adaptation, learning, and affect.* New York: Raven.

Bandura, A. (1990). Reflections on nonability determinants of competence. In R. J. Sternberg & J. Kolligan (Eds.), *Competence considered* (pp. 315–408). New Haven, CT: Yale University Press.

Boggiano, A. K., & Ruble, D. N. (1986). Children's responses to evaluative feedback. In R. Schwarzer (Ed.), *Self-relation cognitions in anxiety and motivation* (pp. 195–227). London: Erlbaum.

Bowlby, J. (1969). *Attachment and loss.* New York: Basic Books.

Bowlby, J. (1988). *A secure base: Parent–child attachment and healthy human development.* New York: Basic Books.

Bretherton, I. (1985). Attachment theory: Retrospect and prospect. In I. Bretherton & E. Waters (Eds.), *Growing points of attachment theory and research* (Monographs of the Society for Research in Child Development, Vol. 50, Serial No. 209, pp. 3–55). Chicago: University of Chicago Press.

Cicchetti, D., Cummings, E. M., Greenberg, M. T., et al. (1990). An organization perspective on attachment beyond infancy. In M. T. Greenberg, D. Cicchetti, & E. M. Cummings (Eds.), *Attachment in the preschool years* (pp. 3–40). Chicago: University of Chicago Press.

Cicchetti, D., & Beeghly, M. (1990). Perspectives on the study of the self in transition. In D. Cicchetti & M. Beeghly (Eds.), *The self in transition* (pp. 1–17). Chicago: University of Chicago Press.

Connell, J. P. (1990). Context, self, and action. A motivational analysis of self-system process across the lifespan. In D. Cicchetti & M. Beeghly (Eds.), *The self in transition* (pp. 61–97). Chicago: University of Chicago Press.

Costanzo, P. R. (1970). Conformity development as a function of self-blame. *Journal of Personality and Social Psychology, 14,* 266–274.

Costanzo, P. R. (1991). Morals, mothers, and memories: The social context of developing social cognition. In R. Cohen & A. Siegel (Eds.), *Context and development* (pp. 91–132). Hillsdale, NJ: Erlbaum.

Costanzo, P. R. (1992). External socialization and the development of adaptive individuation and social connection. In D. N. Ruble, P. R. Costanzo, & M. E. Oliveri (Eds.), *The social psychology of mental health: Basic mechanisms and applications* (pp. 55–80). New York: Guilford Press.

Costanzo, P. R., Coie, J. D., & Dorval, B. (1985). The relative susceptibility of children and adolescents to the opinion pressure of adults and peers. *Proceedings of the Society for Research in Child Development.*

Crick, N. R., & Ladd, G. W. (1993). Children's perceptions of their peer experiences: Attributions, loneliness, social anxiety, and social avoidance. *Developmental Psychology, 29,* 244–254.

Dodge, K. A., & Feldman, E. (1990). Issues in social cognition and sociometric status. In S. R. Asher & J. D. Coie (Eds.), *Peer rejection in childhood* (pp. 119–155). New York: Cambridge University Press.

Dweck, C. S., & Leggett, E. L. (1988). A social-cognition approach to motivation and personality. *Psychological Review, 95,* 256–273.

Eccles, J., Midgley, C., & Adler, T. F. (1984). Grade-related changes in the school environment: Effects of achievement motivation. In J. G. Nicholls (Ed.), *The development of achievement motivation* (pp. 283–332). Greenwich, CT: JAI Press.

Frey, K. S., & Ruble, D. N. (1990). Strategies for comparative evaluation: Maintaining a sense of competence across the lifespan. In R. J. Sternberg & J. Kolligan (Eds.), *Competence considered* (pp. 167–189). New Haven, CT: Yale University Press.

Gore, S. (1992). Social psychological foundations of stress and coping research. In D. N. Ruble, P. R. Costanzo, & M. E. Oliveri (Eds.), *The social psychology of mental health: Basic mechanisms and applications* (pp. 24–54). New York: Guilford Press.

Harter, S. (1987). The determinants and mediational role of global self-worth in children. In N. Eisenberg (Ed.), *Contemporary topics in developmental psychology* (pp. 219–242). New York: Wiley.

Harter, S. (1992). The relationship between perceived competence, affect, and motivational orientation within the classroom: Processes and patterns of change. In A. K. Boggiano & T. S. Pittman (Eds.), *Achievement and motivation* (pp. 77–114). New York: Cambridge Press.

Heider, F. (1944). Social perception and phenomenal causality. *Psychological Review, 51,* 358–374.

Higgins, E. T. (1987). Self-discrepancy: A theory relating self and affect. *Psychological Review, 94,* 319–340.

Higgins, E. T. (1989). Continuities and discontinuities in self-regulatory and self-evaluative processes: A developmental theory relating self and affect. *Journal of Personality, 57,* 407–444.

Holden, G. W. (1983). Avoiding conflict: Mothers as facilitators in the supermarket. *Child Development, 54,* 233–240.

Jones, E. E., & McGillis, D. (1976). Correspondent inferences and the attribution cube: A comparative reappraisal. In J. H. Harvey, W. J. Ickes, & R. F. Kidd (Eds.), *New directions in attribution research* (Vol. 1). Hillsdale, NJ: Erlbaum.

Kopp, C. B. (1982). The antecedents of self-regulation. *Developmental Psychology, 18,* 199–214.

Kopp, C. (1987). The growth of self-regulation: Caregivers and children. In N. Eisenberg (Ed.), *Contemporary topics in developmental psychology* (pp. 34–56). New York: Wiley.

LaFreniere, P. K., & Sroufe, L. A. (1985). Profiles of peer competence in the preschool: Interrelations between measures, influence of social ecology, and relation to attachment history. *Developmental Psychology, 21,* 56–69.

Lepper, M. R., Greene, D., & Nisbett, R. E. (1973). Undermining children's intrinsic interest with extrinsic reward: A test of the "overjustification" hypothesis. *Journal of Personality and Social Psychology, 28,* 129–137.

Lerner, M. J. (1980). *The justice motive.* New York: Plenum Press.

Maccoby, E. E., & Martin, J. A. (1983). Socialization in the context of the family: Parent–child interaction. In E. M. Hetherington (Ed.), *Handbook of child psychology* (Vol. 4, pp. 1–102). New York: Wiley.

Main, M., Kaplan, N., & Cassidy, J. (1985). Security in infancy, childhood, and adulthood: A move to the level of representation. In I. Bretherton & E. Waters (Eds.), *Growing points of attachment theory and research* (Monographs of the Society for Research in Child Development, Vol. 50, Serial No. 209, pp. 66–104). Chicago: University of Chicago Press.

Nisbett, R. E., & Ross, L. (1980). *Human reference: Strategies and shortcomings of social judgment.* Englewood Cliffs, NJ: Prentice-Hall.

Raush, H. L., Barry, W. A., Hertel, R. A., & Swain, M. A. (1974). *Communication, conflict, and marriage.* San Francisco: Jossey-Bass.

Rogoff, B., Malkin, C., & Gilbride, K. (1984). Interaction with babies as guidance in development. In B. Rogoff & J. V. Wertsch (Eds.), *Children's learning in the "zone of proximal development."* San Francisco: Jossey-Bass.

Ruble, D. N., & Frey, K. S. (1991). Changing patterns of comparative behavior as skills are acquired: A functional model of self-evaluation. In J. Suls & T. A. Wills (Eds.), *Social comparison and social justice: Theoretical, empirical, and policy perspectives* (pp. 81–104). Hillsdale, NJ: Erlbaum.

Ruble, D. N., & Thompson, E. P. (1992). The implications of research on social development for mental health: An internal socialization perspective (pp. 81–125). In D. N. Ruble, P. R. Costanzo, & M. E. Oliveri (Eds.), *The social psychology of mental health: Basic mechanisms and applications.* New York: Guilford Press.

Seligman, M. E. P., Abramson, L. Y., Semmel, A., & Von Baeyer, C. (1970). Depressive attributional style. *Journal of Abnormal Psychology, 88,* 242–247.

Schaffer, H. R. (1984). *The child's entry into a social world.* London: Academic.

Simmons, R. G., & Blyth, D. A. (1987). *Moving into adolescence: The impact of pubertal change and school context.* New York: Aldine De Gruyter.

Sroufe, L. A. (1990). An organizational perspective on the self. In C. Cicchetti

& M. Beeghly (Eds.), *The self in transition* (pp. 281–307). Chicago: University of Chicago Press.

Sullivan, H. S. (1965). *Personal psychopathology*. New York: Norton.

Vaughn, B. E., Kopp, C. B., & Krakow, J. B. (1984). The emergence and consolidation of self-control from eighteen to thirty months of age: Normative trends and individual differences. *Child Development, 55*, 990–1004.

Chapter 5

Epidemiology

E. Jane Costello
Adrian Angold

The last comprehensive review of the epidemiology of childhood anxiety, published nearly a decade ago, stated categorically that "no epidemiological data are available regarding anxiety disorders in children" (Orvaschel & Weissman, 1986, p. 70). The authors were forced to rely on surveys of worries and fears. These and other contemporary surveys of childhood maladjustment or deviance tended to find a high rate of symptomatology, which had, however, a relatively low rate of predictive significance (Kanner, 1945; Lapouse & Monk, 1958; MacFarlane, Allen, & Honzik, 1954; Shepherd, Oppenheim, & Mitchell, 1971). The situation is different today, and so is the picture of childhood anxiety presented by recent epidemiological studies. These tend to focus on the prevalence of specific diagnoses as well as symptom counts. They find relatively few cases of any of the multiplicity of *Diagnostic and Statistical Manual of Mental Disorders* (DSM) anxiety disorders but are beginning to link many of them with significant adolescent and adult pathology.

In this chapter we review what recent epidemiological studies can tell us about the causes and course of anxiety disorders. Epidemiology, the study of patterns of disease distribution in time and space (Kleinbaum, Kupper, & Morganstern, 1982), augments clinical research by tracing the effects of exposure to hypothesized risk factors on rates of onset of the disorder in question. Community samples rather than clinical samples are usually necessary for this kind of research, because in the latter, factors affecting reasons for referral for treatment may confuse the picture. For example, in one community study of children aged 7 to 11, black males with only an anxiety disorder—no comorbid diagnoses—were much less likely than were black girls or white children to reach a treatment setting

(Benjamin, Costello, & Warren, 1990). Thus, a study set in this particular treatment setting would give the misleading impression that uncomplicated anxiety disorders are relatively rare in young black males, an impression negated by the community survey.

This chapter reviews a dozen recent epidemiological studies that meet basic standards of data quality: All use reasonably consistent methods of data collection and diagnosis, representative samples, and information from the child as well as parents and/or teachers. Together, these studies paint a reasonably clear picture of age- and sex-specific prevalence for a range of anxiety diagnoses. However, the picture is far from complete. First of all, while prevalence data are available, conclusions are muted by concerns about methodology—the reliability of current assessment instruments for anxiety disorders—and uncertainty about which diagnoses should be included in the broad category of anxiety disorders. Second, there is a serious lack of incidence data, probably because identifying new cases requires multiple waves of data collection. Third, just knowing how many cases there are in the community is not very useful without information linking those rates to rates of exposure to putative risk factors, measures of functional impairment, and assessments of treatment needs. Fourth, there is a complete absence of developmental epidemiological studies of anxiety: studies that link observed continuity and change in risk and rates to causal theory.

This chapter is able to report progress since 1986, but it still has many gaps. Our review is limited to the age group 6 to 17 because there is so little recent community-based research that includes infants and preschool children. The literature on early temperamental predictors of anxiety is largely based on samples of convenience or clinical samples, and the lack of diagnostic data makes it hard to integrate in this chapter. While we report on several longitudinal studies, few analyses enable us to draw conclusions about the developmental course of anxiety disorders. Also, few link the development of anxiety disorders to a pattern of risk factors or propose primary or secondary intervention programs that specifically target anxiety disorders.

PREVALENCE OF ANXIETY DISORDERS

Table 5.1 shows the rates of anxiety disorders reported in a range of recent community studies selected using the criteria listed in the introduction to this chapter. For comparison, 12-month prevalence rates for the 15- to 64-year-old group are included (Kessler, McGonagle, Zhao, et al., 1994). Since overanxious disorder was intended as a childhood variant of generalized anxiety disorder (and is omitted from DSM-IV), these two diagnoses are

TABLE 5.1. Prevalence of Anxiety Disorders in Recent Epidemiological Studies

Study	Location	Sample size	Age	Prevalence	
1. Anderson, Williams, McGee, et al. (1987)	Dunedin, New Zealand	782	11	Any anxiety disorder	7.4%
				OAD	2.9%
				Simple phobia	2.4%
				Social phobia	0.9%
2. McGee, Feehan, Williams, et al. (1990)		943	15	Any anxiety disorder	10.7%
				OAD	5.9%
				Separation anxiety	2.0%
				Simple phobia	3.6%
				Social phobia	1.1%
3. McGee, Feehan, Williams, et al. (1992)		930 (890)	18	Anxiety disorder	12.4%
4. Bird, Canino, Rubio-Stipes, et al. (1988)	Puerto Rico	777 (386)	4–16	Separation anxiety	4.7%
				Simple phobia	2.6%
5. Costello, Costello, Edelbrock, et al. (1988)	Pittsburgh, Pennsylvania	789 (300)	7–11	Any anxiety disorder	15.4%
				OAD	4.6%
				Separation anxiety	4.1%
				Simple phobia	9.1%
				Social phobia	1.0%
				Agoraphobia	1.2%
				Avoidant disorder	1.6%
				Panic disorder	0.0%

(continued)

TABLE 5.1. (continued)

Study	Location	Sample size	Age	Prevalence	
6. Costello, Strouthamer-Loeber, and DeRosier (1993)			12–18	Any anxiety disorder	17.7%
				OAD/GAD	10.8%
				Separation anxiety	3.2%
				Simple phobia	3.6%
				Social phobia	5.1%
				Agoraphobia	2.2%
				Avoidant disorder	1.8%
				Panic disorder	1.1%
7. Costello, Angold, Burns, et al. (in press)	North Carolina	4,500 (1,000)	9, 11, 13	Any anxiety disorder	5.7%
				OAD/GAD	2.6%
				Separation anxiety	3.5%
				Simple phobia	0.3%
				Social phobia	0.6%
				Agoraphobia	0.0%
				Avoidant disorder	0.0%
				Obsessive–compulsive disorder	0.3%
8. Fergusson, Horwood, and Lynskey (1993)	Christchurch, New Zealand	961	15	Any anxiety disorder	12.8% (C 10.8% P 3.9%)[a]
				OAD	C 2.1% P 0.6%
				GAD	C 4.2% P 1.7%
				Separation anxiety	C 0.5% P 0.1%
				Social phobia	C 1.7% P 0.7%
				Simple phobia	C 5.1% P 3.9%
9. Kashani, Beck, Hoeper, et al. (1987)	Missouri	150	14–16	Any anxiety disorder	8.7%
				Separation anxiety	4.1%
				Simple phobia	9.1%

Study	Location	N	Age	Disorder	Girls	Boys
10. Laucht and Schmidt (1987)	Mannheim, Germany	1,444 (399)	8	"Neurotic and emotional disorder"[b]	6.9%[b]	
11. Esser, Schmidt, and Warner (1990)	Mannheim, Germany		13	"Neurotic and emotional disorder"	8.2%	
12. Offord, Boyle, Szatmari, et al. (1987)	Ontario, Canada	2,679	4–16	"Emotional disorder"[b]	9.9%[c]	
13. Offord, Boyle, Racine, et al. (1992)		936	8–16	"Emotional disorder"	15.8%	
14. Velez, Johnson, and Cohen (1989)	New York State	776	10–20	OAD	Girls	Boys
				10–13	15.4%	12.8%
				14–16	14.1%	5.3%
				17–20	13.8%	5.4%
15. Cohen, Cohen, and Brook (1993)				Separation anxiety		
				10–13	13.1%	11.4%
				14–16	4.6%	1.2%
				17–20	1.8%	2.7%
16. Kessler, McGonagle, Zhao, et al. (1994)	United States	8,098	15–64	Any anxiety disorder	17.2%[d]	
				GAD	3.1%	
				Simple phobia	8.8%	
				Social phobia	7.9%	
				Agoraphobia w/o panic	2.8%	
				Panic disorder	2.3%	

Note. Two or more sets of data in the same cell are different waves of data on the same subjects. Numbers in parentheses indicate the number of subjects actually interviewed.
[a]C: child report.   P: parent report.
[b]Neurotic and/or emotional disorders include both anxiety and depressive syndromes.
[c]Among children for whom both wave 1 and wave 2 data were available, the rate of wave 1 emotional disorder was 15.8%.
[d]12-month rates.

counted as alternative forms of the same disorder (except for the Christ-church, New Zealand, study, where reanalysis was not possible).

Despite the variability inherent in comparisons of studies using a wide range of approaches to measurement, taxonomy, and sample selection, some patterns can be clearly seen. First, anxiety disorders considered as a group are not uncommon. Estimates for the presence of any anxiety disorder ranged from 5.7 to 17.7%, with half the estimates lying above 10%. Figure 5.1 shows the prevalence estimates for the studies as a function of the mean age of the subjects surveyed. There is a trend for rates to increase slightly with age (rank order correlation ρ = .29). While this chapter does not extend to a detailed account of the methodological considerations associated with assessing childhood psychopathology (Achenbach, McConaughy, & Howell, 1987; Angold, 1994), it is worth noting that anxiety disorders are consistently reported by children more than by parents about their children.

Rates for *overanxious disorder/generalizied anxiety disorder* (OAD/GAD) show the widest variability, ranging from 2.6% in the North Carolina study to 15.4% in the youngest cohort of the New York State study. The adult rate of GAD was 3.1%, and it was slightly higher in the 15- to 24-year-old cohort than in older groups. None of the studies in Table 5.1 shows evidence of increasing rates of OAD/GAD with age. With two exceptions (the 10- to 13-year-old boys and girls in Cohen's 1992 analyses), rates of *separation anxiety* are below 5% and fall with age. Most studies report rates of *simple phobia* below 5%, but two show rates above

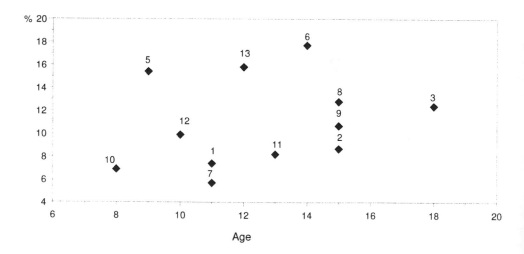

FIGURE 5.1. Prevalence of anxiety disorders by age. Numbers refer to the studies in Table 5.1.

9% (Costello, Costello, Edelbrock, et al., 1988; Kessler et al., 1994). Interestingly, the data give no evidence of a reduction in prevalence with age for simple phobias.

Other anxiety disorders are reported by five or fewer studies and have very low prevalence rates; the conclusions drawn here should be viewed with great caution until other data are published. Only five studies report rates of *social phobia*, and all but one are below 2%. The higher rate is reported by the adolescents themselves in Costello, Stouthamer-Loeber, and DeRosier's 1993 follow-up study. There is no sign of an age trend. Two of the three reports of *agoraphobia* are of 0% prevalence; the other (Costello et al., 1988) found a prevalence of 1.2%. The three reports of *avoidant disorder* give rates of 0% to 1.6%. The two reports of *obsessive–compulsive disorder* are very low, as predicted from clinical studies.

Assessment methods are not yet sufficiently reliable to say to what extent the differences in prevalence rates noted here are the result of real differences in the children sampled or are simply signs of poor measurement techniques. However, the studies show some consistencies as well as variability. OAD/GAD, separation anxiety, and simple phobia are nearly always the most commonly diagnosed anxiety disorders, occurring in around 5% of children, while social phobia, agoraphobia, panic disorder, avoidant disorder, and obsessive–compulsive disorder are rare, with prevalence rates generally well below 2%. The prevalence of anxiety disorder appears to increase slightly with age, but this cannot be observed in any specific disorder; separation anxiety appears to decrease with age.

COMORBIDITY

Comorbidity among Anxiety Disorders

It is clear from Table 5.1 that the use of the DSM-III and DSM-III-R taxonomies results in multiple diagnoses for some children. In our own study of adolescents, using the Diagnostic Interview Schedule for Children (DISC-2.1; Shaffer, Fisher, Schwab-Stone, et al., 1989), only 25 out of 81 anxiety diagnoses occurred unaccompanied by another anxiety diagnosis. So far, community studies have not clarified whether there are patterns of comorbidity between specific disorders. In the North Carolina data, despite a high level of comorbidity among anxiety diagnoses in general, there was no association between phobic disorders on the one hand and the anxiety or panic diagnoses on the other, whereas the latter two groups were closely linked. The Pittsburgh adolescent study actually showed a *negative* association between phobic disorders and the other types of anxiety: OAD/GAD, separation anxiety, and so on were significantly less likely when a phobic disorder was present than when one was absent.

Comorbidity with Other Disorders

Table 5.2 summarizes the data from published studies that permit a review of comorbidity of anxiety disorders with other disorders. The data are presented as odds ratios, the ratio of the rate of anxiety disorders in the presence of the other diagnosis to the rate in its absence. Anxiety disorders are three to four times as likely to be diagnosed in children with depressive disorders as in children with no depression. They occur two to three times as often in children with oppositional or conduct disorders as in those without them. The only study to look at comorbidity with tic disorders and enuresis found anxiety disorders at three times the expected rate. None of the four studies found a significant degree of comorbidity between anxiety disorders and attention-deficit/hyperactivity disorder (ADHD). It is important to bear in mind that while the rates of comorbidity are much higher than expected by chance, the actual numbers in each study are low; much larger studies are needed to confirm the findings.

CONTINUITY OF ANXIETY DISORDERS

Five studies, from New Zealand, Germany, Canada, New York State, and Pittsburgh, have collected more than one wave of data on the same children, at intervals varying from 2 to 5 years. It is not strictly correct to infer continuity of disorder from these studies, since the reference period for each assessment is briefer than the period between the two waves of interviews; there are gaps in the data. However, it is reasonable to infer that children with anxiety disorders at both assessments have at least a greater degree of vulnerability than children with a disorder at only one or at neither time point.

Table 5.3 summarizes the information on continuity. Several of the calculations were made by us, based on the published data, and may be less than precise. Overall, 20 to 30% of children with an anxiety disorder at the later time point also had one at the earlier time point. The coefficients of agreement (κ; Cohen, 1968) are generally within the range defined as poor to fair (Landis & Koch, 1977). However, they point consistently in the same direction: to a moderate level of continuity beyond what might be expected by chance alone. The reliability of the assessment measures used also has to be borne in mind in thinking about continuity. For example, three of the studies used the DISC in one or another of its revisions. The 2-week retest reliability of the earlier version of the DISC

TABLE 5.2. Comorbidity of Anxiety Disorders with Other Diagnostic Groups: Odds Ratios and 95% Confidence Intervals

Study	Depression/dysthymia	Conduct/oppositional	ADHD	Tics/enuresis
Fergusson, Horwood, and Lynskey (1993)	4.6 (2.6–8.0)	3.1 (1.9–5.1)	1.0 (0.4–2.5)	NA
Costello, Costello, Edelbrock, et al. (1988) Pittsburgh, time 1	2.7 (0.4–15.8)	2.3 (1.1–4.8)	2.4 (0.7–8.3)	NA
Costello, Stouthamer-Loeber, and DeRosier (1993) Pittsburgh, time 2	3.4 (1.2–9.5)	2.3 (1.2–4.3)	2.1 (0.9–4.5)	NA
Costello, Angold, Burns, et al. (in press) North Carolina	4.8 (1.6–14.0)	2.1 (1.2–3.7)	2.1 (1.0–4.9)	2.9 (1.6–5.1)

Note. Odds ratios that are underlined indicate a statistically significant difference between rates of anxiety in the presence and absence of another diagnosis.

Table 5.3. Continuity of Anxiety Disorders: Evidence from Longitudinal Studies

Study	n (%) at time 1	n (%) at time 2	n (%) with diagnosis at both times	κ(agreement beyond chance)
Cohen, Cohen, Kasen, et al. (1993) (overanxious disorder)	Mild 125 (17.0%) Moderate 87 (11.8%) 19 (2.6%)	NA	Mild 57/734 (7.7%) Moderate 30/734 (4.1%) Severe 8/734 (1.1%)	Mild κ = .21 Moderate κ = .30 Severe κ = .25
Costello, Stouthamer-Loeber, and DeRosier (1993)	55 (15.4%)[a]	49 (14.4%)	18 (4.8%)	κ = .29
McGee, Feehan, Williams, et al. (1990) (11–15)	49	83	Odds ratio for boys = 2.1 (ns) Odds ratio for girls = 6.2 (p < .05)	
McGee, Feehan, Williams, et al. (1992) (15–18)	87 (9.7%)	83 (9.3%)	31 (3.5%)	κ = .29[d]
Laucht and Schmidt (1987)[b]	22 (6.0%)	20 (5.8%)	3 (0.84%)	κ = .09[d]
Offord, Boyle, Szatsman, et al. (1992)	93 (10.8%)	82 (9.7%)	NA[c] (26.2)	κ = .18[d]

[a]n = actual numbers, rate based on weighted data.
[b]Neurotic and emotional disorders.
[c]Weighted rate only presented.
[d]Estimated from published data.

(Costello, Edelbrock, Dulcan, et al., 1984) in a large clinical sample was $\kappa = .36$ to $\kappa = .54$ for parent-reported anxiety disorders and $\kappa = .27$ to $\kappa = .39$ for child-reported anxiety disorders. For the DISC-2.1, the most recent version for which data are available, agreement above chance for the presence of any anxiety disorder, in a community sample, combining parent and child reports, was $\kappa = .32$ (Jensen, Roper, Fisher, et al., 1994). Thus it appears that the degree of continuity in anxiety disorders across 3 to 5 years reviewed in Table 5.3 is very close to and may have reached a ceiling set by the reliability of the measuring instrument used. However, it is noticeable that the agreement over time found in the three DISC-based studies is higher than the agreement found in the other two studies, one of which used rating scales and the other a "structured psychiatric interview" of unknown reliability.

Two of the longitudinal studies looked at continuity separately by sex, and both note the same thing: The continuity is much more common in girls than in boys. McGee, Feehan, Williams, et al. (1992) found this to be the case for internalizing disorders in general, most of which were anxiety disorders. In the Pittsburgh study, the odds ratio (increase in probability of an adolescent anxiety disorder in those with childhood anxiety over the rate in those without) was much higher for girls (odds ratio 4.0, 95%; confidence interval 2.3–7.2) than for boys (odds ratio 2.4, 95%; confidence internal 1.0–5.7), in whom it was only marginally significant.

RISK FACTORS FOR THE DEVELOPMENT OF ANXIETY DISORDERS

The epidemiological literature is still a long way from defining the set of biological, familial, and environmental factors that put children at risk for specific anxiety disorders. Much of the accepted wisdom about the sociodemographic correlates of anxiety disorders—for example, the larger numbers of Caucasians and girls and the reduction in rates across adolescence—has been based on clinical studies and may be affected by referral bias. Similarly, studies of the genetics of anxiety disorders that use referred children as the starting point are likely to be tapping a highly selected subgroup.

The genetic background of both adult and childhood anxiety disorders is still relatively unknown. Angst, Merikangas, Scheidegger, et al. (1990) found that young adults who had anxiety disorders had parents with high rates of both anxiety and depression. This mirrors findings from a clinical sample (Weissman, Warner, Fendrich, et al., 1990). Kendler, Neale, Kessler, et al. (1992) used a powerful twin design to examine genetic liability for anxiety and depression in adult women. Their conclusion was that the same genetic factors appear to influence liability to both GAD and major depression. The same was not true for environmental risk factors. "Although some of the environmental risk factors for MD [major depression] and GAD are shared in common, a substantial proportion of such factors are unique to each disorder. That is, there must be nonfamilial environmental experiences that are depressogenic without being anxiogenic and vice versa. . . . Common or familial environment played no role in the etiology of . . . GAD" (Kendler et al., 1992, p. 720). It will be interesting to see whether this conclusion is borne out in childhood as well as adulthood.

Historically, it has been accepted that women are at greater risk for anxiety disorders, and this was recently supported in a national survey of the United States population aged 15 to 64 (Kessler et al., 1994), where rates for anxiety disorders were 1.5 to 3 times higher in women. The studies of children reviewed here generally confirm more girls than boys with anxiety disorder of some type. However, when one examines specific diagnoses, the difference quickly disappears for all but global measures of "any anxiety disorder." Only for overanxious disorder was the sex difference at all clear and consistent. Age proves equally elusive as a risk factor when individual disorders are examined. The longitudinal studies listed in Table 5.1 show modest increases in rates from the first to later waves of data collection. However, differences in data collection methods and taxonomy could have affected this. The pattern for specific disorders is uneven. Both the Pittsburgh and New York studies (the only ones where the comparison is possible) showed falling rates of separation anxiety disorders from prepuberty to adolescence. The New York study also showed a fall in overanxious disorders. In New Zealand and Pittsburgh, by contrast, there were modest increases in all anxiety disorders (except for simple phobia in Pittsburgh).

Turning to nongenetic familial and other environmental factors, we once again need longitudinal studies in order to distinguish factors that correlate with anxiety disorders from factors that simply cooccur or are perhaps consequences of the onset of disorder. Unfortunately, few studies go beyond examining risk factors for psychiatric disorder in general to looking for risk for specific disorders or pitting one against another, as Kendler and colleagues did in their genetic study. Cohen and colleagues did do this for the New York State data when they examined the increased risk for a range of diagnoses associated with earlier exposure to a set of family and individual risk factors (Velez, Johnson, & Cohen, 1989). The risk factors for separation anxiety emerged as quite different from those for overanxious disorder. Separation anxiety at ages 11 to 20 was predicted by a history of poverty, low levels of parental education, and parental sociopathy. In these respects it resembled the externalizing disorders. Overanxious disorder, in contrast, was predicted by parental emotional problems, school failure, and stressful life events. In these respects it was similar to depression. In the Pittsburgh longitudinal study, separation anxiety was predicted by family problems and being raised in a single-parent household, as were conduct disorders, whereas overanxious disorder was predicted by poor school performance. Different factors in children's lives at ages 7 to 11 predicted their risk in their teens for phobias, as opposed to overanxious disorder or separation anxiety. All types of adolescent anxiety disorders were predicted by childhood behavioral problems and functional impairment. However, adolescent anxieties were also predicted by number of stressful life events (F 8.3, p = .004), ongoing adversity (F 14.8, p = .0001), and maternal depression in childhood (F 8.0, p = .005), whereas phobias were not. It appears that early adversity had lowered the children's threshold for anxiety disorders later on, but that phobias were not under the same kind of environmental control.

Continuity, thought about in terms of risk, tests the hypothesis that childhood disorder is a risk factor for adolescent disorder. Both the New Zealand and Pittsburgh studies found that childhood internalizing disorders, mainly anxiety, greatly increased the risk of adolescent internalizing disorders in girls, but did not affect their rate in boys. It appears that aspects of the environment may either delay recovery in anxious girls or render them vulnerable to relapse. In the Pittsburgh data, we examined the courses of children with depressive or anxiety disorders in childhood for anxiety and depression in adolescence (Figure 5.2). The trajectories of the boys showed no continuity whereas in the girls anxiety predicted anxiety, depression predicted depression, and depression also predicted anxiety. The association between adolescent anxiety and depression in girls was also highly significant (odds ratio 6.2, 95% confidence interval 2.4–15.5) but not in boys. Thus it appears that for girls, both anxiety and depression in childhood increase the risk of adolescent anxiety disorders.

CONCLUSIONS

This brief review of the current state of epidemiological studies of anxiety disorders shows that considerable progress has been made in the past decade. Diagnosis-based instruments are now available, although the reliability of some limits their usefulness, and reliability appears to be a particular problem in the area of anxiety disorders. There are several good cross-sectional surveys of childhood disorders, and even more important, results are beginning to emerge from the handful of longitudinal surveys around the world. Longitudinal and twin studies are beginning to unravel the tangle of potential risk factors for anxiety disorders, collectively and

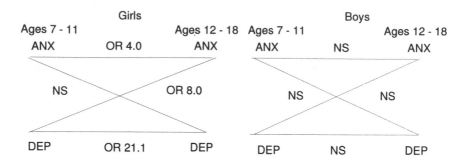

FIGURE 5.2. Continuity of anxiety and depression diagnoses by sex. ANX, any anxiety diagnosis; DEP, any depression diagnosis; OR, odds ratio; NS, not significant. From Costello et al. (1993).

specifically. There are hints of diagnostic specificity in the patterns of prediction, from early adversity to adolescent separation anxiety and from childhood school failure to later OAD/GAD. The sex differences in continuity and change are also extremely interesting. All of these findings, if repeated, will have important implications both for etiological research and for planning interventions.

ACKNOWLEDGMENT

Both authors were supported in part by Faculty Scholar awards from the William T. Grant Foundation and by the Leon Lowenstein Foundation.

REFERENCES

Achenbach, T. M., McConaughy, S. H. & Howell, C. T. (1987). Child/adolescent behavioral and emotional problems: Implications of cross-informant correlations for situational specificity. *Psychological Bulletin, 101,* 213–232.

Anderson, J. C., Williams, S., McGee, R., et al. (1987). DSM-III disorders in preadolescent children: Prevalence in a large sample from the general population. *Archives of General Psychiatry, 44,* 69–77.

Angold, A. (1994). Clinical interviewing with children and adolescents. In M. Rutter, E. Taylor, & L. Hersov (Eds.), *Child and adolescent psychiatry: Modern approaches* (3rd ed., pp. 51–63). Oxford: Blackwell Scientific Publications.

Angst, J., Merikangas, K., Scheidegger, P., et al. (1990). Recurrent brief depression: A new subtype of affective disorder. *Journal of Affective Disorders, 19,* 87–98.

Benjamin, R. S., Costello, E. J., & Warren, M. (1990). Anxiety disorders in a pediatric sample. *Journal of Anxiety Disorders, 4,* 293–316.

Bird, H. R., Canino, G., Rubio-Stipec, M., et al. (1988). Estimates of the prevalence of childhood maladjustment in a community survey in Puerto Rico: The use of combined measures. *Archives of General Psychiatry, 45,* 1120–1126.

Cohen, J. (1968). Weighted kappa: Nominal scale agreement with provision for scaled disagreement or partial credit. *Psychological Bulletin, 70,* 213–220.

Cohen, P., Cohen, J., & Brook, J. (1993). An epidemiological study of disorders in late childhood and adolescence: Vol. 2. Persistence of disorders. *Journal of Child Psychology and Psychiatry, 34,* 869–877.

Cohen, P., Cohen, J., Kasen, S., et al. (1993). An epidemiological study of disorders in late childhood and adolescence: Vol. 1. Age and gender specific prevalence. *Journal of Child Psychology and Psychiatry, 34,* 851–867.

Costello, E. J., Angold, A., Burns, B. J., et al. (in press). The Great Smoky Mountains Study of Youth: Prevalence and correlates of DSM-III-R disorders. *Archives of General Psychiatry.*

Costello, A. J., Edelbrock, C. S., Dulcan, M. K., et al. (1984). *Report on the NIMH Diagnostic Interview Schedule for Children (DISC).* Unpublished manuscript.

Costello, E. J., Costello, A. J., Edelbrock, C., et al. (1988). Psychiatric disorders in pediatric primary care: Prevalence and risk factors. *Archives of General Psychiatry, 45*(12), 1107–1116.

Costello, E. J., Stouthamer-Loeber, M., & DeRosier, M. (1993). *Continuity and change in psychopathology from childhood to adolescence.* Paper presented at the Annual Meeting of the Society for Research in Child and Adolescent Psychopathology, Santa Fe, New Mexico.

Esser, G., Schmidt, M. H., & Woerner, W. (1990). Epidemiology and course of psychiatric disorders in school-age children—Results of a longitudinal study. *Journal of Child Psychology and Psychiatry, 31,* 243–263.

Fergusson, D. M., Horwood, L. J., & Lynskey, M. T. (1993). Prevalence and comorbidity of DSM-III-R diagnoses in a birth cohort of 15 year olds. *Journal of the American Academy of Child and Adolescent Psychiatry, 32,* 1127–1134.

Jensen, P. S., Roper, M., Fisher, P., et al. (1994). *Test–retest reliability of the Diagnostic Interview Schedule for Children (DISC 2.1): Parent, child, and combined algorithms.* Manuscript submitted for publication.

Kanner, L. (1945). *Child psychiatry.* Springfield, IL: C. C. Thomas.

Kashani, J. H., Beck, N. C., Hoeper, E. W., et al. (1987). Psychiatric disorders in a community sample of adolescents. *American Journal of Psychiatry, 144,* 584–589.

Kendler, K. S., Neale, M. C., Kessler, R. C., et al. (1992). Major depression and generalized anxiety disorder: Same genes, (partly) different environments? *Archives of General Psychiatry, 49,* 716–722.

Kessler, R. C., McGonagle, K. A., Zhao, S., et al. (1994). Lifetime and 12-month prevalence of DSM-III-R psychiatric disorders in the United States: Results from the National Comorbidity study. *Archives of General Psychiatry, 51,* 8–19.

Kleinbaum, D. G., Kupper, L. L., & Morgenstern, H. (1982). *Epidemiologic research: Principles and quantitative methods*. New York: Van Nostrand Reinhold.

Landis, J. R., & Koch, G. (1977). The measurement of observer agreement for categorical data. *Biometrics, 33*, 159–174.

Lapouse, R. L., & Monk, M. A. (1958). An epidemiologic study of behavior characteristics in children. *American Journal of Public Health, 48*, 1134–1144.

Laucht, M., & Schmidt, M. H. (1987). Psychiatric disorders at the age of 13: Results and problems of a long-term study. In B. Cooper (Ed.), *Psychiatric epidemiology: Progress and prospects* (pp. 212–224). London: Croom Helm.

MacFarlane, J. W., Allen, L., & Honzik, M. (1954). *A developmental study of the behavior problems of normal children*. Berkeley, CA: University of California Press.

McGee, R., Feehan, M., Williams, S., et al. (1990). DSM-III disorders in a large sample of adolescents. *Journal of the American Academy of Child and Adolescent Psychiatry, 29*, 611–619.

McGee, R., Feehan, M., Williams, S., et al. (1992). DSM-III disorders from age 11 to age 15 years. *Journal of the American Academy of Child and Adolescent Psychiatry, 31*, 51–59.

Offord, D. R., Boyle, M. H., Racine, Y. A., et al. (1992). Outcome, prognosis, and risk in a longitudinal follow-up study. *Journal of the American Academy of Child and Adolescent Psychiatry, 31*, 916–923.

Offord, D. R., Boyle, M. H., Szatmari, P., et al. (1987). Ontario child health study: Vol. II. Six-month prevalence of disorder and rates of service utilization. *Archives of General Psychiatry, 44*, 832–836.

Orvaschel, H., & Weissman, M. M. (1986). Epidemiology of anxiety disorders in children: A review. In R. Gittelman (Ed.), *Anxiety disorders of childhood* (pp. 58–72). New York: Guilford Press.

Shaffer, D., Fisher, P., Schwab-Stone, M., et al. (1989). *The Diagnostic Interview Schedule for Children (DISC 2.1)*. Rockville, MD: National Institute of Mental Health.

Shepherd, M., Oppenheim, B., & Mitchell, S. (1971). *Childhood behavior and mental health*. London: University of London Press.

Velez, C. N., Johnson, J., & Cohen, P. (1989). A longitudinal analysis of selected risk factors of childhood psychopathology. *Journal of the American Academy of Child and Adolescent Psychiatry, 28*, 861–864.

Weissman, M. M., Warner, V., & Fendrich, M. (1990). Applying impairment criteria to children's psychiatric diagnosis. *Journal of the American Academy of Child and Adolescent Psychiatry, 29*, 789–795.

Chapter 6

Assessment

Patricia Stallings
John S. March

ategorical and dimensional approaches support the division of child psychopathology into two broad domains: the *behavioral* (sometimes termed *externalizing*) and the *emotional* (sometimes termed *internalizing*) disturbances (Achenbach, McConaughy, & Howell, 1987). These two broad groupings overlap substantially, and it is common for children to present with symptomatology resulting in the assignment of multiple diagnoses (Cantwell & Baker, 1988). To complicate matters further, children with internalizing psychopathology are better than their parents at reporting symptoms; in those with disruptive behavior disorders the converse is true (Jensen, Traylor, Xenakis, et al., 1988). Other factors shown to influence symptom reporting include patient or parent gender and parental psychiatric status (Weissman, Orvaschel, & Padian, 1980). Although rules have been proposed to resolve diagnostic conflicts stemming from differences in symptom reporting (Reich & Earls, 1987), no clear consensus has emerged. Thus overlaps between diagnostic constructs are confounded by issues involving criterion validity and instrument selection as well as by underlying neurobiological heterogeneity (Fergusson & Horwood, 1993).

In this chapter, we provide an overview of the instruments currently available for measuring anxiety in children and adolescents. We make no attempt to be exhaustive. Our focus rather rests on dimensional and categorical measures of anxiety in young persons that are commonly used in clinical research settings, not on observational or psychophysiological measures. We also omit measures confined to narrow symptom areas, such as dental anxiety. While measures such as these may contribute to a truly developmental understanding of anxiety, they are currently of limited relevance to clinicians and clinical researchers and are constrained by the relative weakness of the descriptive psychopathology literature in any case. Several in-depth discussions of these and other issues are available (Barrios & Hartmann, 1988; Witt, Heffer, & Pfeiffer, 1990; Mash & Terdal, 1988).

BACKGROUND

Fears are ubiquitous among youth; pathological anxieties are presumably less common than normal fears but nonetheless are not rare (Sheehan, Sheehan, & Shaw, 1988). Thus clinicians and researchers interested in childhood anxiety disorders face the task of differentiating pathological anxiety from fears that occur as part of the normal developmental processes. To address this problem, the third edition and the third revised edition of the *Diagnostic and Statistical Manual of Mental Disorders* (DSM-III and DSM-III-R) introduced a subclass of anxiety disorders of childhood and adolescence, linking categorically defined symptom clusters to distress and dysfunction (American Psychiatric Association, 1980, 1987). DSM-IV refines these constructs, while attempting to establish a greater degree of continuity—developmental and nosological—with the adult anxiety disorders (American Psychiatric Association, 1994; also see Part II). Categorical models, however, are not entirely satisfactory approximations of pathological anxiety (Chapter 5), and dimensional measures continue to play a prominent role in attempts by both clinicians and researchers to capture the many faces of pathological anxiety in children (Jensen, Salzberg, Richters, et al., 1993; Barrios & Hartmann, 1988).

Anxiety experienced by young persons is frequently situation-specific, time-limited, and related to normative developmental imperatives. Unfortunately, relatively little is known empirically about the developmental ontogeny of anxiety in children; perspectives as diverse as behavioral inhibition (Chapter 3) and social psychology (Chapter 4) and levels of analysis as different as neuropsychology (Chapter 2) and developmental epidemiology (Chapter 5), have been applied to this area with only the barest hint of integration. For example, fears of small animals and bad weather are common in early childhood; pathological social anxiety may be more common in adolescence. Such fears may be viewed as an adaptive protective mechanism (Chapter 7); only when anxiety is excessive or the context developmentally inappropriate does anxiety become clinically significant (Marks, 1987). Conversely, in obsessive–compulsive disorder (Rapoport, 1991), negative affects may accompany "released" fixed-action patterns that may once have had evolutionary value but have no obvious adaptive value for the afflicted individual. Unfortunately, these and other important dimensions of anxiety in young persons have not been mapped across time, and it is as yet unknown whether they shift attributes or relative importance within gender, ethnic, or cultural groupings (Chapter 5).

Our lack of knowledge in this area in part reflects a want of instrument development, which greatly lags behind that for adults (Jensen et al., 1993). In fact, many scales or categorical measures currently used to assess anxiety symptomatology in young persons are simply age-downward extensions of adult measures. Instruments designed specifically to address anxiety in children and adolescents are helpful for two reasons. First, children appear to undergo a developmentally sanctioned progression in anxiety symptoms, both normal and pathological, characterized by both longitudinal and cross-sectional comorbidities that are quite possibly unique to young persons (Chapter 5). Second, their day-to-day environments differ from those most typically experienced by adults, so the presentation of anxiety also differs, as in "school phobia," for example.

In theory, measures of child and adolescent anxiety can be classified into one of two categories: the state-versus-trait dimension or the global-versus-situation-specific dimension (Roberts, Vargo, & Ferguson, 1989). State measures assess transitory symptoms of anxiety expressed in response to a specific stressor, such as a test or a dental appointment. Trait measures assess symptoms that are stable across various situations or stressors. Global measures assess the child's overall anxiety and make the assumption that anxiety is consistent across situations. Situation-specific measures assess anxiety in particular contexts, for example, social settings. In practice, the state–trait dichotomy has not been well supported in the literature—both states and traits have been construed as representing symptoms that endure for variable periods of time across few or many contexts in response to internal and environmental factors. Thus, with the exception of the simple phobias, most measures attempt to assess relatively stable symptom clusters that are linked to contexts in which the symptoms are most likely to occur. For example, in the development of the Multidimensional Anxiety Scale for Children (MASC; March, Stallings, Parker, et al., 1994), we included discrete questions representing both social anxiety and separation anxiety, expecting that both would exhibit positive correlations with somatic/autonomic anxiety.

Ideally, instruments to assess anxiety in young persons should (1) provide reliable and valid ascertainment of symptoms across multiple symptom domains; (2) discriminate symptom clusters; (3) evaluate severity; (4) incorporate and reconcile multiple observations, such as parent and child ratings; and (5) be sensitive to treatment-induced change in symptoms. With the increasing emphasis on multidisciplinary assessment and treatment strategies, assessment tools also must facilitate communication, not only among clinicians but between clinicians and regulatory bodies such as utilization review committees. Besides advancing clinical utility, access to instruments that offer reliable and valid assessment of anxiety will be a byproduct of and a stimulus to further research.

Despite the fact that no currently available instrument or set of instruments meets these lofty goals, an array of assessment tools is available, and the choice of instruments for evaluating a particular child or adolescent can be daunting. Factors influencing instrument selection include the reasons for the assessment—screening, diagnosis, or monitoring treatment outcome, for example—as well as time required for administration, level of training necessary to administer and/or interpret the instrument, reading level of the child, and cost. We turn now to a discussion of commonly used instruments for assessing anxiety in youth, beginning with semistructured and structured interviews.

SEMISTRUCTURED AND STRUCTURED INTERVIEWS

The interview has long been the mainstay of clinical assessment. While clinician-driven interviews are currently considered acceptable in clinical settings, absence of standardization is problematic for research studies and may not represent optimal clinical practice, either. Thus semistructured interviews, which provide limited opportunities for elaboration as judged appropriate by a clinician examiner, evolved as a means of increasing the reliability of diagnostic assignment. Structured interviews, which severely limit interviewer flexibility, offer the distinct advantage of a standardized method that increases the reliability of diagnoses, especially in epidemiological settings. Structured interviews also can be administered by research assistants with less formal training, thereby reducing costs, although at the expense of validity if not reliability. Computer-driven assessments may serve the same purpose (Baer, Minichiello, Jenike, et al., 1988).

Semistructured Interviews Targeting
Anxiety Disorders

Two semistructured interviews have been developed specifically to evaluate anxiety disorders in youth: the Anxiety Disorders Interview Schedule for Children (ADIS-C; Silverman & Nelles, 1988) and the Children's Anxiety Evaluation Form (CAEF; Hoehn-Saric, Maisami, & Wiegand, 1987). The ADIS, a semistructured interview with both child and parent components, is without doubt the premier instrument for assessing anxiety disorders in youth (Silverman, 1991). Based on the adult ADIS (DiNardo, O'Brien, Barlow, et al., 1983), the ADIS-C relies on DSM-III-R criteria for the anxiety disorders and related disorders and utilizes an interviewer–observer format, thus allowing the clinician to draw information from the interview and from clinical observations. Revisions incorporating DSM-IV criteria are in progress (Anne-Marie Albano, personal communication, March 1994). Each interview—parent and child—requires 1 to 1.5 hours for administration. Items address situational and cognitive cues for anxiety, intensity of anxiety, extent of avoidance, and precipitating events. The parent interview addresses history and effects on the child, while the child interview addresses symptomatology in greater detail. There is considerable overlap between the two versions, with the parent interview focusing more intensively on externalizing disorders, such as attention-deficit/hyperactivity disorder and oppositional defiant disorder. Screening questions allow the interviewer to skip inapplicable portions of the instrument. Composite diagnoses are based on the level of severity endorsed in each interview and the agreement in identification of pathology between the two interviews.

Silverman and Nelles (1988) evaluated the reliability of DSM-III and DSM-III-R childhood anxiety disorder diagnoses. Interrater reliability for the overall category of anxiety was high for child ($\kappa = .84$) and parent interviews ($\kappa = .83$) as well as for the composite diagnosis ($\kappa = .78$). Silverman and Eisen (1992) examined test–retest reliability, showing that overall reliability was high for match on primary diagnosis, symptom scale scores, and overall severity, with an overall kappa coefficient of .75. Specific diagnostic categories of overanxious disorder, simple phobia, and social phobia yielded kappa coefficients of .64, .84, .73, respectively. Matching clinical practice and the research literature, parents tended to report fewer anxiety problems than children themselves reported.

Less well known than the ADIS, the Children's Anxiety Evaluation Form (CAEF) was developed to assess anxiety in nonpsychotic children of normal intelligence (Hoehn-Saric et al., 1987). Somewhat cumbersome to administer and score, the CAEF explores three areas: history suggestive of anxiety by chart review, patient's subjective assessment by semi-structured interview, and observations at interview. Hoehn-Saric et al. (1987) examined the psychometric properties of the CAEF in a sample of 63 children and adolescents admitted to a psychiatric inpatient service. Interrater reliability was assessed by comparing the results in 15 adolescent patients. Pearson correlation coefficients were .81 for the total score, .73 for part I, .86 for part II , and .87 for part III ($p < .01$). The CAEF successfully differentiated the anxiety disorder group from other diagnostic groups, which included oppositional disorder, conduct disorder (aggressive), conduct disorder (nonaggressive), and dysthymic disorder. While the CAEF furnishes a framework that covers all relevant signs and symptoms of anxiety, it currently offers no advantages over the ADIS for internalizing psychopathology, it is not as comprehensive, and it exhibits poorer and less well-documented psychometric properties.

Other Semistructured Interviews

The Schedule for Affective Disorders and Schizophrenia in School-Aged Children (K-SADS; Puig-Antich & Chambers, 1978) was developed by researchers in childhood depression. Parent and child versions are available. Diagnoses generated with the K-SADS are based on clinical judgment rather than on algorithms, thus requiring experienced clinicians to serve as interviewers. Generally before assigning diagnoses, clinicians also review other available materials. The utility of the K-SADS relative to instruments such as the ADIS is presumably weakened by this less objectively operationalized procedure (Hodges, 1993). In this context, Chambers, Puig-Antich, Hirsch, et al. (1985) reported poor reliability for categorically and dimensionally defined anxiety, including overanxious disorder and separation anxiety disorder.

Modeled after a traditional clinical interview, the Child Assessment Schedule (CAS; Hodges & Fitch, 1979) is organized thematically with specific diagnostic items interspersed among more general probe questions. Like the K-SADS, the CAS also provides an opportunity for the interviewer to record behavioral observations. In contrast to the K-SADS, diagnoses are generated by algorithms based on the number of items endorsed in various spheres of functioning. Child and parent versions, both of which require clinician interviewers, are available. Using interrater and test–retest strategies, Hodges, Cools, and McKnew (1989) reported acceptable reliability for the CAS for diagnostic concordance across four diagnostic groups—conduct disorder, depression, grouped anxiety disorders, and attention-deficit disorder.

After a careful review of the relative strengths and weaknesses in respondent-based and interviewer-based approaches to the collection of diagnostic data, Angold, Pendergast, Cox, et al. (in press) designed the Child and Adolescent Psychiatric Assessment (CAPA) to incorporate the strengths of both approaches. In particular, the CAPA attempts to improve standardization, reliability, and meaningfulness of symptoms and diagnostic ratings. The CAPA incorporates child and parent versions and is divided into three phases: the introduction, during which an overall picture of problems is obtained in a nonthreatening conversational style; a detailed symptom review; and incapacity ratings. The central organizing principle of the CAPA is the glossary, which supplies operational definitions of specific symptoms, distress ratings, and frequencies. The CAPA assesses a broad range of child and adolescent disorders and allows scoring DSM-III, DSM-III-R, DSM-IV, ICD-9 and ICD-10 draft criteria sets covering all disorders, family functioning, life events, and service utilization. The authors intend this instrument to be suitable for use in both clinical and epidemiological research, thus pulling these two lines of investigation toward a greater degree of comparability. In assessing anxiety disorders, the CAPA yields kappa coefficients for test–retest and interrater reliability that are comparable to those for the ADIS and better than the DISC, especially for younger children (Angold, personal communication).

Structured Interviews

In contrast to the K-SADS, CAS, and CAPA, the Diagnostic Interview for Children and Adolescents (DICA)—originally modeled after the Research Diagnostic Interview described by Helzer et al. (1981) and later after the National Institute of Mental Health Diagnostic Interview Schedule (DIS)— is a respondent-based (structured) interview that has been widely used for both clinical and epidemiological research. The DICA includes a child interview and a corresponding parent interview. The parent version is a replica of the child version rephrased in parent terminology and includes developmental and medical history questions. The interviews are divided according to 18 DSM-III categories covering both internalizing and externalizing psychopathology, with no particular emphasis on anxiety disorders. Welner, Reich, Herjanic, et al. (1987) found excellent inter-interview agreement; unfortunately, the lowest agreement ratings were reported for the anxiety disorders. Similarly, agreement between clinical interviews and the DICA was poorest for the anxiety disorders ($\kappa = 0.03$), with clinicians reporting fewer diagnoses, perhaps because the DICA reports all endorsed diagnoses while clinicians tend to follow a hierarchical pattern when assigning diagnoses.

In contrast to the DICA, the Diagnostic Interview Schedule for Children (DISC) was developed specifically for use in epidemiological studies (Costello, Edelbrock, Dulcan, et al., 1984; Costello, Edelbrock, & Costello, 1985). In conformity with its roots in epidemiology, the DISC is a structured interview offering the advantage of a standardized order and a standardized wording and coding of signs and symptoms. Aronen, Noam, and Weinstein (1993) compared DISC-C (Child Interview Version) diagnoses with clinician discharge diagnoses, noting that the DISC generated an increased number of anxiety disorder diagnoses as well as a wider range of diagnoses than did clinicians at either admission or discharge. However, agreement between the DISC diagnoses and clinical discharge diagnoses was low for the anxiety disorders ($\kappa = .07$). Conversely, Shaffer, Schwab-Stone, Fisher, et al. (1993) reported reasonable parent–child agreement, test–retest reliability, and internal consistency for anxiety disorders in a psychiatric clinic population. In a separate study, Fisher, Shaffer, Piacentini, et al. (1993) documented adequate sensitivity in identifying obsessive–compulsive disorder. However, Angold and Costello report significantly poorer interrater reliability for the DISC than for the CAPA relative to internalizing but not externalizing psychopathology, especially for younger children (Adrian Angold, personal communication, January 1994). Advantages offered by the DISC are the acceptability of lay administration, the compatibility with DSM-III-R, and the availability of the computerized diagnostic scoring system. However, the instrument's inflexibility, coupled with poor reliability for the anxiety disorders and especially poor sensitivity to internalizing psychopathology during middle childhood, makes the DISC a somewhat problematic choice for clinical research or practice.

PARENT/TEACHER RATINGS

Despite problems with parent–child agreement, parents remain an important source of information on symptomatic anxiety in children (Roberts, et al., 1989). Unfortunately, there are no specific parent or teacher measures of childhood anxiety. There are, however, several parent/teacher behavior inventories that have subscales assessing internalizing symptomatology, including anxiety. We briefly discuss the two most widely used of these instruments, with the caveat that their primarily utility is as screening devices for internalizing and externalizing psychopathology as viewed by adults.

The Conners Parent Rating Scale (CPRS) and Conners Teacher Rating Scale (CTRS) were developed to identify children with disruptive and/or problematic behaviors and to evaluate treatment effectiveness (Goyette, Conners, & Ulrich, 1978). Both the CTRS and CPRS have been used widely in clinical and research settings; numerous studies support high test–retest reliability, interrater reliability, and construct validity of the scales (Conners, 1989), both of which include factors addressing anxiety. For example, the 39-item CTRS contains an anxious-passive factor in addition to measures of learning problems, conduct problems, and hyperactive/impulsive behavior as determined in four separate factor analytic studies in children from different countries, including the United States (Conners, 1969), New Zealand (Werry, Sprague, & Cohen, 1975), and Canada (Trites, Blouin, & Laprade, 1980). New versions of the CTRS and CPRS are currently undergoing national norming, along with the Multidimensional Anxiety Scale for Children (MASC), with shared items providing for clear links between parent-reported and child-reported anxiety in a standardized population.

Another widely used instrument, the Child Behavior Checklist (CBCL; Achenbach & Edelbrock, 1983), assesses the competencies and problems of children of ages 4 to 16 across internalizing and externalizing symptoms, with the former containing items ascertaining anxiety. Like the CTRS, the CBCL includes a teacher version (Edelbrock & Achenbach,

1984) that also encompasses internalizing and externalizing factors. Although the CBCL provides useful information as a screening tool, the lack of an anxiety-specific factor limits usefulness with respect to assessing anxiety or subsets of anxiety symptoms.

MULTIDOMAIN SELF-REPORT MEASURES

As noted earlier, certain anxiety symptoms, such as avoidance of social situations in young persons with social phobia, are readily observable; however, most symptoms are open only to child introspection and thus self-report. For this reason, self-report measures of anxiety, which provide an opportunity for the child to reveal internal or "hidden" experience, have been used widely in both clinical and research settings. In addition, self-report measures are easy to administer, require a minimum of clinician time, and economically capture a wide range of important anxiety dimensions from the child's point of view (Straus, 1993).

While self-report appears to measure a subject's anxiety directly, self-report measures are not without methodological limitations, since social factors may influence the veracity of reporting. For example, some children tend to underestimate or underreport anxiety in the service of presenting a favorable evaluation of themselves or to avoid treatment (Glennon & Weis, 1978); gender and cultural differences also may influence reporting, with females more willing to endorse fearfulness than males (Ollendick, Matson, & Helsel, 1985). The child's ability to read and to understand the questionnaire items also directly influences the validity of responses. Similarly, when help is necessary to read the questions, the expectations of the child regarding the adult helper may set up a response bias that in turn may influence the validity of the data obtained. Despite these limitations, self-report measures of anxiety represent a time-efficient way to capture information about a wide variety of anxiety symptoms; synopses of currently available instruments follow.

Revised Children's Manifest Anxiety Scale

Used in over 40 published studies between 1982 and 1990 (Hagborg, 1991), the Revised Children's Manifest Anxiety Scale (RCMAS; Reynolds & Richmond, 1978) is undoubtedly the most widely used instrument for assessing anxiety in young persons. The RCMAS is a revision of the Children's Manifest Anxiety Scale (CMAS; Castaneda, McCandless, & Palmero, 1956), which in turn was a modification for children of Taylor's Manifest Anxiety Scale (1951). The current RCMAS is a 37-item scale that assesses the level and nature of anxiety in children and adolescents of ages 6 to 19 by self-report. Items are assigned yes or no ratings by the child, and yes responses are used to compute total anxiety and factor scores. To detect "denial" leading to invalid responding, the RCMAS also includes a "lie" scale. The RCMAS Manual (Reynolds & Richmond, 1985) details the construction, administration, scoring, and interpretation of the scale and presents normative data by sex, gender, and age from a large national sample (Reynolds & Paget, 1983).

Reynolds and Richmond (1979) describe three RCMAS factors: physiological manifestations of anxiety, worry and oversensitivity, and fear/concentration. Internal consistency values for the total anxiety score fall in the .8 range (Witt, Heffer, & Pfeiffer, 1990). Reynolds and Paget (1983) reported 3-week test–retest reliability coefficients of .9; Reynolds (1981) reported a 9-month test–retest correlation of .68 in a large group of elementary school children. Reynolds (1980) examined the concurrent validity of the RCMAS with 42 children of ages 6 to 16 referred to a private practice setting for psychological evaluation, showing statistically significant correlations with the trait but not the state scale of the State–Trait Anxiety Inventory for Children (STAIC; Spielberger, 1970), perhaps implying that the RCMAS measures stable or chronic anxiety independent of state or situational anxiety. On the basis of these findings, the author suggested possible use of the RCMAS and the STAIC (trait scale) as alternate measures in pre- and postresearch designs, although actual sensitivity to change in treatment outcome studies remains unclear for both measures. The few studies that assessed the ability of the RCMAS to discriminate between anxiety disorders or between anxiety disorders and other diagnoses have not shown the RCMAS to be promising, a not surprising result due to the substantial confounding of the RCMAS factors with other constructs. For example, the presence of mood, attentional, impulsivity, and peer interactional items clearly confounds both attention-deficit/hyperactivity disorder and major depressive disorder diagnoses (Mattison & Bagnoto, 1987). Similarly, Hoehn-Saric and colleagues (1987) reported that the RCMAS did not differentiate inpatient children with an anxiety disorder from inpatients with other psychiatric diagnoses, and Silverman and colleagues found similar results for overanxious disorder and attention-deficit/hyperactivity disorder (Wendy Silverman, personal communication, March 1993). Thus the RCMAS may be best used to assess general distress, with the accent on anxiety, in mixed psychiatrically disturbed or normal populations.

State–Trait Anxiety Inventory for Children

The STAIC (Spielberger, Edwards, & Lushene, 1973) is composed of two independent 20-item inventories. The state scale purports to assess present-state and situationally linked anxiety; the trait scale addresses temporally stable anxiety across situations. The STAIC includes normative data based on a national sample of children between the ages of 8 and 12 years (Spielberger et al., 1973).

Spielberger and colleagues (1973) reported that the STAIC exhibited better test–retest reliability coefficients for the trait scale (.65 for males and .71 for females) than for the state scale (.31 for males and .47 for females). Similarly, Finch and Nelson (1974) found low but statistically significant correlations between the state (.27) and the trait scales (.54) and the CMAS, raising questions about the validity of the state–trait distinction with emotionally disturbed children. Finch, Montgomery, and Deardorff (1974) found the STAIC to exhibit high internal consistency but low test–retest reliability, causing Spielberger and colleagues (1973) to assert that measures of internal consistency may provide a more meaningful indication of reliability than test–retest correlations. Conversely, others have questioned the validity of the state–trait distinction (Johnson & Melamed, 1979) and the nature of item selection for the STAIC (Finch, Kendall, Montgomery, et al., 1975). Moreover, while Straus, Lease, Last, et al. (1988) reported that overanxious children endorsed increased anxiety on both the state and trait scales to a greater degree than did normal children, Hoehn-Saric and colleagues (1987), found no differences in the STAIC or the RCMAS among five diagnostic groups in an inpatient sample of 63 children and adolescents. Taking these rather confusing findings into consideration and recognizing that the STAIC provides little or no information referrable to the DSM anxiety constructs, Barrios and Hartmann (1988) suggest that the STAIC is best used as a general screening tool or perhaps as a measure of state (in observations) or trait (in treatment outcome studies) anxiety when a general change index is required.

Fear Survey Schedule for Children

Beginning with the work of MacFarlane, Allen, and Honzik (1954), who were among the first to examine the cross-sectional prevalence of normal fears, Scherer and Nakamura (1968) developed the Fear Survey Schedule for Children (FSS-FC) to capture fears in the following categories: school, home, social, physical, animal, travel, classical phobia, and miscellaneous. Comprising 80 items rated on a 4-point Likert scale, the FSS-FC demonstrated reasonable internal consistency but little correlation with the CMAS in initial studies. Factor analysis produced the following factors: fear of failure or criticism, major fears, minor fears–travel, medical fears, fear of death, fear of the dark, home–school fears, and miscellaneous fears, causing the authors to suggest that the scale might be useful to identify specific sources of fear, severity of fearfulness, treatment effects, and individual differences in research studies. Though the original FSS-FC was once widely used in clinical settings, normative data, test–retest reliability, and construct validation data are not available (Ollendick, 1983).

Fear Survey Schedule for Children–Revised

To make the FSS-FC more easily understood by mentally retarded, psychiatrically impaired, and younger children, Ollendick (1983) retained all the original items, believing that they adequately sampled the large variety of fear stimuli reported by children in clinical practice and research settings, but switched the response format from a 4-point to a 3-point Likert scale. Ollendick (1983) then evaluated the psychometric properties of the revised scale, which he termed the Fear Survey Schedule for Children–Revised (FSSC-R), in two normal samples and one clinical sample of children with school phobia. Based on measures of internal consistency in the 0.9 range and test–retest reliabilities ranging from .3 to .5, he concluded that the FSSC-R has high internal consistency and is highly reliable and stable over a 1-week interval but is only moderately stable over a 3-month interval. Exploratory factor analyses resulted in a 5-factor solution closely resembling the factor solution of the original FSS-FC (Ollendick, 1983). Identified factors included fear of failure and criticism, fear of the unknown, fear of injury and small animals, fear of danger and death, and medical fears. Based on a sample of 126 children and adolescents, Ollendick et al. (1985) provided normative data for the FSSC-R for girls and boys of ages 7 to 18. Girls endorsed more fears and an overall higher intensity of fears than boys, indicating that girls show a greater willingness to report fearfulness or greater potential reactivity to fear stimuli. Ollendick (1983) also compared scores of the FSSC-R with scores on the STAIC, the Piers–Harris Children's Self-Concept Scale (SCS; Piers & Harris, 1969), and the Nowicki–Strickland Locus of Control Scale (NSLOC; Nowicki & Strickland, 1973). As expected, higher scores on the FSSC-R were associated with higher levels of trait anxiety; low FSSC-R scores were associated with a better self-concept and an internal locus of control.

Last, Francis, and Strauss (1989) recently examined the ability of the FSSC-R to differentiate subtypes of anxiety disorders in children. Using children and adolescents with DSM-III-R separation anxiety disorder, overanxious disorder, or school phobia, they noted no between-group differences on total FSSC-R score or on the five factor scores, although there were between-group differences in the pattern of reported fears. Interestingly, the school phobia group did not differ significantly from the separation anxiety disorder group in the prevalence of fear of going to school. In fact, only half the school phobia group endorsed an intense fear of going to school, implying that the FSSC-R may be most useful in identifying specific fear sensitivities in individual children.

Social Anxiety Scale for Children

The 10-item Social Anxiety Scale for Children (SASC), which was developed as an aid for studying peer relationships, assesses children's social avoidance, social distress, and fear of negative evaluation (La Greca, Dandes, Wick, et al., 1988). La Greca and colleagues found two factors—fear of negative evaluation (FNE) and social avoidance and distress (SAD)—that showed acceptable internal consistency. Test–retest reliability correlations were $r = .67$ for the total SASC, $r = .70$ for FNE, and $r = .39$ for SAD, with $p < .001$, suggesting that the FNE factor may measure an internalized, stable, or trait aspect of social anxiety that is psychometrically stronger. Both FNE and SAD correlated positively with the RCMAS, with the FNE factor showing the greater correlation.

In a subsequent study of the use of the 22-item revised SASC (SASC-R) with 587 fourth- through sixth-grade children, LaGreca and Stone (1989) noted two factors that were similar to the original FNE and SAD factors. However, the SASC-R SAD factor seemed to reflect social avoidance and distress with new peers and was therefore relabeled SAD–Specific (SAD-S). A third factor captured children's social avoidance and inhibition with peers in general and was labeled SAD–General (SAD-G). While LaGreca (1989) found acceptable test–retest reliability for the three factors of the SASC-R, as did Cabrera (1988; cited in LaGreca, 1989), the somewhat confusing factor structure and lack of normative data renders its place in clinical and research endeavors uncertain at present.

Multidimensional Anxiety Scale for Children

In response to a strong perceived need by researchers working in this area (see, e.g., Jensen et al., 1993, and Fergusson & Horwood, 1993), we recently developed a new scale, the Multidimensional Anxiety Scale for Children (MASC; March, Stallings, Parker, et al., 1994), to address the multidimensional conceptualization of anxiety in a psychometrically rigorous fashion. The MASC is a 45-item 4-point Likert self-report measure comprising four factors and linking six subfactors covering the major domains of self-reported anxiety in children and adolescents. Major factors and associated subfactors include physical anxiety (subdivided into tense/restless and somatic/autonomic factors), harm avoidance (subdivided into perfectionism and anxious coping behaviors), social anxiety (subdivided into humiliation fears and performance anxiety), and separation anxiety. Internal consistency (Chronbach's alpha) falls in the .7 to .8 range for all factors and subfactors; Pearson correlation coefficients averaged .3 to .5 for the within-factor subfactors and .2 to .4 for between-factor subfactor correlations. All correlation coefficients were significant at the .01 level

(Bonferroni correction), suggesting that the particular constructs represented in the factor structure, while subsumed within a latent global anxiety construct, do in fact measure different aspects of childhood anxiety. As expected, females showed more anxiety than males ($p < .01$, Bonferroni correction) for all factors and subfactors. In addition to a national norming study in combination with the newly revised Conners Parent and Teachers Rating Scales (Conners, 1989), we also are evaluating test–retest and interrater reliability, convergent validity, and discriminant validity and have provided the instrument to researchers undertaking a variety of clinical and epidemiological investigations.

MEASURES THAT ASSESS SPECIFIC DIMENSIONS OF ANXIETY

In contrast to the RCMAS, STAIC, and MASC, all of which measure global anxiety plus two or more subfactors, other rating scales attempt to ascertain specific subsets of anxiety symptomatology in children and adolescents. We briefly discuss five such measures—covering social phobia, posttraumatic stress disorder, obsessive–compulsive disorder, and general anxiety—because they are widely used and because they serve as examples of the utility of more narrowly focused assessment methodologies.

Social Phobia Anxiety Inventory for Children

Among the most promising of the new instruments, the Social Phobia and Anxiety Inventory for Children (SPAI-C), which assesses specific somatic symptoms, cognitions, and behavior in a range of social situations, consists of 39 items that are self-rated on a 4-point Likert scale (Turner, Beidel, Dancu, et al., 1989). An initial evaluation of the psychometric properties of the scale indicates that the SPAI-C has good test–retest reliability at 2-week and 10-month intervals (Beidel, Turner, & Morris, 1994). Concurrent validity was shown with the trait subscale of the STAIC, the failure and criticism subscale of the FSSC-R, and the CBCL internalizing scale. In the initial evaluation, the SPAI-C also successfully differentiated socially anxious children from normal controls.

Measures of Posttraumatic Stress Disorder

Although structured and semistructured clinical interviews such as the DISC and CAPA are *de rigueur* for assessing psychiatric problems in children and adolescents, these interviews only recently incorporated posttraumatic stress disorder (PTSD) modules; reliability and validity data for

PTSD are not yet available (Prudence Fisher and Adrian Angold, personal communication, January 1994). In contrast, the Pynoos–Nader version of the Stress Reaction Index (SRI) shows modest empirical support as a semistructured interview (Robert Pynoos, personal communication, 1993) and as a self-report measure (March, Amaya-Jackson, Costanzo, et al., in preparation; Lonigan, Shannon, Finch, et al., 1991) of PTSD. In factor analyses, the SRI captures the major domains of PTSD: reexperiencing, avoidance/numbing, and hyperarousal (Pynoos, Nader, & March, 1990; Chapter 12). In the primary demonstration of construct validity for the SRI, Pynoos and Nader showed that exposure (proximity) was linearly related to the risk for PTSD symptoms (Pynoos, Frederick, Nader, et al., 1987) and that children's memory disturbances, indicating distorted cognitive processing during the event, closely followed exposure (Pynoos & Nader, 1989). However, careful psychometric studies have not been completed, and within- and between-stressor norms are unavailable. Thus PTSD is one area that is ripe for methodological innovation, especially since aspects of the symptom picture vary with child- and stressor-specific factors (March & Amaya-Jackson, in press; Nader, Stuber, & Pynoos, 1991; Kendall-Tackett, Williams, & Finkelhor, 1993).

Two Measures That Assess Obsessive–Compulsive Disorder

Perhaps because of its characteristically stereotypic presentation, obsessive–compulsive disorder (OCD) enjoys a position relatively free of nosologic controversy (March, Johnston, & Greist, 1990). Nonetheless, OCD exhibits substantial subgroup variability (Rettew, Swedo, Leonard, et al., 1992), and scales designed to diagnose or to ascertain the severity of OCD symptoms must take into consideration the range of symptom expression. The primary instrument for assessing OCD is the Yale–Brown Obsessive Compulsive Scale (YBOCS), which assess obsessions and compulsions separately on time consumed, distress, interference, degree of resistance, and control (Goodman, Price, Rasmussen, et al., 1989). A children's version, the CYBOCS, is available (Riddle, Scahill, King, et al., 1992), but in our experience it offers no clear advantage over the standard YBOCS. The YBOCS has been used in pharmacological (DeVeaugh, Moroz, Biederman, et al., 1992; Riddle et al., 1992) and cognitive-behavioral (March, Mulle, & Herbel, 1994) treatment outcome studies, as well as in studies of OCD phenomenology (Rettew et al., 1992). Since the YBOCS is administered and rated by an interviewer, akin to a semistructured interview, it is not suitable for self-report, although preliminary attempts to generate computer (Lee Baer, personal communication, March 1994) and self-report (Warren, Zgourides, Monto, et al., 1994) versions have been reported.

The sole currently available self-report instrument for assessing OCD in children and adolescents is an "epidemiological version" of the Leyton Obsessional Inventory–Child Version (LOI-CU; Berg, Whitaker, Davies, et al., 1988). In 1970, Cooper introduced the Leyton Obsessional Card Inventory for adults, providing a method for the subjective assessment of the number and severity of obsessional traits and symptoms. Berg, Rapoport, and Flament (1986) later modified this instrument as the LOI-CV for use with children of ages 8 to 18. While the LOI-CV, a 44-item scale employing a card-sorting format, demonstrates acceptable psychometric properties, the need for clinician administration and the amount of time required for administration render it unwieldy for use in either research or clinical practice (Berg et al., 1986). Following Snowden (1980), who developed a self-report form of the adult Leyton inventory, Berg and colleagues (1988) developed a 20-item self-report version of the LOI-CV by applying a data-reduction procedure to scores obtained in the earlier study (Berg et al., 1986). Subsequently, from a countywide survey of high school students, Berg and colleagues (1988) reported norms for the 20-item Leyton inventory that showed high internal consistency and greater symptomatology in female than in male respondents. Four factors were identified: general obsessive, dirt/contamination, numbers/luck, and school-related symptoms (Berg et al., 1988). Using semistructured interviews in the second part of a two-stage epidemiological study of OCD in non-referred adolescents, Flament, Whitaker, Rapoport, et al. (1988) evaluated the efficiency of the LOI-CV survey form in identifying OCD, showing acceptable sensitivity (high true-positive rate) and poor specificity (high false-positive rate).

Hamilton Anxiety Rating Scale

Originally developed for use with adults, the Hamilton Anxiety Rating Scale (HARS; Hamilton, 1959, 1969) measures general anxiety in an interview–observational format. Interviewer-administered questionnaires have been found in adult samples to be somewhat more sensitive to the assessment of therapeutic change than have questionnaire measures (Kellner, Kelly, & Scheffield, 1968). Clark and Donovan (1994) recently showed that the HARS is a reliable and valid measure for the assessment of global anxiety when used with adolescents. Interrater reliability and internal consistency were comparable to those reported for adults. Construct and concurrent validities were shown with significant correlations with the STAIC trait subscale, the SPAI-C, and the FSSC-R. The factor structure was similar to that reported earlier for adults. However, norms are unavailable, and reliability of the HARS in assessing anxiety in younger age children requires further exploration.

DISCUSSION

Reliable and valid assessment instruments, which incorporate multiple modalities and reporters, are necessary to enable researchers (and ultimately
clinicians) to address the multiple faces of anxiety in young persons
(Hodges, 1993). Unfortunately, even this brief review makes apparent
the paucity of instrumentation keyed to modern nosologic constructs,
grounded in normal and pathological development, and possessing thoroughly established psychometric properties. While efforts to redress these
weaknesses, as exemplified by the ADIS and the MASC, are underway, a
closer look at assessment issues is imperative if the nascent field of child
and adolescent anxiety disorders is to progress.

ACKNOWLEDGMENT

This work was supported in part by an NIMH Scientist Development Award for
Clinicians (1 K20 MH00981-01) to Dr. March.

REFERENCES

Achenbach, T. M., & Edelbrock, C. S. (1983). *Manual for the Child Behavior
Checklist and Revised Child Behavior Profile.* Burlington, CT: Queen City
Printers.
Achenbach, T., McConaughy, S. H., & Howell, C. T. (1987). Child/adolescent
behavioral and emotional problems: Implications of cross informant cor-
relations for situational specificity. *Psychological Bulletin, 101,* 213–
232.
American Psychiatric Association. (1980). *Diagnostic and statistical manual of
mental disorders* (3rd ed.). Washington, DC: Author.
American Psychiatric Association. (1987). *Diagnostic and statistical manual of
mental disorders* (3rd ed., rev.). Washington, DC: Author.
American Psychiatric Association. (1994). *Diagnostic and statistical manual of
mental disorders* (4th ed.). Washington, DC: Author.
Angold, A., Prendergast, M., Cox, A., et al. (in press). The Child and Adolescent
Psychiatric Assessment (CAPA). *Journal of Psychological Medicine.*
Aronen, E. T., Noam, G. G., & Weinstein, S. R. (1993). Structured diagnostic
interviews and clinicians' discharge diagnoses in hospitalized adolescents.
*Journal of the American Academy of Child and Adolescent Psychiatry,
32,*(3), 674–681.
Baer, L., Minichiello, W. E., Jenike, M. A., et al. (1988). Use of a portable computer program to assist behavioral treatment in a case of obsessive compulsive disorder. *Journal of Behavior Therapy and Experimental Psychiatry,
19*(3), 237–240.

Barrios, B. A., & Hartmann, D. B. (1988). Fears and anxieties. In E. J. Mash & L. G. Terdal (Eds.), *Behavioral assessment of childhood disorders* (2nd ed., pp. 196–262). New York: Guilford Press.

Beidel, D. C., Turner, S. M., & Morris, T. L. (1994). *The SPAI-C: A new self-report inventory for childhood social phobia.* Paper presented at the National Conference of the Anxiety Disorders Association of America, Santa Monica, CA.

Berg, C. J., Rapoport, J. L., & Flament, M. (1986). The Leyton Obsessional Inventory–Child Version. *Journal of the American Academy of Child and Adolescent Psychiatry, 25*(1), 84–91.

Berg, C. Z., Whitaker, A., Davies, M., et al. (1988). The survey form of the Leyton Obsessional Inventory–Child Version: Norms from an epidemiological study. *Journal of the American Academy of Child and Adolescent Psychiatry, 27*(6), 759–763.

Cabrera, D. (1988). *The stability of social states of elementary school children across a two-year period and its relationship to social anxiety, self-perception, and depression.* Unpublished senior honors thesis, University of Miami, Coral Gables, FL.

Cantwell, D. P., & Baker, L. (1988). Issues in the classification of child and adolescent psychopathology. *Journal of the American Academy of Child and Adolescent Psychiatry, 27*(5), 521–533.

Castaneda, A., McCandless, B. R., & Palmero, D. S. (1956). The children's form of the Manifest Anxiety Scale. *Child Development, 27*(3), 317–326.

Chambers, W. J., Puig-Antich, J., Hirsch, M., et al. (1985). The assessment of affective disorders in children and adolescents by semistructured interview: Test–retest reliability of the Schedule for Affective Disorders and Schizophrenia for School Age Children [Present episode version]. *Archives of General Psychiatry, 42,* 696–702.

Clark, D. C., & Donovan, J. E. (1994). Reliability and validity of the Hamilton Anxiety Rating Scale in an adolescent sample. *Journal of the American Academy of Child and Adolescent Psychiatry, 33*(3), 354–360.

Conners, C. K. (1969). A teacher rating scale for use in drug studies with children. *American Journal of Psychiatry, 126*(6), 152–156.

Conners, C. K. (1989). *The Conners rating scales: Instruments for the assessment of childhood psychopathology.* Toronto: Multi-Health Systems.

Cooper, J. (1970). The Leyton Obsessional Inventory. *Psychological Medicine, 1,* 48–64.

Costello, A. J., Edelbrock, C. S., Dulcan, M. K., et al. (1984). *Development and testing of the NIMH Diagnostic Interview Schedule for Children on a Clinical Population: Final report* (Contract RFP-DB-81-0027). Rockville, MD: National Institute of Mental Health, Center for Epidemiological Studies.

Costello, E. J., Edelbrock, C. S., & Costello, A. J. (1985). Validity of the NIMH Diagnostic Interview Schedule for Children. *Journal of Abnormal Child Psychology, 13,* 579–595.

DeVeaugh, G. J., Moroz, G., Biederman, J., et al. (1992). Clomipramine hydrochloride in childhood and adolescent obsessive–compulsive disorder—A multicenter trial. *Journal of the American Academy of Child and Adolescent Psychiatry, 31*(1), 45–49.

DiNardo, P. A., O'Brien, G. T., Barlow, D. M., et al. (1983). Reliability of DSM-III anxiety disorder categories using a new structured interview. *Archives of General Psychiatry, 40*, 1070–1079.

Edelbrock, C., & Achenbach, T. M. (1984). The teacher version of the Child Behavior Profile: Vol. I. Boys aged 6–11. *Journal of Consulting and Clinical Psychology, 52*, 207–217.

Fergusson, D. M., & Horwood, L. J. (1993). The structure, stability and correlations of the trait components of conduct disorder, attention deficit and anxiety/withdrawal reports. *Journal of Child Psychology and Psychiatry and Allied Disciplines, 34*(5), 749–766.

Finch, A. J., Kendall, P. C., Montgomery, L. E., et al. (1975). Effects of two types of failure on anxiety. *Journal of Abnormal Psychology, 84*(5), 583–585.

Finch, A. J., Montgomery, L. E., & Deardorff, P. A. (1974). Reliability of state–trait anxiety with emotionally disturbed children. *Journal of Abnormal Child Psychology, 2*, 67–69.

Finch, A. J., & Nelson, W. M. (1974). Anxiety and locus of conflict in emotionally disturbed children. *Journal of Abnormal Child Psychology, 2*(1), 33–37.

Fisher, P., Shaffer, D., Piacentini, J. C., et al. (1993). Sensitivity of the Diagnostic Interview Schedule for Children, 2nd edition (DISC-2.1) for specific diagnoses of children and adolescents. *Journal of the American Academy of Child and Adolescent Psychiatry, 32*(3), 666–673.

Flament, M. F., Whitaker, A., Rapaport, J. L., et al. (1988). Obsessive compulsive disorder in adolescence: An epidemiological study. *Journal of the American Academy of Child and Adolescent Psychiatry, 27*(6), 764–771.

Glennon, B., & Weis, J. R. (1978). An observational approach to the assessment of anxiety in young children. *Journal of Consulting and Clinical Psychology, 46*, 1246–1257.

Goodman, W. K., Price, L. H., Rasmussen, S. A., et al. (1989). The Yale–Brown Obsessive Compulsive Scale: Vol. II. Validity. *Archives of General Psychiatry, 46*(11), 1012–1016.

Goyette, C. H., Conners, C. K., & Ulrich, R. F. (1978). Normative data on revised Conner's parent and teacher rating scales. *Journal of Clinical Child Psychology, 6*(2), 221–236.

Hagborg, W. J. (1991). The Revised Children's Manifest Anxiety Scale and social desirability. *Educational and Psychological Measurement, 51*, 423–427.

Hamilton, M. (1959). The assessment of anxiety states by rating. *British Journal of Medical Psychology, 32*, 50–55.

Hamilton, M. (1969). Diagnosis and rating of anxiety. *British Journal of Psychiatry: Special Publication, 3*, 76–79.

Helzer, J. E., Robins, L. N., Croughan, J. L., et al. (1981). Renard diagnostic interview: Its reliability and procedural validity with physicians and lay interviewers. *Archives of General Psychiatry, 38*, 393–398.

Hodges, K. (1993). Structured interviews for assessing children. *Journal of Child Psychology and Psychiatry, 34*(1), 49–68.

Hodges, K., Cools, J., & McKnew, D. (1989). Test–retest reliability of a clinical research interview for children: The Child Assessment Schedule (CAS). *Psychological Assessment: Journal of Consulting and Clinical Psychology, 1*, 317–322.

Hodges, K., & Fitch, P. (1979). *Development of a mental status examination interview for children*. Paper presented at the meeting of the Missouri Psychological Association, Kansas City, MO.

Hoehn-Saric, E., Maisami, M., & Weigand, D. (1987). Measurement of anxiety in children and adolescents using semi-structured interviews. *Journal of the American Academy of Child and Adolescent Psychiatry, 28*, 541–545.

Jensen, P. S., Salzberg, A. D., Richters, J. E., et al. (1993). Scales, diagnoses, and child psychopathology: Vol. I. CBCL and DISC relationships. *Journal of the American Academy of Child and Adolescent Psychiatry, 32*(2), 397–406.

Jensen, P. S., Traylor, J., Xenakis, S. N., et al. (1988). Child psychopathology rating scales and interrater agreement: Vol. I. Parents' gender and psychiatric symptoms. *Journal of the American Academy of Child and Adolescent Psychiatry, 27*(4), 442–450.

Johnson, S. B., & Melamed, B. G. (1979). Assessment and treatment of children's fears. In B. B. Lahey & A. E. Kazdin (Eds.), *Advances in clinical child psychology* (Vol. 2, pp. 108–139). New York: Plenum Press.

Kellner, R., Kelly, A. V., & Sheffield, B. F. (1968). The assessment of changes in anxiety in a drug trial: A comparison of methods. *British Journal of Psychiatry, 114*, 863–869.

Kendall-Tackett, K. A., Williams, L. M., & Finkelhor, D. (1993). Impact of sexual abuse on children: A review and synthesis of recent empirical studies. *Psychological Bulletin, 113*(1), 164–180.

La Greca, A. M. (1989). *Social anxiety in children: Scale development and validation*. Paper presented at the Society for Research in Child and Adolescent Psychopathology, Miami, FL.

La Greca, A. M., Dandes, S. K., Wick, P., et al. (1988). The development of the Social Anxiety Scale for Children (SASC): Reliability and concurrent validity. *Journal of Clinical Child Psychology, 17*, 84–91.

La Greca, A. M., & Stone, W. L. (1989). *Social anxiety in children: Relationship to peer, teacher and self ratings*. Unpublished manuscript.

Last, C. G., Francis, G., & Strauss, C. C. (1989). Assessing fears in anxiety-disordered children with the Revised Fear Survey Schedule for Children (FSSC-R). *Journal of Clinical Child Psychology, 18*, 137–141.

Lonigan, C. J., Shannon, M. P., Finch, A. J., et al. (1991). Children's reactions to a natural disaster: Symptom severity and degree of exposure. *Advances in Behavior Research and Therapy, 13*(3), 135–154.

MacFarlane, J. W., Allen, L., & Honzik, M. (1954). *A developmental study of the behavior problems of normal children*. Berkeley: University of California Press.

March, J., & Amaya-Jackson, L. (in press). Post-traumatic stress disorder in children and adolescents. *PTSD Research Quarterly, 4*(4), 1–7.

March, J., Amaya-Jackson, L., Costanzo, P., et al. (1994). *Post-traumatic stress in children and adolescents after an industrial fire.* Manuscript submitted for publication.

March, J., Johnston, H., & Greist, J. (1990). The future of research in obsessive-compulsive disorder. In M. Jenike, L. Baer, & W. Minichello (Eds.), *Obsessive–compulsive disorder.* Littleton, MA: PSG.

March, J., Mulle, K., & Herbel, B. (1994). Behavioral psychotherapy for children and adolescents with obsessive-compulsive disorder: An open trial of a New Protocol Driven Treatment Package. *Journal of the American Academy of Child and Adolescent Psychiatry, 33*(3), 333–341.

March, J., Stallings, P., Parker, T. R., et al. (1994). *The multidimensional anxiety scale for children (MASC): Scale construction and factor structure.* Manuscript submitted for publication.

Marks, I. (1987). *Fears, phobias, and rituals.* New York: Oxford Unversity Press.

Mash , E. J., & Terdal, L. G. (Eds.). (1988). Behavioral assessment of child and family disturbance. In *Behavioral assessment of childhood disorders* (2nd ed., pp. 3–65). New York: Guilford Press.

Mattison, R. E., & Bagnato, S. J. (1987). Empirical measurement of overanxious disorder in boys 8 to 12 years old. *Journal of the American Academy of Child and Adolescent Psychiatry, 26,* 536–540.

Nader, K., Stuber, M., & Pynoos, R. S. (1991). Post traumatic stress reactions in preschool children with catastrophic illness: Assessment needs. *Comprehensive Mental Health Care, 1*(3), 223–239.

Nowicki, S. Jr., & Strickland, B. R. (1973). A locus-of-control scale for children. *Journal of Consulting and Clinical Psychology, 40,* 148–154.

Ollendick, T. H. (1983). Reliability and validity of the Revised Fear Survey Schedule for Children (FSSC-R). *Behaviour Research and Therapy, 21*(6), 685–692.

Ollendick, T. H., Matson, J. L., & Helsel, W. J. (1985). Fears in children and adolescents: Normative data. *Behaviour Research and Therapy, 4,* 465–467.

Piers, E. V., & Harris, D. B. (1969). *The Piers–Harris Children's Self-Concept Scale.* Nashville, TN: Counselor Records and Tests.

Puig-Antich, J., & Chambers, W. (1978). *The Schedule for Affective Disorders and Schizophrenia for School-Age Children (Kiddie-SADS).* New York: New York State Psychiatric Institute.

Pynoos, R. S., Frederick, C. J., Nader, K., et al. (1987). Life threat and post traumatic stress in school-age children. *Archives of General Psychiatry, 44*(12), 1057–1063.

Pynoos, R. S., & Nader, K. (1989). Children's memory and proximity to violence. *Journal of the American Academy of Child and Adolescent Psychiatry, 28*(2), 236–241.

Pynoos, R., Nader, K., & March, J. (1990). Post-traumatic stress disorder in children and adolescents. In J. Weiner (Eds.), *Textbook of child and adolescent psychiatry.* Washington, DC: American Psychiatric Press.

Rapoport, J. L. (1991). Recent advances in obsessive compulsive disorder [see comments]. *Neuropsychopharmacology, 5*(1), 1–10.

Reich, W., & Earls, F. (1987). Rules for making psychiatric diagnoses in children on the basis of multiple sources of information: Preliminary strategies. *Journal of Abnormal Child Psychology, 15*(4), 601–616.

Rettew, D. C., Swedo, S. E., Leonard, H. L., et al. (1992). Obsessions and compulsions across time in 79 children and adolescents with obsessive–compulsive disorder. *Journal of the American Academy of Child and Adolescent Psychiatry, 31*(6), 1050–1056.

Reynolds, C. R. (1980). Concurrent validity of "What I Think and Feel": The Revised Children's Manifest Anxiety Scale. *Journal of Consulting and Clinical Psychology, 48*(6), 774–775.

Reynolds, C. R. (1981). Long-term stability of scores on the Revised Children's Manifest Anxiety Scale. *Perceptual and Motor Skills, 53,* 702.

Reynolds, C. R., & Paget, K. D. (1983). National normative and reliability data for the Revised Children's Manifest Anxiety Scale. *School Psychology Review, 12*(3), 324–336.

Reynolds, C. R., & Richmond, B. O. (1978). What I Think and Feel: A revised measure of children's manifest anxiety. *Journal of Abnormal Child Psychology, 6,* 271–280.

Reynolds, C. R., & Richmond, B. O. (1979). Factor structure and construct validity of "What I Think and Feel": The Revised Children's Manifest Anxiety Scale. *Journal of Personality Assessment, 43*(3), 281–283.

Reynolds, C. R., & Richmond, B. O. (1985). *Revised Children's Manifest Anxiety Scale (RCMAS) manual.* Los Angeles: Western Psychological Services.

Riddle, M. A., Scahill, L., King, R. A., et al. (1992). Double-blind, crossover trial of fluoxetine and placebo in children and adolescents with obsessive–compulsive disorder. *Journal of the American Academy of Child and Adolescent Psychiatry, 31*(6), 1062–1069.

Roberts, N., Vargo, B., & Ferguson, H. B. (1989). Measurement of anxiety and depression in children and adolescents. *Psychiatric Clinics of North America, 12*(4), 837–859.

Scherer, M. W., & Nakamura, C. Y. (1968). A fear survey schedule for children (FSS-FC): A factor analytic comparison with manifest anxiety (CMAS). *Behaviour Research and Therapy, 6,* 173–182.

Shaffer, D., Schwab-Stone, M., Fisher, P., et al. (1993). The Diagnostic Interview Schedule for Children–Revised Version (DISC-R): Vol. I. Preparation, field testing, interrater reliability, and acceptability. *Journal of the American Academy of Child and Adolescent Psychiatry, 32*(3), 643–650.

Sheehan, K. H., Sheehan, D. V., & Shaw, K. R. (1988). Diagnosis and treatment of anxiety disorders in children and adolescents. *Psychiatric Annals, 18,* 146–157.

Silverman, W. K. (1991). *Guide to the use of the Anxiety Disorders Interview Schedule for Children–Revised (Child and Parent versions).* Albany, NY: Graywind.

Silverman, W. K., & Eisen, A. R. (1992). Age differences in the reliability of parent and child reports of child anxious symptomatology using a structured interview. *Journal of the American Academy of Child and Adolescent Psychiatry, 31*(1), 117–124.

Silverman, W. K., & Nelles, W. B. (1988). The anxiety disorders interview schedule for children. *Journal of the American Academy of Child and Adolescent Psychiatry, 27*(6), 772–778.

Snowden, J. (1980). A comparison of written and postbox forms of the Leyton Obsessional Inventory. *Psychological Medicine, 10,* 165–170.

Spielberger, C. D. (1970). *Preliminary manual for State–Trait Anxiety Inventory for Children.* Palo Alto, CA: Consulting Psychologists Press.

Spielberger, C. D., Edwards, C. D., & Lushene, R. E. (1973). *State–Trait Anxiety Inventory for Children.* Palo Alto, CA: Consulting Psychologists Press.

Straus, C. C. (1993). Anxiety disorders. In T. H. Ollendick & M. Hersen (Eds.), *Handbook of child and adolescent assessment* (pp. 239–250). Boston, MA: Allyn & Bacon.

Straus, C. C., Lease, C. A., Last, C. G., et al. (1988). Overanxious disorder: An examination of developmental differences. *Journal of Abnormal Child Psychology, 16*(4), 433–443.

Trites, R. L., Blouin, A. G., & Laprade, K. (1980). Factor analysis of the Conners Teacher Rating Scale based on a large normative sample. *Journal of Counseling and Clinical Psychology, 48,* 615–621.

Turner, S. M., Beidel, D. C., Dancu, C. V., et al. (1989). An empirically derived inventory to measure social fears and anxiety: The Social Phobia and Anxiety Inventory. *Journal of Consulting and Clinical Psychology, 1*(1), 35–40.

Warren, R., Zgourides, G., Monto, M., et al. (1994). *Further assessment of reliability and validity of a self report version of Yale–Brown Obsessive Compulsive Scale.* Paper presented at The Anxiety Disorders Association of America Conference, Santa Monica, CA.

Weissman, M. M., Orvaschel, H., & Padian, N. (1980). Children's symptom and social functioning self-report scales: Comparison of mothers' and children's reports. *Journal of Nervous and Mental Disease, 168*(12), 736–740.

Welner, Z., Reich, W., Herjanic, B., et al. (1987). Reliability, validity, and parent–child agreement studies of the Diagnostic Interview for Children and Adolescents (DICA). *Journal of the American Academy of Child and Adolescent Psychiatry, 26,* 649–653.

Werry, J. S., Sprague, R. L., & Cohen, M. N. (1975). Conners Teacher Rating Scale for use in drug studies with children: An empirical study. *Journal of Abnormal Child Psychology, 3,* 217–229.

Witt, J. C., Heffer, R. W., & Pfeiffer, J. P. (1990). Structured rating scales: A review of self-report and informant rating processes, procedures, and issues. In C. R. Reynolds & R. W. Kamphaus (Eds.), *Handbook of psychological and educational assessment of children: Personality, behavior, and context* (pp. 364–394). New York: Guilford Press.

PART II
Disorders

Chapter 7

Specific Phobia and Generalized Anxiety Disorder

Wendy K. Silverman
Golda S. Ginsburg

T his chapter focuses on specific phobias and generalized anxiety disorder (GAD) in childhood. We begin with a brief historical perspective of these disorders, followed by a summary of models of etiology. Phenomenology, diagnostic criteria, and differential diagnosis using the fourth edition of the *Diagnostic and Statistical Manual of Mental Disorders* (DSM-IV; American Psychiatric Association, 1994) are discussed next. A discussion of related features follows, focusing on cognitive mediators and peer, family, and school problems. The epidemiology, demographics, and natural history of each disorder are then reviewed, as well as assessment and treatment strategies. The chapter closes with a case study of a child who presents with comorbid diagnoses of specific phobia and GAD.

HISTORY AND MODELS

The study of the childhood specific phobias and GAD has important historical significance: Case studies of these problems laid the groundwork for extensive theorizing as well as clinical and empirical study in the areas of psychoanalytic and behavioral psychology. For example, Freud's case of "Little Hans" has come to serve as an important cornerstone of psychoanalytic theory (Freud, 1909/1955). In conceptualizing Little Hans's phobia of horses as arising from his sexual desire for his mother and his wish to do away with his father, the competitor, Freud envisaged flight from internal or instinctual danger (accomplished through repression). Because Hans's repression was incomplete, however, his unconscious anxiety was displaced onto some external object that in some way was related to or symbolic of the unconscious wish. According to Freud, displacement allowed Hans to avoid the phobic object—the horse—rather than his father (Trautman, 1986). Psychodynamic theorists have since broadened this initial conceptualization of Freud by emphasizing aggressive and social conflicts over sexual ones as leading to anxiety in the child (e.g., A. Freud, 1965; Klein, 1932). Because of the unconscious nature of these conflicts, empirical verification of the theory has been difficult. Thus, support for psychoanalytic theory has rested predominantly on inferences drawn from case study reports (see Kazdin & Wilson, 1978, and Rachman & Wilson, 1980, for reviews).

Analogous to the Little Hans case in terms of its impact on theoretical, clinical, and empirical work in the psychoanalytic realm, is that of "Little Albert" in the behavioral realm (Watson & Rayner, 1920). In demonstrating that a young child's fear of a previously neutral stimulus (a rat) could be acquired through contiguous pairing with an aversive stimulus, Watson and Rayner brought to the forefront the potency of learning theory. Learning theorists have since extended this work. For example, Rachman (1977) espoused the importance of direct acquisition (conditioning) as well as indirect acquisition (vicarious exposure and/or the transmission of information or instruction) in the development of phobias. Support for these pathways in the development of fears and subphobias in adults has been provided (e.g., Hekmat, 1987; Murray & Foote, 1979; Ost, 1985; Ost & Hugdahl, 1983; Rimm, Janda, Lancaster, et al., 1977) and recently in a sample of nonclinic-referred children (Ollendick, King, & Hamilton, 1991). Operant factors also play a role in the development of childhood anxiety and phobias; that is, the positive consequences that follow a fearful or anxious response (e.g., avoidance) may initiate and maintain the fearful or anxious response. Finally, the importance of classical conditioning to fear/anxiety acquisition and operant conditioning to fear/anxiety maintenance is the basic premise of the two-factor model (Mowrer, 1939) and its modifications (see Delprato & McGlynn, 1984).

Due in part to the inadequacy of learning theories (see Davey, 1992), cognitive models of childhood phobia and anxiety have also been formulated. In general, these models are based on the assumption that children with excessive fear or anxiety have difficulty in controlling faulty cognitions—cognitions that are irrational, catastrophic, and negative in nature (Kendall, Howard, & Epps, 1988). Although controversies abound as to whether these cognitions are causes or consequences of the fear/anxiety response, there is growing consensus that maladaptive cognitions play some role in the development and/or maintenance of fear and anxiety in youth (e.g., Kendall & Chansky, 1991). The precise nature of that role awaits determination.

Last, based on the accumulation of research findings from family aggregation studies (e.g., Fyer, Mannuzza, Gallops, et al., 1990; Moran & Andrews, 1985; Noyes, Crowe, Harris, et al., 1986; Reich & Yates, 1988; Solyom, Beck, Solyom, et al., 1974; Slater & Shields, 1969; Torgersen, 1979), a genetic or familial model has also been proposed for these disorders. Despite the methodological limitations of this research (e.g., small samples, reliance on retrospective reports), which render it difficult to draw definitive conclusions, the overall findings generally support a familial contribution. Here as well, however, the specific nature of this contribution is unclear. Also unclear is how this contribution varies across specific diagnostic categories (Last, Phillips, & Statfeld, 1987). Clarifying these issues is another important task for future investigations.

PHENOMENOLOGY

DSM-IV (American Psychiatric Association, 1994) indicates that a specific phobia is a persistent fear of a specific stimulus (object or situation) such that the individual avoids the stimulus whenever possible or endures it with intense anxiety. Phobias typically result in interference in functioning in such areas as academic, social or family life. Common phobias of childhood include heights, small animals, doctors, dentists, darkness, loud noises, and thunder and lightning.

Silverman and Rabian (1994) recently reviewed the phenomenology associated with childhood specific phobia along Lang's (1977, 1979) tripartite model (the behavioral, cognitive, and physiological response system). Briefly, in terms of the behavioral system the overt response is typically flight or avoidance, which may occur on immediate exposure to the feared stimulus or on anticipation of exposure. Screaming, crying, or running to a parent or loved one for safety is also common. In terms of the cognitive system, negative self-statements tend to prevail, with a common belief that confrontation with the phobic stimulus will result in personal harm ("the dog will bite"). These thoughts can become intrusive and disrupt the child's concentration and attention. In terms of the physiological system, increased heart rate is widely reported (Beidel & Turner, 1988), as well as shakiness, upset stomach, and sweating.

In contrast to specific phobia, the predominant feature of GAD, as defined by DSM-IV is excessive and preoccupying worry that is not focused on a specific situation or object. Children with GAD report worries across a variety of areas, such as future events, performance, personal safety, and social evaluation. Somatic complaints such as stomachaches and headaches are also not unusual. Children with GAD are markedly self-conscious and frequently seek reassurance from others. These children have been described as "perfectionistic," "eager to please," and "hypermature" (Strauss, 1990).

DIAGNOSTIC CRITERIA

Other than the change of name from simple to specific phobia in DSM-IV, there has been little change in the diagnostic criteria of this disorder since DSM-II (American Psychiatric Association, 1968). The DSM-IV criteria for specific phobia are indicated in Table 7.1. In our experience, criteria D and E are critical, as it is *avoidance* of the feared object or event that tends to result in *interference* in functioning—for both the child and his or her family.

TABLE 7.1. DSM-IV Criteria for a Specific Phobia

A. Marked and persistent fear that is excessive or unreasonable, cued by the presence or anticipation of a specific object or situation (e.g., flying, heights, animals, receiving an injection, seeing blood).

B. Exposure to the phobic stimulus almost invariably provokes an immediate anxiety response, which may take the form of a situationally bound or situationally predisposed Panic Attack. *Note:* In children the anxiety may be expressed by crying, tantrums, freezing, or clinging.

C. The person recognizes that the fear is excessive or unreasonable. *Note:* In children, this feature may be absent.

D. The phobic situation(s) is avoided or else is endured with intense anxiety or distress.

E. The avoidance, anxious anticipation, or distress in the feared situation(s) interferes significantly with the person's normal routine, occupational (or academic) functioning, or social activities or relationships, or there is marked distress about having the phobia.

F. In individuals under 18 years, the duration is at least 6 months.

G. The anxiety, Panic Attacks, or phobic avoidance associated with the specific object or situation are not better accounted for by another mental disorder, such as Obsessive-Compulsive Disorder (e.g., fear of dirt in someone with an obsession about contamination), Posttraumatic Stress Disorder (e.g., avoidance of stimuli associated with a severe stressor), Separation Anxiety Disorder (e.g., avoidance of school), Social Phobia (e.g., avoidance of social situations because of fear of embarrassment), Panic Disorder with Agoraphobia, or Agoraphobia Without History of Panic Disorder.

Note. From American Psychiatric Association (1994, pp. 410–411). Copyright 1994 American Psychiatric Association. Reprinted by permission.

In terms of GAD, an analogous disorder called "overanxious reaction" first appeared as a unique category in DSM-II. Its defining features were subsequently revised for DSM-III. Several problems with the DSM-III-R criteria for overanxious disorder (OAD), and with the disorder itself, existed, however (e.g., Klein & Last, 1989; Silverman, 1992; Werry, 1991). Specifically, OAD was overly diagnosed; its criteria overlapped extensively with those of other disorders, such as social phobia; and some of the criteria were vague (Beidel, 1991; Silverman, 1992; Werry, 1991). Because of these problems, changes were made in DSM-IV. These changes, which include subsuming OAD under the previous "adult" category of GAD, are presented in Table 7.2. As the table indicates, the predominant feature of GAD remains excessive worry (existing more days than not for a period of 6 months), with increased emphasis on physiologic symptoms thought to accompany anxiety (e.g., restlessness).

DIFFERENTIAL DIAGNOSIS

Differential diagnosis of specific phobia and GAD can be complicated and frequently involves distinguishing among other anxiety disorders. In terms of specific phobia, it is important to establish that the fear of the stimulus is unrelated to another anxiety or phobic disorder. Specifically, the child's fear must not be related to having a panic attack as in panic disorder; separation from loved ones, as in separation anxiety disorder; embarrassment or humiliation in social situations, as in social phobia; or not being able to escape from specific places, as in agoraphobia. A youngster may receive more than one of these diagnoses as long as the fears are related to different events or objects.

Also important is differentiation of specific phobia and obsessive–compulsive disorder (OCD). Phobias are similar to obsessions in that they have a repetitive and ruminative quality, especially as the child comes to anticipate future encounters with the feared stimulus (Silverman & Nelles, 1990). However, the diagnosis of specific phobia is not appropriately assigned to a child who displays obsessive fears about contamination, for example, and thereby avoids places with dirt. On the other hand, the diagnosis of OCD does not preclude the diagnosis of specific phobia if the feared stimulus is unrelated to the nature of the diagnosed obsessions. Finally, like specific phobia, posttraumatic stress disorder also involves avoidance of stimuli. However, the stimuli avoided in cases of posttraumatic stress disorder are those that are associated with trauma (American Psychiatric Association, 1994). Thus, a diagnosis of specific phobia would not be appropriate for a child who avoids trauma-related stimuli.

TABLE 7.2. DSM-IV Criteria for Generalized Anxiety Disorder

A. Excessive anxiety or worry (apprehensive expectation), occurring more days than not for at least 6 months, about a number of events or activities (such as work or school performance).

B. The person finds it difficult to control the worry.

C. The anxiety and worry are associated with three (or more) of the following six symptoms (with at least some symptoms present for more days than not for the past six months). *Note*: Only one item is required in children.

  (1) restlessness or feeling keyed up or on edge
  (2) being easily fatigued
  (3) difficulty concentrating or mind going blank
  (4) irritability
  (5) muscle tension
  (6) sleep disturbance (difficulty falling or staying asleep, or restless unsatisfying sleep)

D. The focus of the anxiety and worry is not confined to features of an Axis I disorder, e.g., the anxiety or worry is not about having a Panic Attack (as in Panic Disorder), being embarrassed in public (as in Social Phobia), being contaminated (as in Obsessive–Compulsive Disorder), being away from home or close relatives (as in Separation Anxiety Disorder), gaining weight (as in Anorexia Nervosa), having multiple physical complaints (as in Somatization Disorder), or having a serious illness (as in Hypochondriasis), and the anxiety and worry do not occur exclusively during Posttraumatic Stress Disorder.

E. The anxiety, worry, or physical symptoms cause clinically significant distress or impairment in social, occupational, or other important areas of functioning.

F. The disturbance is not due to the direct physiological effects of a substance (e.g., a drug of abuse, a medication) or a general medical condition (e.g., hyperthyroidism), and does not occur exclusively during a Mood Disorder, a Psychotic Disorder, or a Pervasive Developmental Disorder.

Note. From American Psychiatric Association (1994, pp. 435–436). Copyright 1994 American Psychiatric Association. Reprinted by permission.

In terms of GAD, differential diagnosis can be complex in light of the criteria overlap described earlier. To receive a diagnosis of GAD, the concerns and worries indicated by a child must be unrelated to those of another anxiety disorder. Thus, a diagnosis of GAD would not be appropriate if the focus of the child's anxiety is primarily a specific object or event (as in specific phobia), a social situation (as in social phobia), or separation from a loved one (as in separation anxiety disorder).

In addition to differentiating GAD from other psychiatric disorders, it is also essential to differentiate GAD from physical or organic disorders. For example, it is important to ensure that the "somatic complaints" reported by children with GAD are not in fact part of a larger organic disease process. The complexity of this issue is illustrated by findings that children at a pediatric outpatient clinic who presented with both organic and nonorganic somatic complaints (i.e., recurrent abdominal pain) reported similar levels of anxiety and depression as measured by the State–Trait Anxiety Inventory for Children and the Child Depression Inventory, respectively (Walker & Greene, 1989). These data highlight the difficulty in differentiating diagnoses based on somatic complaints per se and underscore the importance of assessing coexisting organic and psychiatric disorders in the diagnostic workup of the child.

RELATED FEATURES

In this section, a brief summary of the cognitive mediators of specific phobia and GAD is presented. This is followed by a discussion of peer, family, and school problems. Before proceeding, however, the paucity of research in this area should be noted. In addition, the focus has been on "anxious" children or children with "excessive fears or worries," defined by a variety of methods such as parent and teacher assessment and self-ratings. Thus, questions may be raised about the generalizability of this work to clinic samples of children diagnosed with specific phobia and GAD. Nevertheless, some consistent findings have emerged, suggesting future avenues of research.

Cognitive Mediators

A summary of the cognitive mediators must first begin with an important caveat: Work on cognitive mediation relies on methods of cognitive assessment—methods that are fraught with difficulties and controversies. These include the following: whether the methods assess children's cognitions in a reliable, valid, and accurate manner; whether the methods are sensitive to development; whether a relationship exists between assessed cognitions and children's overt behavior. Although it is beyond the scope of this chapter to elaborate on these issues (see Kendall & Hollon, 1981; Kendall & Chansky, 1991), the upshot is that results from cognitive mediation studies are limited by the method used to assess cognitive mediators. For example, if the reliability, validity, or accuracy of a cognitive assessment procedure can be questioned, then the same questions must be asked about the reported cognitive mediators studies (are they reliable, valid, or accurate?). Keeping this caveat in mind, what conclusions can be drawn about the cognitive mediators?

Overall, results from studies examining children's cognitions (e.g., Bell-Dolan & Last, 1990; Kendall & Chansky, 1991; Francis, 1988; Leitenberg, Yost, & Carroll-Wilson, 1986; Prins, 1986; Zatz & Chassen, 1983, 1985) suggest that "anxious" youth tend to report more negative self-statements, off-task thoughts, and negative cognitive errors than their "nonanxious" counterparts. For example, Leitenberg et al. (1986) investigated negative cognitive errors in children with and without self-reported symptoms of depression, self-esteem, and evaluation anxiety. Relevant here are their findings that "highly anxious" children (defined as those who scored more than one standard deviation above the mean on the Test Anxiety Scale for Children; Sarason, Davidson, Lighthall, et al., 1960) engaged in more overgeneralizing in predictions of negative outcomes, personalizing responsibility for negative events, selectively attending to negative aspects of events, and catastrophizing compared to "low anxious" children (defined as those who scored more than one standard deviation below the mean).

In a more recent study, Kendall and Chansky (1991) reported the frequency and usefulness of four different types of cognitions (positive, negative, neutral, and coping/strategic) in a sample of children referred to an anxiety disorders clinic. The sample was divided into two groups (those who met criteria for an anxiety disorder and those who did not) and their responses to self-report questionnaires on cognitions and thought-listing procedures were compared. Results indicated no differences in the overall frequency of each cognition type reported by the two groups. Children diagnosed with an anxiety disorder, however, engaged in an excess of coping cognitions (thoughts aimed at controlling anxiety and completing the task) during exposure to a stressful situation—a finding consistent with other investigations (e.g., Zatz & Chassin, 1985). According to Kendall and Chansky (1991), the excess of coping thoughts in anxious children was unmodulated and interfered with the youngsters' ability to manage their anxiety. Thus, the authors suggest that children with anxiety disorders do in fact possess a reservoir of coping thoughts, but, they may require training in shaping and controlling their thoughts to make them adaptive and useful. Although research on the cognitive mediators of childhood specific phobia and GAD is limited, the tantalizing results discussed indicate the importance of further scientific inquiry in this area.

Peer Problems

Research demonstrating the detrimental effects of poor peer relations on later social and personal adjustment (e.g., Asher & Coie, 1990; Parker & Asher, 1987) highlights the importance of social competence in children. Unfortunately, the impact of having specific phobia or GAD on children's social functioning remains relatively unexplored. One of the few studies to examine peer relations of "anxious" children (Strauss, Frame, & Fore-hand, 1987) involved the classification of 48 elementary school-age children as "highly anxious" or "nonanxious" using teachers' ratings on Quay and Peterson's (1983) Revised Behavior Rating Scale. Classmates provided peer nominations of three children whom they "liked the most" and "liked the least." Peer nominations of the most shy, the most aggressive, and the most socially withdrawn, as well as peer ratings of how much they liked to play with each child in the class, were also obtained. Overall, children in the "highly anxious" group were found to be less popular and were more likely to be nominated as shy and socially withdrawn than their "nonanxious" counterparts.

Using a similar methodology, Strauss, Lahey, Frick, et al. (1988) compared the peer social status of children ages 6 to 13 with an anxiety disorder (separation anxiety disorder, OCD, or OAD; $n = 16$), a conduct disorder ($n = 26$), and a nonreferred control group ($n = 45$). Diagnoses were obtained from structured interviews and social status was based on peer nominations of three children liked most and least. Peer nominations were also obtained for three classmates who fought the most.

The authors found that children with anxiety disorders were less likely to be nominated as most liked than were their nonreferred peers; no differences were found in most liked nominations between the children with anxiety and conduct disorders. Interestingly, when children were classified into three groups, popular, neglected, and rejected, children with anxiety disorders were found to be more socially neglected than either of the other groups.

Despite these differences between anxious and nonanxious children, as Strauss and colleagues (1988) point out, 63% (9 out of 16) of the children with anxiety disorders did not show significant deficits in their peer social status. Therefore, while some proportion of children with anxiety disorders appears at risk for disrupted peer relations, not all such children display difficulties in this area.

It is beyond the scope of this chapter to fully analyze the possible "risk" and "protective" factors for satisfactory peer relations among anxious children. However, one factor worth mentioning here is that of social anxiety. Specifically, research on peer relations in "normal" children indicates that children with high levels of social anxiety suffer in their peer relations (e.g., Asher & Coie, 1990; La Greca & Stone, 1993). To the extent that children with GAD and/or specific phobia also report elevated levels of social anxiety, social anxiety may serve as a mediator in the children's peer relations. Further research examining these relationships is warranted—particularly in light of the potential implications for treatment.

Family Problems

Investigations of family problems among children with specific phobia and GAD vary widely in their methodology, thereby making comparisons and conclusions difficult. Some of these variations include the use of divergent samples (inpatient versus outpatient), the specific facets of family functioning assessed (e.g., discipline practices versus family environment), the particular perspective assessed (child versus parent) and the time frame assessed (past versus present). With these limitations in mind, a brief summary of research findings on family functioning follows.

Early reports of family functioning (or parenting behavior) of children with phobic and anxiety disorders have described the families as showing significant psychopathology, such as overprotectiveness, ambivalence toward the child, and marital dissatisfaction (e.g., Berg, Nichols, & Pritchard, 1969; Eisenberg, 1958). A more recent controlled study on family functioning (Bernstein & Garfinkel, 1986) compared a sample of 6 adolescents referred to an outpatient school phobia clinic (diagnosed with an anxiety disorder of OAD or separation anxiety disorder) with a matched psychiatric group. Parents completed numerous instruments; relevant here are their responses to the revised Family Assessment Measure III (FAM; Skinner, Steinhauer, & Santa-Barbara, 1983), a self-report instrument that assesses various dimensions of general family functioning and dyadic or parent–child relations such as communication, involvement, role performance, control, and affective expression. In contrast to the control group, parents of the adolescents with school phobia scored in the clinical range on the overall dimension of family functioning as well as on dimensions of role performance, affective expression, and communication. These results are consistent with those of other investigators who have found a relation between greater degrees of parental discord/familial disharmony and anxiety in children, using clinic and nonclinic samples (e.g., Dadds & Powell, 1991; Kashani, Vaidya, Soltys, et al., 1990).

Other comparisons between families of "anxious" children and families of children with other psychiatric diagnoses (e.g., depression, conduct disorder) have yielded more mixed results. For example, Bernstein, Svingen, and Garfinkel (1990) examined the family functioning (via the FAM) of 76 children (ages 7 to 17) with "school phobia." Based on independent reviews of clinic charts, the children were classified as depressive disorder only ($n = 22$; diagnoses included major depression, dysthymia, and adjustment disorder with depressed mood), anxiety disorder only ($n = 20$; diagnoses included separation anxiety disorder, OAD, and adjustment disorder with anxious mood), anxious and depressed ($n = 20$), and other psychiatric diagnoses ($n = 14$; diagnoses were predominantly conduct and oppositional defiant disorders). Comparisons among the four diagnostic groups suggested that the anxiety disorder only group was distinct from the other groups by the relative absence of family dysfunction.

Along similar lines, Stark, Humphrey, Crook, et al. (1990) administered the Self-Report Measure of Family Functioning (Bloom, 1985) to four diagnostic groups of children and their mothers (diagnoses were based on responses to the Schedule for Affective Disorders and Schizophrenia for School-Aged Children [K-SADS; Puig-Antich & Chambers, 1978]): (1) depressed only (major depression, dysthymia, or depressive disorder not otherwise specified), (2) anxious only (OAD or anxiety disorder not otherwise specified), (3) depressed and anxious (depressive disorder plus anxiety disorder), and "normal" controls. A comparison among the diagnostic groups indicated that families in the third group, with a depressed and anxious child, reported significantly more family dysfunction than did the other groups, while the anxious only and depressed only groups did not differ significantly from each other.

In summary, the scant information available on family problems of children with anxiety and phobic disorders suggests that these youngsters experience some type of disruption in their family functioning, especially in comparison to children from nonclinic families. On the other hand, a unique pattern of family dysfunction that distinguishes families with an anxious/phobic child from families with a child displaying other psychiatric problems, such as depression, has not been identified. Moreover, to date, the research has focused on mere description of family functioning; investigations of specific mechanisms of transmission of phobias/anxiety have been absent. Such work would seem important to conduct, in light of the research reviewed earlier that indicates a familial contribution to specific phobia and GAD in children.

School Problems

Although a myriad of school problems are likely to arise from excessive childhood anxiety and fear, two problems that are commonly discussed in the literature are school refusal and test anxiety. Children who exhibit school refusal behavior are often labeled as having "school phobia" (a phobia not specified in the DSM classification scheme) and have historically been considered to represent a homogeneous group. However, numerous authors (Atkinson, Quarrington, Cyr, et al., 1985; Bernstein & Garfinkel, 1986; Burke & Silverman, 1987; Ollendick & Mayer, 1984) have noted that these children refuse to go to school for a variety of reasons: fear of a specific stimulus in the school setting (which could suggest the presence of specific phobia); problems with separation from loved ones (which could suggest the presence of separation anxiety disorder); or fear of certain social situations, such as speaking in class (which could suggest the presence of social phobia). Such distinctions are important because they are likely to influence treatment planning (Kearney & Silverman, 1990).

Substantial research has demonstrated the debilitating effects of test anxiety on children's academic performance (e.g., Sarason, 1980). This literature is relevant here because children with elevated levels of test anxiety (as measured by the Test Anxiety Scale for Children) show a higher prevalence of other anxiety and phobic disorders (most commonly OAD and social phobia) compared to children with low levels of text anxiety (Beidel & Turner, 1988). Thus, one might hypothesize that children with anxiety and phobic disorders (social phobia—not necessarily specific phobia, though this requires clarification) show deficits similar to those of children with high test anxiety, deficits such as debilitating off-task and negative self-evaluative thoughts and difficulties with task completion and academic performance (Sarason, Hill, & Zimbardo, 1964; Zatz & Chassin, 1985). Such a hypothesis would also be consistent with findings that teachers report more attentional problems among highly anxious children than among nonanxious children in the classroom (Strauss et al., 1987). It is necessary to test this hypothesis further in future investigations.

EPIDEMIOLOGY, DEMOGRAPHICS, AND NATURAL HISTORY

Estimates on the prevalence of specific phobia and GAD vary according to informant (e.g., parent vs. child), method of obtaining information (e.g., structured versus unstructured interview), sample studied (clinic vs. community), and with respect to GAD, whether an impairment index was included as part of the definition.

Epidemiological data on childhood specific phobia as defined by DSM criteria are rare. Of the few studies that have been conducted using DSM-III criteria (e.g., Anderson, Williams, McGee, et al., 1987; Bird, Canino, Rubio-Stipec, et al., 1988; Kashani, Orvaschel, Rosenberg, et al., 1989; Kashani & Orvaschel, 1990) estimated prevalence rates have been between 2.4 and 3.3%, with a higher prevalence reported for females than males (Anderson et al., 1987). Prevalence rates among diverse child groups, such as African Americans, Native Americans, Hispanics, and Asian Americans, have not been reported.

Although there is much literature on the natural history of "normal" childhood fears (for reviews see Morris & Kratochwill, 1983; Ollendick & Francis, 1988; Silverman & Nelles, 1990), little exists on childhood specific phobia. What does exist is limited methodologically and often failed to assess the children using DSM criteria. Thus, caution is warranted when extrapolating from these studies.

The most frequently cited study is that of Agras, Chapin, and Oliveau (1972). Following a community sample of 30 phobic individuals (10 children under the age of 20 years and 20 adults) over a 5-year period during which none received treatment, 100% of the children were viewed as "improved" compared to 43% of the adults. The authors concluded that many phobic conditions improved without any form of treatment and that child phobics improve more rapidly than their adult counterparts (Agras et al., 1972). However, as Ollendick (1979) has pointed out, the "improved" children in the Agras et al. study were not completely symptom-free, and the majority of them continued to exhibit symptoms of sufficient intensity to be rated between "no disability" and "maximum disability" at the follow-up assessment. Thus, Ollendick's reinterpretation of the Agras et al. (1972) data suggests that phobias, or at least some of the symptoms of phobias, persist over time for a certain proportion of youngsters.

A similar conclusion may be drawn from the results obtained by Hampe, Noble, Miller, et al. (1973). Specifically, the researchers examined 2-year follow-up data obtained from 62 children (6 to 15 years old) who had been treated for phobias. Although 80% of the children no longer exhibited phobias, a small percentage (7%) did. That a certain proportion of individuals retained their phobic symptoms over time is consistent as well with the retrospective reports of adults with phobias (e.g., Abe, 1972; Ost, 1987; Thyer, Parrish, Curtis, et al., 1985). Specifically, when age of onset has been assessed among adults with specific phobia, the ages reported tend to range between 5 and 10 years.

In terms of the epidemiology of GAD, prevalence rates are estimated to range from 2 to 19% (e.g., Anderson et al., 1987; Bowen, Offord, & Boyle, 1990; Kashani & Orvaschel, 1988; McGee, Feehan, Williams, et al., 1990; Velez, Johnson, & Cohen, 1989); studies using stringent diagnostic criteria (based on DSM-III or DSM-III-R; e.g., Achenbach, Connors, Quay, et al., 1989; Anderson et al., 1987; Bowen et al., 1990) report lower (2 to 4%) prevalence rates. In addition, consistent with the general finding in the adult literature on anxiety disorders, GAD, at least from adolescence on, has been diagnosed more frequently in females than males (Bowen et al., 1990; McGee et al., 1990). GAD symptoms are also more prevalent in older children (ages 12 to 19) than younger children (ages 5 to 11) (Strauss, Lease, Last, et al., 1988). Although no information is available on the prevalence of GAD in different ethnic groups, children from middle to upper income families predominate in clinic samples (Last, Perrin, Hersen, et al., 1992; Silverman & Nelles, 1988).

Natural history data on GAD are also sparse and suggest that the disorder, as previously defined by DSM-III-R, is unstable over time. For example, Cantwell and Baker (1989) examined a large sample of children from a speech and hearing clinic over a 4- to 5-year period. Of the 8 children initially diagnosed with OAD, only 25% retained the diagnosis at the follow-up—an equal percentage were considered "well." Moreover, the remaining 50% received an alternative diagnosis.

Another prospective study (Last, Hersen, Kazdin, et al., 1993) followed a sample of children diagnosed with either anxiety or phobic disorders, attention-deficit/hyperactivity disorder, and "never psychiatrically ill" (NPI) over a 1- to 2-year period. The authors found that a majority (65%) of the children diagnosed with anxiety or phobic disorders did not receive any diagnosis at 12- to 24-month follow-ups, though approximately 33% of the youngsters did. Despite the limitations of this study (e.g., a proportion of the children received treatment prior to the follow-up assessments), preliminary evidence suggests that GAD has limited stability over time.

ASSESSMENT

Scales and Interviews

Several child self-report rating scales have been developed to assess childhood fears and generalized anxiety. The most widely used scales include the Fear Survey Schedule for Children–Revised (FSSC-R; Ollendick, 1983); the Revised Children's Manifest Anxiety Scale (RCMAS; Reynolds & Richmond, 1978) and the State–Trait Anxiety Inventory for Children (STAIC; Spielberger, 1973). In general, the psychometric properties of these measures have been well documented. Lacking, however, is a clear demonstration that these measures have discriminant validity—that they are able to differentiate children with specific phobia and/or GAD from children with other types of disorders, either internalizing or externalizing (Hodges, Kline, Stern, et al., 1982; Perrin & Last, 1992). An important exception is the work of Mattison and colleagues (Mattison, Bagnato, & Brubaker, 1988), who showed that scores on the RCMAS one standard deviation above the mean on the worry/oversensitivity subscale could confirm DSM-III diagnoses of OAD but not other disorders.

In addition to discriminant validity, there is the problem of construct validity—whether the FSSC-R and the RCMAS actually measure the constructs that they were designed to measure ("fear," "anxiety"). Indeed, recent reviews of the literature suggest that these measures assess the more diffuse global state of "negative affectivity" (Finch, Lopovsky, & Casat, 1989; King, Ollendick, & Gullone, 1991). Additional research on the utility of these instruments is thus necessary. In the meantime, however, the FSSC-R and the RCMAS continue to be widely used in clinical research, primarily as outcome measures in treatment studies (e.g., Eisen & Silverman, 1993; Kendall, 1994).

Also widely used to assess childhood fears and generalized anxiety are structured interviews, of which a number exist in both child and parallel parent versions, including the K-SADS (Puig-Antich & Chambers, 1978); the Diagnostic Interview for Children and Adolescents (DICA; Herjanic & Reich, 1982); the Interview Schedule for Children (ISC; Kovacs, 1982); the Child Assessment Schedule (CAS; Hodges, McKnew, Cytryn et al., 1982); the Diagnostic Interview Schedule for Children (DISC; Costello, Edelbrock, Dulcan, et al., 1984); the Anxiety Disorders Interview Schedule for Children (ADIS-C; Silverman & Nelles, 1988); and the Child and Adolescent Psychiatric Assessment (CAPA; Angold, Prendergast, Cox, et al., in press).

All of these interviews have undergone revision or modification primarily as a way to improve their diagnostic reliability (see Silverman, 1994). Thus, they all contain sections that cover the DSM criteria for specific phobia and GAD and thereby provide for their diagnosis. However, as reviewed elsewhere (Silverman, 1991), although work has appeared that is encouraging about the diagnostic reliability of these interviews, overall the findings have been uneven. Thus, caution is warranted before assuming that diagnoses obtained using a particular interview schedule are "reliable." In our reliability studies on the ADIS-C and ADIS-P (the parent version), for example, (Silverman & Nelles, 1988; Silverman & Eisen, 1992; Silverman & Rabian, in press), we have found the kappa coefficients to be high for diagnoses of specific phobia but relatively low for GAD.

Little work has been conducted on the validity of these interview schedules. For example, lacking is contrast group validity—whether the interviews can discriminate children with generalized anxiety/phobic disorders from children with and without other psychiatric disorders. In addition, due to the problem inherent in selecting the "gold standard," studies concerned with criterion validity have yielded mixed results (Silverman, 1994). There has also been little validation of interview-based anxiety/phobic diagnoses with respect to etiology, course, prognosis, or treatment responsiveness of these disorders (Edelbrock & Costello, 1984).

Laboratory Measures

The most frequently used laboratory measures of anxiety in children are heart rate and electrodermal activity (e.g., finger or palm sweat; King, Hamilton, & Ollendick, 1988). The complexities of physiological assessment, individual differences in arousal patterns, and the instruments' sensitivity to nonanxiety influences have hindered the establishment of the reliability of these indices with children. One exception is the Palmar Sweat Index (Melamed & Siegel, 1975), a measure of sweat gland activity, used primarily with children who display medical fears. In addition to being reliable, the index is relatively quick and easy to obtain.

In our work with children with specific phobia and GAD, we employ several laboratory measures designed to assess the physiological and behavioral domain, along the lines of Lang's (1979) tripartite model. For example, we concurrently assess the children's heart rate using a computer "heart watch" (that is placed on the child's wrist) during a behavioral exposure task. The behavioral exposure task for GAD is having the child talk for 5 minutes in front of a group of adult strangers. For specific phobia, the child is asked to approach the feared stimulus. Following the exposure task, the child's heart rate signals as measured by the watch are counted by computer. Recent data from our research clinic indicate that this procedure yielded reliable test–retest heart rate scores (Chapunoff, 1992). The ultimate clinical utility of this measure, in terms of its sensitivity as a measure of change in treatment outcome studies, remains to be determined.

TREATMENT

Psychosocial Therapy

In treating children with specific phobia or GAD the same basic ingredient—namely, gradual exposure to the fearful/anxious stimuli—is typically included in psychosocial treatment programs. Gradual exposure provides an opportunity for the child to obtain step-by-step success experiences with the anxious or phobic object or event. In addition to exposure, several facilitative strategies might be used. These strategies are contingency management, modeling, and self-control. Considerably more evidence exists for the utility of these strategies in treating specific phobia than in treating GAD. (Two strategies that are more specific to treating specific phobia but not GAD are systematic desensitization and flooding. For reviews, see King et al., 1988, and Silverman & Eisen, 1993.)

Before summarizing the research findings, the methodological limitations of the research should be acknowledged. As indicated in previous writings (e.g., Silverman & Kearney, 1991; Silverman & Rabian, 1994), work in this area is characterized by a failure to employ (1) controlled experimental procedures, (2) clinical samples, (3) formal diagnostic procedures, (4) multimethod–multisource assessment procedures, and (5) systematic follow-up procedures. In addition, work in this area has failed to adequately address the issue of development and to compare the relative efficacies of strategies. With these limitations in mind, a brief summary of the various facilitative strategies and their utility in treating childhood specific phobia and GAD follows.

Contingency management procedures, based on the principles of operant conditioning, stress the importance of the causal relationship between stimuli and behavior (Morris & Kratochwill, 1983). In our work, we rely on the therapist and the parents to rearrange the environment to ensure that positive consequences follow exposure to the fearful or anxious stimulus and to ensure that positive consequences, such as parental attention, do not follow avoidance behavior (i.e., extinction). Contingency management has been used most frequently to treat children with so-called "school phobia"—a population that, as stated earlier, is highly heterogeneous and may include children with specific phobia, GAD, and other anxiety disorders (e.g., Burke & Silverman, 1987; Last, Francis, Hersen, et al., 1987). Contingency management procedures have also been used to treat children with phobias of heights (Holmes, 1936) and small animals (Obler & Terwilliger, 1970).

Modeling procedures involve the fearful or anxious child observing others handle the feared/anxious object or situation. The models observed may be actual children or adults, children or adults observed on films or videotapes, or symbolic/imaginal models. In our work, we employ the "tagalong" procedure first described by Ollendick and Cerny (1981). In this procedure, the therapist first models appropriate fearless or coping behavior when in the presence of the feared object or event. The child then "tags along," or follows the behaviors of the therapist, with the therapist providing feedback and encouragement. Modeling procedures have been extensively experimentally tested (Barrios & O'Dell, 1989), although the focus has been primarily on dental and medical fears—not clinical phobias or anxieties (e.g., Melamed & Siegel, 1975; Melamed, Yurcheson, Fleece, et al., 1978). In addition to situational fears, modeling procedures have been found to be effective in reducing children's fears of small animals (Bandura, Blanchard, & Ritter, 1969; Bandura & Menlove, 1968; Hill, Liebert, & Mott, 1968), water (Lewis, 1974), heights (Ritter, 1968), and test taking (Mann, 1972).

Self-control procedures stress the important contribution of cognitive processes to behavior change with each child directly involved in regulating his or her own behavior. In our work, we teach children specific thinking styles that they are to apply when confronted with the feared/anxious stimulus. In general, self-control procedures have been effective in reducing children's nighttime fears (Graziano, Mooney, Huber, et al., 1979; Graziano & Mooney, 1980), darkness (Kanfer, Karoly, & Newman, 1975), public speaking (Cradock, Cotler, & Jason, 1978; Fox & Houston, 1981), and bowel movements (Eisen & Silverman, 1991).

The studies just cited primarily have targeted phobias. As indicated in the beginning of this section, there is a paucity of studies where the target has been children who have been carefully diagnosed with OAD using DSM-III or DSM-III-R criteria or with GAD using DSM-IV criteria. One study that did is Kane and Kendall (1989). Specifically, a multiple baseline design was used to evaluate the effectiveness of a 16- to 20-week self-control treatment program of 4 children (ages 9 to 13) with OAD. The program incorporated cognitive self-control strategies, contingency management procedures, and relaxation training. Results indicated significant decreases in children's and parents' ratings of anxiety symptoms between the pretreatment and posttreatment assessment sessions. These gains were generally maintained at 3- and 6-month follow-up.

Kendall (1994) further evaluated the effectiveness of the above treatment program in a controlled study. (In this study, however, the sample comprised not only children diagnosed with OAD [n = 30] but also children diagnosed with separation anxiety disorder [n = 8] and avoidant disorder [n = 9].) All subjects were randomly assigned to either the treatment program or a wait-listed control group. The results supported the efficacy of the treatment: Significant reductions in anxiety symptoms were reported by the children and the parents at posttreatment evaluation and at 1-year follow-up.

Using a multiple baseline design, Eisen and Silverman (1993) compared the efficacy of self-control training, relaxation training, and a combination of both in treating 4 children (ages 6 to 15) diagnosed with OAD. Each of the three conditions, which lasted 6 weeks, included an exposure component. Positive changes from pretreatment to posttreatment were demonstrated by all 4 children and were maintained at 6-month follow-up, based on child and parent reports of anxiety symptoms. Of the three conditions, the combination of self-control training and relaxation training appeared most effective.

In summary, additional controlled clinical trials of treatments of childhood specific phobia and GAD are needed. Although relatively more treatment research has been conducted on specific phobias than on GAD, methodological limitations of the phobia research render it difficult to draw firm conclusions about efficacy. Moreover, no controlled research focuses on the relative effectiveness of the various facilitative strategies. Indeed, we are currently conducting an NIMH-funded study that addresses this issue. In particular, the study compares the relative effectiveness of contingency management procedures and self-control procedures in treating childhood phobias.

Drawing conclusions at this time about the treatment of GAD is also difficult. Certainly, however, the preliminary findings obtained by Kendall and colleagues using their cognitive-behavioral treatment package are promising, and thus the treatment warrants further testing. There is also a need for dismantling types of study, along the lines of Eisen and Silverman (1993). Finally, we are currently evaluating the efficacy of a cognitive-behavioral treatment program conducted in a group format, also with the support of NIMH. In addition to using cognitive-behavioral strategies, the treatment relies on the therapeutic aspects of group processes such as peer modeling, positive and instructive feedback, and social comparisons and support. Taken together, these strategies are expected to be powerful facilitators of change for children with GAD.

Pharmacotherapy

A review of the treatment literature indicates that a wide variety of pharmacologic agents, such as antidepressants, antihistamines, stimulants, and anxiolytics, have been used in the treatment of childhood anxiety disorders (see Gittelman & Koplewicz, 1986). A major difficulty in interpreting this literature, however, is that most of it predates DSM-III, and thus ambiguous terms such as "neurosis," "phobic neurosis," "anxious," or "school phobic," are used to describe the child participants. In addition, most of the literature consists of clinical case studies—most of which lack pretreatment baseline data by which to make comparisons (Gittelman & Koplewicz, 1986).

Given these limitations, what conclusions can be drawn about pharmacological treatment of childhood specific phobia and GAD? Unfortunately, there are not many. Early controlled studies (Gittelman-Klein & Klein, 1971, 1980) employing tricyclic antidepressants with a sample of school refusers—as noted earlier, a group that is likely to contain children with simple phobias and GAD (as well as other disorders)—reported positive outcomes. However, other well-controlled studies employing tricyclics with similar populations (e.g., Berney, Kolvin, Bhate, et al., 1981) found medication to be no more effective than placebo. Clearly additional data demonstrating the efficacy of medication in the treatment of specific phobia and GAD are needed before wide use of these agents can be recommended.

CASE EXAMPLE

Presenting Problem

Jennifer, an 8-year-old Caucasian female, was referred by her pediatrician to the Child Anxiety and Phobia Program at Florida International University, Miami, because of her severe fear of insects, excessive worrying, and somatic complaints. Her pediatrician had ruled out an organic basis for her symptoms. At the time of referral, Jennifer described feeling extremely frightened of insects and reported avoiding places where she had previously seen insects (e.g., the kitchen). She also disclosed worrying a great deal about "not being good enough" (e.g., in her school performance), "making mistakes," "being teased by others," and "being in ac-

cidents" in which she or her parents would be hurt. Concurrent with these
fears and worries, Jennifer reported a number of physiological reactions
such as headaches, stomachaches, sweating, and increased heart rate on
seeing an insect (and when she anticipated seeing an insect) or when worrying. Jennifer's mother described herself as "anxious" and reported that
she too had a fear of insects, though not as severe as her daughter's. She
also stated that her daughter had always been a "worrier," needing constant reassurance.

Assessment and Diagnosis

Jennifer and her mother were administered the ADIS-C and ADIS-P (Silverman & Eisen, 1992; Silverman & Nelles, 1988). In addition, Jennifer
completed several self-report questionnaires, including the FSSC-R, the
RCMAS, and the STAIC. Jennifer's mother completed parent versions of
the FSSC-R and RCMAS. Both Jennifer and her mother indicated that
Jennifer's fearful and avoidant behavior (e.g., refusing to enter the kitchen)
significantly interfered with her daily functioning and was having a negative impact on her social relations. Based on their responses to the interviews, Jennifer was assigned a diagnosis of specific phobia of insects and
GAD. The scores on the self- and parent-report assessment questionnaires
were elevated, supporting the notion that Jennifer experienced excessive
levels of fear and anxiety.

Treatment

Jennifer was enrolled in a 10-week cognitive-behavioral treatment program
in which parent and child are seen individually and jointly each week for a
total of approximately 1.5 hours. Treatment involved imaginal and gradual
in vivo exposure to stimuli along a fear hierarchy, the use of contingency
contracts to reward Jennifer for approach behavior, and the teaching of cognitive self-control strategies. Treatment was aimed at addressing Jennifer's
specific phobia of insects first, then her more generalized anxiety.

Jennifer and her mother were first taught about the nature of fears
and anxiety and common concomitant reactions (subjective–cognitive,
behavioral, and physiological responses). Subsequently, child and mother,
with the therapist's assistance, developed a fear hierarchy pertaining to
Jennifer's fear of insects. Each step on the hierarchy was a structured
gradual exposure task that Jennifer performed either between sessions or
in sessions with the therapist.

To incorporate the use of contingency contracts, the therapist explained the concepts of positive reinforcement and extinction to the child
and her mother, and the three generated a list of rewards (e.g., objects
and activities). Jennifer and her mother were then taught how to formu-

late contingency contracts in which Jennifer was to receive very specific rewards contingent on successfully completing steps or exposure tasks on the hierarchy (e.g., approaching an insect). The use of contingency contracts and rewards was gradually phased out as Jennifer began to master the use of self-control strategies.

In the self-control phase of treatment, Jennifer was taught to examine the specific cognitions that played a role in maintaining her fear of insects (e.g., "the insect is going to bite me"). Using the "STOP" acronym (S stands for "Scared?"; T stands for "Thoughts?"; O stands for "Other thoughts or other things I can do"; and P stands for "Praise") Jennifer learned to recognize when she was afraid or worried, to employ more adaptive coping thoughts and behaviors, and to praise herself for doing so.

During the 10-week treatment program, Jennifer progressed up the fear hierarchy to the point where she was actually able to handle an insect. The strategies were then employed in six additional sessions, which focused on Jennifer's predominant worries (a major feature of GAD). At posttreatment assessment, readministration of the relevant sections of the ADIS-C and ADIS-P revealed that Jennifer no longer met criteria for GAD or specific phobia and that interference in the child's daily functioning and peer relations had ceased. The scores on the questionnaire measures decreased markedly. Follow-up assessments revealed the Jennifer's progress was maintained at 3, 6, and 12 months posttreatment.

SUMMARY

Conceptualizations of specific phobia and generalized anxiety are rooted in early psychoanalytic and behavioral theory, and extensions of these early theories are evident in the subsequent models discussed (e.g., cognitive, familial, etc.).

In terms of specific phobia, the hallmark feature is exaggerated and persistent fear that is focused on a specific object or situation (e.g., a small animal, heights). The predominant feature of GAD is excessive and preoccupying worry that is not focused on a specific object or situation. Common to both disorders is symptomatology that may appear across three response systems: motoric (e.g., avoidance behavior), cognitive (e.g., negative self-statements), and physiological (e.g., stomachaches, sweating).

Diagnostic criteria of specific phobia have remained relatively static over the last 20 years, with little change in DSM-IV. GAD in children, on the other hand, has been revised several times and was previously referred to as OAD in DSM-III-R. For both disorders, however, the challenge of accurate diagnosis depends primarily on differentiating them from other anxiety disorders.

Features of specific phobia and GAD include cognitive mediators, peer, family, and school problems. The cognitive mediators that are likely are an excess of negative self-statements, off-task thoughts, and negative cognitive errors. In addition, a major difficulty appears to be the modulation and application of adaptive coping thoughts. A proportion of "anxious" children display difficulties in peer relations, though not all youngsters do. Research on family problems has not yet been able to identify unique familial characteristics or patterns of interaction that distinguish families with an anxious/phobic child from families with a child with other psychiatric problems. Finally, a myriad of school problems are likely to arise from excessive fear or anxiety. Two problems, school refusal and test anxiety, are both associated with poor academic performance.

Conservative epidemiological estimates on the prevalence of specific phobia and GAD (in primarily Caucasian samples) range between 2 and 4%. Rates among clinic samples are higher, especially for GAD. Existing evidence, albeit sparse, suggests that these disorders are relatively unstable, although some anxious/phobic symptoms appear to persist over time in some children.

Assessment approaches used to diagnose these anxiety disorders tend to address the three response systems (cognitive, motoric, physiological) mentioned earlier. The cognitive system is typically assessed through interviews and questionnaires, behavioral approach tasks assess the motoric system, and physiological measurements include heart rate and sweat gland activity.

Finally, in spite of methodological limitations that plague the treatment literature on specific phobia and GAD, one ingredient considered essential for successful treatment is gradual exposure to the feared object or situation. To facilitate the occurrence of exposure, strategies such as contingency management, self-control training, and modeling have also been used.

ACKNOWLEDGMENT

This chapter was written with the support of NIMH Grants 44781 and 49680.

REFERENCES

Abe, K. (1972). Phobias and nervous symptoms in childhood and maturity: Persistence and associations. *British Journal of Psychiatry, 120*, 275–283.

Achenbach, T. M., Conners, C. K., Quay, H. C., et al. (1989). Replication of empirically derived syndromes as a basis for taxonomy of child/adolescent psychopathology. *Journal of Abnormal Child Psychology, 17*, 299–323.

Agras, W. S., Chapin, H. N., & Oliveau, D. C. (1972). The natural history of phobia. *Archives of General Psychiatry, 26*, 315–317.

American Psychiatric Association. (1968). *Diagnostic and statistical manual disorders* (2nd ed.). Washington, DC: Author.

American Psychiatric Association. (1987). *Diagnostic and statistical manual of mental disorders* (3rd ed., rev.). Washington, DC: Author.

American Psychiatric Association. (1994). *Diagnostic and statistical manual of mental disorders* (4th ed.). Washington, DC: Author.

Anderson, J. C., Williams, S., McGee, R., et al. (1987). DSM-III disorders in preadolescent children. *Archives of General Psychiatry, 44*, 69–76.

Angold, A., Prendergast, M., Cox, A., et al. (in press). The Child and Adolescent Psychiatric Assessment (CAPA). *Psychological Medicine*.

Asher, S. R., & Coie, J. D. (1990). *Peer rejection in children*. Cambridge: Cambridge University Press.

Atkinson, L., Quarrington, B., Cyr, J. J., et al. (1985). Differential classification in school refusal. *British Journal of Psychiatry, 155*, 191–195.

Bandura, A., Blanchard, E. B., & Ritter, B. (1969). Relative efficacy of desensitization and modeling approaches for inducing behavioral, affective, and attitudinal changes. *Journal of Personality and Social Psychology, 13*, 179–199.

Bandura, A., & Menlove, F. (1968). Factors determining vicarious extinction of avoidance behavior through symbolic modeling. *Journal of Personality and Social Psychology, 8*, 99–108.

Barrios, B. A., & O'Dell, S. L. (1989). Fears and anxieties. In E. J. Mash & R. A. Barkley (Eds.), *Treatment of childhood disorders* (pp. 167–221). New York: Guilford Press.

Beidel, D. C. (1991). Social phobia and overanxious disorder in school-age children. *Journal of the American Academy of Child and Adolescent Psychiatry, 3*, 545–552.

Beidel, D. C., & Turner, S. M. (1988). Comorbidity of test anxiety and other anxiety disorders in children. *Journal of Abnormal Child Psychology, 16*, 275–287.

Bell-Dolan, D., & Last, C. G. (1990). *Attributional style of anxious children*. Paper presented at the 24th annual convention of the Association for the Advancement of Behavior Therapy, San Francisco, CA.

Berg, I., Nichols, K., & Pritchard, C. (1969). School-phobia—Its classification and relationship to dependency. *Journal of Child Psychology and Psychiatry, 10*, 123–141.

Berney, T., Kolvin, I., Bhate, S. R., et al. (1981). School phobia: A therapeutic trial with clomipramine and short-term outcome. *British Journal of Psychiatry, 138*, 110–118.

Bernstein, G. A., & Garfinkel, B. D. (1986). School phobia: The overlap of affective and anxiety disorders. *Journal of the American Academy of Child and Adolescent Psychiatry, 25*, 235–241.

Bernstein, G. A., Svingen, P. H., & Garfinkel, B. D. (1990). School phobia: Patterns of family functioning. *Journal of the American Academy of Child and Adolescent Psychiatry, 29*, 24–30.

Bird, H. R., Canino, G., Rubio-Stipec, M., et al. (1988). Estimates of the prevalence of childhood maladjustment in a community survey in Puerto Rico.
Archives of General Psychiatry, 45, 1120–1126.

Bloom, B. L. (1985). A factor analysis of self-report measures of family functioning. *Family Process, 24,* 225–239.

Bowen, R. C., Offord, D. R., & Boyle, M. H. (1990). The prevalence of overanxious disorder and separation disorder in the community results from the
Ontario Mental Health Study. *Journal of the American Academy of Child
and Adolescent Psychiatry, 29,* 753–758.

Burke, A. E., & Silverman, W. K. (1987). The prescriptive treatment of school
refusal. *Clinical Psychology Review, 29,* 570–574.

Cantwell, D. P., & Baker, L. (1989). Stability and natural history of DSM-III
childhood diagnoses. *Journal of the American Academy of Child and Adolescent Psychiatry, 29,* 691–700.

Chapunoff, A. (1992). *Test–retest reliability of heart response in children with
phobic disorder.* Unpublished master's thesis, Florida International University, Miami.

Costello, A. J., Edelbrock, C. S., Dulcan, M. K., et al. (1984). *Report to NIMH
on the NIMH diagnostic interview schedule for children (DISC).* Rockville,
MD: National Institute of Mental Health.

Cradock, C., Cotler, S., & Jason, L. A. (1978). Primary prevention: Immuniza-
tion of children for speech anxiety. *Cognitive Therapy and Research, 2,*
389–396.

Dadds, M. R., & Powell, M. B. (1991). The relationship of interparental conflict and global marital adjustment to aggression, anxiety, and immaturity
in aggressive and non-clinic children. *Journal of Abnormal Child Psychology, 19,* 553–567.

Davey, G. C. (1992). Classical conditioning and the acquisition of human fears
and phobias: A review and synthesis of the literature. *Advances in Behaviour
Research and Therapy, 14,* 29–66.

Delprato, D. J., & McGlynn, F. D. (1984). Behavioral theories of anxiety disorders. In S. M. Turner (Ed.), *Behavioral treatment of anxiety disorder*
(pp. 63–122). New York: Plenum Press.

Edelbrock, C., & Costello, A. (1984). Structured psychiatric interview for children and adolescents. In G. Goldstein & M. Hersen (Eds.), *Handbook of
psychological assessment* (pp. 276–290). New York: Pergamon Press.

Eisen, A. R., & Silverman, W. K. (1991). Treatment of an adolescent with bowel
movement phobia using self-control therapy. *Journal of Behavior Therapy
and Experimental Psychiatry, 22,* 45–51.

Eisen, A. R., & Silverman, W. K. (1993). Should I relax or change my thoughts?:
A preliminary examination of cognitive therapy, relaxation training, and
their combination with overanxious children. *Journal of Cognitive Psychotherapy: An International Quarterly, 7,* 265–280.

Eisenberg, L. (1958). School phobia: Diagnosis, genesis and clinical management.
Pediatric Clinics of North America, 5, 645–666.

Finch, A. J. Jr., Lipovsky, J. A., & Casat, C. D. (1989). Anxiety and depression in children and adolescents: Negative affectivity or separate constructs? In P. C. Kendall & D. Watson (Eds.), *Anxiety and depression: Distinctive and overlapping features* (pp. 171–196). San Diego: Academic Press.

Fox, J. E., & Houston, B. K. (1981). Efficacy of self-instructional training for reducing children's anxiety in evaluative situations. *Behaviour Research and Therapy, 19,* 509–515.

Francis, G. (1988). Assessing cognitions in anxious children. *Behavior Modification, 12,* 267–280.

Freud, A. (1965). *Normality and pathology in childhood: Assessment of development.* New York: International Universities Press.

Freud, S. (1955). Analysis of a phobia in a five-year-old boy. In J. Strachey (Ed. and Trans.), *The standard edition of the complete psychological works of Sigmund Freud* (Vol. 10, pp. 1–149). London: Hogarth Press. (Original work published 1909)

Fyer, A. J., Mannuzza, S., Gallops, M. P., et al. (1990). Familial transmission of simple phobias and fears. *Archives of General Psychiatry, 47,* 252–256.

Gittelman, B., & Koplewicz, H. S. (1986). Pharmacotherapy of childhood anxiety disorders. In R. Gittelman (Ed.), *Anxiety disorders of childhood* (pp. 188–201). New York: Guilford Press.

Gittelman-Klein, R., & Klein, D. F. (1971). Controlled imipramine treatment of school phobia. *Archives of General Psychiatry, 25,* 204–207.

Gittelman-Klein, R., & Klein, D. F. (1980). Separation anxiety in school refusal and its treatment with drugs. In L. Hersov & I. Berg (Eds.), *Out of school* (pp. 321–341). New York: Wiley.

Graziano, A. M., & Mooney, K. C. (1980). Family self-control instruction for children's nighttime fear reduction. *Journal of Consulting and Clinical Psychology, 48,* 206–213.

Graziano, A. M., & Mooney, K. C., Huber, C., et al. (1979). Self-control instruction for children's fear-reduction. *Journal of Behavior Therapy and Experimental Psychiatry, 10,* 221–227.

Hampe, E., Noble, M., Miller, L. C., et al. (1973). Phobic children at two years post-treatment. *Journal of Abnormal Psychology, 82,* 446–453.

Hekmat, H. (1987). Origins and development of human fear reactions. *Journal of Anxiety Disorders, 1,* 197–218.

Herjanic, B., & Reich, W. (1982). Development of a structured psychiatric interview for children: Agreement between child and parent on individual symptoms. *Journal of Abnormal Child Psychiatry, 10,* 307–324.

Hill, J. H., Liebert, R. M., & Mott, D. E. W. (1968). Vicarious extinction of avoidance behavior through films: An initial test. *Psychological Reports, 22,* 192.

Hodges, K., McKnew, D., Cytryn, L., et al. (1982). The Child Assessment Schedule (CAS) diagnostic interview: A report on reliability and validity. *Journal of the American Academy of Child Psychiatry, 21,* 468–473.

Holmes, F. B. (1936). An experimental investigation of a method of overcoming children's fears. *Child Development, 7,* 6–30.

Kane, M. T., & Kendall, P. C. (1989). Anxiety disorders in children: A multiple baseline evaluation of a cognitive-behavioral treatment. *Behavior Therapy*, 20, 499–508.

Kanfer, F. H., Karoly, P., & Newman, A. (1975). Reduction of children's fear of the dark by confidence-related and situation threat-related verbal cues. *Journal of Consulting and Clinical Psychology*, 43, 251–258.

Kashani, J. H., & Orvaschel, H. (1988). Anxiety disorders in mid-adolescence: A community sample. *American Journal of Psychiatry*, 145, 960–964.

Kashani, J., & Orvaschel, H. (1990). A community study of anxiety in children and adolescents. *American Journal Psychiatry*, 147, 313–318.

Kashani, J. H., Orvaschel, H., Rosenberg, T. K., et al. (1989). Psychopathology in a community sample of children and adolescents: A developmental perspective. *Journal of the American Academy of Child and Adolescent Psychiatry*, 28, 701–706.

Kashani, J. H., Vaidya, A. F., Soltys, S. M., et al. (1990). Correlates of anxiety in psychiatrically hospitalized children and their parents. *American Journal of Psychiatry*, 147, 319–323.

Kazdin, A. E., & Wilson, G. T. (1978). *Evaluation of behavior therapy: Issues, evidence and research strategies*. Cambridge, MA: Ballinger.

Kearney, C. A., & Silverman, W. K. (1990). A preliminary analysis of a functional model of assessment and treatment for school refusal behavior. *Behavior Modification*, 14, 340–366.

Kendall, P. C. (1994). Treating anxiety disorders in youth: Results of a randomized clinical trial. *Journal of Consulting and Clinical Psychology*, 62, 100–110.

Kendall, P. C., & Chansky, T. E. (1991). Considering cognition in anxiety-disordered children. *Journal of Anxiety Disorders*, 5, 167–185.

Kendall, P. C., & Hollon, S. D. (1981). *Assessment strategies for cognitive-behavioral interventions*. New York: Academic Press.

Kendall, P. C., Howard, B. L., & Epps, J. (1988). The anxious child: Cognitive behavioral treatment strategies. *Behavior Modification*, 12, 281–310.

King, N. J., Hamilton, D. I., & Ollendick, T. H. (1988). *Children's phobias: A behavioural perspective*. New York: Wiley.

King, N. J., Ollendick, T. H., & Gullone, E. (1991). Negative affectivity in children and adolescents: Relations between anxiety and depression. *Clinical Psychology Review*, 11, 441–459.

Klein, M. (1932). *The psycho-analysis of children*. New York: Grove Press.

Klein, R. G., & Last, C. G. (1989). Anxiety disorders in children. *Developmental Clinical Psychology and Psychiatry*, 20, 76–83.

Kovacs, M. (1982). *The longitudinal study of child and adolescent psychopathology: Vol. I. The semistructured psychiatric interview schedule for children (ISC)*. Unpublished manuscript.

La Greca, A. M., & Stone, W. L. (1993). The Social Anxiety Scale for Children–Revised: Factor structure and concurrent validity. *Journal of Clinical Child Psychology*, 22, 17–27.

Lang, P. J. (1977). Imagery in therapy: An information processing analysis of fear. *Behavior Therapy*, 8, 862–886.

Lang, P. J. (1979). A bio-informational theory of emotional imagery. *Psychophysiology, 16,* 492–512.

Last, C. G., Francis, G., Hersen, M., et al. (1987). Separation anxiety and school phobia: A comparison using DSM-III criteria. *American Journal of Psychiatry, 144,* 653–657.

Last, C. G., Hersen, M., Kazdin, A. E., et al. (1993). *Prospective study of anxiety-disordered children.* Manuscript submitted for publication.

Last, C. G., Phillips, J. E., & Statfeld, A. (1987). Childhood anxiety disorders in mothers and their children. *Child Psychiatry and Human Development, 18,* 103–110.

Last, C. G., Perrin, S., Hersen, M., et al. (1992). DSM-III-R anxiety disorders in children: Sociodemographic and clinical characteristics. *Journal of the American Academy of Child and Adolescent Psychiatry, 31,* 1070–1076.

Leitenberg, H., Yost, L. W., & Carroll-Wilson, M. (1986). Negative cognitive errors in children: Questionnaire development, normative data and comparisons between children with and without self-reported symptoms of depression, low self-esteem, and evaluation anxiety. *Journal of Consulting and Clinical Psychology, 54,* 528–536.

Lewis, S. (1974). A comparison of behavior therapy techniques in the reduction of fearful avoidance behavior. *Behavior Therapy, 5,* 648–655.

Mann, J. (1972). Vicarious desensitization of test anxiety through observation of videotaped treatment. *Journal of Counseling Psychology, 19,* 1–7.

Mattison, R. E., Bagnato, S. J., & Brubaker, B. M. (1988). Diagnostic utility of the Revised Children's Manifest Anxiety Scale in children with DSM-III anxiety disorders. *Journal of Anxiety Disorders, 2,* 147–155.

McGee, R., Feehan, M., Williams, S., et al. (1990). DSM-III disorders in a large sample of adolescents. *Journal of the American Academy of Child and Adolescent Psychiatry, 29,* 611–619.

Melamed, B. G., & Siegel, L. J. (1975). Reduction of anxiety in children facing hospitalization and surgery by use of filmed modeling. *Journal of Consulting and Clinical Psychology, 43,* 511–521.

Melamed, B. G., Yurcheson, R., Fleece, E. L., et al. (1978). Effects of filmed modeling on the reduction of anxiety-related behaviors in individuals varying in level of previous experience in the stress situation. *Journal of Consulting and Clinical Psychology, 40,* 1357–1367.

Moran, C., & Andrews, G. (1985). The familial occurrence of agoraphobia. *British Journal of Psychiatry, 146,* 262–267.

Morris, R. J., & Kratochwill, T. R. (1983). *Treating children's fears and phobias: A behavioral approach.* New York: Pergamon Press.

Mowrer, O. H. (1939). A stimulus–response theory of anxiety and its role as reinforcing agent. *Psychological Review, 46,* 553–565.

Murray, E. J., & Foote, F. (1979). The origins of fear of snakes. *Behaviour Research and Therapy, 17,* 489–493.

Noyes, R., Crowe, R. R., Harris, E. L., et al. (1986). Relationship between panic disorder and agoraphobia. *Archives of General Psychiatry, 43,* 227–232.

Obler, M., & Terwilliger, R. F. (1970). Pilot study on the effectiveness of systematic desensitization with neurologically impaired children with phobic disorders. *Journal of Consulting and Clinical Psychology, 34,* 314–318.

Ollendick, T. H. (1979). Fear reduction techniques with children. In M. Hersen, R. M. Eisler, & P. M. Miller (Eds.), *Progress in behavior modification* (Vol. 8, pp. 127–168). New York: Academic Press.

Ollendick, T. H. (1983). Reliability and validity of the Revised Fear Survey Schedule for Children (FSSC-R). *Behaviour Research and Therapy, 21,* 395–399.

Ollendick, T. H., & Cerny, J. A. (1981). *Clinical behavior therapy with children.* New York: Plenum Press.

Ollendick, T., & Francis, G. (1988). Behavioral assessment and treatment of childhood phobias. *Behavior Modification, 12,* 165–204.

Ollendick, T. H., King, N. J., & Hamilton, D. I. (1991). Origins of childhood fears: An evaluation of Rachman's theory of fear acquisition. *Behaviour Research and Therapy, 29,* 117–123.

Ollendick, T. H., & Mayer, J. A. (1984). School phobia. In S. M. Turner (Ed.), *Behavioral theories and treatment of anxiety* (pp. 367–411). New York: Plenum Press.

Ost, L. G. (1985). Ways of acquiring phobias and outcome of behavioral treatments. *Behaviour Research and Therapy, 23,* 683–689.

Ost, L. (1987). Age of onset in different phobias. *Journal of Abnormal Psychology, 96,* 123–145.

Ost, L. G., & Hugdahl, K. (1983). Acquisition of agoraphobia, mode of onset and anxiety response patterns. *Behaviour Research and Therapy, 21,* 623–631.

Parker, J. G., & Asher, S. R. (1987). Peer relations and later personal adjustment: Are low-accepted children at risk? *Psychological Bulletin, 102,* 357–389.

Perrin, S., & Last, C. G. (1992). Do childhood anxiety measures measure anxiety. *Journal of Abnormal Child Psychology, 20,* 567–578.

Prins, P. J. M. (1986). Children's self-speech and self-regulation during a fear-provoking behavioral test. *Behaviour Research and Therapy, 24,* 181–191.

Puig-Antich, J., & Chambers, W. (1978). *The Schedule for Affective Disorders and Schizophrenia for School-Aged Children.* New York: New York State Psychiatric Institute.

Quay, H. C., & Peterson, D. R. (1983). *Interim manual for the Revised Behavior Problem Checklist.* Unpublished manuscript, University of Miami, Coral Gables.

Rachman, S. (1977). The conditioning theory of fear acquisition: A critical examination. *Behaviour Research and Therapy, 15,* 375–387.

Rachman, S. H., & Wilson, G. (1980). *The effects of psychotherapy.* New York: Pergamon Press.

Reich, J., & Yates, W. (1988). Family history of psychiatric disorders in social phobia. *Comprehensive Psychiatry, 29,* 72–75.

Reynolds, C. R., & Richmond, B. O. (1978). What I Think and Feel: A revised measure of children's manifest anxiety. *Journal of Abnormal Child Psychology, 6,* 271–280.

Rimm, D. C., Janda, H. L., Lancaster, D. W., et al. (1977). An exploratory investigation of the origin and maintenance of phobias. *Behaviour Research and Therapy, 15,* 231–238.

Ritter, B. (1968). The group desensitization of children's snake phobias using vicarious and contact desensitization procedures. *Behaviour Research and Therapy, 6,* 1–6.

Sarason, I. G. (1980). *Test anxiety: Theory, research, and application.* Hillsdale, NJ: Erlbaum.

Sarason, S. B., Davidson, K. S., Lighthall, F. F., et al. (1960). *Anxiety and elementary school children.* New York: Wiley.

Sarason, S. B., Hill, K. T., & Zimbardo, P. G. (1964). A longitudinal study of the relation of test anxiety to performance on intelligence and achievement tests. *Monographs of the Society for Research in Child Development, 29* (7, Serial No. 98).

Silverman, W. K. (1991). Diagnostic reliability of anxiety disorders in children using structured interviews. *Journal of Anxiety Disorders, 5,* 105–124.

Silverman, W. K. (1992). Taxonomy of anxiety disorders in children. In G. D. Burrows, R. Noyes, & S. M. Roth (Eds.), *Handbook of anxiety* (Vol. 5, pp. 281–308). Amsterdam: Elsevier.

Silverman, W. K. (1993). DSM and the classification of anxiety disorders in children and adults. In C. G. Last (Ed.), *Anxiety across the lifespan: A developmental perspective on anxiety and the anxiety disorders* (pp. 7–36). New York: Springer.

Silverman, W. K. (1994). Structured diagnostic interviews. In T. H. Ollendick, N. King, & W. Yule (Eds.), *International handbook of phobic and anxiety disorders in children* (pp. 293–316). New York: Plenum Press.

Silverman, W. K., & Eisen, A. R. (1992). Age differences in the reliability of parent and child reports of child anxious symptomatology using a structured interview. *Journal of American Academy of Child and Adolescent Psychiatry, 32,* 117–124.

Silverman, W. K., & Eisen, A. R. (1993). Phobic disorders. In R. T. Ammerman, C. G. Last, & M. Hersen (Eds.), *Handbook of prescriptive treatments for children and adolescents* (pp. 178–197). Boston, MA: Allyn & Bacon.

Silverman, W. K., & Kearney, C. A. (1991). The nature and treatment of anxiety in school-aged children. *Educational Psychology Review, 3,* 335–361.

Silverman, W. K., & Nelles, W. B. (1988). The Anxiety Disorders Interview Schedule for Children. *Journal of the American Academy of Child and Adolescent Psychiatry, 27,* 772–778.

Silverman, W. K., & Nelles, W. B. (1990). Simple phobia in childhood. In M. Hersen & C. G. Last (Eds.), *Handbook of child and adult psychopathology: A longitudinal perspective* (pp. 183–196). New York: Pergamon Press.

Silverman, W. K., & Rabian, B. (1994). Specific phobias. In T. H. Ollendick, N. J. King, & W. Yule (Eds.), *International handbook of phobic and anxiety disorders in children and adolescents* (pp. 87–110). New York: Plenum Press.

Silverman, W. K., & Rabian, B. (in press). Test–retest reliability of the DSM-III-R childhood anxiety disorders symptoms using the Anxiety Disorders Interview Schedule for Children. *Journal of Anxiety Disorders.*

Skinner, H. A., Steinhauer, P. D., & Santa-Barbara, J. (1983). The Family Assessment Measure. *Canadian Journal Community Mental Health*, *2*, 91–105.

Slater, E., & Shields, J. (1969). Genetical aspects of anxiety. In M. J. Lader (Ed.), *Studies of anxiety* (pp. 62–71). London: Royal Medico-Psychological Association.

Solyom, L., Beck, P., Solyom, C., et al. (1974). Some etiological factors in phobic neurosis. *Canadian Psychiatric Association Journal*, *19*, 69–78.

Spielberger, C. (1973). *Manual for the State–Trait Anxiety Inventory for Children*. Palo Alto, CA: Consulting Psychologists Press.

Stark, K. D., Humphrey, L. L., Crook, K., et al. (1990). Perceived family environments of depressed and anxious children: Child's and maternal figure's perspectives. *Journal of Abnormal Child Psychology*, *18*, 527–547.

Strauss, C. C., Lease, C. A., Last, C. G., et al. (1988). Overanxious disorder: An examination of developmental differences. *Journal of Abnormal Child Psychology*, *16*, 433–443.

Strauss, C. C. (1990). Overanxious disorder in childhood. In M. Hersen & C. G. Last (Eds.), *Handbook of child and adult psychopathology: A longitudinal perspective* (pp. 237–246). New York: Pergamon Press.

Strauss, C. C., Frame, C. L., & Forehand, R. (1987). Psychosocial impairment associated with anxiety in children. *Journal of Clinical Child Psychology*, *16*, 235–239.

Strauss, C. C., Lahey, B. B., Frick, P., et al. (1988). Peer social status of children with anxiety disorders. *Journal of Consulting and Clinical Psychology*, *56*, 137–141.

Thyer, B. A., Parrish, R. T., Curtis, G. C., et al. (1985). Ages of onset of DSM-III anxiety disorders. *Comprehensive Psychiatry*, *26*, 113–122.

Torgersen, S. (1979). The nature and origin of common phobic fears. *British Journal of Psychiatry*, *134*, 343–351.

Trautman, P. D. (1986). Psychodynamic theories of anxiety and their application to children. In R. Gittelman (Ed.), *Anxiety disorders of childhood* (pp. 168–184). New York: Guilford Press.

Velez, C. N., Johnson, J., & Cohen, P. (1989). A longitudinal analysis of selected risk factors for childhood psychopathology. *Journal of the American Academy of Child and Adolescent Psychiatry*, *28*, 861–864.

Walker, L. S., & Greene, J. W. (1989). Children with recurrent abdominal pain and their parents: More somatic complaints, anxiety, and depression than other patient families? *Journal of Pediatric Psychology*, *14*, 231–243.

Watson, J. B., & Rayner, R. (1920). Conditioned emotional reactions. *Journal of Experimental Psychology*, *3*, 1–14.

Werry, J. S. (1991). Overanxious disorder: A review of its taxonomic properties. *Journal of the American Academy of Child and Adolescent Psychiatry*, *30*, 533–544.

Zatz, S., & Chassin, L. (1983). Cognitions of test-anxious children. *Journal of Consulting and Clinical Psychology*, *51*, 524–534.

Zatz, S., & Chassin, L. (1985). Cognitions of test-anxious children under naturalistic test-taking conditions. *Journal of Consulting and Clinical Psychology*, *53*, 393–401.

Chapter 8

Social Phobia

Deborah C. Beidel
Tracy L. Morris

Sociability, a preference for affiliation and the companionship of others rather than solitude, appears to be a basic and consistently identified dimension of personality (Buss & Plomin, 1984; Thomas & Chess, 1984). Shyness, another commonly identified aspect of behavior, is a form of social withdrawal that is characterized by social–evaluative concerns, particularly in novel settings (Rubin & Asendorpf, 1993). Thus, sociability refers to the desire for social affiliation, whereas shyness refers to distress and inhibited behaviors in social interactions. Empirical studies have confirmed that sociability and social withdrawal represent distinct traits (Cheek & Buss, 1981), can be detected at a very early age, and are stable across periods of developmental change (Broberg, Lamb, & Hwang, 1990; Kagan, Reznick, Clarke, et al., 1984). Any individual's social behavior may be characterized according to these two dimensions. For example, those who are low on the sociability dimension may have little desire for and receive very little satisfaction from social interactions with others. Therefore, when in social encounters, they may not interact but nonetheless show (or feel) very little emotional distress. Others may have a strong desire for social encounters but become so distressed when in the company of others that they are unable to engage in rewarding interpersonal interactions. Currently, children who profess a desire for social encounters but who become significantly distressed when doing so may meet diagnostic criteria for social phobia.

The recognition of individual differences in sociability and the labeling of individuals as shy is not a new concept. Case descriptions of those who would appear to meet criteria for social phobia have been documented since the time of Hippocrates (Marks, 1985). More recently, Marks (1970) described the phenomenology of socially phobic adults, and in 1980 this diagnostic condition was codified in the American psychiatric nomenclature with the publication of the third edition of the *Diagnostic and Statistical Manual of Mental Disorders* (DSM-III; American Psychiatric Association, 1980). However, despite this recognition, social phobia initially received very little attention from child researchers. One possible explanation for this omission is the belief that fears in children are considered to be common (Barrios & O'Dell, 1989) and that a number of individuals report being shy as children but subsequently "outgrowing" this condition (Bruch, Giordano, & Pearl, 1986). Another possibility is that although children who were fearful of social encounters could have been given the diagnosis of social phobia, other diagnostic conditions (listed in the child and adolescent section of DSM-III-R) also contained criteria that tapped social–evaluative fears. Thus, until recently (Beidel, 1991; Beidel & Turner, 1988; Francis, Last, & Strauss, 1992; Strauss & Last, 1993), social phobia in children (as a distinct diagnostic entity) was virtually ignored in the scientific literature.

According to DSM-IV, (American Psychiatric Association, 1994), social phobia is "a marked and persistent fear of one or more situations (the social phobic situations) in which the person is exposed to possible scrutiny by others and fears that he or she may do something or act in a way that will be humiliating or embarrassing" (p. 416). Based on adult retrospective reports, the average age of onset of social phobia is early to middle adolescence (Liebowitz, Gorman, Fyer, et al., 1985; Turner, Beidel, Dancu, et al., 1986). Cases of social phobia have been documented in children as young as age 8 (Beidel & Turner, 1988) and Last and her colleagues (Strauss & Last, 1993; Last, Perrin, Hersen, et al., 1992) reported an average age of onset ranging from 11.3 to 12.3 years, based on child and adolescent clinic-referred samples. As noted, the diagnostic schema of DSM-III-R allowed for children with social fears to be assigned a diagnosis of social phobia. However, within the section of the manual devoted specifically to child and adolescent disorders, other disorders contained criteria addressing social fears. For example, avoidant disorder of childhood or adolescence was defined as "excessive shrinking from contact with unfamiliar people, for a period of six months or longer, sufficiently severe to interfere with social functioning in peer relationships" (p. 61). Children with this disorder expressed a desire for social involvement with familiar people and usually had satisfying relationships with them. Several of the diagnostic criteria for overanxious disorder were characteristic of children with social fears: excessive concerns about competence in academic, social, or athletic settings, excessive concern about the appropriateness of past behavior, and marked self-consciousness. Beidel (1991) noted that there were very few significant differences between children diagnosed with social phobia and those diagnosed with overanxious disorder on a number of self-report, daily diary, and psychophysiological measures, although the social phobic children were significantly different from a normal control group. Finally, although the relationship of elective mutism, persistent refusal to talk in one or more major social situations (including school), to social phobia has not been explored, the similarities in diagnostic criteria are obvious.

The diagnostic criteria in DSM-IV (American Psychiatric Association, 1994) group all children with social–evaluative fears under one heading: Social Phobia (Social Anxiety Disorder). The diagnostic criteria are as follows:

A. A marked and persistent fear of one or more social or performance situations in which the person is exposed to unfamiliar people or to possible scrutiny by others. The individual fears that he or she will act in a way (or show anxiety symptoms) that will be humiliating or embarrassing. Note: In children, there must be evidence of the capacity for age-appropriate social relationships with familiar people and the anxiety must occur in peer settings, not just in interactions with adults.

B. Exposure to the feared social situation almost invariably provokes anxiety, which may take the form of a situationally bound or situationally predisposed Panic Attack. Note: In children, the anxiety may be expressed by crying, tantrums, freezing, or shrinking from social situations with unfamiliar people.

C. The person recognizes that the fear is excessive or unreasonable. Note: In children, this feature may be absent. (p. 417)

These criteria have significant implications for our understanding of children with social–evaluative fears. First, it groups all of the children in one category, thus permitting a more accurate determination of the disorder's prevalence. Second, the recognition that the fear is unreasonable is not a necessary criterion. This is important inasmuch as young children may lack the perceptual or cognitive skills to recognize the irrationality of their fears. Third, specific descriptors detailing how the disorder is expressed in children call attention to its presence in this population. This is particularly important in light of the chronic nature of social phobia (Turner & Beidel, 1989), its treatment-refractory nature when the onset is prior to age 11 (Davidson, 1993), and its relationship to alcohol abuse, truancy, and conduct problems (Clark, 1993).

At this point it is important to note that pre-1980 descriptions of shy and withdrawn children bear some similarity to the clinical condition of social phobia. However, appropriate comparisons between those samples and the DSM-III-R or DSM-IV diagnostic categories are difficult due to the likely heterogeneity of the shy group. In addition, the minimal empirical data available for children diagnosed with social phobia means that

crucial data on phenomenology and treatment outcome are lacking. Therefore, data from the shyness literature will at times be used to illustrate
crucial issues, but the discussion will focus primarily on the DSM-III-R
and DSM-IV definitions of the disorder.

PHENOMENOLOGY AND DIFFERENTIAL DIAGNOSIS

Children with social phobia report distress in a broad range of interpersonal encounters including (in order of decreasing frequency in number
of children endorsing the fear) the following: formal speaking (88.8%),
eating in front of others (39.3%), going to parties (27.6%), writing in front
of others (27.6%), using public restrooms (24.1%), speaking to authority figures (20.7%), and informal speaking (13%) (Beidel, 1992). Strauss
and Last (1993) reported a similar range of distressing situations plus a
category called "school," referring to social distress in the school setting.
In both studies, many of the situations describe specific behaviors performed in front of others (writing, eating, speaking) and more general
conversational interactions. Among adults with social phobia, the percentage of those who are anxious only when performing specific activities
(sometimes termed the specific subtype) and those with more generalized
social fears (known as the generalized subtype) is a matter of some controversy, as is the exact procedure used to make this distinction (e.g.,
Turner, Beidel, & Townsley, 1992). The generalized subtype is retained
in DSM-IV. Although such distinctions have not yet been addressed in child
or adolescent populations, based on some preliminary data from our clinic,
children with social phobia endorse an average of 2.3 anxiety-producing
situations. Thus, a substantial number could be considered to suffer from
the generalized subtype (if the subtype distinction is based on the number
of fearful situations).

Children with social phobia have reported that distressful events occur
approximately every other day, significantly more often than for normal
controls (Beidel, 1991). Consistent with Strauss and Last's (1993) observation that school is a fearful setting, 60% of the distressing events occurred at school. Within this setting, the most common distressing event
was an unstructured peer encounter (e.g., having to talk to another child),
followed by taking tests, performing in front of others, and reading aloud.
The socially phobic children were significantly more likely to respond negatively when these events occurred. Physical symptoms included heart palpitations (70.8%), shakiness (66.7%), flushes/chills (62.5%), sweating
(54.2%), and nausea (54.2%) (Beidel, Christ, & Long, 1991). Furthermore, a number of these negative coping responses (8%) involved behavioral avoidance (Beidel, 1991). As noted, although formal speaking situ-

ations are the most universally feared, the most frequent distressful encounter is interpersonal conversation. Thus, in addition to circumscribed phobic situations, clinicians need to be attuned to the potentially anxiety-producing consequences of interpersonal encounters.

Although social phobia can be diagnosed in children and adults, the disorder does not manifest itself identically across different developmental stages. In a comparison of the epidemiological and clinical presentations of social phobia in adults and children, Beidel and Turner (1993) reported similar prevalence rates. In addition, similar coexisting diagnoses (generalized anxiety disorder in adults, overanxious disorder in children, and specific phobia in both adults and children) also were common among individuals with social phobia (Beidel & Turner, 1993; Last, Strauss, & Francis, 1987; Turner, Beidel, Borden, et al., 1991). Both adults and children endorsed distress across a broad range of potentially fearful situations. Formal speaking was the most commonly endorsed event, and the physical complaints characteristic of socially phobic adults also were common for children with this disorder. However, when in anxiety-producing situations, children did not report the occurrence of negative cognitions with the same frequency as adults.

With respect to other clinical correlates of the disorder, socially phobic children and adolescents have significantly higher levels of depression (as measured by the Children's Depression Inventory) and more severe fears of criticism and of failure (as measured by the Fear Survey Schedule for Children–Revised) than normal controls (Beidel & Turner, 1988; Francis, Last, & Strauss, 1992; Strauss & Last, 1993). Beidel (1991) found that children with social phobia had more severe trait anxiety, less confidence in their cognitive abilities, and a strong tendency toward a rigid temperamental style. The last finding is consistent with the obsessive–compulsive personality style found among socially phobic adults (Turner et al., 1991).

A substantial percentage of children and adolescents with social phobia had additional DSM-III-R Axis I disorders, thereby complicating attempts at differential diagnosis. However, much of the current comorbidity has been eliminated with the publication of DSM-IV, because the usual cooccurring conditions were overanxious disorder and/or avoidant disorder. For example, 6.9% of socially phobic children in a community sample had a secondary diagnosis of overanxious disorder, whereas 10% of children with a primary diagnosis of overanxious disorder had a secondary diagnosis of social phobia (Beidel, 1992). Much higher rates of comorbidity have been reported when samples consisted of children referred for treatment to an anxiety disorders clinic. Last et al. (1992) reported that 86.9% of socially phobic children had an additional anxiety diagnosis. Conversely, coexisting social phobia was diagnosed in 19% of children with primary separation anxiety disorder, 56.9% of those with primary overanxious disorder and 55% with a primary diagnosis of major depressive disorder. Finally, 65% of the children with avoidant disorder had a co-occurring diagnosis of social phobia, which is consistent with the overlap between the conditions. Similar comorbidity rates (79% for social phobia, 91% for avoidant disorder, and 100% for social phobia and avoidant disorder) were reported by Francis et al. (1992). The most common comorbid condition was overanxious disorder, present in 58%, 39%, and 83% of the diagnostic groups, respectively.

Despite the overlap among these conditions, social phobia can be differentiated from most other anxiety disorders by closely examining the core fear. For example, most individuals with panic disorder fear the constellation of physical symptoms that define a panic attack. Furthermore, they fear being trapped in a situation where they will be unable to get help should such an attack occur. Marks (1970) offered a useful distinction by noting that panic disorder patients fear crowds whereas social phobics fear the individuals that make up the crowd. In contrast, simple phobias (now referred to as specific phobia in DSM-IV) encompass fears of objects or situations that do not involve social encounters or fear of a panic attack. Strauss and Last (1993) examined the differences between children with social phobia and simple phobia who were referred to a child anxiety disorders clinic. Children with social phobia were older at the time of referral, described significantly more loneliness, fearfulness, and depression on self-report instruments, and were more likely to be diagnosed with avoidant disorder and overanxious disorder than were children with simple phobias. The latter finding is not surprising given the significant overlap of these three diagnostic conditions, which in fact may be describing various aspects of the same core disorder. Thus, the presence of comorbid conditions as a distinction between simple and social phobia could become obsolete with the publication of DSM-IV.

Another important differential diagnosis is that of separation anxiety disorder: excessive concern about separation from a major attachment figure. The child expresses fear that something will happen to himself or herself, parents, or someone else who serves in a major caretaker role. Thus, to some extent separation anxiety disorder is distress over estrangement from others. In contrast, social phobia entails distress over approach or interaction with others (Beidel & Morris, 1993). In reality, however, the distinction is not quite so simple. For example, it is usually assumed that "school phobia" is a result of separation anxiety disorder. However, when the specific fears of social phobic children were examined, fear of school was endorsed by 64% of the group (Strauss & Last, 1993). Thus, school refusal often is as likely to be a symptom of social phobia as it is of fearful separation from an attachment figure.

Within the diagnostic schema of DSM-III-R, the most difficult differential diagnosis was that of overanxious disorder. Similar to social phobia, the DSM-III-R diagnosis of overanxious disorder encompassed fears of a social–evaluative nature—worry about the appropriateness of past behavior, concern about competence in academic, athletic, or social areas, and marked self-consciousness (APA, 1987). A comparison of this description with that of social phobia illustrates the obvious overlap between these two conditions. However, those with social phobia appear to be more significantly impaired. For example, Beidel (1991) reported that whereas social phobics could be differentiated from normal controls based on a number of different criteria, those with overanxious disorder could be distinguished from normal controls only by their significantly higher trait anxiety and an absence of either positive or negative coping responses when faced with an anxiety-producing situation (e.g., they worried, but their anxiety did not seem to interfere with their daily functioning). However, the results of a discriminant function analysis differentiated socially phobic and overanxious children based on trait anxiety scores, baseline pulse rates, and self-perception of cognitive competence. Thus, although overlapping, these conditions were not identical. With the implementation of DSM-IV, the diagnostic criteria for overanxious disorder have been altered, the social–evaluative elements have been eliminated, and the syndrome is subsumed under generalized anxiety disorder. The issue of differential diagnosis with the new diagnostic criteria have not yet been addressed.

RELATED FEATURES

Cognitive Factors

As noted, the mean reported age of onset for social phobia is early to middle adolescence. However, it is unlikely that social fears and social performance deficits spontaneously arise during this age period. In fact, adult social phobics generally describe themselves as having been shy from early childhood. Although others may be able to perceive these children as behaviorally inhibited and socially anxious, young children may lack the metacognitive and verbal skills to ground description of their fears in a social context. A similar argument has been made for the existence of panic disorder in children (Nelles & Barlow, 1988). It is during adolescence that increased social demands and the onset of more formal operational thought processes allow for awareness of discrepancies between the perspectives of others and one's self-view. Such cognitive processes may be critical in the perpetuation of social anxiety, as they facilitate focus on anticipated or actual scrutiny by others (Cheek, Carpentieri, Smith, et al., 1986).

A number of theorists have suggested excessive self-focused attention to be an important factor in the development and maintenance of social anxiety (e.g., Hartman, 1983; Sarason, 1975). Though probably influenced by prior performance, an individual's expectation for future social success and the resultant success or failure attributions may be intimately related to subsequent manifestation and subjective experience of anxiety. The results of several investigations have indicated that in contrast to most normal adults, shy adults accepted more personal responsibility for negative outcomes and less responsibility for positive outcomes (e.g., Teglasi & Fagin, 1984; Teglasi & Hoffman, 1982). In one of the few child studies, Rubin (1985) found that peer-neglected children reported exaggerated feelings of social incompetence. However, an increased frequency of negative cognitions in socially phobic children when in stressful situations has not been demonstrated (Beidel, 1991). Continued work is needed with child and adolescent social phobics to delineate cognitive factors associated with the disorder.

Family Factors

Investigations of the offspring of adults with anxiety disorders indicate that these children are themselves at risk for the development of anxiety disorders (Turner, Beidel, & Costello, 1987; Weissman, Leckman, Merikangas, et al., 1984). At present it is unclear whether genetic or family environment variables exert primary influence, but extant data suggest reciprocal interaction effects. Strong evidence mediating the relationship between parental behaviors and children's social competence has been cited in the developmental literature (e.g., Ladd & Golter, 1988; Parke & Bhavnagri, 1989; Radke-Yarrow & Zahn-Waxler, 1986). Consistent empirical support has been demonstrated for a relationship between infant–parent attachment and subsequent social relationships with peers (for a review, see Putallaz & Heflin, 1990). In the child's early years, opportunities for social interaction are arranged by the parents. Daniels and Plomin (1985) suggested that mothers who are shy avoid exposing their children to varied social situations, which may perpetuate a cycle of social fear. Finnie and Russell (1988) found that during a group play situation, mothers of peer-neglected children provided fewer group-oriented and more materials-oriented instructions to their children, with fewer strategies to assist their child's group entry, than did mothers of popular children. Maternal warmth and engagement has been found to be positively correlated with children's prosocial behavior with peers (Attili, 1989; Hinde & Tamplin, 1983). In an observational study, MacDonald (1987) found that fathers of peer-neglected boys engaged in less affectively arousing play (rough and tumble) than did fathers of popular or peer-rejected boys. With respect to children with DSM-III-R disorders, obsessive–compulsive symptoms are higher in the fathers of socially anxious children than in normal controls, and socially anxious children describe a more restrictive family environment (Messer & Beidel, 1994). Because socially anxious children currently have an anxiety disorder, the role of family factors as precipitants cannot be determined. Further investigation is needed to examine the role of the family environment in mediating the development and expression of childhood social phobia; one such study is currently underway (Turner & Beidel, 1993).

Peer Relationships

Social anxiety impairs the child's ability to establish and maintain friendships (Rubin, LeMare, Lollis, et al., 1990). Conversely, poor peer relationships can foster discomfort in social situations. In retrospective reports, shy adults cite unpleasant experiences with peers as contributing factors in the development of their shyness (Ishiyama, 1984). Peer-neglected children endorse more social anxiety (LaGreca, Dandes, Wick, et al., 1988) and lower perceived social competence (Patterson, Kupersmidt, & Griesler, 1990) than do other children. Children with an anxiety disorder are more likely to be classified as peer-neglected than both psychiatric and nonpsychiatric controls (Strauss, Lahey, Frick, et al., 1988). A recent study of adolescents (Vernberg, Abwender, Ewell, et al., 1992) has provided further support for reciprocal causal relationships between peer experience and social anxiety.

Proposed Developmental Pathway

Temperamental inhibition, insecure attachment, and peer neglect may be markers, as well as propelling pathways, for the manifestation of social anxiety. Temperamentally inhibited infants possess a low threshold for physiologic arousal and impaired ability to adapt to stressful stimuli (Buss & Plomin, 1984; Fox, 1989; Kagan, Reznick, & Snidman, 1987). Caregivers may find it aversive to interact with these highly reactive and difficult-to-soothe infants and subsequently may become nonresponsive or neglectful (e.g., Kagan et al., 1984). This pattern of interaction may foster an anxious–insecure attachment (Ainsworth, Blehar, Waters, et al., 1978; Belsky & Rovine, 1987), and the anxious–insecurely attached child is likely to withdraw from peers within the social milieu (Renkin, Egeland, Marvinney, et al., 1989). Restricted peer interaction leads to impairments in the development of social skills and interpersonal relationships (e.g., Vernberg et al., 1992). The child may then become increasingly anxious and ineffective in social situations. Empirical investigation of potential pathways leading to the development of social phobia will assist in the identification of children at risk for the disorder and may ultimately lead to the formation of early intervention programs.

Course and Outcome

Empirical data on the detrimental effects of childhood social phobia are beginning to emerge. For example, a percentage of children who refuse to attend school do so because of social fears (Last et al., 1991). Additionally, Perrin and Last (1993) noted that among anxious children, social phobia was much more likely to precede the onset of depression than vice versa. Clark (1993) reported that a substantial percentage of adolescents who abuse alcohol meet diagnostic criteria for social phobia. Furthermore, conduct problems, difficulty getting along with peers, and truancy were common behaviors found in this sample of adolescent boys comorbid for social phobia and alcohol abuse. When distress reaches a certain level, children with severe social fears may refuse to engage in certain activities and thereby be perceived by others as oppositional. Similarly, 70% of social phobics reported that their alcohol abuse began after the onset of their social fears (Stravynski, Lamontagne, Lavallee, et al., 1986), probably in an effort to control their social distress. As noted, Davidson (1993) found that conduct problems and truancy were part of the childhood history of adult social phobics and that onset of social phobia prior to age 11 predicted nonrecovery in adulthood. These data must be regarded cautiously because of their preliminary and retrospective nature, but the consistency of the findings documents the pervasive negative outcome when childhood social phobia is unrecognized and untreated.

EPIDEMIOLOGY AND DEMOGRAPHICS

Social phobia appears to affect approximately 1% of the general child and adolescent population. For example, Anderson, Williams, McGee, et al. (1987) reported a 0.9% prevalence rate among a sample of 11-year-olds in New Zealand. Similarly, McGee, Feehan, Williams, et al. (1990) found a 1.1% prevalence rate of social phobia among 15-year-old children. However, the latter rate may be an underestimate because in that study, fear of public speaking was included as a simple phobia. Finally, among children in the United States, a cross-sectional study of children of ages 8, 12, and 17 reported a 1.0% prevalence rate (Kashani & Orvaschel, 1990). Last et al. (1992) reported that 14.9% of a clinic-referred sample had a primary diagnosis of social phobia (2.7% had a primary diagnosis of avoidant disorder). As noted earlier, prevalence rates for social phobia may increase with the new DSM-IV diagnostic schema.

Last et al. (1992) reported that 44.3% of their social phobic sample were female, whereas Beidel and Turner (1992) reported that females comprised 70% of their socially phobic sample. The differences in the male–female ratio may reflect differences in the sampling procedures. However, it should be noted that the Beidel and Turner (1992) ratio was consistent with the Epidemiological Catchment Area data for the general population of adults with social phobia. Thus, samples based on clinic-referred patients may reflect a particular selection bias (those who choose to seek treatment) rather than reflecting the general population.

Strauss and Last (1993) reported that 86% of the children with social phobia who were referred to a specialty treatment clinic were Caucasian. In contrast, among a sample of 8- to 11-year-old school children initially selected as test anxious, 55% of the children who met criteria for social phobia were African American and 45% were Caucasian (Beidel, Turner, & Trager, 1994). When the categories of overanxious disorder and social phobia were combined, 59% of the children were African American and 41% were Caucasian. The discrepancies in the prevalence of these disorders probably reflects differences in referral patterns. A National Institute of Mental Health epidemiological study of childhood mental disorders is currently underway, and the outcome will provide needed prevalence data as well as clarify the sociodemographic characteristics of children with social phobia.

ETIOLOGY AND NATURAL HISTORY

Although etiological data are not available for child or adolescent samples, some information can be gleaned from retrospective reports of adult samples. In a study by Ost (1987), 58% of a sample of social phobics reported that the onset of their disorder followed a traumatic event. A clinic sample of adult social phobics divided into specific and generalized subtypes, 56% and 40% respectively, reported the occurrence of specific traumatic events (Turner, Townsley, & Beidel, 1993). Data on traumatic conditioning events in socially phobic children are not available.

In the latest of a series of publications on the family history of children with anxiety disorders (Last, Hersen, Kazdin, et al., 1992), social phobia and avoidant disorder were significantly more prevalent among the first-degree relatives of anxious children compared to the relatives of the normal controls, but there was no difference in prevalence rates for these disorders between anxiety and attention-deficit/hyperactivity disorder (ADHD) groups. However, the relatives of children with social phobia were no more likely to have social phobia or avoidant disorder themselves than were the relatives of children with ADHD or the normal control group. There are no studies specifically examining the family pathology of children with social phobia. However, a recently published study (Fyer, Mannuzza, Chapman, et al., 1993) indicated a significantly increased risk for social phobia in the adult relatives of adult patients with social phobia compared to adult relatives of normal controls (16% vs. 5%).

Behavioral inhibition describes the consistent tendency to be fearful or to withdraw in situations that are characterized by novelty or unfamiliarity (Kagan et al., 1984). An initial study did not find a significantly higher rate of social phobia and/or avoidant disorder in behaviorally inhibited children than in uninhibited children or in a normal comparison group (Biederman, Rosenbaum, Hirshfeld, et al., 1990, Chapter 3). However, there was a significantly higher rate of overanxious disorder in the behaviorally inhibited children compared to the normal control group. A 3-year follow-up investigation (Biederman, Rosenbaum, Bolduc-Murphy, et al., 1993, Chapter 3) found that significantly more inhibited than not-inhibited children had separation anxiety disorder, avoidant disorder, and agoraphobia. In addition, significantly more inhibited than not-inhibited children had two or more anxiety disorders. When the emergence of anxiety disorders at follow-up was examined using a subsample of inhibited and not-inhibited children who were free of disorders at baseline, significantly more inhibited than not-inhibited children had developed separation anxiety disorder, avoidant disorder, and two or more anxiety disorders.

In another study of the relationship of behavioral inhibition to psychopathology, Rosenbaum, Biederman, Hirshfeld, et al. (1991, Chapter 3) examined the presence of anxiety disorders in the parents and siblings of children who were identified as behaviorally inhibited or uninhibited. Normal control children were also included in the investigation. When compared with parents of uninhibited and normal control children, the parents of children with behavioral inhibition had significantly higher risks for (1) more than two anxiety disorders, (2) the presence of a childhood anxiety disorder, and (3) a continuing anxiety disorder (from childhood through adulthood). Interestingly, these results were accounted for by the presence of social phobia (17.5%, 0%, and 2.9%), avoidant disorder (15%, 0%, and 0%), and overanxious disorder (37.5%, 11.4%, 8.6%) in the inhibited, uninhibited, and normal control children's parents respectively. There were no differences among the three groups for any of the other anxiety disorders. This study provides some of the strongest evidence for a relationship between behavioral inhibition and social phobia. The data suggest the possibility of a familial predisposition toward the development of social fears; however, additional environmental factors yet to be elucidated appear to be implicated in the onset of the disorder.

ASSESSMENT

Clinical Assessment

Children with social phobia normally do not seek treatment on their own volition, and often caregivers are not aware of the severity of the children's distress. A thorough clinical evaluation must include an assessment of physical symptoms, worries, and distressing situations that are characteristic of social phobia. Much of the material to be assessed in a clinical interview has already been presented. However, children do not necessarily cogently describe the symptoms of this disorder. Rather, they may express vague complaints such as headaches or stomachaches or discuss issues that may seem only tangentially related to social phobia. There are several other behaviors that should serve to alert clinicians to the need for a thorough assessment for the presence of social phobia. These include school difficulty and school refusal, test anxiety, shyness, and poor peer relationships.

The relationship of school refusal and social phobia has yet to be determined empirically. However, it has long been recognized clinically that social fears are one of the factors that contribute to "school phobia," or school refusal (Ollendick & Meyer, 1984; Smith & Sharpe, 1970). As noted earlier, Strauss and Last (1993) have identified school as a significant source of distress for socially phobic children. However, in our community (school) sample of children identified with social phobia, only 10% had been referred for or sought treatment, even though all the children (and their mothers) endorsed a significant degree of social distress. In contrast, children who were referred to our clinic for treatment usually were experiencing significant difficulty in school situations, primarily school refusal. Therefore, refusal to attend school (as well as somatic complaints usually occurring on school days), particularly the more severe cases, may be symptomatic of social phobia.

Test anxiety and its relationship to social phobia also has been the topic of empirical studies. Children with test anxiety can be divided into two groups: those whose anxiety is circumscribed around specific testing situations (Type A) and those for whom tests represent just one aspect of a more general social–evaluative state (Type B; Sarason, 1975). Originally identified in college students, similar subtypes have been identified in elementary school children. Beidel and Turner (1988) reported that 24% of a sample of test-anxious children met DSM-III criteria for social phobia (and an additional 24% met criteria for overanxious disorder). These children represent Sarason's Type B category. This finding is quite robust, because in a recent replication of that initial study, 27% of a sample of test-anxious children met diagnostic criteria for social phobia (and an additional 20% met criteria for overanxious disorder; Beidel et al., 1994).

However, the existence of test anxiety alone does not identify children with social phobia; therefore, studies are currently underway to determine if other factors, in combination with a complaint of test anxiety, more clearly identify children suffering from social phobia. The determination of such factors, followed by the education of other professionals (e.g., teachers) about the importance of the factors, may assist in the early identification and treatment of children with social phobia. Until such data are available, clinicians are well advised to assess for social phobia in any child who complains of significant anxiety during examinations.

Although the overlap is intriguing, the relationship of shyness to social phobia has received little empirical attention. In a review of the existing literature, Turner, Beidel, and Townsley (1990) noted that the somatic responses of shy people and socially phobic individuals are similar in terms of specific physical symptomatology and type of negative cognitions; they differ in social and occupational impairment, course of the disorder, overt behavioral characteristics, and age of onset. In children, a body of literature exists on the treatment of children identified as shy, socially isolated/withdrawn, or peer-neglected. The characteristics of these groups suggest considerable overlap with social phobia and avoidant disorder. For example, LaGreca et al. (1988) found that peer-neglected children endorsed the highest social anxiety of any sociometric status group. In addition, children with an anxiety disorder are more likely to be classified as peer-neglected than both psychiatric and nonpsychiatric controls (Strauss et al., 1988). Furthermore, shyness or passive isolation in children (the type associated with social anxiety) and/or low perceived social competence in second grade significantly predicted depression and loneliness in the fifth grade (Rubin & Mills, 1988). Finally, internalizing problems (anxiety, depression, and so on) in middle childhood were significantly predicted by earlier (second grade) childhood difficulties including lower perceptions of social competence, poor peer acceptance, and social isolation, but the predictions were not specific for social fears (Hymel, Rubin, Rowden, et al., 1990). These data illustrate the difficulty in attempting to extrapolate data from samples of shy or socially isolated children as illustrative of social phobia. The term "shy" often is used to describe behavioral reticence in interpersonal situations, and the causes that produce this type of behavior are likely to be heterogeneous. Therefore, although reports that a child is very shy should alert the clinician to assess carefully for social phobia, the concepts of shyness and social phobia are not interchangeable.

Scales and Interviews

There are several structured and semistructured interview schedules that include an assessment of social fears in children. These include the Anxiety Disorders Interview Schedule for Children (ADIS-C; Silverman & Nelles, 1988; Silverman & Eisen, 1991), the Schedule for Affective Disorders and Schizophrenia for Children (K-SADS; Chambers, Puig-Antich, Hirsch, et al., 1985, modified by Last, 1986), the Diagnostic Interview for Children and Adolescents (DICA; Herjanic & Reich, 1982), the Diagnostic Interview Schedule for Children (DISC; Costello, Edelbrock, Duncan, et al., 1984), and the Child Assessment Schedule (CAS; Hodges, 1986). Overall, the K-SADS (as modified by Last, 1986) and the ADIS-C appear to have the highest published interrater reliability coefficients for anxiety disorders, possibly because they were specifically developed for this purpose. However, interrater reliability may also be an effect of the particular interviewer training procedures and clinical skill in addition to the particular interview schedule. Therefore, although some schedules may be constructed in order to enhance the possibility of high interrater reliability, clinical expertise and appropriate training are necessary in order to obtain reliable and valid diagnoses.

In general, although self-report measures such as the Fear Survey Schedule for Children–Revised (FSSC-R; Ollendick, 1983), the Revised Children Manifest Anxiety Scale (RCMAS; Reynolds & Richmond, 1978), and the Modified State–Trait Anxiety Inventory for Children (STAIC-M; Fox & Houston, 1983) discriminate anxious children from normal controls, they do not differentiate anxious children from those with other psychiatric disorders such as ADHD (Perrin & Last, 1993). Therefore, although self-report instruments may be useful in providing clinical information regarding the range, extent, and severity of children's fears, they cannot be used for diagnosis.

Two recently developed inventories specifically assess social fears or social phobia in children. The Social Anxiety Scale for Children–Revised (SASC-R) was developed to assess social evaluative anxiety and social avoidance and distress of elementary school children (LaGreca, 1991). Conceptually, this scale is similar to the Social Avoidance and Distress Scale and Fear of Negative Evaluation Scale used with adults (Watson & Friend, 1969). The SASC-R is a 22-item inventory that consists of three factors: fear of negative evaluation, social avoidance and distress—new (situations), social avoidance and distress—general. Internal consistency coefficients range from .67 to .86. Test–retest reliability was reported to be good, but coefficients were not presented. The subscales of the SASC-R correlate moderately and significantly with general anxiety and with self-perceptions of social acceptance, global self-worth, and behavioral conduct (LaGreca, 1991). To date, studies examining the ability of the SASC-R to differentiate among various diagnostic groups have not been reported. This aspect is particularly worthy of investigation because the adult version of this scale does not possess this discriminative ability.

The Social Phobia and Anxiety Inventory (SPAI; Turner et al., 1989) is an empirically derived self-report inventory that has been demonstrated to have excellent test–retest reliability, and good concurrent, construct and discriminant validity. Recently, the psychometric properties of this inventory were examined in a sample of adolescents of ages 12 to 18 (Clark, Turner, Beidel, et al., 1994). The results indicated that the scale has excellent internal consistency ($\alpha = .97$) with this population. The SPAI social phobia subscale was significantly correlated with the Fear Survey Schedule for Children fear of failure and criticism subscale ($r = .51$) and measures of trait anxiety ($r = .48$), heterosexual interaction ($r = -.45$), and assertiveness ($r = -.29$). Adolescents with social phobia scored significantly higher on the SPAI than those with other anxiety disorders, those with other psychiatric disorders, or normal controls. Thus, although originally developed for use with adults, the SPAI also appears to have utility for the assessment of social phobia in adolescents.

Very recently, a child version of the SPAI, the SPAI-C, has been developed for use with children and adolescents (Beidel, Turner, & Morris, in press). The 26-item empirically derived inventory has been piloted for use with children between the ages of 8 and 17; it assesses distress in a variety of social situations. In addition, like the SPAI, it assesses cognitive and physical symptomatology as well as overt behavior. Preliminary results for the SPAI-C indicate that it has high internal consistency ($\alpha = .95$), good to excellent test–retest reliability for 2-week ($r = .86$) and 10-month ($r = .63$) intervals. Scores on the SPAI-C are significantly correlated with trait anxiety ($r = .50$), the Fear Survey Schedule for Children–Revised fear of criticism subscale ($r = .53$), and the Child Behavior Checklist internalizing subscale ($r = .45$) and social competence subscale ($r = -.33$). Finally, the scale successfully differentiates socially anxious children from normal controls. Studies examining the ability of the SPAI-C to discriminate other anxious groups and other psychiatric groups from socially anxious subjects are currently underway.

Laboratory Measures

There are only limited data on the assessment of autonomic reactivity in a carefully diagnosed sample of socially phobic children. Beidel (1991) compared the pulse rate responses of children with social phobia, children with overanxious disorder, and normal controls when taking a test or reading aloud in front of a small group. Children with social phobia have higher increases in pulse rates when reading aloud before a group or taking a test than overanxious children or normal controls. The increased pulse rate responses of the socially phobic group are consistent with those for socially phobic adults and what would be expected if the child were suffering from a phobic disorder. Although the use of psychophysiological assessment may provide important information about social phobia in children, basic psychometric studies pertaining to the reliability and validity of these measures in these populations are necessary.

PSYCHOSOCIAL TREATMENT

To date, there have been no published treatment studies of children specifically identified as meeting diagnostic criteria for social phobia or avoidant disorder. Despite the lack of empirical data on these specific diagnostic classifications, there has been much written on the treatment of social fears and social isolation in children. In this section we review behavioral procedures commonly used in the treatment of social anxiety.

Cognitive-Behavioral Therapy

Cognitive treatment of social anxiety has primarily focused on the modification of maladaptive self-statements that are thought to contribute to socially avoidant behavior. Negative self-dialogue is common in socially anxious children (e.g., "Everyone is looking at me," "What if I do something wrong"; Stefanek, Ollendick, Baldock, et al., 1987). Test-anxious children have been found to engage in similar negative self-talk (e.g., "I'm stupid, I'm going to fail the test"; Zatz & Chassin, 1983). Cognitive restructuring procedures (based on Lazarus, 1974) are commonly used with older children to promote positive coping and competency statements, in an attempt to facilitate social approach behaviors. To date, there have been no controlled investigations of the use of cognitive procedures with socially phobic children or adolescents.

Respondent-Based Procedures

The behavioral treatment of anxiety and avoidant behavior in children dates to the classic work of Mary Cover Jones and the treatment of "Peter" (Jones, 1924). Wolpe (1958) expanded on this early work and developed the procedure that has become one of the most commonly used treatments for phobias: systematic desensitization. The central assumption of systematic desensitization is that fearful behavior can be reduced by systematically and gradually pairing anxiety-arousing stimuli with competing stimuli, such as food, praise, pleasant imagery, or muscle relaxation.

Systematic desensitization with children consists of three basic steps: (1) training in deep muscle relaxation (see Morris & Kratochwill, 1983, for a description of the progressive relaxation procedure), (2) rank ordering of fearful situations from lowest to highest, and (3) graduated presentation of items in the stimulus hierarchy while the child is in a relaxed state. Such procedures appear to work well with older children and adolescents (see Barrios & O'Dell, 1989, for a review). However, younger children may have difficulty with both the imaginal presentation of fear stimuli and the acquisition of the incompatible muscular relaxation response (Ollendick & Cerny, 1981). With younger children, emotive imagery (e.g., imaginal association between the child and a favored superhero like Raphael the Teenage Mutant Ninja Turtle), combined with *in vivo* presentation of the feared object or event, may be more effective (e.g., Hatzenbuehler & Schroeder, 1978; Lazarus & Abramowitz, 1962; Ultee, Griffiaen, & Schellekens, 1982).

The term "graduated exposure" refers to the process of progressive *in vivo* exposure to fearful stimuli without concomitant use of progressive muscle relaxation. A final respondent-based procedure is reinforced practice, which combines graduated exposure with structured positive reinforcement. In reinforced practice, rewards are provided to the child for remaining in the presence of anxiety-arousing stimuli for progressively longer periods of time (e.g., Leitenberg & Callahan, 1973).

Operant/Contingency Management Procedures

Operant procedures rely on the basic concepts of reinforcement, punishment, and stimulus control articulated by Thorndike (1911) and Skinner (1953). Use of such procedures with socially avoidant children requires assessment of the antecedents and consequences that are maintaining the child's fearful behavior. The operant approach is based on the assumption that socially avoidant children have not been adequately reinforced for social behavior or have been inadvertently reinforced for nonsocial behavior (e.g., refusal to go to a party with peers results in reduction of social anxiety, which reinforces avoidant behavior). Treatment entails arrangement of contingencies in the school and/or home environments to facilitate social interaction, with provision of reinforcement contingent on appropriate social behavior (e.g., Walker, Greenwood, Hops, et al., 1979). An assumption of this approach is that the child possesses the necessary social skills but has not been reinforced adequately for applying them. Children who lack basic skills for successful social interaction require treatment programs incorporating the modeling and skills training approaches described next.

Modeling

Rachman (1977) and Bandura (1986) have presented an observational framework for the acquisition and amelioration of fear and anxiety. Learning and behavior change are said to occur through observation of another individual's behavior and the resulting consequences of the behavior (Bandura, 1969). Modeling procedures are the clinical application of observational learning theory.

Modeling techniques have proven effective in the treatment of anxious and socially avoidant behavior (see Barrios & O'Dell, 1989; O'Connor, 1969). In the procedure, the child observes a filmed or live model demonstrate appropriate coping behavior while in the presence of anxiety-arousing stimuli. Following the demonstration, the child is instructed to imitate the model's performance. Performance trials are repeated and the therapist provides feedback and reinforcement for behavior that approximates that of the model. Participant modeling is a special form of modeling in which the therapist (or nonanxious peer confederate) provides support and physically guides the child through the anxiety-arousing situation. Ollendick (1979) has suggested that participant modeling may be the most effective, filmed modeling is least effective. Furthermore, use of peer models may be preferable to adult models, as vicarious conditioning is enhanced by similarity of models to target subjects.

Social Skills Training

Social skills training (SST) programs may be useful for anxious children who lack the skills necessary for successful social interaction. SST programs have been widely used with socially withdrawn children to facilitate development of social relationships. However, the efficacy of SST programs with children diagnosed specifically with social phobia or avoidant disorder remains to be addressed empirically. In the typical SST program, target children are provided group instruction in the execution of specific behaviors (e.g., smiling, eye contact, initiations, conversational skills). Group leaders model effective behaviors and the children are given practice opportunities accompanied by verbal feedback and reinforcement. Although SST programs have been successful in increasing the frequency of the specific target behaviors (e.g., LaGreca & Santogrossi, 1980), changes in social acceptance by peers have not been demonstrated (Berler, Gross, & Drabman, 1982; Tiffen & Spence, 1986; Whitehill, Hersen, & Bellack, 1980).

Peer-Mediated Approaches

Treatments that incorporate a child's peers have been suggested to be superior over adult-mediated approaches for remediating social isolation (Strain & Fox, 1981). Although peer-mediated procedures have not been used with populations selected specifically for social phobia, research with socially withdrawn children suggests their usefulness in facilitating changes in both social behavior and peer acceptance. The most commonly used peer-mediated approaches provide peers with incentives and/or training to increase their rate of positive social interaction with target children (e.g., Christopher, Hansen, & MacMillan, 1991; Paine, Hops, Walker, et al., 1982; Strain & Odom, 1986). In peer pairing, an alternate peer-mediated procedure, target children are provided opportunities to engage in activities with either "normal" or "popular status" peers. Compared with no-treatment controls, socially withdrawn preschoolers given the opportunity to interact with playmates in free-play sessions were found to increase their frequency of peer interaction (Furman, Rahe, & Hartup, 1979). A recent study of peer-neglected first- and second-grade children (Morris, Messer, & Gross, in press) provides further evidence for the effectiveness of a peer-pairing procedure in increasing both positive social interaction and peer acceptance.

Peer-pairing treatment is conceptualized as the provision and structuring of a facilitative environment conducive to mutually reinforcing social interactional influences. Popular peers function as ideal models of age-appropriate social behavior, as well as salient providers of social reinforcement. Activities requiring verbal interaction with higher-status peers may function as informal "exposure" sessions resulting in habituation or extinction of anxiety responses to social stimuli. Additionally, changes in self-perceptions and cognitions following efficacy experiences with peers may alter the subsequent behavior of socially avoidant children. As peer-pairing procedures are relatively cost-effective and readily implemented, future studies are warranted investigating the utility of the approach with children meeting diagnostic criteria for avoidant disorder or social phobia.

PHARMACOLOGICAL TREATMENT

Although a number of pharmacologic agents have demonstrated utility in the treatment of adults with anxiety disorders, there is a lack of controlled trials evaluating potential efficacy and risks in children. Initial reports indicated that alprazolam may be useful in reducing social avoidance in children with overanxious and avoidant disorders (e.g., Simeon & Ferguson, 1987). Studies examining the long-term effects of benzodiazepine on children are lacking, but the incidence of paradoxic reactions such as disinhibition or aggression has been considered more frequent in children than in adults (Kutcher, Reiter, Gardner, et al., 1992).

Gittelman-Klein and Klein (1971, 1973) report that imipramine improved treatment outcome in a group of formerly treatment-resistant school phobics. Bernstein, Garfinkel, and Barchardt (1990) compared the effectiveness of imipramine, alprazolam, and placebo in the treatment of

24 children with school refusal. Results suggested a trend favoring medication over placebo, with no significant differences noted between imipramine and alprazolam. However, the small sample size may have precluded the detection of more moderate differences between the active medication groups.

Phenelzine, a monoamine oxidase inhibitor, has received some empirical support for the treatment of social phobia in adults. Results of Gelernter, Uhde, Cimbolic, et al. (1991) suggest that phenelzine is superior to alprazolam in therapeutic response and maintenance of treatment gains. Case reports have suggested that phenelzine may be effective in the treatment of children with elective mutism (e.g., Golwyn & Weinstock, 1990). Despite such promise, reports on the use of phenelzine in children with avoidant disorder and social phobia are lacking.

Buspirone is a novel anxiolytic agent with antidepressant effects (Goldberg, 1984; Kastenholz & Crimson, 1984). Clinical trials with adults indicate that buspirone has a relative efficacy similar to the benzodiazepines (Cohn & Wilcox, 1986) with minimal abuse potential (Balster, 1990; Lader, 1987). Case reports (Kranzler, 1988) suggest that buspirone may be useful in the treatment of children with overanxious disorder. The minimal side-effect profile and low abuse potential make buspirone an appealing pharmacologic agent for use with children with avoidant disorder or social phobia. However, controlled investigations of the benefits and risks of buspirone use with children are necessary.

CASE EXAMPLE

David was an 11-year-old boy who presented with a lifelong history of social phobia and avoidance. He never played with more than one other child at a time. When playing with a peer, David would leave if a third child came along. He never played at another child's house and stated that he did not have any friends. Although he attended school almost every day, he always had severe stomachaches during the morning bus ride. In addition, he was unable to eat lunch at school because he felt so sick around the other children in the school cafeteria that he was afraid he would vomit. This was a very significant problem since David was an insulin-dependent diabetic and had to eat six small meals per day. David's avoidance behaviors were pervasive and included refusal to eat at fast-food restaurants and refusal to attend any social activity unless accompanied by a parent. David was an only child. His interactions with his parents were very warm and personable. His mother suffered from panic disorder and his father served as David's only social contact. Both parents were motivated to assist David in overcoming his social fears.

The results of the initial assessment revealed that in addition to his social phobia and avoidance, David had poor social skills and was generally quite anxious. Therefore, the treatment program consisted of three components: relaxation training, social skills training, and *in vivo* practice of basic conversational skills. The first 3 weeks of the intervention were devoted to relaxation training. Between sessions, David practiced once per day at home using a specially designed relaxation tape. Social skills training consisted of verbal and nonverbal skills designed to promote social engagement. David was taught basic conversational skills such as introducing oneself, asking questions to maintain a conversation, and basic endings. In addition, attention was given to correcting inadequate eye contact, voice volume, and so on. One behavior was selected for training for each week. For generalization training, the selection of a site where there were a large number of children available for practice was crucial to the success of the program. A permanent dinosaur exhibit at a local museum of science was ideal. David was escorted to the museum by his therapist where he practiced greetings and made small talk with other children. Only when a particular skill had been acquired successfully in the clinic did he practice it in the generalization setting.

After 12 weeks, David had made some progress, but the self-monitoring data indicated that a more intensive procedure might be more clinically and cost effective. A flooding paradigm was instituted where David was accompanied by his therapist to anxiety-producing situations (such as a fast-food restaurant) and encouraged to stay until his anxiety dissipated. Furthermore, in an effort to increase the number of treatment sessions, David's father accompanied David and the therapist. In this way, David's father was instructed in the exposure procedures and was able to carry out additional sessions independently. After 3 months, self-monitoring and parental report indicated a substantial increase in the number of social encounters in which David engaged. He began attending birthday parties and roller-skating parties. In addition, for the first time in his life, David had a best friend.

SUMMARY AND RESEARCH CONSIDERATIONS

Despite the emerging interest in the assessment and treatment of childhood social phobia, there is a paucity of methodologically sound investigations and many basic research questions remain. First, although DSM-IV appears to be a significant advance over DSM-III-R in terms of clarifying the diagnostic criteria and eliminating the overlapping categories, the clinical correlates of children with social phobia are still in need of investigation. For example, although specific "childhood" descriptors are included in the diagnostic criteria, all have not been derived from empirical investigations. Thus, many of the clinical manifestations of social phobia remain to be elucidated. Second, one of the major impediments to research in this area has been the lack of reliable and valid assessment measures specifically designed for the assessment of childhood social phobia. Clinical assessment of social phobia requires attention to vague complaints and associated features that may signal the presence of this disorder. Of the two currently available self-report instruments, both have acceptable to good reliability and validity, but the SPAI-C (as well as the SPAI) is the only instrument that specifically assesses social phobia. For adolescents, it appears that the selection of either the SPAI-C or the SPAI is appropriate, with the final decision resting on the age and the reading level of the particular adolescent. Third, treatment outcome data are virtually nonexistent. There is a lack of double-blind placebo-controlled investigations that limit conclusions regarding the efficacy of pharmacological treatment. Similarly, there are few carefully controlled single-case designs or group outcome studies of behavioral interventions. In addition, although peer-mediated approaches to the treatment of social anxiety have demonstrated promise, further investigations of their effectiveness with children meeting criteria for social phobia are warranted. In summary, given the impact of social fears on a child's current functioning and its potential devastating long-term outcome, more attention to the identification and treatment of childhood social phobia is necessary.

REFERENCES

Ainsworth, M. S., Blehar, M., Waters, E., et al. (1978). *Patterns of attachment*. Hillsdale, NJ: Lawrence Erlbaum.

American Psychiatric Association (1980). *Diagnostic and statistical manual of mental disorders* (3rd ed.). Washington, DC: Author.

American Psychiatric Association (1987). *Diagnostic and statistical manual of mental disorders* (3rd ed., rev.). Washington, DC: Author.

American Psychiatric Association (1994). *Diagnostic and statistical manual of mental disorders* (4th ed.). Washington, DC: Author.

Anderson, J. C., Williams, S., McGee, R., et al. (1987). DSM-III disorders in preadolescent children. *Archives of General Psychiatry, 44,* 69–76.

Attili, G. (1989). Social competence versus emotional security: The link between home relationships and behavior problems at school. In B. H. Schneider, G. Attili, J. Nadel, et al. (Eds.), *Social competence in developmental perspective* (pp. 293–311). London: Kluwer.

Balster, R. (1990). Abuse potential of buspirone and related drugs. *Journal of Clinical Psychopharmacology, 10,* 31S–37S.

Bandura, A. (1969). *Principles of behavior modification*. New York: Holt, Rinehart, & Winston.

Bandura, A. (1986). *Social foundations of thought and action: A social cognitive theory.* Englewood Cliffs, NJ: Prentice-Hall.

Barrios, B., & O'Dell, S. (1989). Fears and anxieties. In E. J. Mash & R. A. Barkley (Eds.), *Treatment of childhood disorders* (pp. 167–221). New York: Guilford Press.

Beidel, D. C. (1991). Social phobia and overanxious disorder in school-age children. *Journal of the American Academy of Child and Adolescent Psychiatry, 30,* 545–552.

Beidel, D. C. (1992, April). *Social phobia in children.* Presented at the National Institute of Mental Health, Washington, DC.

Beidel, D. C., Christ, M. A. G., & Long, P. J. (1991). Somatic complaints in anxious children. *Journal of Abnormal Child Psychology, 19,* 659–670.

Beidel, D. C., & Morris, T. L. (1993). Avoidant disorder of childhood and social phobia. In H. Leonard (Ed.), *Child and Adolescent Psychiatric Clinics of North America, 4,* 623–638.

Beidel, D. C., & Turner, S. M. (1988). Comorbidity of test anxiety and other anxiety disorders in children. *Journal of Abnormal Child Psychology, 16,* 275–287.

Beidel, D. C., & Turner, S. M. (1993). *Are socially phobic children the same as socially phobic adults?* Manuscript in preparation, Medical University of South Carolina.

Beidel, D. C., Turner, S. M., & Morris, T. L. (in press). The Social Phobia and Anxiety Inventory for Children: Psychometric characteristics. *Psychological Assessment.*

Beidel, D. C., Turner, M. W., & Trager, K. N. (1994). Test anxiety and childhood anxiety disorders in African American and white school children. *Journal of Anxiety Disorders, 8,* 169–179.

Belsky, J., & Rovine, M. (1987). Temperament and attachment security in the strange situation: An empirical rapprochement. *Child Development, 58,* 787–795.

Berler, E. S., Gross, A. M., & Drabman, R. S. (1982). Social skills training with children: Proceed with caution. *Journal of Applied Behavior Analysis, 15,* 41–53.

Bernstein, G., Garfinkel, B., & Barchardt, C. (1990). Comparative studies of pharmacotherapy for school refusal. *Journal of the American Academy of Child and Adolescent Psychiatry, 29,* 773–781.

Biederman, J., Rosenbaum, J. F., Bolduc-Murphy, E. A., et al. (1993). A 3-year follow-up of children with and without behavioral inhibition. *Journal of the American Academy of Child and Adolescent Psychiatry, 32,* 814–821.

Biederman, J., Rosenbaum, J. F., Hirshfeld, D. R., et al. (1990). Psychiatric correlates of behavioral inhibition in young children of parents with and without psychiatric disorders. *Archives of General Psychiatry, 47,* 21–26.

Bromberg, A., Lamb, M. E., & Hwang, P. (1990). Inhibition: Its stability and correlates in sixteen to forty-month-old children. *Child Development, 61,* 1153–1163.

Bruch, M. A., Giordano, S., & Pearl, L. (1986). Differences between fearful and self- conscious shy subtypes in background and current adjustment. *Journal of Research in Personality, 20,* 172–186.

Buss, A. H., & Plomin, R. (1984). *Temperament: Early developing personality traits.* Hillsdale, NJ: Erlbaum.

Chambers, W. J., Puig-Antich, J., Hirsch, M., et al. (1985). The assessment of affective disorders in children and adolescents by semistructured interview: Test–retest reliability of the Schedule for Affective Disorders and Schizophrenia in School-Age Children, Present Episode Version. *Archives of General Psychiatry, 42,* 696–702.

Cheek, J. M., & Buss, A. H. (1981). Shyness and sociability. *Journal of Personality and Social Psychology, 41,* 330–339.

Cheek, J. M., Carpentieri, A. M., Smith, T. G., et al. (1986). Adolescent shyness. In W. H. Jones, J. M. Cheek, & S. R. Briggs (Eds.), *Shyness: Perspectives on research and treatment* (pp. 105–115). New York: Plenum Press.

Christopher, J. S., Hansen, D. J., & MacMillan, V. M. (1991). Effectiveness of a peer-helper intervention to increase children's social interactions. *Behavior Modification, 15,* 22–50.

Clark, D. B. (1993, March). *Assessment of social anxiety in adolescent alcohol abusers.* Presented at the Anxiety Disorders Association of America Annual Convention, Charleston, SC.

Clark, D. B., Turner, S. M., Beidel, D. C., et al. (1994). Reliability and validity of the Social Phobia and Anxiety Inventory for adolescents. *Psychological Assessment, 6,* 135–140.

Costello, A. J., Edelbrock, C., Duncan, M., et al. (1984). *Report on the NIMH Diagnostic Inteview Schedule for Children (DISC).* Unpublished manuscript, University of Pittsburgh.

Cohn, J., & Wilcox, C. (1986). Low-sedation potential of buspirone compared with alprazolam and lorazepam in the treatment of anxious patients: A double-blind study. *Journal of Clinical Psychiatry, 47,* 409–412.

Daniels, D., & Plomin, R. (1985). Origins of individual differences in infant shyness. *Developmental Psychology, 21,* 118–121.

Davidson, J. (1993, March). *Childhood histories of adult social phobics.* Presented at the Anxiety Disorders Association of American Annual Convention, Charleston, SC.

Finnie, V., & Russell, A. (1988). Preschool children's social status and their mothers' behavior and knowledge in the supervisory role. *Developmental Psychology, 24,* 789–801.

Fox, J. E., & Houston, B. K. (1983). Distinguishing between cognitive and somatic trait and somatic state anxiety in children. *Journal of Personality and Social Psychology, 45,* 862–870.

Fox, N. A. (1989). Psychophysiological correlates of emotional reactivity during the first year of life. *Developmental Psychology, 25,* 364–372.

Francis, G., Last, C. G., & Strauss, C. C. (1992). Avoidant personality disorder and social phobia in children and adolescents. *Journal of the American Academy of Child and Adolescent Psychiatry, 31,* 1086–1089.

Furman, W., Rahe, D. F., & Hartup, W. W. (1979). Rehabilitation of socially withdrawn preschool children through mixed-age and same-age socialization. *Child Development, 50,* 915–922.

Fyer, A. J., Mannuzza, S., Chapman, T. F. (1993). A direct interview family study of social phobia. *Archives of General Psychiatry, 50,* 286–293.

Gelernter, C. S., Uhde, T. W., Cimbolic, P., et al. (1991). Cognitive-behavioral and pharmacologic treatments of social phobia: A controlled study. *Archives of General Psychiatry, 48,* 938–944.

Gittelman-Klein, R., & Klein, D. (1971). Controlled imipramine treatment of school phobia. *Archives of General Psychiatry, 25,* 204–207.

Gittelman-Klein, R., & Klein, D. (1973). School phobia: Diagnostic considerations in the light of imipramine effects. *Journal of Nervous and Mental Disease, 156,* 199–215.

Goldberg, H. (1984). Buspirone hydrochloride: A unique new anxiolytic agent. *Pharmacotherapy, 4,* 315–324.

Golwyn, D. H., & Weinstock, R. C. (1990). Phenelzine treatment of elective mutism: A case-report. *Journal of Clinical Psychiatry, 51,* 384–385.

Hartman, L. M. (1983). A metacognitive model of social anxiety: Implications for treatment. *Clinical Psychology Review, 3,* 435–456.

Hatzenbuehler, L. C., & Schroeder, H. E. (1978). Desensitization procedures in the treatment of childhood disorders. *Psychological Bulletin, 85,* 831–844.

Herjanic, B., & Reich, W. (1982). Development of a structured psychiatric interview for children: Agreement between child and parent on individual symptoms. *Journal of Abnormal Child Psychology, 10,* 307–324.

Hinde, R. A., & Tamplin, A. (1983). Relations between mother–child interaction and behavior in pre-school. *British Journal of Developmental Psychology, 1,* 231–257.

Hodges, K. (1986). *The Child Assessment Schedule.* Unpublished manuscript, Eastern Michigan University.

Hymel, S., Rubin, K. H., Rowden, L., et al. (1990). Children's peer relationships: Longitudinal prediction of internalizing and externalizing problems from middle to late childhood. *Child Development, 61,* 2004–2021.

Ishiyama, F. I. (1984). Shyness: Anxious social sensitivity and self-isolating tendency. *Adolescence, 19,* 903–911.

Jones, M. C. (1924). The elimination of children's fears. *Journal of Experimental Psychology, 7,* 382–390.

Kagan, J., Reznick, J. S., Clarke, C., et al. (1984). Behavioral inhibition to the unfamiliar. *Child Development, 55,* 2212–2225.

Kagan, J., Reznick, J. S., & Snidman, N. (1987). The physiology and psychology of behavioral inhibition in children. *Child Development, 58,* 1459–1473.

Kashani, J. H., & Orvaschel, H. (1990). A community study of anxiety in children and adolescents. *American Journal of Psychiatry, 147,* 313–318.

Kastenholz, K., & Crimson, M. (1984). Buspirone, a novel benzodiazepine anxiolytic. *Drug Reviews, 3,* 600–607.

Kranzler, H. (1988). Use of buspirone in an adolescent with overanxious disorder. *Journal of the American Academy of Child and Adolescent Psychiatry, 27,* 789–790.

Kutcher, S. P., Reiter, S., Gardner, D. M., et al. (1992). The pharmacotherapy of anxiety disorders in children and adolescents. *Psychiatric Clinics of North America, 15,* 41–67.

Ladd, G. W., & Golter, B. S. (1988). Parents' management of preschoolers' peer relations: Is it related to children's social competence? *Developmental Psychology, 24,* 109–117.

Lader, M. (1987). Assessing the potential for buspirone dependence or abuse and effects of its withdrawal. *American Journal of Medicine, 82,* 20–26.

LaGreca, A. M. (1991, August). *The development of social anxiety in children.* Paper presented at the American Psychological Association, San Francisco.

LaGreca, A. M., Dandes, S. K., Wick, P., et al. (1988). Development of the Social Anxiety Scale for Children: Reliability and concurrent validity. *Journal of Clinical Child Psychology, 17,* 84–91.

LaGreca, A. M., & Santogrossi, D. A. (1980). Social skills training with elementary students: A behavioral group approach. *Journal of Consulting and Clinical Psychology, 48,* 220–227.

Last, C. G. (1986). *DSM-III anxiety disorders of childhood and adolescence.* Unpublished manuscript, University of Pittsburgh.

Last, C. G., Hersen, M., Kazdin, A., et al. (1991). Anxiety disorders in children and their families. *Archives of General Psychiatry, 48,* 928–934.

Last, C. G., Perrin, S., Hersen, M., et al. (1992). DSM-III-R anxiety disorders in children: Sociodemographic and clinical characteristics. *Journal of the American Academy of Child and Adolescent Psychiatry, 31,* 1070–1076.

Last, C. G., Strauss, C. C., & Francis, G. (1987). Comorbidity among childhood anxiety disorders. *Journal of Nervous and Mental Disease, 175,* 726–730.

Lazarus, A. A. (1974). Cognitive restructuring. *Psychotherapy: Theory, Research, and Practice, 11,* 98–102.

Lazarus, A. A., & Abramowitz, A. (1962). The use of "emotive imagery" in the treatment of children's phobias. *Journal of Mental Science, 108,* 191–195.

Leitenberg, H., & Callahan, E. (1973). Reinforced practice and reduction of different kinds of fears in adults and children. *Behaviour Research and Therapy, 11,* 19–30.

Liebowitz, M. R., Gorman, J. M., Fyer, A. J., et al. (1985). Social phobia. *Archives of General Psychiatry, 42,* 729–736.

MacDonald, K. (1987). Parent–child physical play with rejected, neglected, and popular boys. *Developmental Psychology, 5,* 705–711.

Marks, I. M. (1970). The classification of phobic disorders. *British Journal of Psychiatry, 116,* 377–386.

Marks, I. M. (1985). Behavioral treatment of Social phobia. *Psychopharmacology Bulletin, 21,* 615–618.

McGee, R., Feehan, M., Williams, S., et al. (1990). DSM-III disorders in a large sample of adolescents. *Journal of the American Academy of Child and Adolescent Psychiatry, 29,* 611–619.

Messer, S. C., & Beidel, D. C. (1994). Psychological correlates of childhood anxiety disorders. *Journal of the American Academy of Child and Adolescent Psychiatry, 33,* 975–983.

Morris, R. J., & Kratochwill, T. R. (1983). Childhood fears and phobias. In R. J. Morris & T. R. Kratochwill (Eds.), *The practice of child therapy* (pp. 53–86). New York: Pergamon.

Morris, T. L., Messer, S. C., & Gross, A. M. (in press). Enhancement of the social interaction and status of neglected children: A peer-pairing approach. *Journal of Clinical Child Psychology.*

Nelles, W. B., & Barlow, D. H. (1988). Do children panic? *Clinical Psychology Review, 8,* 359–372.

O'Connor, R. D. (1969). Modification of social withdrawal through symbolic modeling. *Journal of Applied Behavior Analysis, 2,* 15–22.

Ollendick, T. H. (1979). Fear reduction techniques with children. In M. Hersen, R. M. Eisler, & P. M. Miller (Eds.), *Progress in behavior modification* (Vol. 8, pp. 127–168). New York: Academic Press.

Ollendick, T. H. (1983). Reliability and validity of the revised Fear Survey Schedule for Children (FSSC-R). *Behaviour Research and Therapy, 21,* 685–692.

Ollendick, T. H., & Cerny, J. A. (1981). *Clinical behavior therapy with children.* New York: Plenum Press.

Ollendick, T. H., & Meyer, J. (1984). School phobia. In S. M. Turner (Ed.), *Behavioral theories and treatment of anxiety* (pp. 367–411). New York: Plenum Press.

Ost, L. G. (1987). Age of onset in different phobias. *Journal of Abnormal Psychology, 96,* 223–229.

Paine, S. C., Hops, H., Walker, H. M., et al. (1982). Repeated treatment effects: A study of maintaining behavior change in socially withdrawn children. *Behavior Modification, 6,* 171–199.

Parke, R. D., & Bhavnagri, N. P. (1989). Parents as managers of children's peer relationships. In D. Belle (Ed.), *Children's social networks and social supports* (pp. 241–259). New York: Wiley.

Patterson, C. J., Kupersmidt, J. B., & Griesler, P. C. (1990). Children's perceptions of self and of relationships with others as a function of sociometric status. *Child Development, 61,* 1335–1349.

Perrin, S., & Last, C. G. (1993). Do childhood anxiety measures measure anxiety? *Journal of Abnormal Child Psychology, 20,* 567–578.

Putallaz, M., & Heflin, A. H. (1990). Parent–child interaction. In S. R. Asher & J. C. Coie (Eds.), *Children's status in the peer group* (pp. 189–216). New York: Cambridge University Press.

Rachman, S. J. (1977). The conditioning theory of fear-acquisition: A critical examination. *Behaviour Research and Therapy, 15,* 375–387.

Radke-Yarrow, M., & Zahn-Waxler, C. (1986). The role of familial factors in the development of prosocial behavior: Research findings and questions. In D. Olweus, J. Block, & M. Radke-Yarrow (Eds.), *Development of antisocial and prosocial behavior: Research, theories, and issues* (pp. 207–233). Orlando, FL: Academic Press.

Renkin, B., Egeland, B., Marvinney, D., et al. (1989). Early childhood antecedents of aggression and passive-withdrawal in early elementary school. *Journal of Personality, 57,* 257–282.

Reynolds, C. R., & Richmond, B. O. (1978). Factor structure and construct validity of "What I Think and Feel": The Revised Children's Manifest Anxiety Scale. *Journal of Personality Assessment, 43*, 281–283.

Rosenbaum, J. F., Biederman, J., Hirshfeld, D. R., et al. (1991). Further evidence of an association between behavioral inhibition and anxiety disorders: Results from a family study of children from a non-clinical sample. *Journal of Psychiatric Research, 25*, 49–65.

Rubin, K. H. (1985). Socially withdrawn children: An at-risk population? In B. Schneider, K. H. Rubin, & J. Ledingham (Eds.), *Children's peer relations: Issues in assessment and intervention*, (pp. 125–139). New York: Springer-Verlag.

Rubin, K. H., & Asendorpf, J. B. (1993). Social withdrawal, inhibition, and shyness in childhood: Conceptual and definitional issues. In K. H. Rubin & J. B. Asendorpf (Eds.), *Social withdrawal, inhibition, and shyness in childhood* (pp. 3–17). Hillsdale, NJ: Erlbaum.

Rubin, K. H., LeMare, L. J., & Lollis, S. (1990). Social withdrawal in childhood: Developmental pathways to peer rejection. In S. R. Asher & J. D. Coie (Eds.), *Peer rejection in childhood* (pp. 217–249). Cambridge: Cambridge University Press.

Rubin, K. H., & Mills, R. S. L. (1988). The many faces of social isolation in childhood. *Journal of Consulting and Clinical Psychology, 56*, 916–924.

Sarason, I. G. (1975). Test anxiety, attention, and the general problem of anxiety. In C. D. Spielberger & I. G. Sarason (Eds.), *Stress and Anxiety* (Vol. 1, pp. 165–188). Washington, DC: Hemisphere/Wiley.

Silverman, W. K., & Eisen, A. R. (1991). Age differences in the reliability of parent and child reports of child anxious symptomatology using a structured interview. *Journal of the American Academy of Child and Adolescent Psychiatry, 31*, 117–124.

Silverman, W. K., & Nelles, W. B. (1988). The Anxiety Disorders Interview Schedule for Children. *Journal of the American Academy of Child and Adolescent Psychiatry, 27*, 772–778.

Simeon, J., & Ferguson, B. (1987). Alprazolam effects in children with anxiety disorders. *Canadian Journal of Psychiatry, 32*, 570–574.

Skinner, B. F. (1953). *Science and human behavior*. New York: The Free Press.

Smith, R. E., & Sharpe, T. M. (1970). Treatment of a school phobia with implosive therapy. *Journal of Consulting and Clinical Psychology, 35*, 239–243.

Stefanek, M. E., Ollendick, T. H., Baldock, W. P., et al. (1987). Self-statements in aggressive, withdrawn, and popular children. *Cognitive Therapy and Research, 2*, 229–239.

Strain, P. S., & Fox, J. E. (1981). Peers as therapeutic agents for isolate classmates. In A. E. Kazdin & B. B. Lahey (Eds.), *Advances in child clinical psychology* (Vol. 4, pp. 167–198). New York: Plenum Press.

Strain, P. S., & Odom, S. L. (1986). Peer social initiations: Effective interventions for social skills development in exceptional children. *Exceptional Children, 52*, 543–551.

Strauss, C. C., Lahey, B. B., Frick, P., et al. (1988). Peer social status of children with anxiety disorders. *Journal of Consulting and Clinical Psychology, 56*, 137–141.

Strauss, C. C., & Last, C. G. (1993). Social and simple phobias in children. *Journal of Anxiety Disorders, 1*, 141–152.

Stravynski, A., Lamontagne, Y., & Lavallee, Y. (1986). Clinical phobias and avoidant disorder among alcoholics admitted to an alcoholism rehabilitation setting. *Canadian Journal of Psychiatry, 31*, 714–719.

Teglasi, H., & Fagin, S. S. (1984). Social anxiety and self-other biases in causal attributions. *Journal of Research in Personality, 18*, 64–80.

Teglasi, H., & Hoffman, M. A. (1982). Causal attribution in shy subjects. *Journal of Research in Personality, 12*, 431–438.

Thomas, A., & Chess, S. (1977). *Temperament and development.* New York: Brunner/Mazel.

Thorndike, E. L. (1911). *Animal intelligence.* New York: MacMillan.

Tiffen, K., & Spence, S. H. (1986). Responsiveness of isolated versus rejected children to social skills training. *Journal of Child Psychology and Psychiatry, 27*, 343–355.

Turner, S. M., & Beidel, D. C. (1989). Social phobia: Clinical syndrome, diagnosis and comorbidity. *Clinical Psychology Review, 9*, 3–18.

Turner, S. M., & Beidel, D. C. (1993). *Children at Risk for Anxiety Disorders.* Unpublished manuscript, Medical University of South Carolina.

Turner, S. M., Beidel, D. C., Borden, J. W., et al. (1991). Social phobia: Axis I and II correlates. *Journal of Abnormal Psychology, 100*, 102–106.

Turner, S. M., Beidel, D. C., & Costello, A. (1987). Psychopathology in the offspring of anxiety disorders patients. *Journal of Consulting and Clinical Psychology, 55*, 229–235.

Turner, S. M., Beidel, D. C., Dancu, C. V., et al. (1986). Psychopathology of social phobia and comparison to avoidant personality disorder. *Journal of Abnormal Psychology, 95*, 389–394.

Turner, S. M., Beidel, D. C., Dancu, C. V., et al. (1989). An empirically derived inventory to measure social fears and anxiety: The Social Phobia and Anxiety Inventory. *Psychological Assessment: A Journal of Consulting and Clinical Psychology, 1*, 35–40.

Turner, S. M., Beidel, D. C., & Townsley, R. M. (1990). Social phobia: Relationship to shyness. *Behaviour Research and Therapy, 28*, 497–505.

Turner, S. M., Beidel, D. C., & Townsley, R. M. (1992). Socially phobia: A comparison of specific and generalized subtypes and avoidant personality disorder. *Journal of Abnormal Psychology, 101*, 326–331.

Turner, S. M., Townsley, R. M., & Beidel, D. C. (1993). *Potential etiological factors in social phobia.* Manuscript in preparation.

Ultee, C. A., Griffiaen, D., & Schellekens, J. (1982). The reduction of anxiety in children: A comparison of the effects of systematic desensitization *in vitro* and systematic desensitization *in vivo. Behaviour Research and Therapy, 20*, 61–67.

Vernberg, E. M., Abwender, D. A., Ewell, K. K., et al. (1992). Social anxiety and peer relationships in early adolescence: A prospective analysis. *Journal of Clinical Child Psychology, 21*, 189–196.

Walker, H. M., Greenwood, C. R., Hops, H., et al. (1979). Differential effects of reinforcing topographic components of free play social interaction: Analysis and systematic replication. *Behavior Modification, 3*, 291–321.

Watson, D., & Friend, R. (1969). Measurement of social-evaluative anxiety. *Journal of Consulting and Clinical Psychology, 33*, 448–457.

Weissman, M. M., Leckman, J. F., Merikangas, K. R., et al. (1984). Depression and anxiety disorders in parents and children. *Archives of General Psychiatry, 41*, 845–852.

Whitehill, M. B., Hersen, M., & Bellack, A. S. (1980). Conversational skills training for socially isolated children. *Behaviour Research and Therapy, 18*, 217–225.

Wolpe, J. (1958). *Psychotherapy by reciprocal inhibition*. Stanford, CA: Stanford University Press.

Zatz, S., & Chassin, L. (1983). Cognitions in test-anxious children. *Journal of Consulting and Clinical Psychology, 51*, 526–534.

Chapter 9

Separation
Anxiety Disorder
and Panic Disorder

Bruce Black

Separation anxiety disorder (SAD) is a relatively common psychiatric disorder of childhood and early adolescence. Panic disorder is a common psychiatric disorder of adults, but it may also be diagnosed in children and adolescents. SAD and panic disorder appear to be closely related. This chapter reviews what is known about these two common anxiety disorders and the relationship between them.

Separation anxiety has been recognized and studied as a characteristic of normal development and as a symptom for many years (Freud, 1909/1955; Bowlby, 1973). However, it was not treated as a distinct clinical diagnostic category until the publication of the third edition of the *Diagnostic and Statistical Manual of Mental Disorders* (DSM-III) in 1980, which described SAD as one of three distinct Anxiety Disorders of Childhood or Adolescence (American Psychiatric Association, 1980). DSM-III-R and DSM-IV introduced only very minor changes to the diagnostic criteria specified in DSM-III (American Psychiatric Association, 1987, 1994). The most significant change is that DSM-IV requires duration of symptoms for at least 4 weeks, whereas DSM-III and DSM-III-R required only 2 weeks. ICD-9-CM (World Health Organization, 1980) classifies SAD as a subtype of adjustment reaction.

Panic disorder and agoraphobia have been described since ancient times. However, the features of panic disorder that distinguish it from other anxiety disorders and the exact nature of the relationship between panic disorder and agoraphobia were not clearly recognized and described until the early 1960s (Klein, 1964, 1981). The terms "panic disorder" and "agoraphobia with panic attacks" were introduced in DSM-III in 1980. In DSM-IV, the terms were modified to "panic disorder with agoraphobia" and "panic disorder without agoraphobia." Research on the features of panic disorder in children and adolescents did not begin until the late 1980s, and there continues to be some controversy regarding whether or not panic disorder occurs in children prior to puberty (Nelles & Barlow, 1988; Black & Robbins, 1990; Black, Unde, & Robbins, 1990; Moreau & Weissman, 1992; Klein, Mannuzzo, & Chapman, 1992; Abelson & Alessi, 1992; Moreau & Follet, 1993).

DIAGNOSIS AND PHENOMENOLOGY

Diagnostic Criteria and Clinical Features

The DSM-IV diagnostic criteria for SAD are listed in Table 9.1. The primary clinical feature of SAD is excessive anxiety regarding separation from home or from important attachment figures, most often the child's mother or primary caretaker.

Behaviorally, children suffering from SAD may seek to avoid separation from attachment figures. For example, they may resist or refuse to go to school, to be left alone, to sleep apart from attachment figures, or to spend the night away from home, or may follow mother around the house. They may express persistent fears that they will become permanently separated from the attachment figure, particularly by some calamitous event such as the sudden death or disappearance of the attachment figure or the child's abduction. Affected children experience significant distress when separated from attachment figures and may spend much of the time apart anxiously anticipating reunion. When separation is imminent or has occurred, children with SAD may display signs of extreme subjective distress, terror, and autonomic symptoms of anxiety such as palpitations and hyperventilation, and they may actively resist the threatened separation. The resistance may take the form of tenaciously clinging to mother, and/or screaming, crying, begging, or complaining of severe somatic distress, most often in the form of abdominal pain. Children with SAD frequently also report other fears such as fear of the dark, monsters, and kidnappers. Nighttime fears, resistance to going to bed, difficulty falling asleep alone or sleeping through the night alone, and complaints of nightmares are common. Simple phobias, overanxious disorder, depressive disorders, mild behavioral problems, and oppositional behavior and argumentativeness are not uncommon (Last, Perrin, Hersen, et al., 1992).

Reluctance or refusal to attend school is the most common reason for referral of children with SAD to mental health clinicians. Refusal to

TABLE 9.1. Diagnostic Criteria for Separation Anxiety Disorder

A. Developmentally inappropriate and excessive anxiety concerning separa-
    tion from home or from those to whom the individual is attached, as
    evidenced by three (or more) of the following:
    (1) recurrent excessive distress when separation from home or major
        attachment figures occurs or is anticipated
    (2) persistent and excessive worry about losing, or about possible harm
        befalling, major attachment figures
    (3) persistent and excessive worry that an untoward event will lead to
        separation from a major attachment figure (e.g., getting lost or being
        kidnapped)
    (4) persistent reluctance or refusal to go to school or elsewhere because of
        fear of separation
    (5) persistently and excessively fearful or reluctant to be alone or without
        major attachment figures at home or without significant adults in
        other settings
    (6) persistent reluctance or refusal to go to sleep without being near a
        major attachment figure or to sleep away from home
    (7) repeated nightmares involving the theme of separation
    (8) repeated complaints of physical symptoms (such as headaches,
        stomachaches, nausea, or vomiting) when separation from major
        attachment figures is anticipated or involved
B. The duration of the disturbance is at least 4 weeks.
C. The onset is before age 18 years.
D. The disturbance causes clinically significant distress or impairment in
    social, academic (occupational), or other important areas of functioning.
E. The disturbance does not occur exclusively during the course of a Perva-
    sive Developmental Disorder, Schizophrenia, or other Psychotic Disorder
    and, in adolescents and adults, is not better accounted for by Panic
    Disorder with Agoraphobia.
Specify if: **Early Onset:** if onset occurs before age 6 years.

Note. From American Psychiatric Association (1994, p. 113). Copyright 1994 American
Psychiatric Association. Reprinted by permission.

sleep alone or other sleep problems and somatic symptoms are also common presenting complaints. Pediatricians commonly see children with SAD
because of somatic complaints, especially abdominal pain or nausea on
school days.

Apprehension and distress regarding separation from attachment figures, resistance to separation, and protest when separation takes place are
common in normal toddlers and preschoolers. In fact, these feelings and
behaviors generally occur to some degree at some time in nearly all healthy
children. Indeed, distress regarding separation from loved ones or other
familiar persons is a common psychological experience familiar to persons of all ages and may even be regarded as a normal corollary of the

development of healthy interpersonal attachments. It is only when these feelings and behaviors are manifest to an extent that is clearly developmentally inappropriate, prolonged, and causing clinically significant distress or functional impairment that a diagnosis of SAD is warranted. By DSM-IV criteria, SAD is diagnosed only when onset of the disorder occurs prior to the age of 18. In clinical practice, the diagnosis is almost never used beyond midadolescence. However, similar symptom complexes may occasionally be seen in adults (see Case 1 at the end of the chapter).

Panic disorder is characterized by the occurrence of unexpected and recurrent panic attacks. Panic attacks are discrete periods of intense fear or discomfort accompanied by characteristic somatic and psychic symptoms, with a sudden onset and rapid increase of symptom intensity over the course of no more than 5 to 10 minutes. The attacks typically last minutes to hours. With regards to the situational context of the attack, panic attacks may be classified as (1) unexpected (uncued) panic attacks, which occur spontaneously or "out of the blue," with no apparent precipitating event or circumstance, (2) situationally predisposed panic attacks, which occur in situations or circumstances that may frequently but not always precipitate a panic attack, and (3) situation bound panic attacks, which occur in situations or circumstances that always or almost always precipitate a panic attack (American Psychiatric Association, 1994). Panic attacks may occur in association with panic disorder, specific phobia, social phobia, posttraumatic stress disorder, or SAD. In panic disorder, by definition, at least some of the panic attacks are unexpected. Typically, most or all of the panic attacks early in the course of the disorder are uncued panic attacks, while situationally predisposed or situation bound attacks are likely to predominate later in the course of the disorder. (Panic attacks occurring in specific or social phobia are primarily situation bound or situationally predisposed attacks.)

Generalized anxiety between panic attacks, anticipatory anxiety (worry about the future occurrence of panic attacks), and agoraphobia are complications that seem to develop in the great majority of individuals seeking treatment for panic disorder. Agoraphobia is characterized by fear and avoidance of places or situations where the individual fears a panic attack is likely to occur, or from which escape might be difficult or embarrassing, or in which help might not be available in the event of a panic attack. Most individuals with panic disorder seen in clinical settings have some degree of agoraphobia, ranging from mild (e.g., avoidance of going to crowded public places alone) to severe (essentially housebound). The natural history of panic disorder and panic disorder with agoraphobia and the progression from mild panic disorder to severe agoraphobia have been well described elsewhere (American Psychiatric Association, 1994; Klein,

1964, 1981; Klein, Ross, & Cohen, 1987). Psychiatric symptoms and the course of illness in children and adolescents with panic disorder appear to be similar to those seen in adults (Black & Robbins, 1990; Moreau & Weissman, 1992; Last & Strauss, 1989; Macaulay & Kleinknecht, 1989; Bradley & Hood, 1993).

Several studies have found an increased incidence of stressful life events, particularly death or severe illness of a loved one, preceding the onset of panic disorder in adults (Roy-Byrne, Geraci, & Unde, 1986). The same pattern appears to hold true for adolescents with panic disorder (Black & Robbins, 1990; Macaulay & Kleinknecht, 1989; Bradley & Hood, 1993) and children with SAD (Gittelman, 1985a; Costello, 1989a).

Related Features

Studies assessing psychiatric comorbidity have shown that children with SAD may frequently be diagnosed with other psychiatric disorders as well. In clinical samples of children with SAD, approximately one half are diagnosed with another anxiety disorder (most often overanxious disorder or specific phobia) and one third with depression (Last, Hersen, Kazdin, et al., 1987a; Last, Francis, Hersen, et al., 1987; Klein & Last, 1989). Studies of depressed prepubertal children have found concurrent SAD in 40 to 60% of subjects (Ryan, Puig-Antich, Ambrosini, et al., 1987; Kovacs, Gatsonis, Paulauskas, et al., 1989; Keller, Lavori, Wunder, et al., 1992). When SAD and depression are both diagnosed, the SAD precedes the depression in approximately two thirds of cases. Although other anxiety disorders also occur with an increased prevalence in depressed children, SAD is the most common.

A limitation of the comorbidity studies is the lack of assessment of the real impairment associated with the comorbid conditions. In other words, is the observed comorbidity clinically meaningful or is it an artifact of the diagnostic process and criteria? A number of relatively nonspecific symptoms are included among the diagnostic criteria of both SAD and depression (e.g., disturbed sleep, somatic complaints, irritability). Furthermore, it is hardly surprising that children suffering frequent fearfulness and significant impairment due to SAD appear to be unhappy and demoralized. Likewise, it is not surprising that depressed children in psychic pain may cling to their parents and resist separation, as do children with medical conditions associated with recurrent physical pain or procedures.

Two terms that are sometimes inaccurately used interchangeably with SAD deserve discussion. "School phobia" and "school refusal" have never been included in any official diagnostic nomenclature. However, they have been widely used as diagnostic terms both clinically and in the scientific literature, particularly prior to the introduction of the diagnostic category of SAD in DSM-III in 1980 but continuing to this day.

In fact, not all children with school refusal or fear of school suffer from SAD, and not all children with SAD manifest school refusal. In one clinical sample, only 73% of children diagnosed with SAD manifested school avoidance (Last, Francis, et al., 1987). In a study of 63 children with anxiety-based school refusal referred to an anxiety disorders clinic, 38% were given a primary diagnosis of SAD, 30% social phobia, and 14% simple phobia (Last & Strauss, 1990). Children may also refuse school because of depressive disorders, conduct disorder, or family problems. In another study of 24 children with school refusal, 10 were diagnosed with depressive disorder only, 10 with both depressive and anxiety disorder, and only 4 with anxiety disorder only (Bernstein, Garfinkel, & Borchardt, 1990). The term "separation anxiety disorder" should be used as a diagnostic term, describing children who meet DSM-IV or diagnostic criteria for SAD. "School phobia" and "school refusal" may be used descriptively (but not as diagnostic labels), the former to refer generically to children with a fear of school (e.g., due to a simple phobia of some aspect of the school situation, social phobia, or fear of violence in the school), the latter to refer generically to children who refuse to attend school for any reason.

Adults with panic disorder have been shown to have an increased prevalence of depression, substance abuse, and suicide attempts. A high incidence of depression has also been reported among children and adolescents with panic disorder (Black & Robbins, 1990; Bradley & Hood, 1993; Alessi, Robbins, & Dilsaver, 1987; Alessi & Magen, 1988). Separation anxiety disorder may be a common complication of panic disorder for both children and adolescents, but perhaps particularly for children (Bradley & Hood, 1993). An association between earlier age at onset and greater levels of impairment, alcohol abuse, and suicide attempts has been demonstrated (Weissman, 1989).

Differential Diagnosis

The differential diagnosis of children presenting with complaints of school avoidance, school refusal, or excessive separation distress should include, in addition to SAD, generalized anxiety disorder (which subsumes DSM-III-R overanxious disorder of childhood), social phobia, specific phobia, depression, family dysfunction (particularly anxiety disorder, mood disorder, or substance abuse in a parent), substance-induced anxiety disorder (including caffeine and prescription and nonprescription drugs), medical disorders that may produce anxiety, and panic disorder (a fuller description of the relationship of SAD and panic disorder is presented in the last section of this chapter).

The differential diagnosis of children and adolescents presenting with panic attacks should include social phobia, specific phobia, substance-induced anxiety disorder (especially caffeinism), posttraumatic stress disorder, obsessive–compulsive disorder, depression, and medical disorders that may produce anxiety.

Course and Outcome

Separation anxiety may have either an acute or an insidious onset. When the onset is acute, there has frequently been a recent stress, such as a move to a new home or a new school, starting school, or a change in family circumstances. Onset, exacerbation, or recurrence following a school vacation or after the child has been absent from school due to a prolonged physical illness are not uncommon.

There has been little empirical research on the long-term course of children diagnosed with SAD (Keller et al., 1992; Cantwell & Baker, 1989). However, clinical observation suggests that the course is quite variable. Many children seem to recover completely without any apparent sequelae. This may be particularly true for children who manifest the disorder at a relatively early age. Other children experience long periods without significant symptoms interspersed with periodic exacerbations or sudden recurrences, especially during times of increased stress or increased demands for autonomy. For example, a child with separation anxiety and school refusal during the first weeks or months of the first grade may seem to recover and be without symptoms after several months of school, once a certain level of comfort with the school environment has been achieved and attachments to teacher and peers have developed. However, the child may experience a return of symptoms following prolonged school holidays, transfer to a new teacher or classroom, or transfer to middle school or high school. This child may later be at increased risk of developing anxiety symptoms or depressive illness when he or she leaves home to go to college or may develop overly dependent and anxious attachments as an adult.

In other words, vulnerability to excessive distress when attachments are disrupted or threatened may remain as a stable personality trait throughout childhood and adolescence and into adulthood. Symptoms become manifest only when disruption or threat of disruption actually occurs. A heightened vulnerability to behavioral manifestations of separation distress has been shown to be a relatively stable trait in nonhuman primates, as well (Suomi, Kraemer, Baysinger, et al., 1981).

Other children may suffer a more chronic and persistent course. A later age of onset, comorbidity with other psychiatric disorders, and family psychopathology may all be associated with greater risk of chronic illness. Children with SAD who have not been in school for a year or more may be particularly refractory to treatment.

Finally, although adequate prospective studies have not been completed, several studies have found evidence to suggest that children with SAD, particularly girls, are at increased risk of developing panic disorder and agoraphobia during childhood or as an adult (Moreau & Follet, 1993; Gittelman & Klein, 1985; Casat, 1988; Biederman, Rosenbaum, Bolduc-Murphy, et al., 1993b). Up to half of adult agoraphobics may have a history of childhood SAD. Children with SAD may also be at increased risk of suffering from depressive disorders and social phobia as adults.

The longitudinal course of panic disorder in children and adolescents has not been studied. In adults, panic disorder tends to be a chronic and recurrent illness (Breier, Charney, & Heninger, 1986; Keller & Baker, 1992). Comorbid depression, personality disorder, and a history of childhood anxiety disorder are all associated with a more chronic, unremitting course of illness in adults with panic disorder (Pollack, Otto, Rosenbaum, et al., 1992).

Familial Pattern

An increased prevalence of anxiety disorders and of depression has been demonstrated in the families of children with SAD, relative to controls. One study found that 68% of mothers of SAD children had a lifetime diagnosis of an anxiety disorder, while 53% had a lifetime diagnosis of major depression and 47% had a current anxiety disorder diagnosis (Last, Hersen, Kazdin, et al., 1987b). The morbidity risk for anxiety disorder among relatives of anxiety-disordered children is significantly greater in mothers and sisters than in fathers and brothers (Last & Beidel, 1991). Mothers of anxiety-disordered children are particularly more likely to suffer from panic disorder or panic disorder with agoraphobia. The prevalence of childhood-onset anxiety disorders is also increased among mothers of anxiety-disordered children.

Increased rates of SAD have also been demonstrated in the siblings of children with SAD and in the offspring of women with anxiety or depressive disorders (Last & Beidel, 1991). Offspring of parents with panic disorder have been shown to have a threefold increased risk of SAD, while offspring of parents with panic disorder plus major depression have more than a tenfold increased risk (Weissman, Leckman, Merikangas, et al., 1984; Leckman, Weissman, Merikangas, et al., 1985). Agoraphobic women with an early history of SAD are more likely to have children with SAD than are agoraphobic women without a history of SAD.

The increased familial prevalence of the nosological forebears of panic disorder was noted as early as the mid-nineteenth century and was discussed by Freud in 1895 (Freud, 1895/1959; Noyes, Clancy, Crowe, et al., 1978; Cohen, Badal, Kilpatrick, et al., 1951). More recent studies have found a lifetime morbidity risk for first-degree relatives of individuals with panic disorder of 15 to 25%, with female relatives at higher risk than male relatives (Noyes, Crowe, Haris, et al., 1986; Marks, 1986). "Bottom-up" studies have found an increased prevalence of anxiety disorders, including panic disorder, among adult relatives of children and adolescents with anxiety disorders (Last & Strauss, 1989). "Top-down" studies have also found an increased prevalence of anxiety disorders, including panic disorder and separation anxiety disorder, among offspring of adult probands with panic disorder (Last & Beidel, 1991). Behavioral inhibition, a stable temperamental trait, is found in 85% of the offspring of parents with panic disorder and agoraphobia, compared to 15% of the offspring of nonpsychiatric controls (Biederman et al., 1993a). Behavioral inhibition in young children predicts increased risk for development of anxiety disorder during childhood (Biederman et al., 1993b).

Because only small numbers of children or adolescents with panic disorder have been included in these studies, the data are insufficient for drawing firm conclusions regarding the familial patterns of illness specific to children and adolescents with panic disorder (as opposed to all anxiety disorders). However, case reports of children and adolescents with panic disorder have also reported a high prevalence of panic disorder among the subjects' parents (Bradley & Hood, 1993; Moreau, Weissman, & Warner, 1989).

EPIDEMIOLOGY

Many published child and adolescent psychiatric epidemiological studies report rates of anxiety disorders without breakdown of the specific disorders. Studies that do give results for specific anxiety diagnoses vary in methodology and in the age range of the target samples. The reported prevalence of SAD in most studies is in the range of 3.5 to 5.4% (Anderson, Williams, McGee, et al., 1987; Costello, 1989b). The prevalence of reported SAD symptoms without significant impairment is much higher (up to 50% in 8-year-olds) (Kashani & Orvaschel, 1990). Some studies have reported a greater prevalence of SAD in girls compared to boys (Costello, 1989a; Last, Francis, et al., 1987; Anderson et al., 1987), while others have reported no differences between the sexes (Last et al., 1992; Bird, Gould, Yager, et al., 1989). Peak age at onset appears to be in middle childhood, around 7 to 9 years of age (Last et al., 1992; Bird et al., 1989), but the disorder may develop in adolescence as well. One study reported a prevalence in 14- to 16-year-olds of 1.3% (Kashani & Orvaschel, 1988). Lower family socioeconomic status and lower parental education level may be associated with a greater prevalence of the disorder (Bird et al., 1989; Velz, Johnson, & Cohen, 1989).

The lifetime prevalence of panic disorder in the general adult population is about 1.5%, and 6-month prevalence is about 1% (Myers, Weissman, Tischler, et al., 1984). In adults, the disorder is approximately two to three times more prevalent in females (Robins, Helzer, Weissman, et al., 1984). A direct interview study of a nonclinical sample of 5,108 high school students found a lifetime prevalence estimate for panic disorder of 0.6% (girls 0.7%, boys 0.4%) (Whitaker, Johnson, Shaffer, et al., 1990). Less than half of the cases identified had received treatment. The incidence of panic *attacks* (without development of full-blown panic disorder) in young adolescents is much greater and increases greatly with the onset of puberty (Hayward, Killen, & Taylor, 1989; Hayward, Killen, Hammer, et al., 1992).

The prevalence of panic attacks and panic disorder prior to puberty is unknown. However, numerous case reports have made it clear that the disorder does occur prior to puberty (Black & Robbins, 1990; Black et al., 1990; Moreau & Weissman, 1992; Vitiello, Behar, Wolfson, et al., 1990), while retrospective studies of adults with panic disorder have shown that onset during adolescence is common. In a group of 3,000 adults questioned retrospectively about age of onset of their disorder, the peak age of onset was between 15 and 20 years (von Korff, Eaton, & Keyl, 1985). In a retrospective chart review of a group of 62 adult patients with panic disorder without agoraphobia, the mean age of onset was 26.6 years, with 39% of patients reporting onset of symptoms prior to the age of 20 and 13% prior to the age of 10 (Thyer, Parrish, Curtis, et al., 1985). Among 95 patients with panic disorder with agoraphobia, the mean age of onset was 26.3 years, with 29% of these patients experiencing onset prior to age 20 and 4% prior to age 10. In another study, 30 of 100 patients with panic disorder with agoraphobia reported that their first panic attack occurred before the age of 20 and 6 before age 10 (Sheehan, Sheehan, & Minichiello, 1981).

Panic disorder is not uncommon among adolescents presenting to mental health clinicians. It seems to be less commonly diagnosed among children. This may be due to a low prevalence of the disorder in childhood or a missed diagnosis by clinicians or because children with panic disorder are not taken for treatment or are more commonly seen by pediatricians for evaluation of somatic complaints (Nelles & Barlow, 1988; Black & Robbins, 1990; Moreau & Follet, 1993; Joorabchi, 1977; Herman, Stickler, & Lucas, 1981; Herskowitz, 1986).

ASSESSMENT

The assessment of children and adolescents presenting with complaints suggesting a diagnosis of SAD or with panic attack symptoms is similar to the assessment of children with any other type of anxiety complaint. The American Academy of Child and Adolescent Psychiatry Practice Parameters for the Assessment of Anxiety Disorders in Children (American Academy of Child and Adolescent Psychiatry, 1993) provides a useful guide for comprehensive assessment. A variety of structured and semi-structured diagnostic interviews for parents and children are available (Edelbrock & Costello, 1988; Silverman & Nelles, 1988). In routine clinical practice these interviews are generally too long to be administered in their entirety. However, clinicians may find it useful to keep one or more standard interviews handy when interviewing anxious children or their parents and to routinely refer to selected sections of the interviews to clarify portions of the history, to assure a complete review of symptoms, and as an aid in differential diagnosis. General psychiatric symptom rating scales for completion by parents and teachers may also be useful (Gittelman, 1985b, 1985c; Achenbach, 1985). Anxiety symptom scales are available for parents, teachers, and self-rating by children, but they are generally of such poor validity and reliability that they are not clinically useful (Klein & Last, 1989; Klein, Koplewicz, Kanner, 1992).

Several points about the assessment of children with SAD bear special emphasis. First, when school refusal or avoidance is present, a very detailed understanding of how the school avoidance is manifested and how it has unfolded is essential to the development of a successful treatment plan. Exactly when and how did the school avoidance or refusal start? What did the child say? How did the parents respond to the child's complaints? How did the school respond? What have the parents or the school done to try to get the child back into school and how has the child responded to these efforts? What exactly is the current pattern? How does the child spend the day when not in school?

Second, because anxiety or mood disorders are common in the parents of children with SAD and may greatly complicate treatment of the child, a complete family history, assessment of current psychiatric symptoms in members of the immediate family, and assessment of current family functioning are essential (Bernstein, Svingen, & Garfinkel, 1990; Last, Hersen, Kazdin, et al., 1991).

When questioning children about panic attack symptoms, the developmental level of the child must, of course, be taken into consideration, and questions must be framed in simple, understandable terms. Children have a poor sense of time and poor memory for onset or course of symptoms, and may have difficulty distinguishing somatic symptoms from anxious cognitions (Nelles & Barlow, 1988). Children and adolescents with panic disorder and their parents characteristically present complaining of somatic symptoms, separation anxiety, generalized anxiety, specific phobias (e.g., choking or vomiting phobias), and behavioral symptoms rather than of panic attacks (Black & Robbins, 1990; Black et al., 1990; Moreau & Follet, 1993; Joorabchi, 1977; Herman et al., 1981; Herskowitz, 1986). The history of discrete panic attacks leading to secondary symptoms of avoidance, separation anxiety (often including school refusal), and generalized anxiety may become apparent only after careful questioning.

TREATMENT

There is little empirical research demonstrating the efficacy of any type of treatment for SAD. Cognitive and behavioral treatment have been shown to be effective in treating anxiety disorders in adults. Many case studies of successful cognitive or behavioral group treatment of children with SAD have appeared in the literature, but no controlled studies have been completed (Kendall, Chansky, Fridman, et al., 1991; Drobes & Strauss, 1993). However, the existing literature and broad clinical experience suggest that relatively straightforward behavioral treatment approaches will frequently be successful (R. G. Klein et al., 1992).

Benzodiazepines, tricyclic antidepressants, monoamine oxidase inhibitor antidepressants, and selective serotonin reuptake inhibitor antidepressants have all been shown to be useful in the treatment of adults with anxiety disorders, and all have been used in the treatment of children with SAD and other anxiety disorders (Kutcher, Reiter, Gardner, et al., 1992; Allen, Rapoport, & Swedo, 1993). In fact, benzodiazepines and tricyclic antidepressants seem to be commonly prescribed to children with SAD. Only imipramine, clomipramine, and alprazolam have been used in controlled treatment studies, and results have been inconclusive.

An early study of treatment with imipramine in 35 children with "school phobia" at doses of 100 to 200 mg/day found it to be significantly superior to placebo in inducing return to school and on global ratings of improvement (Klein & Gittelman-Klein, 1978). However, a later study of 21 children with SAD failed to find any difference in outcome between imipramine and placebo treatment groups (R. G. Klein et al., 1992). In this study, all subjects were first treated with a program of behavioral psychotherapy for 6 weeks and entered pharmacological treatment only if they continued to meet full DSM-III-R diagnostic criteria for SAD and to suffer significant impairment. It is noteworthy that 24 of 45 children originally considered for inclusion in the study did show enough response to

6 weeks of behavioral treatment that they were not eligible for inclusion in the drug treatment study. Of these 24, about half required no further treatment. The second study differed from the first in targeting children with SAD per se, rather than children with school refusal. Indeed, only 15 of the 21 subjects (71%) in the second study had symptoms of school refusal. Thus, it is possible that the subjects of the second study were less severely affected than the subjects of the first study. However, this did not seem to account for the disparity in results between the two studies, and otherwise the study designs, medication dosage, and length of treatment were similar.

A third controlled study compared three groups of children with school refusal treated with imipramine, alprazolam, or placebo (Bernstein, Garfinkel, & Borchardt, 1990). Only 14 of the 24 children entering the study were diagnosed with an anxiety disorder, and the number with SAD was not reported. Only 18 subjects completed 8 weeks of treatment. Statistically significant differences between groups in treatment response were not demonstrated. Because of the diagnostic heterogeneity of this group, as well as the small sample size and large baseline differences between groups, no conclusions can be drawn regarding the efficacy of these treatments for SAD.

Finally, a study of clomipramine treatment for school refusal did not find beneficial effects, but the doses may have been too low (Berney, Kolvin, Bhate, et al., 1981).

A number of open and controlled studies of benzodiazepines in anxiety-disordered children have reported beneficial results (Kutcher, Reiter, Gardner, et al., 1992; Simeon & Ferguson, 1987; Simeon, Ferguson, Knott, et al., 1992). Two uncontrolled studies of treatment of school refusal with chlordiazepoxide reported positive therapeutic effects (D'Amato, 1962; Kraft, 1965).

Antihistamine medications (mainly diphenhydramine and hydroxyzine) also have been commonly used to treat SAD and other anxiety conditions in children. None has been carefully studied. They probably do nothing more than sedate the child. Because of the lack of demonstrated antianxiety effects and because of potential side effects, they should not be used in the treatment of child and adolescent anxiety disorders.

Monoamine oxidase inhibitor antidepressants and selective serotonin uptake inhibitor antidepressants also have been used to treat children with anxiety disorders with some success reported (Allen et al., 1993). However, neither class of medications has been studied in children with SAD.

Based on the current scientific literature, no firm conclusions can be drawn regarding the usefulness of psychotropic medications in the treatment of children with SAD. Unfortunately, most of the studies cited used school refusal as the defining inclusion criteria rather than SAD. Furthermore, brief duration of treatment and small sample sizes hamper interpretation of all these studies.

For many cases of uncomplicated SAD of relatively brief duration (less than 2 to 4 months), simple instructions to parents and school staff regarding modifying environmental contingencies associated with the behavioral symptoms (particularly school refusal) may lead to a rapid decrease of symptoms. Clinical experience seems to demonstrate that the longer a school-refusing child is out of school, the more difficult it is to get him or her back. Therefore, when school refusal has been of relatively brief duration, treatment should always focus on achieving a prompt return to school.

What parents need most in these situations is ongoing support and reassurance from the clinician that appropriate limit setting is in the child's best interest, despite the child's apparent great distress. Assisting the parents and school to work together to plan and implement the return to school can also be valuable. Many children benefit from a supportive relationship with a psychotherapist, focused particularly on helping the child to identify and master negative affects and cognitions associated with separation. For more complicated, long-standing, or treatment-resistant cases, a carefully implemented program of behaviorial treatment including graduated *in vivo* exposure should generally be considered the treatment of choice for SAD. Medication should probably be reserved for persistently treatment-resistant cases or for children with comorbid conditions for which pharmacotherapy is indicated.

Current family psychopathology or family dysfunction can be a common cause of treatment failure with children with SAD. For example, a severely anxious or depressed mother may be unwilling to allow the child to separate or may have communicated to the child that she needs the child at home for protection or help. Thus, when family psychopathology or dysfunction does exist, it should always be treated concurrently.

A number of antidepressant medications and high-potency benzodiazepines have been shown to be effective in the treatment of panic disorder and agoraphobia in adults (Klein & Fink, 1962; Sheehan, 1985; Ballenger, Burrows, DuPont, et al., 1988; Liebowitz, 1989; Schneier, Liebowitz, Davies, et al., 1990; "Treatment of Panic Disorder," 1991). Case reports suggest that these medications are also effective in the treatment of children and adolescents with panic disorder (Black & Robbins, 1990; Black et al., 1990; Biederman, 1987; Kutcher & Mackenzie, 1988; Ballenger, Carey, & Steele, 1989). However, there have been no controlled treatment studies. Cognitive and behavioral treatments have also proven

⚡ effective in the treatment of adults with panic disorder (Treatment of Panic
Disorder, 1991; Barlow & Cerney, 1988; Beck, Sokol, Clark, et al., 1992),
but cognitive-behavioral treatment of panic disorder in children and adolescents has not been reported.

RELATIONSHIP BETWEEN SAD
AND PANIC DISORDER

Panic disorder and SAD may be related to one another in a number of
ways.

1. Symptomatically, the reactions that children with SAD demonstrate when they are separated from parents or anticipate separation may be characterized as panic attacks (Klein & Fink, 1962).
2. Children with SAD are at increased risk of developing panic disorder and agoraphobia as adults. Preliminary evidence suggests
   that many children with separation anxiety disorder are likely to
   develop panic disorder with agoraphobia during childhood
   (Biederman et al., 1993b).
3. A strong familial relationship between SAD and panic disorder has
   been demonstrated. Offspring of parents with panic disorder have
   more than a threefold increased risk of SAD (Weissman et al.,
   1984; Leckman et al., 1985), and agoraphobic women with an
   early history of SAD are more likely to have children with SAD
   than are agoraphobic women without a history of SAD.
4. The majority of children reported in the clinical literature with
   prepubertal onset of panic disorder also manifested symptoms of
   SAD, and the SAD symptoms were commonly the primary presenting symptoms. Likewise, a significant proportion of adolescents with panic disorder present with symptoms of SAD (Bradley & Hood, 1993).

   In fact, it is not uncommon for individuals with panic disorder at any
age to fear and avoid separation from attachment figures. For adults, these
are most commonly spouses, other relatives, or close friends but may be a
parent, while for children it is usually a parent. As previously suggested
by Black et al. (1990), SAD symptoms may develop in response to panic
attacks and may be viewed as "manifestations of agoraphobia, with specific features (e.g., fear of school, fear of not being able to contact a parent
in the event of a panic attack) that one might expect to see in an agoraphobic child" (p. 835). In fact, it is difficult to imagine how a child could
experience recurrent panic attacks and not develop full-blown symptoms

of SAD. The extreme distress that the child manifests when separation threatens or is imminent may be seen as a situationally predisposed panic attack.

A number of authors have suggested that panic disorder and SAD may be different clinical manifestations of a common underlying disorder (Klein, 1981; Black & Robbins, 1990). Others have gone further and proposed "a formal reformulation of separation anxiety or school phobia . . . as childhood versions of adult panic disorder or agoraphobia" (Abelson & Alessi, 1992, p. 115).

The following case examples illustrate the overlap between panic disorder and SAD.

Case Example 1

A 28-year-old woman presented complaining of panic attacks. The patient had experienced several uncued panic attacks over a 2-month period about 8 months prior to evaluation but then no further uncued attacks. However, for the last 6 months she had been experiencing panic attacks with increasing frequency whenever her husband (a resident physician) was required to work overnight (situationally predisposed panic attacks). At these times, in addition to typical panic symptoms, she reported fearing that her husband would die in an accident and that she would never see him again or that her 2-year-old child would die. She reported severe insomnia whenever her husband was away from home overnight. When she did sleep, she had nightmares that her husband or baby had been killed in an accident. When her husband was home, she was reluctant to be in a room alone and followed him around the house. With the exception of the requirement of onset of symptoms prior to age 18, she met DSM-IV diagnostic criteria for SAD.

The patient also reported a gradual increase in caffeine use over the last several years, to a current daily intake of 6 to 8 cups of coffee. She was advised to taper and discontinue use of caffeine. No other treatment was initiated. After 6 weeks, panic attacks and symptoms of separation anxiety had completely resolved.

Case Example 2

John was an 11-year-old boy with a history of intermittent anxiety and school reluctance since kindergarten but no prior history of overt school refusal and no prior psychiatric treatment. His father suffered from panic disorder and recurrent depression. While playing soccer on a warm spring day, John complained of feeling faint and then became distraught, crying and complaining that he felt he was dying. He had previously been an enthusiastic participant in sports. Following this event, he seemed to look forward to soccer games with his team and would go to the game site with his parents, but then he would tell his parents, "I don't feel well," hold his abdomen, appear frightened, cry, and refuse to play. He also became phobic of hot weather, refusing to go outside when it was too hot, and began to ask to sleep with his parents every night, again complaining, "I don't feel well."

John's pediatrician ordered an upper GI series, which was negative, then prescribed prochlorperazine to relieve nausea before soccer games, without any benefit. John went back to school in the fall without difficulty, but in November he began to call home in the middle of the day, complaining of "having the bad feelings" and wanting to go home. By February this behavior had intensified, and he began to refuse to go to school. Conflicts with his parents over school attendance led to tantrums, with screaming, crying, and turning over and breaking furniture. The pediatrician prescribed alprazolam without any apparent benefit.

In March, after several weeks out of school, John was seen by a child psychiatrist. He reported to the psychiatrist that his "bad feelings" were associated with nausea, dizziness, paresthesias, palpitations, and nervousness, and that "it scares me to be someplace without my parents 'cause I might get those feelings." A behavioral plan was implemented to accomplish a gradual return to school, starting with 5 minutes daily. Simultaneously, treatment with desipramine was begun at 25 mg daily amd gradually increased over 2 weeks to 125 mg daily (4 mg/kg). After 4 weeks all symptoms had resolved, John was spending all day in school without any complaints or signs of anxiety, and he had resumed full participation in soccer.

SUMMARY

SAD and panic disorder are anxiety disorders that appear to be relatively common among young people, may be associated with significant short-term morbidity and disability, and are associated with risk of anxiety disorder in adulthood. Although the prevalence of panic disorder prior to puberty is unclear, it may be more common than is generally appreciated in clinical settings. It is a common disorder in adolescence. The two disorders are closely related, and it appears likely that many children presenting with symptoms of SAD are in fact demonstrating an early manifestation of panic disorder. At the current time, no form of treatment has been empirically demonstrated to be effective for either disorder in this age group. Further research on the relationship between these two disorders and on treatment methods is needed.

REFERENCES

Abelson, J. L., & Alessi, N. E. (1992). Discussion of child panic revisited. *Journal of the American Academy of Child and Adolescent Psychiatry, 31*, 114–116.

Achenbach, T. M. (1985). Assessment of anxiety in children. In A. H. Tuma & J. Maser (Eds.), *Anxiety and the anxiety disorders* (pp. 707–734). Hillsdale, NJ: Erlbaum.

Alessi, N. E., & Magen, J. (1988). Panic disorder in psychiatrically hospitalized children. *American Journal of Psychiatry, 145*, 1450–1452.

Alessi, N. E., Robbins, D. R., & Dilsaver, S. C. (1987). Panic and depressive disorders among psychiatrically hospitalized adolescents. *Psychiatry Research, 20*, 275–283.

Allen, A. J., Rapoport, J. L., & Swedo, S. E. (1993). Psychopharmacologic treatment of childhood anxiety disorders. *Child and Adolescent Psychiatric Clinics of North America, 2*, 795–818.

American Academy of Child and Adolescent Psychiatry. (1993). Practice parameters for the assessment and treatment of anxiety disorders. *Journal of the American Academy of Child and Adolescent Psychiatry, 32*, 1089–1098.

American Psychiatric Association (1980). *Diagnostic and statistical manual of mental disorders* (3rd ed.). Washington, DC: Author.

American Psychiatric Association (1987). *Diagnostic and statistical manual of mental disorders* (3rd ed., rev.). Washington, DC: Author.

American Psychiatric Association. (1994). *Diagnostic and statistical manual of mental disorders* (4th ed.). Washington, DC: Author.

Anderson, J. C., Williams, S., McGee, R., et al. (1987). DSM-III disorders in preadolescent children. *Archives of General Psychiatry, 44*, 69–76.

Ballenger, J. C., Burrows, G. D., DuPont, R. L., et al. (1988). Alprazolam in panic disorder and agoraphobia: Efficacy in short-term treatment. *Archives of General Psychiatry, 45*, 413–422.

Ballenger, J. C., Carey, D. J., & Steele, J. J. (1989). Three cases of panic disorder with agoraphobia in children. *American Journal of Psychiatry, 146*, 922–925.

Barlow, D. H., & Cerney, J. A. (1988). *Psychological treatment of panic.* New York: Guilford Press.

Beck, A. T., Sokol, L., Clark, D. A., et al. (1992). A crossover study of focused cognitive therapy for panic disorder. *American Journal of Psychiatry, 149*, 778–783.

Berney, T., Kolvin, I., Bhate, S. R., et al. (1981). School phobia: A therapeutic trial with clomipramine and short-term outcome. *British Journal of Psychiatry, 138*, 110–118.

Bernstein, G. A., Garfinkel, B. D., & Borchardt, C. M. (1990). Comparative studies of pharmacotherapy for school refusal. *Journal of the American Academy of Child and Adolescent Psychiatry, 29*, 773–781.

Bernstein, G. A., Svingen, P. H., & Garfinkel, B. D. (1990). School phobia: Patterns of family functioning. *Journal of the American Academy of Child and Adolescent Psychiatry, 29*, 24–30.

Biederman, J. (1987). Clonazepam in the treatment of prepubertal children with panic-like symptoms. *Journal of Clinical Psychiatry, 48*(Suppl. 10), 38–42.

Biederman, J., Rosenbaum, J. F., Bolduc-Murphy, E. A., et al. (1993a). Behavioral inhibition as a temperamental risk factor for anxiety disorders. *Child and Adolescent Psychiatric Clinics of North America, 2*, 667–684.

Biederman, J., Rosenbaum, J. F., Bolduc-Murphy, E. A., et al. (1993b). A 3-year follow-up of children with and without behavioral inhibition. *Journal of the American Academy of Child and Adolescent Psychiatry, 32*, 814–821.

Bird, H. R., Gould, M. S., Yager, T., et al. (1989). Risk factors for maladjustment in Puerto Rican children. *Journal of the American Academy of Child and Adolescent Psychiatry, 28*, 847–850.

Black, B., & Robbins, D. R. (1990). Panic disorder in children and adolescents. *Journal of the American Academy of Child and Adolescent Psychiatry, 29*, 36–44.

Black, B., Uhde, T. W., & Robbins, D. R. (1990). Reply to D. F. Klein, R. G. Klein: Does panic disorder exist in childhood? [Letter]. *Journal of the American Academy of Child and Adolescent Psychiatry, 29*, 834–835.

Bowlby, J. (1973). *Separation: Anxiety and anger.* New York: Basic Books.

Bradley, S. J., & Hood, J. (1993). Psychiatrically referred adolescents with panic attacks: Presenting symptoms, stressors, and comorbidity. *Journal of the American Academy of Child and Adolescent Psychiatry, 32*, 826–829

Breier, A., Charney, D. S., & Heninger, G. R. (1986). Agoraphobia with panic attacks: Development, diagnostic stability, and course of illness. *Archives of General Psychiatry, 43*, 1029–1036.

Cantwell, D. P., & Baker, L. (1989). Stability and natural history of DSM-III childhood diagnoses. *Journal of the American Academy of Child and Adolescent Psychiatry, 28*, 691–700.

Casat, C. D. (1988). Childhood anxiety disorders: A review of the possible relationship to adult panic disorder and agoraphobia. *Journal of Anxiety Disorders, 2*, 51–60.

Cohen, M. E., Badal, D. W., Kilpatrick, A., et al. (1951). The high familial prevalence of neurocirculatory asthenia (anxiety neurosis, effort syndrome). *American Journal of Human Genetics, 3*, 126–158.

Costello, E. J. (1989a). Child psychiatric disorders and their correlates: A primary care pediatric sample. *Journal of the American Academy of Child and Adolescent Psychiatry, 28*, 851–855.

Costello, E. J. (1989b). Developments in child psychiatric epidemiology. *Journal of the American Academy of Child and Adolescent Psychiatry, 28*, 836–841.

D'Amato, G. (1962). Chlordiazepoxide in the management of school phobia. *Diseases of the Nervous System, 23*, 292–295.

Drobes, D. J., & Strauss, C. C. (1993). Behavioral treatment of childhood anxiety disorders. *Child and Adolescent Psychiatric Clinics of North America, 2*, 779–794.

Edelbrock, C., & Costello, A. J. (1988). Structured psychiatric interviews for children. In M. Rutter, A. H. Tuma, & I. S. Lann (Eds.), *Assessment and diagnosis in child psychopathology* (pp. 87–112). New York: Guilford Press.

Freud, S. (1955). Analysis of a phobia in a five-year-old boy. In J. Strachey (Ed.), *The standard edition of the complete psychological works of Sigmund Freud* (Vol. 10, pp. 1–149). London: Hogarth. (Original work published 1909)

Freud, S. (1959). On the grounds for detaching a particular syndrome from neurasthenia under the description "anxiety neurosis." In J. Strachey (Ed.), *The standard edition of the complete psychological works of Sigmund Freud* (Vol. 3, pp. 87–116). London: Hogarth. (Original work published 1895)

Gittelman, R. (1985a). Anxiety disorders in children. In B. B. Lahey & A. E. Kazdin (Eds.), *Advances in clinical child psychology* (Vol. 8, pp. 53–79). New York: Plenum Press.

Gittelman, R. (1985b). Parent's questionnaire (modified Conners): Anxiety and mood items added. *Psychopharmacology Bulletin, 21,* 939–943.

Gittelman, R. (1985c). Teacher rating scale (modified Conners): Anxiety and mood items added. *Psychopharmacology Bulletin, 21,* 945–948.

Gittelman, R., & Klein, D. F. (1985). Childhood separation anxiety and adult agoraphobia. In A. H. Tuma & J. Maser (Eds.), *Anxiety and the anxiety disorders* (pp. 389–402). Hillsdale, NJ: Erlbaum.

Hayward, C., Killen, J. D., Hammer, L. D., et al. (1992). Pubertal stage and panic attack history in sixth- and seventh-grade girls. *American Journal of Psychiatry, 149,* 1239–1243.

Hayward, C., Killen, J. D., Taylor, C. B. (1989). Panic attacks in young adolescents. *American Journal of Psychiatry, 146,* 1061–1062.

Herman, S., Stickler, G., & Lucas, A. (1981). Hyperventilation syndrome in children and adolescents: Long-term follow-up. *Pediatrics, 67,* 183–187.

Herskowitz, J. (1986). Neurological presentations of panic disorder in childhood and adolescence. *Developmental Medicine and Child Neurology, 28,* 617–623.

Joorabchi, B. (1977). Expressions of the hyperventilation syndrome in childhood. *Clinical Pediatrics, 16,* 1110–1115.

Kashani, J. H., & Orvaschel, H. (1988). Anxiety disorders in mid-adolescence. *American Journal of Psychiatry, 145,* 960–964.

Kashani, J. H., & Orvaschel, H. (1990). A community study of anxiety in children and adolescents. *American Journal of Psychiatry, 147,* 313–318.

Keller, M. B., & Baker, L. A. (1992). The clinical course of panic disorder and depression. *Journal of Clinical Psychiatry, 53*(Suppl. 3), 5–8.

Keller, M. B., Lavori, P. W., & Wunder, J., et al. (1992). Chronic course of anxiety disorders in children and adolescents. *Journal of the American Academy of Child and Adolescent Psychiatry, 31,* 595–599.

Kendall, P. C., Chansky, T. E., Fridman, M., et al. (1991). Treating anxiety disorders in children and adolescents. In P. C. Kendall (Ed.), *Child and adolescent therapy* (pp. 131–164). New York: Guilford Press.

Klein, D. F. (1964). Delineation of two drug responsive anxiety syndromes. *Psychopharmacologia, 5,* 397–408.

Klein, D. F. (1981). Anxiety reconceptualized. In D. F. Klein & J. Rabkin (Eds.), *Anxiety: New research and changing concepts* (pp. 235–263). New York: Raven.

Klein, D. F., & Fink, M. (1962). Psychiatric reaction patterns to imipramine. *American Journal of Psychiatry, 119,* 432–438.

Klein, D. F., & Gittelman-Klein, R. (1978). Drug treatment of separation anxious and depressive illness in children. *Advances in Biological Psychiatry*, 2, 50–60.

Klein, D. F., Mannuzza, S., & Chapman, T. (1992). Child panic revisited. *Journal of the American Academy of Child and Adolescent Psychiatry*, 31, 112–116.

Klein, D. F., Ross, D. C., Cohen, P. (1987). Panic and avoidance in agoraphobia. *Archives of General Psychiatry*, 44, 377–385.

Klein, R. G., Koplewicz, H. S., & Kanner, A. (1992). Imipramine treatment of children with separation anxiety disorder. *Journal of the American Academy of Child and Adolescent Psychiatry*, 31, 21–28.

Klein, R. G., & Last, C. G. (1989). *Anxiety disorders in children*. Newbury Park, CA: Sage.

Kovacs, M., Gatsonis, C., Paulauskas, S. L., et al. (1989). Depressive disorders in childhood: Vol. IV. A longitudinal study of comorbidity with and risk for anxiety disorders. *Archives of General Psychiatry*, 46, 776–782.

Kraft, I. (1965). A clinical study of chlordiazepoxide used in psychiatric disorders of childhood. *International Journal of Neuropsychiatry*, 1, 433–437.

Kutcher, S. P., & Mackenzie, S. (1988). Successful clonazepam treatment of adolescents with panic disorder. *Journal of Clinical Psychopharmacology*, 8, 299–300.

Kutcher, S. P., Reiter, S., Gardner, D. M., et al. (1992). The pharmacotherapy of anxiety disorders in children and adolescents. *Psychiatric Clinics of North America*, 15, 41–68.

Last, C. G., & Beidel, D. C. (1991). Anxiety. In M. Lewis (Ed.), *Child and adolescent psychiatry: A comprehensive textbook* (pp. 281–292). Baltimore: Williams & Wilkins.

Last, C. G., Francis, G., Hersen, M., et al. (1987). Separation anxiety and school phobia: A comparison using DSM-III criteria. *American Journal of Psychiatry*, 144, 653–657.

Last, C. G., Hersen, M., Kazdin, A. E., et al. (1987a). Comparison of DSM-III separation anxiety disorder and overanxious disorders: Demographic characteristics and patterns of comorbidity. *Journal of the American Academy of Child and Adolescent Psychiatry*, 26, 527–531.

Last, C. G., Hersen, M., Kazdin, A. E., et al. (1987b). Psychiatric illness in the mothers of anxious children. *American Journal of Psychiatry*, 144, 1580–1583.

Last, C. G., Hersen, M., Kazdin, A., et al. (1991). Anxiety disorders in children and their families. *Archives of General Psychiatry*, 48, 928–937.

Last, C. G., Perrin, S., Hersen, M., et al. (1992). DSM-III-R anxiety disorders in children: Sociodemographic and clinical characteristics. *Journal of the American Academy of Child Adolescent Psychiatry*, 31, 1070–1076.

Last, C. G., & Strauss, C. C. (1989). Panic disorder in children and adolescents. *Journal of Anxiety Disorders*, 3, 87–95.

Last, C. G., & Strauss, C. C. (1990). School refusal in anxiety disordered children and adolescents. *Journal of the American Academy of Child and Adolescent Psychiatry*, 29, 31–35.

Leckman, J. F., Weissman, M. M., Merikangas, K. R., et al. (1985). Major depression and panic disorder. *Psychopharmacology Bulletin, 21*, 543–545.

Liebowitz, M. R. (1989). Tricyclic antidepressants and monoamine oxidase inhibitors in the treatment of panic disorder: Brief review. *Psychopharmacology Bulletin, 25*, 17–20.

Macaulay, J. L., & Kleinknecht, R. A. (1989). Panic and panic attacks in adolescents. *Journal of Anxiety Disorders, 3*, 221–241.

Marks, I. M. (1986). Genetics of fear and anxiety. *British Journal of Psychiatry, 149*, 406–418.

Moreau, D., & Follet, C. (1993). Panic disorder in children and adolescents. *Child and Adolescent Psychiatric Clinics of North America, 2*, 581–602.

Moreau, D., & Weissman, M. M. (1992). Panic disorder in children and adolescents: A review. *American Journal of Psychiatry, 149*, 1306–1314.

Moreau, D. M., Weissman, M. M., & Warner, V. (1989). Panic disorder in children at high risk for depression. *American Journal of Psychiatry, 146*, 1059–1060.

Myers, J. K., Weissman, M. M., Tischler, G. L., et al. (1984). Six-month prevalence of psychiatric disorders in three communities. *Archives of General Psychiatry, 41*, 959–967.

Nelles, W. B., & Barlow, D. H. (1988). Do children panic? *Clinical Psychology Review, 8*, 359–372.

Noyes, R., Clancy, J., Crowe, R., (1978). The familial prevalence of anxiety neurosis. *Archives of General Psychiatry, 35*, 1057–1059.

Noyes, R., Crowe, R. R., Haris, E. L., et al. (1986). Relationship between panic disorder and agoraphobia: A family study. *Archives of General Psychiatry, 43*, 227–232.

Pollack, M. H., Otto, M. W., Rosenbaum, J. F., et al. (1992). Personality disorders in patients with panic disorder: Association with childhood anxiety disorders, early trauma, comorbidity, and chronicity. *Comprehensive Psychiatry, 33*, 78–83.

Robins, L. N., Helzer, J. E., Weissman, M. M., et al. (1984). Lifetime prevalence of specific psychiatric disorders in three sites. *Archives of General Psychiatry, 41*, 949–958.

Roy-Byrne, P., Geraci, M., & Uhde, T. W. (1986). Life events and the onset of panic disorder. *American Journal of Psychiatry, 143*, 1424–1427.

Ryan, N. D., Puig-Antich, J., Ambrosini, P., et al. (1987). The clinical picture of major depression in children and adolescents. *Archives General Psychiatry, 44*, 854–861.

Schneier, F. R., Liebowitz, M. R., Davies, S. O., et al. (1990). Fluoxetine in panic disorder. *Journal of Clinical Psychopharmacology, 10*, 119–121.

Sheehan, D. V., Sheehan, K. E., Minichiello, W. E. (1981). Age of onset of phobic disorders: A reevaluation. *Comprehensive Psychiatry, 22*, 544–553.

Silverman, W. K., & Nelles, W. B. (1988). The anxiety disorders interview schedule for children. *Journal of the American Academy of Child and Adolescent Psychiatry, 27*, 772–778.

Simeon, J. G., & Ferguson, H. B. (1987). Alprazolam effects in children with anxiety disorders. *Canadian Journal Psychiatry, 32*, 570–574.

Simeon, J. V., Ferguson, H. B., Knott, V., et al. (1992). Clinical, cognitive, and neurophysiological effects of alprazolam in children and adolescents with overanxious and avoidant disorders. *Journal of American Academy of Child and Adolescent Psychiatry, 31,* 29–33.

Suomi, S. J., Kraemer, G. W., Baysinger, C. M., et al. (1981). Inherited and experiential factors associated with individual differences in anxious behavior displayed by rhesus monkeys. In D. F. Klein & J. Rabkin (Eds.), *Anxiety: New research and changing concepts* (pp. 179–199). New York: Raven.

Thyer, B. A., Parrish, R. T., Curtis, G. C., et al. (1985). Ages of onset of DSM-III anxiety disoders. *Comprehensive Psychiatry, 26,* 113–122.

Treatment of panic disorder. (1991, September 26–27). *NIH Consensus Development Conference Consensus Statement, 9*(2).

Velz, C. N., Johnson, J., & Cohen, P. (1989). A longitudinal analysis of selected risk factors for childhood psychopathology. *Journal of the American Academy of Child and Adolescent Psychiatry, 28,* 861–864.

Vitiello, B., Behar, D., Wolfson, S., et al. (1990). Diagnosis of panic disorder in prepubertal children. *Journal of the American Academy of Child and Adolescent Psychiatry, 29,* 782–784.

von Korff, M. R., Eaton, W. W., & Keyl, P. M. (1985). The epidemiology of panic attacks and panic disorder. *American Journal of Epidemiology, 122,* 970–981.

Weissman, M. M. (1989, May 6). *The epidemiology of panic disorder in adolescents: Implications for diagnosis.* Paper presented at the Annual Meeting of the American Society for Adolescent Psychiatry, San Francisco, CA.

Weissman, M. M., Leckman, J. F., Merikangas, K. R., et al. (1984). Depression and anxiety disorders in parents and children: Results from the Yale family study. *Archives of General Psychiatry, 41,* 845–852.

Whitaker, A., Johnson, J., Shaffer, D., et al. (1990). Uncommon troubles in young people: Prevalence estimates of selected psychiatric disorders in a nonreferred adolescent population. *Archives of General Psychiatry, 47,* 487–496.

World Health Organization. (1980). *The International Classification of Diseases, 9th revision, Clinical Modification (ICD-9-CM).* Washington, DC: Author.

Chapter 10

Selective Mutism

Henrietta Leonard
Sara Dow

T he inclusion of selective mutism in this volume on childhood anxiety disorders represents a change in understanding and studying this unusual and interesting phenomenon. Although selective mutism is classified under "other disorders of childhood" and not as an anxiety disorder in the fourth edition of the *Diagnostic and Statistical Manual of Mental Disorders* (American Psychiatric Association, 1994), current investigations are reevaluating this determination. With the increasing focus on the continuity of anxiety disorders from childhood to adulthood, this phenomenon deserves systematic reevaluation. This chapter reviews the recent reconceptualization of selective mutism in the context of both the early literature and future lines of study.

HISTORY, MODELS, AND ETIOLOGY

Elective or selective mutism was first identified by Kussmaul (1877) as "aphasia voluntaria," although it received little subsequent attention. The term "elective mutism," was used by Tramer (1934) to describe the behavior of children who spoke only in certain situations or only to certain people. Hesselman (1983) suggested that the term "selective mutism" was more descriptive, and this term replaced "elective mutism" in the change from DSM-III-R to DSM-IV (American Psychiatric Association, 1987, 1994).

In reviewing the last 100 years of literature, it appears that the diagnosis of elective mutism described a heterogeneous population. Historically, the disorder was attributed to a response to an early trauma, to a change of environment, or to a manifestation of intrapersonal and family dynamics (Wright, 1985). More recently, selective mutism has been seen as a manifestation of an anxiety disorder, and it is this conceptualization that is under study.

The cause of selective mutism is unknown and probably is multifactorial, as well as differing between individuals. In 1980, Hayden described five different subtypes, and these serve to help understand both different approaches and possible etiologies. Only the subtype "biological mutism," where mutism is a secondary consequence of another disorder (such as autism or deafness) would be excluded under current diagnostic criteria.

Hayden's (1980) first subtype, "symbiotic mutism," suggested that the phenomenon could be explained by the nature of the relationship between the patient and the (enmeshed) mother, where the child uses a "clinging, shy, and sensitive exterior" to manipulate and control her (the child's) environment (p. 123). In the second subtype, "passive–aggressive mutism," the child's "defiant refusal to speak" is a manifestation of her hostility (p. 126). Clearly, ideas of the older literature predominated—the "enmeshed mother," the "oppositional child"—but such were the explanations for most childhood psychiatric symptoms at the time. The third subtype, "reactive mutism," was felt to be the consequence of a traumatic event, such as starting school, emigration, hospitalization, severe or prolonged illness, and early psychological or physical traumatic experiences (which would include physical and sexual abuse). The fourth subtype, "speech phobic mutism," was characterized by the "active fear of hearing one's own voice" (p. 124); this might mirror what socially phobic adults report.

The recent reconceptualization of selective mutism as an anxiety disorder stemmed from several lines of observation. Historically, many reports noted that electively mute children were shy and timid, and Wilkins (1985) wrote that the mutism might be a manifestation of an "underlying anxiety state or depressive equivalent" (p. 202). Certainly the majority of selectively mute children evaluated at the National Institute of Mental Health (NIMH) appeared to be excessively shy and did not have an oppositional quality to their silence (Leonard & Topol, 1993). Second, shyness and reserve have been reported as characteristic of the families of children with selective mutism (Hayden, 1980; Kolvin & Fundudis, 1981; Wergeland, 1979; Wright, 1968), and systematic research has documented the familial transmission of other anxiety disorders (Last, Phillips, & Statfeld, 1987; Weissman, Leckman, Merikangas, et al., 1984).

Research on the biological components of temperament merits specific attention. One model for childhood anxiety, "behavioral inhibition to the unfamiliar," has identified children who are "inhibited" (Biederman, Rosenbaum, Bolduc-Murphy, et al., 1993). These children are identifiable between 2 and 3 years of age, resist challenging or new situations, have a characteristic autonomic nervous system response to foreign (stressful) situations, and are at increased risk for subsequent anxiety disorders (Biederman et al., 1993). Whether selectively mute children are temperamentally inhibited has not yet been studied.

The hypothesis that there is a relationship between selective mutism and either social phobia or panic disorder was first posited by Crumley in 1990. A 20-year follow-up case report of an electively mute child (who had not spoken at all in school until the sixth grade) reported that the patient continued to have great anxiety about facing people and avoided social settings. Crumley noted that it was "difficult to decide which was more the object of fear, the panic or the social scrutiny" and concluded that "future research may show it to be an uncommon manifestation of common familiar disorders" (p. 319). Later that year, Golwyn and Weinstock (1990) described the first successful pharmacologic treatment of an electively mute child, and reported a dramatic clinical response to phenelzine. The child had elective mutism and "associated shyness." Her father had panic disorder that responded to phenelzine. "Her response to pharmacologic treatment for social phobia, her family history of panic disorder, and the shyness and anxiety reported in the selective mutism literature raise nosologic questions about selective mutism and its relationship to social phobia and the anxiety disorders" (p. 385). In our clinic, it was not unusual for the children to have either specifically told their parents—or the parents had no difficulty surmising—that they were afraid to speak in public or to have others hear their voice. Subsequently, Black and Uhde (1992) and Leonard and Topol (1993) have continued to investigate the efficacy of pharmacologic treatments in selectively mute children.

Alternatively, selective mutism may perhaps be viewed as an obsessive-compulsive spectrum disorder: It is difficult to separate the concept of an obsessive fear of speaking from the anxiety involved in doing so. Hayden (1980) reported that some of his patients had ritualistic behavior that would "nullify the effects of the speech, so that they could start talking, keep talking, or talk only about the right things"—although he did not label the behavior as obsessive per se. Several of the selectively mute children evaluated in our clinic had a comorbid obsessive–compulsive disorder (OCD) diagnosis at evaluation, although comorbid selective mutism has not previously been diagnosed in children with primary OCD (Swedo, Rapoport, Leonard, et al, 1989). This line of research continues in the NIMH investigations.

In conclusion, selective mutism is under systematic study at several sites around the country, and from these studies a better understanding of the neurobiology, etiology, and diagnostic classification should emerge.

PHENOMENOLOGY

Parents of a selectively mute child typically report that the child speaks loudly and freely at home but "doesn't say one word at school." The extent to which a selectively mute child speaks varies greatly. Characteristically, the selectively mute child converses freely at home, and some speak in very specific and familiar social situations. Selectively mute children usually do not speak out loud in public where either strangers or less well-known people might hear; thus they will not order food from a waitress or speak with a clerk in a store. However, there are some who speak to strangers in stores and restaurants but persistently do not speak at school or to people who know them. Some children are able to have long conversations with people on the telephone with whom they do not converse in person. There is usually a distinct hierarchy of people to whom the child does and does not speak.

Some individuals who have recovered from selective mutism recall that they were afraid to speak in public or to have others hear their voice. It is not unusual for a child to speak to a best friend in one of their homes but not at school where others might hear his or her voice. Usually parents report that their child "has always been this way" but that they thought the child would outgrow the behavior. Thus, most selectively mute children are not clinically identified until they start either preschool or kindergarten.

Only two systematic reports have compared selectively mute children with contrasting populations. Kolvin and Fundudis (1981) compared 24 electively mute children with a group of speech-retarded children ($n = 84$) and their matched control group ($n = 102$). Wilkins (1985) compared the case notes of 24 children with selective mutism to 24 matched controls with diagnoses of "emotional disorders." The largest case descriptions have included 68 (Hayden, 1980), 27 (Parker, Olsen, & Throckmorton, 1960), 24 (Kolvin & Fundudis, 1981; Wilkins, 1985; Wright, 1968), 21 (Lowenstein, 1979), 20 (Krohn, Weckstein, & Wright, 1992), and 11 children (Wergeland, 1979). Several comprehensive reviews of selective mutism are available (Kratochwill, Brody, & Piersel, 1979, Kratochwill, 1981; Wright, 1985; Leonard & Topol, 1993), and Tancer's (1992) paper serves as an excellent tabular compilation of the literature from the past 15 years.

DIFFERENTIAL DIAGNOSIS

Selective mutism is currently classified in DSM-IV (American Psychiatric Association, 1994) under "Disorders Usually First Diagnosed in Infancy, Childhood, or Adolescence." As to whether systematic research will ultimately recommend that the disorder be classified as an anxiety disorder remains to be determined.

Selective mutism is characterized in DSM-IV by the "consistent failure to speak in specific social situations (in which there is an expectation for speaking, e.g., at school) despite speaking in other situations" (p. 115). The disorder must interfere with educational or occupational functioning or with social communication. The symptoms must have been present for at least a month and cannot be limited to the first month of school.

Generally speaking, in diagnosing selective mutism one would want to distinguish between selective mutism and a developmental disorder or another psychiatric disorder in which mutism is a secondary condition, such as autism, schizophrenia, deafness, and aphonia. In mental retardation, pervasive developmental disorder, and other developmental disorders (including severe expressive language disorder), the child may physically but not psychologically have difficulty in speaking.

The DSM-IV diagnostic criteria state that the symptoms must not be able to be "better accounted for by a Communication Disorder (e.g. Stuttering)" (American Psychiatric Association, 1994, p. 115). It is not known what the rate of either expressive or receptive language disorders is in the selectively mute population, but one would want to rule out any significant difficulty that might secondarily contribute to the child's difficulty and/or self-consciousness about speaking. An expressive or receptive language disability can be diagnosed in addition to the selective mutism, if both are present.

Assigning the diagnosis is more complicated in children from immigrant families who may not wish to speak in the new language or who have had some difficulty in learning two languages early in life. In these cases, the mutism may be due to a lack of knowledge rather than a fear of speaking. According to DSM-IV, the selective mutism diagnosis should not be assigned if there is a "lack of knowledge of, or comfort with, the spoken language required in the social situation" (p. 114).

Excessive shyness or timidity may be mistaken for selective mutism; distinguishing between them is difficult, because selectively mute children are characteristically shy. Comorbid anxiety disorders (social phobia, generalized anxiety disorder, OCD) may be assigned if those diagnostic criteria are met.

RELATED FEATURES

Children with selective mutism have been consistently described as excessively shy (Hayden, 1980; Kolvin & Fundudis, 1981; Wergeland, 1979). The children are "particularly sensitive, shy, afraid of everything strange or new" (Wergeland, 1979, p. 219), and "fearfulness, phobias, and nervous habits [are] extremely common" (Hayden, 1980, p. 128). Although the literature makes frequent reference to the "negativistic, oppositional, controlling and manipulative" stance of these children (Krohn et al., 1992, p. 711), it is our impression that the children are "unable" to speak in the specific social setting; it is anxiety rather than an oppositional stance that inhibits their ability to speak.

Comorbidity with other anxiety disorders has not been systematically assessed, but it is probably common. Some reported associated diagnoses have included depression (Wilkins, 1985), hysteria (Lowenstein, 1979), obsessive–compulsive behaviors (Hayden, 1980; Kolvin & Fundudis, 1981; Wergeland, 1979), and enuresis and/or encopresis (Kolvin & Fundudis, 1981; Wilkins, 1985). The references to obsessive–compulsive behaviors are particularly interesting. Hayden (1980) reported that 18% (12 of 68) of the children in his study had obsessive-compulsive behaviors such as "having things just so" and "lining all the papers up a certain way" (p. 124). Wergeland (1979, p. 221) noted "clear tendencies toward compulsion-neurosis in six" of 11 children, while Kolvin and Fundudis (1981) noted that 2 of 24 (8%) were "seriously obsessional" (p. 226). Whether some of these children have an obsessive fear of hearing their own voice or embarrassing themselves remains to be determined and merits further study.

Some reports described comorbidity of language disorders in children with selective mutism, although none documented systematic speech or language assessment (Kolvin & Fundudis, 1981; Wilkins, 1985; Wright, 1968). Kolvin and Fundudis (1981) found that 12 of 24 (50%) of the children evaluated in their selective mutism clinic had normal hearing but "immaturities of speech and/or other speech difficulties," a percentage the authors estimated to be high compared to the general population. It is still not known what percentage of selectively mute children may have an underlying speech or language difficulty, but this should be specifically evaluated both in individuals and in systematic studies.

EPIDEMIOLOGY, DEMOGRAPHICS, AND NATURAL HISTORY

Although it has been over 100 years since selective mutism was first identified, the literature is limited and has described a diverse group of children. The age of onset is usually 3 to 6 years (Wright, 1985); 70% are referred for diagnosis and treatment during their kindergarten years (Parker et al., 1960). Boys in Hayden's (1980) study were referred an average of 2.3 years earlier than girls, a finding the author attributed to the greater tolerance of reticent behavior in females. Selective mutism is generally thought, however, to be more common in girls than in boys (Hayden, 1980), with a reported ratio of about 3:1 (Wergeland, 1979).

Although selective mutism is considered to be a rare disorder, it may actually be more prevalent, since most cases do not come to medical attention and do resolve with age. Prevalence estimates have ranged from 0.08% (Fundudis, Kolvin, & Garside, 1979) to 0.7% (Brown & Lloyd, 1975). In one of the few epidemiological studies (Fundudis et al., 1979), only 2 (0.08%) selectively mute children were identified in a total city cohort of 3,300 7-year old children. Brown and Lloyd (1975) reported that only 0.7% (42 of 6,072) of the 5-year-olds they studied were not speaking 8 weeks after starting first grade. This suggests that selective mutism in the young child entering school may be transient and resolved on its own. However, in a small percentage the diagnosis and disability is ongoing.

The majority of cases "outgrow" the disorder, although it is not known whether remnants of shyness or anxiety persist. Certainly, most parents can be reassured that the child will outgrow it, although it is not uncommon for the disorder to persist for several years in elementary school. Since some treatments for this disorder appear to be effective, one could argue that interventions might shorten its course.

With the natural course of the illness characterized by spontaneous remissions, it is difficult to assess follow-up reports. Friedman and Karagan (1973) asserted that long-term improvement occurs despite no apparent immediate gains. Wright (1968) reported that at 6-month to 7-year follow-ups for 19 of an initial 24 children, all of the children were talking; 21% (n = 4) were evaluated as having had excellent response, 58% (n = 11) as good, 16% (n = 3) as fair, and 5% (n = 1) as poor (Wright, 1968). Others have reported less optimistic outcomes. Kolvin and Fundudis's (1981) 5- to 10-year follow-up of 24 selectively mute children suggested a poor outcome; only 46% (11 of 24) of the sample showed improvement. They concluded that those who fail to improve by 10 years of age are suffering from a more intractable form of selective mutism.

As a clinician, one might reassure the families of selectively mute children that in the majority of cases the symptoms resolve. However, children with symptoms lasting more than 6 months should be evaluated and treated. Most clinicians would assume that the best prognosis would require early diagnosis and treatment.

ASSESSMENT

Any child with selective mutism should provide a complete medical history and have a physical examination. The assessor should ask about a history of recurrent ear infections and perform a screening hearing examination. Neurological examination should note any "soft signs" or motor delays. A developmental history of motor, language, cognitive, and social milestones should be obtained, which includes the prenatal and perinatal periods. Questions about the child's speech should assess articulation, understanding, and fluency and find out if the child stutters or repeats sounds.

A complete psychiatric assessment for comorbid diagnoses should be completed. Issues of temperament, including quality of inhibition and social interactions, are important to explore. Is the child interested in social relationships and does the child have friends to whom he or she speaks? Often, the child will have several friends whom he or she speak with at home but not in school. Does the child still socially interact and is the child part of the group in school, even if he or she does not speak?

Cognitive and academic skills should also be assessed; typically psychological testing is indicated to formally evaluate these skills. Formal speech and language assessments should also be completed. Parents can audiorecord the child's voice at home for use by the speech therapist in assessing expressive skills. Receptive (comprehension), expressive, verbal, and nonverbal language and oral–motor performance should be noted.

Although there have been occasional reports of selective mutism following an early hospitalization or trauma, evaluations of the patients in our clinic have not suggested that selective mutism is caused by trauma. Certainly, a careful history should be taken, but parents of selectively mute children should not be assumed to be abusing their children. Parents have related stories of how mental health and school systems have confronted them about "presumed abuse." These unfortunate accusations appear to stem from the paucity of available information and the misunderstandings about selective mutism in both the general and the psychiatric communities.

TREATMENT

Historically, treatment for selective mutism has included a variety of behavioral and individual and/or family psychodynamic psychotherapy approaches. Krohn and colleagues' (1992) review reported only five treatment studies that included more than 10 cases (Brown, Wilson, & Laybourne, 1963; Wergeland, 1979; Parker et al., 1960; Kolvin & Fundudis, 1981; Wright, 1968); thus, case reports predominate. For further reading, the reader is referred to several excellent reviews of the treatment literature (Kratochwill et al., 1979; Kratochwill, 1981; Wright, 1985).

Although selective mutism may be difficult to treat (Kolvin & Fundudis, 1981), early intervention has been hypothesized to prevent secondary problems with socializing and learning (Wright, 1968). Wright (1985) recommended that all children with a history of selective mutism longer than 6 months should be referred for treatment. Generally, the literature has suggested that a behavioral approach, either with or without family intervention, is more effective than more traditional dynamic interventions (Kratochwill, 1981; Wright, 1985). Currently, a multidisciplinary approach is often considered, and pharmacotherapy may be indicated.

COGNITIVE-BEHAVIORAL THERAPY

Cognitive-behavioral therapy is generally the first and primary intervention for selective mutism, although it is time consuming and requires the full cooperation of parents, teachers, and other school professionals. Treatment approaches are built around the concept that for the child, anxiety itself about talking inhibits speaking (negatively reinforces the behavior) and that not speaking reduces the anxiety. Labbe and Williamson (1984) noted that most behavioral treatments have used one of two theoretical approaches: either helping the child to recover from anxiety about talking or positively reinforcing the child for speaking. Reed (1963) recommended that the distinction should be made as to whether the mutism is maintained by social reinforcement or by avoiding the anxiety generated by speaking.

Wright (1985) highlighted several principles for treatment. First, the intervention should be in the context of a small group of speaking peers and adults. This "safe" environment uses both peer pressure and peer and adult role models. Second, the staff should be reminded to avoid reinforcing the mutism. Specifically, the staff should maintain "an attitude of expectation of speech and positively reinforce every effort the child makes to speak" (Colligan, Colligan, & Dillard, 1977, p. 10). Third, the family should be involved in the treatment.

Other approaches are based on positively rewarding the desired behavior and encouraging the child to escape or avoid a negative situation by talking. Initially, a behavioral treatment plan might have nonverbal social interactions as the goals and then, as the child becomes part of the group, move on to speaking goals. Thus, one would hope to decrease social anxiety and encourage social interactions. Obviously, small, manageable, incremental goals are important (e.g., raising one's hand, whispering to the teacher). It is a mistake to expect a child to speak loudly in front of others in the beginning of the behavioral plan; the child is likely to be overwhelmed and fail.

Although the long-term outcome of behavioral treatment of selective mutism is not well studied, single-case studies abound (Albert-Stewart, 1986; Cunningham, Cataldo, Mallion, et al, 1983). Krohn (1992) described a behavioral approach using a combination of empathic dynamic interventions, firm behavioral expectations, and close family and school involvement. The reader is directed to some excellent reviews of the literature on behavioral therapy for further details (Labbe & Williamson, 1984; Sanok & Ascione, 1979; Reed, 1963; Kratochwill et al., 1979; Cunningham et al., 1983).

Psychodynamic Psychotherapy

Psychodynamic theories have been based on the hypothesis that the symptom is a manifestation of intrapsychic conflict. Thus the disorder might represent a regression to a preverbal stage of development, a behavior that would compromise separation/individuation, or a manifestation of angry or manipulative affect (Browne et al., 1963). Psychodynamic treatments have focused on identifying the underlying conflict, and typically play therapy and sometimes art therapy were utilized because they enabled the child to express feelings nonverbally. The therapist might also try to involve other family members in the therapeutic process, and family psychotherapy may be needed in specific cases. The majority of the family therapy case reports, as well as the integrated treatment modality reports, emphasize the importance of family involvement in the treatment plan. Meyers (1984) serves as a source for the review of the family therapy literature.

Browne and colleagues (1963) and Wergeland (1979) described 10 and 11 cases, respectively, of electively mute children treated with a psychodynamic approach, and they concluded that the treatment was lengthy and the outcome poor. Psychodynamic therapy would not typically be recommended as the major intervention for the primary symptom, however the modality may provide a supportive role in understanding and encouraging social interaction and addressing any family issues unique to that child.

Psychosocial Interventions

Psychosocial interventions are important components of the treatment plan. In general, efforts to coerce the child to speak are unsuccessful and may make the situation worse as they further increase the child's anxiety. Successful efforts focus on involving the child in peer group activities, emphasizing verbal skills when the child does talk, and encouraging home visits by relatives and friends. Parents should identify several friends who can be regular playmates and should arrange after-school play dates. An increasing number of social interactions and relationships with classmates may indirectly decrease stresses in the classroom. Additionally, the child should be encouraged to partake in nonverbal relationships with adults, to answer questions that require merely a one-word answer, and to participate in nonthreatening activities with strangers.

Of specific note, selectively mute children should remain in a regular classroom and should not be placed in emotionally disturbed or special education classrooms. An individualized behavioral treatment plan can be implemented in a regular classroom setting without great difficulty. Practically, the behavior modification program could be designed by the teacher, speech therapist, and school psychologist. (The reader is referred to Calhoun & Koenig, 1973, for a discussion of classroom modification of selective mutism.) A speech therapist can play an ongoing and unique role in providing a full speech and language workup and implementing treatment in school that might include pragmatically based small group interactions.

Psychopharmacology

The literature on pharmacotherapy for the treatment of selective mutism is preliminary at this point, although interest in this intervention is increasing. In 1990, Golwyn and Weinstock (1990) reported a single case of a 7-year-old girl with a 2-year history of elective mutism and "associated shyness" who responded to phenelzine (at doses up to 2 mg/kg/day) and at 16 weeks spoke freely to others. The phenelzine was tapered and discontinued by week 24, and at 5-month follow-up, the girl was still talking. Black and Uhde (1992) described a 12-year-old girl with elective mutism associated with "social anxiety" who had never spoken a word in school. After failing to respond to placebo or to 10 weeks of desipramine (at doses up to 200 mg/day), she had a good response to fluoxetine (20 mg/day). At 4 weeks, when she returned to school in the fall, she spoke freely for the first time, and follow-up at 7 months (assumably still on medication) noted that her social communication and interactions were normal. Both Golwyn and Weinstock (1990) and Black and Uhde (1992) concluded that the responses to pharmacologic agents for social phobia raised nosologic issues about the relationship of selective mutism to social phobia and other anxiety disorders.

Currently, several sites are systematically investigating the safety and efficacy of various serotonin reuptake inhibitors (SRIs) in the treatment of selective mutism. A recent report of a controlled trial suggested that fluoxetine may be effective for selective mutism (Black & Uhde, 1994). Fluoxetine is approved by the Federal Food and Drug Administration for the treatment of depression in adults, and some pediatric safety and efficacy data are available on its use in treatment of OCD in children and adolescents (Riddle, Scahill, King, et al., 1992).

Despite the limited data on the pharmacotherapy of selective mutism, it would seem reasonable to treat it as an anxiety disorder. Whether one conceptualized it as a childhood form of social phobia, another anxiety disorder, or an obsessive-compulsive spectrum disorder, a SRI would be the logical first pharmacotherapeutic intervention. Fluoxetine and any of the other SRIs offer advantages over phenelzine (a monoamine oxidase inhibitor), which requires dietary restrictions and concern about hypertensive crisis. At this point, no evidence supports trials in selectively mute children of other medications that have been used at times to treat social phobia in adults (e.g., beta-adrenergic blockers). Thus, although the SRIs may eventually play a role in the treatment of selective mutism, response alone does not permit us to conclude anything about the nosology of selective mutism: Drug efficacy does not validate a diagnosis.

In summary, we concur with others (Black & Uhde, 1992; Golwyn & Weinstock, 1990) that a trial of fluoxetine or another SRI (or phenelzine after the SRIs have been tried) should be considered when the symptoms of selective mutism are of long duration or cause significant impairment or if other treatments have been unsuccessful. Clearly further research, particularly controlled studies with long-term outcome evaluations, are required to answer these questions, but preliminary evidence is promising.

CASE EXAMPLE

K. M. is 5 years and 10 months old, in kindergarten, and was brought to us by her parents for evaluation because she did not speak at school to teachers or to peers and had not done so during her two previous years in preschool. Two years ago, K. M. had difficulties being left at preschool, and it took about two months before she could be left without crying. Although she does not talk to the other children, she interacts with them and participates in school activities. She has several friends whom she seems to like and whom she talks about at home. She has two friends in the neighborhood whom she speaks to. She speaks openly to all family members at home but does not speak to them in public if others might hear her.

K. M. says that she does not know why she does not talk, but she has told her mother that she feels "scared." Her mother describes her as shy and as a "worrier." She sometimes is afraid to go into another room by herself, and she is petrified of storms. No specific traumatic or abusive events in K. M.'s life could be identified. Her parents note that she internalizes her worries. They report that the shyness interferes with her making friends, although she has always had one or two special friends.

Developmental history was remarkable for a series of middle-ear infections that required tube placement. She did not consistently speak words until 2 years of age, but when her mother brought this to the pediatrician's attention, a tympanogram done at the time was normal. K. M.'s parents report that she speaks clearly with normal volume and fluency and without articulation difficulties. Her mother is not aware of any specific comprehension difficulties.

On evaluation, K. M. was alert and paid close attention to the questions. She appeared uncomfortable and did not smile at all. She would on occasion shake her head (yes or no) in response to a question, and she clung closely to her parents for most of the examination. Her mood appeared anxious. On psychological testing on the Leiter Performance Scale, she scored at the 6-year 9-months age when she was chronologically 5 years and 10 months. On the Peabody Picture Vocabulary Test (Revised) she scored at the 4-year 8-months age. A detailed speech and language evaluation reported a 6- to 12-month receptive language delay.

Diagnostic impressions included selective mutism, history of separation anxiety disorder, overanxious disorder, and receptive language delay. Recommendations included speech and language therapy within the school system and the development of a behavior modification program to be used at school and at home. No recommendations were made for pharmacotherapy, until the response to ongoing assessment and a behavior modification program could be assessed.

RESEARCH ISSUES

Systematic phenomenological studies are needed to reconsider selective mutism in the light of new developments in the study of childhood anxiety disorders. Recent clinical experience suggests that most selective mutes are not "refusing" to talk (which implies a willful oppositional state) but that they feel unable to do so. Studies of the phenomenology, neurobiology, familial psychopathology, and treatment would provide information to determine whether selective mutism might be well classified as an anxiety disorder. Studies are needed to determine effective treatments, and more work is needed to clarify the efficacy of medications, although they appear promising at this point.

NOTE ON PATIENT ADVOCACY GROUPS

The Foundation for Elective Mutism, a nonprofit national organization, provides support to those who are dealing with children with this disorder and information on the disorder. Organized by two mothers of children with selective mutism, the organization has encouraged research around the country in order to reassess old misconceptions about the disorder. Some areas of the country have local patient and family chapters of the national organization. For information on the national organization, contact the cofounders and codirectors: Mrs. Sue Leszcyk, Foundation for Elective Mutism, P.O. Box 450632, Sunrise, Florida 33345–0632, or Mrs. Carolyn Miller, Foundation for Elective Mutism, P.O. Box 13133, Sissonville, West Virginia 25360.

REFERENCES

Albert-Stewart, P. (1986). Positive reinforcement in short-term treatment of an electively mute child: A case study. *Psychological Reports, 58,* 571–576.

American Psychiatric Association. (1987). *Diagnostic and statistical manual of mental disorders* (3rd ed., rev.). Washington, DC: Author.

American Psychiatric Association. (1994). *Diagnostic and statistical manual of mental disorders* (4th ed.). Washington, DC: Author.

Biederman, J., Rosenbaum, J. F., Bolduc-Murphy, E. A., et al. (1993). Behavioral inhibition as a temperamental risk factor for anxiety disorders. *Child and Adolescent Psychiatric Clinics of North America, 2,* 667–684.

Black, B., & Uhde, T. W. (1992). Elective mutism as a variant of social phobia. *Journal of the American Academy of Child and Adolescent Psychiatry, 31,* 1090–1094.

Black, B., & Uhde, T. W. (1994). Treatment of elective mutism with fluoxetine: A double-blind, placebo-controlled study. *Journal of the American Academy of Child and Adolescent Psychiatry, 33*(7), 1000–1006.

Brown, J. B., & Lloyd, H. (1975). A controlled study of children not speaking at school. *Journal of the Association of Workers for Maladjusted Children, 3,* 49–63.

Browne, E., Wilson, V., & Laybourne, P. C. (1963). Diagnosis and treatment of elective mutism in children. *Journal of the American Academy of Child and Adolescent Psychiatry, 2,* 605–617.

Calhoun, J., & Koenig, K. P. (1973). Classroom modification of elective mutism. *Behavioral Therapy, 4,* 700–702.

Colligan, R. W., Colligan, R. C., & Dillard, M. K. (1977). Contingency management in the classroom treatment of longterm elective mutism: A case report. *Journal of School Psychology, 15,* 9–17.

Crumley, F. E. (1990). The masquerade of mutism. *Journal of the American Academy of Child and Adolescent Psychiatry, 29,* 318–319.

Cunningham, C. E., Cataldo, M. F., Mallion C., et al. (1983). A review and controlled single case evaluation of behavioral approaches to the management of elective mutism. *Child and Family Behavior Therapy, 5,* 25–49.

Friedman, R., & Karagan, N. (1973). Characteristics and management of elective mutism in children. *Psychology in the Schools, 10,* 249–254.

Fundudis, T., Kolvin, I., & Garside, R. (1979). *Speech retarded and deaf children: Their psychological development.* London: Academic Press.

Golwyn, D. H., & Weinstock, R. C. (1990). Phenelzine treatment of elective mutism: A case report. *Journal of Clinical Psychiatry, 51,* 384–385.

Hayden, T. L. (1980). Classification of elective mutism. *Journal of the American Academy of Child and Adolescent Psychiatry, 19,* 118–133.

Hesselman, S. (1983). Elective mutism in children 1877–1981. *Acta Paedopsychiatrica, 49,* 297–310.

Kolvin, I., & Fundudis, T. (1981). Elective mute children: Psychological, development, and background factors. *Journal of Child Psychology and Psychiatry, 22,* 219–232.

Kratochwill, T. R., Brody, G. H., & Piersel, W. C. (1979). Elective mutism in children. *Advances in Clinical Child Psychology, 2,* 194–240.

Kratochwill, T. R. (1981). *Selective mutism: Implications for research and treatment.* Hillsdale, NJ: Erlbaum.

Krohn, D. D., Weckstein, S. M., & Wright, H. L. (1992). A study of the effectiveness of a specific treatment for elective mutism. *Journal of the American Academy of Child and Adolescent Psychiatry, 31,* 711–718.

Kussmaul, A. (1877). *Die Störungen der Sprache.* Leipzig: F. C. W. Vogel.

Labbe, E. E., & Williamson, D. A. (1984). Behavioral treatment of elective mutism: A review of the literature. *Clinical Psychology Review, 4,* 273–294.

Last, C. G., Phillips, J. E., & Statfeld, A. (1987). Childhood anxiety disorders in mothers and their children. *Child Psychiatry and Human Development, 18,* 103–112.

Leonard, H. L., & Topol, D. A. (1993). Elective mutism. *Child and Adolescent Psychiatric Clinics of North America, 2,* 695–707.

Lowenstein, L. F. (1979). The result of 21 elective mute cases. *Acta Paedopsychiatrica, 45,* 17–23.

Meyers, S. V. (1984). Elective mutism in children: A family systems approach. *American Journal of Family Therapy, 12,* 39–45.

Parker, E. B., Olsen, T. F., & Throckmorton, M. C. (1960). Social casework with elementary school children who do not talk in school. *Social Work, 5,* 64–70.

Reed, G. (1963). Elective mutism in children: A reappraisal. *Journal of Child Psychology and Psychiatry, 4,* 99.

Riddle, M. A., Scahill, L., King, R. A., et al. (1992). Double-blind, crossover trial of fluoxetine and placebo in children and adolescents with obsessive–compulsive disorder. *Journal of the American Academy of Child and Adolescent Psychiatry, 31,* 1062–1069.

Sanok, R. L., & Ascione, F. R. (1979). Behavioral interventions for elective mutism: An evaluative review. *Child Behavior Therapy, 1,* 49–67.

Swedo, S. E., Rapoport, J. L., Leonard, H. L., et al. (1989). Obsessive compulsive disorder in children and adolescents: Clinical phenomenology of 70 consecutive cases. *Archives of General Psychiatry, 46,* 335–343.

Tancer, N. K. (1992). Elective mutism. In B. B. Lahey & A. E. Kazdin (Eds.), *Advances in Clinical Child Psychology* (Vol. 14, pp. 265–288). New York: Plenum Press.

Tramer, M. (1934). Elektiver Mutismus bei Kindern. *Zeitschrift fuer Kinderpsychiatrie, 1,* 30–35.

Weissman, M. M., Leckman, J. E., Merikangas, K. R., et al. (1984). Depression and anxiety disorders in parents and children: Results from the Yale Family Study. *Archives General Psychiatry, 41,* 845–852.

Wergeland, H. (1979). Elective mutism. *Acta Psychiatria Scandinavica, 59,* 218–228.

Wilkins, R. (1985). A comparison of elective mutism and emotional disorders in children. *British Journal of Psychiatry, 146,* 198–203.

Wright, H. H. (1985). Early identification and intervention with children who refuse to speak. *Journal of the American Academy of Child and Adolescent Psychiatry, 24,* 739–746.

Wright, H. L. (1968). A clinical study of children who refuse to talk in school. *Journal of the American Academy of Child and Adolescent Psychiatry, 7,* 603–617.

Chapter 11

Obsessive–Compulsive Disorder

John S. March
Henrietta L. Leonard
Susan E. Swedo

Although guiding theories and treatment approaches to obsessive–compulsive disorder (OCD) have varied tremendously, descriptions of the disorder are remarkably consistent across time and the adult literature (Jenike, Baer, & Minichello, 1990). In 1903, Janet described a 5-year-old with obsessive–compulsive symptoms in the following terms: "No reassuring satisfies: the patient must be forever verifying his honesty, cleanliness, sanity, perceptions, and what he did last" (Janet, 1903). While Kanner later reported that children with OCD had "constricted" premorbid personalities and had been raised with an "overdose of parental perfectionism" (Kanner, 1962), Despert noted that children with OCD generally were acutely aware of the abnormality of their thoughts in a way that was not true for schizophrenic children (Despert, 1955), Judd commented on normal premorbid behavior and an absence of obviously intrusive or strict parents (Judd, 1965), and Anna Freud drew a distinction between obsessive–compulsive phenomena and the "pre-ego" repetitions of young children (Freud, 1965, p. 151). More recently, Rapoport and colleagues' groundbreaking series of studies at the National Institute of Mental Health (NIMH), which were widely reported in the lay press after publication of *The Boy Who Couldn't Stop Washing* (Rapoport, 1989), ushered in the modern understanding of OCD in children and adolescents. In this chapter we review the diagnosis and treatment of OCD in young persons. We restrict our discussion to OCD per se, as substantially less empirical information is available regarding the so-called "obsessive–compulsive spectrum" disorders, such as trichotillomania or body dysmorphophobia.

EPIDEMIOLOGY AND DIAGNOSIS

As in adults, OCD in children is substantially more common than once thought. In the Isle of Wight study, the point prevalence of mixed obsessive–compulsive and anxiety symptoms was 0.3% (Rutter, Tizard, & Whitmore, 1970), slightly less that the 0.4% (corrected 1%) found in a community sample of 5000 New Jersey adolescents (Flament, Whitaker, Rapoport, et al., 1988). Among adults with OCD, one third to one half develop the disorder during childhood or adolescence (Rasmussen & Eisen, 1990). Moreover, children with the disorder often go unrecognized. In Flament's epidemiological survey, only 4 of the 18 children found to have OCD were under professional care (Flament et al., 1988). None of the 18 carried a diagnosis of OCD, including the 4 children in mental health treatment, confirming Jenike's characterization of OCD as a "hidden epidemic" (Jenike, 1989).

As in the third revised edition of the *Diagnostic and Statistical Manual of Mental Disorders* (DSM-III-R; American Psychiatric Association, 1987), OCD in DSM-IV (American Psychiatric Association, 1994) is characterized by recurrent obsessions and/or compulsions that cause marked distress and/or interfere in one's life. Obsessions are defined as recurrent and persistent thoughts, images, or impulses that are ego-dystonic, intrusive, and, for the most part, senseless. Obsessions are generally accompanied by dysphoric affects, such as fear, disgust, and doubt, or a feeling of incompleteness, and so they are distressing to the affected individual. Not surprisingly, persons with OCD typically attempt to ignore, suppress, or neutralize obsessive thoughts and associated feelings by enacting compulsions, which are defined as "repetitive, purposeful, and intentional behaviors that are performed in response to an obsession, according to certain rules, or in a stereotyped fashion" (American Psychiatric Association, 1987, p. 245). Generally, then, compulsions, which can be observable repetitive behaviors such as washing or covert mental acts such as counting, serve to neutralize or alleviate anxious discomfort or prevent a dreaded event.

To merit a diagnosis of OCD, an affected youngster may have either obsessions or compulsions, although the great majority have both, and his or her symptoms must "cause marked distress, be time-consuming (take more than an hour a day), or significantly interfere with the person's normal routine, occupational functioning, or usual social activities or relationships with others" (American Psychiatric Association 1987, p. 245). DSM-IV specifies that affected individuals recognize at some point in the illness that obsessions originate within the mind and are not simply excessive worries about real problems; similarly, compulsions must be seen as excessive or unreasonable. The requirement that insight be preserved is waived for children, however, although persons of all ages who lack insight receive the appellation "poor insight type." The specific content of the obsessions cannot be related to another DSM-IV Axis I diagnosis, such as thoughts about food resulting from an eating disorder or guilty thoughts (ruminations) from depression. Despite substantial comorbidity with OCD, Tourette's syndrome (TS) is not an exclusionary criterion and may be an associated diagnosis.

PHENOMENOLOGY

Symptoms

The most common compulsions in children are washing and cleaning, followed by checking, counting, repeating, touching, and straightening (Swedo, Rapoport, Leonard, et al., 1989). Most children experience washing rituals at some time during the course of the illness. Corresponding obsessions include fear of contamination, fear of harm to self, and fear of harm to a familiar person. Among children evaluated at NIMH, the most common rituals were excessive washing (85%), repeating or redoing (51%), checking (46%), touching (20%), counting (18%), ordering/arranging (17%), and hoarding (11%). The most common obsessions were concerns of germs or contaminants (40%), fears that harm would come to self or others (24%), scrupulosity (excessive religiosity or scrutiny of one's thoughts or actions; 13%), and forbidden thoughts (4%) (Swedo, Rapaport, Leonard, et al., 1989). Interestingly, adult washers are more commonly female, as contrasted with checkers who are more commonly male (Rasmussen & Eisen, 1992); for unknown reasons, this may be less the case for children than for adults (Swedo, Rapaport, Leonard, et al., 1989b). In the NIMH cohort, pure obsessives were less common than pure compulsives (Swedo, Rapaport, Leonard, et al., 1989), perhaps reflecting gradual segregation of obsessional mental content from the urge to ritualize. Finally, in a recently completed retrospective analysis, Rettew and colleagues found that symptoms changed over time, although no clear pattern of progression was present (Rettew, Swedo, Leonard, et al., 1992).

Age and Gender Effects

In the NIMH sample, the modal age at onset of OCD was 7 and the mean age at onset was 10.2, implying an early onset group and a group with onset in adolescence (Swedo, Rapaport, Leonard, et al., 1989). The early-onset group was two times more likely to be male and to have a family member with OCD or TS. In children less than 7 or 8 years old, rituals commonly flag the disorder. For example, perseverative behaviors denoted

OCD in an otherwise normal 2-year-old (Swedo, Rapaport, Leonard, et al., 1989). Interestingly, parents of children with OCD recall more early ritualistic behavior than do parents of normal controls (Leonard, Goldberger, Rapoport, et al., 1990). In a similar investigation, Last and Strauss (1989) identified 20 children with OCD among 190 with anxiety disorders presenting to an anxiety disorders clinic. Echoing the NIMH findings, males outnumbered females in the Pittsburgh sample; the opposite was true for other childhood-onset anxiety disorders. In this study, early-onset OCD was also more prevalent in males, again confirming the NIMH findings. On the other hand, in the Flament et al. (1988) epidemiological survey of New Jersey adolescents the ratio of males to females was 1:1, raising the possibility of ascertainment bias in the clinical samples. Ascertainment bias may also color the conclusion that OCD is more common in white than black children in clinical samples.

Developmental Factors

Most if not all children exhibit normative age-dependent obsessive–compulsive behaviors. For example, many young children want things done "just so" or insist on elaborate bedtime rituals (Gesell, Ames, & Ilg, 1974). Such behaviors often can be understood in terms of developmental issues involving mastery and control, and the behaviors have usually been replaced by middle childhood by collecting, hobbies, and "focused interests." Clinically, normative obsessive–compulsive behaviors can be reliably discriminated from OCD on the basis of timing, content, and severity (Leonard et al., 1990). Developmentally sanctioned obsessive–compulsive behaviors occur early in childhood and are rare during adolescence, are common to large numbers of children, and are associated with the mastery of developmental issues. In contrast, OCD occurs somewhat later, appears "bizarre" to adults and to other children, if not to the affected child, and always produces dysfunction rather than mastery.

Comorbidity

Children with a variety of psychiatric disorders exhibit obsessions or ritualistic behaviors, confounding the diagnosis of OCD in some patients. In addition, more than one disorder may be diagnosed in a single patient, since the diagnosis of OCD is not exclusionary. In the NIMH cohort of 70 children and adolescents (which excluded children with mental retardation, eating disorders, and TS), 26% had OCD as the sole disorder at baseline (Swedo, Rapaport, Leonard, et al., 1989). Tic disorders (30%), major depression (26%), specific developmental disability (24%), simple phobias (17%), overanxious disorder (16%), adjustment disorder with depressed mood (13%), oppositional disorder (11%), attention-deficit disorder (10%), conduct disorder (7%), separation anxiety disorder (7%), enuresis (4%), alcohol abuse (4%), and encopresis (3%) were the most common comorbid diagnoses (Swedo, Rapaport, Leonard, et al., 1989). Riddle and colleagues reported similar findings: 38% of the subjects in their study received an anxiety disorder diagnosis, 29% a mood disorder diagnosis, and 24% a tic diagnosis (Riddle, Scahill, King, et al., 1990). Last and Strauss (1989) found comparable results in their clinically derived population, as did Flament et al. (1988) in their epidemiological sample. Interestingly, although the diagnosis of personality disorders in children is obviously problematic, a suprisingly small number, only 11%, exhibited obsessive–compulsive personality disorder (OCPD) in the NIMH sample, perhaps implying that obsessive–compulsive personality traits, while over represented among children with OCD, are neither necessary nor sufficient for the diagnosis (Swedo, Rapaport, Leonard, et al., 1989). Moreover, in children with both disorders, it is often unclear whether OCD is a risk factor for OCPD or whether the opposite is true, especially since OCPD may remit with successful treatment of OCD (Ricciardi, Baer, Jenike, et al., 1992).

Neuropsychological Factors

Adults with OCD frequently exhibit left-sided soft signs on neurological examination and poor visual–spatial processing on neuropsychological testing, implicating right hemisphere and perhaps basal ganglia dysfunction in OCD (Hollander et al., 1990). Like children with other anxiety disorders, young persons with OCD also exhibit subtle neurological impairments (Hollander, DeCaria, Aronowitz, et al., 1991; Chapter 2). Rapoport and her colleagues at NIMH, studying older children with OCD thought to be neurologically normal at intake, found a lack of normal cerebral laterality and a high rate of age-inappropriate synkinesias and left hemibody signs (Behar, Rapoport, Berg, et al., 1984; Rapoport, Elkins, & Langer, 1981). A subsequent, more detailed, investigation documented both neurological (Denkla, 1989) and neuropsychiatric (Cox, Fedio, & Rapoport, 1989) abnormalities, involving poor visual–spatial skills and abnormal speech prosody. For example, on a stressed neurological examination, over 80% showed soft neurological findings, including 8 individuals with left hemisyndrome, 13 cases of neurodevelopmental "immaturity," and 18 cases of choreiform syndrome (Denkla, 1989).

Recently, March Johnston, Jefferson, et al. (1990), reporting the results of a placebo-controlled trial of clomipramine in outpatient children with OCD, speculated that subtle impairments in neurological status may adversely influence the outcome of pharmacotherapy. Hollander, Schiffman, Cohen, et al. (1990) also noted that neuropsychiatric abnormalities were positively correlated with a poor response to treatment with serotonin uptake inhibitors in adults with OCD. Children with OCD who show specific abnormalities in visual–spatial–organizational information processing are at risk for specific learning problems, such as dysgraphia, arithmetic and expressive written language deficiencies, and slow processing speed and efficiency (March & Conners, unpublished data). When poor social skills resulting from weaknesses in the nonverbal processing of social–emotional communication are also present (March, unpublished data), OCD overlaps Asperger's syndrome (Szatmari, Bremner, & Nagy, 1989). Unfortunately, these often subtle neuropsychological and academic impairments are frequently missed and contribute clinically to "treatment-resistant" cases. Conversely, impaired neuropsychological test performance was not associated with specific aspects of OCD phenomenology in the NIMH studies, nor did it predict the outcome of treatment with clomipramine (Swedo, Leonard, & Rapoport, 1990; Leonard & Rapoport, 1989). Clearly, additional research will be necessary to disentangle the complexities of subgroup heterogeneity in this area.

NATURAL HISTORY AND PROGNOSIS

Before the arrival of modern pharmacotherapy and behavior therapy, the long-term outcome of treatment of OCD was dismal. As in many adults (Rasmussen & Eisen, 1990), OCD is in many children and adolescents a chronic mental illness. Warren reported that in a 7-year reevaluation of 15 patients with "obsessive–compulsive state," 2 (13%) had no symptoms, 8 (53%) had mild to moderate symptoms, and 5 (33%) were "severely handicapped" (Warren, 1960). On 1- to 14-year follow-up of 17 patients with severe obsessive–compulsive neurosis, Hollingsworth and colleagues reported that only 30% were symptom free; most remained quite ill (Hollingsworth, Tanguay, & Grossman, 1980). Similar findings held in a largely untreated community population at 2-year follow-up: 31% (5 of 16) of those who had initially met criteria for OCD still did so, and only 12% (2 of 16) had no OCD features of any form (Berg, Rapoport, Whitaker, et al., 1989). Flament, Koby, Rapoport, et al. (1990) reevaluated 25 of 27 (93%) patients 2 to 7 years after their initial NIMH evaluation and reported that 17 (68%) still met criteria for OCD; no baseline predictors of outcome were identified. (Of note here is that many of these patients were evaluated before modern pharmacotherapy with serotonin reuptake inhibitors [SRIs].)

In the largest systematic follow-up study of pediatric OCD, 54 clinical patients at NIMH were re-evaluated 2 to 7 years later (Leonard, Swedo, Lenane, et al., 1993). All patients initially had been treated with an SRI, and had access to maintenance pharmacotherapy; many but not all also had received some form of behavior therapy. Even so, 43% still met diagnostic criteria for OCD; only 11% were totally asymptomatic, supporting previous reports of the chronicity and intractability of the illness. At the time of follow-up, 70% continued to take medication. As a group, they were improved from baseline, although 10 (19%) were unchanged or worse, several because of complicating comorbid disorders that had not been present at baseline. Fewer patients in the NIMH follow-up study met criteria for OCD than in the Flament study, and it is tempting but scientifically untenable without control groups to infer that treatment was specifically responsible for the incremental improvement in outcome. Nevertheless, in light of preliminary evidence that well-delivered treatment with a combination of pharmacotherapy and cognitive-behavioral psychotherapy may improve long-term prognosis (March, Mulle, & Herbel, 1994), it is probably reasonable to conclude that many if not most pediatric OCD patients, with treatment, currently can expect substantial improvement but not complete remission of symptoms over time.

OCD AS A NEUROBEHAVIORAL DISORDER

Esman, reviewing the psychoanalytic understanding of OCD, noted that insight-oriented psychotherapy has proven disappointing at best in ameliorating OCD symptoms (Esman, 1989); it is doubtful whether specific OCD symptoms really represent derivatives of intrapsychic conflicts (Staebler, Pollard, & Merkel, 1993). In contrast, successful treatment of OCD with SRIs provided the initial rationale for a neurobehavioral explanation for OCD in the form of the "serotonin hypothesis" (Goodman, McDougle, Price, et al., 1990). Later, phenomenological similarities between obsessive–compulsive symptoms (washing, balancing, licking), neurobiological findings, and recent studies of trichotillomania led to the hypothesis that OCD is (in some patients) a "grooming behavior gone awry" (Swedo, 1989). Nonetheless, while progress on the treatment front has been relatively rapid, progress in understanding the biological foundations of the disorder has been somewhat slower, and the use of biological markers to differentiate OCD from intercurrent psychiatric disorders with which it shares common features is in its infancy (Swedo & Rapoport, 1990). The interested reader is referred to recent reviews for a more detailed discussion of this topic (Swedo & Rapoport, 1990; March, Gutzman, Jefferson, et al., 1989; Insel, 1992a, 1992c; Chapter 1).

Genetic Studies

Several lines of evidence suggest that genetics plays an important role in OCD, especially in the relationship between OCD and TS. Lenane, Swedo, Leonard, et al. (1990) reported that 20% of first-degree relatives (9% of mothers and 25% of fathers) of 46 pediatric OCD probands met criteria for a lifetime diagnosis of OCD. Riddle, Scahill, et al. (1990) reported similar results, finding that 15 of 21 childhood OCD patients had a parent with either OCD (*n* = 4) or obsessive–compulsive symptoms (*n* = 11). Similarly, tics are clearly more common in OCD probands (Leonard, Lenane, Swedo, et al., 1992), and conversely, the rate of OCD appears elevated in TS patients (Frankel, Cummings, Robertson, et al., 1986; Pauls, Towbin, Leckman, et al., 1986). Finally, Pauls and colleagues reported an increased rate of OCD in the first-degree relatives of TS probands, regardless of the OCD status of the TS proband (Pauls, Raymond, Stevenson, et al., 1991; Pauls et al., 1986). While the magnitude of heritability remains uncertain, it seems clear that what is "transmitted" between generations is the OCD/TS pattern and not a particular OCD subtype (Swedo, Rapaport, Leonard, et al., 1989b). Although the gene has yet to be identified, these findings led Pauls et al. (1986, 1991) to hypothesize that OCD and TS may represent alternate expressions of the same gene(s) through an autosomal dominant mode of inheritance, with variable penetrance and sex-influenced expressivity.

Neuroanatomy

Several lines of evidence, including comorbidity between OCD and various basal ganglia illnesses plus findings from brain imaging studies, implicate abnormalities in cortico-striatal-thalamo-cortical (CSTC) circuitry in OCD (Rapoport, Swedo, & Leonard, 1992). Various central nervous system insults have long been associated with the disorder, including head injury, epileptic seizures, and brain tumors (Insel, Mueller, & Gillin, 1984). OCD occurs at an increased rate in basal ganglia illnesses, among them TS (Pauls et al., 1986), postencephalitic Parkinson's disease (von Economo, 1931), and Huntington's chorea (Cummings & Cunningham, 1992). Moreover, psychosurgical procedures interrupting CSTC circuits result in symptom improvement in a high percentage of patients refractory to less drastic treatments (Mindus & Jenike, 1992).

Recent studies in adults with OCD, utilizing fluorodeoxyglucose positron emission tomographic (PET) scanning (Baxter, Schwartz, Mazziotta, et al., 1988), have found significant elevations in local cerebral glucose metabolic rates in the frontal cortex, orbital gyri, and caudate nuclei of nonmedicated OCD patients compared to depressed and normal controls (Insel, 1992c). Brain imaging studies have now extended these findings to OCD in young persons. Luxenberg, Swedo, Flament, et al. (1988) found smaller caudate volumes on computerized tomography (CT) scans in 10 male adults with childhood-onset OCD compared to those of controls. Swedo reported orbital frontal regional hypermetabolism and alterations in the left anterior cingulate in adults with childhood-onset OCD (Swedo, Schapiro, Grady, et al., 1989). Interestingly, PET changes correlated positively with symptomatic improvement after both pharmacotherapy and behavior therapy (Baxter, Schwartz, Bergman, et al., 1992). However, these results must be interpreted with caution because of considerable "scatter" in the data, requiring sophisticated statistical algorithms to disentangle (Azari, Pietrini, Horwitz, et al., 1993; Insel, 1992c).

Neurophysiology

Neurobiological investigations also implicate neurotransmitter and neuroendocrine abnormalities in the etiopathogenesis of OCD (Chapter 1; Swedo & Rapoport, 1990). Both treatment and challenge studies provide support for the hypothesis that central serotonergic dysregulation lies is at the core of OCD (March et al., 1989). For example, medication trials in adults clearly demonstrate the efficacy of SRIs (Jenike, 1992); challenge studies with metachlorophenylpiperazine (m-CPP), a serotonergic agonist, also support dysregulation of the serotonergic system (Zohar, Insel, Zohar, et al., 1988). Because of the association between OCD and TS (Leonard et al., 1992), exacerbation of OCD symptoms with psychostimulants (Borcherding, Keysor, Rapoport, et al., 1990), and the augmenting effects of dopamine receptor antagonists (McDougle, Goodman, Price, et al., 1990), others have proposed a role for dopaminergic dysregulation in some patients (Goodman, McDougle, & Price, 1992). Unfortunately, cerebrospinal fluid (CSF) studies have shown inconsistent results. In adults, levels of 5-hydroxyindoleacetic acid (5-HIAA), the predominant serotonin metabolite, did not differ between OCD patients and normal controls, although lower levels of 5-HIAA were negatively correlated with treatment outcome (Lydiard, Ballenger, Ellinwood, et al., 1990; Thoren, Asberg, & Cronholm, 1980). Pretreatment 5-HIAA levels were higher in pediatric OCD patients than in disruptive behavior disorder controls (Kruesi, Rapoport, Hamburger, et al., 1990) and were positively correlated with three of seven measures of improvement after 5 weeks of clomipramine (Swedo, Leonard, Kruesi, et al., 1992). For technical and ethical reasons, advances in this area are likely to come from neuroimaging studies using receptor-specific ligands.

Neuroendocrine dysregulation also may play a role in the pathobiology of OCD. In a large epidemiological study, boys with OCD were shorter than both the normal and psychiatric controls and had a flatter growth pattern, hinting at subtle neuroendocrine dysfunction (Hamburger, Swedo, Whitaker, et al., 1989). Consistent with overlaps between OCD and TS, boys are also more likely to have a prepubertal onset of OCD than are girls, who more commonly report onset of OCD symptoms at puberty (Swedo, Rapoport, Cheslow, et al., 1989). These findings might implicate adrenal adrenarchy and gonadal steroidogenesis respectively in the onset of OCD. Interestingly, antiandrogen treatment reduced OCD symptoms in open trials, but the improvement did not persist (Casas, Alvarez, & Duro, et al., 1986). Finally, arginine vasopressin was negatively correlated with OCD severity in the NIMH pediatric CSF study (Swedo, Leonard, Kruesi, et al., 1992). In this study, oxytocin was associated with depressive but not obsessive–compulsive symptomatology, whereas the Yale group, stimulated by Insel's work on oxytocin as a mediator of attachment behaviors (Insel, 1992b), found a significant correlation between OCD and "phobic" OCD in adults (Riddle, 1993).

OCD as an Antibody-Mediated Neuropsychiatric Disorder

"Strep throat" may be a notable risk factor for another subgroup of children with OCD and tic disorders. Prospective data suggest that Sydenham's chorea, an autoimmune inflammation of the basal ganglia triggered by a bacterial (streptococcal) infection, provides a medical model for antineuronal antibody-mediated OCD (Swedo, Leonard, Schapiro, et al., 1993). OCD occurs at an increased rate in pediatric patients with Sydenham's chorea compared with nonchoreic rheumatic fever patients (Swedo, Rapaport, Cheslow, et al., 1989). Antineuronal antibodies, which are formed against group A beta-hemolytic strep cell wall antigens and cross-react with caudate neural tissue, rise parallel with obsessive–compulsive symptoms and caudate swelling on magnetic resonance imaging (MRI); decreases in anticaudate antibodies with acute penicillin treatment or plasmaphereis are accompanied by rapid resolution of obsessive–compulsive symptoms (Swedo, Leonard, & Kiessling, 1994).

CLINICAL ASSESSMENT AND TREATMENT

The nature and impact of OCD vary widely in children and adolescents, and many young OCD sufferers are embarrassed and secretive, despite full awareness that their obsessions are senseless and their ritual excessive. Thus accurate assessment, beginning with the questions asked about the disorder during the initial interview, is essential to skillful diagnosis and treatment (Wolff & Wolff, 1991; Thyer, 1991; Chapter 6). Semi-structured interviews (Kearney & Silverman, 1990), such as the Anxiety Disorders Interview for Children (ADIS-C); scalar measures, such as the Maudsley Obsessional Inventory (Sternberger & Burns, 1990), the Leyton Obsessional Inventory (Berg, Rapoport, & Flament, 1985), and the Yale–Brown Obsessive Compulsive Scale (YBOCS), which is currently considered the instrument of choice for rating OCD symptoms (Goodman, Price, Rasmussen, et al., 1989); and global measures of impairment, such as the Clinical Global Impairment scale and the NIMH global scale, and improvement, such as the Clinical Global Improvement scale, have been usefully applied in assessing OCD in young persons. Since comorbidity may partially predict the nature and outcome of treatment (Dar & Greist, 1992), systematically assessing comorbidities is important, as well. Finally, it is essential to monitor the process and outcome of treatment using measures that sample specific symptom domains, such as washing versus avoidance, functional domains, such as home or school, and symptomatic distress during exposure, such as subjective units of discomfort (SUDS; March, in press).

As illustrated by recent lay publications (Baer, 1991; Foa & Wilson, 1991), cognitive-behavioral psychotherapy has become the psychotherapeutic treatment of choice for adults with OCD. Moreover, since anti-exposure instructions (in which patients are encouraged not to resist their obsessions and rituals) attenuate the effectiveness of drug treatment (Marks, Lelliott, Basoglu, et al., 1988), the combination of drug and behavioral therapies may be the treatment of choice for adult OCD in patients requiring medication (Greist, 1992). Although empirical documentation of the effectiveness of behavior therapy in child and adolescent patients with OCD lags behind that for pharmacotherapy (Rapoport et al., 1992; March, in press), a similar assumption may hold for younger patients as well.

Cognitive-Behavioral Psychotherapy

Not surprisingly, since flexible, empirically supported cognitive-behavioral treatments are now available for many childhood mental illnesses (Kendall, 1991), cognitive-behavioral psychotherapy (CBT) is routinely described as the psychotherapeutic treatment of choice for children and adolescents with OCD (Berg, Rapoport, & Wolff, 1989; March et al., 1994). Unlike other psychotherapies that have been applied to OCD, CBT presents a logically consistent and compelling relationship between the disorder, the treatment, and the specified outcome. Unfortunately, clinicians routinely complain that their child patients do not comply with behavioral treatments; parents routinely complain that clinicians are poorly trained in CBT. Both critiques may avoidable, given an increased understanding of the implementation of CBT for children and adolescents with OCD. We recently developed and presented preliminary data concerning the effectiveness of a manualized treatment protocol (March & Mulle, 1933; March et al., 1994) and in the process carefully reviewed the literature on CBT with child and adolescent OCD (March, in press). The interested reader is referred to these and other excellent reviews (Berg, Rapaport, & Wolff, 1989; Wolff & Wolff, 1991) for additional information.

Depending on the needs of the particular child, exposure-based treatments and anxiety management training are the core elements of most treatment programs (March, in press), including ours (March et al., 1994). Applied to OCD, the exposure principle relies on the fact that anxiety usually attenuates after sufficient duration of contact with a feared stimulus (Dar & Greist, 1992). Thus, a child with phobic symptoms regarding germs must come into and remain in contact with "germy" objects until his or her anxiety extinguishes. Repeated exposure is associated with decreased anxiety until the child no longer fears contact with a particular phobic stimulus. Exposure in child patients is typically implemented in a gradual fashion (sometimes termed *graded exposure*), with exposure targets under either therapist or patient control (March et al., 1994).

Adequate exposure depends on blocking rituals or avoidance behaviors, a process termed *response prevention* (Dar & Greist, 1992). For example, a child with germ worries must not only touch "germy" things but must refrain from ritualized washing until his or her anxiety diminishes substantially. Many children cannot realistically avoid exposure to specific phobic stimuli, such as exposure to bathrooms for the child with contamination fears, and response prevention targets not infrequently can be selected independently of contrived exposure targets.

Because blocking rituals or avoidance behaviors removes the negative reinforcement effect of the rituals or avoidance, response prevention technically is an extinction procedure. By convention, however, extinction is usually defined as the elimination of behaviors through removal of parental positive reinforcement; it is a contingency management procedure. For example, a child with reassurance-seeking rituals may ask parents to refrain from reassurance-seeking. Extinction frequently produces rapid effects, but it can be hard to implement when a child's behavior is bizarre or frequent. As with exposure and response prevention (E/RP), placing extinction targets under the child's control leads to increased compliance and improved outcomes (March et al., 1994).

Finally, a variety of other cognitive-behavioral techniques have been employed to support E/RP. Anxiety management training (AMT)—defined here as a combination of relaxation training, breathing control training, and cognitive restructuring—is an effective treatment for overanxious children and adolescents (Kendall, 1991). AMT may contribute to the successful cognitive-behavioral treatment of younger persons with OCD by (1) targeting comorbidities that might interfere with OCD treatment and (2) facilitating exposure through reducing the amplitude of exposure-related anxiety (March et al., 1994; March & Mulle, in press). Positive reinforcement does not directly alter OCD symptoms, but it helps encourage exposure and so produces a noticeable if indirect clinical benefit. In contrast, punishment (imposition of an aversive event) or response-cost (removal of a positive event) procedures have shown themselves to be uniformly unhelpful in the treatment of OCD (Harris & Wiebe, 1992). Modeling—whether overt (the child understands that the therapist is demonstrating more appropriate or adaptive) or covert (the therapist informally models a behavior)—improves compliance with in-session E/RP and generalization to between-session E/RP homework. Similarly, shaping involves positively reinforcing successive approximations to a desired target behavior. Modeling and shaping also reduce anticipatory anxiety and provide an opportunity for increased constructive self-talk before and during E/RP tasks (Thyer, 1991). Since E/RP has not proven particularly helpful with obsessional slowness, modeling and shaping procedures may be the cognitive-behavioral treatment of choice for children with this OCD subtype (Ratnasuriya, Marks, Forshaw, et al., 1991). Unfortunately, relapse often occurs when therapist-assisted shaping, limit setting, and temporal speeding procedures are withdrawn (Wolff & Rapoport, 1988). For patients with complex, ticlike repeating rituals, such as hair pulling, habit reversal procedures, in which patients and their families are taught thought stopping, visualization, relaxation, competing motoric responses, and relapse prevention strategies sometimes prove helpful alone or in combination with medications (Baer, 1992; Vitulano, King, Scahill, et al., 1992).

Pharmacotherapy

Pharmacotherapy and CBT work well together, and many children with OCD require or would benefit from both CBT and pharmacotherapy (Piacentini, Jaffer, Gitow, et al., 1992). Clinically, pharmacotherapy for children with OCD strongly resembles that for adults in that both rely on SRIs (Rapoport et al., 1992; Jenike, 1992). Of the SRIs, clomipramine (Anafranil, manufactured by CIBA-Geigy) is by far the best studied medication in the pediatric population. Flament, Rapoport, Berg, et al. (1985) reported that clomipramine was significantly superior to placebo in a 10-week (5 weeks of active medication) placebo-controlled double-blind crossover study. In this study, despipramine was chosen as the comparison drug because it is primarily noradrenergic in action but has similar antidepressant and anxiolytic—but not anti-OCD—effects. Only 16% of the patients were unimproved; 75% experienced a moderate to marked improvement during the trial. Plasma concentrations of clomipramine or desmethyl-clomipramine failed to predict response to treatment, nor did extent of depressive symptoms. In a replication of this pioneering study, clomipramine proved clearly superior to desipramine and was generally well tolerated with only mild anticholinergic side effects (Leonard, Swedo, Rapoport, et al., 1989). Patient age and sex, severity and duration of symptoms, concomitant depressive symptoms, and symptom pattern also failed to predict response to treatment in children with OCD (Swedo, Leonard, & Rapoport, 1992).

The NIMH findings were later confirmed in a large 8-week multi-center double-blind parallel comparison of clomipramine versus placebo that led to FDA approval of clomipramine for the treatment of OCD in children and adolescents (DeVeaugh, Moroz, Biederman, et al., 1992). Following are some of the conclusions from the clomipramine multicenter trial.

1. In contrast to pharmacotherapy for children and adolescents with depression (Ryan, 1992), there is little or no placebo effect in patients with OCD.
2. On average, noticeable clinical effects begin at 3 weeks and plateau at 10 weeks.
3. Clomipramine produces about a 30% reduction in OCD symptoms, corresponding to a rating of moderate to marked improvement on a measure of patient satisfaction.
4. Given that subjects on average remained in the mildly to moderately ill range at the conclusion of the trial, clomipramine is clearly not a panacea for all patients.

Side effects—primarily anticholinergic, antihistiminic, and alpha-blocking effects—were comparable to (but milder than) those seen in the adult multicenter trial. No patient developed seizures or clinically untoward electrocardiographic changes. Long-term clomipramine maintenance has not revealed any unexpected adverse reactions (DeVeaugh et al., 1992) (Leonard, Swedo, Lenane, et al., 1991).

Besides clomipramine, several selective serotonin reuptake inhibitors (SSRIs), including fluoxetine (Prozac, manufactured by Lilly), sertraline (Zoloft, manufactured by Pfizer), and paroxetine (Paxil, manufactured by Smith-Kline), which have been approved by the FDA for the treatment of depression in adults, and fluvoxamine (Luvox, manufactured by Solvay), also are likely candidates for effective treatment of OCD in youth (Chapter 15). Fluoxetine, which recently received an FDA indication for the treatment of OCD in adults, has been reported to be safe and effective for

OCD in children and adolescents with OCD (Riddle, Hardin, King, et al., 1990; Riddle, Scahill, King, et al., 1992). In contrast to adults, for whom fluoxetine doses as high as 80 mg/day may be required, amounts as low as 5 mg/day are often effective in younger children, perhaps reflecting unexplained pharmacodynamic differences between adults and children. Although safety and efficacy have not yet been established empirically for the SSRIs, multicenter trials of fluvoxamine and sertraline are underway, and clinical lore and open trials support application of the SSRIs as treatments for OCD.

Clinically, many patients respond early to one of the SRIs. A substantial minority, however, does not respond until 8 or even 12 weeks of treatment at therapeutic doses. The rate of improvement sometimes improves with concomitant CBT; nevertheless, it is important to wait at least 8 weeks at therapeutic doses before changing agents or undertaking augmentation. Approximately one third of patients fail to be helped by SRI monotherapy, sometimes for reasons, such as family or school problems, that have little to do with pharmacotherapy. Some patients benefit from combination therapy, for example a SRI with clonazepam (Leonard, Topol, Swedo, et al., in press). Clinical lore suggests that still others could benefit from the addition of a neuroleptic, such as pimozide or haloperidol, to a SRI when comorbid schizotypal personality disorder or a tic spectrum disorder is present. Parenthetically, although several medications have been reported to be useful as augmentors of the SRIs in adults, only clonazepam and haloperidol have proven effective in controlled trials in adults (Pigott & Rubenstein, 1992; McDougle, Goodman, Leckman, et al., 1994); lithium (Pigott, Pato, L'Heureux, et al., 1991) and buspirone have not been shown to be beneficial (Pigott, L'Heureux, Hill, et al., 1992). Many children require a focused psychosocial intervention, such as a pedagogic or behavioral school program, instead of a second medication, and it is important to distinguish appropriate targets for psychosocial interventions versus pharmacotherapy.

How long should patients who respond continue to take medication? Although periodic discontinuation trials are advisable, many responders require ongoing maintenance pharmacotherapy. In a double-blind desipramine substitution study of long-term clomipramine-maintained responders, 8 of 9 patients who were switched to desipramine relapsed within 2 months compared to 2 of 11 subjects who stayed on clomipramine (Leonard et al., 1991). However, even patients on continued long-term clomipramine maintenance continued to exhibit some obsessive-compulsive symptoms, which varied in severity over time (Leonard et al., 1991). It is important to note, however, that concomitant CBT may improve the outlook for medication discontinuation. In an open study of CBT, where the majority of subjects also were treated with medication (March et al., 1994), the average magnitude of improvement was larger and relapse rates were lower than usually seen with medication alone (DeVeaugh et al., 1992; Leonard et al., 1989). Thus, combining CBT and pharmacotherapy with a SRI, including booster treatments during medication discontinuation, may improve both short- and long-term outcomes in medication-responsive patients, even those for whom ongoing pharmacotherapy proves necessary (Leonard et al., 1993).

Individual, Group, and Family Psychotherapy

Psychodynamic psychotherapy is an ineffective treatment for younger (Hollingsworth et al., 1980) as well as older patients with OCD (Esman, 1989). However, when aimed at comorbidities, such as depression, or DSM-IV Axis II traits, such as excessive dependency needs, focused supportive and/or cognitive-behavioral psychotherapy may benefit patients by increasing compliance with E/RP. Similarly, when normal development has been adversely affected by OCD, insight-oriented psychotherapy coupled with focused cognitive-behavioral interventions, such as assertiveness training or anger coping (Lochman, Lampron, Gemmer, et al., 1987), frequently becomes more important as OCD diminishes.

Although OCD appears familial and probably shares a genetic diathesis with TS in some children, (Riddle, Scahill, et al., 1990; Lenane et al., 1990), family dysfunction is neither necessary nor sufficient for the onset of OCD (Lenane, 1989). Nonetheless, families affect and are affected by OCD, especially if more than one family member has OCD. For example, high "expressed emotion" may exacerbate OCD; a calm supportive family may improve outcome (Hibbs, Hamburger, Lenane, et al., 1991). While cognitive-behavioral treatment for OCD is more commonly administered in an individual rather than in a family setting, a combination of individual and family sessions may prove best for most patients (March et al., 1994). Specific family therapy or marital therapy may be appropriate when family dysfunction or marital discord impedes the application of cognitive-behavioral interventions directed at OCD.

Psychosurgery

A combination of pharmacotherapy, behavior therapy, and, if necessary, family therapy benefit all but a small minority of children with OCD. Rarely, a treatment nonresponsive child may be a candidate for psychosurgery. Up to 80% of neurosurgically treated adults with refractory OCD receive significant benefit (Mindus & Jenike, 1992). There is only one published study that documents the use of psychosurgery in adolescents with OCD. Lopez Ibor and Lopez Ibor-Alino (1975) noted a significant reduction in OCD symptoms in five patients following stereotaxic capsulotomy. While they found few long-term side effects attributable to surgical intervention, postoperative rehabilitation surprisingly took nearly a year. Thus, when the disorder is life-threatening and the patient is highly motivated and resistant to conventional treatments, psychosurgery may be considered for adolescents with severe OCD. Psychosurgery is proscribed for young children because of the potential for irreversible side effects such as seizures, the fluctuating nature of OCD symptoms in young children, and the possibility that an age-related improvement in compliance with multimodal treatment will reduce OCD symptoms and obviate the need for neurosurgical intervention.

CONCLUSION

The diagnosis and treatment of OCD in children and adolescents are substantially similar to the diagnosis and treatment of OCD in adults. Differences derive largely from developmental considerations, especially family dynamics and limitations in insight with younger age. Ideally, children with OCD should receive behavior therapy (E/RP) and, if they are not rapidly responsive to behavior therapy, a SRI. With younger children, some physicians and patients choose medication first, trying to avoid the time, effort, and anxiety associated with behavior therapy. Others prefer to begin with behavior therapy in hopes of avoiding the need for medication and accompanying side effects. Most prefer to combine the two approaches, especially in severely ill patients. Since there is little empirical data favoring one SRI over another (Jenike, Hyman, Baer, et al., 1990; Pigott, Pato, Bernstein, et al., 1990), choice of agent depends on side effect profile, accumulated clinical experience, clinician and patient preference, and ultimately new evidence from controlled studies. Supportive psychotherapy is useful in every case; family therapy is useful when family problems interfere with the implementation of OCD-specific interventions. Although current treatments are not curative in the majority of patients, given a correct diagnosis and the skillful combination of pharmacotherapy and CBT, most children can be helped to live a life largely unfettered by OCD.

ACKNOWLEDGMENT

This work was supported in part by an NIMH Scientist Development Award for Clinicians (1 K20 MH00981-01) to Dr. March.

REFERENCES

American Psychiatric Association. (1987). *Diagnostic and statistical manual of mental disorders* (3rd ed., rev.). Washington DC: Author.

American Psychiatric Association. (1994). *Diagnostic and statistical manual of mental disorders* (4th ed.). Washington DC: Author.

Azari, N. P., Pietrini, P., Horwitz, B., et al. (1993). Individual differences in cerebral metabolic patterns during pharmacotherapy in obsessive–compulsive disorder: A multiple regression/discriminant analysis of positron emission tomographic data. *Biological Psychiatry, 34*(11), 798–809.

Baer, L. (1991). *Getting control.* Boston, MA: Little, Brown.

Baer, L. (1992). Behavior therapy for obsessive–compulsive disorder and trichotillomania: Implications for Tourette syndrome. *Advances In Neurology, 58,* 333–340.

Baxter, L. J., Schwartz, J. M., Bergman, K. S., et al. (1992). Caudate glucose metabolic rate changes with both drug and behavior therapy for obsessive–compulsive disorder. *Archives of General Psychiatry, 49*(9), 681–689.

Baxter, L. J., Schwartz, J. M., Mazziotta, J. C., et al. (1988). Cerebral glucose metabolic rates in nondepressed patients with obsessive–compulsive disorder. *American Journal of Psychiatry, 145*(12), 1560–1563.

Behar, D., Rapoport, J. L., Berg, C. J., et al. (1984). Computerized tomography and neuropsychological test measures in adolescents with obsessive–compulsive disorder. *American Journal of Psychiatry, 141*(3), 363–369.

Berg, C., Rapoport, J., & Wolff, R. (1989). Behavioral treatment for obsessive–compulsive disorder in childhood. In J. Rapoport (Eds.), *Obsessive–compulsive disorder in children and adolescents* (pp. 169–185). Washington, DC: American Psychiatric Press.

Berg, C. J., Rapoport, J. L., & Flament, M. (1985). The Leyton Obsessional Inventory—Child Version. *Psychopharmacology Bulletin, 21*(4), 1057–1059.

Berg, C. Z., Rapoport, J. L., Whitaker, A., et al. (1989). Childhood obsessive compulsive disorder: A two-year prospective follow-up of a community sample. *Journal of the American Academy of Child and Adolescent Psychiatry, 28*(4), 528–533.

Borcherding, B. G., Keysor, C. S., Rapoport, J. L., et al. (1990). Motor/vocal tics and compulsive behaviors on stimulant drugs: Is there a common vulnerability? *Psychiatry Research, 33*(1), 83–94.

Casas, M., Alvarez, E., Duro, P., et al. (1986). Antiandrogenic treatment of obsessive–compulsive neurosis. *Acta Psychiatria Scandinavica, 73,* 221–222.

Cox, C., Fedio, P., & Rapoport, J. (1989). Neuropsychological testing of obsessive–compulsive adolescents. In J. Rapoport (Ed.), *Obsessive–compulsive disorder in children and adolescents* (pp. 73–86). Washington, DC: American Psychiatric Press.

Cummings, J. L., & Cunningham, K. (1992). Obsessive–compulsive disorder in Huntington's disease. *Biological Psychiatry, 31*(3), 263–270.

Dar, R., & Greist, J. (1992). Behavior therapy for obsessive–compulsive disorder. *Psychiatric Clinics of North America, 15*(4), 885–894.

Denkla, M. (1989). Neurological examination. In J. Rapoport (Ed.), *Obsessive-compulsive disorder in children and adolescents* (pp. 107–118). Washington, DC: American Psychiatric Press.

Despert, L. (1955). Differential diagnosis between obsessive–compulsive neurosis and schizophrenia. In P. Hoch & J. Zubin (Eds.), *Psychopathology of childhood*. New York: Grune & Stratton.

DeVeaugh, G. J., Moroz, G., Biederman, J., et al. (1992). Clomipramine hydrochloride in childhood and adolescent obsessive–compulsive disorder—a multicenter trial. *Journal of the American Academy of Child and Adolescent Psychiatry, 31*(1), 45–49.

Esman, A. (1989). Psychoanalysis in general psychiatry: Obsessive–compulsive disorder as a paradigm. *Journal of the American Psychoanalytic Association, 37*, 319–336.

Flament, M. F., Koby, E., Rapoport, J. L., et al. (1990). Childhood obsessive–compulsive disorder: A prospective follow-up study. *Journal of Child Psychology and Psychiatry and Allied Disciplines, 31*(3), 363–380.

Flament, M. F., Rapoport, J. L., Berg, C. J., et al. (1985). Clomipramine treatment of childhood obsessive–compulsive disorder. A double-blind controlled study. *Archives of General Psychiatry, 42*(10), 977–983.

Flament, M. F., Whitaker, A., Rapoport, J. L., et al. (1988). Obsessive compulsive disorder in adolescence: An epidemiological study. *Journal of the American Academy of Child and Adolescent Psychiatry, 27*(6), 764–771.

Foa, E., & Wilson, R. (1991). *Stop obsessing!* New York: Bantam.

Frankel, M., Cummings, J., Robertson, M., et al. (1986). Obsessions and compulsions in Gilles de la Tourette syndrome. *Neurology, 36*, 378–382.

Freud, A. (1965). *Normality and pathology in childhood*. New York: International Universities Press.

Gesell, A., Ames, L., & Ilg, F. (1974). *Infant and child in the culture today*. New York: Harper & Row.

Goodman, W., McDougle, C., Price, L., et al. (1990). Beyond the serotonin hypothesis: A role for dopamine in some forms of obsessive compulsive disorder. *Journal of Clinical Psychiatry, 51*(Suppl.), 36–43.

Goodman, W. K., McDougle, C. J., & Price, L. H. (1992). The role of serotonin and dopamine in the pathophysiology of obsessive compulsive disorder. *International Clinical Psychopharmacology, 1*, 35–38.

Goodman, W. K., Price, L. H., Rasmussen, S. A., et al. (1989). The Yale–Brown Obsessive Compulsive Scale: Vol. II. Validity. *Archives of General Psychiatry, 46*(11), 1012–1016.

Greist, J. H. (1992). An integrated approach to treatment of obsessive compulsive disorder. *Journal of Clinical Psychiatry, 53*(Suppl.), 38–41.

Hamburger, S. D., Swedo, S., Whitaker, A., et al. (1989). Growth rate in adolescents with obsessive–compulsive disorder. *American Journal of Psychiatry, 146*(5), 652–655.

Harris, C., & Wiebe, D. (1992). An analysis of response prevention and flooding procedures in the treatment of adolescent obsessive compulsive disorder. *Journal of Behavior Therapy and Experimental Psychiatry, 23*(2), 107–115.

Hibbs, E. D., Hamburger, S. D., Lenane, M., et al. (1991). Determinants of expressed emotion in families of disturbed and normal children. *Journal of Child Psychology and Psychiatry and Allied Disciplines, 32*(5), 757–770.

Hollander, E., DeCaria, C. M., Aronowitz, B., et al. (1991). A pilot follow-up study of childhood soft signs and the development of adult psychopathology. *Journal of Neuropsychiatry and Clinical Neurosciences, 3*(2), 186–189.

Hollander, E., Schiffman, E., Cohen, B., et al. (1990). Signs of central nervous system dysfunction in obsessive–compulsive disorder [see comments]. *Archives of General Psychiatry, 47*(1), 27–32.

Hollingsworth, C., Tanguay, P., & Grossman, L. (1980). Long-term outcome of obsessive compulsive disorder in childhood. *Journal of the American Academy of Child and Adolescent Psychiatry, 19,* 134–144.

Insel, T. R. (1992a). Neurobiology of obsessive compulsive disorder: A review. *International Clinical Psychopharmacology, 1,* 31–33.

Insel, T. R. (1992b). Oxytocin—a neuropeptide for affiliation: Evidence from behavioral, receptor autoradiographic, and comparative studies [Review]. *Psychoneuroendocrinology, 17*(1), 3–35.

Insel, T. R. (1992c). Toward a neuroanatomy of obsessive–compulsive disorder. *Archives of General Psychiatry, 49*(9), 739–744.

Insel, T., Mueller, E., & Gillin, C. (1984). Biological markers in obsessive–compulsive and affective disorders. *Journal of Psychiatric Research, 18,* 407–423.

Janet, P. (1903). *Les obsessions et la psychiatrie.* Paris: Felix Alan.

Jenike, M. A. (1989). Obsessive–compulsive and related disorders: A hidden epidemic [editorial; comment]. *New England Journal of Medicine, 321*(8), 539–541.

Jenike, M. A. (1992). Pharmacologic treatment of obsessive compulsive disorders. *Psychiatric Clinics of North America, 15*(4), 895–919.

Jenike, M., Baer, L., & Minichello, W. (1990). *Obsessive–compulsive disorders* (2nd ed). Littleton, MA: PSG.

Jenike, M. A., Hyman, S., Baer, L., et al. (1990). A controlled trial of fluvoxamine in obsessive–compulsive disorder: Implications for a serotonergic theory [see comments]. *American Journal of Psychiatry, 147*(9), 1209–1215.

Judd, L. (1965). Obsessive compulsive neurosis in children. *Archives of General Psychiatry, 12,* 136–143.

Kanner, L. (1962). *Child psychiatry* (3rd ed.). Springfield, MA: Charles C. Thomas.

Kearney, C. A., & Silverman, W. K. (1990). Treatment of an adolescent with obsessive–compulsive disorder by alternating response prevention and cognitive therapy: An empirical analysis. *Journal of Behavior Therapy and Experimental Psychiatry, 21*(1), 39–47.

Kendall, P. (1991). *Child and adolescent therapy.* New York: Guilford Press.

Kruesi, M. J., Rapoport, J. L., Hamburger, S., et al. (1990). Cerebrospinal fluid monoamine metabolites, aggression, and impulsivity in disruptive behavior disorders of children and adolescents. *Archives of General Psychiatry, 47*(5), 419–426.

Last, C., & Strauss, C. (1989). Obsessive–compulsive disorder in childhood. *Journal of Anxiety Disorders, 3,* 295–302.

Lenane, M. (1989). Families in obsessive–compulsive disorder. In J. Rapoport (Ed.), *Obsessive–compulsive disorder in children and adolescents* (pp. 237–249). Washington, DC: American Psychiatric Press.

Lenane, M. C., Swedo, S. E., Leonard, H., et al. (1990). Psychiatric disorders in first degree relatives of children and adolescents with obsessive compulsive disorder. *Journal of the American Academy of Child and Adolescent Psychiatry, 29*(3), 407–412.

Leonard, H. L., Goldberger, E. L., Rapoport, J. L., et al. (1990). Childhood rituals: Normal development or obsessive–compulsive symptoms? *Journal of the American Academy of Child and Adolescent Psychiatry, 29*(1), 17–23.

Leonard, H. L., Lenane, M. C., Swedo, S. E., et al. (1992). Tics and Tourette's disorder: A 2- to 7-year follow-up of 54 obsessive–compulsive children. *American Journal of Psychiatry, 149*(9), 1244–1251.

Leonard, H. L., & Rapoport, J. L. (1989). Pharmacotherapy of childhood obsessive–compulsive disorder. *Psychiatric Clinics of North America, 12*(4), 963–970.

Leonard, H. L., Swedo, S. E., Lenane, M. C., et al. (1991). A double-blind desipramine substitution during long-term clomipramine treatment in children and adolescents with obsessive–compulsive disorder. *Archives of General Psychiatry, 48*(10), 922–927.

Leonard, H. L., Swedo, S. E., Lenane, M. C., et al. (1993). A 2- to 7-year follow-up study of 54 obsessive–compulsive children and adolescents. *Archives of General Psychiatry, 50*(6), 429–439.

Leonard, H. L., Swedo, S. E., Rapoport, J. L., et al. (1989). Treatment of obsessive-compulsive disorder with clomipramine and desipramine in children and adolescents. A double-blind crossover comparison. *Archives of General Psychiatry, 46*(12), 1088–1092.

Leonard, H., Topol, D., Swedo, S., et al. (in press). Clonazepam as an augmenting agent in the treatment of childhood-onset obsessive–compulsive disorder. *Journal of the American Academy of Child and Adolescent Psychiatry.*

Lochman, J., Lampron, L., Gemmer, T., et al. (1987). Anger coping intervention with agressive children: A guide to implementation in school settings. In P. Keller & S. Heyman (Eds.), *Innovations in clinical practice: A source book* (pp. 339–356). Sarasota, FL: Professional Resource Exchange.

Lopez Ibor, J., & Lopez Ibor-Alino, J. (1975). Selection criteria for patients who should undergo psychiatric surgery. In W. Sweet, S. Obrador, & J. Martin-Rodriguez (Eds.), *Neurosurgical treatment in psychiatry*. Baltimore: University Park Press.

Luxenberg, J. S., Swedo, S. E., Flament, M. F., et al. (1988). Neuroanatomical abnormalities in obsessive–compulsive disorder detected with quantitative X-ray computed tomography. *American Journal of Psychiatry, 145*(9), 1089–1093.

Lydiard, R., Ballenger, J., Ellinwood, E., et al. (1990). *CSF monoamine metabolites in obsessive–compulsive disorder*. Presented at the annual meeting of the American Psychiatric Association, New York.

March, J. (in press). Cognitive-behavioral psychotherapy for children and adolescents with obsessive–compulsive disorder: A review and recommendations for treatment. *Journal of the American Academy of Child and Adolescent Psychiatry.*

March, J., Johnston, H., Jefferson, J., et al. (1990). Do subtle neurological impairments predict treatment resistance in children and adolescents with obsessive–compulsive disorder. *Journal of Child and Adolescent Psychopharmacology, 1,* 133–140.

March, J., & Mulle, K. (1993). *"How I ran OCD off my land": A cognitive–behavioral program for the treatment of obsessive–compulsive disorder in children and adolescents.* Unpublished manuscript.

March, J., & Mulle, K. (in press). Behavioral psychotherapy for obsessive–compulsive disorder: A preliminary single case study. *Journal of Anxiety Disorders.*

March, J., Mulle, K., & Herbel, B. (1994). Behavioral psychotherapy for children and adolescents with obsessive–compulsive disorder: An open trial of a new protocol driven treatment package. *Journal of the American Academy of Child and Adolescent Psychiatry, 33*(3), 333–341.

March, J. S., Gutzman, L. D., Jefferson, J. W., et al. (1989). Serotonin and treatment in obsessive–compulsive disorder. *Psychiatric Development, 7*(1), 1–18.

Marks, I. M., Lelliott, P., Basoglu, M., et al. (1988). Clomipramine, self-exposure and therapist-aided exposure for obsessive–compulsive rituals. *British Journal of Psychiatry, 152,* 522–534.

McDougle, C., Goodman, W., Leckman, J., et al. (1994). Haloperidol addition in fluvoxamine-refractory obsessive–compulsive disorder. *Archives of General Psychiatry, 51,* 302–308.

McDougle, C. J., Goodman, W. K., Price, L. H., et al. (1990). Neuroleptic addition in fluvoxamine-refractory obsessive–compulsive disorder. *American Journal of Psychiatry, 147*(5), 652–654.

Mindus, & Jenike, M. A. (1992). Neurosurgical treatment of malignant obsessive compulsive disorder. *Psychiatric Clinics of North America, 15*(4), 921–938.

Pauls, D., Raymond, C., Stevenson, J., et al. (1991). A family study of Gilles de la Tourette syndrome. *Human Genetics, 48,* 154–163.

Pauls, D., Towbin, K., Leckman, J., et al. (1986). Gilles de la Tourette syndrome and obsessive compulsive disorder: Evidence supporting a genetic relationship. *Archives of General Psychiatry, 43,* 1180–1182.

Piacentini, J., Jaffer, M., Gitow, A., et al. (1992). Psychopharmacologic treatment of child and adolescent obsessive compulsive disorder. *Psychiatric Clinics of North America, 15*(1), 87–107.

Pigott T. L. F., & Rubenstein, C. (1992). *A controlled trial of clonazepam augmentation in OCD patients treated with clomipramine or fluoxedtine.* Presented at the annual meeting of the American Psychiatric Association, Washington, DC.

Pigott, T. A., L'Heureux, F., Hill, J. L., et al. (1992). A double-blind study of adjuvant buspirone hydrochloride in clomipramine-treated patients with obsessive–compulsive disorder. *Journal of Clinical Psychopharmacology, 12*(1), 11–18.

Pigott, T. A., Pato, M. T., Bernstein, S. E., et al. (1990). Controlled comparisons of clomipramine and fluoxetine in the treatment of obsessive–compulsive disorder: Behavioral and biological results [see comments]. *Archives of General Psychiatry, 47*(10), 926–932.

Pigott, T. A., Pato, M. T., L'Heureux, F., et al. (1991). A controlled comparison of adjuvant lithium carbonate or thyroid hormone in clomipramine-treated patients with obsessive–compulsive disorder. *Journal of Clinical Psychopharmacology, 11*(4), 242–248.

Rapoport, J. (1989). *The boy who couldn't stop washing.* Washington, DC: American Psychiatric Press.

Rapoport, J., Elkins, R., & Langer, D. (1981). Childhood obsessive compulsive disorder. *American Journal of Psychiatry, 138,* 1545–1554.

Rapoport, J. L., Swedo, S. E., & Leonard, H. L. (1992). Childhood obsessive compulsive disorder. *Journal of Clinical Psychiatry, 56,* 11–16.

Rasmussen, S. A., & Eisen, J. L. (1990). Epidemiology of obsessive compulsive disorder. *Journal of Clinical Psychiatry, 53,* (Suppl. 10–3; discussion 14).

Rasmussen, S. A., & Eisen, J. L. (1992). The epidemiology and differential diagnosis of obsessive compulsive disorder. *Journal of Clinical Psychiatry,* 4–10.

Ratnasuriya, R. H., Marks, I. M., Forshaw, D. M., et al. (1991). Obsessive slowness revisited. *British Journal of Psychiatry, 159*(273), 273–274.

Rettew, D. C., Swedo, S. E., Leonard, H. L., et al. (1992). Obsessions and compulsions across time in 79 children and adolescents with obsessive–compulsive disorder. *Journal of the American Academy of Child and Adolescent Psychiatry, 31*(6), 1050–1056.

Ricciardi, J. N., Baer, L., Jenike, M. A., et al. (1992). Changes in DSM-III-R axis II diagnoses following treatment of obsessive–compulsive disorder. *American Journal of Psychiatry, 149*(6), 829–831.

Riddle, M. (1993). *OCD: Comorbidity with Tourette's syndrome.* Presented at the annual meeting of the American Academy of Child and Adolescent Psychiatry, San Antonio, TX.

Riddle, M. A., Hardin, M. T., King, R., et al. (1990). Fluoxetine treatment of children and adolescents with Tourette's and obsessive compulsive disorders: Preliminary clinical experience. *Journal of the American Academy of Child and Adolescent Psychiatry, 29*(1), 45–48.

Riddle, M. A., Scahill, L., King, R., et al. (1990). Obsessive compulsive disorder in children and adolescents: Phenomenology and family history. *Journal of the American Academy of Child and Adolescent Psychiatry, 29*(5), 766–772.

Riddle, M. A., Scahill, L., King, R. A., et al. (1992). Double-blind, crossover trial of fluoxetine and placebo in children and adolescents with obsessive–compulsive disorder. *Journal of the American Academy of Child and Adolescent Psychiatry, 31*(6), 1062–1069.

Rutter, M., Tizard, J., & Whitmore, K. (1970). *Education, health, and behavior.* London: Longmans.

Ryan, N. D. (1992). The pharmacologic treatment of child and adolescent depression [Review]. *Psychiatric Clinics of North America, 15*(1), 29–40.

Staebler, C. R., Pollard, C. A., & Merkel, W. T. (1993). Sexual history and quality of current relationships in patients with obsessive compulsive disorder: A comparison with two other psychiatric samples. *Journal of Sex and Marital Therapy, 19*(2), 147–153.

Sternberger, L. G., & Burns, G. L. (1990). Maudsley Obsessional–Compulsive Inventory: Obsessions and compulsions in a nonclinical sample. *Behaviour Research and Therapy, 28*(4), 337–340.

Swedo, S. (1989). Rituals and releasers: An ethological model of obsessive-compulsive disorder. In J. Rapoport (Eds.), *Obsessive–compulsive disorder in children and adolescents* (pp. 269–288). Washington, DC: American Psychiatric Press.

Swedo, S., Leonard, H., & Kiessling, L. (1994). Speculations on anti-neuronal antibody-mediated neuropsychiatric disorders of childhood. *Pediatrics, 93*(2), 323–326.

Swedo, S. E., Leonard, H. L., Kruesi, M. J., et al. (1992). Cerebrospinal fluid neurochemistry in children and adolescents with obsessive–compulsive disorder. *Archives of General Psychiatry, 49*(1), 29–36.

Swedo, S., Leonard, H., & Rapoport, J. (1990). Childhood-onset obsessive-compulsive disorder. In M. Jenike, L. Baer, & Minichello (Eds.), *Obsessive-compulsive disorder.* Littleton, MA: PSG.

Swedo, S. E., Leonard, H. L., & Rapoport, J. L. (1992). Childhood-onset obsessive compulsive disorder. *Psychiatric Clinics of North America, 15*(4), 767–775.

Swedo, S. E., Leonard, H. L., Schapiro, M. B., et al. (1993). Sydenham's chorea: Physical and psychological symptoms of St. Vitus dance. *Pediatrics, 91*(4), 706–713.

Swedo, S., & Rapoport, J. (1990). Neurochemical and neuroendocrine considerations of obsessive–compulsive disorder in childhood. In W. Deutsch, A. Weizman, & R. Weizman (Eds.), *Application of basic neuroscience to child psychiatry* (pp. 275–284). New York: Plenum Press.

Swedo, S. E., Rapoport, J. L., Cheslow, D. L., et al. (1989). High prevalence of obsessive–compulsive symptoms in patients with Sydenham's chorea. *American Journal of Psychiatry, 146*(2), 246–249.

Swedo, S. E., Rapoport, J. L., Leonard, H., et al. (1989). Obsessive–compulsive disorder in children and adolescents: Clinical phenomenology of 70 consecutive cases. *Archives of General Psychiatry, 46*(4), 335–341.

Swedo, S. E., Schapiro, M. B., Grady, C. L., et al. (1989). Cerebral glucose metabolism in childhood-onset obsessive–compulsive disorder. *Archives of General Psychiatry, 46*(6), 518–523.

Szatmari, P., Bremner, R., & Nagy, J. (1989). Asperger's syndrome: A review of clinical features. *Canadian Journal of Psychiatry (Revue Canadienne de Psychiatrie), 34*(6), 554–560.

Thoren, P., Asberg, M., & Cronholm, B. (1980). Clomipramine treatment of obsessive–compulsive disorder: A controlled trial. *Archives of General Psychiatry, 37,* 1281–1285.

Thyer, B. A. (1991). Diagnosis and treatment of child and adolescent anxiety disorders. *Behavior Modification, 15*(3), 310–325.

Vitulano, L. A., King, R. A., Scahill, L., et al. (1992). Behavioral treatment of children and adolescents with trichotillomania. *Journal of the American Academy of Child and Adolescent Psychiatry, 31*(1), 139–146.

von Economo, C. (1931). *Encephalitis lethargica, its sequalae and treatment.* Rome: Oxford University Press.

Warren, W. (1960). A study of adolescent inpatients and the outcome six or more years later. *Journal of Child Psychology and Psychiatry, 6,* 141–160.

Wolff, R., & Rapoport, J. (1988). Behavioral treatment of childhood obsessive–compulsive disorder. *Behavior Modification, 12*(2), 252–266.

Wolff, R. P., & Wolff, L. S. (1991). Assessment and treatment of obsessive–compulsive disorder in children. *Behavior Modification, 15*(3), 372–393.

Zohar, J., Insel, T. R., Zohar, K. R., et al. (1988). Serotonergic responsivity in obsessive–compulsive disorder: Effects of chronic clomipramine treatment. *Archives of General Psychiatry, 45*(2), 167–172.

Chapter 12

Posttraumatic Stress Disorder

Lisa Amaya-Jackson
John S. March

In recent decades, there has been increasing recognition that traumatic experiences can have a severe and lasting impact on children. In *Post-Traumatic Stress Disorder in Children*, Eth and Pynoos (1985) reviewed the current knowledge regarding the vulnerability of children and adolescents to violence, war, cancer, and sexual abuse. Subsequently, an upsurge in research confirmed that exposure to these and other high-magnitude threats reliably predicts later psychopathology (defined categorically, as in posttraumatic stress disorder [PTSD], or dimensionally, as in effects on peer relationships or self-esteem) in young persons. For example, Reiss, Richters, Radke-Yarrow, et al. (1993) extended the perspective to the specific topic of community violence—its magnitude, effects, and implications for prevention and for treatment. In this chapter, we summarize the literature on child and adolescent PTSD, paying particular attention to elements of the clinical picture that diverge from the adult disorder.

EPIDEMIOLOGY AND NATURAL HISTORY

The Epidemiologic Catchment Area (ECA) studies revealed current and lifetime prevalence rates for PTSD in adults as 0.4 and 1.3%, respectively. An additional 15% experienced many of the PTSD symptoms but failed to meet full *Diagnostic and Statistical Manual of Mental Disorders*, third edition (DSM-III) criteria for the disorder (American Psychiatric Association, 1980; Davidson, Hughes, Blazer, et al., 1991; Helzer, Robins, & McEvoy, 1987). The tendency of PTSD toward chronicity contributes to these high lifetime prevalence rates (Davidson & Fairbank, 1992). Breslau, Davis, Andreski, et al. (1991), using a modified version of the Diagnostic Interview Schedule (DIS; Robins, Helzer, Croughan, et al., 1981), found a 9% prevalence rate in urban young adults, suggesting that incidence may be higher or lower in differing geographical locations or study populations.

While no epidemiological studies look specifically at the general incidence or prevalence of PTSD in children and adolescents, rates of PTSD are clearly higher in youth exposed to life-threatening events, including criminal assault (Pynoos & Eth, 1985; Pynoos & Nader, 1988a, 1988b), hostage taking (Schwarz & Kowalski, 1991), kidnapping (Terr, 1979), combat (Clarke, Sack, & Goff), bone marrow transplantation (Stuber, Nader, Yasuda, et al., 1991), severe burns (Stoddard, Norman, & Murphy, 1989), and marine disaster (Yule, Udwin, Murdoch, 1990; Yule & Williams, 1990). Studies crossing a variety of natural disasters also show elevated rates of posttraumatic stress in disaster victims relative to controls (Burke, Borus, Burns, et al., 1982; McFarlane, 1987; Green, Korol, Grace, et al., 1991).

Terr's description of the Chowchilla school bus kidnapping was one of the first to describe posttraumatic stress symptoms in children. All 25 children involved had moderate to severe PTSD regardless of their prior developmental or psychiatric history, parental relationships, or past trauma (Terr, 1983). Similarly, Pynoos, Frederick, Nader, et al. (1987) found that almost 60% of exposed children continued to meet full criteria for PTSD a year after a schoolyard sniper attack. Of adolescent Cambodian refugees who survived the atrocities of the Pol Pot regime, 50% were found to have PTSD with persistent symptoms accompanied by depression and anxiety 3 years later (Kinzie, Sack, Angell, et al., 1989). While domestic violence and sexual abuse have been shown to be significant public health problems in prevalence and in impact on psychological functioning of affected children (Deblinger, McLeer, Atkins, et al., 1989; Widom, 1989), only recently has PTSD begun to be assessed in affected children as an important adverse outcome of both single-event and chronic trauma. For example, Deblinger et al. (1989) report rates of PTSD at 20%, 7%, and 10% in psychiatric inpatient children who have been sexually abused, physically abused, and nonabused, respectively.

Pynoos and Nader also showed that trauma exposure (proximity) was linearly related to the risk for PTSD symptoms in children (Pynoos et al., 1987) and that memory disturbances, indicating distorted cognitive processing during the event, closely followed exposure (Pynoos & Nader, 1989). Confirming clinical experience, Saigh (1991) later showed that PTSD could result from trauma exposure as a victim, witness, or even learning about a negative life event secondarily, through verbal description. Not surprisingly, choice of threshold for exposure and PTSD symptoms determines the rate of diagnosis (Schwarz & Kowalski, 1991).

While studies clearly show elevated rates of posttraumatic stress in victims relative to controls, they show inconsistent results regarding the chronicity of PTSD, although studies that include child subjects tend to show that the psychological impact on children persists over time (Earls, Smith, Reich, et al., 1988; Kinzie et al., 1989; McFarlane, 1987; Terr, 1983). These studies also reveal that parents tend to underestimate both the intensity and duration of the stress reactions of their children (Bloch, Silber, & Perry, 1956; Burke et al., 1982; Handford, Mayes, Mattison, et al., 1986; Terr, 1983).

DIAGNOSIS AND CLASSIFICATION

Although PTSD entered the diagnostic nomenclature with DSM-III (American Psychiatric Association, 1980), the diagnostic criteria for PTSD were not explicitly applied to children and adolescents until DSM-III-R (American Psychiatric Association, 1987). Nevertheless, the research laboratory now clearly documents that children show a symptom picture consistent with the diagnosis of PTSD in adults (March & Amaya-Jackson, 1993). Moreover, since traumatic events experienced prior to age 11 are three times more likely to result in PTSD (Davidson & Smith, 1990), children may be more sensitive to trauma than are adolescents or adults.

In DSM-IV (American Psychiatric Association, 1994), a diagnosis of PTSD requires exposure to an event that involved actual or threatened death or serious injury (to self or others) and a personal response involving extreme fear and helplessness. Children may express the latter in the form of disorganized or agitated behavior. Recognizing the high prevalence of traumatic events, DSM-IV omits the DSM-III-R caveat that the stressor should lie outside usual human experience. Stressor events (e.g., kidnapping) continue to be specified on Axis IV, typically at the most severe level.

A diagnosis of PTSD also requires the following categorical symptoms for at least 1 month: (1) intrusive reexperiencing of the event, (2) avoidance of stimuli associated with the trauma or numbing of general responsiveness, and (3) persistent symptoms of increased arousal. DSM-IV includes (Criterion F) the new stipulation that the disturbance must cause impairment of function. New subcategories specify acute (less than 3 months) or chronic (greater than 3 months) duration of symptoms. The DSM-IV diagnostic criteria for PTSD are summarized in Table 12.1.

In order to cover acute stress responses, which may predict long-term adverse sequelae, DSM-IV also adds a new diagnosis: Acute Stress Disorder (ASD). The essential features of ASD include the development of severe anxiety, posttraumatic stress symptoms, and dissociative symptoms

TABLE 12.1. Diagnostic Criteria for 309.81 Posttraumatic Stress Disorder

A. The person has been exposed to a traumatic event in which both of the following were present:
   1. the person experienced, witnessed, or was confronted with an event or events that involved actual or threatened death or serious injury, or a threat to the physical integrity of self or others
   2. the person's response involved intense fear, helplessness, or horror. **Note:** In children, this may be expressed instead by disorganized or agitated behavior
B. The traumatic event is persistently reexperienced in one (or more) of the following ways:
   1. recurrent and intrusive distressing recollections of the event, including images, thoughts, or perceptions. **Note:** In young children, repetitive play may occur in which themes or aspects of the trauma are expressed
   2. recurrent distressing dreams of the event. **Note:** In children, there may be frightening dreams without recognizable content.
   3. acting or feeling as if the traumatic event were recurring (includes a sense of reliving the experience, illusions, hallucinations, and dissociative flashback episodes, including those that occur on awakening or when intoxicated). **Note:** In young children, trauma-specific reenactment may occur.
   4. intense psychological distress at exposure to internal or external cues that symbolize or resemble an aspect of the traumatic event
   5. physiological reactivity on exposure to internal or external cues that symbolize or resemble an aspect of the traumatic event
C. Persistent avoidance of stimuli associated with the trauma and numbing of general responsiveness (not present before the trauma), as indicated by three (or more) of the following:
   1. efforts to avoid thoughts, feelings, or conversations associated with the trauma
   2. efforts to avoid activities, places, or people that arouse recollections of the trauma
   3. inability to recall an important aspect of the trauma
   4. markedly diminished interest or participation in significant activities
   5. feeling of detachment or estrangement from others
   6. restricted range of affect (e.g., unable to have loving feelings)
   7. sense of a foreshortened future (e.g., does not expect to have a career, marriage, children, or a normal life span)
D. Persistent symptoms of increased arousal (not present before the trauma), as indicated by two (or more) of the following:
   1. difficulty falling or staying asleep
   2. irritability or outbursts of anger
   3. difficulty concentrating
   4. hypervigilance
   5. exaggerated startle response
E. Duration of the disturbance (symptoms in Criteria B, C, and D) is more than 1 month.
F. The disturbance causes clinically significant distress or impairment in social, occupational, or other important areas of functioning.

Specify if:

       Acute: if duration of symptoms is less that 3 months
       Chronic: if duration of symptoms is 3 months or more

Specify if:

       With Delayed Onset: if onset of symptoms is at least 6 months after the stressor

Note. From American Psychiatric Association (1994, pp. 427–429). Copyright 1994 American Psychiatric Association. Reprinted by permission.

within 1 month following a traumatic event. The DSM-IV diagnostic criteria for ASD are listed in Table 12.2.

CLINICAL FINDINGS

The Stressor

As the changes in DSM-IV show, the definition of the stressor (Criterion A)—what constitutes a "traumatic" experience—has been an area of some controversy (March, 1992). Clearly, exposure to a life-threatening event—either directly or as a witness—is a potent risk factor for a traumatic stress reaction. However, while PTSD in children resembles PTSD in adults, aspects of the symptom picture vary with child- and stressor-specific factors (Nader, Stuber, & Pynoos, 1991; Kendall-Tackett, Williams, & Finkelhor, 1993; Famularo, Kinscherff, & Fenton, 1990). Chronic physical and sexual abuse in childhood often results in severe psychopathology that bears little relationship to the classic PTSD symptom picture (Kendall-Tackett et al., 1993). Although there is clear overlap between the categories, Terr (1991) makes the useful distinction between Type I trauma (sudden, unpredictable, single-incident, that may or may not be multiply repeated) and Type II trauma (chronic, expected, repeated; usually childhood physical and/or sexual abuse).

Children also may develop PTSD symptoms from indirect exposure in a near-miss experience; for example, a child who left the Chowchilla bus before it was kidnapped developed PTSD himself (Terr, 1990). The unwitnessed death or injury of a loved one may precipitate symptoms of PTSD that are exacerbated by the family's retelling of the event, by detailed media coverage (Amaya-Jackson, Caddell, Costanzo, et al., 1992), and by contagion effects within the community.

When human accountability is tied to the stressor, the impact may be more severe and long-lasting (American Psychiatric Association, 1987). When the event is perpetrated by an authority figure close to the child, long-lasting adverse changes in personality may occur, undermining the child's ability to trust or form meaningful relationships (Herman, 1992). Associated symptoms include impaired affect modulation, self-destructive behavior, dissociation, somatic complaints, feelings of ineffectiveness and shame, feeling permanently damaged, feeling constantly threatened, and a loss of previous beliefs (American Psychiatric Association, 1994). The DSM-IV field trials explored these constellations of symptoms as a possible entity distinct from PTSD to be termed Complex PTSD or Disorder of Extreme Stress Not Otherwise Specified (DESNOS; Herman, 1993). However, Complex PTSD was not included in DSM-IV because all field

TABLE 12.2. Diagnostic Criteria for 308.3 Acute Stress Disorder

A. The person has been exposed to a traumatic event in which both of the following were present:
   1. the person experienced, witnessed, or was confronted with an event or events that involved actual or threatened death or serious injury, or a threat to the physical integrity of self or others
   2. the person's response involved intense fear, helplessness, or horror
B. Either while experiencing or after experiencing the distressing event, the individual has three (or more) of the following dissociative symptoms:
   1. a subjective sense of numbing, detachment, or absence of emotional responsiveness
   2. a reduction in awareness of his or her surroundings (e.g., "being in a daze")
   3. derealization
   4. depersonalization
   5. dissociative amnesia (i.e., inability to recall an important aspect of the trauma)
C. The traumatic event is persistently reexperienced in at least one of the following ways: recurrent images, thoughts, dreams, illusions, flashback episodes, or a sense of reliving the experience; or distress on exposure to reminders of the traumatic event.
D. Marked avoidance of stimuli that arouse recollections of the trauma (e.g., thoughts, feelings, conversations, activities, places, people).
E. Marked symptoms of anxiety or increased arousal (e.g., difficulty sleeping, irritability, poor concentration, hypervigilance, exaggerated startle response, motor restlessness).
F. The disturbance causes clinically significant distress or impairment in social, occupational, or other important areas of functioning or impairs the individual's ability to pursue some necessary task, such as obtaining necessary assistance or mobilizing personal resources by telling family members about the traumatic experience.
G. The disturbance lasts for a minimum of 2 days and a maximum of 4 weeks and occurs within 4 weeks of the traumatic event.
H. The disturbance is not due to the direct physiological effects of a substance (e.g., a drug of abuse, a medication) or a general medical condition, is not better accounted for by Brief Psychotic Disorder, and is not merely an exacerbation of a preexisting Axis I or Axis II disorder.

Note. From American Psychiatric Association (1994, pp. 431–432). Copyright 1994 American Psychiatric Association. Reprinted by permission.

trial subjects with the disorder also had classic PTSD, making complex PTSD only a potential subcategory, and because of overlap with borderline personality disorder (DSM-IV field trials, unpublished). It is hoped that ongoing research will further clarify the diagnostically significant sequelae of long-term exposure (and PTSD symptoms) on personality functioning.

Reexperiencing

The traumatic event can be reexperienced in the form of distressing, intrusive thoughts or memories, dreams, and flashbacks. Reexperiencing symptoms set PTSD apart from other psychiatric syndromes; in no other symptom are portions of the traumatic event recapitulated. Reexperiencing occurs both spontaneously and in response to traumatic reminders. Nightmares may depict horrors linked to specific traumatic moments in the event or may generalize to other fears or dangers that threaten the child or someone he loves. These less event-specific threats, for example monsters or "bad guys," may prevent caregivers from recognizing the significance of the traumatic event.

"Traumatic play"—the repetitive acting out of specific themes of the trauma—is often observed in younger children. When children incorporate rescues that lead to a happy ending (intervention fantasies; Pynoos & Nader, 1993), play may represent an attempt at mastery. When traumatic play continues in a monotonous, repetitive fashion, without working through, it is more appropriately viewed as a defensive failure (Terr, 1981). Contagion effects may be noted in peers who become participants in "playground shoot-outs." Traumatic play is clearly maladaptive when it interferes with play's normative uses or leads to risky or aggressive behavior. Reexperiencing that involves unconscious forces (either in play or in everyday life) is more appropriately viewed as reenactment behavior than as play. Counterphobic "acting out" is common in adolescents given their propensity for impulsive risk-taking behavior.

In adults, flashbacks resemble panic attacks in which the mental content of the panic attack is related to an antecedent trauma (Mellman & David, 1985). It has been suggested that children are less likely to experience flashbacks (Terr, 1983), but we have not found this to be true either clinically or in our research on children who went through the Hamlet fire. Indeed, children developed what we have termed "pseudoflashbacks"— recurring images of the event that they concocted from the detailed descriptions they heard or that they imagined on their own. Some children attempt to block these images from their minds by covering their eyes or ears. Other children remain motorically active in an effort to keep their minds otherwise occupied and may resemble nontraumatized children with attention-deficit/hyperactivity disorder.

Avoidance or Numbing

Child trauma victims invariably make conscious attempts to avoid thoughts, feelings, or activities that bring back recollections of the event. Cognitive suppression and distraction are particularly common, as is behavioral avoidance. However, children pay a high price for these survival strategies because the strategies inevitably spill over into other domains of functioning. Children with PTSD often show markedly diminished interest in previously enjoyed activities and sometimes lose previously acquired skills, leaving them less verbal or regressed to behaviors such as thumb sucking or enuresis.

Children with PTSD also may show evidence of restricted affect, accompanying feelings of detachment or estrangement from others. One child survivor of a disaster in which a tornado struck her school cafeteria during lunch, killing and injuring many of her classmates, explained her need to totally shut down her feelings: "It's like my mind is a library with all the books tightly shut. But when I talk about things . . . it's like all the books fall open all at once, and then I can't even think." For this child—and for other PTSD children—there appears to be dysregulation in the ability to modulate both intrusive and avoidant symptoms.

Child victims of trauma are said to develop a "sense of foreshortened future" (American Psychiatric Association, 1987), believing they may never grow up or fulfill other adult tasks (Terr, 1990), and "omen" formations. However, the empirical literature shows little support for these findings as necessary elements of the PTSD symptom picture.

Increased Physiological Arousal

Depending on the nature of the stressor, children with PTSD may show symptoms of increased physiological arousal, such as sleep disturbances, irritability, difficulty concentrating, hypervigilance, exaggerated startle responses, and outbursts of aggression. Somatic symptoms of autonomic hyperactivity may be both tonic or phasic in nature, with the latter occurring more often when the child encounters traumatic reminders. Changes in sleep architecture have been documented in adults with PTSD (Friedman, 1991; Kramer, Kinney, & Scharf, 1982); clinically, sleep disturbances in PTSD children are particularly noteworthy. For example, sleepwalking and night terrors are not uncommon. Sleep problems often impair a child's attention/concentration skills and hence may negatively affect learning and behavior in school.

COMORBIDITY AND DIFFERENTIAL DIAGNOSIS

Traumatized children frequently exhibit symptoms of disorders other than PTSD, and children with other disorders not uncommonly have PTSD as an intercurrent diagnosis (Herzog, Keller, Sacks, et al., 1992; Famularo, Kinscherff, & Fenton, 1992; Pynoos & Nader, 1988a; Goldman,

D'Angelo, Demaso, et al., 1992). Besides true comorbidity, PTSD symptoms are often confounded by spurious comorbidity resulting from overlap between criteria sets (e.g., affective constriction in PTSD overlaps anhedonia in depression); on the other hand, other diagnoses can be confounded by PTSD symptoms (e.g., the child who looks depressed and inattentive because of lack of sleep). In our study of children after the Hamlet fire, we showed that PTSD is weakly associated with disruptive behavior disorders (March, Amaya-Jackson, Costanzo, et al., unpublished data). Similar results were noted after Hurricane Hugo (Lonigan, Shannon, Finch, et al., 1991) and in children suffering from chronic maltreatment (Famularo et al., 1992). Because of the high prevalence of dimensional and transitional symptomatology, it is crucial to include these non-PTSD outcomes as targets for treatment and as predictors of treatment response in treatment outcome studies.

The anxiety spectrum disorders are prominent comorbid conditions following both direct and indirect exposure to traumatic events. Many children experience increased attachment behaviors, such as worries about the safety of family or friends. While this finding may be explained by a constitutional proneness to separation anxiety, it is more likely that children become separation anxious because exposure to PTSD-related threats and symptoms activates attachment bonds. While a diagnosis of separation anxiety disorder is warranted when symptoms of separation anxiety interfere with the child's daily life, it is important to remember the reasonableness of the originating threat. Thus, reconstituting a safe environment must precede otherwise premature attempts to enforce or encourage separation.

Children who do not meet full criteria for PTSD, often because they experienced a lower stressor "dose," frequently manifest symptoms of DSM-IV Generalized Anxiety. It is important to keep the traumatic origin of the anxiety in mind when designing a treatment plan for such children, who may otherwise be at risk for delayed-onset PTSD. Similarly, children often display somatic symptoms as a kind of traumatic reenactment that overlaps with limited-symptom panic and separation anxiety disorder (Chapter 9). Without adequate treatment, these symptoms may progress to panic attacks or to PTSD. Traumatic simple phobias are relatively easy to distinguish from PTSD in that they lack tonic arousal, do not readily generalize to new situations, and so result in less psychosocial dysfunction than PTSD.

Depressive-spectrum symptomology, ranging from simple demoralization to melancholic major depression, is the most common secondary comorbidity in PTSD. Depression can sometimes be distinguished from PTSD by the self-punitive nature of the child's thoughts or by a more pervasive anhedonia than that usually seen with phobically driven affective constriction.

A full depressive syndrome is frequently a normal reaction to the loss of a loved one (Weller & Weller, 1990). Indeed, grief symptoms were found to have a linear relationship across differing exposure groups to severity of PTSD symptoms in children who lost friends and family following the Hamlet fire (Amaya-Jackson, March, & Costanzo, 1993). The trauma response may significantly interfere with normal grieving. Children appear to be especially vulnerable to what Eth and Pynoos (1985) refer to as "the additive demands of trauma mastery and grief work" (p. 179). For example, reminiscing, an essential part of the bereavement process, may be inhibited as the intrusive recollections of the traumatic event disturb the child's ability to recall pleasant memories of the deceased (Eth & Pynoos, 1985). Therefore, the child's traumatic responses must first be addressed so that the normal process of mourning may be adequately resolved.

Obsessive–compulsive disorder (OCD) is readily distinguished from PTSD: OCD usually lacks a PTSD-magnitude precipitant and trauma-specific intrusions. Rarely, symptoms of OCD may develop in the context of PTSD by secondary generalization. For example, children who have been sexually assaulted sometimes develop obsessional thoughts of contamination and may handle the anxiety associated with these thoughts through washing rituals. Checking rituals in response to obsessional concerns about safety issues also occur in PTSD and must be differentiated from OCD. Parenthetically, optimal treatment of such symptoms in both conditions involves anxiety management training and exposure-based interventions (Foa & Rothbaum, 1992; March, Mulle, & Herbel, 1994).

Schizophrenia, the delusional disorders, and brief reactive psychoses are readily distinguished from PTSD by dissimilarities between psychotic intrusive thoughts and PTSD reexperiencing and the presence of otherwise intact reality testing in PTSD.

Sexualized or aggressive play, self-mutilation, and suicidal behaviors may represent traumatic reenactments in child victims of sexual or physical abuse; these symptoms should always prompt a search for traumatic antecedents. When children who have experienced repeated victimization demonstrate contradictory behaviors across different contexts, the diagnosis of dissociative identity disorder (formerly multiple personality disorder) should be considered.

Since PTSD can mimic the disruptive behavior disorders, it is important to rule out PTSD as a cause of deteriorating school performance, poor concentration, irritability, or aggression before diagnosing oppositional defiant disorder, conduct disorder, or attention-deficit/hyperactivity disorder in a child who has experienced a life-threatening event. Preexisting learning disorders may be exaggerated by the child's traumatic reaction; alternatively, learning disorders can render the child less capable of processing the traumatic event. A similar relationship can be seen between trauma and substance abuse.

Not all reactions to traumatic events are necessarily pathological (March, 1991). However, even subsyndromal PTSD may interfere with the child's daily functioning; in this case an adjustment disorder diagnosis is appropriate. In formulating a treatment plan, clinicians should not overlook the significance of subsyndromal symptoms that may be appropriate targets of primary prevention. Mental health professionals should play an active role in utilizing prevention strategies that include teaching and consultation to primary-care physicians who may be the first contacts children have following a traumatic life event.

ETIOLOGY

While the stressor event (DSM-IV Criterion A) is inextricably tied to PTSD, variables other than the stressor contribute to the development of the disorder, including each child's personal characteristics and surrounding environment. However, very little is known empirically about the role and interaction of risk and protective factors (and associated mediating variables) in the development of posttraumatic stress symptoms in young persons (Green et al., 1991). Important child variables include demographic factors (e.g., SES, age, and gender), the presence of psychiatric comorbidity, other life events, social cognition, and each child's coping ability. For example, we found that black race and female gender were important risk factors for PTSD after the Hamlet fire (March et al., unpublished data).

Conaway summarizes a wide variety of social behaviors that have been reported to be abnormal in traumatized children, with problematic social behaviors serving both as a risk factor and an outcome of traumatic experiences (Conaway & Hansen, 1989). Joseph, Brewin, Yule, et al. (1993) point out that locus of control may play a role either in the induction or in the maintenance of PTSD, since lack of personal efficacy is associated with chronic PTSD symptoms. We found similar results in our study of the aftermath of the Hamlet fire (March et al., unpublished data).

Parental reactions to traumatic events have been shown to influence the response of children to the events, particularly those of younger children (McFarlane, 1987). Other family factors that may have mediating effects on the trauma include marital status and stability and education and psychological functioning of the parents. A family's social support network, separately from the child's own social supports, also may influence the family's and hence the child's response to trauma. Previous negative life events are likely mediators of children's response to a current trauma (Coddington, 1972). Referring specifically to PTSD risk, Pynoos & Nader (1988) suggest that the "effects of each episode can be additive and seriously deplete the child's inner resources" but empirical evidence for this proposition is lacking. Garmezy, Cicchetti, and Emde (in Reiss, et al., 1993) provide developmentally aware perspectives regarding risk analyses in trauma survivors. Garbarino cites an emergent model of risk presented by Sameroff, Seifer, Baracas, et al. (1987)—children can cope with low levels of risk in the form of one or two risk factors, but an accumulation of risk factors jeopardizes developmental domains across the board, including IQ scores (Garbarino, 1991). Garbarino also provides a thoughtful review of war trauma in the context of threats to normal development (Garbarino, Kostelny, & Dubrow, 1991).

CONCEPTUAL FRAMEWORKS FOR TRAUMA

Conceptual frameworks as varied as psychoanalytic theory, social learning theory, and/or neurobiology have all been applied to PTSD in youth. Brief summaries of each follow; the astute clinician will pick and choose which serves best for which symptom component and associated treatments.

Psychoanalytic Framework

Freud (1926/1948) conceived of psychic trauma as resulting from a traumatic stimulus overwhelming the ego and rendering it helpless. Indeed, his study of psychological trauma underpins much of psychoanalytic theory (van der Kolk & van der Hart, 1989). Unfortunately, Freud later substituted "repressed childhood wishes" for childhood traumatic experiences as etiologic for the "hysterical neuroses" he saw in his patients, thus denying appropriate attention to posttrauma syndromes. Both Freud and Janet believed that the disturbance resulting from a traumatic insult set in motion such tremendous utilization of energy in the form of psychic defense that the victim essentially was left with all other psychical functions impoverished (Freud, 1920/1959; van der Kolk, 1984). Freud referred to "repetition compulsion" as a victim's attempt to achieve mastery of the trauma by repeating traumatic themes in actions of everyday life and as representing fixation on the trauma. Later writers took a more pessimistic slant, terming traumatic play and other reexperiencing symptoms as "defensive failure" (Terr, 1991). Whichever perspective you might hold, psychodynamically defined defense mechanisms that play a role in PTSD include denial, dissociation, projection, and identification with the aggressor.

Social Learning Framework

Social learning theory frames PTSD as a stimulus-driven anxiety disorder in which both classical and instrumental conditioning play important roles (Kirkpatrick, Veronen, & Best, 1985). This view is in contrast to psychoanalytic theory, where anxiety is seen as a secondary feature. In classical conditioning, the stressor event acts as an unconditioned stimulus that elicits an unconditioned (reflexive) response in the child characterized by extreme fear and the cognitive perception of helplessness. Cognitive, affective, physiologic, and environmental cues accompanying the traumatic event then become conditioned stimuli often called "traumatic reminders." Through stimulus generalization these reminders in turn become capable of eliciting a conditioned response in the form of PTSD symptoms. In instrumental conditioning, children quickly learn by trial and error how to reduce PTSD symptoms through cognitive and behavioral avoidance and sometimes anxiety-dampening rituals. Unfortunately, these behaviors preclude the extinction of trauma-based anxiety and foster stimulus generalization (Fairbank & Nicholson, 1987).

Like psychoanalytic theories, the cognitive-behavioral perspective recognizes that perceived (subjective) as well as actual (objective) threat determine an individual's response. Hence, Foa, Steketee, and Rothbaum (1989) note that individuals with PTSD develop "fear structures" that are conditioned by both the event and the PTSD symptom picture. Fear structures are exceptionally sensitive to activation by internal and external cues reminiscent of the initiating trauma, including thoughts and affects incorporated during and after the event. Moreover, they contain automatic stimulus–response elements, such as verbal, somatic, and behavioral cues, and information regarding the meaning of event. For example, an adolescent victim of rape may lose her sense that the world is a just or a safe place (Taylor, Wood, & Lictman, 1983). These alterations in meaning determine in part whether the event is indeed "traumatic."

Neurobiological Framework

While models for PTSD in adults, largely based on dysregulation in the neurophysiological and neuroanatomic systems regulating the stress response, have become increasingly sophisticated (Giller, 1990), research into the biological underpinnings of childhood PTSD is weak at best, particularly along a developmental matrix. Perry (in press) hypothesizes that the abnormal patterns of catecholamine activity associated with prolonged "alarm reactions" induced by traumatic events during childhood may result in altered development of the central nervous system, with consequent dysregulation of the cardiovascular system, affective lability, behavioral impulsivity, and anxiety and increased startle responses and sleep abnormalities. Furthermore, he characterizes childhood PTSD as a developmental disorder since a child's developing brain is particularly vulnerable to the abnormal patterns of neurotransmitter and hormonal transmission (Perry, in press).

Implicated neurotransmitters in adult studies include norepinephrine, serotonin, dopamine, γ-aminobutyric acid (GABA), excitatory amino acids, corticosteroids and their modulators, and endogenous opioids (Friedman, 1990). Not surprisingly, these neurotransmitters police neuroanatomic regions implicated in PTSD, including brain stem arousal mechanisms, diencephalic modulation of sensory and emotional information, and cortical and limbic modulation of memory and motivation, including selective appraisal of threat (Friedman, 1990; Giller, 1990). Limited data on child patients currently suggests dysregulation in fear-enhanced startle responses (Ornitz & Pynoos, 1989) and in growth hormone regulation (Jensen, Pease, Benset, et al., 1991). Further studies of the neurobiology of PTSD in children and adolescents will require a sound understanding of the neurodevelopmental foundation of the stress response (Amaya-Jackson & March, 1993; Perry, in press).

ASSESSMENT AND TREATMENT

Assessment

A child may present with PTSD under several circumstances, including when referred for triage immediately following a traumatic event, when PTSD is ongoing, or when symptoms arise *de novo* or in the process of treatment for another disorder. As in any thorough evaluation, a multimethod evaluation is preferable, incorporating information from multiple sources. Both parent and child interviews should be done, with additional information obtained from teachers. Parents in general are good evaluators of children's externalizing behaviors; however, they may be less adequate in assessing internalizing symptoms (Costello & Angold, 1988; Herjanic, Herjanic, Brown, et al., 1975; Weissman, Wickramavatne, Warner, et al., 1987). Parents also have been noted to downplay or deny the impact of traumatic life experiences on their children (Bromet, 1990; Handford et al., 1986). Nevertheless, past history of trauma must be assessed because previous stressors may increase a child's risk for a more severe response.

Although they do not test specifically for PTSD, parent/teacher rating scales, such as the Conners Parent and Teacher Rating Scales (Conners, 1985), can be useful adjuncts in understanding a child's pre- and postevent behaviors. Self-report measures, such as the Children's Depression Inventory (Kovacs, 1985) and the Multidimensional Anxiety Scale for Children (MASC; Chapter 6) can be useful in assessing internalizing symptoms. Semistructured clinical interviews, such as the Anxiety Disorders Interview Schedule for Children (ADIS-C) or the Child and Adolescent Psychiatric Assessment (CAPA), have been developed to assess diagnostic psychiatric problems in children and adolescents, some with modules specific to PTSD (Chapter 6). While these instruments are most frequently used in research settings, they can be helpful to the clinician concerned with disentangling PTSD from associated comorbidities. Formulating a diagnosis and comprehensive treatment plan is aided by a thorough developmental history, a physical/neurological exam, and psychological and/or educational testing.

Psychosocial Treatment

Solomon, Gerrity, and Muff (1992) recently reviewed empirical studies of psychotherapeutic, cognitive-behavioral, and drug treatments for PTSD, noting that the literature provides greater support for cognitive-behavioral therapy (CBT) than for the other two treatments. Virtually all the cited studies involve adults; despite the substantial literature on PTSD in younger subjects, the dearth of treatment outcome studies is striking. With few exceptions, the child literature covers unsubstantiated case reports and theories of treatment founded entirely on clinical experience. Based in large part on his own work in the area, Saigh (1987, 1992) has made a persuasive case for the efficacy of cognitive-behavioral psychotherapy (CBT) in treating single-incident trauma. Deblinger (Deblinger, McLeer, & Henry, 1990) also has shown that CBT benefits children with PTSD from sexual abuse. Nevertheless, mental health providers dealing with traumatized children and adolescents are inevitably forced to operate from clinical lore or to "borrow" treatments, such as CBT from overanxious disorder or age-downward extension of trauma work in adults.

The mainstay of treatment is usually a mixture of cognitive-behavioral, supportive, and psychodynamic psychotherapy spread over several phases: brief preventive therapy, long-term therapy, and pulsed intervention. Additional formats include group and family interventions (Pynoos & Eth, 1986). Early preventive interventions are especially important to catch a youngster's symptoms at their most prominent before the sealing over of affect has taken place.

We and others utilize a prevention–intervention model that incorporates triage for acutely exposed children, supporting and strengthening coping skills for anticipated grief/trauma responses, treating other disorders that may develop or become exacerbated in the context of PTSD, and brief, focused psychotherapy for chronic PTSD symptoms (Pynoos & Nader,

1990; Amaya-Jackson & March, 1993). Central to almost all treatment strategies is an emphasis on reexposing the individual to traumatic cues under safe conditions, incorporating reparative and mastery elements in a structured, supportive manner (Lyons, 1987; Saigh, 1987). Since traumatic events and consequent PTSD symptoms frequently impair the child's family life, peer relationships, and school performance, it is important to address the child's current functioning in these areas. Comorbid symptoms, such as grief, guilt, anger, depression, anxiety, and behavioral disturbances, are also appropriate targets for brief psychotherapy.

"Psychological first aid" is especially applicable in crisis centers and in classrooms (Eth, Silverstein, & Pynoos, 1985; March, 1991; Pynoos & Nader, 1988a) and serves both as an intervention and as a screening tool for children who may need further evaluation. Debriefing interviews with teachers and parents can help identify and clarify adults' and childrens' reactions to a traumatic event. Adult caregivers may need assistance with the resurfacing of prior losses or guilt and helplessness over not being able to prevent what happened. Classroom discussion and drawings can be used as a means to express feelings, clarify confusion, and identify needs. Reparative drawings or role-playing vignettes are important components in this process: Tornado-ravaged houses can be rebuilt; injuries can be healed; children whose last view of a dying friend was tarnished by blood can find some relief by drawing their friend whole from the memory of the last time they played or as they imagine them "up in heaven." Children identified as highly exposed or having difficulty adjusting may be referred for further treatment. Additional interventions that may be needed and that can be done through the schools include support and counseling groups for parents or children and consultation–liaison with guidance staff and teachers.

Systematic review of the traumatic event is a key element of the initial interview and subsequent treatment (Pynoos & Eth, 1986)—it is imperative that the treating clinician understand the child's perception of the event, subjective meaning, level of exposure, and attributions of cause. This will often involve active and directive interventions on the part of the therapist. Through the use of precept play, drawings, puppets, and role playing, the child's experience as well as subjective meaning and attributions can be strategically explored. Clinicians must pay close attention to their own countertransference, rescue fantasies, and any tendency to shy away from particularly upsetting aspects of the child's experiences. The therapist's ability to endure the recounting of the event and the affect involved is crucial to the child's ability to utilize the treatment in general and to tolerate exposure in particular. Children's reactions can be normalized, intervention fantasies can be acknowledged, traumatic reminders can be identified, and confusion and distortions can be clarified. Since each session represents an implicit if not explicit exposure task, care must be taken to insure adequate closure at each session in preparation for the week's "homework."

Trauma work can often be conducted as brief psychotherapy, particularly following an acute traumatic event with no premorbid risk factors. Since controlled reexposure to traumatic cues is an essential aspect of treatment (Lyons, 1987; Saigh, 1987), traumatic memories and associated specific reminders must be worked through in their entirety. A key treatment concept necessary for successful "working through" is to approach the trauma as a series of traumatic moments (Pynoos & Nader, 1993). Specific moments are frequently linked to intervention fantasies: Often the "worst moment" occurs at the time of real or fantasized helplessness. Children often rush through their description of key elements of the trauma in an attempt to avoid the intense affect or reexperiencing. Systematically strategizing recall in a play-by-play fashion minimizes cognitive and behavioral avoidance and thus promotes exposure and habituation of anxiety. Response prevention is important in reducing avoidance as well as ritualized behaviors. Traditional cognitive-behavioral techniques, including relaxation, breathing training, and cognitive restructuring, facilitate the exposure/response prevention process.

Associated symptoms of grief, depression, anxiety, somatization, guilt, and behavioral disturbances are also appropriate targets of brief psychotherapy. Since traumatic events and consequent PTSD symptoms invariably affect the child's family relationships, peer relationships, and school performance, monitoring the child's current level of functioning should not be forgotten.

In the face of exposure to a massive amount of violence, intrafamilial homicide or suicide, prolonged abuse, or exposure to repetitively distressing events, brief trauma work may not be enough. The presence of preexisting psychopathology in the child or a parent, prior history of abuse, or ongoing exposure to a disruptive living situation also suggest a need for a more intensive, longer-term intervention. Long-term treatment can occur weekly or as pulsed intervention, based on the child's developmental phase, capacity for response, and clinical issues. In pulsed intervention, brief therapy is suspended (rather than terminated) until further treatment becomes necessary—such as during developmental transitions, changes in living situation, formation of intimate relationships, marriage, and so on. "Pulsing" the treatment helps prevent ongoing helplessness by minimizing dependence on the therapist as "the only one who really understands." Longer-term therapy also may be required to address issues related to character formation and impaired ability to form meaningful relationships. Pulsed intervention should not be confused with intermittent treatment, which may be utilized following brief psychotherapy that necessitates only occasional "booster" sessions. Severe PTSD requires arduous and critical dedication to treatment on the part of both patient and therapist.

Group and family therapy can play an important role as adjunctive or alternative treatments. Family work may be helpful when family members experience difficulty facing the child's distress or lack skills to adequately meet the child's needs. Parents may be preoccupied with their own reactions and not be aware of the child's symptoms. Families can be taught coping strategies, such as how to recognize and deal with traumatic reminders. When there are multiple victims, as after a natural disaster or mass violence, group psychotherapy can be of tremendous benefit following (or concomitant with) individual treatment. Lay support groups help provide emotional sustenance when dealing with traumatic symptoms and can facilitate exposure therapy through shared successes in resisting the urge to avoid traumatic reminders.

Pharmacological Treatment

Given the neurophysiological activation that is common to both acute and chronic stress, psychotropic medication can prove helpful in allowing psychological treatment to move forward. However, other than clinical lore, few data exist to guide the medication of children and adolescents with PTSD. Ideally, medications should decrease intrusions, avoidance, and anxious arousal; minimize impulsivity and improve sleep; treat secondary disorders; and facilitate cognitive and behavioral psychotherapies. In adults, case reports and uncontrolled trials suggest that the benefits of conventional drug treatments in PTSD are modest (Friedman, 1988b). Clinical experience is similar for children and adolescents.

A variety of uncontrolled trials report that standard antidepressants improve PTSD symptoms in adults (Friedman, 1988b). Only five controlled studies of antidepressant medications in adult PTSD have been published. Two report modest decreases in intrusion and anxiety symptoms, with phenelzine performing better than imipramine in one study (Davidson, Walker, & Kilts, 1987; Frank, Kosten, Giller, et al., 1988). Modest decreases in intrusion and anxiety symptoms were also recently reported for amitriptyline (Davidson, Kudler, Smith, et al., 1990). The other two studies were negative. Both were crossover designs utilizing lower doses and shorter treatments (Reist, Dauffmann, Haier, et al., 1989; Shetatsky, Greenberg, & Lere, 1988). Many clinicians find antidepressant therapy helpful in treating PTSD-related sleep disturbances. More recently, there have been reports that the selective serotonin reuptake inhibitor (SSRI) fluoxetine shows promise (Davidson, Roth, & Newman, 1991; March, 1992; McDougle, Charney, & St. James, 1991), particularly in reducing the avoidant symptoms of PTSD, a finding that has been noted to a lesser extent with amitriptiline. A placebo-controlled study of fluoxetine in adults is currently under way (Davidson, personal communication, January, 1994).

Among other drugs, the benzodiazepines suppress generalized anxiety but not the core PTSD symptoms of intrusions and avoidance; alprazolam withdrawal effects may be especially severe. In our experience there can be unpredictable paradoxical disinhibition in using benzodiazepines in children and young teenagers. Alternatively, buspirone has shown promise in targeting anxiety states and affective dysregulation. Lithium and carbamazepine reduce affective instability; carbamazepine also may reduce intrusive symptomatology (Friedman, 1988a), although its effectiveness is probably comparable to standard tricyclic antidepressants. Clonidine decreases startle responses in adult patients with PTSD (Kolb, Burris, & Griffith, 1984) and in children (Ornitz & Pynoos, 1989) and may target other symptoms of physiological "lability" as measured by autonomic arousal (Perry, in press). Similarly, propranolol reduces arousal symptoms in child sexual abuse survivors, presumably by blocking sympathetic nervous system hyperreactivity, although central effects also may play a role (Famularo, Kinsherff, & Fenton, 1988). Neuroleptics are ineffective and are not recommended unless a formal thought disorder is also present. Though little or no controlled data exists to predict treatment response in children and adolescents for any of these medications, we often utilize a regimen consisting of an SSRI frequently coupled to clonazepam, buspirone, or clonidine, modelling current trends in adult anxiety disorders (including PTSD).

SUMMARY

PTSD in children and adolescents is similar to PTSD in adults, with differences primarily in divergent stressors, developmental themes, family issues, and collateral symptoms. Almost wholly unsupported by data-based research, current treatment involves debriefing, brief psychotherapy, and pulsed long-term intervention, all integrating psychodynamic, pharmacological, and cognitive-behavioral treatments.

REFERENCES

Amaya-Jackson, L., Caddell, J., Costanzo, P., et al. (1992). Preliminary results of Hamlet child protocol. In S. Roth (Chair), *Design, implementation, and results of a quick response research project: The Hamlet study*. Symposia conducted at the annual meeting of The International Society for Traumatic Stress Studies, Los Angeles, CA.

Amaya-Jackson, L., & March, J. (1993). Post-traumatic stress disorder in children and adolescents. In H. Leonard (Ed.), *Child and adolescent clinics of North America: Anxiety disorders* (pp. 639–654). Philadelphia: W. B. Saunders.

Amaya-Jackson, L., March, J., & Costanzo, P. (1993). *Psychiatric consequences among children exposed to a community disaster.* Unpublished manuscript.

American Psychiatric Association. (1980). *Diagnostic and statistical manual of mental disorders* (3rd ed.). Washington, DC: Author.

American Psychiatric Association. (1987). *Diagnostic and statistical manual of mental disorders* (3rd rev., ed.). Washington, DC: Author.

American Psychiatric Association. (1994). *Diagnostic and statistical manual of mental disorders* (4th ed.). Washington, DC: Author.

Bloch, D., Silber, E., & Perry, S. (1956). Some factors in the emotional reaction of children to disaster. *American Journal of Psychiatry, 113,* 416–422.

Breslau, N., Davis, G., Andreski, P., et al. (1991). Traumatic events and post-traumatic stress disorder in an urban population of young adults. *Archives of General Psychiatry, 48,* 218–222.

Bromet, E. (1990). Methodological issues in the assessment of traumatic events. *Journal of Applied Social Psychology, 20(20),* 1719–1724.

Burke, J., Borus, J., Burns, B., et al. (1982). Changes in children's behavior after a natural disaster. *American Journal of Psychiatry, 1139,* 1010–1014.

Clarke, G., Sack, W. H., & Goff, B. (1993). Three forms of stress in Cambodian adolescent refugees. *Journal of Abnormal Child Psychology, 21(1),* 65–77.

Coddington, R. D. (1972). The significance of life events as etiologic factors in the diseases of children. *Journal of Psychosomatic Research, 16,* 7–18.

Conaway, L. P., & Hansen, D. J. (1989). Social behavior of physically abused and neglected children: A critical review. *Clinical Psychology Review, 9(5),* 627–652.

Conners, C. K. (1985). The Conners rating scales: Instruments for the assessment of childhood psychopathology. In *Children's Hospital National Medical Center,* Washington, DC.

Costello, E., & Angold, A. (1988). Scales to assess child and adolescent depression: Checklists, screens, and nets. *Journal of the American Academy of Child and Adolescent Psychiatry, 27(6),* 357–363.

Davidson, J., & Fairbank, J. (1992). The epidemiology of post-traumatic stress disorder. In J. Davidson & E. Foa (Eds.), *Post-traumatic stress disorder: DSM-IV and beyond* (pp. 147–169). Washington, DC: American Psychiatric Press.

Davidson, J., Kudler, H., Smith, R., et al. (1990). Treatment of posttraumatic stress disorder with amitriptyline and placebo. *Archives of General Psychiatry, 47,* 259–266.

Davidson, J., Roth, S., & Newman, E. (1991). Fluoxetine in post-traumatic stress disorder. *Journal of Traumatic Stress, 4,* 419–423.

Davidson, J., Walker, J., & Kilts, C. (1987). A pilot study of phenelzine in post-traumatic stress disorder. *British Journal of Psychiatry, 150,* 252–255.

Davidson, R., Hughes, D., Blazer, D., et al. (1991). Post-traumatic stress disorder in the community: An epidemiological study. *Psychological Medicine, 21,* 713–721.

Davidson, S., & Smith, R. (1990, July). Traumatic experiences in psychiatric out-patients. *Journal of Traumatic Stress Studies, 3,* 459–475.

Deblinger, E., McLeer, S. V., Atkins, M. S., et al. (1989). Post-traumatic stress in sexually abused, physically abused, and nonabused children. *Child Abuse and Neglect, 13,* 403–408.

Deblinger, E., McLeer, S. V., & Henry, D. (1990). Cognitive behavioral treat-ment for sexually abused children suffering post-traumatic stress: Prelimi-nary findings. *Journal of the American Academy of Child and Adolescent Psychiatry, 29*(5), 747–752.

Earls, F., Smith, E., Reich, W., et al. (1988). Investigating psychopathological consequences of a disaster in children: A pilot study incorporating a struc-tured diagnostic interview. *Journal of the American Academy of Child and Adolescent Psychiatry, 27,* 90–95.

Eth, S., & Pynoos, R. S. (1985). Interaction of trauma and grief in childhood. In S. Eth & R. S. Pynoos (Eds.), *Post-traumatic stress disorder in children.* Washington, DC: American Psychiatric Press.

Eth, S., Siverstein, S., & Pynoos, R. S. (1985). Mental health consultation to a preschool following the murder of a mother and child. *Hospital and Com-munity Psychiatry, 36,* 73–76.

Fairbank, J., & Nicholson, R. (1987). Theoretical and empirical issues in the treat-ment of post-traumatic stress disorder in Vietnam veterans. *Journal of Clini-cal Psychology, 43,* 44–55.

Famularo, R., Kinscherff, R., & Fenton, T. (1988). Propranolol treatment for childhood posttraumatic stress disorder, acute type. *American Journal of Diseases of Children, 142,* 1244–1247.

Famularo, R., Kinscherff, R., & Fenton, T. (1990). Symptom differences in acute and chronic presentation of childhood post-traumatic stress disorder. *Child Abuse and Neglect, 14*(3), 439–444.

Famularo, R., Kinscherff, R., & Fenton, T. (1992). Psychiatric diagnoses of mal-treated children: Preliminary findings. *Journal of the American Academy of Child and Adolescent Psychiatry, 31*(5), 863–867.

Foa, E., & Rothbaum, E. (1992). Cognitive-behavioral treatment of posttrau-matic stress disorder. In P. Saigh (Eds.), *Post-traumatic stress disorder: A behavioral approach to diagnosis and treatment* (pp. 85–110). Needham Heights, MA: Allyn & Bacon.

Foa, E., Steketee, G., & Rothbaum, B. (1989). Behavioral/cognitive con-ceptualizations of post-traumatic stress disorder. *Behavior Therapy, 20,* 155–176.

Frank, J., Kosten, T., Giller, E., et al. (1988). A randomized clinical trial of phenelezine and imipraine for post-traumatic stress disorder. *American Journal of Psychiatry, 145,* 1289–1291.

Freud, S. (1948). Inhibitions, symptoms, and anxiety. In J. Strachey (Ed.), *The standard edition of the complete psychological works of Sigmund Freud* (Vol. 20, pp. 87–174). London: Hogarth. (Original work published 1926)

Freud, S. (1959). Beyond the pleasure principle. In J. Strachey (Ed.), *The stan-dard edition of the complete psychological works of Sigmund Freud* (Vol. 18, pp. 7–64). London: Hogarth. (Original work published 1920)

Friedman, M. (1988a). PTSD and carbamazepine. *American Journal of Psychiatry, 145,* 281–285.

Friedman, M. (1988b). Toward rational pharmacotherapy for posttraumatic stress disorders: An interim report. *American Journal of Psychiatry, 145,* 281–285.

Friedman, M. (1990). Biological aspects of PTSD: Laboratory and clinical research. *PTSD Research Quarterly, 1,* 1–2.

Friedman, M. J. (1991). Biological approaches to the diagnosis and treatment of post-traumatic stress disorder. *Journal of Traumatic Stress, 4*(1), 67–91.

Garbarino, J. (1991). [Keynote address]. Annual meeting of The International Society for Traumatic Stress Studies, Washington, DC.

Garbarino, J., Kostelny, K., & Dubrow, N. (1991). *No place to be a child: Growing up in a war zone.* Lexington, MA: Lexington Books.

Giller, E. (1990). *Biological assessment and treatment of post-traumatic stress disorder.* Washington, DC: American Psychiatric Press.

Goldman, S., D'Angelo, E., Demaso, D., et al. (1992). Physical and sexual abuse histories among children with borderline personality disorder. *American Journal of Psychiatry, 149*(12), 1723–1726.

Green, B., Korol, M., Grace, M. C., et al. (1991). Children and disaster: Age, gender, and parental effects on PTSD symptoms. *Journal of the American Academy of Child and Adolescent Psychiatry, 30*(6), 945–951.

Handford, M. A., Mayes, S. D., Mattison, R. E., et al. (1986). Child and parent reaction to the Three Mile Island Nuclear Accident. *Journal of the American Academy of Child and Adolescent Psychiatry, 25,* 346–356.

Helzer, J. E., Robins, L. N., & McEvoy, L. (1987). Post-traumatic stress disorder in the general population: Findings of the epidemiologic catchment area survey. *New England Journal of Medicine, 317,* 1630–1634.

Herjanic, B., Herjanic, M., Brown, F., et al. (1975). Are children reliable reporters? *Journal of Abnormal Child Psychology, 100*(3), 307–324.

Herman, J. L. (1992). Complex PTSD: A syndrome in survivors of prolonged and repeated trauma. *Journal of Traumatic Stress, 5*(3), 377–391.

Herman, J. L. (1993). Sequelae of prolonged and repeated trauma: Evidence for a complex posttraumatic syndrome (DESNOS). In J. Davidson & E. Foa (Eds.), *Post-traumatic stress disorder: DSM-IV and beyond* (pp. 213–228). Washington, DC: American Psychiatric Press.

Herzog, D., Keller, M. B., Sacks, N., et al. (1992). Psychiatric comorbidity in treatment-seeking anorexics and bulemics. *Journal of the American Academy of Child and Adolescent Psychiatry, 31*(5), 810–818.

Jensen, J. B., Pease, J. J., Benset, R., et al. (1991). Growth hormone response patterns in sexually or physically abused boys. *Journal of the American Academy of Child and Adolescent Psychiatry, 30*(5), 784–790.

Joseph, S. A., Brewin, C. R., Yule, W., et al. (1993). Causal attributions and post-traumatic stress in adolescents. *Journal of Child Psychology and Psychiatry, 34*(2), 247–253.

Kendall-Tackett, K. A., Williams, L. M., & Finkelhor, D. (1993). Impact of sexual abuse on children: A review and synthesis of recent empirical studies. *Psychological Bulletin, 113,* 164–180.

Kinzie, J. D., Sack, W., Angell, R., et al. (1989, October). *A three year follow-up of Cambodian young people traumatized as children.* Presented at the annual meeting of the American Academy of Child and Adolescent Psychiatry, New York, NY.

Kirkpatrick, D., Veronen, L., & Best, C. (1985). Factors predicting psychological distress among rape victims. In C. Figley (Ed.), *Trauma and its wake.* New York: Brunner/Mazel.

Kolb, L., Burris, B., & Griffith, S. (1984). Propranolol and clonidine in treatment of the chronic post-traumatic stress disorders of war. In B. van der Kolk (Ed.), *PTSD, psychological and biological sequelae.* Washington, DC: American Psychiatric Press.

Kovacs, M. (1985). The Children's Depression Inventory (CDI). *Psychopharmacology Bulletin, 21,* 995–998.

Kramer, M., Kinney, L., & Scharf, M. (1982). Sleep in delayed stress victims. *Sleep Research, 11,* 113.

Lonigan, C. J., Shannon, M. P., Finch, A. J., et al. (1991). Children's reactions to a natural disaster: Symptom severity and degree of exposure. *Advances in Behavior Research and Therapy, 13,* 135–154.

Lyons, J. A. (1987). Post-traumatic stress disorder in children and adolescents: A review of the literature. *Developmental and Behavioral Pediatrics, 8*(6), 349–356.

March, J. (1991). Post-traumatic stress in the emergency setting. *Emergency Care Quarterly, 1,* pp. 74–81.

March, J. (1992). Fluoxetine and fluvoxamine in PTSD. *American Journal of Psychiatry, 149,* 413.

March, J. (1992). The stressor "A" criterion in DSM-IV post-traumatic stress disorder. In J. Davidson & E. Foa (Eds.), *Post-traumatic stress disorder: DSM-IV and beyond.* Washington, DC: American Psychiatric Press.

March, J., Mulle, K., & Herbel, B. (1994). Behavioral psychotherapy for children and adolescents with obsessive–compulsive disorder: An open trial of a new protocol driven treatment package. *Journal of the American Academy of Child and Adolescent Psychiatry, 33*(3), 333–341.

March, J. S., & Amaya-Jackson, L. (1993). Post-traumatic stress disorder in children and adolescents. *PTSD Research Quarterly, 4*(4), 1–3.

McFarlane, A. (1987). Post-traumatic phenomena in a longitudinal study of children following a natural disaster. *Journal of American Academy of Child and Adolescent Psychiatry, 26*(5), 764–769.

Mellman, T., & David, G. (1985). Combat-related flashbacks in posttraumatic stress disorder: Phenomenology and similarity to panic attacks. *Journal of Clinical Psychiatry, 46,* 379–382.

Nader, K., Stuber, M., & Pynoos, R. (1991). Posttraumatic stress reactions in preschool children with catastrophic illness: Assessment needs. *Comprehensive Mental Health Care, 1*(3), 223–239.

Ornitz, E., & Pynoos, R. (1989). Startle modulation in children with post-traumatic stress disorder. *American Journal of Psychiatry, 146,* 866–870.

Perry, B. D. (in press) Neurobiological sequelae of childhood trauma: Post-traumatic stress disorders in children. In M. Murberg (Ed.), *Catecholamines in post traumatic stress disorder.* Washington, DC: American Psychiatric Press.

Pynoos, R., & Eth, S. (1985). Witnessing acts of personal violence. In S. Eth & R. S. Pynoos (Eds.), *Post-traumatic stress in children* (pp. 17–43). Washington, DC: American Psychiatric Press.

Pynoos, R. S., & Eth, S. (1986). Witness to violence: The child interview. *Journal of the American Academy of Child and Adolescent Psychiatry, 25*(3), 306–319.

Pynoos, R. S., Frederick, C., Nader, K., et al. (1987, December). Life threat and post-traumatic stress in school-age children. *Archives of General Psychiatry, 44,* 1057–1063.

Pynoos, R., & Nader, K. (1988a). Psychological first aid and treatment approach to children exposed to community violence: Research implications. *Journal of Traumatic Stress, 1,* 445–473.

Pynoos, R. S., & Nader, K. (1988b). Children who witness the sexual assaults of their mothers. *Journal of the American Academy of Child and Adolescent Psychiatry, 27*(5), 567–572.

Pynoos, R., & Nader, K. (1989). Children's memory and proximity to violence. *Journal of the American Academy of Child and Adolescent Psychiatry, 28*(2), 236–241.

Pynoos, R., & Nader, K. (1990). Mental health disturbances in children exposed to disaster: Prevention intervention strategies. In S. Goldston, J. Yager, C. Heinicke, et al. (Eds.), *Preventing mental health disturbances in childhood.* Washington, DC: American Psychiatric Press.

Pynoos, R. S., & Nader, K. (1993). Issues in the treatment of post-traumatic stress in children and adolescents. In J. Wilson & B. Raphael (Eds.), *The international handbook of traumatic stress syndromes* (pp. 535–549). New York: Plenum Press.

Reiss, D., Richters, J., Radke-Yarrow, M., et al. (1993). *Children and violence.* New York: Guilford Press.

Reist, C., Dauffmann, C., Haier, R., et al. (1989). A controlled trial of desipramine in 18 men with posttraumatic stress disorder. *American Journal of Psychiatry, 146,* 513–516.

Robins, L. N., Helzer, J. E., Croughan, J., et al. (1981). The National Institute of Mental Health Diagnostic Interview Schedule: Its history, characteristics, and validity. *Archives of General Psychiatry, 149,* 475–481.

Saigh, P. (1987). *In vitro* flooding of a childhood post-traumatic stress disorder. *School Psychology Review, 16,* 203–211.

Saigh, P. A. (1991). The development of posttraumatic stress disorder following four different types of traumatization. *Behaviour Research and Therapy, 29*(3), 213–216.

Saigh, P. A. (1992). The behavioral treatment of child and adolescent posttraumatic stress disorder. *Advances in Behavior Research and Therapy, 14,* 247–275.

Sameroff, A., Seifer, R., Barocas, R., et al. (1987). Intelligence quotient scores of 4-year-old children: Social-environment risk factors. *Pediatrics, 79,* 343–350.

Schwarz, E. D., & Kowalski, J. M. (1991, May). Post-traumatic stress disorder after a school shooting: Effects of symptom threshold selection and diagnosis by DSM-III, DSM-III-R, or proposed DSM-IV. *American Journal of Psychiatry, 148*(5), 592–597.

Shetatsky, M., Greenberg, D., & Lere, B. (1988). A controlled trial of phenelzine in post-traumatic stress disorder. *Psychiatry Research, 24,* 149–155.

Solomon, S. D., Gerrity, E. T., & Muff, A. M. (1992). Efficacy of treatments for posttraumatic stress disorder: An empirical review. *Journal of the American Medical Association, 268,* 633–638.

Stoddard, F., Norman, D., & Murphy, J. (1989). A diagnostic outcome study of children and adolescents with severe burns. *Journal of Trauma, 29,* 471–477.

Stuber, M. L., Nader, Y., Yasuda, P., et al. (1991). Stress responses after pediatric bone marrow transplantation: Preliminary results of a prospective longitudinal study. *Journal of the American Academy of Child and Adolescent Psychiatry, 30,* 952–957.

Taylor, S., Wood, J., & Lictman, R. (1983). It could be worse: Selective evaluation as a response to victimization. *Journal of Social Issues, 39,* 19–40.

Terr, L. (1979). Children of Chowchilla: A study of psychic trauma. *Psychoanalytic Study of the Child, 34,* 547–623.

Terr, L. (1981). Forbidden games: Post-traumatic child's play. *Journal of the American Academy of Child Psychiatry, 20,* 741–760.

Terr, L. (1983). Chowchilla revisited: The effects of psychic trauma four years after a school-bus kidnapping. *American Journal of Psychiatry, 140,* 1543–1550.

Terr, L. (1990). *Too scared to cry.* New York: HarperCollins.

Terr, L. C. (1991). Childhood traumas: An outline and overview. *American Journal of Psychiatry, 148,* 10–19.

van der Kolk, B. (1984). *Psychological trauma.* Washington, DC: American Psychiatric Press.

van der Kolk, B., & van der Hart, O. (1989). Pierre Janet and the breakdown of adaptation in psychological trauma. *American Journal of Psychiatry, 146,* 1530–1540.

Weissman, M., Wickramavatne, Warner, et al. (1987). Assessing psychiatric disorders in children. *Archives of General Psychiatry, 44,* 747–753.

Weller, E. B., & Weller, R. A. (1990). Grief in children and adolescents. In B. Garfinkel, G. Carlson, & E. Weller (Eds.), *Psychiatric disorders in children and adolescents* (pp. 37–47). Philadelphia: W. B. Saunders.

Widom, C. S. (1989). Does violence beget violence? A critical examination of the literature. *Psychological Bulletin, 106,* 3–28.

Yule, W., Udwin, O., & Murdoch, K. (1990). The "Jupiter" sinking: Effects on children's fears, depression and anxiety. *Journal of Child Psychchology and Psychiatry, 31,* 1051–1061.

Yule, W., & Williams, R. M. (1990). Post-traumatic stress reactions in children. *Journal of Traumatic Stress, 3,* 279–295.

Chapter 13

Comorbidity of Anxiety Disorders

John F. Curry
Laura Bennett Murphy

The diagnostic nomenclature in the third revised edition of the *Diagnostistic and Statistical Manual of Mental Disorders* (DSM-III-R; American Psychiatric Association, 1987) includes three anxiety disorders specific to childhood and adolescence: separation anxiety disorder (SAD), overanxious disorder (OAD), and avoidant disorder (AD). The central characteristic of SAD is an unrealistic fear of separation from a major attachment figure, and the central feature of OAD is unrealistic worry about the future, the past, and one's own competence (Bell-Dolan & Brazeal, 1993). AD is characterized chiefly by such an excessive avoidance of contact with unfamiliar people that social functioning is impaired. At the same time the child desires or has satisfying relationships with familiar people, such as family members (Beidel & Morris, 1993). This diagnostic system for childhood anxiety disorders has been substantially revised in DSM-IV (American Psychiatric Association, 1994). The revisions will be summarized in the final section of this chapter. However, since the DSM-III-R system formed the basis for studies of comorbidity to date, that system will be used to organize our review.

In addition to these disorders of childhood or adolescent onset, young people may suffer from one of the anxiety disorders that occur in adults. These include simple phobias, social phobia, panic disorder and/or agoraphobia, posttraumatic stress disorder (PTSD), and obsessive–compulsive disorder (OCD). Like the childhood anxiety disorders, each of these syndromes is characterized by a central feature. A simple phobia is the unrealistic fear and avoidance of a circumscribed object or event (Silverman & Rabian, 1993), while social phobia is the persistent fear of situations

in which the individual may be subject to scrutiny by others with potential for humiliation or embarrassment (Beidel & Morris, 1993). Panic
disorder is characterized by discrete episodes of intense anxiety with a
number of physiological symptoms, accompanied by fear of such attacks
in the intervening intervals. Often panic disorder is accompanied by agoraphobia (PDAG), the fear of being in places from which escape might be
difficult or embarrassing (Silverman & Rabian, 1993). PTSD is a reaction to an extremely distressing event outside the usual range of human
experience. The reaction is characterized by intrusive reexperiencing of
the trauma, avoidance, and hyperarousal (Amaya-Jackson & March,
1993). OCD is marked by persistent thoughts, images, or impulses that
are distressing, intrusive, and senseless (obsessions) or by repetitive behaviors performed in response to an obsession (compulsions) (Leonard,
Lenane, & Swedo, 1993).

These disorders have been reviewed in detail in Chapters 7–12. They
are recounted here only to point to the conceptual basis for distinguishing
among the anxiety disorders in the current diagnostic nomenclature. The
DSM-III-R and DSM-IV systems list a large number of fairly narrowly defined disorders. Although such systems have the advantage of conceptual
clarity and precision, the validity of the various disorders remains to be demonstrated, in terms of specificity of natural history, response to treatment,
family history, laboratory findings, and psychopathological features.

One of the apparent disadvantages of the multicategorical diagnostic system of DSM-III-R and its predecessor, DSM-III, has been the phenomenon of high rates of comorbidity, the simultaneous presence of two
or more disorders in the same patient. This phenomenon creates both theoretical and clinical problems. At the most general theoretical level, high
rates of comorbidity call into question the assumption that categories
within the taxonomy are discrete. As Carson (1991) has noted, "The notion
that the patient may simultaneously harbor a plurality of separate disorders
with considerable feature overlap seems on its face to involve enormous
classificatory difficulties" (p. 303). Essentially, the phenomenon implies
that the DSM taxonomy is not what Millon (1991) has termed a classical
set of discrete categories but rather a prototypal or ideal set against which
actual individuals can be compared. Prototypal structures allow for more
heterogeneity within a class or diagnostic group and permit recognition
of fuzzy conceptual boundaries that correspond better with clinical reality (Millon, 1991).

Comorbidity creates several substantive problems in the interpretation of research findings, outlined clearly by Angold and Costello (1992)
with particular reference to childhood and adolescent depression. Two or
more disorders in a single individual may be understood as reflecting a
similar set of underlying pathogenetic processes. As Angold and Costello

note, family history of mental illness, parental marital discord, and negative life events have all been associated with a variety of childhood disorders, but their specific causal contribution to any one disorder is small. Alternatively, one disorder may be seen as the cause of the other. For instance, the emergence of conduct-disordered behavior in a sizable proportion of already depressed youngsters (Kovacs, Paulauskas, Gatsonis, et al., 1988) could be interpreted as a behavioral reaction to the distress and internal frustration generated by years of enduring a mood disorder. Finally, one disorder may be seen as a precursor of another, either directly or through reducing protective factors. For example, some theorists believe that childhood SAD is a direct developmental precursor of adult agoraphobia (Moreau & Follett, 1993).

Comorbidity presents problems to the treating clinician. The first of these is the choice of treatment target: Which disorder should be the primary focus of treatment? Secondary clinical problems of comorbidity include selection of treatment methods and development of a sufficiently comprehensive treatment plan.

Given these preliminary considerations regarding the phenomenon of comorbidity, we turn to what is known about comorbidity of anxiety disorders in children and adolescents as they were conceptualized in DSM-III-R. Initially, we focus on comorbidity among the anxiety disorders themselves. We then focus on the comorbidity of anxiety disorders with other internalizing disorders and then with externalizing disorders. Finally, we discuss implications of comorbidity for the treatment of anxious children and adolescents.

COMORBIDITY AMONG THE ANXIETY DISORDERS

Separation Anxiety Disorder and Overanxious Disorder

Anxiety disorders are the most common psychiatric disorders in children and adolescents, and, among the anxiety disorders, SAD and OAD are the most common (Bell-Dolan & Brazeal, 1993). Kashani and Orvaschel (1990) assessed disorders and symptoms in a community sample of 8-, 12-, and 17-year-olds. The most frequent anxiety disorder was SAD, occurring in 13% of the sample. About half (48%) of the youngsters with SAD had no other diagnosis. Among the other half, the most frequent comorbid anxiety disorder was OAD, which occurred in 33% of SAD youths. The next most frequent anxiety disorder in the SAD group was simple phobias, which was diagnosed in 18% of those with SAD; 7% of those with SAD had both OAD and a simple phobia.

In a study of 5- to 18-year-olds referred to an anxiety disorders clinic, Last, Strauss, and Francis (1987) assigned primary and secondary diagnoses. In this study the primary diagnosis was the chief cause of distress and the primary target of treatment but not necessarily the first disorder to appear. Again, SAD was the most frequent primary diagnosis, occurring in 33% of the referrals. Over half of those with SAD (58%) had no comorbid anxiety disorder. In the others with SAD, OAD was the most common comorbid anxiety disorder, occurring as it did in the community sample of Kashani and Orvaschel (1990) in 33%. Simple phobias and avoidant disorder each occurred in 12.5% of the SAD youngsters and social phobia in 8%. Thus, in comparison with the community sample, this clinical sample had similar rates of comorbidity of OAD and simple phobias with SAD but higher rates of social phobias and avoidant disorder.

More recently, Last, Perrin, Hersen, et al. (1992) reported that SAD occurred as primary diagnosis in 27% of referrals to an anxiety disorders clinic. The most common additional lifetime anxiety disorder was simple phobias, occurring in 37% of SAD youngsters, with OAD occurring in 23%.

In the community study of Kashani and Orvaschel (1990), OAD was nearly as frequent as SAD, occurring in 12% of the sample. About half of those with OAD had no other anxiety diagnosis, but 44% had SAD, 12% had a simple phobia, and 4% had social phobia; 8% of OAD youngsters had both SAD and a simple phobia. Last, Strauss, et al. (1987) diagnosed 15% of referred youngsters with primary OAD, nearly half of whom (45%) had no other anxiety disorder. The most common comorbid anxiety disorders in the OAD group were secondary social phobia (36% of the OAD group) and avoidant disorder (27% of the OAD group). Both SAD and a simple phobia occurred in 9% of the OAD group. These two studies differ in types of samples, diagnostic interviews, and use of a primary diagnostic hierarchy. It is not possible to know which of these factors account most for the discrepant results. In the clinical sample assessed with a primary diagnostic hierarchy, SAD was much less likely to accompany primary OAD, and social anxiety disorders were much more likely to accompany OAD.

In their later publication, Last et al. (1992) reported similar rates of primary OAD (13%) among referred youths. Every other anxiety disorder assessed was present in at least 20% of the OAD sample, with highest rates occurring for social phobia (57%), simple phobias (43%), and SAD (37%).

We are aware of only one longitudinal study of SAD and OAD that assessed their relationship over time. Cantwell and Baker (1989) followed primarily preschool children for a 4- to 5-year period after initial diagnosis. SAD showed a high rate of recovery and a low rate of stability: Only one of the original sample of nine children still had SAD at follow-up.

Three had developed OAD. By contrast, OAD had a low rate of recovery and low stability. Only two of the original eight OAD children maintained that diagnosis at follow-up, while two others developed avoidant disorder.

Several studies indicate that SAD children are likely to be younger than OAD children (Cantwell & Baker, 1989; Last, Hersen, Kazdin, et al., 1987; Kashani & Orvaschel, 1990). In the latter, a cross-sectional study, fears of separation declined and social anxiety increased with increasing age. SAD children have also been found to come from lower socioeconomic backgrounds than OAD children (Last, Hersen, et al., 1987). Slightly over half of both OAD and SAD children are female (Last et al., 1992).

Avoidant Disorder and Social Phobia

Considerably less research has been conducted on these two diagnostic classifications, than on SAD or OAD. Moreover, the bulk of research to date suggests that avoidant disorder cannot be distinguished from social phobia, except by earlier age of onset. Francis, Last, and Strauss (1992) found no significant differences between social phobia and avoidant disorder in gender ratio, racial distribution, socioeconomic background or additional diagnoses, but avoidant-disordered children were younger. Cantwell and Baker (1989) found that avoidant disorder was the most common psychiatric disorder in preschool, language-disordered children, occurring in about 5% of their sample. Among children and adolescents referred for treatment to an anxiety disorders clinic, avoidant disorder (3%) was much more rare than social phobia (15%) and had an earlier age of onset (8 vs. 11 years) (Last et al., 1992). The majority of avoidant-disordered children also had a lifetime diagnosis of social phobia. Nearly half of the children with social phobia also had a lifetime history of OAD; the next most frequent comorbid anxiety disorder was simple phobia (41%; now referred to as *specific phobia* in DSM-IV).

Simple Phobia

In their community study, Kashani and Orvaschel (1990) found that 3% of their sample had a specific phobia. Almost all of these young people had an additional diagnosis, most commonly SAD (5 of 7 cases) or OAD (3 of 7 cases). In clinical samples, the prevalence of a simple phobia ranges from 5% to 20% depending on whether school phobia is included (Last, Strauss, et al., 1987; Last et al., 1992). In the latter sample, almost 40% of children with a simple phobia had lifetime histories of SAD and nearly a third had social phobia. Age of onset of simple phobias is earlier than that of social phobia (8 vs. 11 years).

Panic Disorder

Last, et al., (1992) found primary panic disorder in nearly 10% of their anxiety disorders clinic sample. Panic disorder had on average an adolescent onset (14 years), and the most common comorbid anxiety diagnosis was OAD, which had occurred in 42% of these adolescents. Moreau and Follett (1993) have argued on the basis of retrospective adult reports, case studies, and studies of at-risk children of psychiatrically diagnosed parents that panic disorder occurs in prepubertal children. They have also reviewed the conflicting evidence for a developmental link between childhood SAD and adult PDAG. The association, however, between lifetime OAD and adolescent panic disorder argues in favor of a link between those two disorders rather than between SAD and panic disorder (Last et al., 1992).

Posttraumatic Stress Disorder

PTSD was not assessed in the community sample of Kashani and Orvaschel (1990) and was too rare in the anxiety clinic sample of Last et al. (1992) to permit calculations of comorbid conditions. Amaya-Jackson and March (1993) described possible comorbid conditions for purposes of conducting a differential diagnosis. These may include OAD, SAD, or depression. To date, empirical data on comorbidity of other disorders and PTSD are lacking.

Obsessive-Compulsive Disorder

OCD was diagnosed as the primary disorder in 7% of the young people referred to an anxiety disorders clinic, and the most common additional lifetime anxiety diagnosis was simple phobia, which characterized nearly half of these patients (Last et al., 1992). In pediatric patients evaluated at the National Institute of Mental Health (NIMH) (Leonard et al., 1993), the most common comorbid anxiety disorders were simple phobias (17%), OAD (16%), and SAD (7%).

COMORBIDITY OF ANXIETY AND DEPRESSION

Anxiety disorders and depressive disorders frequently occur simultaneously in children and adolescents (Kovacs, Gatsonis, Paulauskas, et al., 1989; Brady & Kendall, 1992). Estimates of the rates of co-occurrence, however, range widely. From 1 to 69% of children with an anxiety disorder have a depressive disorder (Bernstein & Borchardt, 1991; Brady & Kendall,

1992; Anderson, Williams, McGee, et al., 1987; Bernstein, 1991; Strauss, Last, Hersen, et al., 1988; Costello, Burns, Costello, et al., 1988; Bernstein & Garfinkel, 1986), 40 to 75% of all children with a depressive disorder have a concurrent anxiety disorder (Kovacs et al., 1989; Bernstein & Borchardt, 1991; Kashani, Carlson, Beck, et al., 1987; Weissman, Leckman, Merikangas, et al., 1984).

Methodological and sampling procedures account for these vast differences. First, studies vary in their use of community-based versus clinic-based samples. In general, studies whose subject pool comes from inpatient facilities report higher rates of comorbidity than those drawn from outpatient clinics, which in turn report higher rates of comorbidity than community-based (epidemiological) samples (Brady & Kendall, 1992).

Second, evidence suggests that children with concurrent anxiety and depressive disorders are significantly older at presentation than those with anxiety alone, highlighting the need for a developmental approach to addressing this issue. Bernstein (1991), in a study of 96 school refusers of ages 7 through 17, reported that the pure anxiety group had a mean age of 11.3 (± 2.3), while the mixed anxiety and depression group had a mean age of 13.9 (± 1.9).

Third, depression is more likely to be diagnosed in conjunction with particular types of anxiety disorders (e.g., SAD) as opposed to others (simple phobias) and with those in which there is a higher degree of functional impairment (Kashani & Orvaschel, 1988; Bernstein & Borchardt, 1991). Bernstein (1991) reported that among those with concurrent anxiety and depressive disorders, 50% had a diagnosis of SAD, 29.2% had a diagnosis of OAD, 12.5% had a diagnosis of both SAD and OAD, 4.2% had a diagnosis of panic disorder, and 4.2 percent had a diagnosis of unspecified anxiety disorder. Similarly, in a study of 142 8- to 13-year-olds (Kovacs et al., 1989), among those with comorbid anxiety and depressive disorders 31% were diagnosed with SAD, 16% with OAD, 1% with simple phobias, 2% with OCD, 2% with panic disorder, and 2% with an atypical anxiety disorder.

Fourth, depression is more likely to be diagnosed among children with multiple anxiety diagnoses (Strauss et al., 1988).

Kovacs and colleagues (1989) examined the chronology of disorder among 142 8- to 13-year-old depressed youngsters recruited from a child psychiatric clinic and a general medical clinic. They considered disorders that occurred within 2 months of each other to be contemporaneous. Their findings were that in general, anxiety disorders predated depression in almost two-thirds of the cases. This finding was modified, however, by the type of depressive disorder. Among nine children diagnosed with dysthymia, in only two cases did the anxiety predate the depression. It was six times more likely for anxiety to precede a major depressive disorder than to precede dysthymia.

Little research has addressed the effects of comorbidity on the natural course of an anxiety disorder alone or a depressive disorder alone. Kovacs and colleagues (1989), in their study of 142 youngsters referred for depressive disorders, reported that recovery from comorbid anxiety disorders did not parallel recovery from depressions. When occurring with major depressive disorder (MDD), the chances of the anxiety disorder persisting after the depression remitted were 41%. When occurring with dysthymia, the rate of persistence of the anxiety disorder dropped to about 25%.

COMORBIDITY OF ANXIETY
AND BEHAVIORAL DISORDERS

Much less research has gone into the co-occurrence of anxiety and behavioral disorders. They exist comorbidly less often than do anxiety and the internalizing disorders, and clinically, comorbid anxiety disorders may be underdiagnosed since the problem behavior is viewed as primary. Some have suggested, however, that the recognition of a comorbid internalizing disorder is of utmost importance, as it may reflect the existence of a "subtype" of behavioral disorders that has different family histories and are differentially responsive to treatment (Pliszka, 1989).

Anxiety and Attention Deficit

Again, the rates of comorbidity vary depending on the type of behavioral disorder and sampling and measurement issues. Anxiety and attention-deficit disorder (ADD) are suggested to be coexisting in the following ways: From 17 to 22% of children diagnosed with an anxiety disorder also meet criteria for ADD (Bird, Gould, & Staghezza, 1993; Cantwell & Baker, 1989; Bradley & Hood, 1993), and 8 to 50.8% of children and adolescents with ADD have a comorbid anxiety disorder (Bird et al., 1993; Cantwell & Baker, 1989; Bradley & Hood, 1993; August & Garfinkel, 1993; Biederman, Newcorn, & Sprich, 1991). While the range of comorbidity rates in this second group is wide, most estimates for outpatients range from 30 to 45%.

As previously reported, variability is a function of (1) referral status of the subjects—inpatient, outpatient, community (Woolston, Rosenthal, Riddle, et al., 1989; Biederman et al., 1991)—and (2) the way in which ADD or attention-deficit/hyperactivity disorder (ADHD) is diagnosed. There appear to be higher rates of comorbidity with the DSM-III category of ADD without hyperactivity (Biederman et al., 1991); August and

Garfinkel (1993), in an epidemiological study of 1,490 first- through fourth-graders, found that children with ADD were diagnosed with co-morbid anxiety at higher rates than those with ADHD (57% versus 34%). Similarly, Lahey, Schaughency, Hyrd, et al. (1987) reported that children with ADD have higher rates of emotional disorders (both anxiety and af-fective) compared to children diagnosed with ADHD. Pliszka (1989) de-scribed children diagnosed under the contemporary nosology as ADHD with anxiety to be qualitatively similar to and to have similar areas of deficit as the children reported in the Lahey studies.

Anxiety and Problems of Conduct

Rates of anxiety disorders among youngsters with conduct disorder (CD) or oppositional defiant disorder (ODD) typically range from the low 20s to 40% (Walker, Lahey, Russo, et al., 1991; Kashani et al., 1987; Ander-son et al., 1987; Zoccolillo, 1992), with comorbidity rates tending to be higher for ODD. Bird et al. (1993) reported high rates of CD/ODD among a community sample of children of ages 9 to 16 and 62% comorbidity rate. They did not separate the number of children with ODD from the youngsters with CD, and this diagnostic group represents the highest level of comorbidity in their study.

Anxiety and Substance Abuse

It has been hypothesized that anxiety may play a key role in the abuse of substances by both youngsters and adults. Tension-reduction theories of substance abuse, as well as theories of self-medication, suggest that sub-stances may be taken by people with higher levels of anxiety and distress. Adult studies have supported these hypotheses (Bukstein, Brent, & Kaminer, 1989), and in a survey of high school students, a majority of substance users cited "to relax or relieve tension" as a reason for using alcohol or marijuana (Bukstein et al., 1989). In a study of 111 incarcer-ated youth, Neighbors, Kempton, and Forehand (1992) reported that 22% of alcohol and marijuana users and 38% of polysubstance abusers met diagnostic criteria for an anxiety disorder.

Chronology of Comorbid Anxiety and Behavioral Disorders

Biederman and colleagues (1991) suggested that ADHD and anxiety dis-orders probably transmit independently. Cantwell and Baker (1989) dem-onstrated that the average age of onset in their sample of children drawn from a community speech and hearing center was 5.7 for conduct problems, 5.65 for attentional difficulties, and 5.18 for anxiety disorders. Among the children with anxiety disorders, however, the average age of onset for SAD was 3.6 while the average age of onset for OAD was 7.3. Of 35 youngsters who had an initial "pure" diagnosis of ADHD, two had developed a comorbid anxiety disorder at follow-up 5 years later. Of nine children with an initial "pure" diagnosis of SAD, two later were diagnosed with ADHD and ADD, and one of these two continued to have comorbid SAD. Similarly, among eight children with an initial diagnosis of OAD, three were diagnosed at follow-up with ADHD or ADD. The results of this study suggest that although ADD is rather stable, anxiety disorders are not. There is no clear directionality or chronology of onset for these disorders. None of the children in the Cantwell study initially diagnosed with conduct disorders demonstrated anxiety disorders at follow-up, nor did any of the children with initial "pure" diagnoses of anxiety disorder later develop conduct problems.

Anxiety disorders are typically thought to predate substance abuse difficulties. Zoccolillo and Rogers (1991) reported that the average age of onset of anxiety symptoms predates the average age of onset of substance use. However, some have argued that drug withdrawal may be sufficient to trigger the onset of an anxiety disorder. Neighbors et al. (1992) reported that adolescents are more likely to have multiple diagnoses as they move farther along the substance abuse trajectory. Longitudinal studies and/or retrospective studies are needed to address this issue.

Effect of Comorbidity on the Course of the Disorders

In a study of referred outpatient children meeting the criteria for ADHD, Pliszka (1989) found that those with a comorbid anxiety disorder demonstrated less impulsivity ($p < .05$) and that they tended to be less oppositional. Additionally, on a behavioral observation measure, the comorbid group scored significantly lower on off-task behavior. None of the children in the anxiety/ADHD group had a concurrent diagnosis of CD, a significant difference from the ADHD without anxiety group. Finally, members of the ADHD/anxiety group were significantly less likely to respond to stimulant treatment for ADHD.

Zoccolillo and Rogers (1991) reported no differences in outcomes of criminality, accidents, or pregnancy as a function of comorbid diagnosis of anxiety among 55 adolescent girls diagnosed with CD. However, Walker and colleagues (1991), in a study of 177 boys of ages 7 to 12, reported that boys with a diagnosis of CD without a comorbid anxiety disorder received significantly more sociometric nominations for fighting than boys diagnosed with CD and an anxiety disorder. Additionally, this group received more nominations of meanness than the CD with anxiety disorder group.

TREATMENT IMPLICATIONS

Choosing treatment targets in clinical work with children and adolescents is complicated by the phenomenon of comorbidity. To date, empirical data are not available to guide the clinician in designing a treatment plan. In this section, we outline three sets of critical issues to consider when taking comorbidity into account in designing treatment.

Relationship between Disorders

As noted, the relationship between two comorbid disorders can be conceptualized in at least three ways. Both may be attributed to a common underlying process or set of processes. One may be seen as causing the other. One may be seen as raising the risk of the other or as lowering a protective threshold for onset of the other.

If two disorders are viewed as manifestations of a common underlying process, then the process would be the most logical target for treatment. For example, OAD has been associated in some studies with perfectionism in the child's parents (Bell-Dolan & Brazeal, 1993) and childhood depression with low rates of positive reinforcement by parents (Cole & Rehm, 1986). In certain cases such findings would support the choice of parent training or family therapy as part of the treatment of a child with comorbid OAD and depression.

If one disorder is viewed as the cause of a second, then treatment should focus on the first, in the expectation that successful treatment of that disorder will also ameliorate the other disorder. For example, a youngster who develops a dysthymic disorder secondary to impairment caused by OCD should be treated first for OCD. It is obviously important to assess carefully the actual reduction in the secondary disorder, not just to assume the effectiveness of the primary-disorder treatment on the secondary disorder.

When one disorder seems to have been a precursor to a second, the choice of treatment target is less clear. Comorbid panic disorder and OAD or SAD in an adolescent might present such a case. Here one might assume that the earlier condition (OAD or SAD) lowered the threshold for onset of panic disorder. However, the later condition might be associated with more severe impairment, indicating another set of concerns to be taken into account in choosing treatment targets. Brown and Barlow (1992), citing Klerman (1990), outlined three meanings of the distinction between primary and secondary diagnoses. One disorder may be assessed as having occurred earlier in life than the other; one may be assessed as the cause of the other; or one may be seen as the source of more current impairment than the other. If the "primary" disorder occurred first in the child's lifetime but did not cause the "secondary" disorder, and if the "secondary" disorder in these two senses is the "primary" disorder with regard to impairment, the more incapacitating condition should be the main target of treatment. This guideline would seem to apply, for example, to the treatment of comorbid anxiety and conduct disorder in an adolescent. Even if the anxiety disorder had an earlier age of onset, the conduct disorder demands primary attention because of its negative consequences.

Specificity of Treatment

A second set of issues to consider in designing a treatment plan for the child or adolescent with comorbid disorders is the degree of specificity of the treatments under consideration. Some treatments targeted at theorized underlying common processes are expected to be general in their effects, rather than specifically oriented toward reduction of specific disorders. For example, interpersonal models of group psychotherapy (Yalom, 1985) are designed for intervention with patients who are heterogenous in symptomatology but not severely impaired. Such a treatment model is based on the theory that various symptoms reflect underlying disturbances in interpersonal relationships and that group intervention targeted at relationship capacities and skills will alleviate the presenting symptoms. Similarly, certain medications may be used to treat comorbid anxiety and depression on the assumption that both conditions reflect underlying biochemical abnormalities.

By contrast, most recent developments in treatment methods have been oriented toward specificity of intervention with certain homogeneous groups of patients. These interventions have the advantage of clear theoretical links with a specific disorder, but the phenomenon of comorbidity raises questions about how to implement them in general clinical practice. As Kendall, Kortlander, Chansky, et al. (1992) have stated, treatment of the child with comorbid disorders using specific, manualized treatments requires individualized selection of appropriate treatment components. We suggest that three approaches may be considered in such cases.

First, if the child's primary disorder (in the sense of causality or impairment) can be addressed by a specific, manualized psychosocial treatment or by a specific medication, then that treatment should be chosen first. In practice, there are only a few specific, well-validated treatments for childhood and adolescent disorders; response prevention for OCD in a child with comorbid and secondary depression might be an example.

Similarly, systematic desensitization for a primary phobic disorder would be an appropriate treatment choice.

Second, if the specific, manualized treatments of two comorbid disorders contain certain common elements, then those may be abstracted from the separate treatments and applied in a given case. An example would be relaxation training, communication training, problem solving, and assertiveness training as treatment for adolescents with comorbid depression and substance abuse. These cognitive-behavioral methods have been included in different manuals for the treatment or prevention of substance abuse (Botvin, Baker, Dusenbury, et al., 1990) and depression (Clarke, Lewinsohn, & Hops, 1990).

Third, manualized treatments for two comorbid disorders could be combined to yield a more comprehensive treatment. For example, the most effective treatments for ODD and CD appear to be those that involve parents and that focus, at least in part, on contingencies, discipline methods, and family communication (Alexander & Parsons, 1982). Family treatment combined with individual or group cognitive-behavioral treatment of an anxious, conduct-disordered adolescent may provide more comprehensive, effective treatment than either treatment alone.

Developmental Considerations

Treatment planning may be directed by concerns about developmental psychopathology. There are few well validated findings to date on the developmental sequence of comorbid disorders. However, as noted earlier, in cases of comorbid MDD and anxiety disorder, the anxiety disorder more often develops first. Similarly, with comorbid anxiety and substance abuse, the anxiety disorder more often develops first. Such findings point to the importance of early intervention in the treatment of anxiety disorders. Particularly in the early stages of manifestation of depression or substance abuse, it is critical for clinicians to assess for the presence of an anxiety disorder, which may then become a target for treatment. More generally, the high rates of comorbid anxiety disorders in clinical samples of children and adolescents indicate the need to assess routinely for the full range of anxiety disorders. This is particularly true in inpatient settings where rates of comorbidity are highest.

CONCLUSIONS AND MODIFICATIONS IN DSM-IV

Research to date has yielded basic data describing the phenomenon of comorbidity of anxiety disorders in children and adolescents. High rates of anxiety disorders have been found to be associated with high rates of other anxiety disorders and high rates of other internalizing and externalizing disorders. Research is needed to address a number of issues bearing on the classification of anxiety disorders and, most importantly, on their effective treatment. Research on the categories of avoidant disorder and social phobia, for example, has already shown that it is more parsimonious to consider these as developmentally different manifestations of one disorder. This change has been incorporated into DSM-IV, where avoidant disorder has been subsumed under social phobia. Similarly, the frequent occurrence of OAD as a condition comorbid with other anxiety disorders has raised the question of whether OAD might be better conceptualized as a trait or vulnerability marker for the development of a wide range of specific disorders. Similar questions have been raised about the nosological validity of the adult equivalent of OAD, generalized anxiety disorder (Brown & Barlow, 1992). Generalized anxiety has been retained as a diagnostic class in DSM-IV, but OAD has been omitted as a separate childhood anxiety disorder. Instead, OAD has been subsumed under the category of generalized anxiety disorder. This change, however, does not settle the research issue of whether generalized anxiety is best conceptualized as a trait or a diagnosis.

Treatment implications of comorbidity have not generally been addressed in empirical studies. In our discussion of treatment implications, we outline general issues that have a bearing on the choice of treatment targets and methods. Obviously, such issues as the impact of comorbid disorders on treatment effectiveness, the utility of primary and secondary diagnostic distinctions in treatment planning, and the efficacy of general versus specific treatments for comorbid conditions await empirical evaluation.

REFERENCES

Alexander, J. F., & Parsons, B. V. (1982). *Functional family therapy.* Monterey, CA: Brooks/Cole.

Amaya-Jackson, L., & March, J. S. (1993). Post-traumatic stress disorder in children and adolescents. In H. L. Leonard (Ed.), *Anxiety disorders: Child and adolescent psychiatric clinics of North America* (pp. 639–654). Philadelphia: W. B. Saunders.

American Psychiatric Association. (1987). *Diagnostic and statistical manual of mental disorders* (3rd ed., rev.). Washington, DC: Author.

American Psychiatric Association. (1994). *Diagnostic and statistical manual of mentral disorders* (4th ed.). Washington, DC: Author.

Anderson, J., Williams, S., McGee, R., et al. (1987). DSM-III disorders in preadolescent children: Prevalence in a large sample from the general population. *Archives of General Psychiatry, 44,* 69–76.

Angold, A., & Costello, E. J. (1992). Comorbidity in children and adolescents with depression. In D. P. Cantwell (Ed.), *Mood disorders: Child and adolescent psychiatric clinics of North America* (pp. 31–52). Philadelphia: W. B. Saunders.

August, G., & Garfinkel, B. (1993). The nosology of attention-deficit hyperactivity disorder. *Journal of the American Academy of Child and Adolescent Psychiatry, 32,* 155–165.

Beidel, D. C., & Morris, T. L. (1993). Avoidant disorder of childhood and social phobia. In H. L. Leonard (Ed.), *Anxiety disorders: Child and adolescent psychiatric clinics of North America* (pp. 623–638). Philadelphia: W. B. Saunders.

Bell-Dolan, D., & Brazael, T. J. (1993). Separation anxiety disorder, overanxious disorder, and school refusal. In H. L. Leonard (Ed.), *Anxiety disorders: Child and adolescent psychiatric clinics of North America* (pp. 563–580). Philadelphia: W. B. Saunders.

Biederman, J., Newcorn, J., & Sprich, S. (1991). Comorbidity of attention deficit hyperactivity disorder with conduct, depressive, anxiety, and other disorders. *American Journal of Psychiatry, 148,* 565–577.

Bird, H., Gould, M., & Staghezza, B. (1993). Patterns of diagnostic comorbidity in a community sample of children aged 9 through 16 years. *Journal of the American Academy of Child and Adolescent Psychiatry, 32,* 361–368.

Bernstein, G. (1991). Comorbidity and severity of anxiety and depressive disorders in a clinic sample. *Journal of the American Academy of Child and Adolescent Psychiatry, 30,* 43–50.

Bernstein, G., & Borchardt, C. (1991). Anxiety disorders of childhood and adolescence: A critical review. *Journal of the American Academy of Child and Adolescent Psychiatry, 30,* 519–532.

Bernstein, G., & Garfinkel, B. (1986). School phobia: The overlap of affective and anxiety disorders. *Journal of the American Academy of Child and Adolescent Psychiatry, 25,* 235–241.

Botvin, G. J., Baker, E., Dusenbury, L., et al. (1990). Preventing adolescent drug abuse through a multimodal cognitive-behavioral approach. *Journal of Consulting and Clinical Psychology, 58,* 437–446.

Bradley, S., & Hood, J. (1993). Psychiatrically referred adolescents with panic attacks: Presenting symptoms, stressors, and comorbitiy. *Journal of the American Academy of Child and Adolescent Psychiatry, 32,* 826–829.

Brady, E., & Kendall, P. (1992). Comorbidity of anxiety and depression in children and adolescents. *Psychological Bulletin, 111,* 244–255.

Brown, T. A., & Barlow, D. H. (1992). Comorbidity among anxiety disorders: Implications for treatment and DSM-IV. *Journal of Consulting and Clinical Psychology, 60,* 835–844.

Bukstein, O., Brent, D., & Kaminer, Y. (1989). Comorbidity of substance abuse and other psychiatric disorders in adolescents. *American Journal of Psychiatry, 146,* 1131–1141.

Cantwell, D., & Baker, L. (1989). Stability and natural history of DSM-III childhood diagnoses. *Journal of the American Academy of Child and Adolescent Psychiatry, 28,* 691–700.

Carson, R. C. (1991). Dilemmas in the pathway of the DSM-IV. *Journal of Abnormal Psychology, 100,* 302–307.

Clarke, G. N., Lewinsohn, P. M., & Hops, H. (1990). *Instructor's manual for the Adolescent Coping with Depressive course* (4th ed.). Eugene, OR: Costalia.

Cole, D. A., & Rehm, L. P. (1986). Family interaction patterns and childhood depression. *Journal of Abnormal Child Psychology, 14,* 297–314.

Costello, E., Burns, B., Costello, A., et al. (1988). Service utilization and psychiatric diagnosis in pediatric primary care: The role of the gatekeeper. *Pediatrics, 82,* 435–441.

Francis, G., Last, C. G., & Strauss, C. C. (1992). Avoidant disorder and social phobia in children and adolescents. *Journal of the American Academy of Child and Adolescent Psychiatry, 31,* 1086–1089.

Kashani, J., Carlson, G., Beck, N., et al. (1987). Depression, depressive symptoms, and depressed mood among a community sample of adolescents. *American Journal of Psychiatry, 144,* 931–934.

Kashani, J., & Orvaschel, H. (1988). Anxiety disorders in mid-adolescence: A community sample. *American Journal of Psychiatry, 145,* 960–964.

Kashani, J., & Orvaschel, H. (1990). A community study of anxiety in children and adolescents. *American Journal of Psychiatry, 147,* 313–318.

Kendall, P. C., Kortlander, E., Chansky, T. E., et al. (1992). Comorbidity of anxiety and depression in youth: Treatment implications. *Journal of Consulting and Clinical Psychology, 60,* 869–880.

Klerman, G. (1990). Approaches to the phenomena of comorbidity. In J. D. Masse & C. R. Cloninger (Eds.), *Comorbidity of mood and anxiety disorders* (pp. 13–37). Washington, DC: American Psychiatric Press.

Kovacs, M., Gatsonis, C., Paulauskas, S., et al. (1989). Depressive disorders in childhood: Vol. IV. A longitudinal study of comorbidity with and risk for anxiety disorders. *Archives of General Psychiatry, 46,* 776–782.

Kovacs, M., Paulauskas, S., Gatsonis, C., et al. (1988). Depressive disorders in childhood: Vol. III. A longitudinal study of comorbidity with and risk for conduct disorders. *Journal of Affective Disorders, 15,* 205–217.

Lahey, B., Schaughency, E., Hyrd, G., et al. (1987). Attention deficit disorder with and without hyperactivity. *Journal of the American Academy of Child and Adolescent Psychiatry, 26,* 718–723.

Last, C. G., Hersen, M., Kazdin, A. E., et al. (1987). Comparison of DSM-III separation anxiety and overanxious disorder: Demographic characteristics and patterns of comorbidity. *Journal of the American Academy of Child and Adolescent Psychiatry, 26,* 527–531.

Last, C. G., Perrin, S., Hersen, M., et al. (1992). DSM-III-R anxiety disorders in children: Sociodemographic and clinical characteristics. *Journal of the American Academy of Child and Adolescent Psychiatry, 31,* 1070–1076.

Last, C. G., Strauss, C. C., & Francis, G. (1987). Comorbidity among childhood anxiety disorders. *Journal of Nervous and Mental Disease, 175,* 726–730.

Leonard, H. L., Lenane, M. C., & Swedo, S. (1993). Obsessive–compulsive disorder. In H. L. Leonard (Ed.), *Anxiety disorders: Child and adolescent psychiatric clinics of North America.* Philadelphia: W. B. Saunders.

Millon, T. (1991). Classification in psychopathology: Rationale, alternatives, and standards. *Journal of Abnormal Psychology, 100,* 245–261.

Moreau, D., & Follett, C. (1993). Panic disorder in children and adolescents. In H. L. Leonard (Ed.), *Anxiety disorders: Child and adolescent psychiatric clinics of North America* (pp. 581–602). Philadelphia: W. B. Saunders.

Neighbors, B., Kempton, T., & Forehand, R. (1992). Co-occurrence of substance abuse with conduct, anxiety, and depression disorders in juvenile deliquents. *Addictive Behaviors, 17,* 379–386.

Pliszka, S. (1989). Effect of anxiety on cognition, behavior, and stimulant response in ADHD. *Journal of the American Academy of Child and Adolescent Psychiatry, 28,* 882–887.

Silverman, W. K., & Rabian, B. (1993). Simple phobias. In H. L. Leonard (Ed.), *Anxiety disorders: Child and adolescent psychiatric clinics of North America* (pp. 603–622). Philadelphia: W. B. Saunders.

Strauss, C., Last, C., Hersen, M., et al. (1988). Association between anxiety and depression in children and adolescents with anxiety disorder. *Journal of Abnormal Child Psychology, 12,* 57–68.

Walker, J., Lahey, B., Russo, M., et al. (1991). Anxiety, inhibition, and conduct disorder in children. *Journal of the American Academy of Child and Adolescent Psychiatry, 30,* 187–191.

Weissman, M., Leckman, J., Merikangas, K., et al. (1984). Depression and anxiety disorders in parents and children. *Archives of General Psychiatry, 41,* 845–852.

Woolston, J., Rosenthal, S., Riddle, M., et al. (1989). Childhood comorbidity of anxiety/affective disorders and behavior disorders. *Journal of the American Academy of Child and Adolescent Psychiatry, 28,* 707–713.

Yalom, I. (1985). *The theory and practice of group psychotherapy* (3rd ed.). New York: Basic Books.

Zoccolillo, M. (1992). Co-occurrence of conduct disorder and its adult outcomes with depressive and anxiety disorders. *Journal of the American Academy of Child and Adolescent Psychiatry, 31,* 547–556.

Zoccolillo, M., & Rogers, K. (1991). Characteristics and outcome of hospitalized adolescent girls with conduct disorder. *Journal of the American Academy of Child and Adolescent Psychiatry, 30,* 973–981.

PART III

Treatment

Chapter 14

Cognitive-Behavioral Psychotherapy

Greta Francis
Deborah Beidel

As is evident from the previous chapters in this book, the study of anxiety disorders in children has received increased research attention over the past decade. Although the theoretical and clinical descriptive literatures are extensive, the treatment literature remains sparse and consists primarily of suggestions regarding strategies rather than definitive conclusions regarding treatment efficacy. In this chapter we review the use of cognitive-behavioral psychotherapy to treat anxiety disorders in children and adolescents. The term "cognitive-behavioral" is meant to represent an integration of cognitive, behavioral, affective, and social strategies for change (Kendall, Chansky, Kane, et al., 1992). As such, we review a variety of treatment strategies that are based on principles of learning.

The behavioral treatment of childhood anxiety has illustrious roots. Jones (1924) was among the first to demonstrate the application of learning theory to the treatment of childhood anxiety in her classic study of the deconditioning of a fear in "Little Peter." However, according to Ollendick and Cerny (1981), behavioral treatment of childhood disorders did not begin to gain popularity until the 1960s. By 1979, a new journal, *Child Behavior Therapy*, was founded and a special issue of *American Psychologist* was subtitled *Psychology and Children: Current Research and Practice* (Kazdin, 1979).

Although the last 30 years have been characterized by intense interest in behavioral therapy for childhood disorders, only recently has the interest focused on childhood anxiety disorders. With a small number of notable exceptions (e.g., Graziano & Mooney, 1980), the current cognitive-behavioral treatment literature consists primarily of case reports and single-case studies.

As noted, the common link among all cognitive-behavioral treatment strategies is that they are based on models of learning. Principles of classical conditioning, operant conditioning, cognitive learning theory, and social learning theory are the underpinnings of cognitive-behavioral strategies used to treat childhood anxiety. A number of reviews characterize the relationship of learning theories to the treatment of childhood psychopathology; the reader is referred particularly to VanHasselt and Hersen (1987), Kazdin (1978), and Ollendick and Cerny (1981) for details.

A number of cognitive-behavioral strategies have been used to treat childhood anxiety, including exposure-based interventions such as systematic desensitization, gradual exposure, and flooding; contingency management; modeling; and cognitive strategies. Often these interventions are used in combination, as exemplified by the cognitive-behavioral treatment program for anxious children proposed by Kendall and colleagues (Kendall et al., 1992).

In this chapter, we highlight a number of studies that exemplify the application of cognitive-behavioral therapy to the treatment of childhood anxiety disorders. Applications of exposure-based strategies, contingency contracting, modeling, and cognitive procedures are illustrated, and an overview of Kendall et al.'s (1992) integrated cognitive-behavioral treatment package is provided. This review is not intended to be all-inclusive; for comprehensive coverage, the reader is referred to Ammerman and Hersen's (1993) edited volume entitled *Handbook of Behavior Therapy with Children and Adults.*

EXPOSURE-BASED STRATEGIES

Exposure-based treatments require that the child approach anxiety-provoking situations. Exposure can be conducted imaginably or *in vivo*. In gradual exposure, the child and the therapist generate a list of feared situations in a hierarchy from least to most anxiety provoking. The child then approaches each situation sequentially, moving up the hierarchy as his or her anxiety level permits. It is important to start with situations that produce only minimal anxiety so as to facilitate success.

The literature includes a number of examples of the use of exposure-based strategies to treat childhood anxiety. Francis and Ollendick (1990) described a case study of the use of gradual *in vivo* exposure to treat an adolescent with generalized social phobia. The 16-year-old subject had a long history of school refusal and avoidance of most social situations. She reported intense social–evaluative fears. Treatment was conducted over a 3-month period. First, a fear hierarchy was developed, which ranged from least (going to a shopping mall with someone) to most anxiety provoking (going to school alone and staying all day). Items from the hierarchy were used as homework assignments to be practiced between therapy sessions. Tasks were completed in a gradual fashion, with repeated practice for each one. For example, the youngster practiced riding the bus, going to a shopping mall alone, and going to a movie early and waiting in a crowded line. Although she was unable to return to her regular high school, she did attend an alternative school program, obtain her GED, and enroll in a local community college. By the end of treatment, although she still found some social situations anxiety provoking, she no longer engaged in avoidance behaviors.

SYSTEMATIC DESENSITIZATION

Systematic desensitization consists of three steps: relaxation training, construction of the anxiety hierarchy, and pairing of relaxation with gradual presentation of anxiety-provoking situations (Wolpe, 1958). Progressive muscle relaxation scripts have been developed for use with children. Koeppen (1974) produced a script that teaches progressive muscle relaxation by using imagery. For example, a child is taught to tense and relax muscles in the hands by imagining that he or she is squeezing the juice from a lemon and to tense and relax muscles in the feet and legs by imagining that he or she is stepping into a big gooey mud puddle. Scripts for children differ from those suggested for adults; scripts for children are shorter in length and offer fewer distinctions among the muscle groups. Such modifications appear necessary to ensure attentiveness to the procedure, thereby increasing the likelihood of its effectiveness.

The following two studies illustrate the use of systematic desensitization. Van Hasselt, Hersen, Bellack, et al. (1979) used systematic desensitization to treat an 11-year-old boy with multiple phobias (test taking, blood, heights). Four sessions were spent teaching deep muscle relaxation, and the child was given an audiotape of relaxation instructions to practice with twice daily. Hierarchies were developed for each feared situation. Treatment was conducted using a multiple baseline design, with treatment applied sequentially to fears of heights, blood, and test taking. Changes in behavioral and cognitive indices of fear were associated with the application of treatment. For example, the youngster was able to climb farther up a ladder, come closer to blood, and complete tests in fewer trials per session by the end of treatment. These gains reportedly were maintained at 6-month follow-up.

Hagopian and Ollendick (1993) presented a case study of the treatment of a 9-year-old boy with a severe dog phobia using systematic desensitization plus self-instruction training. The youngster had been attacked by a dog, but not seriously injured, 6 months prior to seeking treatment. The therapist worked with the child and the parents to develop an avoidance hierarchy. For example, the least anxiety-provoking item on the 20-item hierarchy was "You leave the house with your parents and get into the car to go to the store," the tenth item was "You are now walking by the alley where the attack occurred and you can hear the dog barking as you approach," and the most anxiety-provoking item was "You go by the dog, turn around, and go back out of the alley." Initially, the child, accompanied by his parents, was able to complete eight steps of the hierarchy before becoming very anxious.

Treatment consisted of progressive muscle relaxation paired with presentation of items from the hierarchy. Between therapy sessions, the child practiced the steps at home with the assistance of his parents. In the self-instruction training, the therapist first modeled adaptive self-statements while role-playing the steps in the hierarchy (e.g., "Relax, take a deep breath"). The child then practiced the self-statements while the therapist instructed him aloud. This was followed by the child instructing himself aloud while practicing the steps. Finally, the child instructed himself by whispering while practicing the steps.

The child received praise from his parents and the therapist for accomplishing therapeutic tasks. The authors reported that the child was able to go into the alley where the attack occurred and pet the dog that attacked him by the end of treatment. Contact with the child 6 months following completion of treatment revealed that the gains had been maintained.

FLOODING

Flooding involves repeated and prolonged exposure to the feared stimulus with the goal of extinguishing the anxiety response. Such exposure can be conducted imaginably or *in vivo*. Throughout the flooding process, the child is asked to provide anxiety ratings and remains in the presence of the anxiety-provoking stimulus until his or her self-reported anxiety level diminishes. Typically, flooding is used in conjunction with response prevention, which requires that the child not engage in avoidance responses. More than some of the other interventions, flooding and response prevention create distress, at least in the initial stages. Therefore, it is important that the child clearly understand the treatment rationale, which may limit its applicability with younger children.

Flooding has been used primarily to treat obsessive–compulsive disorder, although there are a few examples of the use of this strategy to treat phobic conditions (Blagg & Yule, 1984; Harris & Goetsch, 1990) and post-traumatic fear (Saigh, 1986, 1987a, 1987b, 1987c). McCarthy and Foa (1988) described the use of flooding to treat a 13-year-old boy with obsessive–compulsive disorder. His obsessions included intrusive thoughts about causing injury to family members, failing in school, and being teased by peers. In response to anxiety related to these thoughts, he engaged in excessive rehearsal of test material, ritualistic movements of his head and hands, and repetitions of behaviors that occurred simultaneously with intrusive thoughts. For example, if he was brushing his teeth when an intrusive thought came into his head, he would brush his teeth 20 more times.

Treatment included imaginal flooding, *in vivo* flooding, and response prevention. Fifteen 90-minute sessions were conducted over a 3-week period, followed by 8 hours of home-based intervention during the fourth week of treatment. Imaginal flooding scenes included exposure to anxiety-provoking stimuli and the feared catastrophic consequences associated with failure to complete rituals. Imaginal flooding sessions were audiotaped and the youngster replayed the tapes as homework. *In vivo* flooding sessions required the adolescent to make contact with the feared stimuli. No compulsive behaviors were permitted during *in vivo* flooding. The child's parents participated in monitoring him to ensure that ritualistic behaviors were prevented at home as well.

In vivo exposure exercises also were assigned as homework each day. The authors reported that a reward system was implemented in order to maintain the youngster's motivation to complete treatment assignments. In addition, school personnel were taught how to refrain from reinforcing his compulsive behaviors. The authors reported that the frequency of rituals decreased and treatment gains were maintained at follow-up a year later.

Saigh (1986, 1987a, 1987b, 1987c) conducted a series of single-case studies using imaginal flooding to treat war-related fears in Lebanese children. Chronological trauma scenes were developed and presented. For example, the scenes developed for a 6-year-old boy who had been exposed to a bomb blast included hearing a loud explosion and seeing people injured, approaching the shopping area in which the explosion had occurred, and observing a man carrying an injured child. Each treatment session focused on one scene. Prior to presentation of imaginal flooding, each child relaxed for 10 to 15 minutes. Following presentation of the traumatic scene, which lasted for 24 to 60 minutes, each session concluded with 5 to 10 minutes of relaxation. Saigh reported improvement on a variety of indices, such as self-reported anxiety during probe scenes, self-monitoring of intrusive thoughts, and anxiety questionnaires.

CONTINGENCY MANAGEMENT

Contingency management procedures are used to modify antecedent and consequent events that may influence the acquisition and/or maintenance of fearful or anxious behavior. Operant strategies such as positive reinforcement, shaping, extinction, and punishment fall under the rubric of contingency management. While contingency management can be used in the context of a therapy session, it also can be taught to parents for implementation in the home. At times, parents of anxious children require extensive teaching of operant strategies in order to successfully implement contingency management procedures. The involvement of parents or teachers in administering treatment in the home or school can be vital in facilitating generalization and maintenance of therapeutic gains.

The use of operant strategies was described by Kearney and Silverman (1990) in their study of prescriptive treatment for school refusal. They evaluated seven children and adolescents with school refusal and determined through functional analyses that two of the youngsters were refusing school because of inadvertent positive reinforcement for such behavior. One child was a 9-year-old boy who was anxious about separation and voiced somatic complaints on school days. The other child was a 13-year-old boy who also voiced somatic complaints on school days but was oppositional at home rather than separation anxious.

Treatment consisted of shaping and differential reinforcement for the 9-year-old and contingency contracting for the 13-year-old. Parents of the 9-year-old were taught not to provide any attention to the child if he remained at home. He was required to remain in his room each day (including weekends) and complete homework assignments at night. The child was instructed initially that he could avoid the weekend room restriction if he attended school for 2 days each week. This expectation was increased gradually to 5 days. School attendance was rewarded with previously restricted privileges, such as bike riding.

Treatment of the 13-year-old boy consisted of developing a contingency contract agreed to, signed, and monitored by the child and his parents. Contingencies for appropriate and inappropriate behaviors were defined. For example, his allowance was fined if he failed to attend school, while his curfew was extended if he did go to school.

School attendance improved for both subjects during treatment. The 9-year-old boy missed 11 days during the first 3 weeks of treatment but had perfect attendance during the final 4 weeks of treatment. The 13-year-old boy missed only 1 day of school during nine weeks of treatment. At 6-month follow-up, both youngsters were attending school regularly.

MODELING

Social learning theory tells us that children learn an enormous amount by watching others (Bandura, 1977). An anxious child can benefit from observing a model approach and cope with a feared situation. Variants of modeling include filmed, live, and participant modeling. In filmed modeling, the anxious child watches a videotape of the model, while in live modeling, the model is in the presence of the anxious child. In participant modeling, the live model interacts with the anxious child and guides his or her approach to the feared stimulus.

Modeling has been used extensively to treat common childhood fears (for a review, see Graziano, DeGiovanni, & Garcia, 1979). Johnson and McGlynn (1988) presented a case study of the use of modeling to treat a 6-year-old girl with a simple phobia of balloons. The child became extremely distressed and fearful in the presence of balloons and attempted to avoid situations in which she might encounter balloons. The child's mother indicated that although the fear seemed trivial, in fact it had caused the child to avoid entering a toy store and her classroom, leave a parade, and become very distressed at a wedding. A behavioral approach test (BAT) was conducted in order to gather assessment data.

A participant modeling approach was selected to treat the child's phobia. Treatment sessions were conducted weekly over a 6-week period. Filmed modeling was used first, followed by guided participant modeling. During filmed modeling, the child watched a videotape of a little girl who initially was fearful of balloons but was able to overcome her fear by gradual approach to and play with balloons. The film ended with the model popping a balloon with a pin and receiving a reward for her performance. A postfilm BAT revealed no decrease in fear from that observed during the pretreatment assessment.

Guided participant modeling then was started, with the previously videotaped model as a live model during the initial treatment session. The model encouraged the child to interact with balloons in a playful way. Both the therapist and the model showed the child how balloons were inflated and praised the child's efforts to imitate their behaviors. Subsequent sessions were spent with the child and therapist playing appropriately with balloons. The child's mother terminated treatment after the sixth session, before additional planned trials of self-directed mastery could be conducted. By the time of termination, the child no longer exhibited fearfulness and her parents felt that no further treatment was indicated. Contact with the child 2 years following completion of treatment revealed no further problems with fear of balloons.

COGNITIVE STRATEGIES

Cognitive procedures include a variety of techniques such as self-instruction training, problem solving, and altering maladaptive self-talk. These strategies typically are taught using modeling, exposure, and behavioral rehearsal. Self-instruction training (Meichenbaum & Goodman, 1971) for anxious children was described by Hagopian and Ollendick (1993) as incorporating the following steps: (1) the therapist approaches the feared stimulus while talking aloud about coping, (2) the child approaches the feared stimulus and verbalizes coping statements at the direction of the therapist, (3) the child approaches the feared stimulus while saying coping statements aloud, (4) the child approaches the feared stimulus while whispering coping statements, (5) the child approaches the feared stimulus while thinking the coping statement.

Problem-solving training involves defining the problem, determining an approach to be used to solve the problem, focusing attention, and self-reinforcement or coping statements (Kendall & Braswell, 1985). The child is taught to ask himself or herself a series of questions in order to solve a problem. For example, the child may go through the following sequence: (1) What is the problem? (2) What are all the things I could do about it? (3) What will probably happen if I do those things? (4) Which solution do I think will work best? and (5) After I have tried it, how did I do?

To modify maladaptive self-talk, the child must first learn to identify and monitor self-statements associated with anxiety and avoidance behaviors. Once maladaptive self-talk is identified, the child works with the therapist to generate alternative self-statements that serve to decrease anxiety, facilitate approach behaviors, and improve coping (Kendall et al., 1992).

The use of cognitive strategies to treat childhood anxiety is a relatively recent development. Most, if not all, available studies describe the use of cognitive strategies in combination with other forms of behavior therapy (e.g., Friedman & Ollendick, 1989; Graziano, Mooney, Huber, et al., 1979; Graziano & Mooney, 1980, 1982; Mansdorf & Lukens, 1987). In fact, it has been suggested that self-instruction training in the absence of operant strategies may be of limited usefulness in decreasing fear in children (e.g., Hagopian, Weist, & Ollendick, 1990).

Mansdorf and Lukens (1987) used a cognitive-behavioral approach to treat two separation-anxious children and their parents. Both children were school refusers and had not responded positively to treatment with imipramine. The initial assessment included specification of self-statements made by the children and their parents as well as determination of the existing consequences for nonattendance at school.

Treatment included modifying child self-statements, modifying parent self-statements, and restructuring contingencies so that parental reinforcement became contingent on school attendance. Gradual exposure also was used to facilitate the children's return to school. Cognitive strategies were aimed at promoting the use of coping statements. For example, one child worried that "the kids in school will make fun of me." This maladaptive self-statement was replaced with a statement designed to facilitate coping ("That's their problem, not mine."). Similarly, the parents of this child were taught to replace the thought "My child is sick so I shouldn't push" with a coping self-statement such as "A push is a way to help." Results indicated that the children's school attendance improved dramatically with treatment: Both were remaining in school all day by the fourth week. These gains were maintained at 3-month follow-up.

Graziano and colleagues used cognitive self-control strategies to treat severe nighttime fears in young children. Graziano and Mooney (1980) conducted a group study comparing children with nighttime fears that had persisted for at least 2 years who were being taught self-control strategies to a control group of similar children who were on the waiting list for treatment. Subjects were randomly assigned to experimental ($n = 17$) or control condition ($n = 16$). Children and their parents were seen for five sessions. Assessments were conducted during sessions 1 and 5, and treatment was completed during the remaining three sessions. Before, during, and after treatment, "fearless" nighttime behavior was monitored. Fearless behavior included the child going to bed within 20 minutes of a direction to do so, sleeping in his or her own room with lights and radio off, and not complaining at bedtime or during the night.

Treatment was conducted in separate parent and child groups. During the child-focused group, children were taught to relax, imagine a pleasant scene, and say "I am brave, I can take care of myself when I am alone, I can take care of myself when I am in the dark." Homework was assigned in which the children practiced skills each night and monitored their behavior. In the parent groups, parents learned to initiate their child's homework practice. Parents also were asked to monitor progress and provide immediate reinforcement for brave behavior. Parents gave "bravery" tokens each evening and morning, which were to be cashed in at a later date for a party.

Results indicated that children in the experimental group experienced significant improvement in nighttime behavior compared to children in the control group. Treated children went to bed faster, fell asleep faster, and displayed fewer delay tactics, such as asking for water, than did control group children. At follow-up 3 years later, 23 of 34 children had maintained their improvement, 8 of 34 were described as "still afraid but much less so," and 3 of 34 continued to have significant nighttime fears (Graziano & Mooney, 1982).

INTEGRATED COGNITIVE-BEHAVIORAL PROGRAM

An integrated cognitive-behavioral program for the treatment of childhood anxiety has been promoted by Kendall and colleagues (1992). They outlined three goals of this treatment approach: (1) The child learns to recognize, experience, and cope with anxiety; (2) the child learns to reduce his or her level of anxiety; (3) the child learns to master developmentally appropriate, challenging, and difficult tasks.

The integrated cognitive-behavioral treatment program is divided into two phases, an eight-session skills training phase followed by an eight-session practice phase. In the skills acquisition phase, the child is taught (1) to become aware of his or her physical responses to feelings, specifically anxiety; (2) to recognize self-talk associated with anxiety feelings; (3) problem-solving skills to modify anxious self-talk and promote coping; and (4) self-evaluation and reinforcement. During the practice phase of treatment, the child participates in gradual imaginal and *in vivo* exposure to anxiety-provoking situations. During exposure exercises, the child is encouraged to use the coping strategies that he or she developed during the skills training phase of the program.

Kendall et al. (1992) described a research evaluation of their integrated cognitive-behavioral treatment program for anxious children. Anxiety-disordered children were randomly assigned to a waiting list or treatment condition. Multimethod assessment was conducted pre- and posttreatment. The majority of children in the study were diagnosed with overanxious disorder (86%). Results indicated a decrease in self-reported anxiety over time for children in the treatment condition compared to those in the waiting list control group. Relative to control group children, treated children described themselves and parents described their children as having significantly better coping abilities by the posttreatment assessment. Parent reports of internalizing symptoms showed a significant decrease over time in the treated children compared to the waiting list control children. Teacher ratings of internalizing symptoms were not significantly different for children in treatment versus control group. There were significant changes in the diagnosis of overanxious disorder over the course of treatment for both groups. Using parent-reported diagnoses, 60% of treated cases compared to only 7% of waiting list cases had no diagnosis after treatment. But using child-reported diagnoses, 80% of treated cases and 40% of waiting list cases no longer qualified for a diagnosis of overanxious disorder after treatment. Moreover, at 1-year follow-up, 100% of treated cases no longer met criteria for an anxiety disorder.

CASE EXAMPLE

Leslie was a 13-year-old female of Portuguese descent who was referred to an outpatient clinic specializing in the treatment of childhood anxiety disorders by her pediatrician because of intense separation anxiety. She lived with her biological parents and 20-year-old brother, each of whom worked outside the home. Leslie was bilingual, speaking both English and Portuguese. Her father and brother also were bilingual, while her mother spoke only Portuguese. The relationships among family members were warm and supportive. Leslie attended eighth grade and reportedly was an honors student.

The initial appointment was attended by Leslie, her brother, and her parents. Her brother served as a translator between the mother and the therapist. The parents reported that while Leslie had always been a shy child, she abruptly began to exhibit intense anxiety symptoms following an incident in which she observed a relative having a grand mal seizure approximately 6 months earlier. Leslie started to ask repeated questions about her health and the health of family members. She was hypervigilant about any and all minor injuries and illnesses and reported that she was extremely fearful of herself or a family member dying. Leslie became reluctant to leave home and very clingy with family members; for example, she would not go alone from one room to another in her home. Leslie had a long history of requiring her mother to stay with her until she fell asleep at night. Following her observation of the seizure, she began to have significant problems falling and staying asleep even when her mother remained with her. It was this problem that prompted Leslie's parents to take her to the pediatrician. The pediatrician initially prescribed Atarax in a dose of 20 mg to be taken three times per day. After 6 months with no significant improvement in anxiety symptoms, the pediatrician referred Leslie to the anxiety disorders clinic.

At the initial assessment, Leslie presented as a thin girl with long dark hair and glasses who looked significantly younger than her stated age. She was reluctant to leave her parents in the waiting room and accompany the therapist, but she did so after expressing her anxiety and receiving reassurance that the first visit would be of short duration. During the interview, Leslie avoided eye contact, spoke rapidly in a very quiet tone of voice, was slow to respond to questions, and picked at her clothing with her fingers. Her report of symptoms confirmed the information provided by her parents.

After completion of the initial evaluation, the family was told that Leslie's symptoms were consistent with a diagnosis of separation anxiety. A recommendation was made for individual therapy for Leslie that would include the cognitive-behavioral techniques of *in vivo* gradual exposure and modification of maladaptive self-talk. Although the parents wanted Leslie to discontinue the medication, Leslie was very fearful that she would become more anxious should she do so. It was agreed that the therapist would consult with Leslie's pediatrician regarding the continued use of medication and that no decision would be made without Leslie's input.

A treatment rationale was provided by the therapist and discussed at length with Leslie. The role of learning in the development and maintenance of her anxiety, avoidance behavior, and maladaptive self-statements was highlighted. Examples of how other kinds of fears are learned and maintained were provided.

During the first few therapy sessions, Leslie and the therapist identified situations that currently were anxiety provoking. Leslie self-monitored her thoughts and anxiety level about the situations three times per day. The situations included sleeping alone, being alone in a room in the house, and going upstairs in the house. In addition, Leslie identified self-statements associated with anxiety. For example, she thought that she had cancer after seeing a tiny bump on her arm and thought that her family members would die if she was away from them. Self-monitoring continued throughout the course of treatment.

Leslie participated in ranking her anxiety-provoking situations and developing a hierarchy. From least to most anxiety provoking, the situations were being alone in a downstairs room, going upstairs alone for a brief time, going upstairs alone for a longer time, going to sleep alone, and staying alone in her room after waking up in the middle of the night.

Leslie also was actively involved in developing cognitive coping statements. She was aware that the things she said to herself influenced how she felt and was motivated to identify self-statements that would facilitate her approach to anxiety-provoking situations. Leslie developed the following coping self-statements: "Just because I feel a little scared doesn't mean that anything bad is going to happen," "Each time I practice and see that everything is okay, I feel better," and "If I start to worry, I can think about something fun to take my mind off my worry."

Over the course of five weekly treatment sessions, Leslie practiced confronting situations from the hierarchy while using the coping statements she had generated. During this time, the therapist consulted with Leslie's pediatrician, who expressed a desire to discontinue the medication. Although Leslie maintained a high level of anxiety regarding discontinuing the medication, she agreed to decrease the dose of Atarax from 20 mg three times per day to 20 mg at bedtime.

By the fifth week, Leslie had made considerable progress. She was spending increasing amounts of time alone, both downstairs and upstairs in the house. In addition, she was able to go to sleep alone without her mother having to remain with her. The parents reported a decrease in the frequency of reassurance-seeking questions about her and their health. Furthermore, Leslie described a significant decrease in the number of worries and level of anxiety that she experienced when separated from her parents.

At this time a decision was made by Leslie, her parents, and the therapist to decrease the frequency of sessions to once every 2 weeks. In addition, Leslie agreed to work on stopping the Atarax. Stopping the medication was conceptualized for Leslie as another "experiment," similar to the experiments she had conducted successfully when working on sleeping alone and going upstairs alone. Coping self-statements were generated specific to this task (e.g., "I might feel a little nervous when I stop taking the medicine. If I think about good things or read a book at bedtime, my nervousness will decrease"). Over the course of about 10 days, she successfully discontinued the medication.

After a month of biweekly sessions, the frequency of sessions was reduced to monthly. Leslie was seen for three monthly sessions. During each session, her self-monitoring was reviewed. Only one anxiety-provoking situation occurred over the course of the 3-month period. Leslie became somewhat anxious when her dog became sick and had to be rushed to the veterinarian. At that time, she told herself that "the doctor will help my dog get better," and she reported that her anxiety decreased. In addition, session time was spent reviewing what she could do in the future when faced with anxiety-provoking situations. At the end of 3 months, Leslie was discharged from treatment with the reassurance that she could recontact her therapist if she needed to at any point in the future.

SUMMARY AND FUTURE DIRECTIONS

As is evident from this review, the use of cognitive-behavioral interventions holds significant promise for the treatment of childhood anxiety disorders. However, due to the limited empirical data, few conclusions other than its substantial potential can be made at this time. The lack of a relevant literature by which to guide treatment interventions and treatment decision making can be traced to several factors. First, and perhaps foremost, is the belief that childhood fears are part of normal development and will dissipate without intervention. Although some significant fears do seem to be transitory (Barrios & Hartmann, 1988), others, such as social–evaluative concerns, do not (Achenbach, 1985) and may form a foundation for future disruptive behaviors. Childhood social fears have been associated, for example, with alcohol abuse and truancy and conduct problems (Clark, 1993) and can predict inadequate social adjustment in adulthood (Davidson, 1993). Furthermore, many anxiety disorders have an average age of onset during childhood and adolescence (Last, Perrin, Hersen, et al., 1992; Rettew, Swedo, Leonard, et al., 1992), and many adults report that even when their actual disorder did not appear until adulthood, similar but perhaps milder forms of the behaviors (e.g., shyness, rigid and ritualistic behaviors) often were present from an early age (e.g., Turner & Beidel, 1988). Although much has been accomplished over the past 10 years in increasing public and professional awareness of the complexity and prevalence of childhood anxiety disorders, research efforts directed at the long-term outcome of untreated disorders are needed in order to document fully their detrimental outcome.

A second factor contributing to the limited intervention research is shifting diagnostic criteria. Since 1980, when three categories of childhood anxiety disorders were introduced in the third edition of the *Diagnostic and Statistical Manual of Mental Disorders* (DSM-III; American Psychiatric Association, 1980), revisions were made in DSM-III-R and DSM-IV (American Psychiatric Association, 1987, 1994). Although these revisions represent attempts to refine the diagnostic classification system, it is difficult to conduct a programmatic line of research when the characteristics of the subject population keep changing, even to a small degree. For example, it is difficult to build a data base for the efficacy of a particular intervention when the population characteristics become heterogeneous as a result of changing diagnostic decision rules. Furthermore, some DSM diagnostic categories, such as avoidant disorder and overanxious disorder, have been removed in DSM-IV. The construct validity of avoidant disorder recently has been evaluated empirically and found to be questionable (Francis, Last, & Strauss, 1992). Although construct validity (as the syndrome is currently defined) overanxious disorder appears somewhat suspect (Beidel, 1991), a number of investigators have argued that the category should be retained until sufficient empirical data are amassed (Silverman & Eisen, 1992; Werry, 1991). However, DSM-IV eliminates this diagnostic category, merging some of the criteria into generalized anxiety disorder. Conceptually, this reorganization appears logical; however, we would argue that such changes should have empirical as well as face validity. Furthermore, while the DSM-IV changes are likely to increase diagnostic precision (e.g., all children with social fears will be diagnosed with social phobia [social anxiety disorder] rather than overanxious disorder or avoidant disorder of childhood), the instability of diagnoses makes the results of longitudinal outcome studies difficult, if not impossible, to interpret and limits their utility.

A third factor that may have functioned to limit empirical investigations is the belief that even if anxiety disorders in children do exist, they are not "serious" disorders like conduct disorder or attention-deficit/ hyperactivity disorder (ADHD). It is true that most children with anxiety disorders do not engage in the antisocial behaviors of children with conduct disorders or disrupt classroom settings as do children with ADHD. However, evidence is increasing that untreated social phobia, for example, may be a predisposing factor in substance abuse (Amies, Gelder, & Shaw, 1983; Clark, 1993), truancy (Clark, 1993; Davidson, 1993), conduct problems (Davidson, 1993), clinically significant depression and suicidal acts and attempts (Amies et al., 1983; Schneier, Johnson, Hornig, et al., 1992), and financial dependence on welfare and disability benefits (Schneier et al., 1992). Similarly, it is our clinical experience that childhood obsessive–compulsive disorder often is associated with school refusal and significant parent–child conflict. Thus, there is evidence that these disorders can negatively affect a child's current and future functioning and that they are in critical need of research attention and funding.

A fourth factor may be that the reporting of individual case studies of treatment success with children, coupled with the substantial data on effective behavioral and cognitive-behavioral treatments with adults, has led to the premature conclusion of the effectiveness of such treatments with children and that no further research is therefore necessary. Naturally, one cannot assume that treatment interventions used with adults will be equally effective with children. As noted earlier in this chapter, relaxation scripts for children are usually shorter than the adult versions, involve the differentiation of fewer muscle groups, and for the youngest children, include imagery and examples in order to help them follow the procedures effectively. Similarly, the effectiveness flooding, which has been used very successfully with adults, depends to a great extent on patient compliance, and compliance, in part, depends on understanding the therapeutic rationale. It has been our clinical experience that young children have great difficulty understanding the rationale, making flooding an extremely stressful procedure for children. Therefore, exposure procedures with young children are more likely to use a graduated approach where the intensity of the distress can be moderated. Finally, external reinforcers for compliance with an exposure program are needed more often with children than with adults. In summary, one cannot assume that effective adult interventions can be adopted unmodified for use with children or necessarily will be equally effective in children.

Despite these limitations, the behavioral and cognitive-behavioral treatment of anxiety disorders in children is an area that is ripe for investigation. The most obvious need is for well-controlled clinical trials. If one can extrapolate from studies of adult populations, the placebo response rate for anxiety disorders ranges from 35 to 45% (Barlow, Craske, Cerny, et al., 1989; Beck, Stanley, Baldwin, et al., in press; Turner, Beidel, & Jacob, 1993) with the exception of obsessive–compulsive disorder (Clomipramine Collaborative Study Group, 1991). Therefore, case reports of the effectiveness of these interventions are of only limited utility because one cannot discount the role of factors such as attention and support in determining the outcome.

With respect to the assessment of treatment outcome, there is a need to address the effectiveness of the interventions as well as their efficacy. That is, treatments need to be assessed not just for their ability to decrease symptoms but also for their ability to enhance interpersonal, familial, and academic functioning. This will require the creation of new assessment instruments and strategies and more attention to outcomes that are clinically meaningful, not just statistically significant (Turner, Beidel, Long, et al., 1993). The effort expended will permit a more meaningful evaluation of our therapeutic interventions.

Another area in need of study is the identification of children who are at risk for the development of anxiety disorders. Currently a number of investigations assessing familial factors are completed or underway (e.g., Last, Hersen, Kazdin, et al., 1991; Turner & Beidel, 1993). Similarly, Kagan and Biederman and their colleagues (e.g., Biederman, Rosenbaum, Bolduc-Murphy, et al., 1993) have been following a sample of children identified in infancy as behaviorally inhibited in an effort to determine the long-term outcome of this construct. Studies assessing environmental risks, such as exposure to ongoing community violence (Cooley, Turner, & Beidel, 1993) or specific traumatic events (Richters, in press), also play an important role in the concept of "at risk." The relationship of these events to the development of anxiety disorders has yet to be explicated fully. Furthermore, in conjunction with the determination of those who are at risk for the development of anxiety disorders, there is a need for more information about those who appear to outgrow potential risk factors such as shyness or behavioral inhibition.

To date, the factors that determine who will go on to develop a disorder and who will not remain unclear. Preliminary efforts appear to identify severity of the predisposing condition as one factor (Bruch, Giordano & Pearl, 1986; Biederman et al., 1993), although other factors also are probably involved. The results of all of these efforts will contribute to a database that will enhance our understanding of vulnerability to and risk for anxiety disorders. With such information, immediate intervention and prevention efforts that serve to circumvent the negative outcomes of these disorders can be developed.

REFERENCES

Achenbach, T. M. (1985). Assessment of anxiety in children. In A. H. Tuma & J. D. Maser (Eds.), *Anxiety and the anxiety disorders* (pp. 707–734). Hillsdale, NJ: Erlbaum.

American Psychiatric Association. (1980). *Diagnostic and statistical manual of mental disorders* (3rd ed.). Washington, DC: Author.

American Psychiatric Association. (1987). *Diagnostic and statistical manual of mental disorders* (3rd ed., rev.). Washington, DC: Author.

American Psychiatric Association. (1994). *Diagnostic and statistical manual of mental disorders* (4th ed.). Washington, DC: Author.

Amies, P. L., Gelder, M. G., & Shaw, P. M. (1983). Social phobia: A comparative clinical study. *British Journal of Psychiatry, 142,* 174–179.

Ammerman, R. T., & Hersen, M. (Eds.). (1993). *Handbook of behavior therapy with children and adults.* Needham Heights, MA: Allyn & Bacon.

Bandura, A. (1977). Self-efficacy: Towards a unifying theory of behavioral change. *Psychological Review, 84,* 191–215.

Barlow, D. H., Craske, M. G., Cerny, J. A., et al. (1989). Behavioral treatment of panic disorder. *Behavior Therapy, 20,* 261–282.

Barrios, B. A., & Hartmann, D. B. (1988). Fears and anxieties in children. In E. J. Mash & L. G. Terdal (Eds.), *Behavioral assessment of childhood disorders* (2nd ed., pp. 196–262). New York: Guilford Press.

Beck, J. G., Stanley, M. A., Baldwin, L. E., et al. (in press). A comparison of cognitive therapy and relaxation training for panic disorder: Outcome and treatment specificity. *Journal of Consulting and Clinical Psychology.*

Beidel, D. C. (1991). Social phobia and overanxious disorder in school-age children. *Journal of the American Academy of Child and Adolescent Psychiatry, 30,* 545–552.

Biederman, J., Rosenbaum, J. F., Bolduc-Murphy, E. A., et al. (1993). A 3 year follow-up of children with and without behavioral inhibition. *Journal of the American Academy of Child and Adolescent Psychiatry, 32,* 814–821.

Blagg, N. R., & Yule, W. (1984). The behavioral treatment of school refusal— A comparative study. *Behaviour Research and Therapy, 22,* 119–127.

Bruch, M. A., Giordano, S., & Pearl, L. (1986). Differences between fearful and self-conscious shy subtypes in background and current adjustment. *Journal of Research in Personality, 20,* 172–186.

Clark, D. B. (1993, March). *Assessment of social anxiety in adolescent alcohol abusers.* Presented at the Anxiety Disorders Association of America Annual Convention, Charleston, SC.

Clomipramine Collaborative Study Group (1991). Clomipramine in the treatment of patients with obsessive–compulsive disorder. *Archives of General Psychiatry, 48,* 730–738.

Cooley, M. R., Turner, S. M., & Beidel, D. C. (1993). *Assessing community violence: The children's report of exposure to violence.* Manuscript in preparation, Medical University of South Carolina.

Davidson, J. (1993, March). *Retrospective reports of adult social phobics.* Presented at the Anxiety Disorders Association of America Annual Convention, Charleston, SC.

Francis, G., Last, C., & Strauss, C. C. (1992). Avoidant disorder and social phobia in children and adolescents. *Journal of the American Academy of Child and Adolescent Psychiatry, 31*, 1086–1089.

Francis, G. & Ollendick, T. (1990). Behavioral treatment of social anxiety. In E. L. Feindler & G. R. Kalfus (Eds.), *Casebook in adolescent behavior therapy* (pp. 127–146). New York: Springer.

Friedman, A. G., & Ollendick, T. H. (1989). Treatment programs for severe nighttime fears: A methodological note. *Journal of Behavior Therapy and Experimental Psychiatry, 20*, 171–178.

Graziano, A., DeGiovanni, I. S., & Garcia, K. (1979). Behavioral treatment of children's fears: A review. *Psychological Bulletin, 86*, 804–830.

Graziano, A., & Mooney, K. (1980). Family self control instruction for children's nighttime fear reduction. *Journal of Consulting and Clinical Psychology, 48*, 206–213.

Graziano, A., & Mooney, K. (1982). Behavioral treatment of "night fears" in children: Maintenance of improvement at 2½ to 3 year follow-up. *Journal of Consulting and Clinical Psychology, 50*, 398–399.

Graziano, A. M., Mooney, K. C., Huber, C., et al. (1979). Self-control instruction for children's fear reduction. *Journal of Behavior Therapy and Experimental Psychiatry, 10*, 221–227.

Hagopian, L. P., & Ollendick, T. H. (1993). Simple phobia in children. *Handbook of Behavior Therapy with Children and Adults* (pp. 123–136). Needham Heights, MA: Allyn & Bacon.

Hagopian, L. P., Weist, M. W., & Ollendick, T. H. (1990). Cognitive-behavior therapy with an 11-year-old girl fearful of AIDS and illness: A case study. *Journal of Anxiety Disorders, 4*, 257–265.

Harris, C. V., & Goetsch, V. L. (1990). Multi-component flooding treatment of adolescent phobia. In E. L. Feindler & G. R. Kalfus (Eds.), *Adolescent behavior therapy casebook* (pp. 147–164). New York: Springer.

Johnson, J. H., & McGlynn, F. D., (1988). Simple phobia. In M. Hersen & C. G. Last (Eds.), *Child behavior therapy casebook* (pp. 43–54). New York: Plenum Press.

Jones, M. C. (1924). A laboratory study of fear: The case of Peter. *Journal of Genetic Psychology, 31*, 308–315.

Kazdin, A. E. (1978). *History of behavior modification*. Baltimore: University Park Press.

Kazdin, A. E. (1979). Advances in child behavior therapy: Applications and implications. *American Psychologist, 38*, 981–987.

Kearney, C. A. & Silverman, W. K. (1990). A preliminary analysis of a functional model of assessment and treatment for school refusal behavior. *Behavior Modification, 14*, 340–366.

Kendall, P. C., & Braswell, L. (1985). *Cognitive-behavioral therapy for impulsive children*. New York: Guilford Press.

Kendall, P. C., Chansky, T. E., Kane, M. T., et al. (1992). *Anxiety disorders in youth: Cognitive-behavioral interventions*. Needham Heights, MA: Allyn & Bacon.

Koeppen, A. S. (1974). Relaxation training for children. *Elementary School Guidance and Counseling, 9*, 14–21.

Last, C. G., Hersen, M., Kazdin, A., et al. (1991). Anxiety disorders in children and their families. *Archives of General Psychiatry, 48*, 928–934.

Last, C. G., Perrin, S., Hersen, M., et al. (1992). DSM-III-R anxiety disorders in children: Sociodemographic and clinical characteristics. *American Academy of Child and Adolescent Psychiatry, 31*, 1070–1076.

McCarthy, P. R., & Foa, E. B. (1988). Obsessive–compulsive disorder. In M. Hersen & C. G. Last (Eds.), *Child behavior therapy casebook* (pp. 55–69). New York: Plenum Press.

Mansdorf, I. J., & Lukens, E. (1987). Cognitive-behavioral psychotherapy for separation anxious children exhibiting school phobia. *Journal of the American Academy of Child and Adolescent Psychiatry, 26*, 222–225.

Meichenbaum, D. H., & Goodman, J. (1971). Training impulsive children to talk to themselves: A means of developing self-control. *Journal of Abnormal Psychology, 77*, 115–126.

Ollendick, T. H., & Cerny, J. A. (1981). *Clinical behavior therapy with children.* New York: Plenum Press.

Rettew, D. C., Swedo, S. E., Leonard, H. L., et al. (1992). Obsessions and compulsions across time in 79 children and adolescents with obsessive–compulsive disorder. *Journal of the American Academy of Child and Adolescent Psychiatry, 31*, 1050–1056.

Richters, J. E. (in press). Community violence and children's development: Toward a research agenda for the 1990s. *American Journal of Psychiatry.*

Saigh, P. A. (1986). In vitro flooding in the treatment of a 6 year-old boy's posttraumatic stress disorder. *Behaviour Research and Therapy, 24*, 685–688.

Saigh, P. A. (1987a). In vitro flooding of a adolescent posttraumatic stress disorder. *Journal of Clinical Child Psychology, 16*, 147–150.

Saigh, P. A. (1987b). In vitro flooding of a childhood posttraumatic stress disorder. *School Psychology Review, 16*, 203–211.

Saigh, P. A. (1987c). In vitro flooding of childhood posttraumatic stress disorders: A systematic replication. *Professional School Psychology, 2*, 135–137.

Schneier, F. R., Johnson, J., Hornig, C. D., et al. (1992). Social phobia: Comorbidity and morbidity in an epidemiologic sample. *Archives of General Psychiatry, 49*, 282–288.

Silverman, W. K., & Eisen, A. R. (1992). Age differences in the reliability of parent and child reports of child anxious symptomatology using a structured interview. *Journal of the American Academy of Child and Adolescent Psychiatry, 31*(1), 117–124.

Turner, S. M., & Beidel, D. C. (1988). *Treating obsessive–compulsive disorder.* New York: Pergamon Press.

Turner, S. M., & Beidel, D. C. (1993). *Children at risk for anxiety disorders.* Unpublished manuscript, Medical University of South Carolina.

Turner, S. M., Beidel, D. C., & Jacob, R. G. (1993). *Social phobia: A compari-*

son of behavior therapy and atenolol. Unpublished manuscript, Medical University of South Carolina.

Turner, S. M., Beidel, D. C., Long, P. J., et al. (1993). A composite measure to determine the functional status of treated social phobics: The Social Phobia Endstate Functioning Index. *Behavior Therapy, 24,* 265–275.

VanHasselt, V. B., & Hersen, M. (Eds.). (1987). *Handbook of adolescent psychology.* Elmsford, NY: Pergamon Press.

VanHasselt, V. B., Hersen, M., Bellack, A. S., et al. (1979). Tripartite assessment of the effects of systematic desensitization in a multiphobic child: An experimental analysis. *Journal of Behavior Therapy and Experimental Psychiatry, 10,* 57–66.

Werry, J. S. (1991). Overanxious disorder: A review of its taxonomic properties. *Journal of the American Academy of Child and Adolescent Psychiatry, 30,* 533–544.

Wolpe, J. (1958). *Psychotherapy by reciprocal inhibition.* Stanford: Stanford University Press.

Chapter 15

Pharmacotherapy: Approaches and Applications

Stan Kutcher
Sharon Reiter
David Gardner

R ecent advances in the identification, diagnosis, and biological understanding of child and adolescent-onset anxiety disorders (Gittelman, 1986; Last, 1989; American Psychiatric Association, 1987) have led to the application of pharmacological treatments borrowed in part from successful strategies applied in adult populations with similar disorders (Simeon & Ferguson, 1985; Kutcher, Reiter, Gardner, et al., 1992; Reiter, Kutcher, & Gardner, 1992). Psychopharmacological interventions are becoming increasingly beneficial in the treatment of a variety of anxiety disorders and are recognized as an essential part of comprehensive clinical intervention in these disorders in children and adolescents.

However, careful consideration of the exact role of pharmacological treatments needs to be made for both individual disorders and particular patients. Most studies of medications specifically for use in child and adolescent anxiety disorders have only recently been conducted, and only a few of the potentially useful compounds have undergone careful evaluation. Thus, the demonstrated efficacy of pharmacotherapy for specific anxiety disorders is limited by the number of investigations reported in the literature to date (Kutcher et al., 1992; Reiter, et al., 1992). Further difficulties arise in the quality of available information on psychotropic treatments because of the nature of some of the available studies. Unlike the adult literature, few properly conducted double-blind placebo-controlled studies that adequately evaluate the efficacy and risks of specific medications exist in the child and adolescent literature. Many studies are open trials or have been conducted in patient populations that are insufficently characterized. Often standardized diagnostics have not been implemented and objective outcome measures are either undefined or are not specific for the disorders under investigation. Additionally, the well-known heterogeneity of patient populations who meet diagnostic criteria for any one anxiety disorder and the common comorbidity of various anxiety disorders with each other and with other Axis I diagnoses (such as major depressive disorder or attention-deficit/hyperactivity disorder [ADHD]) can make selection of a specific psychotropic agent in any one case a difficult proposition.

More recent studies tend to be of high scientific merit and generally can be considered to properly evaluate the various aspects of pharmacological treatments in well-defined populations. Given the caveats noted, a general consensus supported by reasonable clinical trials of the use of various compounds in these populations has begun to emerge.

PSYCHOPHARMACOLOGICAL MANAGEMENT

Good clinical treatment of child and adolescent anxiety disorders necessitates the application of specific psychopharmacological principles in the prescription and monitoring of medications. While medications are often useful in ameliorating the symptoms of various anxiety disorders, additional treatments are often needed to address the patient's social and academic functioning, which may have been adversely affected by months or even years of an ongoing anxiety disturbance. Medications should thus be prescribed as part of an overall treatment strategy, which may include some of the following interventions: cognitive or behavioral therapy, family therapy, and school liasion. Additionally, the successful psychopharmacological approach includes the use of standardized diagnosis, objective and subjective symptom evaluation, objective and subjective side effect assesment, education about the disorder and the medication, and supportive psychotherapeutic interventions.

Overall Treatment Strategy

The clinical management of anxiety disorders must ensure that three distinct areas of dysfunction in the patient are addressed: primary symptoms, anticipatory anxieties, and behavioral disturbances that have arisen in the patient or the patient's environment as a result of the primary symptoms or anticipatory anxieties. Pharmacological interventions are clearly indicated in the treatment of the primary symptoms but often need to be combined with specific psychotherapeutic interventions, such as cognitive therapy, to deal with anticipatory anxiety that has arisen from the initial disturbance. For example, the adolescent suffering from panic disorder who has experienced one or more panic attacks in the school setting may describe intense anticipatory anxiety prior to leaving for school. A young child who has experienced a panic attack at bedtime may show disturbances in behavior during the "going to bed" routines. School-age children with social phobia may be unduly concerned about the possibility of peer ridicule or public embarassment and avoid class parties, school athletics events, and similar activities. These anticipatory symptoms should ideally be addressed psychotherapeutically concurrently with pharmacological interventions.

Similarly, behavioral disturbances arising secondary to the anxiety disorder are frequent and may involve not only the child/adolescent but also the family. For example, children who are worried or fearful may be clingy or very demanding. At times they can be frankly aggressive, as in the case of a child with obsessive–compulsive disorder (OCD) when a parent or sibling refuses to comply with a ritual. The decrements in social adaptation and subjective well-being of children and teenagers with anxiety disorders often place great stress on the family and may alter interpersonal relationships in the family. Additionally, because of the well-established aggregation of anxiety and other Axis I disorders in families of anxious children and teenagers (Last, Hersen, Kazdin, et al., 1991), one or more family members may be suffering from an anxiety disorder or other psychiatric disturbance (such as depression or alcoholism). Successful intervention for the child or adolescent in that case often includes appropriate pharmacological treatment of the other family member(s), usually a parent. Thus, in the pharmacological management of child and adolescent anxiety disorders, intervention in family functioning is often necessary for optimal treatment outcome.

Additionally, the child or adolescent may have developed other disordered behaviors, often the result of phobic avoidance. For example, the adolescent with panic disorder may avoid going to parties or other social functions. Similarly, the child with social phobia may isolate himself in the schoolyard, away from other children. In these cases, while pharmacological interventions may ameliorate many of the underlying symptoms, other therapeutic techniques, such as behavioral or cognitive therapies are necessary to improve social functioning.

Diagnosis

Although a review of diagnostic procedures is beyond the scope of this chapter and is found elsewhere in this text, the clinician must be familiar with current diagnostic constructs that can be used to direct treatment. Concepts such as "emotional disorder" or "neurotic behavior" have no place in modern diagnostic nomenclature and offer no utility in defining treatment. Clinicians may wish to use diagnostic interviews developed specifically for anxiety disorders (Hoehn-Saric, Maisami, & Wiegand, 1987; Silverman & Nelles, 1988; Chapter 6) once a tentative diagnosis of an anxiety disorder is made in order to carefully and comprehensively characterize the specific disorder. However, the use of a more global diagnostic interview such as the Kiddie Schedule for Affective Disorders and Schizophrenia (K-SADS; Chambers, Puig-Antich, Hirsch, et al., 1985), the Diagnostic Interview for Children and Adolescents (DICA; Herjanic & Reich, 1982), or the Diagnostic Interview Schedule (DIS; Costello, 1983, 1987) is most helpful in the initial diagnostic evaluation. Careful diagnostic assessment should not only properly characterize the specific anxiety disorder but also identify any comorbid states.

Symptom Evaluation

Following appropriate diagnosis, an accurate documentation of specific symptoms, both objective and subjective, should take place and should include symptom type, severity, and frequency. Additionally, measures of global functioning and functioning in specific areas such as school, work, and social activity are necessary in monitoring treatment outcome. For most anxiety disorders a baseline measurement period of at least one to two weeks is necessary prior to initating treatment. Prescribing medications prior to adequate baseline symptom assessment is to be avoided, even though the patients or their parents may exert pressure to start treatment at first consultation.

For panic attacks, a panic attack diary (Figure 15.1) is indispensable. The diary should include a daily record of each panic attack experienced. Additionally, ratings of severity, length of the attack, and number of symptoms should be recorded. Each panic attack should also be categorized as either spontaneous or situational, important information that can be used in ancillary psychological interventions.

In OCD, the Yale–Brown Obsessive Compulsive Disorder Scale (YBOCS; Goodman, Price, Rasmussen, et al., 1989) is a useful tool in assessing both symptom severity and symptom diversity. It can be used for patients of all ages and provides a reliable method of monitoring symptom change.

PANIC ATTACK DIARY

Name: _____

Date: _____

Number	Severity (1–3)	Duration (mins)	Spontaneous	Situation (describe)	Symptom Nos.	Symptom List
1						1. Fear of dying
2						2. Fear of losing control
3						3. Fear of doing something crazy
4						4. Short of breath
5						5. Dizzy or faint
6						6. Heart racing or skipping
7						7. Trembling or shaking
8						8. Sweating
9						9. Choking
10						10. Feeling unreal
						11. Numbness or tingling
						12. Flushes or chills
						13. Chest pain or discomfort
						14. Upset stomach or nausea

FIGURE 15.1. Patient panic attack diary. For each date, the patient records the number of the attack; its severity (1, mild; 2, moderate; 3, severe); duration in minutes; whether it was spontaneous (yes/no) or situational (describe); and the numbers of the symptoms present during the attack.

345

Baseline anxiety ratings can be obtained using various scales, such as the Hamilton Anxiety Rating Scale (Hamilton, 1959) or the Speilberger State–Trait Anxiety Inventory (Spielberger, 1973). These show good test–retest reliability and provide a useful tool for measuring severity changes in various anxiety symptoms. A visual analogue scale (10 centimeters) with a clearly defined low end (no anxiety) and high end (intense anxiety) is of value for younger children who do not have the reading or comprehension abilities necessary for written scales. All these scales can be used with the patient or can be administered to a parent for the parent's perception of symptom severity. It must be remembered however, that these scales are not diagnostic instruments; they are merely symptom rating scales that are sensitive to symptom change over time. Furthermore, as patients, parents, and other informants (such as teachers) can vary in their perception of various symptoms and behaviors, it is desirable to have two or three reliable informants (including the patient) whenever possible to provide a comprehensive evaluation.

Global functioning can be assessed using the Global Assessment Scale of the third revised edition of the *Diagnostic and Statistical Manual of Mental Disorders* (DSM-III-R; American Psychiatric Association, 1987) or a visual analogue scale. Similarly, specific areas of functioning, such as school, peer relationships, and family conflicts, can be monitored using a visual analogue scale (Figure 15.2). Finally, the Symptom Checklist—58 (Derogatis, Litman, Rickels, et al., 1974) provides a useful self-report assessment of a variety of symptoms related to anxiety disorders and can be used by patients who read at sixth-grade level.

ASSESSMENT: SPECIFIC FUNCTIONING

School   0 ------------------------------------- 10

Social   0 ------------------------------------- 10

Family   0 ------------------------------------- 10

Peers   0 ------------------------------------- 10

FIGURE 15.2. Visual analogue scale for assessing anxiety in specific areas of functioning. 0, no anxiety; 10, intense anxiety.

Side Effect Monitoring

Anxiety disorders are characterized by somatic symptoms that are often similar to those that can be induced by medications (e.g., headaches, nausea, gastrointestinal distress, diarrhea, and various aches and pains). These symptoms must be identified and evaluated prior to starting treatment with medications. This evaluation helps identify "true" side effects that emerge as a result of treatment. Furthermore, it helps patients and their families to objectively evaluate somatic symptoms that occur during treatment and encourages measured consideration of the often unexpected negative side effects to treatment with medications.

In many cases, this careful approach can mean the difference between a patient persisting with an effective treatment or premature discontinuation of medications as a result of negative preconceptions or prejudices regarding their effects. For example, if headaches are reported and evaluated as to frequency and severity prior to treatment, headaches during treatment are unlikely to be due to medications if their frequency and severity are about the same as they were before treatment—even though the patient or the patient's family identifies the headaches as "caused by the pills." Indeed, scores on side effect evaluation scales tend to decrease with successful medication treatment as the anxiety symptoms abate.

A side effect scale (SES) should be constructed for each specific medication used. An example of a clinically useful side effect scale developed for use with the selective serotonin reuptake inhibitors (SSRIs) is found in Figure 15.3. Ideally, an SES should be completed at least three times during the baseline symptom evaluation in order to obtain a valid profile of somatic symptoms which often fluctuate over time.

Education about the Disorder and the Medications

Children and teenagers with anxiety disorders or their parents are often concerned about treatment with medications. Educating the patient and family about the disorder and the medications used in its treatment is an essential part of psychopharmacological management. Following diagnosis, a sufficient period of time should be dedicated to full and frank discussion of the diagnosis and the differential diagnoses; the clinician's understanding of the biological, social, and interpersonal aspects of the disorder(s); the natural history and course of the disorder; the expected outcome with and without treatment; the various treatment options available (including their risks, benefits, and demonstrated efficacies); the potential role of medications in treating the specific disorder (including risks and benefits); and the expected length of treatment. Once these issues are

SSRI ANTIDEPRESSANT MONITORING
SIDE EFFECTS

Patient name _____   **Blood Pressure: Sitting** _____/_____

Date _____   **Standing** _____/_____

Interviewer _____   **Heart Rate:** beats/minute

Please circle the number of the response that best describes how you have experienced each of the following possible side effects over the past week.

Side effect	Never		Somewhat		Constantly
Nausea	0	1	2	3	4
Vomiting	0	1	2	3	4
Diarrhea/loose stools	0	1	2	3	4
Constipation	0	1	2	3	4
Stomach pains/cramps	0	1	2	3	4
Dry mouth	0	1	2	3	4
Sweating	0	1	2	3	4
Drowsiness	0	1	2	3	4
Fatigue	0	1	2	3	4
Insomnia	0	1	2	3	4
Restlessness/agitation	0	1	2	3	4
Tremor	0	1	2	3	4
Headache	0	1	2	3	4
Difficulty concentrating	0	1	2	3	4
Dizziness	0	1	2	3	4
Decreased appetite	0	1	2	3	4
Increased appetite	0	1	2	3	4
Impotence	0	1	2	3	4
Increased energy	0	1	2	3	4
Increased mood	0	1	2	3	4
Suicide/self-harm ideation	0	1	2	3	4
Impulsivity	0	1	2	3	4
Suicidal acts*	0	1	2	3	4
Other: _____	0	1	2	3	4
Other: _____	0	1	2	3	4

*Describe: _____

FIGURE 15.3. Side effects for selective serotonin reuptake inhibitors.

discussed, the patient and family can be offered pharmacological interventions. Some patients agree to pharmacotherapy at the outset of treatment; others forgo medications in preference for other types of treatment. The pharmacotherapist should support the direction the patient chooses and assist in the development of a strategy that will identify points during treatment when the use of medications is reevaluated depending on symptom improvement.

Once a medication approach is chosen, it is imperative to fully describe and document the potential side effects of the compound(s) to be used. The dosage pattern and the relationship between expected side effects and dosage changes should be described. The importance of a period during which the medication is gradually raised to an expected therapeutic level must be discussed. Many patients conceptualize the treatment course of any medication on the model of pain relief with analgesics, so it is important to describe the expected course of symptomatic improvement. This is particularly important when a lag time is expected between initiation of treatment and the onset of symptomatic relief, as in the use of buspirone in treating the symptoms of overanxious disorder (OAD). A patient or family expecting immediate symptom resolution may terminate potentially effective medication in the mistaken belief that "it is not working."

The clinician must be equally clear about the anticipated benefits of medication use. Expected degrees of symptomatic improvement must be identified prior to initiating medication treatment and unrealistic expectations openly identified and discussed. For example, a decrement of 70 to 80% in panic attack frequency may often be accepted as maximal improvement with medications, while in many cases a 50% decrease in compulsive behaviors may identify the limit of medication effect in OCD. While this degree of symptomatic change does not constitute symptom resolution, it may lead to vastly improved social and academic functioning and may enhance and even speed up certain psychological interventions. Similarly, patients and their families must be informed that not all medicines help everybody and that a period of medication trial and error may be necessary to find the medication that is most helpful. In some cases, particularly where very strong antimedication sentiment is present or where significant conflict exists between the patient and a parent regarding the use of medication, but pharmacological treatment is nonetheless being sought, a single-blind placebo/active medication trial may be indicated (Kutcher, 1986).

Drug interactions with other medications (including over-the-counter compounds) should be identified. Because illicit drugs or alcohol can render treatment ineffective or confuse the clinical picture in such a way as to make it impossible to evaluate the efficacy of medications, patients must be advised to refrain from using these compounds. As this often may be an issue with adolescents, some of whom may self-medicate in response to symptom-based distress, information about substance abuse must be presented in an accurate, concise manner, with the risks clearly described but not exaggerated.

Finally, a point during treatment should be identified at which the patient's symptoms and functioning will be comprehensively reevaluated and further decisions about the treatment process made. It is necessary that this assessment point be chosen to allow enough time for expected symptom improvement. In some cases, such as the use of the benzodiazepine clonazepam for panic disorder, four weeks from treatment initiation may be sufficient. For other cases, for example, the use of clomipramine for OCD, 8 or 10 weeks is more appropriate.

USEFUL MEDICATIONS

Antidepressants

The potential role of various antidepressants in treating anxiety disorders arises from the hypothesized role of specific neurotransmitters, particularly noradrenaline and serotonin, in the pathogenesis of anxiety states. Although studies in child and adolescent populations are lacking, various paramaters of dysregulated central nervous system (CNS) noradrenergic and serotonergic functioning have been described in adults with anxiety disorders.

The noradrenergic system may be associated with the pathophysiology of a number of anxiety disorders. For example, stimulation of the locus ceruleus may lead to panic states (Charney, Heninger, Breier, 1984). Some but not all studies have demonstrated a relationship between basal levels of plasma catecholamines of 3-methoxy-4-hydroxyphenylglycol (MHPG) and anxiety symptoms (Wyatt, Portnoy, Kupfer, et al., 1971; Hamlin, Lydiard, Martin, et al., 1983; Sweeney, Mass, & Heninger, 1978; Uhde, Joffe, Jimerson, et al., 1988). Urinary excretion of noradrenaline metabolites is reported to be decreased in panic disorder, and some investigators have described significantly different changes in peripheral noradrenergic functioning in response to a variety of pharmacological challenges in anxious probands compared to normal controls (Charney & Heninger, 1986; Nutt, 1989; Liebowitz, Gorman, Fyer, et al., 1985). Thus, noradrenergic-system-affecting agents such as tricyclic antidepressants (TCAs) or monoamine oxidase inhibitors (MAOIs) may exert their anxiolytic effects primarily through influences on catecholamine functioning (Potter, Rudorfer, Pickar, et al., 1987).

Serotonin system dysfunction may also be associated with anxiety states (Kahn, van Praag, Wetzler, et al., 1988; File, 1984). Although the evidence for serotonin system dysfunction in OCD is perhaps best known (Winslow & Insel, 1990; Hollander, Concetta, Nitescu, et al., 1992, Charney, Goodman, Price, et al., 1988), some evidence for CNS dysregulation in other anxiety disorders has been found as well (Charney & Heninger, 1986). Thus both the TCAs (which are known to effect serotonin functioning at the presynaptic autoreceptor site) and the SSRIs may exhibit therapeutic effect in OCD and other anxiety states (Den Boer, Westenberg, Kamarbeck, et al., 1987).

Tricyclic Antidepressants

Treatment studies of TCAs such as imipramine, desipramine, nortriptyline, and clomipramine have been reported involving a variety of child and adolescent anxiety disorders, including separation anxiety disorder and OCD. A number of TCAs have also been evaluated in clinical populations of children and adolescents in which a high prevalence of anxiety states is found (namely school refusers).

Imipramine Treatment for School Refusal

Gittelman-Klein and Klein (1971, 1973) reported a double-blind placebo-controlled trial of imipramine (IMI) in 35 children and young adolescents (ages 7 to 15) diagnosed as school refusers. These were treatment-resistant children who had been unable to return to school following an adequate trial of behavioral therapies. Imipramine was given at a mean daily dose of 159 mg per day for 6 weeks and behavioral treatments continued throughout the study. By the study end, 81% of the imipramine-treated group compared to 47% of the placebo-treated group had successfully returned to school. Furthermore, while the subjects in the placebo-treated group continued to report distressing anxiety symptoms, the imipramine group experienced subjective improvements in anxiety. Both treatment groups complained of medication side effects including drowsiness, dizziness, tremor, and constipation. Only dry mouth occurred significantly more frequently in the imipramine-treated group.

Berney (1981) did not demonstrate similar efficacy in a 12-week trial of clomipramine (CMI) in a population of 46 school refusers (19 male, 27 female) of ages 9 to 15. Dosages used were subtherapeutic, however, with 9- and 10-year-olds receiving 40 mg daily, 10- and 11-year-olds 50 mg daily, and 13- to 15-year-olds 60 mg daily. Insufficient information was presented to permit proper evaluation of possible clomipramine adverse effects.

Bernstein, Garfinkel, and Barchardt (1990) compared imipramine (IMI) to the benzodiazepine alprazolam combined with extensive psychosocial treatment (school reentry program) in both open ($n = 17$) and double-blind placebo-controlled ($n = 24$) studies of school refusers (Bernstein & Garfinkel, 1986; Bernstein et al., 1990). While results tended to favor the medication-treated group, particularly in the open trial, insignificant differences between medication and nonmedication groups were found in the double-blind placebo study. Serum levels of IMI showed adequate medication dosage, and the mean alprazolam dose was 1.8 mg daily. Neither medication showed superiority over the other in either improvement of anxiety symptoms or clinically significant side effects. Two important factors, however, limit the findings of this study. First, the numbers studied were too small to show anything except a very large treatment effect, so the study has a high likelihood of exhibiting a type 2 error. Second, because a medication was added to what was possibly by itself an effective psychosocial treatment, it is impossible to determine what independent effect medication might have in a treatment-naive population of school refusers.

However, although again limited by small sample size, a more recent study by Klein, Kopelwicz, and Kanner (1992) also was unable to demonstrate a significant IMI-treatment effect in 20 children and young adolescents (ages 6 to 15) diagnosed with separation anxiety disorder. Following a 1-month trial of behavior therapy, subjects were randomly assigned to IMI (mean dose of 153 mg per day) or placebo treatment for 6 consecutive weeks. In each treatment group, 50% of the patients improved. Furthermore, there were no significant group differences in either subjective reports of side effects or electrocardiogram changes.

Taken together, these studies show a possible role for the use of imipramine in the treatment of school refusal, although it is not clear what specific anxiety disorders may have underlain the school-refusing behavior of the subjects in these studies. Because other Axis I disorders (e.g., depression) may lead to school refusal, tricyclic antidepressants should not be used in the routine treatment of school refusers. A potentially useful role for tricyclics with school refusers may be as an adjunct to ongoing behavioral therapies in a treatment-resistant subgroup.

Clomipramine Treatment
for Obsessive–Compulsive Disorder

Tricyclic treatment of OCD in children and adolescents has been relatively well studied (Piacentini, Jaffer, Gitow, et al., 1992). The initial double-blind placebo-controlled crossover design study of CMI use with OCD demonstrated that in the short term, CMI at a mean daily dose of 141 mg per day was significantly more effective than placebo (Flament, Rapoport, Berg, et al., 1985). However, while mean group OCD scores showed a clearly positive medication response, fewer than 50% of the subjects reported a minimum of 50% symptom improvement from baseline, and only 10% experienced total symptom relief. This finding suggests that while CMI may be an effective pharmacological intervention in the treatment of OCD, not all patients experience full symptomatic resolution.

Further support for CMI effectiveness with OCD was reported by DeVaugh-Geiss, Landau, Katz, et al. (1989), who described an 8-week double-blind trial of CMI and placebo in 60 patients with OCD. At a maximal daily dose of 3 mg/kg 37% of the CMI group compared to 8% of the placebo group demonstrated a positive treatment response. However, the CMI/OCD findings taken together suggest that while some patients experience significant symptomatic improvement with CMI, many retain some degree of symptom severity, although their social functioning and psychological distress may be somewhat improved.

The specificity of the antiobsessive response to the more serotonergic TCAs is suggested by the study of Leonard, Swedo, Rapoport, et al. (1989), which compared the efficacies of CMI and desipramine (DMI) in the treatment of child and adolescent OCD. Using a crossover design, the study demonstrated that not only was CMI significantly better than DMI in reducing obsessive symptoms in the short term, but the majority of those patients initially treated with CMI relapsed when blindly switched to DMI.

A similar finding was reported by Leonard, Swedo, Lenane, et al. (1991) in a longer-term study of 26 children and young adolescents with OCD. In this group, patients who had been treated for a mean of 17 months with CMI were assigned to two different medication groups; one continued to receive CMI, the other was blindly switched to DMI. During the 2-month study period, 89% of the DMI-substituted group relapsed compared to only 18% of the continuously CMI-treated group—a statistically and clinically significant difference. All probands who relapsed during DMI substitution showed remission of their OCD symptoms within a month of return to CMI treatment. However, even in the continuously CMI-treated group, many probands continued to report OCD symptoms that waxed and waned, often in response to environmental stressors. This chronic, fluctuating pattern of OCD symptoms, even with optimal CMI treatment, is further supported by Swedo and Rapoport (1989), who found that 65% of children with OCD followed up 2 to 5 years after onset of treatment still demonstrated clinically significant symptoms. Similar results have been reported by Rettew, Swedo, Leonard, et al. (1992), but DeVeaugh-Geiss et al. (1989) found that uninterrupted treatment with CMI over a 1-year follow-up led to continued symptomatic improvement.

Furthermore, studies of CMI-treated OCD children and adolescents have lent support to the serotonin hypothesis of OCD. For example, treatment response to CMI in OCD children has been associated with changes in serum prolactin levels, changes in CNS cerebral spinal fluid levels of 5-hydroxyindoleacetic acid, and decreases in platelet serotonin concentrations (Hanna, McCracken, & Cantwell, 1991; Swedo, Leonard, Kruesi, et al., 1992; Flament, Rapoport, Murphy, et al., 1987). These findings support the hypothesis that the serotonin selectivity of CMI may be related to its antiobsessional effects.

Taken together, the CMI/OCD studies indicate that CMI is the tricyclic of choice in treating OCD, even though children and adolescents with subtle neurological impairment may show an attenuated treatment response to CMI (March, Johnson, Jefferson, et al., 1990). However, OCD appears to be a relatively refractory disorder, even with pharmacotherapy with CMI. Some patients in our clinic have experienced greater treatment success with a combination of CMI and a low dose (1 to 2 mg per day) of clonazepam. Additionally, the disorder is chronic and tends to wax and wane, perhaps in association with environmental factors. These issues need to be discussed with patients and their families before starting CMI treatment in order to keep treatment response expectations in perspective. Finally, although no valid controlled studies are available to date, some evidence for the potential efficacy of behavioral treatments in this age group has been demonstrated, suggesting that combined pharmacological and behavioral treatments may be superior to either one alone.

Treatment of Attention-Deficit/Hyperactivity Disorder with Tricyclic Antidepressants

Further studies have evaluated the efficacy of tricyclics in comorbid attentional and anxiety disorders. Cox (1982) described decreased hyperactivity and increased attention span in 14 boys of ages 7 to 11 diagnosed with attention-deficit disorder and comorbid anxiety and treated with IMI. Unfortunately no evaluation of changes in anxiety symptoms was specifically reported. Similarly, Pliszka (1987, 1989) and Biederman, Baldessarini, Wright, et al. (1989b) have noted that boys with ADHD comorbid with anxiety show a better response to TCAs than to stimulant medication. Garfinkel, Wender, Sloman, et al. (1983) demonstrated that ADHD probands with anxiety responded better to both clomipramine and desipramine than to methylphenidate or placebo.

These findings suggest that children and adolescents with comorbid ADHD and anxiety may show a preferential response to TCAs, at least for symptoms of hyperactivity and attention span. However, given the early stages of investigations in this area, it is unclear if anxiety symptoms show similar improvements. In any case, TCAs may have a useful therapeutic role in this subgroup.

Efficacy of Tricyclic Antidepressants with Panic Disorder

Although studies in adult populations have identified the efficacy of TCAs in treating panic disorder (Nurnberg & Coccaro, 1982; Pohl, Berchou, & Rainey, 1983), no studies to our knowledge are available for children and adolescents. Our clinical experience, however, indicates that TCAs, particulary IMI, may be useful agents in alleviating panic attacks in adolescents. The usual therapeutic dose ranges from 75 to 150 mg daily, given in divided doses, with most teenagers responding to doses between 100 to 150 mg daily.

Side Effects of Tricyclic Antidepressants

Although several studies are now available describing the potential use of tricyclics with child and adolescent anxiety disorders, much yet remains unknown about the optimal use of these compounds. For example, dose-response studies remain essentially unreported, so treatment remains largely clinically directed. As well, the clinical relevance of tricyclic plasma levels in anxiety disorders remains unclear—to both therapeutic response and toxicity. Wide variations in plasma levels at similar doses of tricyclics have been reported for depressed children and adolescents (Puig-Antich, Perel, Lupatkin, et al., 1979), yet neither symptomatic improvement nor cardiovascular events have been clearly shown to be related to either dose or plasma level (Kutcher, Boulos, Ward, et al., 1994; Geller, Cooper, McCombo, et al., 1989; Preskorn, Weller, & Weller, 1987; Puig-Antich et al., 1979; Puig-Antich, Perel, Lupatkin, et al., 1987; Ryan, Puig-Antich, Cooper, et al., 1986).

Cardiovascular Effects. Cardiovascular side effects of TCAs may occur more frequently in children and adolescents than in adults, and clinically significant conduction abnormalities may be related to prexisting cardiological abnormalities (Biederman et al., 1989; Ryan, Puig-Antich, Cooper, et al., 1987; Wilens, Biederman, Baldessarini, et al., 1992). However, the clinical significance of cardiac conduction changes as measured by the electrocardiogram is unclear. Sinus tachycardia is the most commonly reported effect of tricyclics on cardiac functioning, and widening of the PR interval and QRS complexes is often seen. Sudden death has been reported in a small number of children treated with desipramine (Biederman, 1991), but the exact relationship (if any) between the possible cardiotoxic effects of this compound and these cases is unclear (Elliott, Popper, & Fraizer, 1990; Popper & Elliott, 1990). Where cardiovascular instability is a factor and antidepressants are the preferred medication choice (e.g., as in treating patients with OCD), a SSRI may be a useful alternative to CMI (Glassman & Preud'homme, 1993). In any case, where the clinician is uncertain about the use of any particular compound, a cardiology consultation prior to initiating treatment may be of benefit.

IMI-associated systolic or diastolic hypertension has been reported in a small group of adolescents treated at doses of 0.4 to 3.6 mg/kg per day (Kuekes, Wigg, Bryant, et al., 1992). Although not clinically significant, it was found more frequently in younger adolescents (ages 13 to 15) than in older adolescents (ages 16 to 17). Furthermore, while a number of other studies have reported blood pressure changes in nonanxiety-disordered children and adolescents treated with various TCAs, the clinical importance of this finding is unclear (Donnelly, Zametkin, Rapoport, et al., 1986; Greenberg & Yellin, 1975; Biederman et al., 1989a). A recent study of older depressed adolescents (mean age 17.2 years) showed no significant differences in either systolic or diastolic blood pressure measures between desipramine and placebo-treated groups (Kutcher et al., 1994). Age may be an important predictor of the vulnerability of child and adolescent populations to this effect, with younger patients more susceptible. However, the clinical relevance of this finding, if any, is not known.

Before initiating tricyclic treatment in children or adolescents, the clinician must complete a full clinical examination including sitting and standing blood pressures and a baseline EKG (Ryan, 1992). Patients with significant cardiac conduction abnormalities or recent (within 2 weeks) use of MAOIs or SSRIs (except fluoxetine, where 5 weeks are needed) are not candidates for TCA treatment. Dosages should be started at low levels (about 10 mg of IMI or equivalent daily) and the amount increased by the starting dose amount every 4 to 7 days. As doses increase, larger increments can be made (25 mg) to a target of about 125 to 150 mg of IMI or equivalent per day in divided doses. At about 3 mg/kg per day, a steady-state serum level should be drawn to direct further dosage increases. The reason for this conservative dosing schedule is that a significant number of anxiety-disordered (particularly panic-disordered) patients experience an increase in anxiety symptoms if dosage is begun too high or if dosage adjustments are too large. When this occurs, patients sometimes refuse to continue with a potentially helpful medication. The value of routine EKG monitoring is not known, but another EKG should probably be taken when higher doses (greater than 3mg/kg per day) are used.

Once a steady-state dose of approximately 3mg/kg per day is reached, the dose should be maintained for 14 to 21 days to determine clinical efficacy (for OCD patients, eight to ten weeks may be required). For patients with a good therapeutic response, the medication should be continued for up to six months prior to reevaluation by gradual dosage reduction. Failure to obtain a therapeutic response at maximal doses should lead to gradual medication discontinuation and institution of an alternative treatment.

Overdose Effects. During treatment with TCAs, particular importance must be paid to overdose, either accidental, as in the case of young children (patients or siblings), or deliberate, as with impulsive adolescents. If taken in sufficent quantity, all tricyclics can cause cardiotoxic events, reduced seizure threshold, and CNS depression (Goodman Gilman, Goodman, Rall, et al., 1985). Because suicide attempts are known to be associated with panic disorder, and because adolescents are at high risk for suicide attempts (Weissman, Klerman, Markowitz, et al., 1989), practitioners considering TCAs for panic-disordered adolescents must carefully weigh the risks and benefits for each patient. An adolescent with panic disorder and a history of impulsivity or substance abuse and previous suicide attempts is not a good candidate for tricyclic treatment.

Adverse Reactions at Therapeutic Doses. Common adverse reactions at therapeutic doses include dry mouth, constipation, nausea, dizziness, sedation, insomnia, and weight changes. Often these symptoms are transitory and can be managed by slower dosage increases or small dosage reductions. TCA-induced manic symptoms have been described in populations of depressed children and teenagers (Geller, Fox, & Fletcher, et al., 1993), although the applicability of these data to anxiety-disordered youngsters is unknown. In patients with comorbid depressive symptoms and a history of bipolarity in first-degree relatives, it is important to carefully monitor mood as well as anxiety symptoms. Reiter (1994) has described three adolescents with primary OCD who developed hypomania following initiation of CMI treatment. A few patients have exhibited signs of irritability, agitation, and even increased aggressivity when treated with TCAs (Alarcon, Johnson, & Lucas, 1991). Behavioral toxicity must be clearly distinguished from anxiety symptoms, as the proper management in these situations is medication withdrawal as opposed to dosage increase.

Withdrawal Effects. When withdrawing TCAs—for reasons of insufficent therapeutic response or intolerable side effects or for determining if further TCA treatment is needed following a period of adequate symptom resolution—gradual dosage decrement is a useful strategy. Rapid tricyclic withdrawal may be associated with a variety of symptoms, including nausea, sweating, restlessness, insomnia, irritability, and vivid dreams, as well as other symptoms that suggest cholinergic overdrive. Young children may be especially sensitive to rapid TCA withdrawal, and nausea, vomiting, and diarrhea can lead to fluid-electrolyte disturbances. Thus TCA withdrawal should be gradual with total reduction accomplished over two to three weeks. In severe cases of withdrawal symptoms, judicious use of an anticholinergic agent such as benztropine may be of value.

If a switch to another antidepressant is contemplated, care must be taken to permit a sufficent washout period, as potentially problematic drug–drug interactions can occur between various classes of antidepressants (e.g., hypertensive crises with the combination of TCAs and MAOIs or the serotonin syndrome in combined TCA and SSRI therapy). Five half-lives of the TCA used is generally regarded as an acceptable washout period.

Selective Serotonin Reuptake Inhibitors

Although a growing literature on the effectiveness of SSRIs in a variety of adult anxiety disorders (panic disorder, OCD) exists, little is currently available on children and adolescents. Clinician experience in our anxiety disorders clinic suggests that in some cases an SSRI (particularly if begun with a low dose) provides effective treatment for adolescents with panic disorder. Riddle, Scahill, King, et al. (1992) reported that fluoxetine at a daily dose of 20 mg was significantly more effective than placebo in a short-term trial of children and adolescents with OCD. This finding supports a number of small open studies reporting similar positive results. Additionally, fluoxetine in doses up to 40 mg daily has been reported as successful in treating the obsessions and rituals of children and young adolescents with combined OCD and Tourette's syndrome. No significant side effects were reported and no increases in tics were noted (Como & Kurlan, 1991; Riddle, Hardin, King, et al., 1990). Finally, Simeon, Thatte, and Wiggins (1990) have described using combined low-dosage CMI and fluoxetine in treating a small number of patients with OCD who had experienced minimal response to CMI alone. In this sample of four patients, adverse effects were reportedly less frequent and severe with the combined treatment than with CMI alone. This combination of medications, however, may induce a serotonin syndrome (Sternbach, 1991) and should be reserved for treatment-resistant patients and provided in specialized clinics where careful monitoring is available.

Generally, although the child and adolescent literature is limited, the SSRIs appear to be well tolerated in this population, particularly if dosing is initiated with low amounts and gradually increased. For example, if fluoxetine is being used, dosage should be initiated with 5 mg daily and gradually raised by 5 mg every 3 to 4 days until a level of 20 mg is reached.

The patient should be maintained at this dose for two to three weeks (in OCD patients, 6 to 8 weeks) to determine therapeutic efficacy.

Subjective side effects tend to be mild, short-lived, and dose related. The more commonly reported side effects include nausea, tremor, sweating, insomnia, and headaches. In studies of SSRIs, however, less than 5% of subjects have withdrawn because of side effects (contrasted to rates of up to 20% in studies of some TCAs). Side effects tend to be similar for most SSRIs, but in our clinical experience, fluvoxamine has been more likely to cause sedation or nausea. SSRIs tend to be better tolerated than TCAs and show further advantages, including minimal clinical cardiovascular effects and safety in overdose (Riddle, Brown, Dzubinski, et al., 1989). Although efficacy studies suggest relatively similar response rates between TCAs and SSRIs in adult populations, comparable studies of children and adolescents are as yet unavailable.

Potential drug–drug interactions must be kept in mind when using SSRIs. Fluoxetine in particular may decrease the clearance of antipsychotics, carbamazepine, and other antidepressants through its hepatic enzyme-inhibiting effects (Ciraulo & Shader, 1990a). This may be of clinical importance where comorbidity of anxiety and other disorders results in the concurrent use of a variety of pharmacological agents.

Of the available SSRIs, fluoxetine may be more likely to induce a type of akathisia or psychomotor restlessness in some patients at treatment onset, particularly if doses greater than 5 mg daily are used to initiate therapy (Riddle et al., 1990). In spite of some concern, however (King, Riddle, Chappell, et al., 1991), there is no demonstrated increase in impulsive or suicidal behaviors with the use of fluoxetine (Boulos, Kutcher, Gardner, et al., 1992; Jain, Birmaker, Garcia, et al., 1992), and all available data to date show that fluoxetine use in at-risk populations is associated with decreases in suicidality (Beasley, Dornseif, Bosanworth, et al., 1991; Fava & Rosenbaum, 1991). Mania or hypomania following the use of fluoxetine has been described in adolescents treated for depression (Venkataraman, Naylor, & King, 1992; Boulos et al., 1992; Jain et al., 1992) and in a small number of teens treated for OCD (Reiter, 1994). A family history of bipolar disorder and premorbid features of attention-deficit disorder, affective instability, or psychotic depression may be risk factors for fluoxetine-induced manic states.

In adolescent patients, some of the SSRIs may be associated with disordered sexual functioning, such as anorgasmia, delayed orgasm, or ejaculatory delay. Given the importance of sexual issues to adolescents, their anxiety about sexual concerns, and the self-esteem variables involved in sexual performance, care must be taken both to discuss these issues prior to treatment and to inquire about potential difficulties during treatment.

When SSRIs are being discontinued, a gradual withdrawal over a week is preferred, although fluoxetine may be stopped more quickly because of its long half-life. If the patient is to be treated with another antidepressant, it is advisable to have a washout period prior to introducing the new compound. This is particularly important if a patient is being switched from an SSRI to a MAOI, where a washout period of five half-lives of the SSRI should be given to minimize serotonin syndrome side effects. In the case of fluoxetine, the washout period may be as long as 5 weeks.

Monoamine Oxidase Inhibitors

Little information is available about the use of MAOIs compounds in children and adolescents with anxiety disorders. The difficulties with the use of the traditional MAOIs is well known, and cardiovascular side effects have been reported in adolescents treated for major depression with traditional MAOIs (Ryan, Puig-Antich, Rabinovich, et al., 1988). Similarly, use of tranylcypromine in our adolescent outpatient clinics has resulted in significant numbers of teenagers exhibiting distressing cardiovascular side effects (primarily orthostatic hypotension). The specific monoamine oxidase A inhibitor moclobemide, with its minimal risk of cardiovascular pressor response to tyramine loading and a side effects profile that in large part is indistinguishable from placebo (Fitton, Faulds, & Goa, 1992; Amrein, Hetzel, Stabl, et al., 1992; Liebowitz, Hollander, Schneier, et al., 1990), has recently been introduced for treatment of depression and various anxiety disorders and will require careful evaluation in children and adolescents with anxiety disorders. At this time only one study of the use of this compound with children has been reported that we are aware of, a study of 12 children treated for attention-deficit disorder (Trott, Friese, Menzel, et al., 1992). The applicability of the data to anxiety disorders is unclear, and the use of moclobemide in treating anxious children and adolescents should at this time be considered experimental.

Benzodiazepines

Benzodiazepines may be the most commonly prescribed psychotropic agents used in treating children and adolescents, although the extent of their use in treating anxiety disorders in this population is unknown (Dugas, Zarifian, Leheuzey, et al., 1980). In contrast to information about their common clinical use, however, there is a lack of both pharmacodynamic and pharmacokinetic information on these compounds with children and adolescents (Coffey, 1990). The information that is available suggests that children may have an increased ability to metabolize and eliminate some of these compounds (Coffey, Shader, & Greenblatt, 1983).

The anxiolytic activity of the benzodiazepines has been related to their ability to enhance CNS inhibition by activating the benzodiazepine/gamma-aminobutyric acid (GABA) receptor complex. GABA is the major ubiquitous CNS inhibitory neurotransmitter, and one of the two GABAergic receptor subtypes, $GABA_A$, is coupled to chloride ion channels containing the CNS benzodiazepine receptor. The actions of benzodiazepines through the benzodiazepine/GABA receptor complex decrease membrane excitability, leading to an inhibitory effect on CNS neurotransmission (Drugan & Holmes, 1991). However, the benzodiazepines may also exert their anxiolytic effects by additionally decreasing CNS serotonin turnover or by decreasing noradrenergic activity in the locus ceruleus (Dantzer, 1985; Gray, 1981; Hommer, Skolnick, & Paul, 1987; Shibata, Kataoka, Comita, et al., 1982; Young & Kuhar, 1979). In addition to their anxiolytic effects, the benzodiazepines suppress Stage IV sleep and possess sedative, hypnotic, anticonvulsant, and muscle relaxant properties that may or may not be related to their anxiolytic properties (Goodman Gilman et al., 1985). Although the efficacy of the benzodiazepines in a variety of anxiety disorders in adults is well established (Greenblatt & Shader, 1987), studies of child and adolescent populations are to date few, and the research evidence supporting their use in this group is not yet fully available.

Studies of adults have shown that the benzodiazepines all possess relatively equivalent efficacy in treating a variety of anxiety disorders, although some, such as clonazepam and alprazolam, may have greater specificity in panic disorder (Goodman Gilman et al., 1985; Greenblatt & Shader, 1974; Rickels & Schweizer, 1987). The benzodiazepines may be classified by their potency (high potency: alprazolam, clonazepam, lorazepam, triazolam; low potency: chlordiazepoxide, diazepam, temazepam, flurazepam), but another clinically useful classification utilizes their pharmacokinetic profiles as these influence duration of action, side effects and risk of withdrawal phenomena (Greenblatt & Shader, 1987). Benzodiazepines with longer half-lives or active metabolites (diazepam, flurazepam, clorazepate, chlordiazepoxide, clonazepam) are less frequently associated with withdrawal symptoms. Longer half-life agents, however, may be associated with increased cognitive or motor impairments (Koeppen, 1984; Smiley, 1987). In contrast, short half-life compounds (alprazoplam, triazolam, oxazepam) may be associated with fewer motor and cognitive difficulties but concurrently increase the number and severity of discontinuation symptoms and lead to interdose rebound phenomenon.

Low-Potency Benzodiazepines

Chlordiazepoxide (CDPZ) has been the most frequently studied benzodiazepine used with children (Petti, Fish, Shapiro, et al., 1982). Krakowski

(1963) used 15 mg of CDPZ per day to treat 51 diagnostically diverse patients of ages 4 to 16 (many were concomitantly treated with a variety of other medications). Improvement in 67% of this group was considered moderate or considerable, and side effects were described as mild and infrequent. Kraft (1965) reported an open trial of 130 clinic patients of unknown diagnostic categories (ages 7 to 17) treated with variable doses of CDPZ (30 to 60 mg daily) for variable lengths of time. In this heterogeneous sample, 40% were considered to show either good or excellent treatment response. While anxiety symptoms were not specifically assessed, the greatest improvement (77%) was found in a group of patients with school phobia, a group that may have included a large number of children and young adolescents with anxiety disorders. D'Amato (1962) reported similar results in treating 9 school-refusing children (ages 8 to 11) with 10 to 30 mg of CDPZ daily for 2 consecutive weeks compared to another school-refusing group of 11 patients treated with psychosocial methods. By the end of the treatment period, 88% of the CDPZ group compared to 18% of the psychosocially treated group were able to return to school. Frommer (1967) described a double-blind crossover trial of CDPZ plus phenelzine versus phenobarbital plus placebo in 32 depressed and 15 symptomatically phobic children. The CDPZ-plus-phenelzine group reportedly received the most benefit, but given the heterogeneity of the groups, the lack of a pure placebo control, the neglect to measure anxiety symptoms, and the conjoint use of CDPZ with phenelzine, this study is difficult to evaluate. Petti et al. (1982) treated 9 boys of ages 7 to 11 with CDPZ in doses ranging from 15 to 120 mg per day. The researchers reported that 66% of the group showed at least moderate improvement and that the most responsive symptoms were anergia, anxiety, depression, and a withdrawn state. However the mixed nature of this group (not one had a primary anxiety disorder diagnosis) makes any extrapolation to anxiety disorders impossible.

Diazepam was studied by Lucas and Pasley (1969) in a diagnostically heterogeneous group of 15 inpatients of ages 7 to 17 treated with doses ranging from 5 to 20 mg per day. Compared to placebo, diazepam showed no significant treatment effect. Five patients reported feeling drowsy and one became disinhibited. This seemingly negative study cannot be interpreted, however, because of its serious methodological limitations, including a patient population in which not one proband may have actually met criteria for an anxiety disorder.

High-Potency Benzodiazepines

Studies of high-potency benzodiazepines generally show methodological superiority over studies of low-potency benzodiazepines. Pfefferbaum,

Overall, Boren, et al. (1987) reported on the use of alprazolam in ameliorating anticpatory anxiety and panic in 13 patients of ages 7 to 14 being treated for cancer. Total daily doses of 0.35 to 3.0 mg per day were associated with a significant improvement in a variety of anxiety and dysphoric states. Side effects were minimal; mild drowsiness was the most frequently reported.

Use in Treating Anxiety Disorders. Simeon and Ferguson (1987), using a case-controlled design, treated 12 patients (ages 8 to 16) with alprazolam (0.25 to 1.5 mg daily). All subjects met DSM-III-R criteria for OAD or avoidant disorder. Alprazolam was significantly superior to placebo on the Clinician Global Impression (CGI) and the Brief Psychiatric Rating Scale (BPRS) scores of anxiety, depression, and psychomotor agitation. Parents reported improved sleep patterns, and cognitive testing showed a significant improvement in paired associate learning. Patients, however, did not self-rate anxiety symptoms as significantly better with alprazolam. Side effects were minimal and medication withdrawal was not associated with any rebound or withdrawal effects.

In a follow-up study, Simeon, Ferguson, Knott, et al. (1992) used a double-blind placebo-controlled design of 4 weeks' duration to treat 30 patients with DSM-III-R OAD ($n = 21$) and avoidant disorder ($n = 9$), using a mean daily dose of alprazolam of 1.57 mg. The medication was well tolerated with no significant side effects reported; again, no rebound or withdrawal effects were noted. The CGI scores showed a treatment-positive trend for alprazolam compared to placebo. No negative cognitive findings were noted in the alprazolam-treated group, and patients taking alprazolam showed an increased beta rhythm on resting EEG.

Although the results of the studies of these diagnostic groups suggest that alprazolam may have an anxiolytic effect, these trials may have used doses of alprazolam below those needed to produce maximal anxiolysis. Similarly, the low doses may have contributed to the low incidence of side effects.

Klein (personal communication, 1992) treated 18 subjects with DSM-III-R separation anxiety disorder (ages 6 to 17) in an open trial of alprazolam (0.5 to 6.0 mg daily). Ratings of anxiety and overall functioning by physicians and mothers showed improvements from baselines of 89% and 82% respectively. Teacher reports and child self-reports, although comparatively less marked (64% and 65% respectively), showed a similar pattern of response. Side effects were infrequent; only 11% of the children were judged to suffer from moderate or severe medication effects. No withdrawal symptoms were noted on gradual discontinuation of the medication.

Another high-potency benzodiazepine, clonazepam, has been studied in children and adolescents with panic disorder. Biederman (1987) treated three children (ages 8 to 11) who exhibited "paniclike symptoms" with 0.5 to 3.0 mg of clonazepam daily. All were reported improved and no clinically significant side effects were noted. Kutcher and Mackenzie (1988) treated adolescents with DSM-III-R panic disorder using 1.0 to 2.0 mg of clonazepam daily. The mean frequency of panic attacks fell from three to less than one per week. The mean Hamilton Anxiety Scale score fell from 30 to 6 over the treatment period. Side effects were minimal, with mild and transitory daytime drowsiness most commonly reported. In a more recent report using a double-blind placebo-controlled treatment design, clonazepam at a dose of up to 2.0 mg per day was found to be significantly better than placebo in decreasing panic attack frequency and daily anxiety ratings in 12 adolescents with DSM-III-R panic disorder (Kutcher, 1990). Side effects were minimal. Similarly, Reiter and Kutcher (1992) found statistically significant reductions in Hamilton Anxiety Ratings Scale scores and significant improvements in school and social functioning in 17 teenagers treated with clonazepam at a mean dose of 1.72 mg per day (range 1.5 to 2.5 mg daily).

Although the studies reviewed offer no absolute guidelines for the use of benzodiazepines with children and adolescents, they demonstrate that some child and adolescent anxiety disorders respond to high-potency benzodiazepines. Alprazolam may be useful in treating the overanxious or avoidant child and clonazepam the adolescent with panic disorder. Of interest is that no child/adolescent study has demonstrated the clinical problems of medication rebound that are documented in the adult literature. Whether this is due to different effects of high-potency benzodiazepines in children and teens compared to adults or to other factors (e.g., dosage, length of continuous treatment, and so on) is unknown. However, it is clear that no study of anxious children and adolescents to date has documented deleterious effects of high-potency benzodiazepines on cognitive functioning nor has any clear evidence of withdrawal or addiction been reported (Simeon & Ferguson, 1985, 1987; Simeon et al., 1992).

Dose and Course Guidelines

In the absence of studies of the entire gamut of possible anxiety disorders and with the lack of dose-finding studies, benzodiazepine treatment guidelines must remain tentative and conservative. Patients treated with high-potency benzodiazepines should be started on a low dose that is gradually increased, allowing time for the patient to adjust to sedative side effects. Table 15.1 provides guidelines that should be adapted to specific patient needs. Maximal daily doses may be increased if full clinical efficacy is not obtained with the ones in the table and the side effects are mild.

Benzodiazepine treatment should be initiated following the comprehensive pharmacotherapy assessment noted earlier. Doses should be increased every 3 to 4 days until the suggested minimally effective therapeutic dose level is reached. The patient should then remain on this dose for a minimum of 1 week to determine its anxiolytic potential. If therapeutic effect is not achieved after this time and side effects are tolerable, the dose can again be gradually increased on a weekly basis.

Once a therapeutic treatment response is obtained, the dose should be maintained for 4 to 6 months. Patients will need to be educated about the waxing and waning nature of anxiety disorders and the danger of relapse if treatment is withdrawn too quickly. A drug-free trial may be warranted, once the extension phase is complete, to determine the persistence of symptoms that may be medication responsive. When this occurs, the dose should be tapered gradually by no more than 25% of the maintenance amount every 3 to 5 days.

If adequate therapeutic response is not obtained at maximum doses or if side effects limit use, the medication should be tapered and alternative treatments begun. If rebound or withdrawal symptoms occur when patients are being withdrawn from a short-acting benzodiazepine, a useful strategy is to switch to an equivalent dose of a longer half-life compound (e.g., from alprazalom to clonazepam; Albeck, 1987; Herman, Rosenabum, & Brotman, 1987). The longer half-life medication can then

TABLE 15.1. Suggested Benzodiazepine Dosing Guidelines for the Treatment of Child and Adolescent Anxiety Disorders

Medication	Starting daily dose (mg)	Maintenance daily dose (mg)	Maximum daily dose (mg)
Clonazepam	0.250–1.00	1.00–4.0 (b.i.d.–t.i.d. dosing)	4.0–6.0
Diazepam	1.000–5.00	5.00–20.0 (t.i.d.–q.i.d. dosing)	20.0–40.0
Lorazepam	0.250–1.00	1.00–4.0 (b.i.d.–t.i.d. dosing)	3.0–4.0
Alprazolam	0.125–0.25	0.25–2.5 (t.i.d.–q.i.d. dosing)	3.0–4.0

Note. These dosages are approximate guidelines only. Actual dosages used will vary depending on clinical effect and presence of side effects. b.i.d., twice a day; t.i.d., three times a day; q.i.d., four times a day.

be gradually withdrawn with fewer negative effects on the schedule outlined.

Withdrawal and Side Effects

Although not reported in the child and adolescent literature on anxiety disorders, withdrawal symptoms are a potential hazard when benzodiazepines are discontinued. Patients should be counseled not to stop these medications abruptly. Withdrawal symptoms may be minor (gastrointestinal cramps, anxiety, concentration and memory difficulties, ataxia, flulike illness, perceptual disturbances) or major (seizures, psychosis, delirium). The risk of seizures is highest with abrupt discontinuation of high-potency and short-acting benzodiazepines, especially alprazolam (Albeck, 1987; Breier, Charney, & Nelson, 1984; Brown & Hange, 1986; Busto, Sellers, Naranjo, et al., 1986; Herman et al., 1987).

When withdrawing benzodiazepines, the clinician must differentiate among withdrawal symptoms (emergence of previously unreported symptoms presumed to arise secondary to the medications' CNS effect), rebound (amplification of original symptoms), and relapse (recurrence of initial symptomatology). Treatment of these states differs: Withdrawal and rebound respond to more gradual medication tapering; relapse requires reinstitution of therapy. Patients from two groups may be at risk for medication withdrawal symptoms: those treated for long periods of time at therapeutic doses and those treated for short periods of time at supratherapeutic doses. Studies of adults who have been long-term, high-dose benzodiazepine users suggest that in this group, extremely gradual withdrawal carried out over a long period of time may be necessary (Allgulander, Borg, Vikander, 1984; Department of Health and Human Services, 1986).

During treatment, the side effects of the benzodiazepines tend to be dose related and may include daytime drowsiness, ataxia, slurred speech, diplopia, and tremor. Unusual or paradoxical reactions including irritability, verbal or physical assaultiveness, and temper outbursts have been associated with benzodiazepine use. Deitch and Jennings (1988) reviewed aggressive dyscontrol associated with benzodiazepine use and concluded that these reactions occurred in less than 1% of adult patients and that no patient characteristics could predict which patient would be at high risk of developing benzodiazepine-induced dyscontrol. Gardner and Cowdry (1985) have found that adults with borderline personality disorder often exhibit increased impulsivity and self-destructive behaviors when treated with therapeutic doses of alprazolam. This may be of clinical importance when considering using these compounds to treat the impulsive and self-destructive teenager who complains of severe anxiety.

The exact incidence of paradoxical or dyscontrol reactions such as disinhibition or aggression with benzodiazepine use with children and adolescents is not known but is thought to be more common than that found in adults. Reiter and Kutcher (1991) reported on a number of adolescents with a variety of clinical diagnoses who exhibited severe paradoxical reactions to therapeutic doses of clonazepam. Clinical impressions in our group and as reported by others (R. Klein, personal communication, 1992), however, suggest that up to 30% of teenagers treated with a high-potency benzodiazepine at generally recognized therapeutic doses may develop a paradoxical reaction if milder forms such as temper outbursts and increased irritability are considered. In our clinic, we have estimated that when doses of clonazepam over 2 mg per day are required, the incidence of paradoxical reactions increases substantially, up to as much as 50%.

Some studies of benzodiazepine use with adults have suggested a relationship between benzodiazepine treatment and the onset of depression (Cohen & Rosenbaum, 1987; Pollach, Tessor, Rosenbaum, et al., 1986). This "treatment-emergent depression" has not been adequately characterized, however, and may simply reflect either an "unmasking" of previously unrecognized depressive symptoms following improvement in anxiety symptoms or the comorbidity of depression in anxiety states. Alternatively, some adult studies have suggested that both alprazolam and clonazepam may be effective antidepressants (Kishimoto, Kamata, Sugihara, et al., 1988; Rickels, Feighner, Smith, et al., 1985). To our knowledge, no data regarding these issues are available for children and adolescents.

With appropriate dosage, high-potency benzodiazepines in children and adolescents seem to cause little or no cognitive or motor impairment, and some evidence suggests that these compounds might improve cognitive functioning in anxious probands, presumably through their anxiolytic effects (Simeon et al., 1992). However, a recent review of psychomotor effects of benzodiazepines in adults concludes that they exert some impairments in motor function, particularly in reaction time (Smiley, 1987). The significance of this effect in children is unclear, but it may be of importance in teenagers who are learning to drive.

Benzodiazepines are relatively safe in overdose, particularly compared to older anxiolytics such as barbiturates and to propranediols or TCAs. Benzodiazepines do increase the sedative effects of other CNS depressants including alcohol, neuroleptics, antidepressants, narcotic analgesics, and antihistamines (Edwards, 1981). This cross-reactivity is a potential problem, particularly with adolescents who use alcohol recreationally. Accordingly, care and time must be taken to provide the necessary education about potential medication/alcohol interactions. Counseling to help the anxious teen deal with the peer pressures of drinking is often required.

Benzodiazepines with a rapid onset of action, such as diazepam and triazolam, may be more likely to create transient euphoric effects, which may be associated with increased abuse potential (American Psychiatric Association, 1990). However, significant abuse of benzodiazepines by anxious children and adolescents has not been reported (Simeon & Ferguson, 1985). Nevertheless, our clinical experience suggests that some adolescents, especially those with premorbid substance abuse or a family history of substance abuse, may be at risk for benzodiazepine abuse.

Buspirone

Buspirone is an azapirone and a novel anxiolytic agent with possible antidepressant qualities (Gardner & Kutcher, 1990; Goldberg, 1984; Kastenholz & Crimson, 1984; Robinson, Rickels, Feighner, et al., 1990; Fabre, 1990). Buspirone is not GABAergic and does not bind to the benzodiazepine receptor complex. Its anxiolytic effect is thought to be mediated through its central serotonergic activity. It is a partial serotonin agonist and may selectively stimulate the serotonin somatodendritic autoreceptor 5-HT 1a, which inhibits neuronal firing in the CNS regions thought to be associated with anxiety modulation—particularly the dorsal raphe nuclei (Marsden, 1990). Buspirone does not seem to decrease noradrenergic activity in the locus ceruleus, thus precluding side effects of drowsiness and impaired cognition (Eison & Temple, 1986). Unlike the benzodiazepines, buspirone has no significant muscle relaxant, sedative, hypnotic, or anticonvulsant properties, nor is its use associated with withdrawal phenomena. In studies of adult populations, buspirone has demonstrated anxiolytic effects similar to those of the benzodiazepines, with a benign side effects profile when used in the treatment of generalized anxiety disorder (GAD; Bond, Lader, Shrotriya, et al., 1983; Cohn & Wilcox, 1986; Gardner & Kutcher, 1990; Goldberg, 1984; Kastenholz & Crimson, 1984; Riblet, Taylor, Eisen, et al., 1982; Skolnick, Paul, & Weissman, 1984; Taylor, Eisen, Riblet, et al., 1985).

Both animal and clinical studies have demonstrated that buspirone has minimal abuse potential (Balster, 1990; Griffith, Jasinski, Casten, et al., 1986; Hendry, Balster, & Rosencrans, 1983; Lader, 1987), although its anxiolytic onset may require up to 2 weeks from the initiation of treatment. The relative paucity of serious side effects and low abuse potential (Bond et al., 1983; Cohn & Wilcox, 1986; Gardner & Kutcher, 1990; Goldberg, 1984; Kastenholz & Crimson, 1984; Riblet et al., 1982; Skolnick et al., 1984; Taylor et al., 1985) make buspirone an attractive medication to use with children and adolescents with OAD, avoidant disorder, social phobia, or GAD.

Given the qualities of buspirone, the lack of studies in the child and adolescent population is surprising. Krantzler (1988) reported the successful treatment of a young adolescent with overanxious disorder with 10 mg of buspirone daily. In our clinics, adolescents with GAD/OAD without panic attacks have been successfully treated with buspirone at doses ranging from 30 to 90 mg daily. One teenager with severe catastrophic anxiety reactions and high baseline anxiety following a closed head injury experienced symptomatic relief leading to improved functioning on a dose of 130 mg daily, combined with a variey of other medications. Minimal side effects were identified.

Simeon et al. (1992) reported an open trial of buspirone with 15 children of ages 6 to 14 with a mixture of anxiety disorders diagnosed using DSM-III-R criteria as separation anxiety disorder, OAD, and OCD. A number also had comorbid attention-deficit disorder. Buspirone treatment over four weeks at a mean dose of 18.6 mg daily was associated with significant improvement in a variety of scales measuring anxiety and depressive symptoms. Side effects were mild; the most commonly reported were sleep difficulties and fatigue.

The pharmacokinetics of buspirone in children and adolescents have not to our knowledge been reported and are apparently not available. However, adult data suggest extensive first-pass hepatic elimination of the drug, with an average oral bioavailability of about 4%. Mean reported elimination half-lives have ranged from 2 to 11 hours in healthy adults. Buspirone is highly protein bound and has one active metabolite (1-pyrimidinylpiperazine), which is not known to have significant clinical effects. *In vitro* studies have not found significant interactions between buspirone and other highly protein-bound drugs, including propranolol, phenytoin, warfarin, and digoxin. Animal studies have not shown buspirone to affect hepatic enzyme activity; however, the addition of buspirone to ongoing neuroleptic treatment may lead to increased neuroleptic levels. Reports of increased blood pressure in several patients who combined buspirone with MAOIs have led to the recommendation that this compound be avoided by patients who are using MAOIs; the serotonergic properties of buspirone may potentiate the hypertensive effects of MAOIs. Buspirone does not appear to potentiate the CNS depressant effects of alcohol, benzodiazepines, or amitriptyline (Gammans, Mayol, & Labudde, 1986; Newton, Casten, Alous, et al., 1982; Mattila, Aranko, & Sepalla, et al., 1982; Moskowitz & Smiley, 1982; Goa & Ward, 1986; Bristol-Myers Squibb, 1989).

The most common side effects of buspirone are gastric upset, dizziness, headache, and insomnia. At therapeutic doses, buspirone causes sedation at a rate similar to that of placebo and has a wide margin of safety, with, to date, no reported cases of fatal overdose when taken alone (Newton et al., 1982; Schrabel, 1987; Bristol-Myers Squibb, Canada, personal communication).

Although buspirone may be effective in treating children and adolescents suffering from OAD, GAD, avoidant disorder, or social phobia, dosage requirements for anxiolytic control in this population have not been established, and the following suggestions must be regarded as tentative. The average daily dose for teens should be about 30 mg given in divided doses, three times a day (t.i.d.). Maximum doses should probably not exceed the recommended upper adult daily limit of 60 mg, although exceptional cases may benefit from higher amounts (higher doses may be associated with dysphoria and gastrointestinal distress). In older children (ages 10 to 12), dosage should be started at 5 mg daily and raised to 5 mg t.i.d. over 2 to 3 days. Dosage should then be maintained for a minimum of two weeks and further increments made thereafter according to therapeutic response. Adolescents may be started on 10 mg per day and raised to 10 mg t.i.d. over 2 to 3 days. In younger children (9 years old and younger), dosage should begin at 2.5 mg daily and then be raised as noted. A maximal daily dosage has not been identified in this age group but should be dictated by clinical response and side effects.

Buspirone has a later onset of anxiolytic action than the benzodiazepines—some 2 to 4 weeks. If at 6 weeks continued use at maximum dosage has not had therapeutic response, treatment should be discontinued. If necessary, this can be accomplished fairly rapidly—in about 4 days—by halving the dose on day 1 of discontinuation and stopping the medication entirely on day 4. As with all other pharmacological agents, if buspirone is effective in relieving symptoms of anxiety, ancillary therapies should be instituted to deal with the social, interpersonal, and vocational/academic consequences of the disorder. Pharmacological treatment should be continued for 4 to 6 months following symptomatic resolution prior to determining the need for ongoing pharmacological intervention. Long-term effects of buspirone in the child and adolescent population are not at this time known.

Of possible relevance to clinical decision making are the reports of adult studies in which patients initially treated with benzodiazepines showed a decreased anxiolytic response to buspirone treatment compared to a benzodiazepine-naive group (Olajide & Lader, 1987; Schweizer, Rickels, & Lukil, 1986). Thus, pharmacological treatment for OAD (or GAD) may be best initiated with buspirone then switching nonresponders to a benzodiazepine. No washout period is required for switching from buspirone to a benzodiazepine or vice versa.

Propranolol

Propranolol is a highly lipophilic beta blocker with both central and peripheral activity. Elimination occurs primarily through hepatic conjugation and in adults, the single-dose half-life is four to 6 hours. A competitive antagonist of both norepinephrine and epinephrine, propranolol's exact anxiolytic mode of action is not known, but it is thought to include both central beta-1 and peripheral beta-1 activity (Goodman Gilman et al., 1985).

Studies of adults have not clearly demonstrated the efficacy of propranolol as a primary pharmacological treatment for anxiety disorders (Rickels & Schweizer, 1987). Propranolol may, however, have therapeutic indications in the treatment of situational anxiety or as an adjunct to low-potency benzodiazepines. Although some evidence suggests that propranolol may partially ameliorate some of the somatic features of anxiety states, its therapeutic effect on the emotional components of anxiety has not been clearly demonstrated.

In children and adolescents, Joorabchi (1977) reported a positive therapeutic response in a small number of patients with "hyperventilation syndrome" treated with 30 to 60 mg of propranolol daily. Following treatment discontinuation, the majority of patients relapsed. Similar results were reported by Famularo (1988) of a 4-week open trial of propranolol in 11 children (mean age 8.5 years) with a DSM-III diagnosis of acute posttraumatic stress disorder. Dosage was titrated to diastolic blood pressure (55 mm of mercury) or heart rate (55 beats per minute) to a maximum of 2.5 mg/kg per day given in three divided doses. Symptomatic improvements were followed by a relapse to pretreatment symptom severity within a week of medication discontinuation. Side effects in both studies were reportedly minimal. A pilot study of propranolol in childhood posttraumatic stress disorder has also been reported (Famularo, 1988).

Although these few studies suggest possible therapeutic efficacy, given the available data, propranalol cannot be recommended for use as the primary pharmacological treatment of children or adolescents with anxiety disorders. Further, its side effect profile—sedation, bradycardia, faintness, dizziness—and its bronchoconstrictor qualities do not support its routine first-line use for childhood anxiety disorders. If it is used as an adjunctive treatment, careful medical monitoring is essential.

Barbiturates

Although some evidence exists that barbiturates may be useful in ameliorating anxiety symptoms in children and young adolescents (Frommer,

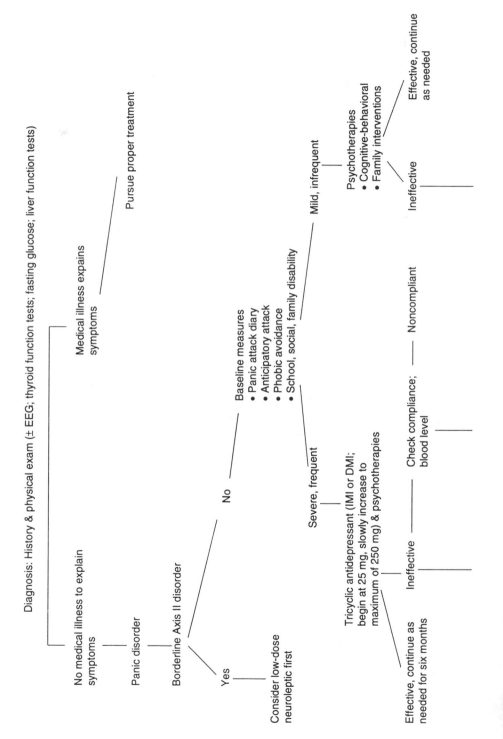

Diagnosis: History & physical exam (± EEG; thyroid function tests; fasting glucose; liver function tests)

No medical illness to explain symptoms

Medical illness expains symptoms

Pursue proper treatment

Panic disorder

Borderline Axis II disorder

Yes — Consider low-dose neuroleptic first

No — Baseline measures
• Panic attack diary
• Anticipatory attack
• Phobic avoidance
• School, social, family disability

Mild, infrequent — Psychotherapies
• Cognitive-behavioral
• Family interventions

Ineffective

Effective, continue as needed

Severe, frequent — Tricyclic antidepressant (IMI or DMI; begin at 25 mg, slowly increase to maximum of 250 mg) & psychotherapies

Effective, continue as needed for six months

Ineffective

Check compliance; blood level

Noncompliant

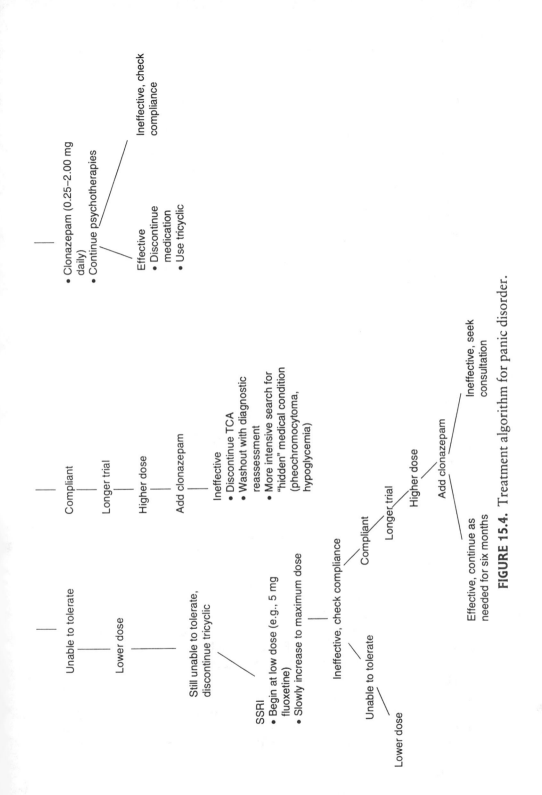

FIGURE 15.4. Treatment algorithm for panic disorder.

373

1967), no convincing clinical or research data supports this practice. Barbiturates at low doses, like benzodiazepines, enhance GABAergic activity in the CNS and increase chloride ion conductance at the benzodiazepine/GABA receptor complex. However, at higher doses barbiturates inhibit the release of excitatory neurotransmitters and mimic the actions of GABA, resulting in profound depression of CNS activity. This dose-dependent effect of CNS depression can lead to serious untoward reactions, including excessive sedation, impairment of motor skills, respiratory depression, coma, and death (Hommer et al., 1987; Goodman Gilman et al., 1985). Thus, the dangerous safety profile, the lack of demonstrated efficacy, and the availability of other effective and safer agents should eliminate the barbiturates as an option in the treatment of anxiety disorders in children and adolescents.

Neuroleptics

Several studies of a variety of neuroleptics in treating anxiety symptoms in populations of diagnostically heterogeneous children and adolescents have been reported (Abe, 1975; Eisenberg, Gilbert, Cytryn, et al., 1961; Fish, 1968; Lucas & Pasley, 1969). However, given the inconclusive results of these studies—their serious methodological limitations, the lack of clear-cut evidence of efficacy of these agents in the treatment of primary anxiety disorders, and the potentially serious side effects of these medications—there is at this time no indication for the use of neuroleptics in the treatment of primary anxiety disorders in children and adolescents.

Antihistamines

Although antihistamines may occasionally be prescribed for the treatment of various child behavioral disorders (Effron & Freedman, 1953; Fish, 1960), we find no clear indication in the literature for their use in treating child and adolescent anxiety disorders. While they may have some minor anxiolytic effect in this population, their use is limited by their sedative properties and other side effects. Further, their use may be associated with lowered seizure threshold, anticholinergic side effects, excessive drowsiness or hangover effects, and other side effects. Another concern regarding the use of antihistamines in treating anxiety is the growing realization that these agents are being abused by teenagers for the mildly derealizing and euphoric effects they produce when taken in excess (Gardner & Kutcher, 1993). Thus, they should not be a medication of choice in treating child or adolescent anxiety disorders.

CONCLUSIONS

Pharmacological management has an important role to play in the comprehensive treatment of child and adolescent anxiety disorders. In most cases, pharmacological treatments should begin concurrently with other therapies, as combined treatment approaches are needed to effectively ameliorate the variety of difficulties found in patients with anxiety disorders. An illustrative algorithm is offered (in Figure 15.4) as a clinical aid to the approach and treatment of a child or adolescent with a panic disorder. This algorithm illustrates the complexity of pharmacotherapeutic management of patients with this disorder. In treating any anxiety disorder with medications, however, the clinician is advised to apply the principles of pharmacotherapeutic management described at the beginning of this chapter.

To date, the available data suggest that high-potency benzodiazepines have clinical utility in panic disorder and may be of value in treating patients with OAD or avoidant disorder. The antidepressants may be of value in treating a variety of anxiety disorders, but cardiovascular side effects and patient tolerability can be limiting factors in their use. Buspirone is a potentially useful agent in OAD disorder (GAD), and its relatively benign side effects profile and low abuse potential make it an attractive choice for adolescents. Other agents have a smaller role, if any, to play, but combinations of various compounds may be useful in treatment-resistant cases. In any case, the further systematic investigation of all these compounds should be a priority in treatment research in the anxiety disorders of children and adolescents.

ACKNOWLEDGMENT

Our thanks to Mrs. B. Rychlewski for manuscript preparation.

REFERENCES

Abe, K. (1975). Sulpiride in school phobia. *Psychiatric Clinics, 8,* 95–98.

Alarcon, R. D., Johnson, B. R., & Lucas, J. P. (1991). Case study: Paranoid and aggressive behaviour in two obsessive–compulsive adolescents treated with clomipramine. *Journal of the American Academy of Child and Adolescent Psychiatry, 30,* 999–1002.

Albeck, J. (1987). Withdrawal and detoxification from benzodiazepine dependence: A potential role for clonazepam. *Journal of Clinical Psychiatry, 48*(Suppl.), 43–48.

Allgulander, C., Borg, S., & Vikander, B. (1984). A 4–6 year follow-up of 50 patients with primary dependence on sedative and hypnotic drugs. *American Journal of Psychiatry, 141*(12), 1580–1582.

American Psychiatric Association. (1987). *Diagnostic and statistical manual of mental disorders* (3rd ed., rev.). Washington, DC: Author.

American Psychiatric Association. (1990). *A task force report: Benzopdiazepine dependence, toxicity and abuse.* Washington, DC: Author.

Amrein, R., Hetzel, W., Stabl, M., et al. (1992). RIMA: A safe concept in the treatment of depression with Moclobemide. *Canadian Journal of Psychiatry, 37*(Suppl. 1), 7–11.

Balster, R. (1990). Abuse potential of buspirone and related drugs. *Journal of Clinical Psychopharmacology, 10,* 31S–37S.

Beasley, C. M., Dornseif, B. E., Bosanworth, J. C., et al. (1991). Fluoxetine and suicide: A meta-analysis of controlled trials of treatment for depresson. *British Medical Journal, 303,* 685–692.

Berney, T. (1981). School phobia: A therapeutic trial with clomipramine and short term outcome. *British Journal of Psychiatry, 138,* 110–118.

Bernstein, G., & Garfinkel, B. (1986). School phobia: The overlap of affective and anxiety disorders. *Journal of the American Academy of Child and Adolescent Psychiatry, 25,* 235–241.

Bernstein, G., Garfinkel, B., Barchardt, C. (1990). Comparative studies of pharmacotherapy for school refusal. *Journal of the American Academy of Child and Adolescent Psychiatry, 29,* 773–781.

Biederman, J. (1991). Sudden death in children treated with a tricyclic antidepressant—A commentary. *Biological Therapies in Psychiatry Newsletter, 14,* 1–4.

Biederman, J. (1987). Clonazepam in the treatment of prepubertal children with panic-like symptoms. *Journal of Clinical Psychiatry, 48*(Suppl.), 38–41.

Biederman, J., Baldessarini, R., Wright, V., et al. (1989a). A double-blind placebo controlled study of desipramine in the treatment of attention deficit disorder: Vol. II. Serum drug levels and cardiovascular findings. *Journal of the American Academy of Child and Adolescent Psychiatry, 28,* 903–911.

Biederman, J., Baldessarini, R., Wright, V., et al. (1989b). A double-blind placebo controlled study of desipramine in the treamtent of ADD: Vol. 1. Efficacy. *Journal of the American Academy of Child and Adolescent Psychiatry, 28,* 777–782.

Bond, A., Lader, M., Shrotriya, R. (1983). Comparative effects of a repeated dose regime of diazepam and buspirone on subjective ratings, psychological tests and the EEG. *European Journal of Clinical Pharmacology, 24,* 463–467.

Boulos, C., Kutcher, S., Gardner, D., et al. (1992). An open naturalistic trial of fluoxetine in adolescents and young adults with treatment-resistant major depression. *Journal of Child and Adolescent Psychopharmacology, 2,* 103–111.

Breier, A., Charney, D., & Nelson, J. (1984). Seizures induced by abrupt discontinuation of alprazolam. *American Journal of Psychiatry, 141,* 1606.

Bristol-Myers Squibb. (1989). *Information for the health care professional— Buspar* [Product information pamphlet]. Canada: Author.

Brown, J., & Hange, K. (1986). A review of alprazolam withdrawal. *Drug Intelligence and Clinical Pharmacy, 20,* 837–844.

Busto, U., Sellers, E., Naranjo, C., et al. (1986). Withdrawal reaction after long-term therapeutic use of benzodiazepines. *New England Journal of Medicine, 315,* 854–856.

Chambers, W. J., Puig-Antich, J., Hirsch, M., et al. (1985). The assessment of affective disorders in children and adolescents by semistructured interviews. Test–retest reliability of the K-SADS-P. *Archives of General Psychiatry, 42,* 666–672.

Charney, D. S., Goodman, W. K., Price, L. H., et al. (1988). Serotonin function in obsessive–compulsive disorder. *Archives of General Psychiatry, 45,* 177–185.

Charney, D., & Heninger, G. (1986). Serotonergic function in panic disorder. *Archives of General Psychiatry, 43,* 1059–1063.

Charney, D. S., Heninger, G. R., & Breier, A. (1984). Noradrenergic function in panic anxiety. Effects of yohimbine in healthy subjects and patients with agoraphobia and panic disorder. *Archives of General Psychiatry, 4,* 75–82.

Ciraulo, D. A., & Shader, R. I. (1990a). Fluoxetine drug–drug interactions: Vol. I. Antidepressants and antipsychotics. *Journal of Clinical Psychopharmacology, 10,* 48–50.

Ciraulo, D. A., & Shader, (1990b). Fluoxetine drug–drug interaction. Vol. II. *Journal of Clinical Psychopharmacology, 10,* 213–217.

Coffey, B. (1990). Anxiolytics for children and adolescents: traditional and new drugs. *Journal of Child and Adolescent Psychopharmacology, 1,* 57–83.

Coffey, B., Shader, R., & Greenblatt, D. (1983). Pharmacokinetics of benzodiazepines and psychostimulants in children. *Journal of Clinical Psychopharmacology, 3,* 217–225.

Cohen, L., & Rosenbaum, J. (1987). Clonazepam: New uses and potential problems. *Journal of Clinical Psychiatry, 48* (Suppl.), 50–55.

Cohn, J., & Wilcox, C. (1986). Low-sedation potential of buspirone compared with alprazolam and lorazepam in the treatment of anxious patients: A double-blind study. *Journal of Clinical Psychiatry, 47,* 409–412.

Como, P. G., & Kurlan, R. (1991). An open-label trial of fluoxetine for obsessive–compulsive disorder in Gilles de la Tourette's syndrome. *Neurology, 41,* 872–874.

Costello, A. (1983, October). *A report on the NIMH Diagnostic Interview Schedule for Children (DISC).* Paper presented at the Research Forum: Structured diagnostic instruments in child psychiatry, American Academy of Child Psychiatry, San Francisco, CA.

Costello, A. (1987). Structured interviewing for the assessment of child psychopathology. In J. Noshpitz (Ed.), *Basic handbook of child psychiatry: Advances and new directions* (pp. 317–328). New York: Basic Books.

Cox, W. (1982). An indication for use of imipramine in attention deficit disorder. *American Journal of Psychiatry, 139,* 1059–1060.

D'Amato, G. (1962). Chlordiazepoxide in management of school phobia. *Diseases of the Nervous System, 23,* 292–295.

Dantzer, R. (1985). Benzodiazepines and the limbic system, In M. Trimble & E. Zarifiam (Eds.), *Psychopharmacology of the limbic system* (pp. 148–163). Oxford: Oxford University Press.

Deitch, J., & Jennings, R. (1988). Aggressive dyscontrol in patients treated with benzodiazepines. *Journal of Clinical Psychiatry, 49,* 184–188.

Den Boer J., Westenberg, H., Kamarbeck, W., et al. (1987). Effect of serotonin uptake inhibitors in anxiety disorders: A double-blind comparison of clomipramine & fluvoxamine. *International Clinical Psychopharmacology, 2*, 21–27.

Department of Health and Human Services, Public Health Service. (1986). *Seizures associated with alprazolam.* Washington, DC: Food and Drug Administration Center for Drugs and Biologics.

Derogatis, L. R., Litman, R. S., Rickels, K., et al. (1974). The Hopkins Symptom Checklist (HSCL): A self-report symptom inventory. *Behavioral Science, 19*(1), 1–15.

DeVeaugh-Geiss, J., Landau, P., & Katz, R. (1989). Preliminary results from a multicenter trial of clomipramine in obsessive–compulsive disorder. *Psychopharmacology Bulletin, 25*, 36–40.

Donnelly, M., Zametkin, A., Rapoport, J., et al. (1986). Treatment of childhood hyperactivity with desipramine: Plasma drug concentration, cardiovascular effects, plasma and urinary catecholamine levels and clinical response. *Clinical Pharmacology Therapy, 39*, 72–81.

Drugan, R., & Holmes, P. (1991). Central and peripheral benzodiazepine receptors: Involvement in an organism's response to physical and psychological stress. *Neuroscience and Behavioral Reviews, 15*, 277–298.

Dugas, M., Zarifian, E., Leheuzey, M.-F., et al. (1980). Preliminary observations of the significance of monitoring tricyclic antidepressant plasma levels in the pediatric patient. *Therapeutic Drug Monitoring, 2*, 307–314.

Edwards, J. (1981). Adverse effects of antianxiety drugs. *Drugs, 22*, 495–514.

Effron, A. S., & Freedman, A. M. (1953). The treatment of behavioral disorders in children with Benadryl. *Journal of Pediatrics, 42*, 261–266.

Eisenberg, L., Gilbert, A., Cytryn, L., et al. (1961). The effectiveness of psychotherapy alone and in conjunction with perphenazine or placebo in the treatment of neurotic and hyperkinetic children. *American Journal of Psychiatry, 117*, 1088–1093.

Eison, A. S., & Temple, D. L. (1986). Buspirone: Review of its pharmacology and current perspectives on its mechanism of action. *Journal of the American Medical Association, 80*(Suppl. 3B), 1–9.

Elliott, G., Popper, C., & Fraizer, S. (1990). Tricyclic antidepressants: A risk for 6–9 year olds, *Journal of Child and Adolescent Psychopharmacology, 2*, 105–106.

Fabre, L. F. (1990). Buspirone in the management of major depression: A placebo-controlled comparison. *Journal of Clinical Psychiatry, 51*(Suppl. 9), 55–61.

Famularo, R. (1988). Propranolol treatment for childhood post traumatic stress disorder, acute type: A pilot study. *American Journal of Diseases of Children, 142*, 1244–1247.

Fava, M., & Rosenbaum, J.F. (1991). Suicidality and fluoxetine: Is there a relationship? *Journal of Clinical Psychiatry, 52*, 108–111.

File, S. (1984). The neurochemistry of anxiety. In G. Burrows, T. Norman, & B. Davis (Eds.), *Anti-anxiety agents* (pp. 28–34). Amsterdam, The Netherlands: Elsevier.

Fish, B. (1960). Drug therapy in child psychiatry: Pharmacological aspects. *Comprehensive Psychiatry, 1*, 212–227.

Fish, B. (1968). Drug use in psychiatric disorder of children. *American Journal of Psychiatry, 124,* 31–36.

Flament, M. F., Rapoport, J. L., Berg, C. J., et al. (1985). Clomipramine treatment of children with obsessive compulsive disorder. *Archives of General Psychiatry, 42,* 977–979.

Flament, M. F., Rapoport, J. L., Murphy, D. L., et al. (1987). Biochemical changes during clomipramine treatment of childhood obsessive–compulsive disorder. *Archives of General Psychiatry, 44,* 219–225.

Frommer, E. (1967). Treatment of childhood depression with antidepressant drugs. *British Medical Journal, 1,* 729–732.

Gammans, R., Mayol, R., & Labudde, J. (1986). Metabolism and disposition of buspirone. *American Journal of Medicine, 80,* 41, 51.

Gardner, D., & Cowdry, R. (1985). Alprazolam induced dyscontrol in borderline personality disorder. *American Journal of Psychiatry, 142,* 98–100.

Gardner, D. M., & Kutcher, S. (1990). Buspirone—A novel anxiolytic. *Family Practice Newsletter, Sunnybrook Health Science Centre, 9,* 1–4.

Gardner, D. M., & Kutcher, S. (1993). Dimenhydrinate abuse among adolescents. *Canadian Journal of Psychiatry, 38,* 113–116.

Garfinkel, B., Wender, P., Sloman, L., et al. (1983). Tricyclic antidepressant and methylphenidate treatment of attention deficit disorder in children. *Journal of the American Academy of Child and Adolescent Psychiatry, 22,* 343–348.

Geller, B., Cooper, T., McCombo, H., et al. (1989). Double-blind placebo controlled study of nortriptyline in depressed children using a "fixed plasma level" design. *Psychopharmacology Bulletin, 25,* 101–108.

Geller, B., Fox, L. W., & Fletcher, M. (1993). Effect of tricyclic antidepressants on switching to mania and on the onset of bipolarity in depressed 6- to 12-year-olds. *Journal of the American Academy of Child and Adolescent Psychiatry, 32,* 43–50.

Gittelman, R. (Ed.). (1986). *Anxiety disorders of childhood.* New York: Guilford Press.

Gittelman-Klein, R., & Klein, D. (1971). Controlled imipramine treatment of school phobia. *Archives of General Psychiatry, 25,* 204–207.

Gittelman-Klein, R., & Klein, D. (1973). School phobia: Diagnostic considerations in the light of imipramine effects. *Journal of Nervous and Mental Disease, 156,* 199–215.

Glassman, A. H., & Preud'homme, X. A. (1993). Review of the cardiovascular effects of heterocyclic antidepressants. *Journal of Clinical Psychiatry, 54,* 16–22.

Goa, K. L., & Ward, A. (1986). Buspirone: A preliminary review of its pharmacological properties and therapeutic efficacy as anxiolytic. *Drugs, 32,* 114–124.

Goldberg, H. (1984). Buspirone hydrochloride: A unique new anxiolytic agent. *Pharmacotherapy, 4,* 315–324.

Goodman Gilman, A., Goodman, L., Rall, T., et al. (Eds.). (1985). *The pharmacological basis of therapeutics.* New York: Macmillan Publishing.

Goodman, W. K., Price, L. H., Rasmussen, S. A., et al. (1989). The Yale–Brown obsessive compulsive scale: Vol. I. Development, use, and reliability. *Archives of General Psychiatry, 46,* 1006–1011.

Gray, J. (1981). *The neuropsychology of anxiety: An enquiry into the functions of the septohippocampal system.* Oxford: Oxford University Press.

Greenberg, L., & Yellin, A. (1975). Blood pressure and pulse changes in hyperactive children treated with imipramine and methylphenidate. *American Journal of Psychiatry, 132,* 1325–1326.

Greenblatt, D., & Shader, R. (1974). *Benzodiazepines in clinical practice.* New York: Raven.

Greenblatt, D., & Shader, R. (1987). Pharmacokinetics of antianxiety agents. In H. Meltzer (Ed.), *Psychopharmacology, the third generation of progress* (pp. 1377–1386). New York: Raven.

Griffith, J., Jasinski, D., Casten, G., et al. (1986). Investigation of the abuse liability of buspirone in alcohol dependent patients. *American Journal of Medicine, 80,* 30–35.

Hamilton, M. (1959). The assessment of anxiety states by rating. *British Journal of Medical Psychology, 32,* 50–55.

Hamlin, C., Lydiard, R., Martin, D., et al. (1983). Urinary excretion of noradrenaline metabolite is decreased in panic disorder. *Lancet, ii,* 740–742.

Hanna, G. L., McCracken, J. T., & Cantwell, D. P. (1991). Prolactin in childhood obsessive–compulsive disorder: Clinical correlates and response to clomipramine. *Journal of the American Academy of Child and Adolescent Psychiatry, 30*(2),173–178.

Hendry, J., Balster, R., & Rosecrans, J. (1983). Discriminative stimulus properties of buspirone compared to central nervous system depressants in rats. *Pharmacology, Biochemistry and Behavior, 19,* 97–101.

Herjanic, B., & Reich, W. (1982). Development of a structured psychiatric interview for children: Agreement between child and parent on individual symptoms. *Journal of Abnormal Child Psychology, 10,* 307–324.

Herman, J., Rosenbaum, J., & Brotman, A. (1987). The alprazolam to clonazepam switch for treatment of panic disorder. *Journal of Clinical Psychopharmacology, 7,* 175–178.

Hoehn-Saric, E., Maisami, M., Wiegand, D. (1987). Measurement of anxiety in children and adolescents using semistructured interviews. *Journal of the American Academy of Child and Adolescent Psychiatry, 26,* 541–545.

Hollander, E., Concetta, M., Nitescu, A., et al. (1992). Serotergic function in obsessive–compulsive disorder. *Archives of General Psychiatry, 49,* 21–28.

Hommer, D., Skolnick, P., & Paul, S. (1987). The benzodiazepine/GABA receptor complex and anxiety. In H. Meltzer (Ed.), *Psychopharmacology, the third generation of progress* (pp. 977–983). New York: Raven.

Jain, U., Birmaher, B., Garcia, M., et al. (1992). Fluoxetine in children and adolescents with mood disorders: A chart review of efficacy and adverse effects. *Journal of Child and Adolescent Psychopharmacology, 4,* 259–266.

Joorabchi, B. (1977). Expressions of the hyperventilation syndrome in childhood. *Clinical Pediatrics, 16,* 1110–1115.

Kahn, R., van Praag, H., Wetzler, S., et al. (1988). Serotonin and anxiety revisited. *Biological Psychiatry, 23,* 189–194.

Kastenholz, K., & Crimson, M. (1984). Buspirone, a novel benzodiazepine anxiolytic. *Drug Reviews, 3,* 600–607.

King, R. A., Riddle, M. A., Chappell, P. B., et al. (1991). Emergence of self-destructive phenomena in children and adolescents during fluoxetine treatment. *Journal of the American Academy of Child and Adolescent Psychiatry, 30*(2), 179–186.

Kishimoto, A., Kamata, K., Sugihara, T., et al. (1988). Treatment of depression with clonazepam. *Acta Psychiatrica Scandinavica, 77,* 81–86.

Klein, R., Kopelwicz, H., & Kanner, A. (1992). Imipramine treatment of children in the separation anxiety disorder. *Journal of the American Academy of Child and Adolescent Psychiatry, 31*(1), 21–28.

Koeppen, D. (1984). Memory and benzodiazepines: Animal and human studies with 1, 4-benzodiazepines and clobazam (1, 5 benzodiazepine). *Drug Development Research, 4,* 555–566.

Kraft, I. (1965). A clinical study of chlordiazepoxide used in psychiatric disorders of children. *International Journal of Neuropsychiatry, 1,* 433–437.

Krakowski, A. J. (1963). Chlordiazepoxide in treatment of children with emotional disturbances. *New York State Journal of Medicine, 63,* 3388–3392.

Kranzler, H. (1988). Use of buspirone in an adolescent with overanxious disorder. *Journal of the American Academy of Child and Adolescent Psychiatry, 27,* 789–790.

Kuekes, D., Wigg, C., Bryant, S., et al. (1992). Hypertension is a risk in adolescents treated with imipramine. *Journal of Child and Adolescent Psychopharmacology, 2,* 241–248.

Kutcher, S. (1986). Assessing and treating attention deficit disorder in adolescents: The clinical application of a single-case research design. *British Journal of Psychiatry, 149,* 710–715.

Kutcher, S. (1990, December 10–14). *High potency benzodiazepines in child and adolescent anxiety disorders.* Presented at the American College of Neuropsychopharmacology 29th Annual Meeting, Puerto Rico.

Kutcher, S., & Mackenzie, S. (1988). Successful clonazepam treatment of adolescents with panic disorder. *Journal of Clinical Psychopharmacology, 8,* 299–301.

Kutcher, S., Reiter, S., Gardner, D., et al. (1992). The pharmacotherapy of anxiety disorders in children and adolescents. *Psychiatric Clinics of North America, 15,* 41–68.

Kutcher, S., Boulos, C., Ward, B., et al. (1994). Response to desipramine treatment in adolescent depression: A fixed dose, placebo controlled trial. *Journal of the American Academy of Child and Adolescent Psychiatry, 33,* 686–694.

Lader, M. (1987). Assessing the potential for buspirone dependence or abuse and effects of its withdrawal. *American Journal of Medicine, 82,* 20–26.

Last, C. (1989). Anxiety disorders of childhood or adolescents. In C. Last (Ed.), *Handbook of child psychiatric diagnosis* (pp. 156–169). New York: Wiley.

Last, C. G., Hersen, M., Kazdin, A., et al. (1991). Anxiety disorders in children and their families. *Archives of General Psychiatry, 48*(10), 928–934.

Leonard, H. L., Swedo, S. E., Lenane, M. C., et al. (1991). A double-blind desipramine substitution during long-term clomipramine treatment in children and adolescents with obsessive–compulsive disorder. *Archives of General Psychiatry, 48,* 922–927.

Leonard, H. L., Swedo, S. E., Rapoport, J. L., et al. (1989). Treatment of obses-sive–compulsive disorder with clomipramine and desipramine in children and adolescents. *Archives of General Psychiatry, 46,* 1088–1092.

Licbowitz, M. R., Gorman, J. M., Fyer, A. J., et al. (1985a). Lactate provocation of panic attacks: Vol. II. Biochemical and physiological findings. *Archives of General Psychiatry, 42,* 709–713.

Liebowitz, M. R., Gorman, J., M. Fyer, A. J., et al. (1985b). Social phobia: Review of a neglected anxiety disorder. *Archives of General Psychiatry, 42,* 729–736.

Liebowitz , M., Hollander, E., Schneier, F., et al. (1990). Reversible and irre-versible monoamine oxidase inhibitors in other psychiatric disorders. *Acta Psychiatrica Scandinavica, 82* (Suppl. 360), 29–34.

Lucas, A., & Pasley, F. (1969). Psychoactive drugs in the treatment of emotion-ally disturbed children: Haloperidol and diazepam. *Comprehensive Psychia-try, 10,* 376–386.

March, J., Johnson, H., Jefferson, J., et al. (1990). Do subtle neurological impair-ments predict treatment resistance to clomipramine in children and adoles-cents with obsessive-compulsive disorder? *Journal of Child and Adolescent Psychopharmacology, 2,* 133–140.

Marsden, C. A. (1990). The pharmacology of new anxiolytics acting on 5-HT neurones. *Postgraduate Medicine, 66*(Suppl. 2), S2–S6.

Mattila, M., Aranko, K., & Sepalla, T. (1982). Acute effects of buspirone and alcohol on psychomotor skills. *Journal of Clinical Psychiatry, 43,* 56–61.

Moskowitz, H., & Smiley, A. (1982). Effects of chronically administered buspi-rone and diazepam on living-related skills performance. *Journal of Clinical Psychiatry, 43,* 45–55.

Newton, R., Casten, G., Alous, D., et al. (1982). The side effect profile of buspi-rone in comparison to active control and placebo. *Journal of Clinical Psy-chiatry, 43,* 100–102.

Nurnberg, H. G., & Coccaro, E. F. (1982). Response of panic disorder and resis-tance of depression to imipramine. *American Journal of Psychiatry, 139,* 1060–1062.

Nutt, D. J. (1989). Altered central alpha2-adrenoceptor sensitivity in panic dis-order. *Archives of General Psychiatry, 46,* 165–169.

Olajide, D., & Lader, M. (1987). A comparison of buspirone, diazepam, and placebo in patients with chronic anxiety states. *Journal of Clinical Psycho-pharmacology, 7,* 148–152.

Petti, T. A., Fish, B., Shapiro, T., et al. (1982). Effects of chlordiazepoxide in disturbed children: A pilot study. *Journal of Clinical Psychopharmacology, 2,* 270–273.

Pfefferbaum, G., Overall, J. E., Boren, H. A., et al. (1987). Alprazolam in the treatment of anticipatory and acute situational anxiety in children with cancer. *Journal of the American Academy of Child and Adolescent Psychia-try, 26,* 532–535.

Piacentini, J., Jaffer, M., Gitow, A., et al. (1992). Psychopharmacological treat-ment of child and adolescent obsessive compulsive disorder. *Psychiatric Clinics of North America, 15,* 87–107.

Pliszka, S. (1987). Tricyclic antidepressants in the treatment of children with attention deficit disorder. *Journal of the American Academy of Child and Adolescent Psychiatry, 26,* 127–132.

Pliszka, S. (1989). Effect of anxiety on cognition, behavior, and stimulant response in ADHD. *Journal of the American Academy of Child and Adolescent Pscyhiatry, 28,* 882–887.

Pohl, R., Berchou, R., & Rainey, J. M. (1983). Tricyclic antidepressants and monoamine oxidase inhibitors in the treatment of agoraphobia. *Journal of Clinical Psychopharmacology, 2,* 399–407.

Pollach, M., Tesor, G., Rosenbaum, J., et al. (1986). Clonazepam in the treatment of panic disorder and agoraphobia: A one-year follow-up. *Journal of Clinical Psychopharmacology, 6,* 302–304.

Popper, C., & Elliott, G. (1990). Sudden death and tricyclic antidepressants: Clinical considerations for children. *Journal of Child and Adolescent Psychopharmacology, 1,* 125–132.

Potter, W., Rudorfer, M., Pickar, D., et al. (1987). Effects of psychotropic drugs on neurotransmitters in man. *Life Sciences, 41,* 817–820.

Preskorn, S., Weller, E., & Weller, I. R. (1987). Depression in children: Relationship between plasma imipramine levels and response. *Journal of Clinical Psychiatry, 43,* 81–89.

Puig-Antich, J., Perel, J., Lupatkin, W., et al. (1979). Plasma levels of imipramine (IMI) and desmethylimipramine (desipramine) and clinical response in prepubertal major depressive disorder. *Journal of the American Academy of Child and Adolescent Psychiatry, 18,* 616–627.

Puig-Antich, J., Perel, J., Lupatkin, W., et al. (1987). Imipramine in prepubertal major depressive disorders. *Archives of General Psychiatry, 44,* 81–89.

Reiter, S. (1994). *Co-morbidity of obsessive–compulsive disorder and bipolar affective disorder in adolescents.* Manuscript in preparation.

Reiter, S., & Kutcher, S. (1991, August). Disinhibition and anger outbursts in adolescents treated with clonazepam [Letter to the editor]. *Journal of Clinical Psychopharmacology, 11,* 268.

Reiter, S., & Kutcher, S. (1992, May). *Treatment of panic attacks in teenagers with clonazepam.* New Clinical Drug Evaluation Unit Presentation.

Reiter, S., Kutcher, S., & Gardner, D. (1992). Anxiety disorders in children and adolescents: Clinical and related issues in pharmacological treatment. *Canadian Journal of Psychiatry, 37,* 432–438.

Rettew, D. C., Swedo, S. E., Leonard, H. L., et al. (1992). Obsessions and compulsions across time in 79 children and adolescents with obsessive–compulsive disorder. *Journal of the American Academy of Child and Adolescent Psychiatry, 31,* 1050–1056.

Riblet, L., Taylor, D., Eison, M., et al. (1982). Pharmacology and neurochemistry of buspirone. *Journal of Clinical Psychiatry, 43,* 11–16.

Rickels, K., Feighner, J., & Smith, W. (1985). Alprazolam, amitriptyline, doxepin and placebo in the treatment of depression. *Archives of General Psychiatry, 42,* 134–141.

Rickels, K., & Schweizer, E. (1987). Current pharmacotherapy of anxiety and panic. In H. Meltzer (Ed.), *Psychopharmacology, the third generation of progress* (pp. 1193–1204). New York: Raven.

Riddle, M. A., Brown, N., Dzubinski, D., et al. (1989). Fluoxetine overdose in an adolescent. *Journal of the American Academy of Child and Adolescent Psychiatry, 28(4),* 587–588.

Riddle, M. A., Hardin, M. T., King, R., et al. (1990). Fluoxetine treatment of children and adolescents with Tourette's and obsessive–compulsive disorders: Preliminary clinical experience. *Journal of the American Academy of Child and Adolescent Psychiatry, 29(1),* 45–48.

Riddle, M. A., Scahill, L., King, R. A., et al. (1992). Double-blind crossover trial of fluoxetine and placebo in children and adolescents with obsessive–compulsive disorder. *Journal of the American Academy of Child and Adolescent Psychiatry, 31,* 1062–1069.

Robinson, D. S., Rickels, K., Feighner, J., et al. (1990). Clinical effects of the 5-HT-IA partial agonists in depression: A composite analysis of busiprone in the treatment of depression. *Journal of Clinical Psychopharmacology, 10,* 67S–76S.

Ryan, N. (1992). The pharmacological treatment of child and adolescent depression. *Psychiatric Clinics of North America, 15,* 29–40.

Ryan, N., Puig-Antich, J., Cooper, T., et al. (1986). Imipramine in adolescent major depression: Plasma level and clinical response. *Acta Psychiatrica Scandanavica, 73,* 275–288.

Ryan, N., Puig-Antich, J., Cooper, T., et al. (1987). Relative safety of single dose versus divided dose imipramine in adolescent major depression. *Journal of the American Academy of Child and Adolescent Psychiatry, 26,* 400–406.

Ryan, N., Puig-Antich, J., Rabinovich, H., et al. (1988). MAOIs in adolescent major depression unresponsive to tricyclic antidepressants. *Journal of the American Academy of Child and Adolescent Psychiatry, 27,* 755–758.

Schrabel, T. (1987). Evaluation of the safety and side effects of antianxiety agents. *American Journal of Medicine, 82*(Suppl. 5A), 7–13.

Schweizer, E., Rickels, K., & Luckil, I. (1986). Resistance to the antianxiety effect of buspirone in patients with a history of benzodiazepine use. *New England Journal of Medicine, 314,* 719–790.

Shibata, K., Kataoka, Y., Comita, Y., et al. (1982). Localization of the site of the anti-conflict action of the benzodiazepines in the amygdaloid nucleus of rats. *Brain Research, 234,* 442–446.

Silverman, W., & Nelles, W. (1988). The anxiety disorders interview schedule for children. *Journal of the American Academy of Child and Adolescent Psychiatry, 27,* 772–778.

Simeon, J. D., Dinicola, V. F., Ferguson, H. B., et al. (1990). Adolescent depression: A placebo-controlled fluoxetine treatment study and follow-up. *Progress in Neuro-Psychopharmacology and Biological Psychiatry, 14,* 791–795.

Simeon, J., & Ferguson, B. (1985). Recent developments in the use of antidepressant and anxiolytic medications. *Psychiatric Clinics of North America, 8,* 893–907.

Simeon, J., & Ferguson, B. (1987). Alprazolam effects in children with anxiety disorders. *Canadian Journal of Psychiatry, 32,* 570–574.

Simeon, J., Ferguson, B., Knott, V., et al. (1992). Clinical, cognitive and neuro-physiological effects of alprazolam in children with overanxious and avoidant disorders. *Journal of the American Academy of Child and Adolescent Psychiatry, 31*, 29–33.

Simeon, J. G., Thatte, S., & Wiggins, D. (1990). Treatment of adolescent obsessive-compulsive disorder with a clomipramine–fluoxetine combination. *Psychopharmacology Bulletin, 26*(3), 285–290.

Skolnick, P., Paul, S., & Weissman, B. A. (1984). Preclinical pharmacology of buspirone hydrochloride. *Pharmacotherapy, 4*, 308–314.

Smiley, N. (1987). Effects of minor tranquilizers and antidepressants on psychomotor performance. *Journal of Clinical Psychiatry, 48*, 22–28.

Spielberger, C. (1973). *Preliminary manual for the State–Trait Anxiety Inventory for Children.* Palo Alto, CA: Consulting Psychologists Press.

Sternbach, H. (1991). The serotonin syndrome. *American Journal of Psychiatry, 148*, 705–713.

Swedo, S. E., Leonard, H. L., Kruesi, M. J. P., et al. (1992). Cerebrospinal fluid neurochemistry in children and adolescents with obsessive–compulsive disorder. *Archives of General Psychiatry, 49*, 29–36.

Swedo, S. E., & Rapoport, J. L. (1989). Phenomenology and differential diagnosis of obsessive compulsive disorder in children and adolescents. In J. L. Rapoport (Ed.), *Obsessive compulsive disorder in children and adolescents* (pp. 13–32). Washington, DC: American Psychiatric Press.

Sweeney, D., Moss, J., & Heninger, G. (1978). State anxiety, physical activity and urinary 3-methoxy-4-hydroxyphentylene glycol excretion. *Archives of General Psychiatry, 35*, 1418–1422.

Taylor, D., Eison, M., Riblet, L., et al. (1985). Pharmacological and clinical effects of buspirone. *Pharmacology, Biochemistry and Behavior, 23*, 687–694.

Trott, G., Friese, H., Menzel, M., et al. (1992). Use of moclobemide in children with attention deficit hyperactivity disorder. *Psychopharmacology, 106*, Sl34–136.

Uhde, T., Joffe, R., Jimerson, D., et al. (1988). Normal urinary free cortisol and plasma MHPG in panic disorder: Clinical and theoretical implications. *Biological Psychiatry, 23*, 575–597.

Venkataraman, S., Naylor, M. W., & King, C. A. (1992). Case study: Mania associated with fluoxetine treatment in adolescents. *Journal of the American Academy of Child and Adolescent Psychiatry, 31*(2), 276–281.

Weissman, P. I., Klerman, G., Markowitz, J. S., et al. (1989). Suicidal ideation and suicide attempts in panic disorder and attacks. *New England Journal of Medicine, 321*, 1209–1214.

Wilens, T., Biederman, J., Baldessarini, R., et al. (1992). Developmental changes in serum concentrations of desipramine and 2-hydroxydesipramine during treatment with desipramine. *Journal of the American Academy of Child and Adolescent Psychiatry, 31*, 691–698.

Winslow, J. T., & Insel, T. R. (1990). Neurobiology of obsessive–compulsive disorder: A possible role for serotonin. *Journal of Clinical Psychiatry, 51*(Suppl.), 27–31.

Wyatt, R., Portnoy, B., Kupfer, D., et al. (1971). Resting plasma catecholamine levels in patients with depression and anxiety. *Archives of General Psychiatry, 24*, 65–70.

Young, W., & Kuhar, M. (1979). Auto radiographic localization of benzodiazepine receptors in the brain of humans and animals. *Nature, 280*, 395–397.

Chapter 16

Psychodynamic Psychotherapy

Charles Keith

The emergence of anxiety and its vicissitudes during the sequential phases of child development has been a central theme in psychoanalytic developmental and clinical theory since the 1920s. Anxiety arising from its biological anlagen at 6 to 8 months and its subsequent development has been viewed as a primary organizing experience shaping character and defensive structures that the child's mind (ego) uses to contain and master the anxiety. Many forms and symptoms of psychopathology are understood as a relative failure of a child's coping defensive patterns that permits the experiencing of the painful affect of anxiety, which in turn forces the child to institute additional symptoms and behaviors to reduce the painful affect surges and to draw caretakers into anxiety-reducing caretaking behaviors. The ubiquity of these phenomena in normal and psychopathological development has been one among several reasons that there has been a relative lack of urgency among psychodynamic clinicians to carefully define and delimit anxiety syndromes as in the various editions of the *Diagnostic and Statistical Manual of Mental Disorders* (DSM).

ONTOGENY OF ANXIETY FROM A PSYCHODYNAMIC DEVELOPMENTAL PERSPECTIVE

A brief review of the development of anxiety and its typical psychopathological sequelae provides a necessary background for describing the psychodynamic psychotherapy of anxiety syndromes in children.

- *Early infancy* (0–5 months). The neonate and young infant can easily become overwhelmed with stimuli, resulting in flushed skin, painful crying, sweating, and rapid pulse rate. However, there is little evidence that these events are experienced as anxiety. (Throughout this chapter, it is apparent that anxiety can only be defined using both subjective and objective criteria. In other words, autonomic arousal alone probably cannot define anxiety when the subject is unable to communicate the internal experience). Therapy during these first few months of life for developmentally damaging and overwhelming stimuli is the provision of adequate caretaking, and it often occurs on an emergency basis. Innate sensitivity to stimuli and ease of autonomic arousal may be factors in infants with difficult temperaments.

- *Later infancy* (about 6 months). The central nervous system has developed enough so that the infant can now experience subjective signs of anxiety that can be observed by others (Emde, 1988). This "starting up" of anxiety—the first fears within central nervous system pathways—is also observed at analogous ages in primates (Kalin, 1993). The well-known phenomenon of stranger anxiety can now take place.

- *Attachment* (10–18 months). Forerunners of attachment configurations can be observed in early infancy, for example, preferential social smiling at the primary caretakers. At about 10 to 18 months, these attachment behaviors coalesce into the formation of an internal concept of a psychologic love object. Thus infants of 18 months of age become concerned about the presence or absence of the love object, and so is created one of the great dangers of childhood and the primary source of separation anxiety, that is, loss of and separation from the primary caretaker. This anxiety can easily become overwhelming, leading to what observers have called "annihilation anxiety." This anxiety can be damaging to early ego structures and may be one of the etiologies of the borderline syndrome in which infants are extremely sensitive to the presence or absence of a caretaking object. Another etiology of early separation disturbances can be innate developmental defects that make it difficult for the infant to tame anxiety even with sufficiently good caretaking. Neuromaturational imbalances and lags may be examples of such inborn defects (Fish, Marcus, Hans, et al., 1992).

- *Loss of the caretaker's love* (15–36 months). Once children have sufficiently mastered separation anxiety vis-à-vis the primary caretaker, there then emerges anxiety over loss of the caretaker's love and approval, typically during the second and third year of life. A fairly common personality structure may develop around these issues, namely the "anxious, inhibited child." Children appear to be primed for behavioral inhibition by autonomic hyperarousal, which may have genetic roots (Chapter 3). Girls appear more vulnerable to this condition, in which the child main-

tains high levels of anxiety concerning the presence or absence of the caretaker and/or to any behaviors that might lead to disapproval and withdrawal of the caretaker's love and care. The child typically develops multiple fears, such as of the dark, animals at the bedroom windows, leaving
the house, and so on. The child's mind is normally capable of externalizing or projecting dangerous impulses such as anger toward the love object
onto outside forces such as animals or the robber in the bushes. These
"external" fears are quite real to the young child due to the lack of reality
testing and magical thinking. The learned distinction between "internal
anxiety" and real "external fears" is usually meaningless to a young child.

A major developmental task for the young child during this period is
mastering signal anxiety, that is, using small doses of anxiety to mobilize
sublimatory, coping mechanisms and defenses, which enables the child to
move forward in development. The more disturbed the child, the more
likely it is that signal anxiety can become immobilizing, overwhelming,
flooding anxiety that leads to the multiple symptoms and separation fears
of behavioral inhibition and more severe psychopathologies of early childhood.

• *Castration anxiety or fear of loss of body parts* (2.5–5 years). Once
the earlier stages are sufficiently mastered, a child's primary source of anxiety becomes castration or fear of loss of body parts, resulting in concerns
about bodily damage. Boys appear more vulnerable than girls to this anxiety due, in part, to their more easily observable external genitals. This
anxiety, if not well contained and sublimated, can lead to multifarious
psychopathologies, perhaps the most insidious of which is inhibition in
which the child unconsciously curtails normal aggressive, assertive
sublimatory behaviors. A most striking outcome of this is seen in children
who become unable to perform competitively in school, a frequent and
often severe problem most commonly manifested by boys who have normal and above normal intelligence yet underachieve in school. When performance inhibition is severe, it can curtail after-school and weekend activities, leaving the child essentially emotionally paralyzed. It is unfortunate
that this syndrome of "academic inhibition" is not recognized in DSM-
IV. On the contrary, this widespread, extremely destructive psychopathological outcome of insufficiently mastered castration anxiety severely dam-
ages mental development.

Aggressive, assertive urges leading to castration anxiety and the resulting inhibition can manifest itself in a diagnostic interview as follows.

A 5-year-old boy put several small dolls on a toy fire truck and had
them put out fires with imaginary hoses on the play table in the
diagnostician's office. The boy then drove the dolls on the truck over
to the wall and with a doll in each hand had them climb up the wall

to look at some disturbance "up there." They carried their imaginary hoses up the wall and squirted them over the landscape. They suddenly saw a monster on the wall and ran back to the fire truck in fright. The dolls then went back up the wall with their fire hoses squirting all the time to "put out" the monster. They thought their hoses did the trick, but suddenly the monster reappeared, and the dolls quickly returned to the fire truck in great fright. The diagnostician was sitting in a chair close to the boy's play, putting into words the emerging metaphoric story. The second time the dolls faced the monster, the boy became overtly anxious after returning the dolls to the truck. He got up and walked across the room to sit on his father's lap while sucking his thumb. In spite of the diagnostician's verbalizations and encouragements, the boy remained clinging to his father the remainder of the diagnostic hour.

In this play sequence, the squirting of hoses on dangerous objects suddenly was interrupted by anxiety ("play interruption," as described by Erik Erikson), resulting in the child regressing to a clinging, thumb-sucking behavior requiring the physical presence of the father. As the diagnostician and father discussed the boy's play, the father realized that the sequence of assertiveness followed by regression and clinging behavior occurred many times each day in the boy's family life. Incidentally, the father initiated the diagnostic evaluation because his son's interest in performing seemed to be decreasing, resulting in worries on the father's part about whether the boy would be able to function adequately in the forthcoming first grade.

The discerning reader will have noticed by now that the psychodynamic formulation involving

urge (e.g., aggression) → anxiety → protective defenses →
→ breakthrough of anxiety → further elaboration of defenses, etc.

can be depicted in a behavioral conditioning framework as long as one takes into account positive and negative feedback from internal and unconscious sources as well as more easily observable external sources.

- *Loss of approval from the conscience, or superego* (3–5 years). The crystalization of the conscience at ages 3–5 indicates that many of the externally experienced dangers from previously developmental stages are now increasingly internalized. The voice of conscience is now ready to warn the child that certain thoughts and activities will be bad, resulting in lowered self-esteem, guilt, and possible depression. Anxiety can also play a prominent role in this developmental phase since the child can come to dread the disapproval of the conscience as much as the loss of a parent's approval.

However, some children slip over into depression during this phase. Some may continue to show mostly anxiety symptoms whereas others show a mixture of anxiety and depression. What factors might tip the scales toward anxiety, depression, or a mixture thereof? One factor might be actual losses which could lead to a symptom pattern of depression. There may be central nervous system or neural-hormonal sensitivities which may push symptomatology toward anxiety or depression. Of course, if the child enters this phase with high levels of anxiety from earlier developmental levels, anxiety symptoms can override depression resulting from the loss of a superego approval.

• *Loss of social approval* (6–10 years). During the latency developmental period, many children who have not sufficiently mastered the earlier anxiety conflicts become prey to the dread of social disapproval. This anxiety—fear of being in the social spotlight, stage fright, and the resulting fear of performing—can further cement patterns of inhibition. Excessive use of this defense against anxiety can severely damage a child's mastery of crucial developmental tasks during this age period, such as becoming a member of social groups, playing by group rules, and having to be part of a larger whole within the classroom, scouts, church groups, and so on.

The preceding list briefly describes the major biopsychosocial dangers for the child during the preadolescent years of development. With each passing year, these psychological dangers are increasingly internalized, encrusted over and take on a life of their own in the child's mind behind at times almost impermeable defenses. These internalized "life stories" of perceived dangers and anxieties in relation to primary relationships can remain persistent sources of fuel for malleable, changing, overt symptoms. Thus, psychopathology can be ongoing in the subjective self while objective symptoms and behaviors shift and change through succeeding developmental phases (Zeanah et al., 1989). Because the child is constantly preoccupied with anxieties, he or she naturally brings them into the diagnostic and psychotherapy setting via play, verbalizations, and interactions with the therapist. How to help the child communicate anxiety issues will be described in the next section.

How does the psychodynamic clinician view the role of the primary caretakers in the creation of these maladaptive symptoms and defenses? Eruption of maladaptive symptoms can occur within the context of good enough, normal parenting. Often normal parents are caught up in trying to relieve the child's anxiety, thereby unwittingly fostering the child's problems. To the psychodynamic clinician, these normal parents are at one end of a parent spectrum; at the other end are parents who themselves are struggling with poorly mastered anxiety disorders from their own past. At times, the parent's problems can engulf a child of basically normal endowment to the point that the child's development is severely compromised. Evaluating and addressing these parental issues in a supportive, therapeutic manner is fundamental to a successful outcome of psychotherapy with the child. To phrase it somewhat differently, the establishment and maintenance of a parental alliance is fundamental for the successful outcome of child psychotherapy. Failure to maintain this alliance and to take into account parental vulnerabilities accounts for the vast majority of psychotherapeutic failures in psychotherapy as well as in all treatment modalities of child and adolescent anxiety disorders.

It has been a common misperception that psychodynamic clinicians blame parents for the child's psychopathology. If parent blaming does occur, it attests to lack of skill and deficiencies in interpersonal sensitivities on the part of some clinicians. Psychodynamic theory and many of its clinicians fully accept the fact that the child brings vulnerabilities to the child–parent interaction. These vulnerabilities range from biological, central nervous system issues such as hyperarousal of frontothalamic circuits to the often neglected important issue of the early onset of maladaptive defensive behaviors, which can reduce even the best parents to discouragement and helplessness.

EVALUATING ANXIETY-DISORDERED CHILDREN FOR PSYCHODYNAMIC PSYCHOTHERAPY

In assessing a prospective patient, the psychodynamic clinician attempts to carry out the kind of thorough, general psychodiagnostic evaluation described by authors throughout this volume. Additional diagnostic investigation becomes important if the psychodynamic clinician has in mind psychodynamic psychotherapy as a treatment possibility. The diagnostician should help the child do a "piece" of psychotherapy during the diagnostic hours. The child should be encouraged to play and talk spontaneously for enough time to develop a theme. Almost without exception, if a child has the capacity for spontaneous play and verbalization, the nuclear anxiety issues emerge in the play metaphors, for example, the case referred to earlier of the 5-year-old boy with the fire truck who was attempting but could not quite face the monster on the wall. This child experienced momentary anxiety, became inhibited and stopped his play, and went to his father for comfort. At this point, the diagnostician can verbalize the play theme and the anxiety in the metaphor. At times, the diagnostician can even interpret the defense against it; in the case of the boy with the fire truck, the play stopped and the child went to his daddy (avoidance and inhibition) because the dolls apparently could not hose down (master) the monster on the wall.

During diagnostic sessions, it is important for the clinician to spell out how psychotherapy will work by making statements such as "Through playing and talking together, we can figure out the monster, how to hose it down and make it work for us." If the child is curious, reassured, and interested in the interpretations, the child will spontaneously return to the play theme or one similar to it, that is, move the theme forward. The diagnostic sessions also provide important clues as to how supportive parents will be in the psychotherapy process. In the case of the boy with the fire truck, the diagnostician noticed that the father was supportive as his child returned to face the monster.

The psychodynamic clinician usually understands the frightening monster as an amalgam of childhood impulses, such as anger or rage and normal strivings for autonomy, that have become confused with destructiveness and gathered up by the child's mind and externalized onto the outside world. The child gathers up these issues and places them outside the bedroom window or onto the wall to avoid or get away from the anxiety-arousing thoughts, feelings, and images. However, since these externalizations are a product of the child's mind, the child really cannot get away from them; they will be there to stir up anxiety the next time the child goes to bed. If the child can work with the diagnostician as described, the chances are good that the child can benefit from well-conducted psychodynamic psychotherapy. However, if the child becomes more anxious and disorganized, clings even more tenaciously to a parent, runs out of the room, and so on, the child may not be ready for psychodynamic psychotherapy and may need a period of supportive treatment to bolster ego functions before psychodynamic psychotherapy is considered. The basic issue here is that the goal of psychodynamic psychotherapy is not to suppress or "chase away" anxiety-arousing issues but to understand and master them in the psychotherapeutic process; the child must be able to bring the anxiety-arousing danger situations into the therapeutic process, and master them with the help of the therapist through play and talk. To summarize, the best way to decide whether a child and parent can use psychodynamic psychotherapy is to try it during the diagnostic evaluation. Unfortunately, many children and parents are referred for psychodynamic psychotherapy without clinical evidence that they can utilize it.

Basic questions the clinician must also answer are whether the child's anxiety symptoms and defenses are within normal bounds, are serious but transitory, or signify enduring psychopathology requiring treatment. If the child's symptomatology meets DSM-IV criteria for one of the anxiety disorders, the clinician can feel justification in recommending treatment. If the child's overall development is becoming delayed and/or damaged, then treatment is even more urgent. Will the child's symptoms recede with time? If the symptoms are of recent onset, then the clinician can safely suggest a waiting period and advise and encourage parents concerning how to understand and better help the child manage the anxiety. Such watchful waiting and periodic parent interviews can themselves be a powerful intervention.

PROCESS OF PSYCHODYNAMIC PSYCHOTHERAPY WITH ANXIETY DISORDERS

Inaugurating Therapy

The following conditions are necessary to inaugurate a course of psychodynamic psychotherapy.

- As noted, the child should demonstrate that he or she can utilize the treatment and that the parent/caretaker can support and ally with the treatment process.
- Since psychodynamic psychotherapy cannot be conducted in a brief time period, such as 8 to 12 sessions, there must be adequate environmental stability over a sufficient length of time to allow for the open-ended nature of the psychotherapeutic process. It is impossible to predict *a priori* how long a particular child will require to master anxiety conflicts in psychotherapy; the therapy can only proceed at the child's pace. The child must at all times feel in control of the process so that the danger of anxiety outbursts is reduced to a minimum. The best way to guarantee child control is to make it clear from the beginning that the therapist will work with material the child brings in and that the therapist will not introduce topics from the outside world, which can easily override the child's coping defenses. Psychotherapy usually cannot be conducted when the child is moving in and out of foster homes or institutions or is in the midst of a family breakup.
- A therapist trained in psychodynamic psychotherapy must be available. Therapists sufficiently trained in psychodynamic psychotherapy too often are not available in mental health clinics or practitioner's offices.
- Payment for the therapy must be possible. This issue is particularly critical now with the severe cutbacks in mental health and insurance funding. At times, psychodynamic psychotherapy is inaugurated only to have it interrupted prematurely when the clinician and the parents realize that the regular payment of fees was not adequately addressed at the beginning.

Conducting Therapy

The basic guiding principles for the therapist and the child (as well as the parent) are as follows (Glenn, 1978).

- The child produces the material in each session through play and the accompanying verbalizations. This guarantees as much as possible that therapy will proceed at the child's pace and will provide the child a sense of control over the process.
- The therapist listens to the material with the following three frameworks in mind.
  1. *Defenses*. What psychological defenses does the child's mind (ego) use to grapple with anxiety-arousing dangerous situations? Some of the more common defenses follow.

     Inhibition: not moving forward toward the dangerous situation.
     Avoidance: actively staying away or moving away from the dangerous situation.
     Repression: not allowing the mind to think about the danger.
     Counterphobic defenses: "diving into" dangerous material to show self and others that there is no anxiety or fear.
     Externalization: projecting dangerous situation onto the external world.

     These defenses operate automatically, that is, out of the child's awareness. When brought into consciousness, they are generally viewed by the child as important protections against experiencing painful anxiety. As these defenses emerge in a pattern over the sessions, the therapist becomes increasingly aware of them and can verbalize them using metaphors for how these defenses "keep us away from scary feelings."
  2. *Wishes and impulses*. Wishes and impulses are the psychosocial fuel for persistent anxiety symptoms. For example, a child may believe that his or her angry thoughts toward parents may lead to their disappearance or death. Persistently holding onto this piece of magical thinking can result in regression to clinging behaviors and separation fears in which the child constantly needs the reassurance of the parents' presence to demonstrate that nothing bad has happened to them. The therapist must repeatedly interpret the child's magical thinking and demonstrate the reality that angry thoughts and wishes do not make someone go away or die.
  3. *Transference*. When the above issues become lived out by the child onto the person of the therapist then transference interpretations become possible and an important part of the treatment. Interpretations around the person of the therapist gives these issues an immediate and powerful impact. For instance, as the child develops a relationship with the therapist, there may occur separation fears around the therapist's vacations or ab-

sences due to illness. During the therapist's absence in reality, there can be a recurrence of old anxiety symptoms in the sessions or in the family setting. In this situation, it often turns out that the child believes the therapist went away because he or she does not love the child anymore due to the child's rambunctious or aggressive behavior in the sessions prior to the therapist's departure.

Course of Therapy

As the child plays out and masters anxiety issues, the initial symptoms (e.g., sleep disturbances, phobias, and excessive clinging) usually drop away. In well-conducted two-to-four-times-weekly psychotherapy sessions, the presenting symptoms usually recede in 3 to 6 months. Why should psychotherapy continue at this point, particularly if the child appears symptom free? It usually is obvious to both the therapist and the parents and sometimes even to the child that psychological vulnerability for the eruption of anxiety symptoms is still present in the form of the old maladaptive defenses and islands of magical thinking inappropriate to the child's chronological age. These issues need repetitive working through and resolving in the psychotherapy sessions, even though symptoms outside of the therapy have mostly disappeared. Resolving psychological vulnerabilities may help prevent future eruptions of symptoms, and this is what accounts for the lengthy nature of psychodynamic psychotherapy.

Termination occurs when a child is largely free of symptomatic suffering, has demonstrated sufficient mastery of the nuclear anxiety conflict through play and words, and is back on the developmental track if the anxiety symptoms leading to treatment had delayed or damaged development. It is a well-known phenomenon that the anxiety symptoms that brought the child into treatment usually recur during the final weeks of psychotherapy because of the impending loss of the relationship with the therapist. Rather than being cause for concern, the recrudescence of symptoms usually provides an opportunity for a final working through of issues at a time when the child's ego has been greatly strengthened. In the termination period, the child can often gain insights into his or her conflicts that would have been impossible at the beginning of psychotherapy.

PSYCHOTROPIC MEDICATIONS DURING PSYCHODYNAMIC PSYCHOTHERAPY

Some clinicians have viewed psychotropic medication and psychodynamic psychotherapy as almost mutually exclusive. Sometimes the belief arose from the clinician's ignorance concerning medications; at other times the belief arose from the assumed efficacy of psychodynamic psychotherapy and the assumption that the use of medication represents a failure of psychotherapy. In recent years, psychodynamic clinicians working with children and adolescents have generally become more sophisticated about the availability and usefulness of the wide range of psychotropic medications, the increasing acceptance of the use of medications with children, and the more realistic appraisal of the strengths and limitations of psychodynamic therapy and psychotropic medications (Showalter, 1989). Antianxiety medications affect primarily the neurobiological substrates of anxiety, whereas psychodynamic therapy works primarily with the psychological constructs of defenses and beliefs arising out of anxiety conflicts. Thus, antianxiety medications and psychodynamic therapy "look" at the child's mind and brain through two separate but overlapping windows. Antianxiety medications may be particularly helpful during the initial stages of psychodynamic therapy when the symptoms may be acute and damaging to the child's psychological and environmental stability. As symptoms remit under the impact of both medication and psychotherapy, then the medication can often be reduced and/or discontinued. The psychodynamic psychotherapist has a somewhat unique opportunity to track the child's beliefs about medication. Medication may represent unwanted parental control and obtrusiveness if the parent administers the medication; the medication may represent feared damage, the child or adolescent saying, in effect, "I have always been afraid I am damaged. The fact that they want to prescribe medication for me is now proof of one of my most dreaded fears." These are just some of the many beliefs that can accrue around the administration of medication and become caught up in a child's ongoing anxious belief systems. It is important that parents, with the therapist's help, become aware of such beliefs in their child so that they can verbalize these concerns as parents and thus remain firm in their resolve to properly complete the course of psychotropic medication.

PARENT THERAPY

Another common stereotype concerning psychodynamic psychotherapy is that the parent is an appendage to the treatment process, merely taking the child for appointments and paying the fees. To the contrary, the parent is the foundation of psychodynamic psychotherapy with children. In this discussion, the parent is defined as the significant caretaking adult who makes psychotherapy possible for the child by not only delivering the child to the sessions and paying the fees but also participating actively with the therapist in the treatment process. Without a firm parental alliance developed through parent therapy, psychodynamic psychotherapy of children is nearly always doomed to fail. In fact, the vast majority of premature terminations and treatment failures are due to the clinician not paying sufficient attention to the vital role of the parent in the treatment process.

The term "parent therapy" means establishing an ongoing process with the parent in which the parent feels allied with the therapist and the psychotherapy, is knowledgeable about what is happening in the child's therapeutic process, and feels increasingly comfortable about handling issues in the child's daily life as well as events immediately surrounding the psychotherapy sessions. The parents of children with anxiety disorders fall into a broad range of readiness for participating in the children's psychotherapy. Parents toward the more normal end of the spectrum of psychopathology come ready to form an alliance and make rapid moves with the child in the home setting as well as to inaugurate the formal psychotherapy sessions. In fact, such parents and often their children tend to do well in any psychological treatment modality. At the other end of the spectrum are parents who bring psychopathology of their own into the treatment process. These parents may have poorly mastered childhood anxiety issues of their own, leading to separation fears that result in the parent not allowing the child to enter treatment due to the dread that the child may become more autonomous and thus move away from the parent. These parents can easily become fearful and suspicious of the therapist's recommendations and find many reasons to terminate the treatment prematurely. These parents often need intensive parent therapy, sometimes for a lengthy period, before the child is seen by the therapist. The basic principle for child therapy applies to parent therapy, particularly with the more disturbed parent: The therapist must go at the parent's pace so that the parent feels in control of the process, not flooded with anxiety.

It is crucial in parent therapy to constantly strengthen parental identities, that is, to foster and support the parent's strengths and help a parent deal with anxieties and fears that may lead to premature disruption of the child's treatment. Time and time again, psychodynamic therapists make the mistake of challenging parental defenses too soon and too forcefully, such as demanding that the parent stop sleeping with the child in the beginning phase of therapy or stirring up marital or family conflicts before the parent can tolerate the attendant anxieties, which leaves a parent, particularly a more disturbed parent, no choice but to flee from therapy. Being human, the therapist often ascribes such an unhappy ending to the parent's "lack of motivation" or to the parent being "too sick." In actuality, the unhappy ending is almost always caused by a technical error on the part of the therapist—moving too rapidly and failing to cement a parental alliance before asking the parent to make major changes. As with psychodynamic child psychotherapy, parent therapy cannot be rushed or pushed.

Once the parent has achieved sufficient stability and mastery of anxiety in relation to the child and has established an alliance with the therapist, various kinds of parent training techniques can be introduced. Often parents bring up their own ideas about how they can help their child master anxiety in the home setting. To paraphrase the old Chinese proverb, "One idea brought up and enacted by a parent is worth a hundred therapeutic suggestions by the therapist." One further caveat. When a parent is in mental or emotional difficulty, it is tempting for the therapist to suggest other treatment modalities such as marriage therapy, family therapy, or individual psychotherapy to the parent for getting through a therapeutic logjam. Frequently the parent interprets such a suggestion as discouragement and rejection on the part of the therapist. One major treatment modality at a time is challenge enough for a parent. Introducing another major treatment modality often overloads the parent's capacities, leading to increased parental anxiety and premature interruption of the child's treatment.

CONCLUSION

Where does psychodynamic psychotherapy fit into the spectrum of available treatments for childhood anxiety disorders? Critics say that the question is becoming irrelevant in the rapidly changing medical economics of the mid-1990s, as many psychiatric treatment modalities for children, particularly open-ended psychotherapy, are being curtailed. Setting aside questions of economics, what are the clinical indications for psychodynamic psychotherapy vis-à-vis various cognitive-behavioral therapies? For rapid symptom relief with healthier parents and children, the time-limited cognitive-behavioral therapies are certainly effective and economical. However, for parents and children with more severe, long-standing psychopathology psychodynamic psychotherapy should be seriously considered (Target & Fonagy, 1994).

Are there definitive studies proving that psychodynamic psychotherapy is effective compared with other psychotherapies, such as the cognitive-behavioral modalities? Such studies are complex to carry out, and to my knowledge, none has been done that meets rigorous research criteria. However, some recent studies have made a start. Moran et al. (1991) compared psychodynamic psychotherapy with supportive management in the treatment of diabetic children who were frequently in diabetic acidosis requiring repeated hospitalizations. Anxiety about bodily illness and body image resulting in denial and defensive noncompliance was a central psychotherapeutic issue. In this carefully controlled study, the diabetic children undergoing psychodynamic psychotherapy demonstrated a dramatic reduction in frequency of hospitalization during the follow-up period compared with the children who were treated with supportive casework techniques. This is an important study, but it did not compare psychodynamic psychotherapy with other psychotherapies such as the cognitive-behavioral modalities as described in Chapter 14. A recent review of the treatment of childhood anxiety disorders suggests that psychodynamic psychotherapy is probably effective and should continue to be considered as one of the primary treatment modalities (American Academy of Child and Adolescent Psychiatry Official Action, 1993).

Can the psychodynamic viewpoint assist the cognitive-behavioral therapist? Certainly there are several commonalities in the two approaches. Both emphasize the need for a treatment alliance with the parent and child. Both place value on helping the child develop an "observing ego" so that the child and therapist can be active partners looking together at the sources of the anxiety.

In spite of the sincere wish for relief of anxiety, the parent and/or the child may also wish to maintain the status quo and may indeed greet any psychotherapy with resistance and defensiveness, that is, be unable to engage in the process or learn new insights and even prematurely interrupt treatment. Gentle, timely identification of these defenses and their associated affects is the "bread and butter" of the psychodynamic psychotherapist. The cognitive-behavioral therapist might adopt this approach for parents and children who are resisting and/or threatening to interrupt the skill-based treatment approach. The cognitive-behavioral therapist could call a "time out" from the structured approach to spend some sessions with the parent, child, or family addressing their anxieties about the treatment itself.

The psychodynamic perspective emphasizes the necessity of repeatedly "working through" the anxiety defense constellations. The appreciation of the working-through process and the length of time it requires has encouraged many cognitive-behavioral therapists to provide repeated "booster" treatments, sometimes spanning several years. This should not be a cause for concern but instead a testimony to the conservativeness and tenacity of the human mind in its ability to hold onto anxiety-laden thought patterns.

In conclusion, well-conducted psychodynamic psychotherapy carried out by properly trained therapists has an important place in the spectrum of treatment modalities for anxiety-disordered children and their parents, particularly for those who do not benefit from short-term treatment.

REFERENCES

American Academy of Child and Adolescent Psychiatry Official Action. (1993, September). Practice parameters for the assessment and treatment of anxiety disorders. *Journal of the American Academy of Child and Adolescent Psychiatry, 32,* 1089–1098.

Emde, R. (1988). Development terminable and interminable: Innate and motivational factors from infancy. *International Journal of Psycho-Analysis, 69*(1), 23–42.

Fish, B., Marcus, J., Hans, S., et al. (1992). Infants at risk for schizophrenia: Sequelae of a genetic neurointegrative defect. *Archives of General Psychiatry, 49,* 221–235.

Glenn, J. (Ed.). (1978). *Child analysis and therapy.* New York: Jason Aronson.

Kalin, N. H. (1993, May). The neurobiology of fear. *Scientific American,* pp. 94–101.

Moran, G., Fonagy, P., Kurtz, A., et al. (1991). A controlled study of the psychoanalytic treatment of brittle diabetes. *Journal of the American Academy of Child and Adolescent Psychiatry, 30,* 926–935.

Showalter, J. E. (1989, September). Psychodynamics and medication. *Journal of the American Academy of Child and Adolescent Psychiatry, 28,* 681–684.

Target, M., & Fonagy, P. (1994, March/April). Efficacy of psychoanalysis for children with emotional disorders. *Journal of the American Academy of Child and Adolescent Psychiatry, 33*(3), 361–371.

Zeanah, C. H., Anders, T. F., Seifer, R., et al. (1989, September). Implications of research on infant development for psychodynamic theory and practice. *Journal of the American Academy of Child and Adolescent Psychiatry, 28*(5), 657–668.

Chapter 17

Family Therapy

Karen C. Wells

U ntil recently, the family therapy field was dominated largely by a constituency of theorists and clinicians who maintained an antiempirical bias and eschewed rigorous evaluations of family therapy approaches. Because of this bias, there are many compelling but unscientific descriptions in the literature of clinical cases treated with family therapy. Over the last 10 years, research-oriented family psychologists have begun to take up the challenge to evaluate empirically the claims of family therapists of treatment effectiveness with specific psychiatric disorders. A small but growing number of articles in the research literature report experimental evaluations of marital or family therapy as a primary or adjunctive treatment modality for adults suffering from major depression (Jacobson, Dobson, Fruzzetti, et al., 1991), bipolar disorder (Miklowitz & Goldstein, 1990), and schizophrenia (Goldstein, Rodnick, Evans, et al., 1978) and for children and adolescents displaying oppositional and aggressive behavior disorders (Wells, in press) and substance abuse disorders (Szapocznik, Murray, Scopetta, et al., 1989).

This research generally has demonstrated the effectiveness of specific, psychoeducational or symptom-focused family therapy programs for these disorders. In addition, three meta-analyses of family therapy outcome studies have recently been conducted. Taken together, these meta-analyses show that the family therapies are effective relative to control conditions and that they seem to be more effective than alternative treatments for some disorders. In addition, patients receiving primary treatment for a psychiatric disorder whose families also receive family therapy show lower relapse rates than patients who do not receive family therapy (Hazelrigg, Cooper, & Borduin, 1987; Markus, Lange, & Pettigrew, 1990; Shadish, 1990).

While these nascent research efforts in the field of family therapy are encouraging, most of the conclusions regarding the effectiveness of family therapy are based on studies of children and adolescents with disruptive behavior disorders; research efforts have not yet extended to the arena of childhood anxiety disorders. A recent review of the literature on empirical foundations of family therapy contained only one paragraph on internalizing problems of children and concluded that "no controlled evaluations of family therapy with child internalizing problems have appeared in the last decade" (Henggeler, Borduin, & Mann, 1993). This statement remains true one year later as this chapter is being written. This state of affairs is somewhat surprising given that many of the theoretical models of childhood anxiety disorders include heavy emphasis on family (especially mother–child) relationships as one set of etiological events for these disorders, and almost every description of clinical treatment for anxious children contains a statement about the importance of attention to parents and family relationships in the overall treatment approach.

Due to the state of the literature on family therapy with childhood anxiety disorders, this review is based primarily on case studies of family therapy as a primary treatment approach for these disorders. In addition, a few recent reports of successful multimodality treatment, including parent or family intervention, have appeared, and presentation of family components from these treatment programs are included. Even though the experimental designs of these studies did not isolate the primary or unique additive effects of family therapy, several authors concluded that family therapy seemed to be an especially important component of the overall treatment. I hope that a review of this sort, emphasizing putative family processes and treatments for childhood anxiety disorders, will serve a heuristic function to stimulate empirical research in this area.

In this chapter, I use the term "family therapy" rather broadly. It includes traditional definitions of family therapy that involve family-based treatment, usually anchored in systems or social learning theories, when a child is presented as the identified patient. It also includes interventions targeted at parents or other family members, designed to change their behavior or emotional responses as part of the overall treatment of the child. Therefore, reports of individual therapy that describe adjunctive interventions with parents deemed important by the authors are included in this chapter. Although purists would not call the latter true family therapy, I think it is important to describe these interventions since we have no empirical guidelines in this area and since one goal is to stimulate the development and evaluation of potentially effective interventions with family members of a child with an anxiety disorder.

It should be noted that much of the literature that includes family therapy for childhood anxiety disorders involves treatment of children with "school phobia" (usually conceptualized as a specific aspect of separation anxiety disorder) and children with obsessive–compulsive disorder

(OCD). While these disorders are relatively rare in epidemiological samples, they have captured the attention of clinicians because of their compelling and highly maladaptive symptoms and the extent to which they interfere with the child's normal developmental course if left untreated. Behavioral treatments based on social learning models and including work with parents have tended to be directed to "school phobia," simple phobias (referred to as specific phobia in DSM-IV), and social phobia. The reader should bear in mind that much of the theorizing about family processes and family treatment of childhood anxiety disorders has developed in the context of the four named disorders and may or may not be relevant to the other anxiety disorders of childhood and adolescence.

THEORETICAL MODELS OF FAMILY RELATIONSHIPS IN CHILDHOOD ANXIETY DISORDERS

Psychodynamic Models

Early theorists writing from a psychodynamic perspective emphasized that anxiety aroused by separation from a parent (usually the mother) was the primary dynamic involved in the avoidance of school by "school phobic" children. Furthermore, this separation anxiety was conceptualized in the context of an intense ambivalent relationship between mother and child, with separation as difficult for the mother as for the child. The ambivalent nature of the relationship accrued from an intense, unresolved, mutual dependency that provoked a rebound hostility when the child's inevitable developmental strivings for independence and self-gratification led to feelings of rejection in the mother.

Although focusing on the mother–child dyad, some early theorists also described a more extended family system in which the marital relationship was weak and the father was a peripheral figure. The mother–child relationship remained intense and primary in the family long past the child's infancy. Furthermore, multigenerational processes were described in which the mother's relationship with her own mother was one of unresolved dependency. Grandmother was described as intrusively involved with the child's mother, undermining her feelings of self-worth in her adult, parental role (Crumley, 1974; Eisenberg, 1958; Skynner, 1974).

Even before the advent of communication theories of family dysfunction and symptom development, Eisenberg (1958) described mismatched communication from mother to child, arising out of the mother's ambivalent feelings, as the catalytic agent in generating separation anxiety. Mismatched communication resulted when mother's verbal admonishments to go to school were coupled with contradictory nonverbal messages such as quavering voice and tremulous gestures. In such scenarios, nonverbal communication took precedence and the child obeyed mother's covert messages not to go to school.

Eisenberg (1958), in his typically eloquent prose, provided behavioral descriptions of the mother–child interactions of a series of 26 cases of "school phobia" referred to a children's therapeutic school or a children's psychiatric service. Behavioral descriptions showed mothers (and in two cases, fathers) who were more anxious than their children at the moment of separation and who communicated this anxiety to their children. Children often took the cue and became anxious and tearful, but if they did not, mother's hostility surfaced ("How do you like that? She doesn't even seem to care!"). Eisenberg concluded that while "school-phobic" children probably display an "intrinsic anxiety proneness," their separation anxiety was acquired and maintained in the context of dysfunctional family interactions.

Empirical attempts to validate the uncontrolled observational studies of interactions in families of separation-anxious, "school-phobic" children are few in number and questionable in methodology and have produced equivocal results (Bernstein, Svingen, & Garfinkel, 1990; Berg & McGuire, 1974; Waldron, Shrier, Stone, et al., 1975). Some studies have found no evidence of family dysfunction in "school-phobic" samples, where others found evidence to support some aspects of the putative dysfunction in these families.

In these studies, samples of "school-phobic" children have been heterogeneous, with little attempt to classify subsamples that might affect results. For example, Ollendick and Mayer (1984) reviewed evidence that "school phobia" is not always anchored in separation anxiety but is heterogeneous in its fundamental mechanisms. Some children refuse to attend school due to fear of separation from the caregiver, but other children display fear of some aspect of the school situation itself (e.g., fear of failure, fear of test taking, fear of a critical teacher). Children in the latter group may be accurately characterized as displaying a specific or social phobia, and the family interaction patterns may be quite different from those in families of separation-anxious children. In general, it is safe to say that, while uncontrolled descriptions of the mutual dependency and anxiety in parent–child interactions of "school-phobic" children (and by extension, of children with separation anxiety disorder) seem compelling, adequate experimental methods have not been brought to bear on the question of family dysfunction in these children, and the issue remains an open question.

Systems Models

Theorists writing from a systems theory perspective have emphasized that a child's symptoms of anxiety or fear are acquired and maintained in the context of ongoing interactions with the child's social system, most immediately the family but including the larger social context as well (e.g., grandparents, peers, school). In systems theory based on a cybernetics model (Von Bertalanffy, 1968), families are viewed as systems that strive to maintain equilibrium or balance. Whenever the family system is disturbed, it initiates moves to return to a homeostatic balance. Viewed in this context, symptomatic behavior by the child serves the cybernetic function of returning the family to equilibrium; that is, symptoms are homeostatic mechanisms (Wells, 1988).

Viewed in the context of cybernetics and general systems theory, developmental, maturational, or situational events may challenge a family system in a way that disturbs the ongoing equilibrium. The family can react by facing the challenge and adapting to it, reaching a new homeostatic balance in the process. On the other hand, the family can create ways to avoid confronting the challenge, thereby maintaining the present homeostatic balance. In this way, families maintain outmoded patterns of behavior that once worked but no longer are functional (Wells, 1988).

Some systems theorists (e.g., Haley, 1976) have viewed systems models of family functioning in the context of a structural model of family organization (Minuchin, 1974). In this model, families are viewed as having a structure characterized by *hierarchy*, which defines the power relationships among members; by *subsystems*, which define groups of people in the family who join together to perform various functions (e.g., the parental subsystem or the sibling subsystem); and by *boundaries*, which define the degree of emotional closeness among the different members and subsystems in the family.

Haley (1976) presented a systems/structural theory of child problems in a family context in discussing a case of a child with a specific phobia. In this model, there is usually an enmeshed dyad (usually one parent and the child) that crosses generational boundaries and is involved in an overintense relationship and a disengaged and peripheral second parent/spouse. While stating that the most common pattern was an enmeshed mother–child dyad and a disengaged father, Haley acknowledged that sometimes the father was enmeshed and the mother peripheral or a grandmother was enmeshed and the mother peripheral. In this theoretical model, the child is characteristically disengaged from his peer group.

In the context of this structure, family interactions are described as having a homeostatic function. If mother is enmeshed and overprotective, the child's fear provides a focus for the mother's overconcern. If wife and husband are disengaged, the child's fear serves as a reason for communication. Spouses who cannot deal with each other on other issues can be held together as parents because of their mutual concern for the child and his fears. If husband and wife are in open but unresolved marital conflict, the child and his symptoms give them something to argue about other than their marital problems. Because systems theorists believe that the best explanation of a phenomenon is its description (Nichols,1984), Haley goes no further than describing the family structure and interactions in explaining his theory of child anxiety problems.

Innovative systems theorists of more recent vintage (White, 1986; White & Epston, 1990) have emphasized that children's anxiety symptoms occur because their families have been unable to find effective solutions to the problems. Furthermore, the solutions that the families have attempted perpetuate the very problems they were intended to solve; the attempted solutions become part of the problem. Family members continue to apply these ineffective, symptom-maintaining solutions because they are restrained from discovering alternative solutions by the presuppositions, premises, and expectations that make up the family members' map of the perceptual "world."

In families of a child with separation anxiety, phobia, or OCD, family members frequently perceive the child's symptoms as an integral part of the child him- or herself, as being powerful, and perceive themselves as being helpless in the face of the symptoms. These premises and expectations dictate certain family responses to the symptoms that serve to maintain them rather than solve them. For example, when a symptom occurs, parents may become frantic and focus anxious attention on the child as they attempt to understand his thoughts and feelings at that moment, reassure him, and assist him in responding to the consequences of his anxiety. Although anchored in cybernetics, White's (1986) theory, relying on cognitive–perceptual processes in family members to explain symptom-maintaining family behavior, bears a resemblance to and extends individual cognitive theories of anxiety and depression (Beck, Rush, Shaw, et al., 1979; Beck, Emery, & Greenberg, 1985).

I know of no empirical studies that address these interaction processes in families of children and adolescents with anxiety disorders. Once again, the theory has developed based on clinical observations of its authors. However, recent research by Gavazzi and colleagues (Gavazzi & Sabatelli, 1990; Gavazzi, Anderson, & Sabatelli, 1993; Sabatelli & Anderson, 1991) has supported components of the general family system model and its relationship to adolescent adjustment. In these studies, greater parental intrusiveness (enmeshment) with the adolescent was associated with lower levels of psychosocial maturity and with greater levels of presenting problem severity in a general clinical sample. Interestingly, lower levels of intrusiveness were associated with greater perceived family supportiveness in this adolescent sample.

Social Learning Models

The social learning theory of the acquisition and maintenance of anxiety and fears, involving operant, respondent, vicarious, and cognitive learning processes, will not be reviewed in entirety here since this theory has been presented in Chapter 14 (see also Shaffer, 1986; Wells & Vitulano, 1984). However, regarding family processes, it is important to note that conditioning, modeling, and cognitive learning imply a social context in which the environment that supplies the contingencies or models for fearful behavior and cognitions usually comprises other people. Often these contingency suppliers and models are other family members.

Studies of behavioral therapy for children with anxiety and phobic disorders often describe parents who positively reinforce fearful and avoidant behavior by rewarding it with attention and other environmental contingencies (e.g., permitting the "school-phobic" child to stay home and watch television, play, or go out with mother) or who negatively reinforce the symptoms by facilitating the child's escape/avoidance responses (e.g., picking the child up from school and bringing her home when she becomes anxious). Also, parents can serve as models of anxious, fearful behavior and cognitions through their own verbalizations and behavioral manifestations of anxiety. Studies showing a higher familial concordance for anxiety disorders in parents and children than would be expected by chance (Turner, Beidel, & Costello, 1987; Weissman, 1988; Weissman, Leckman, Merikangas, et al., 1984) may reflect genetic transmission but may also partially reflect social learning processes.

FAMILY THERAPY FOR CHILDHOOD ANXIETY DISORDERS

Systems/Structural Family Interventions

The goals of treatment in systems approaches to family therapy for children with anxiety disorders arise out of the systems model presented. Various authors have described specific goals of therapy as (1) reinstating a normal family hierarchy in which the roles of parent and spouse are clearly delineated from that of the child, (2) assisting the adults to become more involved with each other, (3) decreasing the involvement in the enmeshed dyad, (4) increasing the involvement between the symptomatic child and the peripheral parent, (5) increasing the involvement of the child with the peer world, and (6) interrupting the problem-maintaining solution behaviors of the family members (Baideme, Kern, & Taffel-Cohen, 1979; Crumley, 1974; Dalton, 1983; Fife & Gant, 1980; Haley, 1976;

O'Connor, 1983; White, 1979). Because of his emphasis on perceptual processes that govern family members' behaviors, White (1986) would add to this list of goals (7) replacing family members' problem-saturated view of their world with an alternative story that contains new solutions. In the case of "school phobia," a primary goal is to return the child to school as soon as possible.

Reframing

Systems therapists use a variety of tactics to achieve these goals. An opening tactic often employed in systems therapy is the use of a technique called reframing. This involves the development of an explanation of the problem that is acceptable to the family and that provides opportunities and incentives for family members to make necessary changes in their relationships (White, 1979).

Good reframing often places a positive connotation on the problem in order to reduce resistance and increase motivation among family members for solving the problem. For example, White (1979), in treating a hospitalized "school-phobic" boy, reframed the boy's problem thus: Because the boy saw himself as so central in the parents lives, he felt that his parents could not cope if he progressed normally through adolescence and eventually left home. The purpose of his school refusal was to keep him standing still developmentally so that his parents would not have to face an "empty nest."

By reframing the problem in this way, the task of the parents became to convince the boy that his worry about them and sacrifice for them was not necessary. In addition, the family's new understanding of the reason for the symptom shifted the perceptual field from one in which the boy was a helpless victim of his fear of attending school, to one in which the boy was making a choice not to attend to school on behalf of his parents. If he could choose not to attend school because he was needed at home, then presumably he could choose to attend school if he was no longer needed at home. It can also be seen how this frame sets the stage for work on the other goals of systems therapy.

Directives

In attempting to address the goals of systems therapy, family therapists often use therapeutic directives designed to achieve the desired outcome. For example, in his work with a child with a specific phobia of dogs, Haley (1973) gave a series of directives. First, father and son were directed to talk with each other in therapy sessions about dogs and about how to manage dogs. Mother was encouraged to remain on the periphery during these discussions. Later, father and son were given an out-of-session directive to obtain a puppy for the boy and bring it home. However, it was not to be just any puppy. It should be a puppy that was afraid of people, and father and son were to cure the puppy of its fear.

These two directives served the obvious purpose of reinvolving the peripheral parent with the symptomatic child and disengaging the enmeshed parent. The nature of the second task also created a subtle perceptual shift in the boy's relationship to fear. Now he was not the victim of fear; he was to be the master of fear in his puppy. Although not emphasized by Haley, White (1986) would have suggested that this shift in perception from one of helplessness to one of control over fearful symptoms had a great deal to do with the success of the therapy. Family and puppy came to the next therapy session, which was spent with father instructing the boy how to train the puppy.

The next directive addressed the marital goals. The parents were told that they were doing so well helping their son with his fear that they should reward themselves with a weekend vacation without the children. While the parents and therapist planned the vacation in the session, the boy and his sister withdrew to a corner and played appropriately as siblings, thus establishing a generational boundary in the session.

This directive is typical of Haley's approach of not tackling marital goals head on but keeping them in the context of the work with the child. However, as often happens, the directive brought to the fore buried marital issues that the couple themselves now raised as something they wished to address. The final sessions focused on marital counseling designed to consolidate the reemerging closeness between the spouses/parents, and the boy's phobia resolved.

Other authors have used directives to facilitate goals of reinvolving the symptomatic child in the world of siblings and peers and strengthening the generational boundary between parents and children. Baideme et al. (1979) directed two siblings (one a "school-phobic" child) to spend regularly scheduled time every day in a mutually enjoyable activity. White (1979) enjoined the aid of an older brother of a "school-phobic" child to "introduce him to the world of the adolescent," while directing mother to pursue individual interests.

Prescribing the Symptoms

Another tactic frequently used by systems family therapists is the use of paradoxical interventions, notably, prescribing the symptom. This intervention directs the patient to engage in symptomatic behavior but under controlled circumstances. For example, White (1979) advised a "school-phobic" child to vomit as much as possible on the way to school and di-

rected the father to encourage the boy to be ill. Furthermore, the child
was instructed to "practice his pain" every morning for 15 minutes with
his father. Baideme et al. (1979) directed a "school-phobic" child to be
afraid and cry and scream every morning before her parents took her to
school. The child was also to spend 15 minutes every morning on the way
to school telling her father her worries. (This followed a directive in which
father, rather than mother, was instructed to take the child to school immediately after her directed crying and screaming session).

Paradoxical intervention also has been used in family therapy for
children with obsessive–compulsive symptoms. O'Connor (1983) asked
a child who had obsessions about vomiting to sit in a kitchen chair for
one hour daily, think hard about trying to vomit, and mop up the vomit
when he was sick. In addition, if obsessions about vomiting occurred at
other times during the day, the boy was to defer those thoughts to the
prescribed hour by saying to himself, "I'll think and worry about it then."
Parents were not to interfere with the obsession practice sessions by offering any observations or reassurances. Dalton (1983) asked a boy with
several cleaning and checking rituals to have a 10-minute handwashing
time each morning.

On the surface, it is not clear why asking a patient to engage in his
symptomatic behavior should reduce the symptoms. Systems theorists
would view the explanation as deriving from the systems model. At one
level of analysis, prescribing the symptom has a powerful impact on inter-
dicting the ongoing family reactions to the symptom that have become a
part of the symptom-maintaining complex. Since the therapist is telling
the patient to have the symptom, the parents and other family members
need not become so frantic and anxiously reassuring when the symptom
occurs under the therapist's control. Some therapists facilitate this outcome by directly instructing parents to stay out of the way, to merely
observe or monitor but not comment while the child is practicing his symptom. Taken even farther, the parents may be instructed to encourage the
child to continue practicing the symptom if the child stops before the
prescribed time limit. Rather than being helpless in the face of the symptom, parents have taken charge of the symptom, thus restoring an appropriate family hierarchy. In White's (1986) view, the function of prescribing the symptom is that it changes the symptom from being a powerful
victimizer over which the patient has no control to being an issue the
patient can volunarily master and control.

As mentioned in the introduction to this chapter, there have been no
controlled investigations of the effectiveness of systems family therapy for
children and adolescents with anxiety disorders. Rather, the literature is
characterized by promulgations of theory and case descriptions of family

therapy using principles and techniques described here. The reports usually state that the patient was free of symptoms at the end of therapy, and
several articles report that patients remained symptom free at 1- or 2-year
follow-up. However, while compelling, it is impossible to know whether
these interventions would be proven effective when subjected to the rig-
ors of the scientific method.

Behavioral Family Interventions

The goals of behavioral family interventions arise out of the social learning
model and focus on how parents may be modeling or reinforcing fearful,
anxious, or avoidant behaviors; how the parents can change their inadvertent reinforcement of the problem; and how parents can model and/or reinforce competent, confident behavior. Interventions at the level of the family have almost always occurred with the parent(s), and dyadic reinforcement
or modeling processes are emphasized. Triadic interactions and the impact
of other family relationships on the symptoms of the target child are rarely
considered in behavioral family interventions for anxiety problems in children, although such relationships have been considered for other behavior
disorders of childhood and adolescence (McMahon & Wells, 1989).

Interestingly, one of the first studies in the behavioral literature on
anxiety disorders in childhood is the only study in which intervention at
the family level constituted the primary or only treatment of the child
(Kennedy, 1965). Most studies are anchored in an individual model in
which treatment is directed toward the child and treatment of the parents
is adjunctive. Consequently, the reports of behavior therapy with anxious
children place emphasis on describing the individual work with the child,
and relatively less attention is given to describing how the parents were
included in the therapy. Nevertheless, some information can be gleaned
from these studies.

Carlson, Figueroa, and Lahey (1986), March (in press), and Wells
and Vitulano (1984) have reviewed behavioral approaches to childhood
anxiety disorders including simple and social phobias, "school phobia,"
and OCD. Specific behavioral treatments have included systematic desensitization and its variants, flooding and implosion therapy, modeling, reinforced practice, and cognitive procedures. In the case of obsessive-compulsive behaviors, the most successful behavioral treatments seem to be
those that combine exposure-based intervention with response prevention
to block the occurrence of the rituals while in contact with the feared
stimuli. In the case of "school phobia," treatment usually involves rapid
reintroduction to school without permission to return home in the middle
of the school day and a rearrangement of the environmental contingencies that were rewarding the avoidance of school.

Kennedy (1965) was among the first to publish a report of behavioral therapy for "school phobia" emphasizing work with parents. In a series of 50 cases of Type I "school phobia" involving a multicomponent treatment plan, the emphasis was on working with parents to facilitate rapid reintroduction to school. A structured interview with the parents was conducted, emphasizing the transient nature of the school refusal and the importance of returning the child to school despite protestations and somatic and anxiety complaints. Parents were told to plan for school reintroduction on Monday morning and not to discuss school attendance or phobic symptoms over the weekend. On Monday morning there also was to be no discussion of anxiety or why the child did not like school. The child was simply to be taken to school by his father. The parents were then asked to compliment the child on going to school and staying there, no matter how resistant the child had been, no matter how many times the child vomited, cried, or started to leave. The two goals of the parent interview were to outline the plan in a confident manner and to convince and reassure the parents of the importance of rapid reintroduction.

The two behavioral principles involved in this treatment are extinction of anxiety responses and reinforcement within the context of a shaping program of gradually more competent school attendance (differential reinforcement of other behavior [DRO]). By having the parents eliminate all conversation about anxiety, phobias, somatic complaints, and not liking school, a powerful reinforcer (parental attention) for anxiety is removed (extinction). By having the parents compliment the child for gradually more competent forms of school attendance, the same reinforcer, parental attention, is now given for the adaptive behavior.

Kennedy (1965) reported that in 50 consecutive cases of "school phobia," this approach with parents (in the context of a six-component treatment plan) resulted in rapid elimination of school refusal in all 50 cases, confirmed by 2- to 8-year follow-up. Moreover, this groundbreaking report set the stage for the use of extinction and DRO procedures in subsequent anxiety treatment.

One of the first controlled evaluations of the effects of behavior therapy with children was conducted with children displaying "monophobias and multiphobias" (Miller, Barrett, Hampe, et al., 1972). In fact, 69% of the children in this sample displayed "school phobia." Although much of the behavioral treatment was directed to the child and will not be described here, parents were involved as models in sessions and as contingency managers at home. For example, in sessions, parents and children together learned the relaxation strategy that precedes systematic desensitization so that parents could become relaxation models for their children. At home, parents were instructed to "restructure contingency schedules"; for example, eliminating television watching during school hours (extinction) for a "school-phobic" child. Miller et al. (1972) reported no differences between behavior therapy and psychotherapy in this study; symptom reduction occurred in both groups. However, of interest was the fact that, while individual treatment of the children in the two groups in this study was quite different, treatment of the parents (instructing them to rearrange contingencies for fearful behavior) in both groups was very similar. Therefore, the similar (positive) outcomes achieved with both treatments may have been a function of the interventions with the parents in both groups.

Subsequent studies of behavioral therapy with children with anxiety disorders have built on and extended the early classic studies employing parent-implemented modeling, extinction, shaping, and DRO (Fine, 1973; MacDonald, 1975; Mansdorf & Lukens, 1986; March, Mulle, & Herbel, 1994; Morelli, 1983). For example, MacDonald (1975) treated a boy with a severe specific phobia of dogs with "multiple impact behavior therapy." The treatment involved many elements, and MacDonald recognized early that other family members had altered their behavior to accommodate the fear in ways that were reinforcing its continued occurrence. The parents also displayed conditioned anxiety about their son resulting in cues for his anxious feelings and prompts to avoid possible contact with dogs. In meeting with the parents, MacDonald instructed them to refrain from cueing their child to be afraid (extinction), to begin praising him for any appropriate reaction to animals (DRO), and to develop reward programs for more competent, mature behavior. The parents required considerable work to eliminate their cueing of anxious behavior. The boy's phobia of dogs diminished dramatically with the multicomponent treatment plan.

Mansdorf and Lukens (1987) incorporated cognitive procedures in their work with the parents of two "school-phobic" adolescents. An analysis was made of the parents' cognitions in interactions with their avoidant children that were thought to be functionally related to their inability to impose on their children appropriate expectations for school attendance and consequences for nonattendance. These cognitions were changed in cognitive restructuring sessions. The parents were taught tó eliminate reinforcement for school refusal and to provide reinforcement for greater amounts of time in school. Both adolescents were attending school full time within 4 weeks. The authors reported that altering the parents' maladaptive cognitions was an essential prelude to contingency management.

A few studies have reported work with parents in the treatment of children with symptoms of OCD. In most cases, the family is involved in interrupting the child's rituals at home. This is often essential, since many children incorporate their parents (and parents allow themselves to be incorporated) into the child's compulsive rituals. Fine (1973) treated two children by assisting the parents in refusing to participate in the child's rituals and keeping calm when the child became anxious and angry about their refusal. For one child, who was missing school due to early morning rituals, the parents were supported in taking him to school at the appropriate time even if he was not completely dressed. Morelli (1983) taught the mother of an adolescent boy to observe all instances of ritualistic behavior, to send the boy back to the stimulus setting with instructions to substitute an appropriate response instead, and to then praise the appropriate behavior (DRO). As in the Mansdorf and Lukens (1987) report, the mother was treated with cognitive restructuring prior to her implementation of interventions with her son. The boy's compulsive rituals lessened dramatically within 15 days of treatment outset.

Desmarais and Lavallée (1988) treated a 10-year-old boy with multiphobias, obsessions, and compulsive rituals. This boy had incorporated his parents into many of his rituals, and if they refused to perform their parts he became anxious and upset. The treatment included working with the parents to refrain from acquiescing to the boy's requests to repeat certain words on demand and to permit repetitions at predetermined times of the day independent of the boy's demands (shaping). Later, the scheduled rituals were faded out. In addition, father was given the task of working with the boy in this shaping program, since most of the ritualistic behavioral interactions had involved the mother. This direction had the effect of removing the primary reinforcing agent—the mother—from the context of the rituals (extinction). The boy's compulsive rituals gradually diminished, and 3-year follow-up revealed maintenance of the symptom reduction.

March et al. (1994) recently reported the development and initial evaluation of a manualized protocol for behavioral treatment of children and adolescents with OCD. The behavioral elements of the treatment package include graded exposure and response prevention, anxiety management training, and family intervention. The entire treatment program occurs in a framework developed by Michael White (White & Epston, 1990), in which OCD is "externalized" as the enemy. The therapist, child, and family become allies together against OCD, and the child and family are given tools for "bossing back" the obsessions and compulsions. Story methodology also is used to facilitate the therapy process and to monitor the effects of treatment. The family component of this protocol involves incorporating the parents in response prevention. In addition, parents are given information and tools for managing their own responses to the child's OCD symptoms. Considerable encouragement is given to parents to stop giving advice, stop insisting on inappropriate exposure tasks, and stop reinforcing performance of rituals with attention or acquiescence to the rituals.

In a series of single-subject designs, March and colleagues showed dramatic reduction in symptoms in 12 out of 15 subjects. Because most children also received medication and because family intervention was only one component of the behavioral treatment package, it is not possible to isolate the unique or additive effects of family intervention in this study. Nevertheless, this systematic series using a manualized treatment approach shows great promise as a treatment for young OCD patients, and component analyses should clarify the contribution of the different treatment elements, including the family intervention.

As can be seen from this selective review of the literature, behavioral treatments of childhood anxiety disorders that involve the parents of the anxious child have been based on functional analyses of the parents' reinforcement patterns in relationship to the child's symptoms. These analyses have shown that parents accommodate to phobic and obsessive–compulsive symptoms in ways that reinforce rather than diminish the symptoms. This effect is unintended by the parents, who often believe that they are doing the right thing; they have to be shown that they are inadvertently reinforcing the very behaviors and emotions they are trying to help the child improve. Treatment involves gaining the parents' cooperation in removing attention and other powerful reinforcers for symptomatic responses (extinction), helping parents to stop complying with the child's anxious demands to participate in the phobic symptoms or compulsive rituals (response prevention/extinction), and helping parents learn to reinforce more competent alternative behaviors (DRO).

Although there are no studies isolating the effects of the family intervention component of behavioral treatments for childhood anxiety disorders, several authors have noted the apparent importance of including parents in treatment. Further research on component analyses of apparently effective treatments are needed to evaluate precisely the contribution of behavioral family interventions.

CONCLUSIONS

This chapter selectively reviews the literature on family processes and family therapy in childhood and adolescent anxiety disorders. This literature is neither extensive nor experimentally rigorous. In addition, most studies of treatment of anxiety in children emphasize the individual treatment of the child; even when family intervention is done, it is not described as carefully as individual treatment modalities. Therefore, what we glean from the literature on family treatment must be considered descriptive rather than confirmatory. Some of the treatments are derived from theoretical models of anxiety and anxiety treatment that have received empirical support in the adult literature (e.g., exposure and response prevention). To the extent that parents are incorporated into the implementation of procedures based on those principles, we may be able to place more credence in the validity of those family treatments. However, the extent to which incorporating parents and family members into treatment has a significant additive or synergistic effect remains to be demonstrated.

Some of the treatments derived from different theoretical models resemble one another. For example, in systems family therapy, paradoxical maneuvers designed to change the pattern of family members' reactions to the child's symptomatic behaviors resemble extinction procedures taught to parents in behavioral family therapy. The fundamental mechanism of action of such procedures may be identical, even though they arise out of different theoretical models.

Systems therapists, more than behavioral therapists, have addressed themselves to the problems of resistance to therapeutic directives, indicating that the two schools of therapy may have much to learn from each other. March and colleagues (1994) have developed the first systematic protocol for treatment of childhood anxiety disorders that incorporates tenets and techniques from each model in a manner that preliminary evidence suggests is highly successful. At this early stage of family treatment development, one hopes that other researchers, as well, will be able to set aside personal and theoretical biases in the service of broad-based treatment approaches that succeed.

Finally, in spite of the interest in family therapy, there remains a lamentable lack of empirical research on both the process and the outcome of systems and behavioral family therapy for anxiety disorders in children. The need for such work is evident in the calls to document the effectiveness of all forms of psychotherapy, and one hopes that the future will find family therapists increasingly more interested in submitting their ideas and strategies to the empirical test.

REFERENCES

Baideme, S. M., Kern, R. M., & Taffel-Cohen, S. (1979). The use of Adlerian family therapy in a case of school phobia. *Journal of Individual Psychology, 35,* 58–69.

Beck, A. T., Emery, G., & Greenberg, R. L. (1985). *Anxiety disorders and phobias.* New York: Basic Books.

Beck, A. T., Rush, A. J., Shaw, B. F., et al. (1979). *Cognitive therapy of depression.* New York: Guilford Press.

Berg, I., & McGuire, R. (1974). Are mothers of school-phobic adolescents overprotective? *British Journal of Psychiatry, 124,* 10–13.

Bernstein, G. A., Svingen, P. H., & Garfinkel, B. D. (1990). School phobia: Patterns of family functioning. *Journal of the American Academy of Child and Adolescent Psychiatry, 29,* 24–30.

Carlson, C. L., Figueroa, R. G., & Lahey, B. B. (1986). Behavior therapy for childhood anxiety disorders. In R. Gittelman (Ed.), *Anxiety disorders of childhood* (pp. 204–232). New York: Guilford Press.

Crumley, F. E. (1974). A school phobia in a three-generational family conflict. *Journal of the American Academy of Child Psychiatry, 13,* 536–550.

Dalton, P. (1983). Family treatment of an obsessive–compulsive child: A case report. *Family Relations, 22,* 99–108.

Desmarais, P. & Lavallée Y. (1988). Severe obsessive–compulsive syndrome in a 10 year old: A 3 year Follow-up. *Canadian Journal of Psychiatry, 33,* 405–408.

Eisenberg, L. (1958). School phobia: A study in the communication of anxiety. *American Journal of Psychiatry, 114,* 712–718.

Fife, B. L., & Gant, B. L. (1980). The resolution of school phobia through family therapy. *Journal of Psychiatric Research, 18,* 13–16.

Fine, S. (1973). Family therapy and a behavioral approach to childhood obsessive–compulsive neurosis. *Archives of General Psychiatry, 28,* 695–697.

Gavazzi, S. M., Anderson, S. A., & Sabatelli, R. M. (1993). Family differentiation, peer differentiation, and adolescent adjustment in a clinical sample. *Journal of Adolescent Research, 8,* 205–225.

Gavazzi, S. M., & Sabatelli, R. M. (1990). Family system dynamics, the individuation process, and psychosocial development. *Journal of Adolescent Research, 5,* 500–519.

Goldstein, M. J., Rodnick, E. H., Evans, J. R., et al. (1978). Drug and family therapy in the aftercare of acute schizophrenics. *Archives of General Psychiatry, 35,* 1169–1177.

Haley, J. (1973). Strategic therapy when a child is presented as the problem. *Journal of the American Academy of Child Psychiatry, 12,* 641–659.

Haley, J. (1976). *Problem-solving therapy.* San Francisco: Jossey-Bass.

Hazelrigg, M. D., Cooper, H. M., & Borduin, C. M. (1987). Evaluating the effectiveness of family therapies: An integrative review and analysis. *Psychological Bulletin, 101,* 428–442.

Henggeler, S. W., Borduin, C. M., & Mann, B. J. (1993). Advances in family therapy: Empirical foundations. In T. H. Ollendick & R. J. Prinz (Eds.), *Advances in clinical child psychology* (pp. 207–241). New York and London: Plenum Press.

Jacobson, N. S., Dobson, K., Fruzzetti, A. E., et al. (1991). Marital therapy as a treatment for depression. *Journal of Consulting and Clinical Psychology, 59,* 547–557.

Kennedy, W. A. (1965). School phobia: Rapid treatment of fifty cases. *Journal of Abnormal Psychology, 70,* 285–289.

MacDonald, M. L. (1975). Multiple impact behavior therapy in a child's dog phobia. *Journal of Behavior Therapy and Experimental Psychiatry, 6,* 317–322.

Mansdorf, I. J., & Lukens, E. (1987). Cognitive-behavioral psychotherapy for separation anxious children exhibiting school phobia. *Journal of the American Academy of Child and Adolescent Psychiatry, 26,* 222–225.

March, J. S. (in press). Behavioral psychotherapy for children and adolescents with obsessive–compulsive disorder: Vol. I. A review of the literature. *Journal of the American Academy of Child and Adolescent Psychiatry.*

March, J. S., Mulle, K., & Herbel, B. (1994). Behavioral psychotherapy for children and adolescents with obsessive–compulsive disorder: An open trial of a new protocol-driven treatment package. *Journal of the American Academy of Child and Adolescent Psychiatry, 33,* 333–341.

Markus, E., Lange, A., & Pettigrew, T. F. (1990). Effectiveness of family therapy: A meta-analysis. *Journal of Family Therapy, 12,* 205–221.

McMahon, R. J., & Wells, K. C. (1989). Conduct disorders. In E. J. Mash & R. A. Barkley (Eds.), *Treatment of childhood disorders* (pp. 73–134). New York: Guilford Press.

Miklowitz, D. J., & Goldstein, M. J. (1990). Behavioral family treatment for patients with bipolar affective disorder. *Behavior Modification, 14,* 457–489.

Miller, L. C., Barrett, C. L., Hampe, E., et al. (1972). Comparison of reciprocal inhibition, psychotherapy, and waiting list control for phobic children. *Journal of Abnormal Psychology, 79,* 269–279.

Minuchin, S. (1974). *Families and family therapy.* Cambridge, MA: Harvard University Press.

Morelli, G. (1983). Adolescent compulsion: A case study involving cognitive-behavioral treatment. *Psychological Reports, 53,* 519–522.

Nichols, M. (1984). *Family therapy: Concepts and methods.* New York: Gardner Press.

O'Connor, J. J. (1983). Why can't I get hives: Brief strategic therapy with an obsessional child. *Family Relations, 22,* 201–209.

Ollendick, T. H., & Mayer, J. A. (1984). School phobia. In S. M. Turner (Ed.), *Behavioral theories and treatment of anxiety* (pp. 367–412). New York: Plenum Press.

Sabatelli, R. M., & Anderson, S. A. (1991). Family system dynamics, peer relationships and adolescents' psychological adjustment. *Family Relations, 40,* 363–369.

Shadish, W. R. (1990). *Novel statistical methods in meta-analysis: An application.* Paper presented at the meeting of the American Psychological Association, Boston.

Shaffer, D. (1986). Learning theories of anxiety. In R. Gittelman (Ed.), *Anxiety disorders of childhood* (pp. 157–167). New York: Guilford Press.

Skynner, A. C. R. (1974). School phobia: A reappraisal. *British Journal of Medical Psychology, 47,* 1–16.

Szapocznik, J., Murray, E., Scopetta, M., et al. (1989). Structural family therapy versus psychodynamic child therapy for problematic Hispanic boys. *Journal of Consulting and Clinical Psychology, 57,* 571–578.

Turner, S. M., Beidel, D. C., & Costello, A. (1987). Psychopathology in the offspring of anxiety disorder patients. *Journal of Consulting and Clinical Psychology, 55,* 229–235.

Von Bertalanffy, L. (1968). *General systems theory.* New York: George Braziller.

Waldron, S., Shrier, D. K., Stone, B., et al. (1975). School phobias and other childhood neuroses: A systematic study of the children and their families. *American Journal of Psychiatry, 132,* 802–808.

Weissman, M. M. (1988). The epidemiology of anxiety disorders: Rates, risks and familial patterns. *Journal of Psychiatric Research, 22,* 99–114.

Weissman, M. M., Leckman, J. F., Merikangas, K. R., et al. (1984). Depression and anxiety disorders in parents and children. *Archives of General Psychiatry, 41,* 845–852.

Wells, K. C. (1988). Family therapy. In J. Matson (Ed.), *Handbook of treatment approaches in childhood psychopathology* (pp. 45–61). New York: Plenum Press.

Wells, K. C. (in press). Parent management training. In G. P. Sholevar (Ed.), *Conduct disorders in children and adolescents: Assessment and intervention* (pp. 281–308). Washington, DC: American Psychiatric Press.

Wells, K. C., & Vitulano, L. A. (1984). Anxiety disorders in childhood. In S. M. Turner (Ed.), *Behavioral theories and treatment of anxiety* (pp. 413–433). New York: Plenum Press.

White, M. (1979). Distant family treatment: A case of school phobia. *Australian Paediatric Journal, 15,* 187–189.

White, M. (1986). Negative explanation, restraint, and double description: A template for family therapy. *Family Relations, 25,* 169–183.

White, M., & Epston, D. (1990). *Narrative means to therapeutic ends.* New York: W. W. Norton.

Chapter 18

Organizing
an Anxiety
Disorders Clinic

John S. March
Karen Mulle
Patricia Stallings
Drew Erhardt
C. Keith Conners

s shown in the preceding chapters, heightened awareness of the
childhood-onset anxiety disorders arose in part from focused
and sophisticated assessment and treatment protocols administered within a subspecialty clinic framework (Last, Hersen,
Kazdin, et al., 1991; Silverman & Eisen, 1992; Rapoport, Leonard, Swedo,
et al., 1993; Klein, Koplewicz, & Kanner, 1992). With the caveat that local
culture has a profound impact on clinical services, this chapter addresses
the pragmatics of setting up an anxiety disorders clinic by briefly describing one such program, the Program in Childhood and Adolescent Anxiety Disorders (PCAAD) at Duke University Medical Center. PCAAD spe-
cializes in the comprehensive evaluation and treatment of anxiety disorders
in children and adolescents, especially patients with diagnostically complex conditions and patients who have not responded well to previous
treatments. To provide a comprehensive database with which to compare
children with internalizing and externalizing psychopathology and to
better manage diagnostic and treatment overlaps, PCAAD is linked closely
to the Duke University Medical Center (DUMC) Attention-Deficit Disorders Program (Keith Conners) and the Neuropsychopharmacology Pro-

gram (John March). Trainees from a variety of settings and practicing psychiatrists and psychologists from North Carolina and communities around the nation rotate through or visit all three subspecialty clinics, so we frequently receive questions about how to establish an anxiety disorders clinic serving young patients.

FRAMEWORK

Purpose

Prior to setting up a specialty program, it is important to establish a set of clear goals, beginning with the purpose of the program. PCAAD is explicitly organized as a clinical research program; every youngster is simultaneously a clinical patient and a research subject. Conversely, since only a minority of our patients participate in formal research protocols, our central goal is the provision of first-rate clinical services.

Developmental Orientation

Child psychiatrists and psychologists are fond of speaking developmentally but in practice sometimes pay less than adequate attention to developmentally based models of psychopathology when assessing or treating mental illnesses in child patients. We use a readily comprehensible developmental model adapted from the learning disabilities (Pennington, 1991), cognitive neuroscience (Posner, Petersen, Fox, et al., 1988), and developmental psychopathology (Robbins & Rutter, 1990) literatures to guide clinical practice (Conners, Wells, March, et al., 1994). We assume that children normally acquire increased social–emotional (self and interpersonal) and academic competencies across time. The failure to do so, relative to age, gender, and culture-matched peers, may reflect capacity limitations, individual difference in the rate of skill acquisition for specific competencies, environmental factors, and/or the development of a mental illness.

Thus three broad domains are seen to influence the likelihood of psychopathology: genetic risk, neurocognitive competence, and environmental input in the form of risk and protective factors and their associated mediating and moderating variables. Neurocognitive competencies specify abilities/disabilities on specific cognitive functions as measured by neuropsychological tests. In addition to basic competencies, such as short-term orienting of attention, neurocognitive competencies include functions closely related to psychiatric symptomatology, such as recognizing facial affects or defining the threshold for attentional orienting to threat cues. Environmental input—such as family factors, life events, school performance, social support, coping style, and socioeconomic status—can modify or be influenced by both genetic factors and neurocognitive competencies. For example, severe trauma and associated posttraumatic stress disorder (PTSD) may modify both symptoms and basic neuropsychological competencies (McNally, English, & Lipke, 1993), with the result being that PTSD resembles panic disorder on some neurocognitive measures (McNally, Riemann, Louro, et al., 1992).

Neurocognitive competence, genetic risk, and environmental input generally do not covary monotonically. Dyslexia nicely illustrates this process: A neurocognitive deficit (poor auditory–linguistic information processing) linked to a specific brain region (left temporal–parietal damage/dysfunction) brings about a psychiatric disturbance (developmental reading disorder) that can be accelerated or inhibited by environmental input (such as family/educational support). In this model, the task of the mental health practitioner is to understand the presenting symptoms in the context of constraints to normal development and to devise a treatment program that ameliorates those constraints so that the youngster can resume as normal as possible a developmental trajectory. For most children with anxiety disorders, this requires a careful multimodal evaluation and some combination of cognitive-behavioral, psychopharmacological, and in many cases, behavioral or pedagogical academic interventions (Conners et al., 1994). In our experience, leaving out one or more legs of this three-legged stool is a common cause of so-called "treatment resistance." Since few practitioners possess all the essential skills and because reimbursement schedules increasingly constrain practice patterns, such complex assessment and treatment regimens are best delivered in a multidisciplinary "team" milieu.

Organization

Once a set of clear goals has been established in the context of a developmental model of child psychopathology, the next task is to set up an organizational framework designed to meet the goals. Plainly, however, clinical services depend not only on goals but also on management issues. For example, what is the expected patient flow? What are the funding sources for patients? Private insurance? Externally funded protocols? What of patients who are unable to pay? Who will handle billing? Are support staff available for data entry and transcription? Are most patients likely to move from assessment to treatment, or will a significant number of patients be referred for consultation only? What providers, such as the inpatient unit and other clinics such as the Attention-Deficit Disorders Program in our case, require links to the subspecialty clinic, and will these links be reciprocal or unidirectional? Who will deliver services, and how will service providers be recompensed? The answers to these questions decide the range of services, set the staffing requirements, and determine if sufficient resources are available to implement a clinical research program.

Special Programs

In addition to providing specialized clinical care, PCAAD educates mental health personnel from a variety of disciplines about anxiety disorders in young persons. As part of this effort, PCAAD staff provide training for a variety of DUMC health care professionals; PCAAD faculty are also available to speak to professional and lay audiences regionally, nationally, and internationally.

Research is a vital element in PCAAD; PCAAD staff conduct research into the biological, psychological, and social aspects of anxiety disorders in children and adolescents. Continued research is necessary to clarify diagnostic issues, determine underlying causes, and identify and validate the best prevention and treatment strategies for children suffering from anxiety disorders. Active research protocols include double-blind medication trials, open and single-subject investigations of cognitive-behavioral therapy (CBT) with obsessive–compulsive disorder (OCD), questionnaire development, application of chronometric models borrowed from cognitive neuroscience to children with anxiety disorders and attention-deficit/hyperactivity disorder (ADHD), and epidemiological and treatment studies of PTSD. Although the participation of parents and children in PCAAD research protocols is important, involvement in a formal research protocol is not a requirement for clinical evaluation and treatment. Not surprisingly, time committed to educational and research endeavors constrains the clinical enterprise, which of course is essential to the conduct of research. Balancing these intertwined objectives can present a noteworthy conundrum.

EVALUATION

Telephone Contact

Table 18.1 lists the disorders most frequently seen in our clinic. Referral sources include physicians, psychologists, other mental health professionals, schools, advocacy groups, and patients and their families. By the time they reach us, many of our patients are remarkably sophisticated regarding the diagnosis and treatment of anxiety disorders in youth. For example, we have recently seen several patients with OCD who learned about our program on the mental health forum of CompuServe Information Service, a commercial computer bulletin board.

TABLE 18.1. Anxiety Disorders

Generalized anxiety disorder
Generalized social phobia
Obsessive–compulsive disorder
Panic disorder
Posttraumatic stress disorder
School phobia
Separation anxiety disorder
Simple phobias
Specific social phobia
Trichotillomania (hair pulling)

In some programs, an administrative assistant or research assistant determines whether referral is appropriate, discusses financial considerations, and coordinates scheduling. Because we receive far more inquiries than we have patient slots, our administrative assistant gathers data regarding the referral source and presenting complaint, and prospective patients are then prescreened for suitability by a PCAAD faculty member. For example, we do not routinely see children with affective disorders as the presenting complaint and take attention-deficit disorder (ADD) or psychopharmacology referrals only from the Attention-Deficit Disorders Program. Accepted patients are scheduled for an intake evaluation; the remainder are referred to other treatment providers.

Preevaluation

To speed and concentrate the evaluation process, we gather a sizable amount of data prior to the patient's initial visit. In addition to requesting psychiatric/psychological, neuropsychological, hospitalization, and school records, we ask patients and family members to complete a packet of materials designed to assess important domains of psychopathology in the context of the patient's presenting concerns. In this way, we adjust the assessing clinician's "prior probabilities" relative to the major domains of anxiety and estimate the likelihood of complicating comorbidities. By focusing on the primary diagnosis and the "rule-outs" of differential diagnosis, we instantiate a "medical model" in which patients are seen as "OK" and psychiatric illness is framed as the object of treatment. Included in the patient/family packet is a brochure describing PCAAD, our fee schedule, information about the first appointment, and a map showing the location of our office. Parents are asked to mail the questionnaires back to us before the initial visit and are informed that the patient will not be seen if the material is not completed. Table 18.2 summarizes the information ob-

TABLE 18.2. Developmental Questionnaire

Demographics
History of presenting problem
Previous treatment
Medication history
Birth and pregnancy history
Early developmental history
School history/learning problems
Peer relationships
Family psychiatric history
Family medical history
Patient medical history
Open comments

tained in the PCAAD/ADDP Developmental Questionnaire; Table 18.3 lists the rating scales we typically obtain from child and parents.

First Appointment

Each patient first receives an extensive clinical evaluation (lasting 1.5 hours) by a child psychiatrist or psychologist. The initial visit includes a clinical interview of the child and his or her parents covering Axes I–V of the fourth edition of the *Diagnostic and Statistical Manual of Mental Disorders* (DSM-IV; American Psychiatric Association, 1994), careful consideration of the rating scale data and the PCAAD/ADDP Developmental Questionnaire, school records and previous mental health treatment records; a formal mental status examination; and in some cases, a specialized neurodevelopmental evaluation. Patients presenting with OCD are evaluated using the symptom checklist from the Yale–Brown Obsessive Compulsive Scale (YBOCS; Goodman, Price, Rasmussen, et al., 1989) and are assigned a baseline score on the YBOCS and the National Institute of Mental Health (NIMH) Global Obsessive–Compulsive Scale.

TABLE 18.3. Rating Scales

Children's Depression Inventory
Conners Parent Rating Scale
Conners Teacher Rating Scale
Leyton Obsessional Inventory
Mood and Feelings Questionnaire
Multidimensional Anxiety Scale for Children (MASC)
Revised Children's Manifest Anxiety Scale
Social Phobia Anxiety Inventory–Child

Ideally, a structured interview, such as the Anxiety Disorders Interview Schedule for Children (ADIS-C; Silverman & Eisen, 1992), should be part of every diagnostic assessment. Unfortunately, we currently lack the staffing resources to complete an ADIS-C, which requires separate 1-hour interviews of the child and one parent. Since we routinely use the ADIS-C with children enrolled in formal research protocols, we feel fairly confident that we cover all the major domains of psychopathology in the clinical interview, especially since information from the clinical interview is tempered by the rating scale data. However, the clinical research function of PCAAD is unquestionably compromised by the absence of interview-supported diagnoses, so development of reliable, valid, and cost-effective instrumentation is a topic of some interest to us.

At the end of the initial visit, the parent(s) and child are given a brief summary of the diagnostic impressions, including treatment implications, and are scheduled for neurocognitive testing and, if necessary, a medical evaluation and laboratory testing with their family doctor or pediatrician. Formal treatment planning waits for the "feedback session," which integrates all the information obtained in the questionnaire screening, the clinical interview, and the neurocognitive battery. In the face of a clinical crisis, such as recent-onset "school phobia," we usually initiate cognitive-behavioral psychotherapy and sometimes pharmacotherapy at the first visit.

Neurocognitive Battery

Despite abundant data linking abnormalities in brain function to psychopathology, operational criteria for identifying mental disorders in children and adolescents have largely relied on behavioral symptoms. For example, the diagnostic criteria for ADHD do a poor job of operationalizing sustained attention, distractibility, or difficulty delaying impulsive responding, all of which overlap to some extent with the anxiety disorders. Computerized models of neurocognitive functioning borrowed from cognitive neuroscience begin to address this deficit by linking behaviorally defined constructs, such as distractibility, with neuropsychological measures assessing short-term orienting of attention (Swanson, Posner, Potkin, et al., 1991). Furthermore, the anxiety disorders literature contains hints that patients with these conditions exhibit impairments relative to normal controls in functions often attributed to the right hemisphere (Chapter 2; March, Johnston, Jefferson, et al., 1990; March & Conners, unpublished data). Using a variety of neurocognitive measures programmed in Microexperimental Language (MEL), we are currently conducting a study using computerized and pen-and-pencil neuropsychological measures of attention, reading, and visual–spatial skills; memory; executive functions; and ability to recognize nonverbal affects in subjects with anxiety disorders,

OCD, Tourette's syndrome, ADHD, and normal controls. Clinical patients receive a subset of these measures, which screen for attentional dysfunction, signal-processing style, poor impulse control regulation, reading difficulties, and visual–spatial–organizational impairments.

Feedback and Treatment Planning

At this point, the patient and his or her parents meet with the treating psychiatrist or psychologist (or both) for one hour to discuss the results of the evaluation and to decide on a treatment plan. During this "feedback" visit, the child's presenting problems are summarized in terms of DSM-IV diagnoses, which are linked to a neurodevelopmental model of anxiety and to reinforcing environmental contingencies. We then make recommendations in each of the following categories: (1) additional assessment procedures, if required, (2) cognitive-behavioral psychotherapy, (3) pharmacotherapy, and (4) behavioral and/or pedagogic academic intervention, if necessary. Unlike evaluations that concentrate solely on story elements, we attempt to implement interventions that present a logically consistent and compelling relationship between the disorder, the treatment, and the specified outcome. In particular, we attempt to keep the various treatment targets (the "nails") distinct with respect to the various treatment interventions (the "hammers") so that aspects of the symptom picture that are likely to require or respond to a psychosocial as distinct from a psychopharmacological intervention are kept clear insofar as is possible (Maletic, March, & Johnston, 1994). This method allow us to review in detail the indications, risks, and benefits of proposed and alternative treatments, after which parents and patient generally choose a treatment intervention consisting of CBT alone or CBT in combination with an appropriate medication.

TREATMENT

The chapters in Part II, Disorders, and Part III, Treatment, plainly set forth the treatment approaches that are commonly used with children and adolescents with anxiety disorders. We do not reprise this material here but instead outline our approach to treatment, which the interested reader can find discussed in somewhat more detail elsewhere (Maletic et al., 1994; March, in press; March, Mulle, & Herbel, 1994; Conners et al., 1994).

Cognitive-Behavioral Psychotherapy

Cognitive-behavioral treatment for anxiety disorders is well supported in the research literature and available in manualized form (March et al.,

1994; Kendall, 1991; Barlow & Craske, 1989). Unfortunately, CBT is probably underutilized in most settings (Goisman, Rogers, Steketee, et al., 1993). Parents complain that practitioners are undertrained in CBT techniques for treating anxious children; clinicians complain that children do not comply. Despite these qualifiers, the sole invariant element of PCAAD treatment consists of individualized cognitive-behavioral psychotherapy, usually lasting for 10 to 16 sessions over 3 to 4 months. Our reasoning regarding the relative positioning of pharmacotherapies depends on several "findings": (1) Successful CBT alone may carry the best long-term prognosis (Marks, Lelliott, Basoglu, et al., 1988); (2) antiexposure instructions (in which patients are encouraged not to resist their phobic symptoms) attenuate the effectiveness of drug treatment (Marks et al., 1988); (3) the combination of drug and behavioral therapies may be more effective than drug therapy alone; and (4) under some circumstances, CBT may reduce relapse in patients undergoing medication discontinuation trials.

To increase compliance with CBT, we borrow an intervention from *How I Ran OCD Off My Land,* our CBT manual for OCD in children (March & Mulle, 1993), that clearly makes the disorder the problem and thwarts blaming. More specifically, the therapist asks the child to give the disorder a nasty nickname and subsequently uses this name to refer to the child's symptoms. In this way, the child can begin to ally with the therapist in order to "boss back" the disorder. Since confronting anxiety-provoking material is intrinsically anxiety provoking, we also provide each child with a "tool kit," consisting of skills to self-manage anxiety that facilitates treatment and promotes mastery of anxiety. In doing so, we loosely follow Kendall's (1991) appproach to anxiety management training (AMT) and/or Barlow's model for panic control treatment (PCT; Barlow & Craske, 1989), as presented in our OCD manual. AMT, which enhances positive coping and may facilitate exposure-based interventions, includes progressive muscle relaxation, breathing training, and cognitive restructuring. Once AMT is mastered, a short form can be taught for use during exposure and response prevention (E/RP). Fear thermometer scores (equivalent to subjective units of discomfort [SUDS] ratings) are used to monitor the effects of anxiety management training and graded exposure.

Regardless of the particular disorder, controlled reexposure to anxiety-provoking stimuli forms the core of treatment for phobic symptoms (Foa & Kozak, 1985). Exposure can be implemented in a gradual fashion or through flooding, with exposure targets under either therapist or patient control. Flooding involves prolonged exposure to the most anxiety-provoking stimuli in order to shorten treatment and maximize benefit. However, in our experience young persons with phobic symptoms abhor disagreeable surprises, and the intensity of flooding or mistargeted graded exposure is almost always surprising. Failure in an exposure task reinforces anxiety and not infrequently disrupts the therapeutic relationship. Moreover, what appears to be graded exposure to the therapist may turn out to be flooding for the child, necessitating a mechanism for negotiating graded exposure that keeps the process largely under the child's control. We frequently use cartographic metaphors to negotiate just such a mechanism, and we find that placing E/RP targets under the child's control leads to increased compliance and improved outcomes (March, in press; March et al., 1994).

In some children, angry affects commingle with fear in anxiety-provoking situations. For these children, we use elements of the anger coping program developed by Lochman, Lampron, Gemmer, et al. (1987) to address cognitively mediated aggression in children with both internalizing and externalizing symptoms. Anger coping incorporates a cognitive problem-solving approach, including exercises to improve perspective-taking skills (or understanding the view of other people involved in an interaction) and role-playing exercises to improve the child's ability to competently enact the appropriate strategies (Lochman et al., 1987). We also incorporate elements of social skills training, habit reversal, modeling/shaping, differential reinforcement of other behavior, and parent training where indicated (Thyer, 1991; Vitulano, King, Scahill, et al., 1992; Erhardt & Baker, 1990; March, in press). Finally, as treatment winds down, we focus on fading out therapist support, generalization training, and relapse prevention, noting that patients can always return for booster sessions if symptoms recur.

Pharmacotherapy

As noted earlier, most children present to mental health settings because of problematic behaviors, either in relationships or in the school setting, and the clinician's task is to understand these behaviors in the context of the constraints to normal development that underlie them. While many behaviors are in some sense problematic, not all behaviors, even symptomatic behaviors, are appropriate targets for medication management. Thus, it is crucial to clearly define the target symptoms for psychopharmacological as contrasted to psychosocial interventions. We have found that taking a neurocognitive or "information processing" approach (Voeller, 1991) facilitates this distinction (Maletic et al., 1994). For example, standing patiently in line is an appropriate target for contingency management in the child with ADHD, whereas decreased sensation seeking and increased vigilance may be more appropriate targets for medication management. Setting realistic goals in the context of a careful assessment and ongoing monitoring of desired and undesired outcomes—treating each child as an informal single-subject design, if you will (Kazdin, 1982)—fits in well with this approach. A placebo-controlled blinded stimulant trial in the child with ADHD is a good example of a clinically relevant single-subject design with medication; a within-subject multiple-baseline design often works well for CBT in the anxious child (March & Mulle, in press), but a "hypothesis testing" strategy is appropriate for all interventions (Conners et al., 1994). We also find that multimodal interventions are more successfully administered in a multidisciplinary "team" environment. In our program, a child psychiatrist attends to psychopharmacology and a child psychologist or behavior therapist implements cognitive-behavioral psychotherapy. A comprehensive summary of the various classes of medications used to treat anxiety diatheses in young persons is presented in Chapter 15. In PCAAD, the great majority of patients receive monotherapy with a serotonin reuptake inhibitor (SRI), typically clomipramine or sertraline. Less commonly, monotherapy with a short-acting benzodiazepine or with buspirone is the pharmacothereuptic strategy; more commonly, these medications are administered on an adjunctive basis to patients already taking an SRI. Patients with comorbid ADHD are given Dexedrine, usually the spansule. Although we see many patients who have "failed" multiple medication trials, it is our experience that returning to standard well-delivered pharmacotherapy plus CBT plus necessary academic intervention converts nonresponders to responders more reliably than polypharmacy.

Academic Interventions

As noted earlier, young persons with anxiety disorders are not uncommonly comorbid for learning disabilities (Cantwell & Baker, 1987). As described primarily in the neurological and neuropsychological literatures (Chapter 2), such children often exhibit a specific pattern of academic deficits characterized by dysgraphia, dyscalculia, slow processing speed and efficiency, and impoverished expressive written language despite adequate spelling and reading skills. Clinically, DSM-IV ADHD, inattentive subtype (characterized by inattention, disorganization, daydreaming), is present in many patients with comorbid learning and anxiety disorders. Many but not all have higher verbal than performance scores on IQ testing. When impairments in the pragmatics of nonverbal social–emotional communication are also present, a wide variety of diagnostic labels have been applied, including Asperger's syndrome, high-functioning autism, nonverbal learning disabilities, and social–emotional learning disabilities, for example (Voeller, 1990).

Unless these often subtle pedagogical and behavioral deficits are identified and addressed, school can become an increasingly frustrating and aversive experience in which academic underachievement is incorrectly attributed to the anxiety disorder or to laziness. Once identified, simple remedies such as overlearning (such as tutoring/drill) or bypass strategies (such as a calculator and/or word processor) have the potential to improve academic performance and to dramatically decrease school-related anxiety. Identification and remediation of these deficits is a relatively specialized task (the interested reader is referred to Pennington, 1991, for additional information), and the availability of a neuropsychologist/psychoeducational consultant is a definite plus.

Other Treatments

At least for OCD (Hollingsworth, Tanguay, & Grossman, 1980), insight-oriented psychotherapy appears to be an ineffective treatment, especially when considered in light of the successes of CBT (March, in press; March et al., 1994). However, supportive psychotherapy may benefit some patients by increasing compliance with AMT and E/RP. Similarly, when normal development has been adversely impacted by an anxiety disorder, insight-oriented psychotherapy coupled to focused cognitive-behavioral interventions, such as assertiveness training or anger coping (Lochman et al., 1987), frequently becomes more important as the anxiety disorder diminishes (Chapter 16). We have found that group social skills training also is helpful in those patients for whom nonverbal learning disabilities interfere with the pragmatics of social–emotional communication (Voeller, 1990).

While anxiety disorders tend to run in families (Last et al., 1991; Riddle, Scahill, King, et al., 1990), family psychopathology is neither necessary nor sufficient for the genesis of anxiety disorders in youth (Last et al., 1991; Lenane, 1989). Nonetheless, families affect and are affected by a child's anxiety disorder. For example, high "expressed emotion" exacerbates OCD; a calm supportive family improves outcome (Hibbs, Hamburger, Lenane, et al., 1991). Thus, while CBT is more commonly administered in an individual setting, a combination of individual and family sessions may prove best for most patients (March, in press; March et al., 1994; Chapter 17). However, formal family therapy or marital therapy is appropriate only when family dysfunction or marital discord impedes the application of cognitive-behavioral interventions (Chapter 17).

Follow-Up

Most children are seen weekly during initial treatment and monthly to every 3 months during maintenance treatment. When treatment is concluded, children are not discharged. Because anxiety disorders tend to wax and wane spontaneously and in response to environmental events such as losses or normative developmental transitions, and because longitudinal comorbidity between the various anxiety disorders is common (see Chapter 13), we use a pulsed intervention model, where children are seen prophylactically for booster CBT sessions and early during relapses to limit downstream psychiatric morbidity. With appropriate consent, PCAAD staff provide a comprehensive report to the patient's referral source, school personnel, or other concerned treatment providers.

Monitoring the Outcome of Treatment

As noted earlier, insofar as possible we try to distinguish the treatment targets for psychosocial and pharmacological therapies (Maletic et al., 1994). In the process of generating a stimulus hierarchy, we evaluate specific anxiety symptoms and their triggers and consequences, after which the patient is assigned a baseline score on one or more outcome measures appropriate to the particular anxiety disorder (Chapter 6). In addition, each patient is rated on a measure of clinical global improvement and clinical global impairment. This is particularly important, as children frequently improve markedly and also fail to normalize on the clinical global impairment scale. We use a visual analogue fear thermometer to rate our patient's expected or actual SUDS to imaginal or *in vivo* exposure or response prevention targets, which in turn define symptom baselines for evaluating outcome (Kendall, 1991). When comorbidities are present, we add rating scales, such as the parent and teacher Conners scales (Conners, 1989), designed to tap specific dimensions of psychopathology. Taken together, these measures provide for a continuous reevaluation of extant psychopathology and ascertainment of change due to treatment.

CONCLUSION

In summary, anxiety disorders subspecialty programs have proven viable in both academic and community settings. Establishing a subspecialty clinic depends on establishing clear goals, perhaps including both clinical services and clinical research, leading to a feasible organizational structure. Treatment depends on a multimodality assessment procedure and almost always incorporates one or more cognitive-behavioral procedures along with pharmacotherapy and (behavioral and pedagogical) academic interventions in a substantial minority if not the majority of patients. Treatment is usually best administered in a mix of individual and family sessions, but formal family therapy is necessary only if family problems constrain implementation of treatment that is specific for the patient's anxiety disorder or disorders. Where possible, distinguishing the targets for psychosocial and pharmacological interventions is helpful. Finally, the assessment and treatment procedures outlined in this chapter require a combination of skills that are rarely found in a single individual. Thus most subspecialty programs involve a multidisciplinary assessment and treatment team.

ACKNOWLEDGMENT

This work was supported in part by an NIMH Scientist Development Award for Clinicians (1 K20 MH00981-01) to Dr. March.

REFERENCES

American Psychiatric Association. (1994). *Diagnostic and statistical manual of mental disorders* (4th ed.). New York: Author.

Barlow, D., & Craske, M. (1989). *Mastery of your anxiety and panic.* Albany: Graywind.

Cantwell, D. P., & Baker, L. (1987). Prevalence and type of psychiatric disorder and developmental disorders in three speech and language groups. *Journal of Communication Disorders, 20*(2), 151–160.

Conners, C. K. (1989). *The Conners rating scales: Instruments for the assessment of childhood psychopathology.* Toronto: Multi-health Systems.

Conners, C., Wells, K., March, J., et al. (1994). Methodological issues in the multimodal treatment of the disruptive behavior disorders. In L. Greenhill (Ed.), *Psychiatric clinics of North America: Disruptive behavior disorders* (pp. 361–378). Philadelphia: Saunders.

Erhardt, D., & Baker, B. L. (1990). The effects of behavioral parent training on families with young hyperactive children. *Journal of Behavior Therapy and Experimental Psychiatry, 21*(2), 121–132.

Foa, E., & Kozak, M. (1985). Emotional processing of fear: Exposure to corrective information. *Psychological Bulletin, 90,* 20–35.

Goisman, R. M., Rogers, M. P., Steketee, G. S., et al. (1993). Utilization of behavioral methods in a multicenter anxiety disorders study. *Journal of Clinical Psychiatry, 54*(6), 213–218.

Goodman, W. K., Price, L. H., Rasmussen, S. A., et al. (1989). The Yale–Brown Obsessive Compulsive Scale: Vol. II. Validity. *Archives of General Psychiatry, 46*(11), 1012–1016.

Hibbs, E. D., Hamburger, S. D., Lenane, M., et al. (1991). Determinants of expressed emotion in families of disturbed and normal children. *Journal of Child Psychology and Psychiatry and Allied Disciplines, 32*(5), 757–770.

Hollingsworth, C., Tanguay, P., & Grossman, L. (1980). Long-term outcome of obsessive compulsive disorder in childhood. *Journal of the American Academy of Child Psychiatry, 19,* 134–144.

Kazdin, A. (1982). *Single-case research designs: Methods for clinical and applied settings.* New York: Oxford University Press.

Kendall, P. (Ed.). (1991). *Child and adolescent therapy*. New York: Guilford Press.

Klein, R. G., Koplewicz, H. S., & Kanner, A. (1992). Imipramine treatment of children with separation anxiety disorder. *Journal of the Academy Child and Adolescent Psychiatry, 31*(1), 21–28.

Last, C. G., Hersen, M., Kazdin, A., et al. (1991). Anxiety disorders in children and their families. *Archives of General Psychiatry, 48*(10), 928–934.

Lenane, M. (1989). Families in obsessive–compulsive disorder. In J. Rapoport (Eds.), *Obsessive–compulsive disorder in children and adolescents* (pp. 237-249). Washington, DC: American Psychiatric Press.

Lochman, J., Lampron, L., Gemmer, T., et al. (1987). Anger coping intervention with agressive children: A guide to implementation in school settings. In P. Keller & S. Heyman (Eds.), *Innovations in clinical practice: A source book* (pp. 339–356). Sarasota, FL: Professional Resource Exchange.

Maletic, V., March, J., & Johnston, H. (1994). Child and adolescent psychopharmacology. In J. Jefferson & J. Greist (Eds.), *Psychiatric clinics of North America: Annual of drug therapy* (pp. 101–124). Philadelphia: Saunders.

March, J. (in press). Cognitive-behavioral psychotherapy for children and adolescents with obsessive–compulsive disorder: A review and recommendations for treatment. *Journal of the American Academy of Child and Adolescent Psychiatry,*

March, J., Johnston, H., Jefferson, J., et al. (1990). Do subtle neurological impairments predict treatment resistance in children and adolescents with obsessive-compulsive disorder. *Journal of Child and Adolescent Psychopharmacology, 1,* 133–140.

March, J., & Mulle, K. (1993). *"How I ran OCD off my land": A cognitive-behavioral program for the treatment of obsessive–compulsive disorder in children and adolescents.* Unpublished manuscript.

March, J., & Mulle, K. (in press). Behavioral psychotherapy for obsessive-compulsive disorder: A preliminary single case study. *Journal of Anxiety Disorders,*

March, J., Mulle, K., & Herbel, B. (1994). Behavioral psychotherapy for children and adolescents with obsessive–compulsive disorder: An open trial of a new protocol driven treatment package. *Journal of the American Academy of Child and Adolescent Psychiatry, 33*(3), 333–341.

Marks, I. M., Lelliott, P., Basoglu, M., et al. (1988). Clomipramine, self-exposure and therapist-aided exposure for obsessive–compulsive rituals. *British Journal of Psychiatry, 152,* 522–534.

McNally, R. J., English, G. E., & Lipke, H. (1993). Assessment of Intrusive cognition in PTSD: Use of the modified stroop. *Journal of Traumatic Stress, 6*(1), 33–42.

McNally, R. J., Riemann, B. C., Louro, C. E., et al. (1992). Cognitive processing of emotional information in panic disorder. *Behaviour Research and Therapy, 30*(2), 143–149.

Pennington, B. (1991). *Diagnosing learning disorders*. New York: Guilford Press.

Posner, M., Petersen, S., Fox, P., et al. (1988). Localization of cognitive operations in the human brain. *Science, 240,* 1627–1631.

Rapoport, J. L., Leonard, H. L., Swedo, S. E., et al. (1993). Obsessive compulsive disorder in children and adolescents: Issues in management. *Journal of Clinical Psychiatry, 54*(Suppl.), 27–29; discussion 30.

Riddle, M. A., Scahill, L., King, R., et al. (1990). Obsessive compulsive disorder in children and adolescents: Phenomenology and family history. *Journal of the American Academy of Child and Adolescent Psychiatry, 29*(5), 766–772.

Robbins, L., & Rutter, M. (1990). *Straight and devious pathways from childhood to adulthood.* Cambridge: Cambridge University Press.

Silverman, W. K., & Eisen, A. R. (1992). Age differences in the reliability of parent and child reports of child anxious symptomatology using a structured interview. *Journal of the American Academy of Child and Adolescent Psychiatry, 31*(1), 117–124.

Swanson, J. M., Posner, M., Potkin, S. G., et al. (1991). Activating tasks for the study of visual–spatial attention in ADHD children: A cognitive anatomic approach. *Journal of Child Neurology, 6*(Suppl.), S119–S127.

Thyer, B. A. (1991). Diagnosis and treatment of child and adolescent anxiety disorders. *Behavior Modification, 15*(3), 310–325.

Vitulano, L. A., King, R. A., Scahill, L., et al. (1992). Behavioral treatment of children and adolescents with trichotillomania. *Journal of the American Academy of Child and Adolescent Psychiatry, 31*(1), 139–146.

Voeller, K. (1990). Right hemisphere deficit syndrome in children: A neurological perspective. *International Journal of Pediatrics, 5*, 163–170.

Voeller, K. K. (1991). Toward a neurobiologic nosology of attention deficit hyperactivity disorder. *Journal of Child Neurology, 6*(Suppl.), S2–S8.

Index